THE THEORY
OF
ARCHITECTURE

CONCEPTS
THEMES
&
PRACTICES

Paul-Alan Johnson

VAN NOSTRAND REINHOLD
New York

To Susan and Lorne
with Love

Copyright © 1994 by Van Nostrand Reinhold
Library of Congress Catalog Card Number 93–21234
ISBN 0–442–01344–2

I(T)P Van Nostrand Reinhold is an International Thomson Publishing company.
ITP logo is a trademark under license.

Printed in the United States of America.

Van Nostrand Reinhold
115 Fifth Avenue
New York, NY 10003

International Thomson Publishing
Berkshire House, 168-173
High Holborn, London WC1V 7AA
England

Thomas Nelson Australia
102 Dodds Street
South Melbourne 3205
Victoria, Australia

Nelson Canada
1120 Birchmount Road
Scarborough, Ontario
M1K 5G4, Canada

International Thomson Publishing GmbH
Königswinterer Straβe 418
53227 Bonn
Germany

International Thomson Publishing Asia
221 Henderson Building #05-10
Kim Tian Plaza
Singapore 0315

International Thomson Publishing Japan
Kyowa Building, 3F
2-2-1 Hirakawacho
Chiyoda-ku, Tokyo 102
Japan

ARCFF   16 15 14 13 12 11 10 9 8 7 6 5 4 3 2

Library of Congress Cataloging in Publication Data

Johnson, Paul-Alan.
    The theory of architecture : concepts, themes, and practices /
Paul-Alan Johnson.
        p.   cm.
    Includes bibliographical references and index.
    ISBN 0-442-01344-2
    1. Architecture—Philosophy.   I. Title.
NA2500.J65   1993
720'.1—dc20   93–21234
                                                     CIP

CONTENTS

FOREWORD

If this opus isn't the capstone to all architectural theory, past, present and most probably future, then I'll eat all five orders simultaneously. At once the most extraordinary compendium of historico-theoretical thinking from Vitruvius to (and beyond) Derrida; it is singular in its usefulness for culturists of all conceits: architects, historians, theorists alike will benefit from its encyclopedic breadth—but that's just the beginning.

It lays open once and for all the jargon-laden halls of architectural academe (as well as its arcane traces) for all to see (and, if they wish, to scrutinize). Its chapters delineate the several ways theory impinges on practice; define architecture from the position of contemporaneity; situate architects within the continuum of establishment; reveal mores and conceits; establishes ethical, hierarchical and authoritarian conditions in and about architecture; and finally present conceptual, relational, and expressionistic modes of the building discipline! And as if that weren't enough to whet the palate, each and every one of these presentations is interrelated, elaborated, validated (through monumental footnoting) and interpreted. It is a tome of intimidatingly gargantuan proportions, and it is worth it all!

Dr. Johnson has done what no other architecturally inclined theorist has ever dared; he has simultaneously presented architecture *and* its theoretical underpinnings as both intrinsic *and* extrinsic, and as such establishes architecture's frightening dialectical dilemma. By being committed at once to "reflecting the epoch" as well as "showing a better way," architecture is a discipline in search of both itself and everything else. Its frustrations at these unresolvably quixotic quests are debated throughout this text by invoking the exegetical energies of the collective voices of its propogandists throughout time.

Whatever baggage one brings to this reading, one discovers that architecture's complexities are far beyond what one imagines. Admittedly, none of this would have been possible before the literary phenomenon of Deconstruction, but this mammoth text is necessary if we are to try to "Put Humpty-Dumpty back together again," for there is an innate optimism evident in each of its parts, as well as the whole; appropriately enough, since architecture *is* the constructive art.

In many ways *The Theory of Architecture* is a modest title, for the not-so-subtle subtext is that theory and architecture interrelate; this is really the definitive work of architecture (of which theory is its decoded, naked significant other). This is a "how to" book, every bit as much as it is a "travel guide." The subject is at once the mind as well as the actualization of things. Separated for far too long, these ostensibly polar opposites are inextricably intertwined in this work, once and for all establishing architecture's process and product as ineluctable.

The Siamese connection that reconnects the mind and the hand is what reduces this otherwise overwhelming work to a kind of thrilling believability; it is finally reassuring to have "proof positive" that architecture and theory are inextricably linked and to know that those who don't position themselves from that cojoined viewpoint operate partially.

Stanley Tigerman
1994

ACKNOWLEDGEMENTS

This book would not have been possible without the support and encouragement of a number of people. Foremost among them is Jon Lang, my colleague at the University of New South Wales. Jon saw the potential in my lecture notes and encouraged me to expand them into a book. My debt and gratitude to Jon for his professional advice and for keeping me on the mark as the work proceeded are immeasurable.

I especially appreciate the support of Stanley Tigerman who has written the very generous foreword. His enthusiasm for the idea and his complimentary remarks on the rough draft upon our first meeting confirmed the direction of the book at a vital stage.

I took leave from teaching in the second half of 1991 to prepare a first draft; in early 1992 I visited a number of schools of architecture across North America to speak with design and theory teachers. My thanks goes to all those I met during that visit for their friendliness and willingness to share their time, thoughts, and hospitality. I especially want to thank the following architectural academics for their advice: George Terrien at Boston Architecture Center; Gary Brown, Clare Cooper-Marcus, Roger Montgomery, and Ralf Weber at University of California, Berkeley; Sam Aroni, Eugene Kupper, Jurg Lang, George Stiny, and Richard Weinstein at University College Los Angeles; Richard Becherer, David Lewis, and Agus Rusli at Carnegie Mellon University; Jay Chatterjee, Dan Friedman, David Gosling, Brenda Lightner, Wolfgang Preiser, David Sale, Gordon Simmons, and Barry Stedman at the University of Cincinnati; Kenneth Frampton, Steven Holl, and Mary McLeod at Columbia University; K. Michael Hays, Gerald McCue, Bill Mitchell, Peter Rowe, and Mack Scogin at Harvard University; Stanley Tigerman and Catherine Ingraham at the University of Illinois at Chicago; Stanford Anderson, John de Monchaux, and Roy Landau at Massachusetts Institute of Technology; Urs Gauchat, Michael Mostoller, Tony Schuman, and Leslie Weisman at New Jersey Institute of Technology; David de Long, Marco Frascari, and David Leatherbarrow at the University of Pennsylvania; Ralph Lerner, Robert Maxwell, Francisco Sanin, and Georges Teyssot at Princeton University; Marc Angelil, Dana Cuff, Robert Harris, and James Steele at the University of Southern California; and Frances Downing, Dan MacGilvray, Malcolm Quantrill, Andrew Seidel, Alan Stacell, Walter Wendler, and David Woodcock at Texas A & M University.

For their collegiality and spirited discussions while I was a visiting scholar during 1991 at the Key Centre of Design Quality, University of Sydney, I would like to thank Keith Billings, Richard Coyne, John Gero, John Lansdown, Marylou Maher, Sid Newton, Michael Rosenman, Fay Sudweeks, and the graduate students.

To my friends and colleagues at the University of New South Wales who have contributed directly and indirectly to my understanding through innumerable discussions about architecture and the theoretical concepts that abound in the discipline, I extend my sincerest gratitude. I wish especially to thank John Cooke, John Gamble, Bruce Judd, Peter Kohane, L. Peter Kollar, Desley Luscombe, and particularly the late Richard Apperly. To the Head of School, John Ballinger, goes my gratitude both for making the school's resources available unstintingly and for freeing me from corporate duties to allow the most efficient use of my time for writing between teaching commitments. It goes without saying that I have also been challenged to order my thoughts about architecture by the countless students who have both provoked argument and endured my preoccupations over many years.

To my editors at Van Nostrand Reinhold, Wendy Lochner, Sherrel Farnsworth, and Elizabeth Gehrman, and to Kelly Francis, I offer my heartfelt appreciation for a thoroughly professional relationship.

While the clarity of mind and extensive knowledge of all these people has assisted me beyond measure, I would not want them to feel in any way accountable for any misinterpretations, lack of understanding, wayward opinions, or errors in the book; for these I alone must bear both the responsibility and the consequence.

Finally, my beleaguered family. To my parents Val and Ron, love and thanks for support and encouragement through years of study. To my son Lorne, thank you for your love and caring despite my being a distracted father. And to my dear wife Susan, I owe you so much for understanding, support, and criticism during many years of being driven completely around the twist by my demands on time and family—thank you for your love, humor, insight, and faith.

PREFACE

"Hey there, lusty one," said the oxen, "what recklessness led you to spurn the grassy bank and make for that steep and thoroughly inaccessible path? Don't you know that it is better to fill yourself on sweet succulent grass than to crave rough stubble and the bitter fruit of the wild fig tree? Not least of all, you should take care that you don't learn to regret such precarious travel on the cliff's edge." **Leon Battista Alberti.** Quoted in Jarzombek (1989):101-102.

The Plight Facing Architects After the Demise of Modernism

During the late 1960s and early 1970s the last and most serious criticisms of the ideology of modernism began to emerge as buildings, many of them regarded as icons of modernism, showed serious flaws in their fabric, their environment, their performance, and their appeal. But the flaws were deeper and of longer standing than their physical manifestation. What was becoming clear was that the social agenda of modernism was flawed also, or rather that the relation between that agenda and its physical embodiment was fundamentally misguided, especially in the crucial area of public housing. It was not a matter of getting the right 'mix' of age groups and placing them in distinctive family or aged persons' building types on housing estates in order to achieve harmony. It was not a matter of providing deck housing with easy shopping access and convenient child minding at appropriate levels as English architects Alison and Peter Smithson did at Sheffield or James Stirling did at Milton Keynes. People were not enthralled with the social collectives of Le Corbusier, his *Unité d'Habitation* as a modern *phalanstère,* a liner in the landscape, bettered only by the montage images of Archigram, and by the normal suburban housing estate. The experiment was over, although the laboratory remained.

It was not the attack on the buildings that was unsettling so much as the questioning of the assumptions underlying them. There were three primary assumptions: that a building was an expression of its function; that exposing the structure or using materials in their brute state was an 'honest' esthetic; and that architecture and social engineering went hand in hand to better future lifestyle and reform degenerating cities. It came as both a shock and an affront when architects heard murmurings that these hallowed values were not believed, that people actually disliked much of the work in which architects had made such psychical investment. Instead of being praised for their clever manipulation of numbers and ingenious mass production, architects were severely criticized. Most damning were accusations that they were forgetting people. The daily press focused on the lack of joy and individuality in many modern buildings, on the dispiriting repetition of dwelling units both on the ground and as 'human filing cabinets' in the sky, and on the dreary esthetic of office buildings in the central business districts of major cities.

The modernist experiment did not produce the didactic exemplars architects intended for the spiritual and esthetic guidance of people. Rather than being appreciated for their simplification of complexities or applauded for their valiant attempts at social reconstruction or for their inventive building techniques, architects were simply dismissed. No tangible improvement in public taste or appreciation followed from their esthetic reforms. Despite there being many good modern buildings and many architects sensitive to people's needs and wants, disillusionment set in. The absence of a fail-safe design canon meant that the same kinds of buildings continued to be built but were dressed up to make them *seem* less joyless, less unconcerned, less uniform. The shift to postmodernism was underway, energized by a nervous individualism that placed heavy demands on years of mediocrity and on an incipient monumentalism based in a bereft classicism or grossly distorted *bibelots*. As a stylistic undertaker, postmodernism resurrected the hoary arguments about decoration and crime. Many architects educated under modernist dictums took umbrage or preferred to remain *in vacuo* for reasons of comfort and defense, because to now agree that embellishment was acceptable or, worse, to be obliged to admit that there might have been a decorative component in modern architecture all along, would have been to admit they had been gullible participants in a giant deceit. The laboratory was back in business.

The proliferation of architectural publications in the past twenty years has fueled an intensely competitive drive among architects to keep abreast, if not stay ahead, of the kaleidoscopic range of work now being undertaken throughout the world. This explosion of exposure has made it almost impossible to comprehend which of the many forces at play are worthy of attention, let alone emulation. Individuals adrift in this fermenting sea turn to their education, to professional awards, to known adjudicators and critics, and ultimately to their own predilections in order to cope. And what do they find — a lack of coherence among the critics, some arguing for traditional values, continuity and conservatism, others appearing to be wantonly provocative, idiosyncratic and obscure, the very same polarity as prevailed when modernism began its conquest of architectural thought earlier in the twentieth century. Yet there seems to be a difference, perhaps because insights become more acute in the midst of change; as familiar things slip away, what takes their place seems alien yet tame, threatening with every new idea yet comforting because it lacks the drive and reformist verve once thought imperative. Nowhere is this more evident than in the impenetrability of some of the ideas being written about and talked over in relation to each new invention by a current starlet, yet relieved by the insouciance of the greater mass of everyday architectural invention.

Although it seemed for a while that 'anything goes', it has turned out, as it always does, that only an intrepid few and some inexperienced young are making new strides. The rest are content to stand still or prefer to side with the reactionary views of Charles, Prince of Wales (1989), or with the rising influence of oil-rich traditional societies seeking emblems of their power, or with strategically placed Third-World cultures whose traditional architectural values still provide a tantalizing drawcard to commercial success. Architects are slowly settling in to having to rethink not only the ideas and values painfully acquired over five generations but also new value systems created over less than one. Just when a new creed seems set it is attacked by critics for not delivering what it promises or for being too shallow. So far this period of interrogation and criticism has offered nothing as all-encompassing and as embracing of the everyday house-architect, as modernist dogma. The sleepwalkers lament.

However, debate is more alive than it ever was and it seems to matter more and work better in the confluence, in the moment of encounter. Then it evaporates—it does not endure. This book tries to capture some of these ephemera and place them in relation to more enduring concerns of architecture.

Recent Works on Architectural Theory

There are remarkably few books on architectural theory that present a comprehensive view of the field and none that review its concepts, themes, and practices in the manner of a compendium as this book does. One that attempts to present theoretical issues in a semi-encyclopedic way is a rewritten dissertation by Necdet Teymur, *Environmental Discourse* (1982), and, despite it being in many respects an obfuscating and frustrating work, material is here to be had if you grapple with idiosyncrasies of the index. The comprehensive range of Teymur's book is symptomatic of the problem of arranging a topic in a way that covers the ground, facilitates dissemination, enables a reader to assimilate material cogently, yet does not structure it so that it appears as a coherent body of knowledge—which architectural theory, or in this case environmental discourse, is not. Another by Pierre von Meiss, *Elements of Architecture: From Form to Place* (1986), arrays 'generic themes of composition' around the themes of order and disorder, measure and balance, fabric and object. It discusses 'architectural principles' teased out from the author's own experiences and practice and reapplied in a phenomenological study of space- and place-related urban issues, although it does not interrogate these principles or issues to any substantial extent.

Anthony Antoniades, in *Architecture and Allied Design: An Environmental Design Perspective* (1986) and *Poetics of Architecture: Theory of Design* (1990), presents a wide range of ideas on architecture by making them into a personal journey. As a teacher he imbues his writing with a didactic tone and a sense of authority that relies on the reader's acceptance of his credentials rather than a deep interrogation of the issues. On the other hand, Peter Rowe's *Design Thinking* (1987) offers a range of insights into many theories of topical and recurring concern, if at times leaving issues begging for further explanation. Jon Lang's *Creating Architectural Theory* (1987) is one of the few books that has attempted to structure behavioral science material in an ordered and instructive way, wherever possible questioning concepts to distill from them any utility. Sketch-texts such as *Architecture: Form, Space and Order* by Francis D. K. Ching (1979) are informative and popular with students but are rudimentary in their theory because material is simply and graphically presented with only minor elaboration or evaluation of the content of ideas.

Chronicles like those of Geoffrey Broadbent (1973), Charles Jencks (1971, 1973, 1977, 1980, 1982), Joseph Rykwert (1982), Alan Colquhoun (1986, 1989), William Mitchell (1990), or Colin Rowe (1976) thematize certain of their historical or technical material into theoretical frames that, while they are learned, absorbing, and illuminating as pieces, are not always comprehensive in their coverage of theoretical issues. They reflect the personal research and professional interests of their authors rather than a wider agenda, and are extremely valuable for that.

From these books one must then either explore discrete subject areas inside architecture (or more fashionably nowadays, outside), absorb manifestos or biographies on individual architects and their works, or make a dramatic leap into the ephemera of compilations, often from conferences or workshops, in search of snippets that might be relevant to one's individual agenda, in the hope that somehow, some way, some day, it will all come together as a meaningful brew. Among the many compilations, Marco Diani and Catherine Ingraham's "Restructuring Architectural Theory" (1988) and John Whiteman, Jeffrey Kipnis, and Richard Burdett's *Strategies in Architectural Thinking* are representative of the new breed of theoretical exploration tapping a wide range of literature, much of it from disciplines other than architecture.

A Moment of Reflection

Few of the writers above mention the difficulties they might have with the concept of theory governing architecture, either because they believe it does, or because they have adopted a softer view of theory than does Stanley Fish in *Doing What Comes Naturally*

(1989). I find Fish's ideas refreshing, and his proffering of theory as politicizing 'theory-talk' in literary and legal studies strikes a chord in relation to architectural theorizing, so much so that I was tempted to call this book *The Theory-Talk of Architecture.* While Fish's 'theory-talk' is provocative and challenging, to have called the book that would have required me to sustain the pejorative and somewhat Orwellian flavor of 'theory-talk' throughout, emphasizing the negative in many concepts and no doubt thereby making the book a somewhat depressing read.

A less dramatic title contemplated was *The Rhetoric of Architecture,* rhetoric at least holding the promise that while there is talk there might well be action consequent upon it. But this too carries conceptual baggage that would need to be unpacked to rid it of those angles of interpretation prevalent in literary studies or, more particularly, in pictorial studies such as Jencks's eighty-page ramble in *Late-Modern Architecture* (1980). But this would have amounted to a critique of Jencks and deflected my intention to write a broad-based compendium.

On another occasion I entertained the title *The Shadow of Architecture,* partly in deference to Vitruvius's admonition that "those [architects] who relied only upon theories and scholarship were obviously hunting the shadow, not the substance" (1960:1.1.2) and partly to T. S. Eliot, who wrote in *"The Hollow Men":*

> Between the idea
> And the reality
> Between the motion
> And the act
> Falls the Shadow

This appeals to me as a neat way of placing theory in relation to architecture without giving it a generative role.

In the end I settled on *The Theory of Architecture* because there is still much that is positive in the wide-ranging literature coming under that rubric and because from the seemingly solid ground of established theory it is possible to probe its crevices and margins gradually, without immediately threatening the whole field with a subversive title. While 'theory' as a generic term will be used unemphasized throughout the book, it should be in quotation marks whenever it is encountered and considered as 'design-talk' in light of the qualifications and concerns being outlined here.

The Underlying Agenda

Lurking beneath almost any writing or pronouncements on architecture, especially those aspiring to theory, is frequently a quest for some overarching construct of the world that will guide and be reflected in architecture. Behind every aphorism, maxim, and dictum, if not every rule of thumb, is some nascent Grand Theory. One of the ubiquitous qualities in such a quest is the belief that socially, politically, and culturally, architecture makes, has made, or will make a difference. Once formulated, the Grand Theory will align architects with inexorable universal forces and make them fit to govern their newly founded world by design, as Platonic philosopher-kings. The sheer audacity of this claim by the foundation modernists and by those who still subscribe to the modernist agenda today is both breathtaking and inspiring. The Grand Theory is of course misguided.

No such claim is made here, though inevitably there is an agenda: to reduce architectural notions to the point of a minimal or bare, if not essential, conception of them. What might be achieved by this? Subjecting architectural concepts, themes, and practices to close scrutiny empowers those who are attempting to comprehend them over and against those who profess to be already 'in-the-know'. This is typically an educative agenda, one that attempts to explicate notions in a straightforward way to facilitate the assembly of a working knowledge. In espousing this agenda I am conscious of the temptation toward some brighter architectural future in which more are informed and fewer are deceived by rhetoric. I suppose the book might therefore be seen by some as anti-foundationalist and that certain of its stances presume some 'theory hope', to use Stanley Fish's term for the push toward some revisionist or newly grounded ideas. My saying that this is not my intention may not be enough to preclude me from either falling into that trap or being accused of it. Nevertheless, this is not my intention.

I have had and continue to have concerns that too much is taken for granted or is presumptuous or pompous in architectural writing and theorizing; the demystification of writing and theorizing remains an active agenda in my own teaching and is no doubt influential both in my choice of matters addressed and in their explication. It is for others—students of architecture and design in particular—to decide whether my agenda is close to theirs or what to do with the outcome. I offer no reconciliation for anything I perceive as fallacious or misdirected, or for matters that are ignored or are left untouched, or that remain somewhat disheveled as a result of my tinkering.

My stance and technique are quite simple. I have selected notions that I think need to be or can be examined, and briefly analyzed them to show their intentions, contradictions, and inconsistencies. Of themselves these qualities are not problematic. Merely to show that they exist makes it impossible for such notions to continue untainted by doubts. Just which notions I select to interrogate is a matter of personal preference, and I run the gauntlet of having my selections and my comments considered trivial or important, consequential or pedantic, current or outmoded, depending on whether the critic holds equivalent or opposing opinions. I care little about this risk, trusting a judgment built up through teaching over many years and through the discourse I have encountered in doing so, knowing that others undoubtedly share some of my frustrations and may enjoy working through some of them with me. Almost any architect or designer with critical pretensions could assemble a similar book, engaging in their own way with the issues I raise or following other lines of thought entirely.

To say that I am 'deconstructing' such notions is portentous, privileged as the term is in current theorizing. 'Deflating' I find less charged. Yet, to the extent that certain oppositions exist in architectural thinking generally and deflating them reduces their potency, I am deconstructing in the way that Stanley Fish remarks of it: "One deconstructs an opposition not by reversing the hierarchy of its poles but by denying to either pole the independence that makes the opposition possible in the first place" (1989:211). I would like to think my deflations are affirmative of architecture rather than negative, derogatory, or nihilistic.

The Structure of This Book

The Theory of Architecture presents concepts, themes, and practices as they feature in architectural discourse using the model of a compendium or glossary but arranged in a conceptual order. It steers a path through the literature with the traditional and predictable notions on one side and the somewhat treacherous terrain of recent architectural writing on the other, the choice of route reflecting personal concerns accumulated over twenty years of teaching. In this respect it is not unlike the journeying of the chroniclers mentioned earlier; its themes and topics may seem idiosyncratic at times, though, I hope, nonetheless relevant. How to arrange the concepts for presentation in some logical and easily accessible form became an immediate and, as it turned out, continuing issue when I set about structuring the book, and prompted me to examine certain well-known if not all well-proven systems.

Aristotle's ten Categories, those classes into which he divided the objects of thought, was one of the earliest bases for systematizing knowledge and even today resonates with a range of architectural issues: Substance, Quantity, Quality (disposition, natural capacity, sensibility, and form/figure), Relation (connection by subject, by object, and by comparison), Action (immanent or transitive), Passion, Place, Time, Position, and Habit. Certainly the synonyms attaching to 'quality' are tantalizingly architectural, although there might be some difficulties in placing generalized statements about what architecture is into this system, unless it was assigned to 'passion'.

The Jansenist theologian Antoine Arnauld (1612–1694) criticized these categories when, in his 1662 *La Logique, ou l'Art de Penser,* he wrote, "To speak the truth, they are themselves of very little use; they help but slightly in the formation of judgment, the true end of logic. Indeed, they often hinder this formation considerably. . . . " Arnauld in his turn was to structure his book around only four topics: Conceiving, Judging, Reasoning, and Ordering. The *logic* was intended as 'useful' for humankind, hence its interest in human processes, the *-ings,* rather than in setting up abstract and detached categories.

Then there is the seven-fold Cartesian categorization of existence cited by Arnauld:

Mens, mensura, quies, motus, positura, figura
Sunt cum materia cunctarum exordi rerum.
Mind, measure, rest, motion, position, shape
Are with matter all the kinds of things (1662:44)

As with Aristotle, it is possible to utilize Arnauld's categories in classifying architectural concepts and themes if 'mind' is taken to include a notion like 'spirit', and if 'rest' is used for a notion like 'balance'. But his categories are perhaps too abstract to receive broad definitional or axiomatic statements about architecture.

Pollitt (1974) groups writers on art and artists in the ancient world into four: *compilers of tradition* like the encyclopedist Pliny and the antiquarian traveler Pausanias; *literary analogists,* who used analogies of the visual arts in their rhetoric and poetry; *moral estheticians* like Plato, Aristotle, and later philosophers; and *professional critics,* the artists, sculptors, and painters who wrote formal and technical treatises of whom Vitruvius is perhaps the best known. Pollitt also discerns four basic stances in art criticism allied with these: that of the professional artist concerning form and design; that of the moral and epistemological value of artistic experience by artist and public; that arising out of literary criticism and concerned with style; and that of the marvelous and magical qualities of art (1974:9–12). A similar structuring of architectural thought would be possible, especially since Pollitt suggests, while organizing the book's glossary alphabetically, a regrouping of terms under three divisions and sets of subheadings to facilitate access. His arrangement (114–115) shows how "architecture" can substitute for "art" or "painting":

A. The nature and methods of "architectural" representation
    1. General
    2. "Architecture"
B. The nature of the "architect"
    1. (His) perception and attitude
    2. Individual styles
    3. (His) technique and skill
    4. (His) reputation
C. The nature of the work of "architecture"
    1. Properties of form and composition
    2. Finish and detail
    3. Color and draftsmanship
    4. Subject matter
    5. General qualities of style
    6. Value and reputation of works of "architecture"

Not only are there similarities between the art-critical stances of the ancient world that Pollitt outlines and the critical writings on architecture over the past two or three centuries, but the categories he proposes for examining the terminology have some validity too. However, naturally enough, there is still an "art-like" ring about his structuring.

Finally, there are literary thesauruses, such as *Roget's,* in which words are arranged according to the ideas they embrace. By the Third Edition of *Roget's* in 1962, words were organized under 1,040 'categories' grouped under various subclasses within eight major 'classes': Abstract Relations, Space, Physics, Matter, Sensation, Intellect, Volition, and Affections. Careful perusal of these elicited certain groupings useful to the architectural approach being envisaged.

Out of these investigations emerged ten headings that sufficiently covered the range of theoretical concepts, themes, and practices used in architectural discourse and literature: Identification, Definition, Power, Attitudes, Ethics, Order, Authority, Governance, Relationship, and Expression. In the event, Identification splits between the introduction, where theory is clarified broadly, and chapter 1, which identifies specific issues of theory as a form of practice. Perusal of the contents gives an idea of the detailed structure, although it should be noted that the arrangement of chapters is no more essential to the order of reading the book than it has been to writing it; they could have been set out differently and not have materially affected the content.

Each chapter begins with an overview, which sets out certain contextual issues of the chapter theme. Each chapter has two parts broadly, but not always, separating general concepts from applied concepts, under which specific topics are gathered. To keep the book to a manageable length, most topics are dealt with in three to four pages, and all have the same format: quotations from texts around the concept or theme at the head of each topic; a "trace" giving the etymology of the key concept words (see chapter 2) of the topic and a brief history of architectural application; a commentary on the topic, raising key issues and airing certain conceptual difficulties, errors, or faults; and a cross-referenced listing of further sources not already referred to in the text or quotations. Full references are found in the bibliography except in the case of quotations for which a source is listed.

Major Sources of Reference

Meanings and etymologies are drawn principally from *The Shorter Oxford English Dictionary on Historical Principles* (1973; SOED) and *Chambers Twentieth Century Dictionary* (1972; CTCD) as well as several other standard dictionaries where further clarification was needed. Etymologies and meanings of key art-historical and architectural terms and their ancient Greek and Latin usage come from Pollitt (1974) and from Onians (1951). Latin roots and spellings have been crosschecked with Lewis (1891) and Greek spellings were checked with *Divry's New English-Greek and Greek-English Handy Dictionary* (1978). For ease of reading, Greek in etymologies has been Anglicized, even though this might lead to some inaccuracy or loss of precision.

A number of quotations come from *The Oxford Dictionary of Quotations* (1977) and *The Oxford Book of Aphorisms* (Cross 1987). Both *Collins Dictionary of Religious & Spiritual Quotations* (Parrinder 1990) and Knevitt (1986) have been invaluable in tracking down the sources of many quotations. I also must mention the limited edition by Kipnis (1990b), even though I have not drawn upon it here.

On the issue of the authority and status of etymology and on the whole idea of definition giving transparency to the meaning of words, there is much that might be said about the pointlessness of being too pedantic about the fixity and force of meanings. The preoccupation with etymologies, the seeking of a greater degree of certainty of meaning by knowing a word's derivation and subsequent history, is in many respects a traditional preoccupation, one always found in the writings of traditional science (Coomaraswamy 1977; Guènon 1958). It is also a formalist and foundationalist preoccupation, one that dogs the legal system and architectural theorizing. "Formalism ... is not merely a linguistic doctrine, but a doctrine that implies, in addition to a theory of language, a theory of the self, of community, of rationality, of practice, of politics. A formalist believes that words have clear meanings ..." (Fish 1989:6), consequent upon which are a string of attendant beliefs that Fish outlines with remarkable clarity. It goes without saying that word meanings vary with use, context, and culture; so, the etymologies herein are mainly intended to give some 'leverage' to the concepts, themes, and practices under discussion and to prompt some creative edge when dealing with them.

The overview to chapter 2, The Definition of Architecture, expands a little upon some of the conceptual difficulties of definition. For the moment it is worthwhile to quote from Jacques Derrida's *The Truth in Painting* (1987) about a course of instruction or seminars in art:

> ... Traditionally, a course begins by the semantic analysis of its title, of the word or concept which entitles it and which can legitimate its discourse only by receiving its own legitimation from that discourse. Thus one would begin by asking oneself: What is *art?* Then: where does it come from? What is the origin of art? This assumes that we reach agreement about what we understand by the word *art.* Hence: What is the origin of the meaning of "art"? For these questions, the *guiding thread* ... will *always* have been the existence of "works," of "works of art."
>
> This protocol of the question installs us in a fundamental presupposition, and massively predetermines the system and combinatory possibilities of answers. What it begins by implying is that art—the word, the concept, the thing—has a unity and, what is more, an originary meaning, an *etymon,* a truth that is *one* and *naked* ..., and that it would be sufficient to unveil it

through history. It implies first of all that "art" can be reached following the three ways of word, concept, and thing, or again of signifier, signified, and referent, or even by some opposition between presence and representation. (Derrida 1987:20).

A course of instruction on the 'theory of architecture' might start in the same way: with a semantic analysis of its title, of the words 'theory' and 'architecture'. We might ask: What is theory? What is architecture? Where do these come from? What are their origins? The guiding thread might be works of theory and works of architecture and works of theory of architecture. The protocol of such questions would imply that the word, concept, thing, has a unity and that an *etymon* might give the clue to its internality. This is the view adopted here, but it is qualified in the sense that Georges Bataille's project was to loosen rather than tighten the grip of architecture. The following quotation comes from Denis Hollier's "Introduction: Bloody Sundays" in *Against Architecture: The Writings of Georges Bataille:*

> There is something anachronistic in associating Bataille, a writer who died even before people started to talk about structuralism, with poststructuralism. The connection, however, is justified if one recalls how insistently throughout the sixties etymology was called upon to make a connection—via the Latin verb *struere,* construct—between structuralist inspiration and architecture. The student uprising of May 1968 has often been described as a revolt against the structuralist establishment. There is a desire to loosen the symbolic authority of architectures in poststructuralism, and in retrospect it is possible to see Bataille as the precursor of this critical view of architecture. (Hollier 1989:ix).

When I began to write this book, certain questions kept recurring about the relevance and authority of each concept under discussion, especially about how it should be presented. I have considered the concepts as a textual equivalent of the neurologist's homunculus; concepts, themes, and practices to be placed in the conceptual space, rather than in the physiognomy of the brain, of an architectural innocent, a robotic *tabula rasa* awaiting programming. The name of this naïf is obviously *Disse,* prompted by dissemination, and its initial questions, like those of many students, might be: "Who am I? What are my beliefs about fundamental issues of architecture? What are my own capabilities? To whom do I owe my allegiances? What bearing do the world views I hold have on what I think, say, and do? Where do I see the world, architecture, myself, as having been or now heading? Where am I now in my architectural understanding? What do I see as important in architecture? What do I see as relevant to the situation with which I am confronted? What stance am I to take concerning this situation? How am I to apply myself to the task at hand? What do I intend my involvement in this situation to achieve? By what means and within which restrictions will I undertake this task?"

Despite or perhaps because of trying to keep these issues conceptually in a first-person focus—I, the 'thinking subject', try to grapple with it, the 'thought object', with a view to some kind of reconciliation or arbitration that will benefit me and others as well as the task at hand. The subject-object paradox emerges in the first utterance, even though for the most part the first person appears in the text only in occasional anecdotes. One of the book's premises is that this paradox is inevitable; I am so fully embedded in the world of my contemplation that I cannot separate myself from it even with the most impersonal mode of writing, just as you cannot remove yourself from your embeddedness when reading this. For that insight alone Stanley Fish is refreshing reading; he says it time and again, and it cannot be said too often in relation to architecture.

This book is intended as text for use in theory courses and seminars at all levels of architectural and design teaching, particularly in vocational degree courses. It is also intended as a reference for architects, designers, and academics who, like me, did not study Ancient Greek or Latin during their formal education, or who, because modern Greek, Italian, German, or French are not their first language, find reading many theoretical texts a stumble through the learnedness of the authors via passages quoted in the original.

For this reason *The Theory of Architecture* depends, unashamedly, upon English-language sources and relies on English translations of ancient or foreign-language architectural texts. This dependence has partly meant using readily accessible works, favoring books over journals because they endure and because they offer either greater elaboration of a theme or the opposite—a more succinct summary of the literature. It is also my experience that journal articles are notoriously difficult to find, especially in the less accessible journals outside the country of origin, and that certain of the more popular journals frequently disappear from collections or deteriorate from overuse, thereby making them totally inaccessible (of necessity, some journal articles have been used, but sparingly). Recent translations of standard texts are given preference wherever possible (for example, Rykwert, Leach, and Tavernor's 1991 translation of Alberti), although no concept or theme examined here is so critical that it depends entirely on such scholarly works, no matter how intriguing these newer and closer readings of standard or obscure texts might be.

It has been impossible to read and to keep in mind what some might see as 'key' writings among journal articles pertaining to a topic. Therefore, book references have been sought as the most efficient way to gain access to detailed arguments, leaving it to readers to track down specific references from bibliographies and footnotes and to supplement these entries with further references of their own. In fact, this book should be used precisely that way, as a pointer to the literature; it does not attempt to be the definitive work. It does, however, attempt to present in a straightforward manner certain ideas raised by some difficult English-language works that are in many cases based on the even more impenetrable works of French or German philosophers of the last generation or two. I am keen to receive comment and supplementary references from readers that might assist in future revisions.

Quotations inhabit these pages just as they have occupied niches in the minds of architects and designers for generations. Their truth-seemings collectively form a collage of architectural themes and concepts that to all intents constitute architectural theory. The occasional maverick among them is a sign of the rising oppositions in architecture today and of the skirmishes occurring in the landscape of ideas. For most architects, mental niches are safe havens lined with traditions and orthodoxies. It is just such coziness that the itinerant theoretical marauder believes needs to be disturbed, and to that end leads the odd raiding party to upset. Consequently, some may see a contradiction and a potential criticism in the book adopting what appears to be a rigid structure of bringing meanings under some sort of systematic scrutiny, a not-so-latent positivistic and rationalist agenda. But, be assured, marauding is the text's main intention.

Any rigidities or contradictions are already in the discourse and literature; they inhabit the quotations and aphorisms as the subtext, and surface frequently throughout the main text. In some ways, just reading the quotations will show that they drag their traces with them without needing to be formally structured; all the reader need do (and probably will do) is wander about the pages, resting at random. Considering the way the book is likely to be read—piecemeal rather than straight through—the book's architectonics should be a help rather than a problem; the reader's mental niches will, as always, fill with fragments in random clusters anyway.

Paul-Alan Johnson
Sydney, 1994.

INTRODUCTION

What Is Theory in Any Discipline?

An architect does not arrive at his finished product solely by a sequence of rationalizations, like a scientist, or through the workings of the *Zeitgeist*. Nor does he reach them by uninhibited intuition, like a musician or a painter. He thinks of forms intuitively, and then tries to justify them rationally; a dialectical process governed by what we may call his theory of architecture, which can only be studied in philosophical and ethical terms. **Peter Collins.** 1965:16.

Discussing intellectuals and power with Deleuze in 1972, Foucault declared that the masses don't need intellectuals to know. Therefore, the role of the intellectual is no longer to provide theory for the enlightenment of the masses; and the role of theory, in turn, changes: it is no longer a striving to attain consciousness but simply a struggle "for undermining and capturing authority." Theory is not like a pair of glasses; it is rather like a pair of guns; it does not enable one to see better but to fight better. **José G. Merquior.** 1985:85.

When we affirm a theory, we also propose its logical implications . . . all those statements that follow from it—as well as those further implications which result from combining this theory with other theories which we also propose or assume. But this means that the informative content of any theory includes an infinity of unforeseeable nontrivial statements; it also makes clear that the content of an idea is far from identical with some particular person's thoughts about it. For there are infinitely many situations, themselves infinitely varied, to which the theory may be applicable. Yet many of these situations have not only not even been imagined at the time the theory is proposed; they are also, literally, *unimaginable* at that time, in terms of the information then available. **William W. Bartley III.** 1973:178–179.

For me theory is the understanding of the use and meaning of objects, their idiosyncrasies, characteristics and effects. **Rob Krier.** 1988:8.

Polemic is propaganda or advocacy: the attempt to justify or discredit one or another style, or way of doing things, with whatever tools come to hand, from invective to argument. Theory seeks to discover by critical inquiry what actually happens, to show how things work. Polemic is interested, in the sense that it promotes certain interests; theory is disinterested and does not seek to persuade people to do this or that, though in the course of showing how things work it will certainly show that certain ways of doing things *do not* work, do not actually happen or do not produce the results which they are claimed to produce. Architects have difficulty in distinguishing polemic from theory. **Tom Heath.** 1991:18.

. . . the theory of any branch of knowledge is simply the critical assessment of it *as* a branch of *knowledge.* What is pertinent to that assessment may depend in part on the kind of knowledge it is, or claims to be: on whether, for example, it is supposedly *a priori* knowledge, like mathematics and logic, or is empirical knowledge, like any of the natural sciences. But for the rest and mainly, it will be the same general type of examination which is called for in any theory-of, and directed to the same kind of question: the certification of this branch of learning as a valid cognitive procedure, capable of yielding cognitively valid results. **Clarence I. Lewis.** 1969:17–18.

Before answering the question, what is theory in any discipline? it is necessary to clarify what a 'discipline' is. Resort to a dictionary begins with the archaic definition "instruction imparted to disciples or scholars; teaching; learning; education" from the Latin *discere,* to learn, and proceeds to tell us that it is "a branch of instruction; a department of knowledge" and, unrewardingly, "the training of scholars and subordinates to proper conduct and action by instructing them and exercising them in the same; mental and moral training." Variations follow relating to military or religious instruction or control and penal correction. Common to all these meanings is the notion of constraint, boundedness, limitation, and restriction. This constraint shows itself in one of two ways. The first is the way in which knowledge is passed on—a 'disciple' or 'follower' is someone already tied to a person (a leader), group (a school), or particular view. The second type of constraint is the mental or moral precepts by which such knowledge is acquired—they do not digress, do not deviate, are kept within bounds, kept on 'the straight and narrow path', focused, and so forth. Constraint enables continuation and advancement. So, a discipline participates in the *alignment* of ideas and knowledge, and various combinations of alignments form the separate disciplines. What determines and maintains any alignment, what gives it its singularity and delimits its boundaries, what assists in adjudicating its decisions, is its *theory.*

The grounds or foundations of any branch of knowledge or discipline can be studied apart from the branch or discipline itself. The way Lewis (1969) considers the foundations of ethics as answering the question, "How do you know that what this principle dictates is imperative to do?" is equally applicable to architecture in that the principles and axioms that supposedly inform architecture may be subjected to the same interrogation—how do we know that what any architectural principle dictates is imperative to do? There is little to argue with about Lewis's statement that a correlative metastudy of any discipline that questions the grounds or validity of that discipline is a 'theory of' or a 'philosophy of' whatever the discipline might be. However, there will be those who would disagree when he also says that such questions do not belong to the discipline itself and cannot use its methods or appeal to findings from the discipline to support any answers. Instead, he maintains, "one must appeal to critical reflection, and if there is any branch of study which might be pertinent to such critical investigations . . . it would be logic and epistemology" (17). It seems then that any 'theory of' or 'philosophy of' architecture is similarly situated — any questions it prompts do not belong to architecture, and architectural methods or findings cannot be utilized for its support. Like its cousins, architectural theory is critical reflection and belongs in the realm of logic and epistemology.

In its Latin and earlier Greek usage, *theory* originally involved the idea of a spectator contemplating an event. While this notion of theory is now obsolete, the stance of the theorist as a spectator still infects the idea of theory in the sense of it being a way of viewing or construing matters as if from outside or beyond a discipline or set of practices. Close examination of the use of the word over two centuries shows that it has run the full gamut of notions, from the principial to the idiosyncratic (see chapter 1). In its looser sense, as (mere) hypothesis — a supposition made as a basis for reasoning, without assumption of its truth — or as starting-point for further investigation from known facts, theory aligns with Jon Lang's view that "Successful theories consist of simple but powerful generalizations about the world and how it operates that enable us to predict accurately future operations. . . . A theory cannot be proved. It stands until it is disproved. . . . Theory must address issues of practice. . . . If theory does not do this, it is irrelevant" (Lang 1987:14–15). The notion of theory as power over the world and its generalizing practice is not universally agreed on, though, and neither is it clear just how the connection with practice works, although it is thought to be a disciplining relationship.

One thrust of the philosopher Michel Foucault's *Discipline and Punish: the Birth of the Prison* (1977a) is that discipline has four co-requisites: spatial distribution, usually by segregation; control of activity, usually through the imposition of routines; exercise, mainly physical and occasionally mental; and strategy, the tactical manipulation and ordering of people (Merquior 1985). There is a close parallel here with architecture as a discipline and the acquisition of its skills and norms through education and training; and, since theory is the mark of discipline, as I later discuss, one manifestation of its power is its attempt to control practice or production. Thus, just as "The web of discipline aims at generalizing the *homo docilis* required by 'rational', efficient, 'technical' society: an obedient, hardworking, conscience-ridden, useful creature, pliable to all modern tactics of production and warfare" (Merquior 1985:94), so theory may be seen as domesticating an area of knowledge and, by normalizing its exponents, producing 'useful creatures' whose performance is mediated by certain punishments ingrained during education and carried on in professional life.

With a characteristic inversion, Foucault has remarked that theory "does not express, translate, or serve to apply practice: it is practice. But it is local and regional . . . not totalizing . . . It is not to 'awaken consciousness' that we struggle . . . but to sap power . . . it is an activity conducted alongside those who struggle for power, and not their illumination from a safe distance" (from *Language, Counter-Memory, Practice*, cited in Boyne 1990:132).

On the other hand, Lewis's definition of theory as critical assessment of a branch of knowledge *as such* does not admit any instrumental aspect for theory, only that it is to do with procedures of thinking and argumentation; with imperatives of direction, and not with the direction itself.

Paradoxically, while theory construed as if one were a spectator or onlooker may now be unacceptable, thinking about theory in this way is still common among critics, if not among theorists, and among those who look to critics and theorists to place theory or themselves "outside" whatever is being examined. In the most obvious case, people try to unravel the so-called language of a designer embedded 'in' a work from a position assumed as 'outside' it such that they might, in reading it, get 'inside' the work the better to understand it. The more private a language appears to be, the more intense they become at wanting to know. They seek meanings or messages from all kinds of stances where there might not be any, in an attempt not to be left in the cold, and they do so without realizing that the whole issue of the opposition of intrinsic and extrinsic is problematic.

The trouble with this kind of mind-wrenching is, as Stanley Fish repeatedly cautions in his collection of essays *Doing What Comes Naturally* (1991), that our very embeddedness in any context prevents us from ever being outside it or being able to construe matters *as if* we might be. We are therefore faced with trying to pursue theory (of communication, in this case) when its meaning is not at all transparent, which is beyond definition by any virtue of what it enables, if it enables at all, and which defies clarification because we cannot detach ourselves sufficiently from it to be able to talk 'objectively' about it. And yet, common sense tells us that theory exists and is utilized by architects, apparently to practical ends. Any meaning of theory we choose to adopt is fraught with this errant variability and frustrating elusiveness.

How Architectural Theory Sits in the World of Theorizing

The core of theory as philosophy is the recognition (or not) that there are conjoint worlds, the central debate of philosophy being over the dialogue between them. One is the external world, 'out there', the *cause celebre* of science, the world of thing-objects in Husserl's terms, assumed as given and potentially knowable. The other is the hypothetical or internal world of our thoughts, imaginings, and interpretations, the world of psychology. The internal world houses our conceptions of the external, molded by notions handed down or across generations persuading and convincing; it is the realm of our rehearsals, associations, ideals, expectations, and hopes for it, a world of no-things—just as 'things' are positive and tangible, it is suggested there is a positive world of 'no-things' (or 'nonthings')—potentials and possibilities—rather than mere negative connotation of 'nothings'. For idealist philosophers like Berkeley, Kant, and Hegel, and for certain philosophies such as the Buddhist Madhyamaka and Vijnanavada, the internal world is all there is and need be.

Architectural theory inhabits this internal world constituted by our assumptions, concepts, ideas, attitudes, intentions, history, and creations. It is a world that in many respects appears dualist in the mind/body connections it makes, but is monist because it is knowable only by our constructs of it and from our 'experience' of it. Unlike materialist or positivist philosophers who deny the metaphysical, architectural theorists tend to embrace the metaphysical in their explanations of creativity and in the mystique they assign to architectural exemplars. For example, creativity in design is traditionally likened to the First Act of Creation in its claims to primacy and in its esotericism. And, like science, architecture is one discipline that has had and continues to have its share of creationists espousing doctrines in which belief in God or a Supreme Being of some kind is a prerequisite to architectural wisdom. What Emanuel Swedenborg said of the philosopher is seen by architectural creationists to apply equally to the *true* theorist:

> For without the utmost devotion to the Supreme Being, no one can be a complete and truly learned philosopher. True philosophy and contempt of the Deity are two opposites. Veneration for the Infinite Being can never be separated from philosophy; for he who fancies himself wise, whilst his wisdom does not teach him to acknowledge a Divine and Infinite Being, that is, he who thinks he can possess any wisdom without a knowledge and veneration of the Deity, has not even a particle of wisdom. **Emanuel Swedenborg.** 1846. The Principia, volume 1:35.

The reason much architectural theory has the flavor of religious dogma is that those who write it do so with a proselytizing agenda. While direct theological inclinations and references abound in the writings of nineteenth-century theorists, notably John Ruskin, such inclinations are harder to find in later and recent theoretical works, even though the proselytizing remains. Unlike the unfettered Christian theology professed over a century ago, where faith was paraded and accepted for the essential role it was seen to play in architectural beliefs and doctrines, recent theoretical pieces mostly fail to admit any such agenda, while at the same time they utilize concepts that rely on faith or make sense only in a theological context. Also, recent architectural treatises have rarely admitted that their arguments are provisional. Instead, they proceed unquestioningly from assumptions whose precedence is as taken for granted as classical canons once were. Such writings make theoretical contributions to the 'intersubjectivity' of discourse where individuality is relished for its difference; but they frequently use terminology dependent upon long-held universalist premises on the assumption that theory, if it is to be theory, must be expounded in these terms.

For example, architect Louis Kahn's notion of letting a building or material 'be what it wants to be' proposes an immanence of form that depends on some *a priori* holism concerning that building or material—some predestination. Architect Frank Lloyd Wright's use of 'the nature of' materials or of a program as exemplifying something innate to the material or program was similar in its immanence. More recently, the 'turn to textuality' (Hays 1988) still relies on the idea of architecture as language, and issues challenges to interpreting meaning, if meaning is not actually conveyed in the old sense of *architecture parlante*, because it presumes that architecture is something that can be read for guidance or edification, as one might a sacred text through exegesis. Only occasionally may an architectural text be read for enjoyment. Through the mysticism, idealism, and narrative runs the string of rationalism. Though rationalism has undergone many shifts of emphasis since the Enlightenment, it is still opposed to empiricism. "The conflict between rationalism and empiricism is one between two concepts of knowledge (or science), that define it as *a priori* or *a posteriori*," writes Alan Colquhoun. "To the extent that knowledge is held to be *a priori*, empirical knowledge appears to be random, unfounded and subject to contingency. To the extent that knowledge is held to be *a posteriori*, the terms are reversed and it is *a priori* knowledge that becomes unsure and dependent on authority, received ideas, or habit. The history of architectural theory during the last two hundred years has been the history of conflict between these two concepts of architectural knowledge" (Colquhoun 1991:58).

A posteriori knowledge is empirical; it is based on how things are or were, and in architecture this knowledge is gained from experience, the consequences of which from my earlier exposition via Lewis, cannot be 'strictly' theoretical. Because *a priori* knowledge by definition does not require reference to experience for its understanding, 'strictly' speaking it and it alone is the province of theory. Returning to Colquhoun, "Innate ideas must be thought of as implanted by God, and, as such, they may be enshrined in a wisdom that has been revealed to mankind in the past and that constitutes valid authority."

Therefore, theory, 'strictly' speaking, is already and always about the mind and ways of God, despite there being those who will maintain that religious beliefs and architectural disposition are entirely separate affairs. What then of the atheist architect? How might a theory of architecture look that makes no reference to a tripartite (spirit-mind-body) view of man, has no need of a Prime Mover in its cosmology, and does not adopt terms that derive from or implicate theology?

Philosophically, belief in a Creator places the architect in a uniquely subservient position in relation to creation as a human act, and arguably makes design more difficult. Issues about the source of creativity and whether design is a manifestation of *a priori* forms become quite vexing for deeply religious students, and the conflicts are at times visible. For instance, a student of mine recently wrote that, as a Christian, design for him was both an act of witness and an act of supplication, which made him almost schizophrenic in attempting to celebrate his own creativity while maintaining humility in the face of it. While the opposite belief removes some of these dilemmas, it generates others; for example, the worth of seeking inspiration from nature or science as evidence of structures in the world useful to architecture. One is immediately confronted by the issue of whether the structure exists in nature before it is 'discerned' and thus orders its physical manifestation, or whether the structure is superimposed as our means of comprehending what exists.

Empiricists like Locke and Hume argued that our ideas and concepts can be known only from experience, while rationalists like Descartes and Leibniz argued for the innate and for the authority of eternal principles. Accepting this division, it is clear that most architects would say they have a foot in both worlds, with principles guiding action and experience confirming the rightness of such action and in turn the principles behind it—a rational and scientific approach. Treating design as a scientific problem though prompts a different kind of theory in Strasser's view, a theory that "would first of all have to *precede* the act of design. Secondly, it would have to lead directly to the act of building in much the same way that the purely intuitive process, regardless of its shortcomings, does generate an end product. In other words it would have to *generate* designs rather than just explain them. And thirdly, it would have to be *general* enough to permit its applicability to an endless variety of individual circumstances . . . it would have to be compatible and congruent with the freedom and creativity necessary to produce a work of *art*" (Strasser 1963:8).

It seems then you cannot have it both ways; theory supporting a rationalist approach to design would be quite different from theory supporting an empiricist approach. And for a theory of either persuasion to be sustained, it "must be able to withstand the objections which people from the most divergent everyday worlds of life may raise against it and, positively, it must be based on proofs possessing universal convincing force" (Strasser 1963:107). Consequently, you cannot remain neutral about *how* the worlds of discipline and practice meet, or merely argue that their reconciliation occurs in the mind of the architect because, 'strictly' speaking, they are irreconcilable. Theory becomes contradictory and meaningless when it is construed as a guide to future action, where the derivation and explication of innate ideas and of principles serves only to guide actions, the success or failure of which reconfirms the principles. Not the least difficulty is that if theory precedes designing yet is dependent on experience for its affirmation, neither theory nor designing can start. In this situation we are faced with the same philosophical dilemma as faced Plato with the Forms. Commonly known as the Third Man Argument, the dilemma arises because a Form and its manifestation need another Form to explain their relationship, and in turn another Form is needed to explain that relationship, and so on to infinite regress. The degree of 'strictness' with which we hold on to architectural theory as an instrumental artifice is but one dimension of the dilemma.

The Practical Application of Architectural Theory

There has long been the view that an imperative operates in architecture and that it induces some 'force' to action, or generates a 'presence' in works. One recent expression of this occurred at a conference sponsored by the Graham Foundation at Harvard Graduate School of Design in 1989, when architect Peter Eisenman reacted to critics of his work who believed they perceived a change in his built work which for them showed it no longer had 'a theoretical charge'. Eisenman challenged them "to go see any of my built work and say there is not a charge in them" (Hays and Burns 1990:131). Eisenman's 'charge' is one demonstration of the force permeating architecture; it impels him to action and it remains in his work after he has departed, just as it does in the work of other architects to greater or lesser degrees. A form of vitalism, this force has its soulmate in the belief that 'theory' is the channel through which distinct architectural beliefs, values, and attitudes are transmitted or actions are filtered, and out of which arise any qualities architecture is seen as having. Commenting on K. Michael Hays's paper on the work of Eisenman at the same conference, Alan Colquhoun observed "it would have been even more interesting if he had questioned the relation between theory and practice in Eisenman's work, which I find to be problematic in some respects, and had then, perhaps, gone on to ask in what way is it possible to conceive of an architecture of negation, pure and simple" (Hays and Burns 1990:134). The theory-practice relation has become a fundamental issue in architecture currently as Hays himself prompted in another context. We need to understand, he argues, "the subtle ways in which ideology inscribes itself in the very forms of architecture" before architects and critics accuse theorists of subverting architecture as Sylvia Lavin (1990) did in an essay on the uses and abuses of theory to which Hays and Jeffrey Kipnis vehemently responded (Hays 1990; Kipnis 1990a). Lavin's critique is discussed further in 1A.1, Design-Talk.

This dialectic is far from trivial. It has been a belief for so long now that it has become the orthodoxy that architecture has two realms—practice and discipline—and that they are concomitant: application-through-solution defines practice and theory-as-guide defines discipline. For many architects, discipline and practice form a tedious couplet in no need of further explanation, yet the relation between them is as ill-understood now as it ever was. In this equation, discipline is seen as effectively the 'hidden client' to practice—its conscience and prescience. To say that any principle of architecture inhabits discipline is certainly unexceptionable, but it is a dramatic step to say then that theory, as the set of principles of architecture, guides and informs practice or that it has practical consequences, without first justifying the separation between theory and practice and then demonstrating how any interaction works.

As an example of the kind of shift occurring in theory, take Jeffrey Kipnis's admission of an interest in design above all else, even above theory, in his 1988 essay "Forms of Irrationality" published in Whiteman, Kipnis and Burdett (1992). When he wrote it, he believed that architectural theory and history "always operate . . . in the service of a design agenda," though by the time the book was published he was heavily qualifying its thrust, saying in a footnote that his thinking had changed substantially on "architectural meaning, the form of architectural theory and the relationship between theory and design." His shift in three years is indicative of how quickly architectural theory is changing, and seems to have resulted from his becoming more circumspect in his investigations and not wanting to be seen as having denigrated or debased architecture or its many talented practitioners—a political act in the best sense, to be sure. Certainly this is the tenor of the reply he makes to Sylvia Lavin's critique of contemporary theory raised earlier, in which he chastises her for violence against "the heart of the discipline" (Kipnis 1990a). Though he did not explain exactly how he thought theory and design related in his 1988 essay, he alluded to processes of negotiation as theory's primary task, and appears to be persisting with this view in his recent commentaries. It is a view of theory that is maintained in this book.

Notwithstanding his qualifications, some of what Kipnis said earlier has great appeal. First, the imputation that (for him and no doubt for many architects) design adumbrates theory is a useful way of placing theory in a subordinate position and sets the scene for his transactional proposition. Second, his criticism of the quest to define and maintain an 'idealized occupant' as the recipient of whatever is being designed as misguided and probably fallacious serves as a reminder that there is a lingering modernist agenda still at work. Trying to get closer to the core of designing, Kipnis maintains that the history, context, and program of designed objects seen in retrospect are unable to also determine the object in prospect. This denial suggests that the 'force' of architecture cannot be found in these aspects but must derive from elsewhere. Kipnis suggests that the architect's 'intention' or motivation is one prominent determinant of the content of a work. But intention is confounded by being circumscribed, as it is, by unintended and unwanted interpretations so strong that a work becomes detached from its author yet still 'lives'. The force of a work so interpreted is in effect decentered, but the compulsion to exist remains.

Again we might ask, what is this force that drives architecture, that all designers engage as they design, and that keeps architecture alive during its birth and afterward? What is it that gives a work 'presence', that makes it assertive, that makes it "significant *to someone*, rather than, or in addition to, being symbolic *of something*" in Michael Benedikt's terms (1987:38)? Kipnis has no ready answer, and though he suggests that it probably lies in the way architectural theory deals with the relation between discourse and practice, between *absurd* and *surd* processes, how it negotiates or manages the irrational and the rational, it more fruitfully inhabits the realm of what Hays in his response to Lavin calls 'mediation', a conciliation in particular circumstances between ideas fighting for supremacy. Both negotiation and mediation rely on talk, and the continuing transaction is process; therefore theory is discursive process. But to say this is simply so is too glib, and it will require the rest of this book to elaborate.

It is clear then, from the contemporary view that Kipnis and other recent writers put forward, that those who have been led to a certain well-known theoretical view have misunderstood theory as something tangible, and as a result are misleading if they declare particular notions as the core of architecture without which it ceases to exist or have vitality, value, or meaning. For example, the historico-theoretical stances of Bruno Zevi's 'space', Siegfried Giedion's 'space/time', Nikolaus Pevsner's historicism, Reyner Banham's 'technic', and particularly Louis Sullivan's 'functionalism' and all its variants, are frames of reference within which several generations of architects have struggled to think, write, and design.

Not only is there a circularity of reasoning here that is a direct result of not recognizing the critical assessment role of theory for which Lewis argues as outlined above, there is also a failure to clarify just how these notions inhere and inform designing. They do not present or support conditions for mediation. As Kipnis says in one of those generalizations he seems to be apologizing for:

> . . . *no architectural design has ever actualized the content of any theory as second order application* . . . architectural design is not and has never been a case of applied philosophy, applied science, or applied art, applied social or political theory, etc. Architectural design has never actualized any other body of ideas. The problem, therefore, is not that traditional architectural theory has always been a second order theory, but that it is a second order theory in form but never in fact (Whiteman, Kipnis, and Burdett 1992:158).

It is of course fair to say that negotiation is a common experience, if not a commonly held theoretical view, and that attitudes arising from personal negotiational experience of architecture and developed out of and alongside education and practice, are influential in that they inform methods or provide shorthand canons that aid implementation. Some would call these attitudes 'theories' even though they are frequently uncritical, mostly affirmative, often populist, usually entrepreneurial (good for business), and beg questions about method, the state of architecture, and progress. Attitudes born of reflection about the state of architecture, ethics, and morality generate ideas as the basis for comprehension if not application. Some would call these 'true' theories because they are mostly critical, radical, disruptive, and progressive, and in the main become didactic discourse, though of late frequently at the hands of entrepreneurial historico-theorists. But because either attitude may be so individualistic as to be incapable of generalization or so universalized as to be of little or no assistance in the immediacy of day-to-day concerns, and because there is no common agreement as to what theory is, neither approach is satisfying in any deeply conceptual way.

Architectural Theory Reinterpreted as Theory-Talk

This dilemma raises a profoundly disturbing doubt that what we have been accepting as architectural theory, whether of the static or the transactional kind, actually does not exist in the way we think or, even more disturbingly, that it may not exist at all. Lord Llewellyn Davies, for instance, strongly repudiated the idea of there being such a thing as 'the theory of architecture' (Whiffen 1965:3). If theory does not exist, then what we have been calling theory is *merely* talk, what Geoffrey Scott identified as 'chatter' three quarters of a century ago when he said that " 'theory'—the attempt to decide architectural right and wrong on purely intellectual grounds—is precisely one of the roots of our mischief. Theory, I suppose, was what made the chatter on the scaffolding of the Tower of Babel. It is the substitute for tradition . . . " (Scott 1924:259–260). Even though this is a neat throwaway of three generations ago, it is almost exactly what Stanley Fish says about theory as the *rhetoric* of legal and literary studies; not theory apart from practice but theory as the 'talk' of practice. In fact, the 'merely' used above is no pejorative but is the clue to the whole problem; it is the means for the 'dedicated scrutiny' that Kipnis (1990a) advocates, the guns of Merquior, the critical assessment of Lewis, and the currency of mediation.

Mark Linder is less charitable about the talk of theory in his piece "Architectural Theory Is No Discipline" (Whiteman, Kipnis, and Burdett 1992:167–169); he writes that "the most we can say about contemporary architectural theory is that it can be called architectural theory," which he labels a 'marginal discourse' because of its recourse to the ideas and techniques of seemingly more stable disciplines outside architecture, such as philosophy, science, or mathematics. He contends that architectural theory "is not a theory that is architectural, but is an attempt to make architecture theoretical"; he proceeds to a 'constrained definition' of theory that is architectural in that it aligns itself with practice by asking what it is that architects *do* and not what architecture *is,* basing it in the work of the American pragmatists.

As much as it appeals to want to establish a link between theory and practice of which Linder writes, and no matter how much the pragmatic tradition might tug at the common sense, there are many conceptual hurdles to overcome before committing to a full-fledged 'theory of doing', the main strategy of which is to convince others of its efficacy by *talking it through.* Indeed, this is not only our fetish of late, but seems to have possessed the architect whenever a moral agenda was sought. Michael Benedikt (1987) muses upon our tendency to find meaning in a reality that offers nothing of the sort, and suggests that we have yet to find our peace with the world or, by implication, with architecture: "We seem to fear that unless we keep talking and calling upon the world to talk, we will be overcome by the dread muteness of objects and by the heedlessness of nature, that we might awaken to our 'true' condition as 'strangers in a strange land.' " Benedikt's prompt alone is no doubt insufficient to convince us that meanings do not exist or that we might find a less arrogant way to attain some connection with the world.

On the other hand, one beneficial outcome of reading Stanley Fish is that he offers a salutary lesson in humility, but of the kind that is like having a two-by-four about the head. His writings concerning theory and its consequences are applicable across any discipline and can be applied most acutely to architectural theory. Fish defines theory narrowly, and somewhat paradoxically, considering his views on the situatedness of theory within practice, as "an abstract or algorithmic formulation that guides or governs practice from a position outside any particular conception of practice. Theory, in short, is something that practitioners consult if they wish to perform correctly, with the term "correctly" here understood as meaning independently of their "preconceptions, biases, or personal preferences." Fish admits that the word is often used less precisely "to designate high-order generalizations, or strong declarations of basic beliefs, or programmatic statements of political or economic agendas, or descriptions of underlying assumptions," but that such inclusiveness makes everything theory "and if one does that there is nothing of a *general* kind to be said about theory." Fish sees only the strongest idea of theory as having the power to take precedence over practice, and since in his view this kind of theory does not exist, "the relationships that *do* exist between theory and practice (and there are many) are no different from the relationships between any form of talk and the practice of which it is the component" (1989:378). He makes this relationship quite clear in his introduction:

> The distinction between theory and theory-talk is a distinction between a discourse that stands apart from all practices (and no such discourse exists) and a discourse that is itself a practice and is therefore consequential to the extent that it is influential or respected or widespread. It is a distinction between the claims often made for theory—that it stands in a relationship of governance or independence to practice—and the force that making those claims (which are uncashable) may have acquired as the result of conditions existing in an institution . . . In short, when theory has consequences, they will be rhetorical, not theoretical . . . (1989:14).

This is a salutary conception of theory, considered in relation to architecture because while Fish suggests a link with practice with which most architects would agree, he does so only by also saying that any consequences theory might have for practice are not practical but rhetorical. In other words, the consequences of theory are "political rather than theoretical" (331). In Fish's conception, theory can be consequential only when it becomes a set of instructions of a quite universal kind "for reaching correct or valid interpretive conclusions" (329), so that decisions can be reached by anyone, lay and expert alike. But just as Fish is not convinced that such a prescription about judgment exists in the literary and legal fields, contemporary opinion is that a similar situation prevails in architecture. Architecture has never had a single, comprehensive, totalizing theoretical prescription about design and, if you accept that theory is precisely what enables a statement like this to be made, then architecture never *can* have such a prescriptive basis. Anything approaching instructions for correct decision-making (Tzonis 1972; Mitchell 1991) tends toward method and is already framed within a theoretical view of architecture; it is a way of leading an already persuaded architect or designer (that is, not just anyone and certainly *not* a layperson—a point to be discussed in the main body of text) to a resolved outcome. Any appeal someone's architectural approach or method might have is already the result of its having been talked through and its value in application agreed to; in other words, the negotiation has already occurred and any outcome does not result directly from some inherently persuasive theoretical logic. The inexorability of theory as action's guide evaporates once it is recognized and accepted as a form of rhetoric; as a form of rhetoric, theory mediates the choices and actions of practice.

Among many another service Fish does for theory from an architectural viewpoint is to show that making a judgment or resolving an issue is quite different from the account of it, and that *theory* as it is commonly conceived has to do with the story. Interestingly, Fish illustrates this with an example from design used by Donald Schön of how the 'theory of pumpoids' developed for the making of a better paintbrush (Fish 1989:374–376). Rightly, in my view, he concludes that any untidiness in the doing is dissolved in the process of retelling to make it seem cogent, and it is these homogenized accounts that for most people constitute theory. But by this very procedure theory has become theory-talk or rhetoric; or, for the purposes here, *design-talk*. To convey the doing *ex post facto* and to make whatever distinctive phases there might have been seem clear, the retelling arranges and organizes and sequences matters in ways unrelated to the doing purely in order to better communicate the story. Such stories are often the mode of the teacher, too. When construed as retelling, theory presents an intractable difficulty for students because they find they cannot replicate the act in the way the story is presented. It is therefore neither universal enough to be a theory nor specific enough to be a method. Instead, students find they must revert to their own thoughts and manners to achieve a result, and in turn contrive their own stories of their exploits.

My own long-standing concerns that what I hear, read, and see taught as architectural theory may not be theory at all in the sense of broad and all-encompassing generalizations about architecture have led me to suspect that, contrary to what Kipnis says above, what is called theory has more to do with certain arguments and ideas aimed at persuading others to particular beliefs and values. In other words, *any* purported architectural theory is nothing more than 'local and regional', to repeat Foucault, exceeding the bounds of the specific out of which it arises and capable of incorporating within its embrace the inevitable contradictions found in the multifarious situations to which it might relate. By way of example it is useful to consider three theories that have held sway in architecture for many years now, two having a behavioral base—Oscar Newman's 'defensible space' and Roger Barker's 'behavior setting' theory—and the third having a semantic base, the theory of signs by which architecture is construed as a language consisting of a vocabulary arranged according to a grammar by which meaning is conveyed.

Three Entrenched Theories in Architecture

Since Oscar Newman first developed his theory of defensible space for high-rise public housing estates, it has been applied to a wide range of situations but, powerful though it is, the theory is effective only for those who can control and change their situations or environment. Defensible space is "a surrogate term for the range of mechanisms—real and symbolic barriers, strongly defined areas of influence, and improved opportunities for surveillance—that combine to bring an environment under the control of its residents" (Newman 1972:3). It reaches its limit when attempts are made to use it to construe how the wider public domain of cities might be designed for control, a situation in which policing power is also stretched to the extreme or exceeded. It is not readily applied by politically powerless or marginal groups in society in any controlling way with the exception that by temporarily colonizing other people's or no people's domains, the homeless may be said to be applying their version of defensible space in their own way to those domains. A similar argument may be made to explain the actions of those maverick groups who vandalize or plunder the vacant buildings, streets, and parks of cities by leaving their graffiti as marks of possession.

While it may be possible to design large public parks and building complexes with spaces capable of being colonized by the homeless, this means relinquishing control and management of those spaces, and is inimical to the notion of ownership; indeed, designers knowingly providing such spaces might well become a matter for litigation if as a result some damage occurs through arson or assault. I have yet to see such an approach to design, which consciously provides for the marginal in society as part of a corporate undertaking. Vagrants and vandals remain disenfranchised and powerless against those who own or control such places and spaces and who see 'design' as a weapon, of which the creation of defensible space is one armament. Only time will tell whether the actor Dennis Hopper's recent design strategy to remodel his Venice Beach home as 'urban guerrilla architecture' following the L. A. riots, with its designer graffiti and fitted broken windows, will be successful. Will he be left alone by vagrants because his house looks like it has been junked already, or will there be attempts to possess it further for the same reason? In either case, if this inversion of Newman works, perhaps Hollywood is the last place left for Oscar.

Turning to Barker, the behavior setting is a robust concept and has had a long run in architecture. It still underlies much design thinking, not the least being Christopher Alexander's 'pattern language', many patterns of which rely on behaviorally determinable settings. Whether couched in strict behaviorally determinist terms, or in the phenomeno-logical language of *life-events* or *place ballets,* and the descriptive language and narratives that emanate from these concepts, the idea of there being some fixity to human activities and a link with and hence replicability in their spatial encapsulation is the conventional wisdom of designing. In fact, it is almost impossible to imagine designing without these fixities and links, the use of building types for instance being one not-insubstantial precedent. The limit of behavior setting theory is reached, not at the scale of the city—Barker (1968) analyzed a small town in Iowa to show how his settings might be used—but at the point that the maverick meets the norms of the city. Because it is normalizing, Barker's behavior setting theory cannot accommodate aberrant behavior such as that of the vandal, drug user, or street person. There are difficulties too in trying to apply the theory to the design of buildings or public spaces having multiple uses in which specific behavior settings collide and must be adjudicated. Further problems arise in applying it to dynamic situations like the most extreme examples of the individualism of Mainstreet USA so beloved of Robert Venturi. A theory that does not encompass all behavior settings, no matter their lack of propriety or conviviality, is not universal enough to be called a theory in Fish's terms, or at best is only local in its reach.

Mentioning Venturi brings me finally to arguably the longest-standing set of ideas in architectural theory and one already touched upon: the linking of the theory of signs to the notion of architecture as language. Beginning with the rediscovery of Vitruvius (1960:1.1.3) and the classical manners of three centuries, continuing through the experiments with *architecture parlante* in the nineteenth century, the idea still persists today not only in the recent dalliance with postmodernist revivalism, but in architectural education. Pedagogies abound that are built around historical analyses, spatial experiments, and compositional studies as the means for students to acquire a design 'vocabulary' or repertoire. Some architects believe that design principles can be distilled from these, while others see conventions acting together with compositional rules to form a grammar, each utilizing and supplementing the developing 'vocabulary'. Yet no assembly of architectural elements can replicate the simplest conception of a human language, not even as a crude approximation, although there are some candidates:

> "Within the semiotic universe," writes Douglas Graf, "certain basic building blocks have been proposed: phonemes, lexemes, sememes, classemes, choremes, myththemes, morpho-semes, metasemes, morphemes, and just plain old phemes and semes. From a brief survey of the literature, it seems that these classifications reflect nothing more than personal attempts to understand the nature of language. This should encourage others to make the same effort. In this spirit, a morpheme sounds like the perfect building block for architecture, but modesty of scope requires that we pursue first the sub-morphemic units, the eames, of which there are two: rayeames, or elements, and charleseames, or configurations. The eames, thus, constitute a framework for a minimal structure in architecture" (Graf in Whiteman, Kipnis, and Burdett 1992:95).

To this witty spoof Dug-alas Graf might have contrived, as with a cryptic crossword, a deeper temporal connection by adding another 'seme' in the form of the rearranged entrails of a pharaoh (Ra(mese)s) along with roots (dug) from the Edenic garden and thereby (alas) perhaps kept the (graf)lex *in camera*. However, with such contrivances it is almost impossible not to be seen as narcissistic; then again, why hide all that cleverness when you have gone to so much trouble. Even with the most elaborate contrivance, not half as much *haver* can be had in architecture; there is no latter-day architectural equivalent of the finesse of a rheme, phoneme, morpheme, or morphon and all the play that goes with elision or with the punning that was so characteristic of the Renaissance and the baroque period. Despite the use of the word 'language' in architectural titles (Summerson 1964; Prak 1968; Hesselgren 1972) and the studies of the theory of signs, of meaning, and of language (Jencks and Baird 1969; Jencks 1977; Broadbent 1977; Broadbent, Bunt and Jencks 1979), no language of architecture has been established. Gillo Dorfles recognized the difficulty during the heyday of structuralism in architecture, and tried to suggest a direction:

> ". . . if we want to systematize architectural analysis from a semiological standpoint, we shall have to say that there is a twofold semiological distinction: one kind of semiological analysis based on the elements of notational language (in a certain way similar to certain primitive ideographic writings) and another kind linked to the work itself and to its constitutive elements (spaces, rhythms, volumes). These last elements can undergo an analysis according to the linguistic patterns we tried to define, but cannot by any means, be reduced to schemes typical only for the verbal language . . ." (*Structuralism and Semiology in Architecture;* cited in Jencks and Baird 1969:48).

This reduction to notation and constituent by Dorfles is similar to Colquhoun's figural and formal division, about which he wrote in his 1977 essay of the same name (Colquhoun 1986). Nonetheless, there are certain architectural qualities that have traditionally carried meaning and are manipulated by architects as they design. Certain geometries and shapes, for instance, are accepted as having a history of use and a symbolism by which their adoption brings particular meanings to a work of architecture, whether intended or not. So much is this the case that shapes such as the cruciform, the pyramid and ziggurat, the aedicule, the helix, and the dome are brimful of meaning arising particularly from their use in religious buildings across cultures (Kollar 1972; Lord Raglan 1964; Rapoport 1969; Thiis-Evensen 1989). These shapes are almost inviolate to the extent that, for some, the equivalent of desecration occurs if they are used without due reference or reverence. In most cases, though, the effect is less dramatic; as Norberg-Schulz notes, "The dome originally *portrayed* heaven, and only later became a conventional sign with a more general sacred character, assigning a certain 'dignity' to the architectural solution" (1965:170). The meanings such elements carry is a product of the associative power of the figural in architecture; they do not necessarily show a language at work, that universal ability of "describing something outside itself, but with no particular agenda or purpose" (P. Rowe 1987:176), notwithstanding work on the formal and figural in language carried out to date or the existence of vernacular and other conventions. Rather, they are the reverse, associations working in much the same way that quotations do, large chunks of already assembled meanings, about which Colquhoun wrote in "Form and Figure" in 1977 (Colquhoun 1986). They inhabit a work and are no different *in effect* from the deliberate strategies used in the work of Robert Venturi or Charles Moore, in which "figural elements or motifs from outside the rest of the work itself are deliberately introduced either to qualify or to offer additional commentary" (P. Rowe 1987:181). If there is a language of architecture it would need to explain both the figural aspect and 'the work itself' (probably the formal) to which both Rowe and Dorfles allude. This 'work on the language' of architecture shows that there has been little advance beyond Broadbent's suggestion in 1969 (Jencks and Baird 1969) that large built elements may be construed as the 'syntagms' and structural elements as the 'morphemes' of architecture. In other words, the theory of architecture as language has reached both its local and temporal limits, even though the wish for an architectural language lingers and is used uncritically in the Summersonian sense, that is, in the form of 'talk' in architecture as though the idea were natural and transparent.

Existing Conceptions of Architectural Theory

Having said that theory is not what many writers have thought it to be, it is nonetheless worthwhile to examine some specific matters raised by these theoretical conceptions. What is presented as the basis for architecture generally and designing in particular usually lacks the rigor, testability, reaction to failure (not fitting the facts) and accountability that hypothesis demands. This is the crux. Most of what is called theory in architecture is either hypothesis incapable of being tested, or is a model of such simplicity that it lacks explanatory power. Without its suppositions, its instrumental aspects, and its attendant responsibilities being open to deep scrutiny, any course of theoretical instruction, any theoretical proposition about the world, any presentation of principles purporting to explain the essence of what we do as architects—if its relevance to the practice, understanding, and appreciation of architecture cannot be demonstrated—is not worth the telling, according to some notable writers (Rossi 1978; Scruton 1979; Lang 1987).

Perhaps the worth of theory does not lie in it being directly instrumental, for, if Wigley's assertion that theory may be supplanted by the 'loaded object' (see 1A.1, Design-Talk) is nearer the mark, it might best be theory's task to nurture and revitalize architecture by *interrogating* it. This is close to what Kipnis (1990a) maintains: "Though unlikely, it is conceivable that, for all its pretensions and novel techniques, contemporary theory may not revise one single canon of the architectural tradition. However, unless that tradition is tested, unless its vitality is affirmed again and again by the most dedicated scrutiny each generation can bring to bear, it will certainly atrophy. That is the use of theory." Not altogether different is the way hermeneutics sees the event in dialogue with its context through interpretation or the way Hays (1990) sees contemporary architectural theory as illuminating the preconceptions, socio-historical aspects, authorities and values within which architecture is embedded, where theory's vocation is "as a *mediating* practice."

Because architectural concepts and terms infest the very language we use, we are immediately presented with another of the many dilemmas of language: how might we discuss architectural theory without resorting to architectural terms that already carry certain meanings? To talk of the construction or structure of architectural theory, for instance, is already to be architectural, and presupposes notions of order, hierarchy, essence, metaphor—in other words, the very issues under discussion. And if we accept Lewis's definition, to use the terms and concepts of a discipline in an exposition of it does not assist in bringing clarity to the discussion. This presents a difficulty for what follows and, because there is no easy way around it, means heading off or showing up trouble as and when it appears.

Another aspect is our approach to understanding the world and how it informs or affects any concept of architectural theory. It is possible to project theories from almost any viewpoint offered by epistemology, philosophy, sociology, psychiatry, or psychology. When combined with various 'in-house' approaches to architecture, the combinations can become bewildering, although in point of fact most writers are inclined to reduce the number of categories to a comprehensive yet manageable range. Witness Bruno Zevi (1948), who offered nine ways of construing architectural theory: political, philosophical-religious, scientific, economic-social, materialist, technical, physio-psychological, formalist, and spatial, of which the last is his favorite (see his chapter 5 for the expansion of these categories; see also his annotated bibliography). Witness also the unselfconscious, conscious, self-conscious, activist, intuitive, logical, and idealist traditions into which Jencks (1971) dissected architecture and his later multidimensional charting of pictorial imagery (1980) already mentioned. Witness Kenneth Frampton's five *Isms* of contemporary architecture published the same year, indicating the 'ideological set' and the governing principles from which certain works appear: Neo-Productivism (technical), Neo-Rationalism (formal), Structuralism (anthropological), Populism (contextural) and Regionalism. Witness the four positions Peter Rowe (1987) discerned: functionalist, populist, conventionalist, and formalist. If we just take Zevi's philosophical-religious grouping, it is possible to discern at least six positions, some of which embrace the categories developed by later writers: rationalist, empiricist, structuralist, pragmatic, phenomenological, and chaotic (these are adopted for the sake of the discussion from a matrix assembled by Frances Downing of Texas A&M University in 1988 extending one developed by John Archea [1975]). The first and second we have already encountered and tend to underscore the other four, and all six in some combination are likely to be found at play in any particular theoretical approach.

Finally, in a focused study that seeks a framework for incorporating the behavioral sciences into architecture, Jon Lang (1987) prompts two stances basic to the formation of any 'theory-of' human endeavor and of broad sweep. One deals with the world as it is and the other posits the world as it might be. *Positive,* or 'descriptive', theory consists of statements and assertions describing and explaining reality and capable of extension into predictions of future reality, although it is not positivistic in insisting upon only verifiable or falsifiable truths. The aim of positive theory is "to enable people to derive a large number of descriptive statements from a single explanatory statement," an economical and strategic shorthand to make sense of the myriad complexities of the world. Lang maintains that "an explicit positive theoretical base is necessary for any discipline if it is to respond to the issues that face it, conduct the research necessary for its progress, develop logical normative statements for its actions, and understand the limits of its understanding." *Normative* theory involves prescriptions for action through standards (or *norms*), manifestos, design principles, and philosophies stemming from an ideological position on what should prevail in the world; it is quite clearly value-laden. The logic of normative theory is not that of science because science does not deal with creation. Rather, Lang says, "Normative theories are built on positive ones" even though "the professed normative position of a designer often differs from its behavioral correlate—practice."

Lang maps these two theoretical orientations in a two-by-two matrix, with two components dealing with their operation and content (see the figure below). *Procedural* issues are concerned with praxis and process, and deal with creativity, analysis, synthesis, evaluation, and research. *Substantive* issues are concerned with phenomena, environmental qualities and functions, esthetics, behavior, and the determination of the emphasis on these. Lang sees the emphasis on theory in architectural education as focusing on the designer as creator and on the acquisition of action prescriptions—by which, Lang says, citing Robert Gutman, is usually meant "the set of principles that guides the architect in making decisions about the complex problems that arise in translating a brief into the design of a building." Such design principles, Lang says, center on developing a system of environmental logic rather than one of human needs, which are seen as ancillary to purely architectural matters. It is possible to disagree with Lang here because there are other schools of thought in which the theoretical approach concentrates on human concerns almost to the exclusion of abstract architectural matters. One might well allocate a *process* orientation to the former and a *product* orientation to the latter.

	Orientation of Theory	
Subject Matter of Theory	*Positive*	*Normative*
Procedural		Professed
		Practiced
Substantive		Professed
		Practiced

FIGURE 1-1. *Theory Matrix (from Lang 1987).*

Theory as a Disturbing Influence on
Authority and Tradition

Something also needs to be said about the likely impact of any newly invented 'theory of' on an existing field of knowledge, especially one already under the sway of a powerful 'grand theory' of the human condition or of primary texts informing its status and genealogy. Fortunately, architecture is less constrained as a field than, say, certain of the sciences, though this means that it is perhaps more susceptible to the vagaries of fashion than some might wish. But it does have its favored discourses and its orthodoxies that for years sat firmly within the discipline but that suffered severe depredation about a generation back when modernism was found wanting; when it was found to be unlovely. Nevertheless, there is still a predominant inclination among architects toward conservatism and toward a modernist 'tradition' loosely defined but rooted in time-honored principles. Good architecture has been seen largely as either working within a context or circumventing it, depending on which principles are adopted and where the cutting edge is perceived. Recent criticism of 'modern' buildings by Charles, Prince of Wales (1989), precipitated and focused debate on the issue and polarized the architectural profession for a time in the United Kingdom, and to a lesser extent elsewhere, into opposing camps. In a rearguard reprisal, the traditional camp has used popular support, conservative authority, and the royal critique to menace the contemporary camp, whose strident retorts emanate from deep within the protective armor of architectural creativity and artistic autonomy. Theories of a sort are emerging to help consolidate and justify one or the other as the reigning orthodoxy or desired future. As with all saber-rattling, everything remains much the same as before.

In a far more threatening manner, on the other hand, Foucault explores deviant attitudes and behaviors through his writings, using deviant ways to undermine and throw into doubt those systems of power and knowledge privileged by reason and science. He thereby exposes the social and political implications of texts in their most comfortable state, a state in which such considerations are almost forgotten because they are so commonly practiced; he does this to ask the question that he believes should perpetually be asked— what is it that modern society or politic has become or is becoming? Foucault and Derrida not only want to disturb authority and tradition; they are intensely curious about what lies beyond authority and tradition. Paradoxically, because they condemn the speaking for others that authority itself musters, they believe it is in society's interest to confront what lies beyond its faith in authority and tradition (Philp 1985).

At its most charged, architectural theory as rhetoric is able to undermine and throw into doubt those conservatives whose privileged positions on architecture are at their most comfortable, thereby stimulating invention and abjuring complacency. The Modern Movement began its agenda by an outright confrontation in rejecting the Beaux Arts orthodoxy.

In the turmoil of its formation it developed a formidable dynamic, the diversity and conflict of which became its driving force. It was only after the Modern Movement was seen to have established itself as a viable alternative that complacency set in once again and a new and debased orthodoxy overwhelmed it, creating a haven for mediocrity. Now, more than three score and ten years later, there is a new charge in the air; the lusty ones are grazing near the cliff's edge and the limits of bearing are being prodded.

The Relation Between Theory and History

This is not the place to raise the multifarious issues of history, historiography and its historical stances, or the many schools of historical thought—these are the subject of another book—though it is inevitable that we will be confronting history in almost every page that follows. It is therefore proper that before venturing into the themes of the present book, some clarification be made as to how history and theory might relate; whether history informs theory or whether they are separate endeavors.

Schools of architecture may be divided among those who assume a conjunction of history and theory; those who see them as independent; those who, like Walter Gropius at the Bauhaus, see no reason for teaching history at all; and, like those at University College in London "for a bit," those who see no value in teaching theory at all. "Our reasons for being pragmatic about theory are purely pragmatic ones," writes Reyner Banham, "we could find very little useful in there that an architect needs or can work with" (Whiffen 1965:93). On the other hand, Sibyl Moholy-Nagy sees theory as "generalized principle, analyzing reality" and, as such, any stylistic rootedness it gathered from history made of it an exercise in futility "for learning or practicing architects." She writes: "The whole vast body of generalized principle, from Vitruvius to Banham, refers *backward* to established architectural facts. It can never refer forward to future design solutions." She goes on of course to propose the "shaping of a new link," her own version of history/theory as "a comprehension of historical concepts, fused into an amalgam in which historical and contemporary are synonymous" (Whiffen 1965:40-41). On the other hand, Sir John Summerson (1957) saw value in deriving theory from history chronologically as the history of ideas.

So, there appear to be very few who do not see theory as needed or as operating in some manner, whether as a highly wrought philosophy replete with a textual armory, or as sets of rules-of-thumb operating, as required, at the studio level only. The teaching of theory and history in an integrated way tends toward a history of theory and a reliance on historical determinism to show the relevance of the so-called lessons of history. Separating out theory from history tends to precipitate a focus on ideological and philosophical material, with a view to theory's potential for application in some way. It also tends to more readily embrace the array of disciplines into which theory reaches and on which architecture is inclined to depend for much of its own regimen.

If this separation is accepted, the question still to be answered is whether theory and history are in some way contrary to yet connected with each other, whether they form the poles of some theory-history spectrum, much in the sense that theory and practice have been considered as opposed in the past but are now seen as interlocutory. In an era when boundaries between distinct disciplines are seen to overlap and in many cases merge to the point of almost dissolving conceptually, if not yet practically, the attempt here to keep them apart may be thought retrograde. However, even a casual viewing of the literature reveals a substantial commitment to maintaining architectural history as a separate entity from architectural theory, whether it be on what is, for some, the outmoded basis of style or chronology, or the more pragmatic basis of archaeology, heritage studies, or biography. Where history and theory begin to merge is at the level of interpretation; sources, intentions, meanings, and influences are teased out of what exists or out of newly discovered connections, and attempts are made to integrate the pragmatics into some thematic schema. The issue comes into sharpest focus with recent histories such as Heinrich Klotz's *History of Postmodern Architecture* (1984), which purports to hang what is largely a stylistic review on an approach to contemporary architecture as "a history of its decisions and its unintended or intended contents and symbolizations" (3), themes that beg a host of theoretical matters.

The way theory is considered here in relation to history is not so much as if they were in polar opposition but rather as if they were in a figure-ground relationship; one helps to define the other. On this admittedly simplistic analogy, theory is the figure and history is the ground (just as history is the figure and theory the ground from a historian's view), though the analogy ought not to be taken as implying that theory is grounded in history. For theory as it is being considered here to have a grounding in history would be a nonsense, the seeking of surety from a history of specific design mediations, as yet to be written outside the experience of the individual, or from the accumulated practices of theory generally that, as they have been written about thus far, shows little consistency. This is not to say that there are no persuasive individual accounts or practicable generalizations of theory, or that these cannot be viewed in some historical way (that is, through some perspective that would amount to a theory of the history of theory). The analogy attempts to illustrate a reciprocity between theory and history that is varying and dynamic rather than precise and static. A parallel may be made with the difference between English and Marxist historical method made clear by Carr:

> The tradition of the English-speaking world is profoundly empirical. Facts speak for themselves. A particular issue is debated 'on its merits'. Themes, episodes, periods are isolated for historical study in the light of some undeclared, and probably unconscious, standard of relevance. . . . All

this would have been anathema to Marx. Marx was no empiricist. To study the part without reference to the whole, the fact without reference to its significance, the event without reference to cause or consequence, the particular crisis without reference to the general situation, would have seemed to Marx a barren exercise (Carr 1961:159–160).

Architectural theory as design-talk cannot be studied without reference to the broader talk of architecture or rhetoric generally, the marks of individuality without reference to the conventions of society, the 'marked' quality without reference to those qualities left unmarked (see chapter 4, Overview), or the architectural event without reference to the physical, cultural, and political contexts that envelop it.

We began with the question "How do you know that what this principle dictates is imperative to do?" We end with a statement of agenda for the rest of the book:

[Theory] cannot help but borrow its terms and its contents from that which it claims to transcend, the mutable world of practice, belief, assumptions, point of view, and so forth. And, by definition, something that cannot succeed cannot have consequences, cannot achieve the goals it has set for itself by being or claiming to be theory, the goals of guiding and/or reforming practice. Theory cannot guide practice because its rules and procedures are no more than generalizations from practice's history (and from only a small piece of that history), and theory cannot reform practice because, rather than neutralizing interest, it begins and ends in interest and raises the imperatives of interest — of some local, particular, partisan project — to the status of universals (Fish 1989:321).

Theoretical Positions

Overview

Congruence is a continuous state of being at rest; it has to do with agreement, accord, conformity. *Confluence* is a momentary state in a moving setting, the meeting of separate streams, the point of unification between otherwise divergent or disconnected forces. They exemplify what are arguably the two fundamental stances in architecture: congruence, the traditional view, unchanging, timeless qualities forming the ways of doing, becoming, and being; confluence, the avant-garde view, experimental, transitory, serendipitous qualities informing the moment. Together they define architecture, structure its agenda, write its text, delimit its boundaries, and set its pace. The dialogue between them *is* architecture, and the unity perceived in any outcome necessarily partakes of both. The extent of each discerned in a work of architecture is one measure of its 'disposition', as well as that of the architect and the culture within which the work and the architect are situated. The idea of there being architectural 'positions', placements within a spectrum of views about architecture, raises the issue of the personal inclinations of architects, their 'dispositions' if you like, their temper, their angle of view, and their adoption of particular stances.

But there are other factors that dispose or incline a work of architecture or an architect toward one or another mode of expression and enable a work to come into being in the first place. One of the most prominent among these is what psychologists call *Weltshmerz* or 'world-pain', that view of the world that says, "here is a world problem that I perceive as my problem." Pollution, hunger, disease, poverty, injustice, lack of basic human rights, inequity, discrimination, and so forth, whether seen globally or locally, are one context within which architectural dispositions, like any other dispositions, are developed. It may not take such humanitarian problems to prompt an architectural view; more likely it will be the world as perceived through architectural glasses, depletion or renewability of resources leading to energy audits as the basis for selecting materials and products, affordability as a determinant of housing type and arrangement, or recycling to minimize waste as the basis for a degree of selfsufficiency with its constructional and lifestyle implications.

There are sociopolitical factors; power is the most influential—who has it, how it is wielded, upon whom, and with what effect. Class and social position affect perceptions of the kinds of issues warranting emphasis in an architectural task, and even the very definition of the task itself. Concern over achieving equity of access in the planning of cities or the provision of public housing, for instance, has led architects to act as advocates on behalf of underprivileged groups in dealing with authorities. Occasionally such involvement will precipitate an educative agenda in which architects forgo their professional élitism as experts in favor of those for whom they design or act as agent, in order that they might become sufficiently empowered to act alone. Concern over equity in sharing the amenity of settings through the strategic placement of buildings has led architects to participate in city planning commissions and local council advisory groups, and to public advocacy on behalf of professional bodies, public and private interest groups, and so on. On the other hand, the power of corporate clients is substantial and many architects depend on their patronage. At the same time architects operate under a professional duty of care to the public at large, the so-called 'hidden client' or third party to design, which they accept as a more or less understood given within any program.

Then there are those community mores that dictate matters of decorum, propriety, behavior, and taste in the public sphere, matters of cultural expectation and social history. Over and against these are professional esthetic standards at an individual and group level, frequently tacit but arising from monitored education, mutual aspiration, and self-reflection. It happens that some cultures are sufficiently sensitized to esthetic matters that they are dealt with in the normal course of events. In other cultures architects and planners have abrogated this responsibility, and as a result their urban environments are suffering loss of visual cohesion or substantial environmental discomfort if not degradation because of massive developments dramatically altering the scale and relationships between people, buildings, and neighborhoods. Often, in the process, microclimates are altered through reduced solar access to the streets and wind patterns are altered as well. In these situations, architects and planners are faced with the task of clawing their way back to a position of leverage in order to regain some of the quality lost.

Heritage issues loom large in many urban settings where economic pressure wills to demolish and rebuild rather than restore and reuse. Not that an architect or planner is always Good

Queen Bess (Carr 1961:45–46) in such situations; all too often it is not an impending loss of heritage that motivates action but the fear that its replacement will be vapid and mean-spirited.

All of which is a preliminary to the question: How do architects acquire whatever dispositions about the world and architecture that they have? And in what way might such dispositions be opened up to scrutiny so that others might gain? One way to explore these kinds of questions is to examine definitional statements about architecture, the 'architecture is' syndrome, reflecting (as it appears to) some internalized arrangement of an architect's disposition toward the external world. There is, however, a difficulty that is not unlike the notion of expressionism, that somehow what is said reflects the state of mind of the sayer.

It is worth examining for a moment just what positions there are in architecture. One writer divides what he calls 'normative' positions in architecture into four classes or orientations: functionalist, populist, conventionalist, and formalist (Rowe 1987). A normative position, it may be recalled from the introduction, involves prescriptions for action through agreed norms, manifestos, design principles, and philosophies arising from an ideological position about what ought to be (Lang 1987). Rowe's normative positions each follow the Hegelian triad of thesis, antithesis, synthesis, which for Rowe are (1) the identification of a contentious problem or issue, (2) an assessment of these matters in current practice and of their missed potential, and (3) a counterproposal resolving them. These three positions range along a continuum from doctrinaire to categorical.

In Rowe's terms, the functionalist orientation focuses on enclosing activities and seeks the expressive potential of uses, circulation, technology, construction, and materials. The populist orientation concentrates on the user; everyday practices, user behavior, and funky imagery. The conventionalist position draws upon the idea of a psychological engagement with people through historical reference, convention, or type. And the formalist position looks to certain autonomous qualities such as composition, language, meaning, and morphology, and is primarily self-referential (Rowe 1987:115–134). Rowe stresses that these categories are not absolute and that there are some architects whose works combine two or more approaches.

As to which approach one might adopt, Rowe is more circumspect. He examines their claims to legitimacy and observes that they are all substantiated on "a widely held view of man and his world" that comes down to two elemental ideas: a 'foundational' view of humanity that reduces to certain common denominators, such as rationality; and a 'relativist' view wherein humanity's embeddedness in culture and tradition is dominant (134–143). To reduce the four positions to either foundationalist or relativist says little for their productive value as design strategies, so Rowe offers another approach: "Instead of regarding architectural positions as arguments with proposals linked solely to some deep-seated view of man and his world, we can regard them as essentially teleological doctrines, or doctrines about means" based on an idea of what it is 'good' or 'right' or 'proper' to do.

Rowe, however, gets himself into a knot when he says, "Suppose one had to choose between 'imageability', functional conformance, and structural innovation; how might one assign the priorities among these three categories in designing a building? An essential feature of *theory that purports to guide practical action* [emphasis added] is the provision of some basis for assigning such categorical priorities" (145). These are primarily moral questions and Rowe endeavors to show a way of handling them by urging what are in fact five methods for making judgments—intuition, a single overriding principle, a multiplicity of principles, prudential judgment, and lexical ordering—advocated by the jurist John Rawls in his *Theory of Justice* (1971). Rowe ends this portion of his discussion by questioning the centrality and comprehensiveness any positions should have and offers, in effect, several prescriptions for theory. Regarding their centrality, the "most compelling" theoretical positions "seem to address the important issues of the moment" and this focus is what "good theory" has. He concludes that theory "is mainly concerned with that which lies outside the urcorpus [the primitive or earliest corpus, unanimously agreed as given] of knowledge." As for comprehensiveness, "architectural theory should attempt to comprehensively address and define the realm of architecture," at the same time suggesting that disagreement at times may arise over the urcorpus itself, thereby throwing such definitions into disarray (147–149).

In the very last section of the chapter Rowe insists on two things of any position: "First, a position must show that the guiding idea of good and the ensuing prescription of means is fundamental at the moment and that substantiation can be sustained between moments. . . . Second, the theoretical position must exhibit a character of completeness by embracing other fundamental dimensions of architecture that it does not directly address" (149). A tall order so far. He goes on to ask what his discussion has to do with "the guidance of practical inquiry, design thinking, or professional action." He answers thus: "normative positions . . . *as well as those that are more idiosyncratic and personal* [emphasis added], do in fact provide direction for action"; a balance must be struck between "aloof abstractions" and "concrete prescriptive principles." When sufficient substantiation is not provided, he maintains that theoretical positions become exposed and practice impaired, and from the resulting multiplicity of positions guidance becomes "merely a matter of personal taste."

What we come away with from Rowe's analysis is a confounding idea of what in his terms theory is or does. If normative theory is an agreement about what ought to be, then it cannot be 'outside' the urcorpus, which is already unanimously agreed. If it is a personal manifesto, then it is not normative. However, it may be that there is sufficient overlap or correspondence among a set of individual positions that might be 'agreed', thereby constituting them as normative. In other words, the normative is a political and dialogic act. That theory cannot be 'outside' its own terms of reference is almost recognized by Rowe in his remarks on the disruption occurring if the urcorpus is questioned, but he turns away from its full implication. In this sense theory *is* its urcorpus, as well as its momentary attention.

To admit that both normative and idiosyncratic positions guide action is to deny the whole idea of the normative as a guide to action, and reduces the issue to one of competing discourses, of design-talk. What is fundamentally at issue is that Rowe, and many another architect, argues from a base that assumes theory is a 'thing that guides' rather than a discourse that mediates; he therefore seeks to define and explain the impossible. The balance Rowe seeks between abstraction and concreteness is precisely what theory as mediation provides; it is not a matter of one or the other belonging to separate realms. His own words provide the clue for the error of this kind of thinking: theory, even construed as a guide to practice, is always already a matter of personal taste.

The reason for this prolonged consideration of Rowe's thesis is that it provides a number of lessons for architectural education. It is an often unstated tenet of architectural education that students will, once having participated in a course of instruction and experiment, emerge with a position; it is presumed that they want to achieve the status of having a position and that a position is something worth having. In other words, an architectural position is not one to be taken in relation to nonarchitectural matters but that concerns other architectural positions already assumed to be in position. "What is your position?" is a theoretical question; it seeks to place you in a field or space whose vectors are as yet undeclared coordinates of speculation about architecture defining some continuous realm. The alternative notion is preferred here: that the realm might consist only of menhirs of speculation jostling for a place in the light. As with conceptions of the physical construction of the universe, it is impossible to imagine this space or field from a position outside; there are only degrees of proximity, neither inside nor outside its conception.

There is also a more intimate geography once a position is declared; using certain prepositions or adverbs—above, at, beside, beyond, far, near—determines the intensity with which the position is held or justified. To not have a position is anathema. To not have a position means either that you are still finding your way toward or among the menhirs; you have lost your bearings and have not arrived at the realm or are confused by the shouting; or that you actually have a position, but its field is other than the one on which the lights are focused, a field thought to be chaos by those aiming the lights.

All of which shows that the pursuit of an architectural position is a political act, one that involves active participation in the discourse. The only way to provide an educational base is to show students the trends of the discourse and the basis of specific positions. The choice is theirs as to which position or amalgam of positions to adopt, which will be for them the most strategic for whatever view they might have about the practice of architecture. If students choose to agree with certain views purely because it might give them leverage in future employment, that is fine. If they choose to adopt certain views for ideological reasons, that is also fine. Changing position is always an option, of course, and one frequently pursued by researchers and theorists as well as by students. There is nothing absolute about adopting an architectural position, and there need not be any impediment to changing position if one chooses to do so. Doctrinaire views about architecture may be what attracts students to an institution, creates interest in an architect, or entices readers to a book, but the choice of position is always the inquirer's to make.

A. The Reach and Limits of Theory

1. The Way of Theory, or Design-Talk

Theory . . . is the ability to demonstrate and explain the productions of dexterity on the principles of proportion. **Vitruvius.** 1486:1.1.1.

The Renaissance produced no theory of architecture. It produced treatises on architecture: Fra Giocondo, Alberti, Palladio, Serlio, and many others, not only built, but wrote. But the style they built in was too alive to admit of analysis, too popular to require defence. They give us rules, but not principles. They had no need of theory, for they addressed themselves to taste. **Geoffrey Scott.** 1924: on "The Romantic Fallacy."

Theory of design argues about reasons that can explain, dictate or prove a design decision, such as the adoption or the creation of a shape in an architectural work. It is related more to the investigations of systems of decision making in design than to the verbalization of different design decisions as such. **Alexander Tzonis.** 1972:16.

I assert that the first principle of a theory is the necessity to persist with the same themes and I believe that it is the nature of artists and particularly architects to focus in on the theme to be developed, to choose a method of analysis internal to architecture and to try always to solve the same problems. . . . What I believe to be the basic principle of a theory of architectural education and therefore of design . . . [is] the necessity to persistently hold only to one theme. . . . The formation of a theory of design constitutes the objective of an architecture and its priority over any other research is unquestionable. **Aldo Rossi.** Cited in Bandini 1982:14, n12.

Architectural theory consists in the attempt to formulate the maxims, rules and precepts which govern, or ought to govern, the practice of the builder. . . . Such precepts assume that we already know what we are seeking to achieve: the *nature* of architectural success is not at issue; the question is, rather, how best to achieve it. A theory of architecture impinges on aesthetics only if it claims a *universal* validity, for then it must aim to capture the essence, and not the accidents, of architectural beauty. But such a theory is implicitly philosophical, and must be judged accordingly; we will wish to know whether it succeeds in establishing its claims *a priori,* by a consideration of the phenomena in their most abstract and universal guise. **Roger Scruton.** 1979:4.

All great theories of architecture reflect such understanding [that is, a "deep intellectual and intuitive understanding of past and present conditions"] and only they contain truly creative possibilities. **Wojciech Lesnikowski** and **Calli Spheeris.** 1987:39.

. . . the traditional status of theory has changed. No longer is it some abstract realm of defense that surrounds objects, protecting them from examination by mystifying them. Architectural theory generally preempts an encounter with the object. It is concerned with veiling rather than exposing objects. With these projects, all theory is loaded into the object: propositions now take the form of objects rather than verbal abstractions. What counts is the condition of the object, not the abstract theory. Indeed the force of the object makes the theory that produced it irrelevant. **Mark Wigley.** In Johnson and Wigley 1988:19.

To the extent that it has a community of subscribers, theory represents a corpus of principles that are agreed upon and therefore worthy of emulation. **Peter Rowe.** 1987:115.

TRACE The word 'theory' comes from the Latin *theoria,* in turn adopted from the Greek *theoros,* which means 'spectator, envoy'. Its base, *theasthai,* means to 'look upon, contemplate', while the English meaning of it is as a conception or mental scheme of something to be done, or of the method of doing it, and a systematic statement of rules or principles to be followed. A clear distinction between theory and practice emerged by the beginning of the seventeenth century, when theory also described "that department of an art or technical subject which consists in the knowledge or statement of the facts on which it depends, or of its principles or methods, as distinct from the practice of it" (SOED). By the end of the eighteenth century the word embraced both the mathematical sense of an organized system of principles or theorems and the looser sense of 'a hypothesis proposed as an explanation'. The somewhat derogatory connotations of the latter included 'a mere hypothesis, speculation, conjecture', through to 'an idea or set of ideas about something', and finally 'an individual view or notion'.

The range of classical architectural theory is reviewed by the historian Dora Wiebenson (1983) so it will not be arrayed here except to say that Vitruvius and Alberti still live in the minds of many contemporary theorists. Concerning twentieth-century works on architectural theory, the best compilation is Dennis Sharp's *Sources of Modern Architecture: A Critical Bibliography* (1981). Few theoretical works of the last three-quarters of a century have been as influential on modern practicing architects (as against theorists) as Le Corbusier's *Vers une architecture (Towards an [a New] Architecture)* of 1923, the *Bauhaus* books by Walter Gropius, or Frank Lloyd Wright's *An Organic Architecture: The Architecture of Democracy* (1939), for the period to 1949; and Le Corbusier's *Le Modulor* (1950) and *Modulor 2* (1955), Gropius's *The Scope of Total Architecture* (1956), Robert Venturi's *Complexity and Contradiction in Architecture* (1966), and Christopher Alexander's *A Pattern Language* (1977), for the period after 1950. In devoting almost half of two hundred pages to theory (a quarter of which advance 'an integrated theory of architecture'), Norberg-Schulz's *Intentions in Architecture* (1965) is one of the few works of recent years to attempt a coordinated account of theoretical notions, even though significant portions lacked clarity.

COMMENTARY   The introduction defined theory broadly as a process of discourse mediating design ideas, rather than as a stand-alone notion prior to and governing design, and raised a number of theoretical issues relating to theory's province. This clears the way to discussing a few specific matters concerning the processes of mediation. It is not an extravagant claim to say that theory as design-talk has achieved a far higher status and volume of writing in architecture in the past few years than in almost any previous era. Why is this the case and what are its effects? The dramatic increase in critical literary theory and the changes in discourse that have accompanied it has prompted the literary and legal theorist Stanley Fish to remark of declarations by literary theorists that theory's claims over change and redirection "are not disputed but are made the basis of a fear by those who see in theory the specter of frivolous and value-subverting change and hope . . . that when the rage for theory abates, 'the study of literature can continue its uninterrupted course without having suffered any permanent damage'" (Fish 1989:154).

Such 'theory-fear' is paralleled in architecture by historian Sylvia Lavin (1990) in a short article on the 'uses and abuses' of theory; it is her essay that provides the basis for much of this section. Berating the 'theory frenzy' and its imperial ambitions, Lavin rails against its militancy, its 'subversion', its assumption of 'strategic arms', and its 'radical weaponry'. But we need not fear, for Lavin is really scoffing at theory's supposed revolutionary influence. All is to no avail, she asserts, because the revolution is only 'attempted', turned out in an 'Armani suit'; the 'seeds of failure' are cast about on 'verbal quicksand'. The theory revolution is debased by being turned into an architectural commodity; it is ironic rather than serious, and therefore it cannot be counted as a threat any longer.

A path through the battlefield now properly cleared by Lavin, the way is open for a return to theory remaining benignly theoretical and architecture being safely architectural, except for one final remark: ". . . generating architecture's will to theorize seems to be the idea that by using the radical power of theory, which contains within it the sum of all human discourse, architecture will become both revolutionary and universal. This has an ominously familiar ring. It would seem in fact that critical theory has seduced architecture into thinking it can realize the failed goals of the Modern Movement" (Lavin 1990:179). With this comment, Lavin adds an extra tag to her body bag of critical theory: a failed revival of ignominious modernism, the architectural equivalent of calling it Hitler.

This harangue of Lavin's need not have been written at all if, instead of theory being considered a *thing*, it had been thought of as design-talk. Once admitted, Lavin's critique could have proceeded without fear of marauding theory, enabling her to speak freely about her real agenda: the Modern Movement. For, far from the failed Titan being a standard for dismissing theory, Lavin sees in contemporary architectural theory's "yearning to return to the heroic security of Modern ambitions" a reduction of those ambitions to "mere representations and shallow caricatures of their former selves." In other words, the cause Lavin is trumpeting presumably is the hope of a revitalized Modern Movement, or at least the revitalized hope of a functionalism not-yet-dead. Surely it will no longer distress too many architects to declare once again that the Modern Movement's functionalist ambitions *were* mere representations and shallow caricatures long before contemporary theory transformed them into the post-functionalist concern for a dialectic of form (Eisenman, in Emanuel 1980).

What this critique shows is the emotional and intellectual investment in theory, the privileging of one kind of design-talk over another. Such is the way of theory, it seems, that it has been and is still seen as a colonizing creature; dormant for years, it periodically erupts with the force of Ripley's alien. But, as Fish (1989) has remarked of deconstruction and any other theoretical pronouncement, "it announces a rationale for practices already in force; it provides a banner under which those who are already doing what it names can march; it provides a visible target for those who have long thought that things are going from bad to worse." Any change or threat of change thought to have been caused by theory is misunderstood because, while there may be a new rush of articles, symposia, and journals, "theory does not cause change on the level claimed by those who either see it as a means of salvation or fear it as the subverter of values" (155). If there is a criticism of 'critical theory', it is that theory cannot be self-conscious and does not oblige explication of its assumptions beyond its own embeddedness any more than any other kind of talk does. Like its reciprocal, history, "Theory is a form of practice, as rooted in particular historical and cultural conditions as any other . . . the extent to which its introduction will or will not give rise to changes, small and large, cannot be determined in advance" (Fish 1989:156).

Another consideration in the idea of theory as a colonial power is the belief many architects have that it is both possible and desirable for there to be one grand theory of architecture. The pursuit of a unified theory has occupied only a few writers openly over the past three or four generations, but has been a hidden agenda in much architectural writing, especially during the foundation years of modernism. The signals are quite evident among the key writers cited in the Trace above and among many less popular writers, either in reporting the immanence of such a goal, proclaiming it is in their sights as it were, or in their arrival at some totalizing concept. Only in a very few writers over the last quarter of the twentieth century can a progressive working agenda on theory be detected. Perhaps the American theorist and architect Christopher Alexander comes closest to having explored theory most assiduously. His 'pattern language' approach has had and still has an enormous impact on architects and architectural education, despite its idiosyncrasy and his own claims to its unsatisfactoriness, most probably because it has been one of the few to theorize graphically as well as conceptually.

It is the main thesis of this book that if theory is construed as design-talk it can be seen to permeate all architectural endeavor. Theory's role in the practice of architecture has been thought to *guide* practice, but its effect has actually been to *mediate* the day-to-day decisions of practice through discourse, either on the broad level of architectural media or the intimate level of the special dialogue that occurs between designer and artifact. It mediates the practice of architecture by intervening between a proposal or concept and the history of all previous proposals and concepts, whether fictional, unbuilt, or built. Design-talk has developed its own language and has undergone stylistic changes in the manner of its discourse, certain phrases, themes, and concepts finding favor at one moment and being discarded at the next. And it has created its own mythos, the heroes and villains of architecture, the privileged great architects and great works, the marked as against the vast array of the unmarked.

FURTHER SOURCES   Allsopp 1977; Antoniades 1990; Banham 1962; Diani and Ingraham 1988; Frascari 1988,1991; Hays 1990; Ingraham 1991; Kahn 1991; Kipnis 1990; Lang 1987; Lavin 1990; Zambonini 1989.

2. Theory and Architectural Practice

When theory and practice are united in one person, the ideal condition of art is attained, because art is enriched and perfected by knowledge . . . **Giorgio Vasari.** "Life of Alberti." Cited by Leopold D. Ettlinger in Kostof 1977:97.

Theory and practice form the counterpoint of architecture. *Ratio-cinatio* and *Fabrica,* or *ars* and *scientia,* or design and building, it is always out of this bi-polarity that architecture can be comprehended, that the story of architecture as idea and reality can be told. **Adolf K. Placzek.** In Wiebenson 1983:Foreword.

But for his *pragma* architectural man needs his *theoria:* the ever-loved Orders, the constant search for ideal proportions, the concepts of symmetry, harmony, perfection. **Adolf K. Placzek.** In Wiebenson 1983:Foreword.

Theory can change practice by legitimizing usages condemned by previous theories. **Juan Pablo Bonta.** 1979:64.

Praxis ceases to have theoretical ballast: each social practice runs its own show, and the 'theoretical practice'—the intellectuals' job—would be just one of them, were it not for the fact that, in a sense, it is bound to be an unhappy practice, doomed to self-suspicion and bad consciousness. **Jose G. Merquior.** 1985:85.

. . . whether the turn to textuality is considered an expansion of architectural practice into new critical realms, a closing down of the practice into new forms of formalism, or . . . an emerging attempt to construct a countermemory of the architectural avant-garde's radical but failed past, will depend on one's construction of the ideological trajectory of modernism into the present as much as the personal politics of these practitioners or their critics. **K. Michael Hays.** 1988.

Transgression does not belong to the same space as the idea, except as something that subverts it. That is why transgression is a matter not for theory but for practice. **Denis Hollier.** 1989:25.

In short, theory is not consequential even when the practitioner is himself a theorist. Indeed, the practitioner may cease to be a theorist or may wake one morning (as I predict we all will) to find that theory has passed from the scene and still continue in his life's work without ever missing a beat. **Stanley Fish.** 1989:335.

Architecture tends to make an absolute separation between theory and practice, between analysis and synthesis. This difference, however, could be better expressed in the difference between discourses: an analytical, exploratory, critical discourse and a normative discourse. Most theories are developed within the first category, while practice falls into the latter. **Diana Agrest.** 1991:1.

TRACE In use from the end of the fifteenth century, the English word 'practice' superseded the late medieval 'practic' adopted from the Latin *practicus* and from the Greek *praktikos,* 'record, action', from *prattein,* to 'do, act'. The term *praxis* stems from the same root but has become an affectation in architectural writing of late. Related to the legal use as 'a deed', from the sixteenth century, practice meant 'the habitual doing or carrying on of something; customary or constant action; action as distinct from profession, theory, knowledge; conduct' (SOED). By distinguishing it from theory, contemplation, or speculation, the dictionary definition underscores the main thesis of this book—that theory is a form of practice. Practice also had the meaning of scheming and underhand dealings, conspiracy, intrigue, and collusion, or the results therefrom, such as a scheme, plot, intrigue, maneuver, or artifice.

As to the relation between theory and practice, the ancient Greeks used *akribeia* "as a term in professional criticism used primarily to assess the degree of precision with which an artist had translated theory into practice (or in Vitruvian terminology *ratiocinatio* into *opus*). The term was perhaps also used to evaluate exactitude in the rendering of small details" (Pollitt 1974:124-125). Its Latin translations are *diligens* and *diligentia,* which were used also in relation to complexity of detail as well as precision. "Vitruvius's mention of a *ratio* of *symmetria* to which architects should adhere *diligentissime* (passage 1 [Vitruvius 3.1.1]) is remarkably similar in language to Pliny's comment on Lysippus, and since this passage occurs in the portion of the *De Architectura* which is most deeply indebted to Greek architectural theory and its terminology, it seems possible that here too *diligentissime (akribestata)* refers not simply to a general diligence but rather to precision in the application of theory to technique" (Pollitt 1974:355). Theory and practice were "most sharply defined and most perfectly interwoven" between the fifteenth and eighteenth centuries after the rediscovery of Vitruvius in 1414 and his publication in 1485 (although beaten to print the year before by Alberti) followed by a succession of writings by theoretician-cum-practitioner architects such as Serlio, Palladio, Vignola, and Scamozzi and a multitude of writers of lesser fame (Placzek in Wiebenson 1983).

COMMENTARY   Architectural design-talk resides in the subjective, in Husserl's 'world-for-us'. Architectural theory at times falsely assumes an absolute sense because of our tendency to solidify life's events by isolating, identifying, naming, ordering, classifying, and sequencing, so that complexities may be more readily pinned down and comprehended. Such processes reflect the Cartesian scientific method, which presupposes there is an order to the world that we today believe essential to our understanding of the world, to our control of our situation within the world, to the *power* we exercise over it. But these constructions of ours are of little or no relevance to the world *per se* that is the object of our attention, a view that may be criticized for its lack of acknowledgment of a separate and superordinate metaphysical explanation of the world, for its separation of subject and object, and for its construing of a *per se* for the world even though such a concept is not at all clear.

These criticisms are largely irrelevant, however, to theory as a mediating practice in architecture, because the mediation proceeds no matter which stance we adopt. In other words, the outcome of any mediation will be independent of our way of construing a task, even though the outcome depends totally on our ushering it into existence by our construing; our buildings, once built, become detached from our theorizing about them. As Philip Johnson wrote in response to the moralizing at the end of Australian architect and critic Robin Boyd's *The Puzzle of Architecture* in 1966, "I believe architecture, even present architecture, just happens. Rationalizations are interesting; Mies (less is more), Kahn (servant spaces) have interesting minds and their theories illuminate their work. But architecture will have immortality for different reasons that are hard for contemporaries to fathom. . . . History will tell" (Johnson 1979:133).

The precise relation between theory and practice is most elusive, though there appears to be some relation between linking text and imagery, concept and percept. Vitruvius's *De architectura* was first published by the Latin grammarian Fra Giovanni Sulpitius, but did not impact theory and practice until the first illustrated editions appeared some twenty-five years later. Aimed at a nonscholarly readership, the illustrations in these editions were "inexact attempts to make Vitruvius's Latin text comprehensible." Critical treatises followed, annotating and supplementing the Vitruvian text and improving the scholarship of the illustrations. By the end of the eighteenth century theory and practice were united in professional treatises that brought together rules of mathematics, proportion, ordering, geometry, and classical history with empirical studies and improved mechanical and technological understanding. By the end of the eighteenth century and on into the nineteenth, architectural studies included "the extreme statements of unrealizable projects reflecting the individual philosophies and ideals of the architects who designed them, specifically those of Boullée . . . and of Ledoux, who developed a universal style based on the architectural expression of new social ideals and scientific discoveries. With the work of these men . . . theory and practice were severed" (Wiebenson 1983). Of most interest is that illustration now far outstripped text and achieved an autonomy that persisted until well into the twentieth century. Over the past fifteen years, despite or perhaps because of the continuing commodification of the image, text has been sharply on the rise and the theory-practice division is once more the agenda.

One way to understand the relationship between theory and practice is to pick up on the notion of 'ushering'. The word 'usher', from the Old French *uissier* (hence huisher, husher), which in turn derives from the Latin *ostiarius*, 'door-keeper', is potent with associations for architecture and for theory. An ostiary is the keeper of the opening or door *(ostium)* and so is a janitor, from *Janus* the Roman deity to whom was ascribed "the origin of all things, the introduction of the system of years, the change of season, the ups and downs of fortune, and the civilization of the human race by means of agriculture, industry, arts, and religion." Janus was the god of "good beginning", and for the Romans "great stress was laid on the circumstances attending the commencement of any project. Janus opened and closed things. He sat, not only on the confines of the earth, but also at the gates of heaven." Janus has two faces, one of a youth representing the beginning, the other of an old man indicating the end. He is depicted with a key in one hand for the opening and closing of circumstances and a scepter in the other as "a sign that he controls the progress of every undertaking" (Murray 1874:132–134). The temple to Janus in the Roman forum had its gates open in time of war and closed in time of peace.

There is neat concurrence between these ideas and the word 'hush', which certainly has onomatopoeic connection with usher or 'husher' and as a verb means to make silent, to still or quiet, especially after prolonged noise. In northern English dialects it is a mining term meaning the rush of water used to expose ore or bedrock. The connection with the act of designing as a tumultuous and at times noisy affair, the mediating role of theory as design-talk laying bare the bedrock of a solution, and the quietude and peace of mind attendant upon a successful outcome is undeniable, if romantic.

The thrust of architectural education makes an alignment with practitioner priorities inevitable through certification of the schools in the first place and through the subsequent viability of graduates in the marketplace. Even if voice can be given to those priorities, it is a mistake; rather than reflecting 'reality' they represent an ideology, a transformation of reality (Teymur 1982:177) differing from that of academe; each perpetuates certain fictive and mythic qualities of the architectural profession. Any claim by practitioners to 'knowing their own mind' vis-a-vis academics, or vice versa, is a misnomer. What takes place between the practitioners and educators are discourses of varying political clout. The practicing architect most frequently claims that graduates lack production skills of immediate benefit as 'units' in practice. While educators usually claim that they teach such skills, their major emphasis is always on the conceptual processes of designing—on design-talk—an ability not immediately utilized by first employers until after they get the young graduate past the not-to-my-standard-of-skill hurdle. Recent cries of "Why aren't students at least taught theory any more?" by some practitioners, by which they seem to mean either design principles or working methods of one kind or another as a basis for decision-making, seem to be just another variation on the criticism that students emerge from universities as 'empty vessels'.

FURTHER SOURCES   Grabow 1983; Strasser 1963; Wiebenson 1983.

3. Theory and Architectural Criticism

He only moves towards perfection of his art whose criticism surpasses his achievement. **Leonardo da Vinci.** Knevitt 1986:#276

The critic has special responsibilities toward the art of his own age. He must ask not only whether it represents a technical advance or refinement, and whether it adds a twist of style or plays adroitly on the nerve of the moment, but what it contributes to or detracts from the dwindled reserves of moral intelligence. What is the measure of man this work proposes? **George Steiner.** 1967:28.

In the traditional approach, designers are not supposed to listen to the feedback of criticism any more than actors in the midst of a play are expected to engage in a conversation with their audience. In fact, designers very seldom acknowledge having been influenced by the writing of critics and historians. **Juan Pablo Bonta.** 1979:231.

When a work departs from culturally established patterns, it always requires a collective effort of clarification. Architecture becomes incorporated into culture as a result of the work of critics, no less than that of designers. **Juan Pablo Bonta.** 1979:138.

The distinctive high culture that predicted the object . . . validates the critic and the critical journal in a cycle of affirmation that maintains rigidly and defined disciplinary boundaries, dominant institutions, and disengaged modes of practice. **K. Michael Hays.** 1988:40.

Every ideal of the critic corresponds to an ideal of the reader; that maxim is alone sufficient to lead us to look on the pretensions of more recent semiotic criticism with suspicion. **Roger Scruton.** 1983:27.

The critic's responsibility is to contain and limit revisionism and keep alive the revolutionary values. I believe in creativity and if you want to call that permanent revolution, I have no objection. I am the Trotsky of art and architecture? I am honoured! **Bruno Zevi.** In Dean 1983:91.

The critic is the link between people and buildings that make the public realm; the critic's view of the art of architecture must embrace the policy and the culture that are inseparable from it. It is the repeated messages and small improvements in these relationships that make the difference. There is a critical responsibility to keep an eye unwaveringly on the values and quality that cannot survive compromise. . . . **Ada Louise Huxtable.** 1986:xvi-xvii.

Critical work today can be done only in the realm of building: to engage with the discourse, architects have to engage with building; the object becomes the site of all theoretical inquiry. Theorists are forced out of the sanctuary, practitioners are roused from sleepwalking practice. Both meet in the realm of building, and engage with objects. **Philip Johnson** and **Mark Wigley.** 1988:19.

TRACE   While the word 'critic' entered the English language in the middle of the sixteenth century, it derives from the Greek *kritikos* (Latin *criticus*), from *krites* meaning 'judge'. Pollitt (1974) shows that the ancient Greeks possessed a critical tradition based primarily around the concepts of idealism and naturalism with which the ancient world came to be viewed during the Renaissance, although other critical principles coexisted with them from time to time. Evidence of an antique critical tradition is gleaned from words scattered throughout ancient literature, emanating principally from four sources: compilers of tradition, literary analogists, moral estheticians, and professional critics.

Vitruvius's *De architectura* is the only substantial architectural work of the ancient writers to survive to the present day, though it was only one of an apparently extensive body of critical writings that seem to have dealt "primarily with problems of engineering . . . [and] may also have treated questions of form and proportion" (Pollitt 1974:12). Critical writing in the modern architectural sense appeared in earnest, however, only from the late-eighteenth century on and reached a level of refinement and scope with John Ruskin. This body of critical thought was not to advance until the hortatory writings of the key exponents of the early Modern Movement.

COMMENTARY   Pollitt briefly examines the critical tradition around Vitruvius and discerns one broad theory he shares with art criticism, the *decor* theory or 'the rational theory of appropriateness' which he describes as "the principle by which one judges whether the form of a building is appropriate to its function and location and whether the details of the building are appropriate to its total form" (Pollitt 1974:68–70). It is not surprising, considering the foundational importance of Vitruvius to architecture since the Renaissance, that criticism has differed little up to recent times. Norberg-Schulz in 1965 declared that "criticism generally limits itself to the 'judgement' of more or less arbitrarily chosen properties of the work in question." For him theory "offers the terminology," as was the case with the ancient Greeks; "the analytical methods" and the relation between theory and criticism is a 'semantical' one:

What the theory tells us about the architectural quality is of basic importance to criticism. The semantical correspondence between task and means, for instance, is essential. A work of architecture is above all judged by investigating if the form 'fits' the task, or if the solution has to be characterized as 'formalistic'. If a satisfactory semantical correspondence is lacking, the criticism may be considered complete if it points out this state of affairs. But if the correspondence exists, one has to go on investigating whether the task has been defined properly and the form articulated adequately. . . . The criticism, in other words, should ask whether the solution is a real *solution* to the task in question, or if it is only more or less pleasant, but irrelevant (Norberg-Shulz 1965:214–215).

Norberg-Schulz's comments are very much the manner of the day, before the modernist agenda was proclaimed to have failed. He is saying that the critic must relate the work to the theory of the work—the design-talk—and test its consistency. The critic, he continues, "should be without preconceived ideas and possess a complete theoretical insight"; but he does not clarify exactly how complete, or what this insight comprises, or whether the critic's own theory of architecture should intercede. The architect and historian Bruno Zevi maintains that it should: "Every critic should feel it his duty to state clearly what he believes in and what he stands for—and against. . . . At least it gives you something to disagree with at a time when most critics neither agree nor disagree, but simply 'explain'" (Dean 1983:91). Beliefs and stands do not of themselves amount to theory, so the relation remains unclear. Reyner Banham points up the intellectual dilemma:

> . . . the production of a properly generalized theory of architecture really involves leaving out the particulars. . . . But, presented with a particular building on a particular site, criticism, evaluation, history cannot proceed in absence of such particulars as the designated function of the building. Practically every critic, . . . historian, . . . journalist who is in the business, in fact, changes gear persistently between the one and the other mode of operation, general and particular (Whiffen 1965:92).

Banham suggests that one answer to this dilemma is to base the criticism in the original brief or program, especially when dealing with buildings that are less formally constrained or rule-governed, and are not traditional types such as housing. He claims that by the critic being so embedded, an experiential or 'situationist' criticism will result, a kind of biography of the decisionmaking in the project, and that value judgments will arise from this process in "finding exemplified in the building, the consistent working out of a personal response to the commission" (Whiffen 1965:102). What is remarkable here is that Banham reiterates what Norberg-Schulz was writing at the time. Leaping forward a quarter-century we find the critic David Kolb remarking that "it is possible to escape the details of individual preference [in criticism] without demanding rational universality . . . by studying the processes of discipline [as in a craft] leading to graceful skill and insight . . . [so] that we might come to understand what it means to be a developed person or society" (Kolb 1990:58). Kolb, like Banham, suggests taking on board the 'processes of discipline', or in other words, theory.

Professionals like the former architecture critic of the *New York Times,* Ada Louise Huxtable (1986), see their role as 'universal consciousness-raising': she writes of "an awakening awareness of the components, and the effects, of what and how we build" (xv), even though she couples this with a sense of despair that critics overall make little difference to architecture. Her successor, the architect Paul Goldberger (1983), feels the same about the power of the critic but is more explicit about the role: "It is to argue critically for a set of values and standards without trying to shape a city or profession in one's own image. It is to evaluate works of design realistically, harshly, and honestly without coming to them with an overpowering ideological bias" (4). Both are pedagogical in relation to the public and not a little cautious in relation to the professionals responsible for building. The New York architect and former critic Michael Sorkin (1990) sees the critic's role slightly differently, opting to 'keep the bastards honest' as it were, and hopefully inventive and exacting, no matter who they are and especially if they are Paul Goldberger (101–108). All seem to agree that there is a responsibility to make public the values revered by the critic, designer, authorities, or professions involved, and to sheet home blame or congratulation to them or sometimes across society. Regarding literary criticism, Roger Scruton sees three kinds of critic:

> I have described three kinds of critic—the critic of skill, the critic of metalanguage, and the critic, as one might express it, of 'common culture'. To each critic there corresponds an ideal reader. Only in the third case does it seem obvious that the critic addresses his remarks to readers of literature who are not also professionals. This is the reason why I can see hope for the defence of the objectivity of criticism only in the postulate of the this third ideal. The critic must have certain general capacities to respond to works of literature, and be capable of entering into cultural relation with the uninitiated reader (1983:29).

Substitute *architecture* for *literature* in this extract, and the first kind of architectural critic services professional journals and awards, the second builds a reputation as a writer for 'critical' academic journals, and the third contributes to the popular press. The transposition seems valid; each of the quotations at the head of this section may be so classified. If Scruton is correct about the third, the second and first will probably need to be architects if they wish their criticism to relate to theory. In any case, there are two critical modes: *interrogative*, or *dialogic*, in which there is exchange between designer and critic, or in which there is a situation that makes adjustment to the work possible; and *static*, or *independent*, in which the critique is aloof from the work or is separated in time. Each mode is an interpretation of a work that assists in placing the work retrospectively in some scheme of things. Static criticism is the basis for history and theory because it is written. No mechanism exists for static criticism to affect the production of a work, and therefore it is of marginal consequence to a designer except by inference, however important it might be to the historian or theorist.

A designer might try to second-guess what criticism a work is likely to attract once it is completed on the basis of what a critic has said previously about that designer or about that kind of work. Or a designer might acquiesce in certain judgments about various bodies of work and thereby attempt to align a new work with what the designer perceives to be a consensus about certain matters in relation to such work with the desire of being embraced by that consensus. Interrogative criticism takes place if a designer makes a tentative statement during the initial phase of design in a tactical exercise to rehearse reactions, and in an effort to determine where the consensus or contentions might lay. This can be informal through peer group association and discussion, or formal through critique. The closest static criticism comes to being interactive in practice is through competition, whether staged or not. Interrogative criticism occurs in 'participatory design' and in education through the convention of studio critique and other feedback.

Just as theory does not guide or inform practice, neither does it guide criticism. If theory as the practice of design-talk mediates design and building practice, then it moderates critical practice, keeps it within limits. Criticism inevitably remains beyond the *conceptual* act of designing. The difficulty for theory as mediator is how to accommodate criticism as an operative. Any attempt to apply criticism to design and building practice is nonsense, and any attempt to make theory a 'critical' mediating practice is a tautology.

FURTHER SOURCES   Bonta 1979; Fitch 1976; Ghirardo 1991.

4. The Language of Architectural Theory

History is captivating . . . for it holds out the hope of various novelties. Poetry . . . delights the feelings of the reader, and leads him smoothly on to the very end of the work. . . . But this cannot be the case with architectural treatises, because those terms which originate in the peculiar needs of the art, give rise to obscurity of ideas from the unusual nature of the language. **Vitruvius.** Book V, Introduction:§1–2.

. . . man is a discursive function among complex and already-formed systems of language, which he witnesses but does not constitute. As Lévi-Strauss has said, "Language, an unreflecting totalization, is human reason which has its reason and of which man knows nothing." It is this condition of displacement which gives rise to design in which authorship can no longer either account for a linear development that has a "beginning" and an "end"—hence the rise of the atemporal—or account for the invention of form—hence the abstract as a mediation between pre-existent sign systems. **Peter Eisenman.** In Emanuel 1980:231.

[one] ideal of the critic . . . is that of a man possessed not of a certain skill but of a certain language. This language is not shared with any reader of literature who is not himself a critic: nor is it one recognized by the writer. It is a 'metalanguage', which is designed purely for the interpretation, and not for the composing, of primary texts . . . criticism must be as available as the works that it

criticizes. It cannot take refuge in a 'metalanguage' which has only texts as its field of reference and unauthorized jargon as its terms. **Roger Scruton.** 1983:26–27.

Art as palliative is an indulgence not permitted painters, architects, or sculptors. Metaphysical speculation, insight into man's soul, and understanding of the arch-aesthetic are anathema to their purpose. There is no need for them to be concerned with potentially rebellious thoughts. The architect's world has to be governed by rational discourse that upholds the fiction of a perennially stable society. **Mark Jarzombek.** 1989:155.

Despite the often difficult terminology and abstruse constructions employed in those discussions [analyzing professional boundaries], they are not hermetic exercises in arcane academic self-indulgence. Rather, they aspire to a direct and informative discourse with design and professional practice. **Jeffrey Kipnis.** 1990a:99,158.

Architects may always have felt little sympathy for verbal analysis; but never before the Modern Movement, and never again since, has intellectual discourse been so openly and unabashedly despised. **Juan Pablo Bonta.** 1990:13.

Manifestos are a form of orthodoxy. In the newborn twentieth century, protectors of the arts are rare and the state is weak. The *word* becomes prince, and manifestos become the guides that will guard and counsel . . . the architectural manifesto takes on a particular perverse dimension. It determines the distance between two realities: that of the intended object, building or city, and that of the individual, architect or otherwise. Like love-letters, manifestos create an erotic distance between the desiring parties. **Bernard Tschumi.** 1990:38–39.

TRACE   As shown in 1A.3, Criticism, the genesis of art criticism is to be found in the language of early Greek texts, and it was Vitruvius who brought to architecture its special language. Although available in various Latin translations from 1485, and in French, German, and Spanish from 1521, Vitruvius was not available in English until John Shute's *The First and Chief Groundes of Architecture* (1563) became the first book on architectural theory. Utilizing the writings of Vitruvius, Serlio, and Philander, Shute introduced the words 'architect', 'architecture', 'Orders', the names and parts of the Orders, and the word 'symmetry' to English society (Hughes and Lynton 1962:305).

Sir Henry Wotton's *The Elements of Architecture* (1624) was to immortalize the Vitruvian triad of "firmeness, commoditie and delight." Alberti instigated the modern notion of architecture as a learned profession in his *De re aedeficatoria* printed in 1585 and exemplifying the model of the architect as *uomo universale*. The book was written "not so much as a practitioner to other practitioners, but as a humanist explaining to the important and rich people of his day about the exalted profession of architecture and its place in public life" (Kostof 1985:407). Since becoming, in Alberti's terms, the master of a universal law that God applies in nature, "the architect in his pursuits approaches the divine

... [which] kind of talk made lodge masons extremely uneasy [because] they were being demoted by a bookish breed of men who knew Latin and Greek and had gone to Rome to look at ruins ... but who could not dress a stone or turn a vault. And the contempt was mutual" (408).

Feeding on the new language about architecture, this bookish breed began to analyse, categorize, and systematize architecture. Serlio reduced church plans to twelve types, Palladio recommended seven room shapes in harmonic proportion in order to create a 'fugal' system of universal import (Wittkower 1973:128), and Blondel's *Encyclopedie* dealt with three key theoretical concepts: method, process, and complexity (Harrington 1985:143). In the twentieth century, architectural writers tried to abandon Beaux Arts terminology by denigration, ornament became a crime, and composition was to undergo a series of rises and falls in favor. Most recently, postmodernism has continued to invent terms, not through the denial of timeless concepts, but through parody and irony.

COMMENTARY   This section is not about the language of architecture in the sense of architecture as a communicative medium (for which see chapter 10), but about its conceptual language, the unauthorized jargon of Scruton's 'metalanguage', the language that enables talk *about* architecture, the language that informs theory, the vocabulary of design-talk. When we talk about architecture, certain terms are conventions and others are invented for the discussion, in time becoming the convention, or else being lost. At first deriving from art and sculpture via Vitruvius, the theoretical aspirations of architects have seen concepts usurped from other disciplines to create an amalgam metalanguage. Terms specific to physics, mathematics, biology, anthropology, psychology, sociology, genetics, literature, and electronics are colonized by architecture, while architectural terms are in turn plundered by philosophy, literature, history, and computer science in a merry chicken-and-egg dance. Words transferred from other disciplines bring with them their antecedent meanings but begin to lose their former specificity in favor of their meaning in their newfound discipline.

For instance, the adoption of concepts like 'selection', 'crossover', and 'mutation' from genetics to describe certain processes in studies of how artificial intelligence might operate in designing describe what a design science researcher *conceives* certain AI processes to be *without* the fullness of their genetic history and usage. Peter Collins (1965) has written about architecture's usurpation by analogy of words from biology, mechanics, gastronomy, and language (!) for use as and as an influence in architectural concepts. He has also remarked on the imprecision of analogies, especially the biological but applicable to all, saying, "It would seem as if the analogy must always be general and poetic" (153). Such imprecision applies today to the incorrect analogy between philosophical deconstruction and architectural deconstructivism. Operative words in other disciplines are selected for their near equivalence to an architectural concept, decontextualized, initially made descriptive in architecture, and may eventually become operative but in a way quite unrelated to their origins.

The transportability of words belies their transparency, because upon close examination some words do not convey what may be intended at a particular time or conceived in their selection; their genealogy "gets in the way" and they need readjustment. The difficulty architects have in declaring some unity in the term 'architecture', for instance, seems not to inhibit its use in computer science, history, or the media. Architectonic terms already exist in other disciplines—the 'foundations' of philosophy, the 'construction' of a legal case, the 'building' of empires, the 'edifice' of government, the 'windows' of opportunity in politics or space shots, the 'threshold' of a new era, the turning of a 'corner' in one's life—trivial examples, perhaps, but indicative of the reach of architectural metaphors. Historians, computer scientists and news commentators seem perfectly at ease with using 'architect' as meaning some holistic embrace of the context to which it is applied, in relation to a war, a computer assembly, or a fiscal policy, for example; indeed they seem wholly oblivious to the architectural debate.

What is it that makes 'architect(ure)' so transparent for these groups but not for architects? English biographer and critic Lytton Strachey's remark in *Eminent Victorians* is appropriate here: "Ignorance is the first requisite of the historian, ignorance which simplifies and clarifies, which selects and omits" (cited in Carr 1965:14). Architectural theoreticians too can simplify and clarify concepts by steadfastly selecting and omitting words from other disciplines and remaining ignorant of their use, a liberty that does not always pertain to their readers. While importing words from other disciplines to architecture may initially be helpful in tagging elusive concepts, if words are not employed for their constancy of meaning, then exploiting them by changing contexts only exacerbates their inconstancy and frustrates clarity.

Just as the continuity of legal judgment through precedent maintains faith in the law, we have a natural inclination and a cultural investment in perpetuating the meanings of words in the everyday world; otherwise communication would be difficult. But, as we know, language is a living and dynamic thing and change of meaning, albeit slow, is inevitable. Words and phrases are subject to fashion and to political manipulation; they are incorporated into the language and leave behind merely a trace, a colonized prior meaning, or, occasionally, a new meaning, once the fashion or compulsion has passed. One recent example of manipulation is the push to turn declared negative connotations into positive connotations to meet antidiscrimination laws, prompting a new crop of euphemisms: the 'disabled' are now 'differently abled', the 'aged' are now 'experientially advantaged', racial differences are minimized by saying 'people of color', and so on. Words and phrases also arise because new events occasion them and existing vocabularies do not suffice. Language changes to meet the circumstances; new words are created.

In our search for ways of talking about architecture, words often are unable to keep pace with changes occurring in current practice, so mismatches occur. The relative constancy of words (that is, their slower rate of change), especially in professional disciplines, imparts a constancy into talk about architecture that is perhaps unwarranted because practice is changing more quickly. Moreover, an assumed constancy plays havoc with design-talk because the use of etymology to array and anchor meanings ensures that theory as a mediating procedure is a drag on current architecture, always asking it to justify itself in pre-existent terms. Just as history is trapped in the present, so theory is trapped in the past; their words make them so. Could it be that the notion of theory guiding practice reflects this structural displacement in the language, that it is a misunderstanding arising from an assumed constancy, and therefore precedence, in the words used in design-talk, and that, in fact, the words are lagging behind design? Could this retardation in fact be a constraint that theory applies to practice, a natural conservatism, and that in the usual formulation, theory does not guide practice but practice paces theory? To construe theory as mediating talk, a dialogue with designing from a conservative position, and not as some *a priori* prescription or *a posteriori* description, makes a lot of sense.

Finally, a useful if cynical analysis of certain fallacies of reasoning in architecture is that of the Australian architect and critic Tom Heath (1991). Heath puts forward what he calls "traps in architectural discourse": definition, substituting words for thought; poetry, fine phrases that bypass critical thought; objective/subjective, evasion of discussion by denial of the public and objective and support of the private and subjective; reductionism, distilling singularity out of intolerable plurality; and relativism and its acceptance in the case of function or rejection in the case of esthetics. One trap he does not mention is that of the hermeneutic circle, the hermeneutical position being that we are all embedded in our world and cannot extricate ourselves in order to be 'objective' about matters like criticism or theory. This means that we become ensnared by the words used to describe architecture; the words infuse architecture and the theorist ends up bonded to both. What is needed in architecture is a word to describe the study of the writing of architectural theory, just as 'historiography' and 'historiology' describe the art or employment of writing history and the knowledge or study of history. The clumsy terms *theoreography* and *theoreology* are contenders; are there any others?

FURTHER SOURCES   Chapter 10B; Banham 1962, 1975; Blake 1977; Brolin 1976; Hesselgren 1972; Kuhn 1970.

5. Theory as Architectural Myth Maker

More and more people want to determine their own parameters of behaviour. . . . People are becoming more interested in people and reality, rather than in feeding mythical systems.

Unfortunately, however, in terms of doing your own thing, architecture is clearly not working. **Michael Webb** and **David Green.** Knevitt 1986:#285.

Myth explains the why and how of the here and now. The explanation given is not only authoritative, because it is given in the form of a myth, it is true to say that a myth has authority, because it offers an explanation. **T. P. Van Baaren** quoted in Dundes 1984:223.

. . . a theory may be inconsistent with the evidence, not because it is incorrect, *but because the evidence is contaminated*. . . . It is this *historico-physiological character of the evidence*, the fact that it does not describe some objective state of affairs *but also expresses subjective, mythical and long-forgotten views* concerning this state of affairs, that forces us to take a fresh look at methodology. It shows that it would be extremely imprudent to let the evidence judge our theories directly and without any further ado. A straightforward and unqualified judgement of theories by 'facts' is bound to eliminate ideas *simply because they do not fit into the framework of some older cosmology.* **Paul Feyerabend.** 1988:52–53.

Architects make architecture, historians make history and what they both make is myth. **Charles Jencks.** Jencks and Baird 1969:265.

TRACE   Contrary to the usual dictionary definition of myth as "a purely fictitious narrative" and its attendant derogatory connotations, Doty (1986:11) presents a complex working definition of myth, the first paragraph of which may be related to the conventional understanding of architectural theory, and the second paragraph to theory as design-talk, by substituting 'theory' for 'myth' and its derivatives:

A mythological corpus consists of (1) a usually complex network of myths that are (2) culturally important (3) imaginal (4) stories, conveying by means of (5) metaphoric and symbolic diction, (6) graphic imagery, and (7) emotional conviction and participation, (8) the primal, foundational accounts (9) of aspects of the real, experienced world and (10) humankind's roles and relative statuses within it.

Mythologies may (11) convey the political and moral values of a culture and (12) provide systems of interpreting (13) individual experience within a universal perspective, which may include (14) the intervention of suprahuman entities as well as (15) aspects of natural and cultural orders. Myths may be enacted or reflected in (16) rituals, ceremonies, and dramas, and (17) they may provide materials for secondary elaboration, the constituent mythemes having become merely images or reference points for a subsequent story, such as a folktale, historical legend, novella, or prophecy.

It is difficult to say precisely when the mythic content of architecture was recognized, and harder still to say when architecture was perceived as the content of myth. The ancient ziggurat and pyramid are symbols of an attempt to intersect with the divine, to recreate the Edenic garden atop the cosmic mountain, the desire of man to once again touch heaven, has been with us since recorded time. "The form originally used to attempt to reach heaven, the ziggurat, has its textual origin in the opening verses of Genesis, where, in describing creation, each verse is longer than the next" writes Stanley Tigerman, citing in support R. E. Clements's statement from his *God and Temple* (1972) that "the structure of the text resembles a pyramid; each succeeding day is accorded more space than its predecessor" (Tigerman 1988:29). Tigerman connects architecture with the moment oral tradition became written text, the covenant in the ark protected by the tent and tabernacle. He sees evidence of the persistence of formal representations of the tabernacle in John Wood's *The Origin of Building or the Plagiarism of the Heathens Detected* (Bath, 1741), Andre le Notre at Marly, Thomas Jefferson at the University of Virginia, and in Le Corbusier's drawings of it. Tigerman argues that the sparsity of Le Corbusier's sketches "reinforces his involvement in the tabula-rasa attitudes that emerged after World War I" (39).

COMMENTARY   Of two methods of seeking paradise, the oral and the written, the "written tradition creates heaven through the use of language and requires architecture to establish its *metaphorical case* [emphasis added]," writes Stanley Tigerman. "A divine ratio has been struck: the oral tradition is to the heavenly garden (the architecture of God) as the written tradition is to the ark containing the covenant (the architecture of man). Examples of both conditions abound throughout the history of architecture." The fixity and placedness of architecture is, for Tigerman, equivalent to reading the divine text committed to writing, and to human parity with God: "A heavenly union is joined and a cosmic intersection concretized. Architecture makes an offering gesture to God" (1988:43). What Tigerman relates may be interpreted as scriptural text requiring an architecture to contain it, the recording of scriptural text inspiring later architectures, which then call out as metaphorical texts for reinterpretation. Many of the elements of Doty's definition of myth are at work.

The mythic power of words, their inability to present constant meanings, and their ability to dissemble make of design-talk a disheveled process. To try to maintain consistency while talking about a work of architecture in the making is foolish, and "a foolish consistency is the hobgoblin of little minds" (Emerson, *Self-Reliance*). A work is neither consistent nor complete while it is being designed—it is fragmentary and experimental, it comes together only during and because of the doing. So any talk about a work of design can be only fragmentary. As Tschumi (1990) says "architecture, when equated with language, can only be read as a series of fragments which make up architectural reality" (58). And because we do not have any other way to relate to architecture, even 'envisaging' it in the doing or by direct experience, we must resort to words to make our relation known.

Any totalizing concept of architecture—trying to understand it by making sense of the fragments—cannot be factual. It can only be partial and necessarily imaginal if it pretends to completeness; in this sense it becomes its shadow and thus is mythic by definition. It is mythic too because it sustains itself against all comers. It does exactly what Van Baaren says myth does: it attempts to explain the why and how of things, often with more than human authority. When conflict occurs, theory gives way or adapts to practice; and the advent of writing in the form of the printed and disseminated text has so fixed theory that its flexibility is transferred to its exegesis, to the ways and means of doing, just as in the religions based on textual authority. Theory as a story of architecture that guides practice is one of its greatest myths; design-talk is its exegesis, only in the mediative is partiality recognized because that is the way concepts are integrated into the doing.

Theory can be added to Jencks's statement that "architects make architecture, historians make history, and what they both make is myth": separately, the three constitute myth. This is not to say that being mythic is a negative thing; any claim the design fields, including architecture, have to credibility rests on the power of their rhetoric to persuade and, since theory sustains so well, it is obviously persuasive. Slogans and aphorisms are the simplest forms of myth and are easily assimilated, so they become the most direct mode of disseminating ideas about architecture. Whether they are 'true' is immaterial as long as they seem convincing; they need only appear to be true to be utilized. If they seem to show a way or to resolve a difficulty, slogans and aphorisms flourish, though their success is largely fortuitous. Functionalism in the form of the aphorism that 'form follows function' is perhaps the most illustrious example of a professional myth that has achieved wide currency. Almost its equal was the assertion that industrial emancipation would lead to egalitarianism, what Porphyrios (1982) calls "the oracular myth of Modernism" (51-52).

Roland Barthes in his essay "Myth Today" (*Mythologies,* 1957) puts forward the structuralist notion of myth as a type of speech, a means of communication similar to the conception of theory as design-talk. Barthes's concept of myth means it cannot possibly be an object, a concept, or an idea; it is a mode of signification, a form, though he describes an intrinsic difficulty: "It can be seen that to purport to discriminate among mythical objects according to their substance would be entirely illusory: since myth is a type of speech, everything can be a myth provided it is conveyed by discourse. Myth is not defined by the object of its message, *but by the way in which it utters its message* [emphasis added]: there are formal limits to myth, there are no 'substantial' ones" (Barthes 1957:117). This is precisely the case with theory and with what Heidegger says about the created 'work': "Everything brought forth surely has this endowment of having been brought forth, if it has any endowment at all. Certainly. But in the work, createdness is expressly created into the created being, so that *it stands out from it,* from the being thus brought forth, *in an expressly particular way* [emphasis added]" (Heidegger 1936:181–182). This 'standing out', this 'expressly particular', this 'bringing forth' is not defined by the object of its message but by the way it utters, by the design-talk that mediates the work.

In other words, creativity in architecture is not the object created but is the *record* of the way it was created, of the decisions taken, of its relational properties, the attitudes that have enabled it to be. Just as it is myth's insubstantiality and formality that are important to Barthes's discussion, it is precisely the elusive qualities of architecture, its insubstantiality and its formality as a created work, that mark its creativity. As Denis Hollier says in *Against Architecture: The Writings of Georges Bataille* (1989), what remains after the functional and pragmatic are taken care of is the poetry of architecture.

In architecture, theory becomes the script of both canon and myth, just as Paul Feyerabend points out in discussing method in science. He suggests that one of the first steps in criticizing commonly used concepts is to import a new conceptual system "from outside science, from religion, from mythology, from the ideas of incompetents, or the ramblings of madmen" (Feyerabend 1988:53–54). It is impossible to 'import' such a system as Feyerabend suggests, but it *is* possible to 'invent' one, which seems to be more or less what he meant. The one thing students of architecture can do is to invent their own mythic realms. Some might say such realms hold too much sway in students and should be removed as soon as possible; I would say, on the contrary, stay with them for as long as they serve to inspire.

FURTHER SOURCES   Lévi-Strauss 1969.

B. Social Aspects of Theory

1. The Relevance of Social Concerns

There is, on the one hand, a dangerous trend towards limiting architecture to an aesthetic experiment detached from life, and, on the other, towards making technology an end instead of a means. It would be preferable to see the architect develop varied forms and expressions, not always meant to live too long, not always taken too seriously, but rather an architecture that is more alive and can add delight to our environment. A *divertimento* mood seems to be lacking in architecture today. The majority of buildings we see around us are a result of careful and factual but dull analysis. **James J. Sweeney** and **Josep L. Sert**. *Antoni Gaudí.* 1960:173–174.

The most fundamental questions address *what is built for whom:* expenditures for museums, skyscrapers, concert halls, and other objects of bourgeois gratification come at the expense of important and necessary social services, not to mention adequate housing at modest prices. Architects quietly design for the very same public-private partnerships that are responsible for razing masses of low-income housing . . . an ideological mask has been provided for developers, real estate interests, and government officials at all levels. **Diane Ghirardo.** 1991:15.

As individuals, most American architects sincerely assert that they are deeply concerned about issues of social and economic justice. Yet, over the past twenty years, as a profession they have steadily moved away from engagement with any social issues, even those that fall within their realm of professional competence, such as homelessness, the growing crisis in affordable and appropriate housing, the loss of environmental quality, and the challenge posed by traffic-choked, increasingly unmanageable urban areas. **Margaret Crawford.** "Can Architects Be Socially Responsible?" Ghirardo 1991:27.

What is so badly needed is for architects, and the developers who employ them, to be more sensitive to the deep-rooted feelings of 'ordinary' people and to find ways of integrating their opinions and their needs into the creative processes from which new buildings emerge. **Charles, Prince of Wales.** 1989:12.

TRACE   The notion of 'society' as an holistic or collective entity would appear to be lost in time, yet the word appears in English only from the mid-sixteenth century. As associations of like-minded individuals offering mutual support, formal societies seem to have appeared during the same period, although they existed in the form of guilds in continental Europe from the eleventh century and as merchant and craft guilds in England after the Norman Conquest in 1066. The 'social contract' as a voluntary agreement between individuals and government in which certain personal liberties are surrendered in return for an orderly society may be traced back to the sophist Lycophron (Flew 1979). The notion of 'society' as a distinct organization was systematically formulated later in the sixteenth century as a democratic opposition to the authority of the divine right of kings. The political-philosophical writings of Thomas Hobbes and John Locke in the seventeenth century were to further distinguish civil society from the state, and anticipated what was to later become the focus of sociology, as did the philosophies of history by Vico and of social change by Hegel.

The late eighteenth century saw model settlements develop as philanthropic land owners and manufacturers put into practice their socially conscious ideas. An architect-theorist like Claude-Nicolas Ledoux was able to partially implement a prototype socio-industrial ideal at the Royal Saltworks at Chaux, the final vision appearing only in published form in 1804. In England, village 'improvements' were conceived more as adornments to the picturesque surroundings of a gentleman's estate than as serious attempts to improve living conditions, while in the cities, social reform in the Georgian housing estates of the 1790s was largely seen as a matter of class-segregation. Architecture's social conscience began to reach out to a wider audience, if not directly address the wider problems, with pattern books on cottage architecture concerned with revamping housing on the basis of utility and economy, with a degree of social conscience expressed by those books geared to helping the lower classes like John Wood the Younger's *A Series of Plans for Cottages or Habitations of the Labourer* published in 1781. Woods's book "was one of several contemporary publications on the house that recognized the squalid state of the housing of the poor [and] was offered to landowners who wished to improve the condition of tenant housing" (Bradley Barker in Wiebenson 1983:III–D–35).

The social-corrective agenda continued to grow into the nineteenth century with benevolent practical settlements like Robert Owen's New Lanark in Scotland, utopian conceptions like Charles Fourier's *phalanstère* of 1834, and the experimental live-and-work *familistère* at Guise built from 1859 by Jean-Baptiste Godin. In the early twentieth century, Tony Garnier conceived his Industrial City as a model industrial-socialist society. Tony Schuman contends that the projects of Ledoux, Godin, and Garnier "share a belief in the perfectibility of human society and in the role of architecture as intrinsic to this transformation" (Ghirardo 1991:235-236).

The term 'sociology' was coined by the French positivist philosopher Auguste Comte in 1838 to describe the positive study of social structures and development; influential sociopolitical writings appeared by theorists such as Claude-Henri de Rouvroy, Comte de Saint-Simon, Alexis de Tocqueville, and Karl Marx, and by mid-century governments were legislating to improve social and health conditions in the industrializing cities. By the late nineteenth century moralizing was reaching deep into the minutiae of architectural theory with the writings of Ruskin and Viollet-le-Duc, and social conscience was inextricably bound to the personal moral agenda of every architect. Curtis (1982) sees the social theorizing and experimentation continuing in a direct line to the Modern Movement, while Manfredo Tafuri cautions that the relationship "between the utopias of Fourier, Owen, and Cabet and the theoretical models of Unwin, Geddes, Howard, or Stein, on the one hand, and those of the Garnier–Le Corbusier current, on the other, are but suppositions in need of careful verification" (Tafuri 1976b:44).

COMMENTARY   In the introduction to his *Theory and Design in the Second Machine Age* (1990), Martin Pawley sees a great weakness in the failure of the age—the thirty years since Reyner Banham wrote his . . . *First Machine Age*—that it has not produced any unifying theories of design at all. He finds this failure all the more remarkable because it occurred during a writing explosion following the proclamation of the death of modern architecture, "a failure so conspicuous that it might be argued that all the writing, theorizing and televising . . . has had the opposite effect: it has not so much explained architecture as buried its driving force, the social purpose of building, a purpose that in the Modern era generated a model relationship between theory and practice."

In an attempt to reclaim architecture's social agenda, the Pratt Institute organized a 'survey exhibition' at the Schaffler Gallery, Brooklyn, in February 1993 under the auspices of The Socially Conscious Design Project and having the theme *What is socially conscious design? A survey of alternative design education in the '90s*. The call for exhibitors sought submissions worldwide of student work "that explores issues of social responsibility and social change; work that challenges traditional formalistic dominant architectural values

. . . design thinking about creating just and equitable environments" (David Chapin and Stephen Marc Klein, "Call for Entries," May 1992).

The premise of the Pratt Institute exhibition is the antithesis of the sponsor, that there is out there 'socially unconscious' or, rather, 'anti-socially conscious' design being undertaken. Specifically, the flyer suggested that "much current design glides over social issues in favor of esthetic or formalistic concerns," with the further expectation that the survey would "reveal unrecognised energy and creativity," the kind that the majority of practitioners no doubt feel they participate in compared with the factional concerns of the lauded few. Not the first, and certainly not the last, calls such as this are the tip of an iceberg of irritable professional sentiment.

Returning to Pawley, he contends that architects today are no longer ideologically oriented but are visually oriented; "they are not in the sociology business but in the imaging business," a business in which "the old world of historical time has been telescoped . . . into a kind of illustrated catalogue of the built environment" (Pawley 1990:4). Because of the power of technology and media, and the overweening opinions against an 'art and science of building design' by the Prince of Wales, in Pawley's gloomy purview we appear to have reached the end of history and to be facing the prospect of architecture as a doomed profession. "Indeed," he writes, "for those with eyes to see there is already one visible pattern of destruction that could dissolve the ancient discipline of architecture within the lifetime of the future King. Even as 'architecture' is stretched thinner and thinner over a skeleton of serviced floor space, the increasingly confident use of the term by the computer industry suggests that it could end up under 'computer' in the dictionaries of the twenty-first century" (6).

Naturally enough, those who are unimpressed or untouched by fashionable rhetoric, radical chic, or the colonizing potential of high technology, the not-so-great-unwashed architects, feel somewhat intimidated by the constant calls these matters make on their attention, though it is doubtful that the profession at large is ready to accede to the Pratt Institute teaching or labeling its work 'alternative design', formerly the province of some fringe minority. If there is a way to access the unvoiced voice of the 'silent majority', the Pratt Institute exhibition may well be the answer.

Another perspective on the state of humanity is put by George Steiner, who made the following comment while writing *Language and Silence* (1967) under the specter of nuclear annihilation (so his sentiment is understandable); picking up the quotation from where it leaves off in 1A.3:

What is the measure of man this work proposes? It is not a question which is easily formulated, or which can be put with unfailing tact. But our time is not of the ordinary. It labours under the stress of inhumanity, experienced on a scale of singular magnitude and horror; and the possibility of ruin is not far off. There are luxuries of detachment one should like to afford, but cannot. . . .

The global nuclear threat may have passed but nuclear threat at a regional level was resurrected with Iraqi innuendo during the Gulf War, and most recently with the knowledge that the Right in South Africa has a nuclear capability. Less dramatic than impending holocaust but no less significant to Steiner's sentiments, daily reports of human disaster from the war in Bosnia, famine in Somalia, floods in India, volcanic eruption in the Philippines, and their equivalents almost anywhere in the world, are such that it is just as appropriate today to say that we "labor under the stress of humanity." Equally we might ask of any work of architecture today "What is the measure of man this work proposes?"—but we don't.

Even housing, which can be the most sanctimonious of social realms, is something of a dead duck in what it offers by way of reward for architects in the First World. Unless it has mechanismic possibilities or the chance for a gimmick, housing is rarely a top-charter in today's architectural press—it is the ubiquitous backdrop it ever was, amid which might be found an occasional glorying experiment, not a means for pro-active concern for the future of society. The era of social engineering has been replaced by sartorial engineering, with the architect as its *ingenium,* no doubt soon to displace the architect as darling of media reportage with 'archineer' or 'enginect' or 'compusciarchitist'.

But for some architects, at least in Europe, architecture continues to be a vehicle for social statement. Ricardo Bofill and the Taller de Arquitectura's Les Arcades du Lac housing project of 1975–81 at Saint-Quentin-en-Yvelines outside Paris, during the heyday of British architectural empiricism, offered not just good, dignified housing, but symbolically attempted a third French revolution by appropriating Versailles for the people. Bofill has since raided history at Montpelier and Marne-la-Vallée, finding forms suitable for the 'proletarian aristocrat' (Schuman in Ghirardo 1991). Herman Hertzberger continues his earlier experiments, of which Centraal Beheer is a landmark, in finding ways of making buildings a social statement about work practices or the power of the people over brute matter or bureaucracy. Ralph Erskine and Lucien Kroll are still pursuing the images of consumer participation and ways of flaunting bureaucracy, although not with quite the same gusto or leeway as the seventies permitted them.

The intense architectural focus on urbanism throughout the eighties, with its concentration on place, order, form, and the eking out of character, while primarily esthetic and compositional, is nevertheless rooted in human appreciation, instruction, and betterment, if avoiding openly admitting any attempt at social rectification, and is therefore clearly a resurgence of human values in the city (Krier 1979, 1988). The seeking of a 'poetics' of architecture today, that contemplative mode of making that the Greek word *poiesis* entails and about which the Italian philosopher of history Giambattista Vico (1744) and more recently the theorist Anthony Antoniades (1990) wrote, is returning the emphasis of architecture to people again, albeit sometimes at the expense of mind, body, or gender, as the designer challenges whether the people 'get it' (Al-Sayed *et al.* 1988; Agrest 1991). The invention of architecture as 'the critical art of contemporary culture' in the late eighties confirmed its shift "out of the world of social practice and into the realm of art," a move vehemently drubbed by Diane Ghirardo in her introduction to *Out of Site* (1991).

Such preoccupation with self can be blinding, even though the priests don't dare say so any more except High Priest Charles, Prince of Wales. In a quaint inversion of royal supplication, princedom is being offered to the plebs in the form of a votive offering, Dorchester, the people's town. The agenda for Dorchester is to redress 'dangerously unbalanced' architecture and to establish a recuperative social agenda by means of "environments in which people can prosper psychologically, as human beings, not merely as cogs in a mechanical process" (Charles 1989:156). Undoubtedly with the best will, Prince Charles is essentially giving vent to matters prompted by his social conscience, even if it is a misguided and particularly avuncular one according to some. Nevertheless, it is the same social conscience that is the architect's nagging doubt, that keeps architects questioning whether their concern at any particular moment is at all relevant. Social engineering, of a sort, is alive and well.

FURTHER SOURCES   Chapter 3, chapter 4B; Vidler 1992.

2. The Social Comprehension and Assimilation of Architecture

A society can be defined as a group of individuals competing for conventional prizes by conventional means. **V. C. Wynne-Edwards.** Cited in Ardrey 1970:88.

[Society is] a group of beings in which communication carries understanding. And where communication—a mutual understanding of signals—drops off to a minimum, there one encounters the social border. **Stuart Altmann.** Paraphrased in Ardrey 1970:89

The language of architecture is formed, defined and left behind in history, together with the very idea of architecture. In this sense the establishment of a 'general grammar' of architecture is utopia. What one can do is recognise and describe syntaxes and 'codes' that are historically defined, useful as 'ideal types' in historiographical analysis. **Manfredo Tafuri.** 1976:228.

. . . the task of history is the recovery, as far as possible, of the original functions and ideologies that, in the course of time, define and delimit the role and meaning of architecture. That this recovery is always subjective does not constitute a real problem. **Manfredo Tafuri.** 1976:228–229.

Accordingly, nothing in the human world can be *merely* utilitarian: even the most ordinary buildings organize space in various ways, and in so doing they signify, issue some kind of message about society's priorities, its presuppositions concerning human nature, politics, economics, over and above their overt concern with the provision of shelter, entertainment, medical care, or whatever. **Terence Hawkes.** 1977:134.

Societies create great architectures only to the extent that they value certain ways of life. The present coldness and ugliness of many modern cities is the concrete expression of our social ills. **René Dubos.** 1981:61.

In general we no longer understand architecture. . . . We have grown out of the symbolism of lines and figures. . . . [A] feeling of inexhaustible significance lay about the [symbolic] building like a magic veil. Beauty entered this system only incidentally, without essentially encroaching upon the fundamental sense of the uncanny and exalted, of consecration by magic and the proximity of the divine. **Friedrich Nietzsche,** 1878:1, §218.

TRACE   Contemporaneous understanding of ancient Greek and Greco-Roman architecture, according to Hersey (1988), was a matter of playing associational games, especially in temples, where the names given to ornament and parts of the building were connected to the terminology and acts of sacrifice as a matter of everyday speech. Hersey deduces the origin of temples from the worship of and rituals around sacred trees or groves that were considered the abodes of gods. Trees were "often decorated with the gear and materials used in sacrifice and with the victims remains: bones, horns, urns, lamps, fruit and vegetable relics, flowers, and weapons" (13). In chapter 2 of *The Lost Meaning of Classical Architecture,* Hersey gives a charged account of ancient Greek architecture and sacrifice, especially in the section "Sacrificial Terminology in Architecture," where many key classical terms are arrayed in their full-blooded glory.

Such literal and figural transference is not the rule. Though there is a link between timber and stone forms and decoration in Indian architecture similar to that of ancient Greek architecture (Zimmer 1960:259–265), rather than adopting sacrificial tropes, Indian decoration is largely narrative and motivated by decorum, "only things covered with ornament are beautiful . . . the simple appearance without ornament is 'not enough' [*alam-kar,* 'to adorn, to decorate' is literally 'to make enough']; it is poor, disgraceful, shocking, except in the case of an ascetic" (236). Religious buildings were offerings by devotees, and "to present an offering without profuse decoration would be an insult to the divinity and would bring to the donor disaster."

Another socio-architectural tradition is the living anthropomorphic relation between the Maori and the *whare whakairo,* or carved meeting house, described by Michael Linzey (1991b). A Maori orator on the *marae,* or ceremonial ground, speaks directly to the meeting house, personifying it as the ancestral presence, before addressing the people; at other times the orator talks of it in the first person. The meeting house "is often profusely decorated with human figures both realistic and abstract . . . [but] this carved timber is no mere ornament added on to the architecture, as it might be interpreted in a European sense." Linzey contrasts the Platonic duality of life inherent in Western European thought that obliges a 'speaking about' things, with the unity of life of the Maori that enables a 'speaking to' the house: "Usually the house itself is named for a specific ancestor and it actually is in its whole construction the *embodiment* of that person; so that the ridge beam is his or her spine, the rafters are the ribs, the interior space is the belly, the outstretched bargeboards, *raparapa*, are the arms with the fingers extended in greeting" (51).

Such sacrificial, expiatory, and decorous sentiments as have been and still are expressed about architecture in many cultures of the world show that there is a connection between a society and its architecture. From a social perspective, this connection amounts to buildings and cities being tropes of political power, social attitudes, and cultural values; from an individual perspective, buildings and cities amount to ideological, spiritual, or psychological statements, in the way Jung's country retreat at Bollingen, near Zurich, concretized his unconscious—"a kind of representation in stone of my innermost thoughts," he wrote (cited in Rybczynski 1989:191). The individual perspective motivated the Modern Movement, which assumed a social perspective as individuals conspired and agreed to create momentous change.

COMMENTARY   Ardrey (1970) reconciles the Wynn-Edwards's view of society as conventionalized competition with the Altmann view of communication establishing a social border, both quoted earlier, in this way: "Through means of mutual understanding, a group regulates the competition among its members so that we strive for symbolic prizes according to rules and regulations presumably fair to all. Beyond the border where communication fails, however, the prizes galvanizing our society may lie beyond another's comprehension" (90). Any assignment of a social role to architecture, the theoretical concerns arising from this role, or the basis for a society's understanding of its architecture, presupposes a connection between society and architecture and an ability of architecture to carry society's impress. It is suggested above, by sheer example, that the relation was somehow obvious or 'natural'.

The Altmann definition argues for a boundedness to a society such that its 'prizes', those things or matters of mutually agreed value, are discernible from outside that society and are able to be read (or misread). If there were architectural equivalents of a society, presumably they would be capable of a similar reading, depending upon what the architectural 'prizes' were determined to be. In other words, there would be a boundary to any local content, beyond which it is not understandable; or rather, this local content would help to differentiate one society from another. No doubt there are certain qualities common to all societies that would be the background against which the 'prizes' would be seen, and that would equate with the commonalities of architecture's materiality and human embrace.

The question for the present discussion is, What is it that is comprehended in the architecture? The commonality or the prizes? How does architecture become the medium of social conveyance, comprehension, interpretation, or expression? The question might be rephrased: what do people perceive in architecture that reflects the constancies or differences in societies, and how is this perception achieved? Does architecture instantiate a society's prizes? Or is it merely the backdrop for society's enactments? It is clear that traditional or monolithic societies with quite rigid social structures and strict mores are inclined to have an architecture that is consistent and monolithic in its tectonics and guided by strict rules of assembly and distribution. Which is not equivalent to saying that inclusive and pluralist societies, with their highly generalized mores and gross (as against fine) tolerances so necessary for maintaining the variety and individuality of their component subsocieties, are similarly inconsistent and multifaceted in their tectonics and are not guided by strict rules, or that 'anything goes'. Evidence for an unequivocal answer may appear to be available for traditional societies, but it is neither easy to find nor expressed in direct and unambiguous terms for pluralist societies.

That traditional daily life and its artifacts and buildings are informed by sacred rite, social custom, or mythic narrative is exemplified in Marcia N. Lehman-Kessler's "The Myth Within" (Linzey 1991:271–281), concerning the *numayma,* or clan house, of the Kwakiutl indigenes of coastal British Columbia, for whom "the concept of architecture as the embodiment of cultural knowledge through physical manifestation of myth" is evident. This study reveals Kwakiutl architecture "to have been the vehicle through which symbols of lineage and wealth were demonstrated. . . . The display of iconographic symbols representing the distribution of wealth served to validate the status of the individuals in a society in which distribution, rather than accumulation, of wealth was important." She concludes that "The numayma house served as a physical link between past and present; the corporeal and supernatural; and the individual and the larger social order." A similar idea pertains in Indonesia where, among the Toraja highland people of South Sulawesi, the *tongkonan,* or noble origin-house, acts as substitute for the written history of a people without written script (Waterson, in Linzey 1991a:501–511). For the ancient Greeks, for certain religious castes in India, for the Maori, and for numerous indigenous societies, architecture is integrated with culture.

In a relatively homogeneous Western culture like that of Catholic Spain, there is a discernible modern tectonic quality that began with the complex integration of structure, surface, color, and allusion in the work of Antoni Gaudí. It is unclear whether this integration was an expression of Gaudí's inner self or of the *genius loci,* the spirit of place of Catalonia (see 9B.5, Place), or of the *Zeitgeist,* the spirit of the age (see chapter 7A), or whether it was a largely unspoken sensibility in which Spanish society, art, structure, and architecture are comprehended together. More broadly, the recent worldwide tendency to ornament in architecture seen in the work of the postmodernists serves to make architecture comprehensible in a way that unadorned modernist forms could not.

Indeed, unadornment is a contradiction in postmodern terms because the forms are frequently utilized primarily for their allusive power, any formal properties being mostly a residual of their troping, as is the case with Charles Moore's *Piazza d'Italia.* The explosive forms of the deconstructivists, while not so obviously ornamented, nevertheless serve to counterpoint the formal and ornamental qualities of their settings or of the ghosts that accompany them. Coop Himmelblau's Viennese rooftop alteration achieves its power only because it erupts unexpectedly from the traditional roofscape, thereby corrupting a nineteenth-century assemblage. Bernard Tschumi's *Parc de la Villette* pavilions achieve their power only by contrast with the ghosts of historic garden pavilions or with what these pavilions might have been in the hands of some other architect.

Because these works exist at all, certain qualities have been recognized by and can be declared about the societies that spawned them. The presence of highly individual works suggests a tolerance of individuality and artistry, whereas a more homogeneous or totalitarian society demanding compliance would not allow such works to exist. The current preoccupation with textuality in architecture, presumably to correct perceived intellectual deficiencies of the recent past, may be unwarranted, because social comprehension of architecture, if it can occur at all in any other than a localized way in pluralist Western societies, will occur only through consensus; current architecture will reflect only those qualities society agrees should pertain.

Yet architecture as an embodiment of a society's prizes may not be a matter of conscious (verbal, vocal, written) communication at all; it may have everything to do with nonverbal communication and the associational content of meaning as Rapoport (1982) believes; certainly, however social comprehension and assimilation of architecture works, it is not philosophical, it is historical. At the risk of further mystifying the relationship, it is possible that the relation between a society and its architecture may be closer to what Giambattista Vico urged two hundred and fifty years ago as the basis for his *New Science*—not intellectual refinement, not reflections of civilized natures, but poetry like that created by the earliest peoples, "poets who spoke in poetic characters," whose poetics arose from a "poverty of language and [a] need to explain and be understood" (Vico 1744:s34). Deconstruction and textuality may only confound comprehension because they over-subscribe to language, though they may well remain substantial preoccupations with theorists who *talk about and within* architecture. Few are concerned today with the *talking to* that Linzey remarks upon and that society needs to achieve if its architecture is to assimilate—the poetics, the transitive act that unites Heidegger's woodcutter and the tree, the artisan and the artifact (see chapter 4, Overview).

FURTHER SOURCES   Chapter 3; Hollier 1989; Macrae-Gibson 1985; Oliver 1969; Vidler 1992.

3. Theory and Environment-Behavior Studies

It was in vain that I asked him [Le Corbusier] to put himself in the place of the prospective purchasers, whose eyes are accustomed to decorative effects, even though they may be of the most discreet kind. . . . **Henry Frugès.** Boudon 1969:7.

One could build beautifully designed houses, always provided the tenant was prepared to change his outlook. **Le Corbusier.** Boudon 1969:63.

. . . although it is unlikely that we shall ever possess a precise formula for living (a neat list of human needs that could be catered for in our homes), it remains none the less true that both the way in which we live and the homes we live in are products of the human mind and as such are subject to constant modification. From this it follows that they cannot be defined in terms of past achievements. But they can be illumined by experiment, and it is the lessons learned from the Pessac experiment that I have tried to convey. **Philippe Boudon** 1969:2.

The city dweller is constantly coming up against the absolute mysteriousness of other people's reasons. **Jonathon Raban.** 1974:162.

. . . when the environmental code is known, behavior can easily be made appropriate to the setting and the social situation to which it corresponds. **Amos Rapoport.** 1982:59.

. . . there is explanatory theory, which is based on research and supported by empirical data and which leads to understanding and prediction, and then there is "theory," which is really nothing more than opinion, ideology, and the like . . . the construction of explanatory theory cannot begin until there is sufficient empirical data to suggest directions and to constrain such theory construction. **Amos Rapoport.** 1982:241. Epilogue written in 1989.

I get very upset at the standard student approach now which supposes that, if you interview enough housewives in a housing project, and write down what they like best about where they live, you'll know what the solution ought to be. **Charles Moore.** In Cook and Klotz, 1973:235.

In our times, the most important contribution to the philosophy of design has been the recognition that the external forms we give to our environments reflect some aspects of our inner psychological states. **René Dubos.** 1981:61.

TRACE   Behavior combines the prefix 'be-', in the sense of 'thoroughly, soundly, conspicuously, to excess, ridiculously' as we find in bedeck, bejewel, bedazzle; and 'haver, havoir, havour', from the Old French *aver* 'possession, property' and *avoir* 'to have', in combination meaning literally 'having possession of or property over (oneself) to the fullest extent' or 'maintaining oneself'. It implies management or regulation or conduct according to some standard, with due recognition of the standards of others, with propriety, with decorum. Behavior studies would therefore look to studying conduct in relation to certain standards and would logically seek those standards as either an implicit or an explicit code. In the case of environment-behavior studies (EBS), the implicit codes are rarely discussed, much store being put on explicit cues, those found *in the acoutrements* of behavior, in the environment, and in architecture.

Following nearly two decades of survey and experiment that aligned the behavioral sciences with architecture, by 1980 Rapoport (1982) was seeing EBS as a new discipline "at once humanistic and scientific, concerned with developing an explanatory theory of environment-behavior relations (EBR)." Helping consolidate the status of EBS during this time has been the emerging subdiscipline of post-occupancy evaluation (POE) (for a brief history of which see Preiser, Rabinowitz and White 1988); however, neither POE nor any of its chief protagonists rate a mention by Rapoport, even in his epilogue of 1989. Together, EBR and POE are represented as much in the literature as historical and ideological writings, except that the latter seem to grab the attention and imagination of popular architectural culture and students.

COMMENTARY Notwithstanding the nihilistic prognosis by Pawley (1990) outlined in 1B.1, Relevance, EBS has yielded a wealth of information about how people react in and to buildings that is arguably as close to a 'scientific' knowledge base in architecture as we are likely to get, within the reservations expressed below. The emphasis has shifted of late but the concern for affordability in housing, quality management in buildings generally, the push for reliable human data by 'smart technology' interests, and the amount of funding such research commands, is ensuring that EBS remains on the agenda in one form or another. It only remains for it to breach the agenda of the architectural awards systems around the world for social consciences to stay pricked.

The definition of behavior as conduct related to standards invoked by environmental cues leads naturally to considering architecture as a *determining or delimiting accoutrement* whereas, from the previous section, architecture is a social outcome, a result of the history of values prized by society. Yet, according to Rapoport (1982), reactions by people to buildings, the meanings they impute to buildings, are the result of association, personal constructs evolved from their self-history. As a result, the studying of behavior in select environments becomes an inherently circular proposition, which you might say is as it should be because behavior *is* moderated by reference to a closed system of desirable behaviors. *But such a self-referential system of desirable behaviors can be taught,* as it has been and still is taught formally in many spheres of social activity requiring decorum (social etiquette, diplomacy, and so forth), and as it is in the everyday world of parental and peer guidance. In other words, what EBS say is that buildings offer cues *above and beyond any taught behaviors.* Yet so far there seems to be no evidence that buildings can offer additional cues to refine or fine-tune taught behaviors and, furthermore, buildings certainly *cannot and do not of themselves teach appropriate behavior.* Unfortunately, so much person-environment research and architectural discussion about the relation between buildings or cities and people still follows an outmoded and 'naive stimulus-response model of human behavior' (Lang 1987:viii).

Inherent in people-building studies is the basic assumption that studying the behavior of people in relation to buildings can elicit knowledge about their relationship capable of generalization to the level of conventional theory and universal rules for future application. There is a conceptual danger here, as there is with all behavioral research prompting future correction or modification, of violating Hume's Law concerning the *naturalistic fallacy,* of incorrectly deducing an 'ought' from an 'is' without also explaining *why* there is an obligation to carry forward into the future what already is. What is at stake and cannot be admitted by person-environment researchers faced with this difficulty for fear of having nothing to do or say, is that EBS attend to matters that are largely trivial to future designing. With the exception of territorial behavior, about which there has been much clarification, most of what arises from EBS is already generally known. This general knowledge is therefore not greatly modified as a result of the research, and is no more helpful—indeed it can be less helpful—than it was to designing beforehand. There are few, if any, grand ideas that have emerged from EBS sufficient to carry the weight of major design decisions. There are very few dictums flowing from EBS to help focus the mind on people when designing. Almost nothing has emerged from EBS that is reducible to simple design axioms that are then capable of being expanded again to the wealth of information gathered.

When architects say that people must be taken into account in designing, they are saying almost nothing; they are making some vague experiential claim involving themselves. Most certainly, architects are not bringing an armory of EBS to bear on design situations. This may be because much of the research reported in the literature is too dense or too abstract, too localized, too methodologically bound, or too culturally diffuse. Or it may be merely that architects never bother to read the research because it is rarely reported outside academic journals (Johnson 1989). It is mainly in their education that architects are exposed to EBS, and for this purpose the model espoused by Jon Lang (1988), and raised in the Introduction, as a theoretical framework within which EBS information may be fitted is a useful vehicle for interpolating behavioral research. In Lang's model, EBS fits within the 'positive-substantive-person' theory slot, although it is possible to argue that EBS informs the others as well. In terms of Lang's conventional stance on theory (as against the view of theory being put forward in this book), positive theory describes what is; normative theory presents what ought to be and is informed by positive theory. Unfortunately, Lang's valiant scheme is frustrated by EBS because very little of the research is 'positive' in the sense of economizing thought to enable people "to derive a large number of descriptive statements from a single explanatory statement" (Lang 1987:14). Hence it is difficult for positive theory to provide sufficiently generalizable conditions to enable, with proper justification, normative theory statements about what ought to be.

Perhaps the greatest difficulty for EBS in architectural education occurs at the time students are asked to justify what they are designing in human terms. An answer in person-environment terms is usually an *affective* one: the environment will or won't facilitate this or that behavior or fulfill certain perceived 'needs'. The trouble is that neither the student nor the tutor can know whether this is the case until after the design is built and occupied; at best they are guessing, no matter what the experience and knowledge of each may be. The presumption is that *if all goes as before,* assuming *the present situation is approximately the same as previous situations,* then certain behaviors will be enabled and certain needs will be satisfied. We rely on there being a constancy of environment-behavior relations and human needs in designing at the same time we seek through EBS any constancies to facilitate such prediction! We can never achieve what we are setting out to achieve in EBS, so all designing is experimental and is, of itself, either affirmative or not of what we have presumed. Le Corbusier is correct in the sense that designing is a reciprocal affair, but the conundrum is that a Pessac of the tenant kind could never have been designed by Le Corbusier.

FURTHER SOURCES   Altman 1975; EDRA conferences; Preiser 1973,1989; Rapoport 1982; Teymur 1982.

4. Theory and Individuality: Impact on Society and Architecture

Only through a specific social heritage, beginning with the art of language, can individuation arise. The individual, left to himself, is not a source. **Lewis Mumford.** 1938:456.

The bane of the nineteenth century was the celebrity-architect: the Renaissance idea of the individual glorified over the Renaissance sense of artistic unity. And architecture cannot afford to be an affair of the individual. It is only when the individual innovation becomes assimilated into a regional tradition that it can be regarded as culturally valid. **J. M. Richards.** "The condition of architecture and the principle of anonymity." In Martin, Nicholson and Gabo. 1971:184.

The need to give one's personal stamp is as important as the inclination to be unobtrusive. . . . Something becomes our possession because we make a sign on it, because we give it our name, or defile it, because it shows traces of our existence. **N. J. Habraken.** 1971:12.

The building of tall blocks without any intrinsic message (they are merely units of accommodation) devalues the identity of the city and robs it of meaningful symbols. In a mass society the identity of the individual is a precious responsibility, to be reinforced at every stage. **Theo Crosby,** *How to Play the Environment Game* (1973).

A work of art has no importance whatever to society. It is only important to the individual. **Vladimir Nabokov.** *Strong Opinions* (1974).

To be an individual one must win the recognition of others. But the greater the conformity to their expectations, the less one is a distinctive individual. . . . The self is individual and it is social. But the requirements of individuality are in conflict with the demands of sociability in a way that does not seem immediately capable of solution. **Roberto Unger.** *Knowledge and Politics.* 1975. Cited in Fish 1989:409–410.

The cancerous growth of the creative individual expressing himself at the expense of the spectator and/or consumer has spread . . . even into design. No longer does the artist, craftsman, or in some cases the designer, operate with the good of the consumer in mind; rather, many creative statements have become highly individualistic, auto-therapeutic little comments by the artist to himself. **Victor Papanek.** *Design for the Real World.* 1977:41.

Every society is for the individual a basic given pattern to which he is subsidiary. Everyone is doomed to be the person he wants the others to see. That is the price that the individual pays to society in order to remain an insider. **Herman Hertzberger.** In Suckle 1980:48.

"Your house doesn't look much like the other houses on the island," he remarked after looking through my sketches. "Of course not," I answered, thinking that this was a naive reaction—I had hoped for something more insightful. "This is my own design. It's a modern house—it's not supposed to look the same." "But why not?" he asked. "Why shouldn't your house look like the others?" I tried to respond—something about originality and creativity—but he remained unconvinced. **Witold Rybczynski.** 1989:81. Conversation with English painter Michael Shaw.

TRACE   Theories of sociality and individuality "clustered around the dogmas of private property and individual liberty that had taken shape in the eighteenth century" according to Mumford, but continued through the nineteenth as a sinister subterfuge for control and power by governments, élites, and monopolies, all of which "were equally oppressive to good society" (Mumford 1938:455). There are those who maintain much the same today. What is of deeper significance is what is understood by the term 'individuality'.

Individuality is enigmatic because, apart from any obvious numerical unity, it is a separation from some collectivity by virtue of certain indivisible qualities peculiar to itself, yet it also embraces collectivity by virtue of certain features common to members of a group that make it cohere. Individuals can also be taken more narrowly as relating to particulars, namings, which raises the further specter of universals, classes of namings. Flew (1979) says simply that things are particulars and their qualities are universals; for example, a certain red as against the quality of redness. But this distinction is over-simple, as Strawson (1971) illustrates by dividing nouns into three groups—material-names, substance-names, and quality/property-names—and compares them to show how particulars and generals come about (see his chapter 2). He maintains that we need criteria of *distinctness* and *identity* to have an idea of a particular instance of something general.

COMMENTARY   The conundrum of individual-collectivism or collective-individualism suggests that individuality can only be a reciprocal quality, something to do with the relation between matters. It is well known that individual actions have moral, ethical, and legal ramifications for society at large; these have been well studied and are clearly defined in terms of responsibility and accountability at law and in social mores. In architecture the issue of individual action vis-a-vis collective will or status is not so clear, although individuality is believed essential to originality, without which there can be no progress, no new ground broken.

Victor Papanek's railing against selfish individuality denying 'consumer good' quoted earlier opposes the designer as smug 'individualist' to the consumer or world as deserving 'collectivist' in a bitter swipe at élitism by someone who has devoted a life to the 'service' of others. It is symptomatic of the view that individual and collective are in opposition. Yet the pursuit of style and image being decried by Papanek and others as the antithesis of pressing social needs has always been not only the mark of connoisseurship but the very core of design-as-object, *correct style and image are primary to the idea of social transformation by design.* Design is the universal that unites the efforts of individual designers. The theoretical and practical concerns of the design fields, including architecture, have changed little over time; they are still possessed of the same intentions, the same dilemmas and paradoxes, and dogged by the same calls for social relevance.

The architect and theorist Dana Cuff observes that the idea of the creative and original architect-as-individual begins in architectural education: "The principal social relation in school—that between studio instructor and student—is cast as a relation between unique individuals" and that "the primacy of the individual is then carried into practice, promoting the explanation of everyday occurrences as matters of personality, talent, creativity, and convictions" (Cuff 1991:45). Cuff sees the emphasis on individualism as a myth in need of change but not of elimination, because the individual will remain central to architecture as it will in most professions.

Cuff argues for a more inclusive approach to practice and to teaching. She suggests teaching include collaboration; vertical integration of studios; comprehensively structured design problems; design juries augmented by consultants; instruction in negotiation, interpersonal relations, and leadership; and case studies of successful hero collaborations like that of the entrepreneur Henry Frugès and Le Corbusier, or Louis Kahn and the structural engineer August Komendant. For the profession, she suggests external review of buildings beyond or supplementing present in-house awards systems and publication of nonprofessional critical reviews. These prescriptions are similar to Unger's 'love thy neighbor' transformative thought, which seeks complementarity rather than opposition, thereby encouraging the fuller emergence of both individual and community (Fish 1989:409–410).

Strawson maintains that "We bring a particular into our discourse only when we determine, select, *a point of application* for such criteria [distinctness and identity] . . . and no theory of particulars can be adequate which does not take account of the means by which we determine such a point of application *as* a point of application for these criteria" (36). He elaborates a definition of a general thing as being a singular expression, referring to its uniqueness "solely by the meaning of the words making up the expression" and of a particular thing as not being so referred to. In other words, generals *float* or are *unplaced,* and particulars are *placed.*

The importance for architecture and conventional theory of what Strawson says is that *generalizable meaning does not attach to architecture in the particular,* only in the generality; and any theory of architecture as a universalized thing can be made particular only by finding a point of application, certain distinctive features and identifying characteristics to animate the theory, and by declaring how we do so. In other words, conventional theory would need to particularize architecture at the moment of its application. Since any distinctness or identity in a situation must necessarily pre-exist the application of the theory by being identifiable and thus must be *declared,* such declarations must be a form of talk, words, or *specifics,* and therefore are themselves instantiations of generalities. So, if we are to avoid a vapidly circular reasoning, theory is not some generalized formula guiding practice, but is a local and particularized practice in the form of mediating talk.

The social consequence is that design-talk is the only way architecture is known about, and it is the political strength of individual discourse that decides what society says of architecture and what individual architects find dear in society. Every country has its hero architects who have either written or been written about—Le Corbusier, Walter Gropius, Alvar Aalto, Louis Kahn, Aldo Rossi, Tadao Ando, Leon and Rob Krier, Harry Seidler—all of them noted for their individual efforts. In Australia, the most popular book of recent years among the lay readership is Philip Drew's *Leaves of Iron* (1985) about the architect Glen Murcutt, winner in 1992 of the Alvar Aalto Medal. *Leaves,* by virtue of its individuality, is the point of application for one large section of Australian society regarding architecture, albeit architecture seen in distinctly Murcuttian terms, and is cited frequently in the daily press and among students. Reciprocally, architects use it directly and indirectly, and the many other writings on *individual* architects or buildings around the world, to locate themselves in society, to assist in bringing distinction and identity to the points of application of their individual works.

FURTHER SOURCES   7A.2, Progress; Antoniades 1990.

5. Theory and Community: Social Implications for Architecture

. . . people who hate cities . . . are surely right when they interpret them as the enemies of decent family life, of community constraints, of 'public morals'. It is possible, however, to prefer the freedom of a place like this [Earl's Court], with all its hazards, to the forced constrictions of the small town or organically conceived suburb. No-one in their right mind would see anything utopian in Earl's Court: its freedom is badly scarred, commercially exploited, licentious. It affords indifference not tolerance; it is a tribal wilderness not a community. **Jonathon Raban.** 1974:206

We need design and layout which positively encourage neighbourliness, intimacy and, where possible, a sense of shared belonging to a recognisable community. **Charles, Prince of Wales.** 1989:156.

The street is a community room. The meeting house is a community room under a roof. . . . Human agreement is a sense of rapport, of commonness, of all bells ringing in unison—not needing to be understood by example but felt as an undeniable inner demand for a presence. It is an inspiration with the promise of the possible. **Louis Kahn.** 1971. "The room, the street, and human agreement." In Latour 1991:266.

The world with its many people, each one a singularity, each group of different experiences revealing the nature of the human in varied aspects, is full of the possibility of more richly sensing human agreement from which new architecture will come. **Louis Kahn.** 1971. "The room. . . . " In Latour 1991:268.

The city is made up of institutions—that which has been established and is supportable by all men. Education, government, the home are such institutions. When an architect begins his work, the building he is about to design must present itself as belonging to an institution. Even before satisfying the client's specific needs, the forces of the institution in society should be the background of his architectural decisions. **Louis Kahn.** 1971. "Not for the Fainthearted." In Latour 1991:260–261.

TRACE   *Community* is a variant of the Middle English word *comunete* or 'commonty', deriving from the Latin *communis* for common, and having connections with the commonalty, the common people, the common good, commonwealth, and so on. In sociological terms, community entails fellowship and is not a homogeneous concept but one that depends on scale and interest. Multiple interlocking and overlapping communities of interest exist within any given grouping or society based on kin, religious, political, economic, ethnic, geographic, educational, civil, recreational, or other affiliations. Communities vary in size, frequency of contact, and spatial distribution, but have many organizational features in common, such as goals, norms, controls, and rankings. Taken together, communities constitute society.

Just when the notion of community started is difficult to ascertain, but by the Middle Ages the idea was well advanced. Communes had long been a means of countering the prevailing social order, many of the earliest being religious. According to Viollet-le-Duc (1872:I, 262–263), in the twelfth century the citizens of certain Gallic cities tried "to reconquer their ancient privileges and took the communal oath." From about 1160 A.D., the church sought to take advantage of developing secular communes to regain power lost to the abbeys by erecting "vast edifices in which the citizens might assemble around the episcopal throne" in the building of which the lay craft-guilds were called, thereby "entering fully into the views of the bishops." In this way the church inveigled itself into the core of the community, as Mumford explains: "One must think of the [Medieval] church, indeed, as one would now think of a 'community center': not too holy to serve as a dining-hall for a great festival, as a theatre for a religious play, as a forum where the scholars in church schools might stage oratorical contests and learned disputes on a holiday, or even, in the early days, as a safe-deposit vault, behind whose high altar deeds or treasures might be deposited, safe from all but the incorrigibly wicked" (1961:352).

COMMENTARY   It is easy to slip into construing community as a monolith, as happens if we speak of 'the community', 'people', 'architects', or 'the environment' (as one Australian radio station did recently in reporting that a ruptured oil tanker was towed 'beyond the environment' to protect the coastline!). However monolithic the architectural profession might seem while discussing it, monolithicity does not apply to the contradistinctive 'nonarchitectural profession' world that remains. Such imprecision only exacerbates an already loose agenda while designing, especially among students. A monolithic view also entrenches the idea that change can be imposed on a community from outside, whereas it is clear that the boundedness of a community necessary for its definition does not apply to all conceptions of it. There is no outside opposed to an inside if we consider change, as Stanley Fish explains: "When a community is provoked to change by something outside it, that something will already have been inside, in the sense that its angle of notice—the angle from which it is related to the community's project even before it is seen—will determine its shape, not *after* it has been perceived, but *as* it is perceived" (Fish 1989:147).

Change in the community of architects occurs from within by virtue of inclinations already present, as happened when deconstructivism was formally celebrated in the Deconstructivist Architecture exhibit at New York's Museum of Modern Art in 1988 and Mark Wigley, in the book accompanying it, wrote of the modernist 'dream of pure form' being disturbed by contaminated forms that "emerge from within the architectural tradition and happen to exhibit some deconstructive qualities." These qualities arise from repressed impurities within pure form arrayed on Wigley's consulting room couch, "drawn to the surface by a combination of gentle coaxing and violent torture" using 'interrogation' as a kind of poultice (Johnson and Wigley 1988:11). Kuhn (1970) makes similar though less dramatic claims in his discussion of change as an internal 'paradigm shift' in the sciences.

Shifting to the social implications of conventional theory and community, we find a conceptual monolithicity and determinism still at work in visions of the role of 'architecture' in making community like those of Prince Charles above and where he says: " . . . I believe that the lessons they've worked out at Seaside have very serious applications both in rural areas and in our cities. The founders certainly believe that a sense of real community will grow here; that people will *live* here. I wish them well. But—even with sensible regulations—a sense of community is not easily achieved. Living together also requires an act of the spirit" (Charles 1989:146). It is remarkable to have to repeat yet again that neither 'sensible' regulations, design, and layout, nor 'the right sort of surroundings', create community because it is not a physical thing; it is a mental and social alignment that has physical and political manifestations. New Zealand architect Ian Athfield became aware of what community meant to the slum people of Manila on his visit to the Philippines for the first time after winning an international competition to replace the slums. There, the community feeling was far stronger than any quality he imagined he was creating with his design and it was at the moment he sensed this that he realized what architects and planners could *not* do (film *Architect Athfield.* 1977. New Zealand, New Zealand National Film Unit and Television One).

It is circular reasoning leading to a self-fulfilling fallacy to first conceive of architecture as setting physical limits that thereby define a group of people and set them apart from their surroundings, as the now much-decried megastructure has done for housing in many parts of the world, and to then say, as Ada Louise Huxtable did after visiting the 1978 Camden Borough Council Housing in London, that "a heroic effort has been made to create a distinctive community instead of just packaging a specified number of dwellings in no particular context" (1986:235). Not surprisingly, even the more enticing and heretic megastructures of Ricardo Bofill fail to exhort their occupants to higher self-esteem or greater communality, despite being ingested by great architectural symbols or X-rayed by classical rules of composition (Schuman in Ghirardo 1991). What architects have so consistently misunderstood about community because of their emphasis on visual and formal manifestations, just as planners have done with their consensual view of community as social and geographical solidarity (Bailey 1973), is that community is most decidedly *not* distinctive. Community is a hidden structure, any geophysical boundaries of which are *incidental* and not definitional to the community; they do not mark out a territory.

This ephemerality of community is so obviously the case in what is now the age of 'community without propinquity' (Melvin Webber in Proshansky, Ittelson and Rivlin 1970) firmly established through television, satellite communications, and computer networking, that it is arguable whether architecture has ever had any social relevance at all, other than creating for architects and planners a warm inner glow. What architects have begun to realize is that they do have a *duty of care* toward known users and anonymous others in designing buildings, and that conventional theory, as the discourse of design, intervenes on their behalf while designing. Architectural discourse still needs to evolve ways to mediate the social norms, dislocations, injustices, and imbalances that impinge on all designing, ways "to reconnect architecture to social and economic questions [through] a thorough reformulation of both theory and practice in order to avoid repeating the well-intentioned but mistaken strategies used by modernist reformers and sixties radicals" (Margaret Crawford in Ghirardo 1991). Doing that will enable the community to take care of itself.

FURTHER SOURCES   3B.4, Community.

6. Theory and the Utopias of Architects

Nor do there seem to be big-name architects in Ecotopia. People themselves design and build structures for their living groups or enterprises. . . . The community governments have design staffs for public buildings . . . but architecture is not at all the preserve of experts. **Ernest Callenbach.** *Ecotopia.* 1978:134.

He [the modern architect] was helping to establish and to celebrate an enlightened and a just society; and one definition of modern architecture might be that it was an attitude towards building which was divulging in the present that more perfect order which the future was about to disclose. **Colin Rowe** and **Fred Koetter.** 1978:11.

Utopias afford consolation: although they have no real locality there is nevertheless a fantastic, untroubled region in which they are able to unfold; they open up cities with vast avenues, superbly planted gardens, countries where life is easy, even though the road to them is chimerical . . . utopias permit fables and discourse: they run with the very grain of language and are part of the fundamental dimension of the *fabula.* **Georges Teyssot.** "Heterotopias and the History of Spaces," *A + U Architecture + Urbanism,* October 1980:81.

It is perhaps the fate of fudged and ill-considered utopias to end in squalor quickly. But the speed with which Gropius' slab skyscraper in the park, which seemed such a splendid ideal to a Western European and even American haute-bourgeoisie only twenty or thirty years ago [this was written c1974], decayed into the horrific square miles of Lefrak towers has left planners breathless: the shabby utopia had become the exemplar for the biggest boom in world history. . . . **Joseph Rykwert.** 1982:104.

. . . the great Central European urbanistic projects of the 1920s (the *Siedlungen,* or workers' housing in Berlin, Frankfurt, and Vienna) touch their other in the seemingly "extrinsic" obstacle of financial speculation and the rise in land and property values that causes their absolute failure and spells an end to their utopian vocation. **Fredric Jameson.** In Ockman 1985:62, 64.

Architecture bears the seed of the reversal of its own sign. In challenging divine ideals, in attempting, through metaphor, to replicate a pure state, architecture is dialectical. . . . Buildings, gardens, and cities are all grist for human concerns about cosmic union. The most common way to achieve that union is to reminisce about origins—spiritually and geometrically. Ideal geometry has mythic implications that call out to convey human spirituality to God. **Stanley Tigerman.** 1988:46.

Humans distance themselves from the site of the only home they know—the present. Unable to return to the location of their desires defined by memory, and unable to predict or to measure a mute state of anticipation, exiles wander without even the comfort of the earth to which they are destined to return. . . . Exiles are placed in no place, isolated from their own production and dislocated from their belief systems. They look elsewhere for gratification. **Stanley Tigerman.** 1988:152.

TRACE   Utopia is (or was) a neologism concocted from the Greek *ou,* not, and *topos,* place, and meaning 'no-place', to describe the imaginary state in Sir Thomas More's Latin political romance *Utopia,* published in 1516, "incorporating many traits of contemporary England" (Rosenau 1959:41). Since then, its meaning commonly describes any imaginary state of ideal perfection or indefinitely remote region, country, place, state, or condition and, derogatorily, those impossibly so; less strictly, utopia applies to any concept or application aspiring to an ideal. What is not made clear by dictionary definitions, however, is that utopia is primarily a *social* construct, not an architectural one; it is largely indifferent to its physical manifestation. As recently as the 1940s an American scientific research and development company, Technology Inc., under its director Bertram Bogardus, was proposing a new vision for society based in atomic physics.

Colin Rowe and Fred Koetter (1978) discern two versions of the utopian idea, the *classical utopia,* 'an object of contemplation' with the ideal city as its architectural equivalent, and the *activist utopia,* 'a blueprint for the future' or 'an instrument of social change', its architectural equivalent being almost every architectural or planning invention since the Enlightenment aspiring to some kind of perfection. Reyner Banham detects at least three utopias in the Jürgen Joedicke introductory essay, "Reality and Utopia in Town Planning", to a special edition of *Bauen + Wohnen* (January 1964): traditional utopias like More's, trying "to overturn the real facts simply by reversing the present polarities of men and society"; the New Utopianism of professional futurologists, "which often amplifies present trends in society"; and what Joedicke calls 'blind visions', "unrelated to known or anticipated condition of man or his society" (Banham 1976:79). It is not my intention to discuss the nuances of these variations here or to provide a detailed array of examples—for these, the literature is plentiful (see, for example, Rosenau 1959, 1983; Banham 1976; Rowe and Koetter 1978; Frampton 1980)—except to say that Banham counters utopia and the ideal city, saying that utopia "is often obsessional about the proposed social system, but not too concerned about architectural form. Only in the nineteenth century . . . did the two kinds become conflated (as in the vision of a Bellamy or a Howard), and only in the twenties was social Utopia confused with 'architectural adventurism' " (Banham 1976:80).

COMMENTARY   Architectural writers today continue to use 'utopian' either supportively or dismissively as a generalization for anything urban or architectural that is unusual, different, or inventive, and then mostly visually so. In fact, more than a generation ago Banham thought it an abused word and criticized Conrads and Sperlich (*Fantastic Architecture,* 1960) for their "conventionally sloppy use of the word 'Utopia' as meaning little more than visionary or improbable; few of the projects under discussion [t]here were seriously engaged in the task of proposing a radical new and perfected social order" (Banham 1976:79).

Continued abuse since has turned 'utopia' into a *brimborium,* a mouthing of platitudes about the future with no working agenda, even blinder visions than Joedicke's. Stanley Fish is more scathing. He sees no difference between resignation, utopianism, and idolatry, believing they each resist change and reinforce the status quo. "The resigned man," he says, "sees no alternative to the imperatives of his own social and political situation. . . . The utopian man sees that there exists a mode of being more full and satisfactory than that which he now knows, but he believes that his vision of the ideal is wholly discontinuous with the present state of things. . . . And the idolater . . . will naturally regard dissent as evil and change as corruption, and will fall easily into conservative politics" (Fish 1989:412). Despite such cynicism, the architect-visionary is ever the optimist and always willing to see the future as architecture-led.

Architectural interpretations of utopias, though, as well as utopian interpretations of architecture, invariably end up as semblances of a physical place quite contrary to the name *utopia* and contrary to its intention as a social construct, to trope a realm distinctly 'other' with which to stir the heart and mind. Indeed, this is precisely the criticism Constant Niewenhuys, a member of the *Internationale Situationniste* group and later the inspiration for Superstudio, received from his fellow members in response to his illustrating the 'sectors' of his early sixties *Neo-babylone* vision and described them with 'bourgeois practicality', a fatal error because "his building of actual models only served to excuse the *techniciens de la forme architecturale,* while the attempt to propose actual mechanisms for *la vie ludique* merely played into the hands of a consumer economy" (Banham 1976:83). The children of utopia are apparently to be heard but not seen, or read but not depicted—except privately.

But, since architects are voracious consumers of form, they leave nothing to chance or to the imagination, because that is *their* province. The visuality of architects gets in the way, though, of saying anything visionary, as it did with the megastructure of the sixties and all the riotous fun of Archigram about which Banham is unequivocal, "megastructures were ideal cities containing other people's Utopias," a stage for "*Homo ludens,* the archetypal 'man at play' " about which Constant Niewenhuys was concerned, for whom Cedric Price's Fun Palace (1962) was designed, and around whose movements Montreal Expo's Man the Producer pavilion was structured (Banham 1976).

Architecture as a stage upon which social visions are enacted coincides with the idea of utopia as a *ludibrium,* a dramatic fiction or parable, as Dame Frances Yates develops it in *The Rosicrucian Enlightenment* (1972), citing Bacon's *New Atlantis,* a term deriving from the Latin *ludere* (to play). The utopian Johann Andreae used *ludibrium,* in the sense of a 'play-scene', in alluding to the Rosicrucian Fraternity with which his utopian city *Christianopolis* (1619) is closely associated (Yates 1972:141–147). What has therefore been concealed by loose adoption of the term 'utopia' is this magical and mysterious quality, a quality that still drives architectural thinking today. Just as Ben Jonson's masque of 1625, *The Fortunate Isles,* is cited by Yates for its descriptions of a winged building on wheels encapsulating a Rosicrucian emblem, so might we wonder at the wings, the wheels, and the walls of John Hejduk's Berlin and Lancaster/Hanover Masques, as well as many other of his *ludic* ephemera.

Stanley Tigerman comments that "We are in a state of exile. Postmodern Americans, like their Renaissance predecessors, yearn for another, simpler time. America is a land of foundlings and orphans, who are detached from their proper parenthood and wander in search of legitimacy in a world of other histories of longer periods of time" (Tigerman

1988:154). Australia too, a far younger country than North America, has this yearning for a simpler time, taunted by the presence of a decimated but living aboriginal culture; the Aborigines are the "last custodians of ageless wisdom and harmony" (McLachlan 1989:301), preoccupied with the mythical 'Dreaming', a future-present, not the past, whose centeredness and connection with the earth is still largely incomprehensible to the modern Western sensibility. Utopia is alive in architecture, not as a conventional idealized future but as an exilic present, a no-place here and now that design-talk is trying to assemble, unfamiliar words attempting to massage unfamiliar architectures into likely candidates for a consummate future.

FURTHER SOURCES   Jameson 1988; Mumford 1922; Tafuri 1976b; Team 10 1962; Vidler 1992.

CHAPTER

The Definition of Architecture

Overview

. . . the proper definition of architecture, as distinguished from a piece of sculpture, is merely "the art of designing sculpture for a particular place, and placing it there on the best principles of building." **John Ruskin.** 1854. Addenda:§61.

What is architecture? Will I define it with Vitruvius as the art of building? No. This definition contains a crass error. One must conceive in order to make. Our forefathers only built their hut after they had conceived its image. This production of the mind, this creation is what constitutes architecture, that which we can now define as the art to produce any building and bring it to perfection. The art of building is thus only a secondary art that it seems appropriate to call the scientific part of architecture. **Etienne-Louis Boullée.** *Architecture, essai sur l'art* (c1799). Cited in Tschumi 1990:16.

When we come across a mound in the woods, six feet long and three feet wide, heaped up with a spade into a pyramid, then we become serious and something inside us says: here someone lies buried. *That is architecture.* **Adolf Loos.** *Architecture* (1910).

. . . for architecture is an undeniable event that arises in that instant of creation when the mind, preoccupied with assuring the firmness of a construction, with desires for comfort, finds itself raised by a higher intention than that of simply being useful, and tends to show the poetic powers that animate us and give us joy. **Le Corbusier.** 1930:218–219.

A bicycle shed is a building; Lincoln Cathedral is a piece of architecture. Nearly everything that encloses space on a scale sufficient for a human being to move in is a building; the term architecture applies only to buildings designed with a view to aesthetic appeal. **Sir Nikolaus Pevsner.** 1943:15.

... *architecture really does not exist.* Only a work of architecture exists. Architecture does exist in the mind. A man who does a work of architecture does it as an offering to the spirit of architecture ... a spirit which knows no style, knows no technique, no method. It just waits for that which presents itself. *There* is architecture, and it is the embodiment of the unmeasurable. **Louis Kahn.** 1964. In Latour 1991:168.

After more than half a century of scientific pretence, of system-theories that defined it as the intersection of industrialization, sociology, politics and ecology, architecture wonders if it can exist without having to find its meaning or its justification in some purposeful exterior need. **Bernard Tschumi.** 1974. In Tschumi 1990.

Definitions are schizophrenic creatures. Any dictionary will say that defining a word brings it to an end (*de* + *finire,* finish), delimits its boundaries, describes its properties, or fixes its meaning, all with a degree of precision that is intended to get at the 'truth' of the word. Most dictionaries will supplement definitions with etymologies, the derivation of a word, the original truth (from the Gk. *etymos,* truth) and signification that occasioned its birth as a word. Yet all dictionaries will say they are attempting to reflect *changes* in a *living language,* that they embrace literary and colloquial usage, that they include obsolete, archaic, and dialectical words and uses, and admit that influences are so diverse that foreign, technical, scientific, and specialist words are always being imported into a language. The more comprehensive dictionaries will give the history of a word, how it has been used over the years since its birth, and the adjustments or extensions to its original meaning wrought by fashion and favor as a result of circumstance and social and political use.

So, the fixity that the definition of 'definition' implies is in fact quite illusory; the meaning of a word is transitory, if changing slowly. A dictionary therefore offers no more, or less, than the history of society's use of words up to a point in time, and a way of comprehending that society; it is not a source of universal truth. As William James remarked of the way we use words, "Our nouns and adjectives are all humanized heirlooms, and in the theories we build them into, the inner order and arrangement is wholly dictated by human considerations, intellectual consistency being one of them" (1907:112).

There are four kinds of definition relating to the meaning of truth, called here for clarity a 'concept-word'—as against a description-word like 'bird' (it is of course arguable that all words embody concepts)—that are widely applicable: *atomic,* in which a concept-word is eliminated by substituting a synonym; *contextual,* whereby a concept-word in a sentence is eliminated by conversion to a synonymous sentence that does not contain it; *implicit,* whereby a commitment to a set of principles fixes the meaning of a concept-word;

and *use definition,* whereby a schema involving a concept-word is accepted without evidence and thereby legitimates any instantiation of the concept-word (Horwich 1990:34–37). Architecture embraces the implicit definition of truth, the truth of 'unity' being an example, and the use definition of truth, of which the truth of 'spirit' is an example, especially in the above quotation from Louis Kahn.

Antony Flew (1979) separates *descriptive* definition, a present established meaning, from *prescriptive* definition, a meaning proposed for the future, and maintains that definitions may be *ostensive,* explained by pointing or showing, or *verbal,* by saying something in alternative words. Flew offers *contextual* definition (meaning definition *in use*), where meaning is formed implicitly by the context and not explicitly spelled out; and also *recursive* definition, where examples of the class represented by the word are used with rules for generating further examples. Flew also highlights the adoption by previous generations of *nominal* as opposed to *real* definitions, whereby a term may acquire its meaning through existing verbal usage but there is assumed to be a universal meaning of the word common to all applications of it and perhaps beyond full human comprehension. A special case of the 'real' is the *persuasive* definition, where a concept-word is at the same time vaguely descriptive and richly evocative, or where degrees of the concept are suggested by the use of 'real' and 'true'. Such distinctions are frequently found in art and literature, for instance; a difference in truth is drawn between artist and 'true artist', art and 'real art', meaning and 'proper meaning' (there are several instances below). The persuasive definition slips readily into everyday professional discourse, though only occasionally now in the architectural literature, unlike in the nineteenth and early twentieth centuries when such notions were given pause for thought.

In selecting an appropriate concept-word, it is the concept we apprehend that we try to approximate with a word; and when we meet with a concept-word we seek to apprehend the concept of which it is the approximation. The concept appears to be apprehended independently of the word, the sense of it is intuited and the focus of it is emotive (Empson 1951); some would say the concept exists *a priori.* The most appropriate word for a concept is one that brings *transparency* to that concept or that acts as a conduit to it. The aim of transparency is to provide an 'unmediated account' of the concept, something that the philosopher Ludwig Wittgenstein desired in his striving for what Boyne (1990) describes as "a universal language which would be a perfect reflection of the real world" (91); that the philosopher Edmund Husserl sought to achieve through the interior monologue of phenomenology—"a place where expression exists in a pure state, freed from the noise of indication" (93); and that Derrida demolished through his critique of an originary *presence* (Boyne 1990:chapter 4).

It is characteristic of times of rapid change that deep connections are hard to maintain and that certainty becomes an apparition, just as it did earlier in the century and during the sixties. It also seems clear that the desire for certainty does not disappear at such times, but in fact underwrites and mediates change. The changes of the sixties were far less traumatic architecturally than they appeared, or when compared with the heroic period of modernism, because they drew comfort from what was by then the modern tradition, especially the agenda of social responsibility. The certainty of the sixties and seventies was that the architectural experiments then being undertaken were of their time. That this desire for certainty emerged again during the eighties in parallel with the gradual decline of modernist tradition suggests that now the desire for certainty is focusing on something longer lasting; the forces of convention are gathering.

Such convention suggests too that, unlike the polemic of the early modern movement, which sought to break completely with the past, current architectural discourse (which is decidedly historical) may be in a classical and foundational trap. The recent widespread quest for meaning in architecture rooted in historical allusion, architectural asides, or supposed principles opposes the quest for an architecture that tries to deconstruct such things and theorists who are cynical that an *etymon* can deliver any originary sense untainted into the present. For the former, concept-words and their history of use (or 'trace', as it is called here) are meaningful and help to bring certainty and clarity; for the latter these can only be an archaeological curiosity, any authority they might bring to discussion being tentative; both depend on dialectical agreement, the one less forcefully than the other. Hence, any meaning a concept-word may convey can only be by mutual agreement, and even then can occur only at the moment of its utterance, a sensible appearance (Gk. *phainomenon*) agreed between the utterers, as against what Kant called the intellectual intuition (Gk. *noumenon*).

In either case, meaning may be supplanted by what Georges Bataille calls the *besogne,* the drudge work ('job') certain words do or the effects they induce, not in terms of usage, which is historically tied to meaning, but in 'tone' or attitude—similar to Empson's notion of Emotion. 'Formless' is one such word because its job is to denigrate whatever it attaches to as lacking form (just as the job of 'real' and 'true' is to supply some superordinate form and thereby denigrate the nouns they attach to), even though it defies comprehension because as a concept it needs to be linked with the idea, the form (Gk. *eidos*). Yet to define 'formless' in terms of 'lacking form' is to not define it at all (Hollier 1989:29–31). The only way 'formless' can be used and comprehended is through convention, not through any intrinsic sense of truth about lack of form. And so it is with many architectural concept-words.

Architects have been and still are inclined to believe that they are the pursuers, purveyors, interpreters, and protectors of truth in matters of design, that they are the caretakers of clarity and meaning, that conceptual transparency is available only to architects, and by means of it they manifest architecture. Architectural metaphors abound in literature— structure, façade, plan, pillar, keystone, foundation, and so on—but such terms tend to mitigate against any clarity of meaning for the concept-word architecture *itself* (the 'itself' here is the lens to transparency). Architecture is not a word immediately transparent to architects, no matter how it may appear to others who use it. Apprehension of architecture is provided, rather, by the job it does and by the metaphors that accompany its use, prompting Hollier to remark, "Never mind if the proper meaning of architecture remains subject to discussion. What is essential is that it always does its job." And the job it does is described by Hollier as "whatever there is in an edifice that cannot be reduced to building . . . whatever is aesthetic about it . . . [which supplement] finds itself caught from the beginning in a process of semantic expansion that forces what is called architecture to be only the general locus or framework of representation, its ground" (Hollier 1989:31–32).

So, to seek or speak of the 'foundations' or 'cornerstones' of architecture or any other architectural topic using terms that are already architectural tends to obscure meaning rather than elucidate it, and inclines the discussion to circularity. If transparency is to attend architectural concepts, which Jacques Derrida claims cannot be the case because of the absence of any abiding *presence,* then theory cannot be the device by which transparency might be achieved, because universalized notions of the kind conventional theory pretends to *would themselves be transparent* and would not require explanation. So, what pertains in architecture, it seems, is not unmediated transparency but *mediated transparency*—the words get in the way of concepts and it is only by working through the words that meaning can be tapped. Theory as unmediated transparency, as illuminating principle, as universal reason, is therefore an impossibility and must be construed instead as rhetoric; rhetoric is mediation between words and their concepts, theory (design-talk) is mediation between architectural concept-words and their manifestation in practice.

Definitions assist in the mediation but are contingent, and they are required because architects, unlike painters, work with a highly technical language (Hollier 1989:27). Which rather begs the question, How can any communication take place at all if a word has only incidental value, a value of the moment, if it lacks precision honed over time, or if it has such overtones that its meaning may be supplanted? The answer seems to lie in the transaction, in the way it 'can legitimate its discourse only by receiving its own legitimation from that discourse'. Only in discourse do words and concepts have any meaning at all; they do not stand over and beyond the discourse. Hence, any words presented here as definitions in the form *Architecture is art,* or 'service', 'people', 'space', or 'science', can be understood only within the context of a discourse around the key words themselves.

Despite such difficulties, succinct, reductionist, and purportedly essential statements persist by way of definitions of architecture. Noting the unease the philosopher G. W. F. Hegel felt in his *The Philosophy of Fine Art* (1928) about an architectural paradox, Bernard Tschumi asks the question in 1975: "Were the functional and technical characteristics of a house or a temple the means to an end that excludes those very characteristics? Where did the shed end and architecture begin? Was architectural discourse about whatever did not relate to the 'building' itself? Hegel concluded . . . [that] architecture was whatever in a building did not point to utility. Architecture was a sort of 'artistic supplement' added to the simple building" (Tschumi 1990:15-16). Hegel's declaration parallels the search for architectural autonomy and, thereby, self-definition—a point Tschumi echoes in the quotation earlier. The essence of architecture for some is what it wants to be; the totality of architecture is the world just as architects see it.

Qualities thought to animate architecture as if natural or pertaining to certain fundamentals, usually called 'essences' or 'natures' and the core of the many definitions already discussed, are examined in part A. The second part looks at the architecture as a totality, why holism features so strongly in architectural thinking, what constitutes a whole and a partial work, and the relation between parts and wholes. It also explores the abiding question of unity and multiplicity that has absorbed both philosophers and architects for several centuries.

A. The Essence of Architecture

1. What Is the Essence of Architecture?

. . . insofar as purpose is the essence of architecture, architecture is its material manifestation. **Paul Frankl.** 1914:158.

Space is the most difficult aspect of architecture, but it is its essence and the ultimate destination to which architecture has to address itself. **Sir Denys Lasdun.** *RIBA Journal,* September 1977:367.

. . . there is no greater error in the study of human things than to believe that the search for what is essential must lead us to what is hidden . . . In short, when talking of the 'essence' of design, we are not talking of something lying behind appearances, but of the appearances themselves. **Roger Scruton.** 1983:189–190.

It is a persistent philosophical error to hold that the distinction between essence and accident is identical with, or inextricably bound up with, that between substance and property, so that you reach the essence of something by 'stripping away' its qualities. There is hardly a philosopher now who would fall victim to such a confusion. . . . Architecture, when successful, belongs to that *Lebenswelt* of thought and action; its essence, like the essence of almost every human being, lies in its elaboration. **Roger Scruton.** 1983:190.

. . . the central, most destructive characteristic of the Utopian period [has been] the intuitive abstraction of so-called essence from form, and, in turn, the abstraction of essential form from place. As a result buildings became abstracted "essences" set down on little slices of utopia, like canapés for a feast at the end of the world. **Gavin Macrae-Gibson.** 1985:xiv.

When we no longer know whether the "thing" dominates or the force which possesses it, says Nietzsche, the thing is becoming its essence. **John Knesl.** "Architecture and laughter." In Al-Sayed *et al.* 1988:n34.

Architectural theorists spend too much time looking for essences in order to be able to issue norms. We should look instead for continuities and discontinuities of practice and interpretation in which we find ourselves already involved, and which we can use or modify by metaphorical moves. **David Kolb.** 1990:129.

TRACE   Deriving from the Latin *essentia* (from the stem *esse,* to be) and Greek *ousia,* essence is the quality of which the facticity of something is the instantiation, either conceptually or actually, that quality by which something is what it is, the being that *is* the doing. The notion of essence arises from Aristotle's dictum "there is knowledge of each thing only when we know its essence" (*Metaphysics:* 1031, b7) from which it comes that a definition of something expresses its essence. Antony Flew (1979) clarifies essence as "the notion of a fixed and timeless possibility of existence" and lists 'essentialism' as entertaining three philosophical positions: Plato's doctrine of Forms, a defined property of something, and the characteristics necessary for something to be what it is. This last he terms its 'modality', which may be logical, temporal, moral, epistemic, and so on, and which tends to proliferate. For Plato, geometry reflected the essential universals behind manifestation.

   In architecture, the pursuit of essence is akin to the biochemical extraction from plants of some pure or elemental fluid or oil, some vivifying element 'distilled' from a circumstance or concept that is or is to be reduced or concentrated in built form. Primitive though this may seem, it was common throughout the nineteenth century and persisted late into the twentieth. The modern masters of Platonic essence have been Mies van der Rohe and Louis Kahn, the idealism of Mies being described by Jencks (1973) thus: "Universal essences may underlie all appearances, contrary to what the nominalist believes, but the idea that they are all geometric rectangles or even geometric is farcical . . . his world, like that of farce, is based on the radical reduction of things to a few simple formulae and rigid laws which are made to stand for a richer reality" (107). Twenty years later, remarks are still being made about architecture being the last bastion of outmoded Platonic thought.

COMMENTARY   The North American pragmatist philosopher John Dewey commented in *Art as Experience* (1934) that the fallacy of definition is that it pretends to absolute accuracy. "A definition is good when it is sagacious, and it is that when it so points the direction in which we can move expeditiously toward having an experience." Compared with the sciences, he believed art and literary theorists lagged far behind because they were "still largely in thralls to the ancient metaphysics of essence according to which definition, if it is 'correct', discloses to us some inward reality that causes the thing to be what it is as a member of a species that is eternally fixed. Then the species is declared to be more real than an individual, or rather to be itself the true individual" (216).

Later in the book Dewey declares that essence, in everyday terms denoting the *gist* of something, is highly equivocal: "We boil down a series of conversations or of complicated transactions and the result is what is essential. We eliminate all irrelevancies and retain what is indispensable. All genuine expression moves, in this sense, toward 'essence'. Essence here denotes an organization of meanings that have been dispersed in and more or less obscured by incidents attending a variety of experiences. What is essential or indispensable is also so in reference to a purpose" (293). And so it has been until recently in architecture; essence is what architecture taps in resolving a situation, or rather, it is what 'true' architecture taps.

It is no accident that most of the recent quotations above do not favor essence, for the discovery of the last generation, exemplified in the writings of Charles Jencks, has been that essences are neither fundamental to a satisfying architecture nor even fundamental. But modernist architectural ideology was founded on the search for truth and its embodiment in essential built form; truth was thought to lie in the expression of function, structural forces, materials, and the spirit of the age, as well as more abstract concerns and a host of lesser matters. And, just as modernism itself is repeatedly killed off only to rise again, belief in an essential and mystical quality informing architecture is also hard to dissuade and it too keeps resurrecting. Perhaps this is the sign we all keep missing! This essentialist agenda has so permeated architecture that even now it is difficult to talk about architecture without using terms that invoke the intangible. The flinty sharpness of Charles Jencks's earlier writings also softened enough to engage semiology only four years later (Jencks 1977) and the *'spirit* of tradition' after a decade (Jencks 1983).

There must be something fundamentally appealing about essences, idealism, and mystical notions that they continue to hold an attraction for many architects and designers despite substantial moves against them. That there is a huge investment in ego among architects that does not allow them to admit being other than sensitive in understanding and therefore influential, grand interpreters of natural and uncanny forces and deliverers from obscurity, is perhaps part of the answer. It is arguable that architects' will to power may well guide their will to truth, a truth in which they have a territorial claim by means of which, by couching that truth in essential and spiritual terms to which only they have the key, they remain unassailable. Friedrich Nietzsche raised this sort of argument against metaphysical philosophy and philosophers in general in *Beyond Good and Evil* (1885) in part 1, "On the Prejudices of Philosophers." The views architects have of essences may well only be a form of narcissism, a self-congratulation.

For Nietzsche in *Twilight of the Idols* (1888), essence is an unavoidable product of idealization that is the human feeling of increased strength and fullness in a conception. "Let us get rid of a prejudice here," writes Nietzsche, "idealizing does not consist, as is commonly held, in subtracting or discounting the petty or inconsequential. What is decisive is rather a tremendous drive to bring out the main features so that the others disappear in the process. . . . A man in this state transforms things until they mirror his power—until they are reflections of his perfection. This *having to* transform into perfection is—art" (Cited in Dal Co 1990:106). Dal Co comments on this passage that "the ultimate end of representation is therefore the *absolutely essential* that is manifest in *form.*" Now, it may be that the 'main features' or essences of a work are like Sleeping Beauty awaiting the kiss of the architect-designer Prince, but using metaphor in this way merely teases the issue. "A concept expresses the essence of something, but what is it, really, to state the essence of something— *what* it is—if it is not to draw a creative analogy and say what it is *like*? What is the essence of something, if not a metaphor taken literally?" (Madison 1988:88). All statements on the essence of architecture use metaphors: architecture *is* purpose or architecture *is* space, as the above quotations show. What such statements do *not* say is that the essence of architecture *is* what I, the architect, choose it to be.

Architects professing contact with essences therefore are only demonstrating their will to power by favoring certain qualities in a work over others, and in doing so they are merely offering up their opinion, albeit couched in universal terms. Practitioners, more than academics, tend to react angrily to anyone who dares question their opinions, for that is what their professional life is built upon, and their professional power and position are threatened when they are criticized or called to explain. Since philosophical truth is held by idealists to originate in antinomies—such as "rationality in irrationality, the sentient in the dead, logic in unlogic, disinterested contemplation in covetous willing, living for others in egoism, truth in error"—antinomies with which Nietzsche takes issue (1885:Aphorism 2 and Commentary), it is easy to see how architects convinced of the value of service to humankind ('living for others') could sublimate their egos by assuming they have access to the truth of a situation through some vision of its essence.

Such transcendence reinforces their professional self-definition in one sense, but in the end, if accepted in all its exemplification, it is inimical to professionalism because "if one is operating from within what we might call an ideology of essences—a commitment to the centrality and ultimate availability of transcendent truths and values—one will necessarily view with suspicion and fear activities and structures that are informed by partisan purposes (the spirits of advocacy and vanity) and directed toward local and limited (that is, historical) goals. Anti-professionalism, in short, follows inevitably from essentialism" (Fish 1989:221).

But, for all the derogation of essence in the quotations above, remove essentialism from the architecture profession and with it goes a set of vital fictions crucial to professional beliefs and performance. The design premises architects are then left with would be only 'facts' capable of verification or refutation, the very antithesis of *architecture* as that extra something, that magical and mysterious supplement we *know* it to be! Roger Scruton poses a question similar to the title of this section in chapter 3 of *The Aesthetics of Architecture* (1979)—"Has architecture an essence?"—where he discusses architecture from five viewpoints, each with their own body of theory: function, space, *Kuntsgeschichte* (art history), *Kunstwollen* (artistic intention), and proportion. He concludes that none of these views is sufficiently inclusive or formally descriptive enough to warrant the status they claim as the essence of architecture; they each ignore some intentional and centrally significant aspect.

This notion of an inclusive centrality presents the greatest difficulty for idealist architects. For if the essence of any situation is considered a 'within' to be 'penetrated', how do architects or designers know when they are 'in', and once in, how do they transfer the essence to the 'outside' to make it the all-embracing 'expression'? And if essence can be expressed as a comprehensive outward and visible sign, is it any longer essence? Since thinking of essence in this way ignores the embeddedness of the architect and designer in its conception, and while it may help keep the mind focused on the job at hand and therefore can't be all bad, essence is mainly a convenient fiction for a political faction.

FURTHER SOURCES   Hejduk 1985; Kollar 1983; Lakatos 1978.

2. What Is 'the Nature of' Architecture?

Poesy was ever thought to have some participation of divineness, because it doth raise and erect the mind, by submitting the shows of things to the desires of the mind; whereas reason doth buckle and bow the mind unto the nature of things. **Francis Bacon. 1605.** *Advancement of Learning,* Book II.iv.2.

. . . architecture must conform to the nature of the materials. **Carlo Lodoli.** c1750. Cited in Mitchell 1990:206.

. . . the programme being satisfied and the structure determined, what have we to do in proceeding from the simple to the compound? 1st, We must know at the outset the nature of the materials to be employed. . . . **Eugène-Emmanuel Viollet-le-Duc.** 1877. Lecture X:462.

Consider, first, what kinds of ornaments will tell in the distance and what near, and so distribute them, keeping such as by their nature are delicate, down near the eye, and throwing the bold and rough kinds of work to the top. . . . **John Ruskin.** 1855. "The Lamp of Sacrifice":§12.

Now, there is a nice question of conscience in this, which we will hardly settle but by considering that, when the mind is informed beyond the possibility of mistake as to the true nature of things, the affecting it with a contrary impression, however distinct, is no dishonesty, but, on the contrary, a legitimate appeal to the imagination. **John Ruskin.** 1855. "The Lamp of Truth":§7.

. . . the first sign of serious change was like a low breeze, passing through the emaciated tracery, and making it tremble. It began to undulate like the threads of a cobweb lifted by the wind. It lost its essence as a structure of stone. . . . This was a change which sacrificed a great principle of truth: it sacrificed the expression of the qualities of the material. . . . **John Ruskin.** 1855. "The Lamp of Truth":§24.

. . . let the iron be tough, and the brickwork solid, and the carriages strong . . . Railroad architecture has, or would have, a dignity of its own if it were only left to its work. **John Ruskin.** 1855. "The Lamp of Beauty":§21.

We should develop the new forms from the very nature of the new problems. **Ludwig Mies van der Rohe.** 1922.

Create forms out of the nature of our tasks with the methods of our time. This is our task. **Ludwig Mies van der Rohe.** 1923.

An object is defined by its nature. In order, then, to design it to function correctly—a container, a chair, or a house—one must first of all study its nature; for it must serve its purpose perfectly, that is, it must fulfill its function usefully, be durable, economical and 'beautiful'. **Walter Gropius.** 1926. In Conrads 1964:95.

They [designers of 'things for use'] really have no free will nor choice at all—they are just the helpers and servers of their machines, blunderingly, slowly, but very surely unwinding the wrappings from mystery after mystery, towards a fuller and fuller understanding of the nature of things and of what has been always there, waiting to be recognised, controlled, exploited. They are the exploiters, not the creators. **Clough Williams-Ellis.** 1929:89.

Gropius taught at the Bauhaus that in order to design an object correctly, one must first study its *nature*. . . . A few years earlier, Mies had expressed a similar idea. **Juan Pablo Bonta.** 1979:32.

A philosopher's prime concern is with the *nature* of our interest in architecture. **Roger Scruton.** 1979:1.

TRACE   To say that something has a 'nature' is to suggest that it was 'born' with special qualities that make it individual, or that it is by virtue of these qualities an individual and distinctive existence. The nature of something is also believed to be the dominant and sustaining power by which it attains its character, achieves its action, and fulfills its potential; its vital force or functions. In humans the Latin *ingenium* refers to a person's innate qualities (active or passive), what they possess 'by nature' as against by experience, their natural capacities; it was used by Vitruvius to mean "natural ability, talent." In comparison with the qualifications necessary for all undertakings, Protagoras's "venerable and widely used Greek triad" of *askesis, physis,* and *episteme* promulgated in the fifth century B.C., Vitruvius's *ingenium* loosely accords with *physis* (Pollitt 1974:388–389). And *physis* suggested 'generation' in ancient usage, where it was also associated with 'root' and 'seed' according to Onians (1951:253).

From his investigations into the mechanics of building elements and materials, the eighteenth-century Franciscan friar-architect Carlo Lodoli postulated a basis for ornament in architecture through "the invention of new ornamental forms based on the *nature of materials* to use the cant modern phrase" (Rykwert 1982:121). Collins (1965:205) contends that 'the nature of materials' concept was given wide circulation in the nineteenth-century journal *Revue Générale de l'Architecture,* anticipating by some years Viollet-le-Duc who, along with John Ruskin, adopted a stern stance concerning the 'proper' use of materials in architecture: materials must utilize their inherent qualities, their 'nature', their modes of availability, and the opportunities and limitations that their constitution presents in transformation or utilization. Frank Lloyd Wright, too, identified the 'nature of materials' as one of a set of qualities informing his designing; Henry-Russell Hitchcock wrote, with Wright's imprimatur, *In the Nature of Materials* (1942), in which he mentions materials extensively in relation to particular works, but curiously does not talk of their 'nature'.

COMMENTARY   Very much like essence, the 'nature of' art or architecture is deemed some quality or set of qualities inhabiting the task, and then the work answering that task, capable of transcending the work and therefore of being comprehended by viewing or by thinking about it. The 'nature of' something, however, is used to describe these qualities in a more focused way by comparison with 'essence' which is generalized and global. For example, the essence of a school may be to provide knowledge through education, while the nature of a school might be to do so by encouraging social responsibility and accountability, schools with differing natures providing education differently. Mind you, we are dealing here with degrees of imprecision, obliging a distinction where perhaps there is none; but (un)common use of these terms suggests that people do perceive a difference between them. It is not always clear though just what the evidential quality is that is engaged if the 'nature of' is used or whether it is even able to be discerned by anyone other than the person attempting to elucidate it. Like essence, it is frequently so casually used that it is a haven for obscurantists.

The 'nature of' in modern usage supposedly brings us closer to the discriminating qualities of a thing, setting, or circumstance, although in all but the most obvious cases the notion does little to illuminate whatever qualities are implied. For instance, when architects speak of the 'nature of' a site, materials, light, or architecture, nothing is clarified; they still need further explanation. Yet using the 'nature of' in architectural texts is intended to foreground notions supposedly needing to be made obvious before discussion can proceed, except that discussion is more often obscured by this maneuver. The question is, does any situation to which the 'nature of' is applied possess a quality, force, or power that can be elucidated at all, apart from a full and complete description of the situation or any actions pertaining to it? I suspect not.

Because trying to discuss the 'nature of' a work of art or architecture depends upon an understanding of the very qualities being evoked, to say that there is some *other* particular set of qualities comprising and empowering these qualities as the 'nature of' above and beyond their particularity, to the nonidealist, only begs the question. This move also violates a basic philosophical tenet, Ockham's Razor, that ontologies must be economical. Further, to argue in defense of the existence of the 'nature of' something by appealing to the obviousness that this 'nature of' brings to the very definition of the work is at best vapid and circular. Is there another way to be specific about the qualities of a work without using the 'nature of'? Fortunately, there is. By just eliminating 'nature of' wherever it is used, the fuller sense of something will usually be immediately more obvious and even transparent. But what happens if this is done? Is some degree of understanding about a work lost? For example, John Burgee says "We deliberately used carved stone at AT&T. Why not exploit the very nature of the material? Its intrinsic quality is such that it can be carved" (in Diamonstein 1985:34). Remove the 'nature of' and Burgee is saying no more than "Stone can be carved, so we carved it."

Juan Pablo Bonta (1979) highlights the contradiction and elusiveness of the issue: "When Wright said that his forms follow the nature of the materials, they were in fact following the nature of the material *as understood by Wright*. Wood, for example, was not used in the same ways by Wright and Aalto—although they both claimed in good faith to have been following the 'nature of the material'. . . . The mythical 'natural' essential shapes the creators of the Modern Movement were striving for did not belong to the realm of nature, *but to the realm of culture*. They were subject to history, and therefore they could not possibly be eternal" (44). And they were and are subject to personal interpretation, which also means they cannot be eternal, unless one believes there is a quality that unites the nature-seeking of Wright and Aalto, which they both missed.

Harking back to Vitruvius, the term 'nature of' was used in connection with propriety or appropriateness (*decor*), one of his six fundamental architectural principles. Sites for sacred precincts and the building of temples, he said, were to be chosen only if they were "very healthy places with suitable springs of water," whereby it was expected that "the divinity will stand in higher esteem and find his dignity increased, all owing to the *nature of* his site" (1486:1.2.6). The 'nature of' here may be interpreted as meaning simply the naturalness or natural qualities of the site and not some superordinate qualities. But in using 'very' and 'suitable' instead of saying "healthy places with springs of water," Vitruvius perhaps implied that there was more than just the normal life-sustaining qualities of the site at stake, that superior qualities like excellence of place (very) and of water (suitable—for a god) were involved. The implication was that these would supplement the divinity, that through the *coalescence* of these desirable qualities a site became sufficiently potent to enhance the divinity to whom the temple on the site was dedicated.

This is hardly surprising—it would be an impoverished people who would choose an inferior site for a god! But, as for Wright and Aalto with timber, the qualities perceived by Vitruvius (very and suitable) were seen to be influential *in themselves* rather than because of any objective evidence of their 'nature' in the sites. Also reflexively, the perception of specific qualities in certain sites, to which an aboriginal culture might attribute spiritual significance and around which religious and social beliefs, rituals, and taboos are generated, is likewise a perception of that culture rather than necessarily inherent in the 'nature of' the sites themselves.

Finally, Viollet-le-Duc was less inclined to use the phrase 'nature of', and was more precise in his exposition on the architectural implications of using specific materials than was Ruskin. Ruskin danced around the phrase on many occasions and wrote a lot of whimsy about the nature of materials as he interpreted them. But then so did Adrian Stokes (1978), suggesting that materials should proclaim their 'hard substance'. Especially quaint were Ruskin's admonitions against the artificiality of 'the grainer', in support of which he remarked that marble is "providentially distributed, in a manner particularly pointing it out as intended for the service of man" (1853:2.§XLI, "Early Renaissance"). Also, the embedded 'historical language' ('theological language', he goes on to say) of marble's veins and Ruskin's claim that where marble is not to be found, "Nature has supplied other materials, — clay for brick, or forest for timber, — in the working of which she intends other characters of the human mind to be developed. . . " (§XLIV) show how the nature of materials could be given a moral spin. What would John Ruskin say of the science of artificial lighting today, in the face of claiming then that "we would not wantonly . . . mock the sunbeams with artificial and ineffective light" (§XLVII)?

One might reasonably ask "So what?" Is such pedantic criticism really warranted? Does it matter if a site or a work does not 'actually' have such a nature? If a culture believes there to be such a nature and this assists in the operation and progress of that culture, then surely this is what matters, not the factualness of the belief. Perhaps so. But it is in my nature to be pedantic.

FURTHER SOURCES   10A.4, Character; Antoniades 1990; Coomaraswamy 1977, vol.1; Dal Co 1990; Hitchcock 1942; Kollar 1983; Latour 1991; Wright 1939, 1943, 1954.

3. Naturalism and Natural Architecture

. . . I suppose there is no conceivable form or grouping of forms but in some part of the universe an example of it may be found. But I think I am justified in considering those forms to be *most* natural which are most frequent . . . and assume that which is most frequent to be *most* beautiful: I mean, of course, *visibly* frequent. **John Ruskin.** 1855. "The Lamp of Beauty":§3.

In nature there is no independent problem of appearance; hence, there is nothing in opposition to the forms dictated by fitness for purpose. This occurs only in mankind. The essential problem of applied art is clearly that of appearance. **Hugo Häring.** 1927. In Conrads 1964:103.

Free rein must be given to the expression of the laws of nature . . . the unassailable physical truth of statics. Richness of expression can result from such a search, which will have that irreplaceable quality of longevity, of remaining valid, being born of the immutable and irrevocable truth of nature. **Harry Seidler.** 1986. Theme address to the Third International Conference on Tall Buildings. Chicago, January.

TRACE   Naturalism is "the philosophical belief that what is studied by the non-human and human sciences is all there is, and the denial of any explanation of the world extending beyond or outside the Universe" (Flew 1979), an attendant aspect of which is that only natural laws and forces—as against supernatural or spiritual—operate, and that the world is self-sustaining. Naturalism is thus the opposite of idealism. The presumption that phenomena can be explained without reference to divine forces or purpose is called The Stratonician Presumption after Strato of Lampsacus (d. 269 BC), the successor but one to the headship of the Lyceum after Aristotle. Stratonician atheism was exemplified by the naturalism of the Scottish philosopher and historian David Hume (1711–1776). The philosopher Huston Smith regards naturalism (but not himself) as a product of what he terms the Modern Western Mindset, the quest for control over nature, as a consequence of which "an epistemology that aims relentlessly at control rules out the possibility of transcendence in principle" (1989:200, 150).

In ancient Greek art "to represent nature as it really is (or at least to simulate our optical experience of it) . . . [any perceived] progression toward naturalism has been felt by some to be not only a *fact* of Greek art but also its *aim*" (Pollitt 1974:5, 6). Naturalism continues to be a view of art in which subjects are rendered as naturally and objectively as possible; the term is often interchanged with 'realism'. In architecture, however, naturalism is not a term usually encountered; there is no stylistic equivalent to its use in art, and its philosophical meaning is only implied in relation to terms like 'natural' or 'naturalistic'. An architecture is only termed 'natural', and therefore is seen as subscribing to a kind of naturalism, if there is seen to be an unselfconsciousness in its working out, as so-called vernacular architecture achieves, or if a peculiarly apt or symbiotic relationship is achieved between a task and its architectural resolution. It is this synergy of the self and the unself to produce naturalistic architecture that intrigues.

COMMENTARY   For Huston Smith (1989), naturalism is that world view that places nature at the center, a world of space, time, and matter, an outlook spawned by science in which "nothing that lacks a material component exists, and that in what does exist it is its physical component that has the final say" (145). Smith maintains that empiricism, or the scientific method, initially augmented human control over nature, and the increased pleasure gained from this power inclined us to privilege this kind of knowledge, which then merged with the experience of our thoughts and feelings to give naturalism. In excluding the transcendence of superior values from another realm, naturalism recognized that natural superiority arises only after the inferior, which in fact controls it, and that "accounting must proceed from inferior to superior, from less to more . . . higher forms come after and out of the lower" (151); and in some instances from nothing comes something. The term for this order of precedence from below is *reductionism;* all higher and more complex things may be reduced to their lower and less complex predecessors.

Architects are control orientated—some would say obsessed—and the modern movement in particular has shown *function* to be a prime form of naturalism, a concept that is highly rationalizable and facilitates control over most aspects of human action and building performance, yet utterly malleable to personal idiosyncrasy. It could accommodate everything from hard-edged rationalism and materialism to extreme swings of fantasy, such as those exemplified by Paul Scheerbart, Bruno Taut, and the Crystal Chain gang early on; to the promises of glory arising from the new 'spirit' of an age of machines and technology, the term 'spirit' being used quite loosely to mean, not traditional spiritual notions or forces emanating from some supernatural realm, but progress sourced in the hum of electricity and the buzz of sheer human industry and inventiveness, and above all reveling in and glorifying human control. This was no new age of spiritualism wherein supplication before an Almighty was to apologize and plead the case for human existence, this was naked human ambition; architects and designers broke through the traditional values and religious convictions that surrounded them in so many other spheres of life.

But there is another way of thinking and doing that accords more closely to a naturalistic vision in which symbiosis is uppermost. This is allied with what Reyner Banham called "the mystique of the engineer as the noble savage of the machine age: a mystique owed partly to Adolf Loos (like so many radical myths of our time) who always admired what he believed to be unselfconsciousness in design, and partly to the Futurist Movement (like so many more of our myths) who professed to see in engineers the outlines of an alien culture 'the gift of mechanical prophecy, the flair for metals' " (1975:44). This peculiar skill of engineers, a very human mastery in fact, to understand and then capture (rather than reveal) the forces of nature in structural form, is seen not only by architects but by engineers themselves as the vitality of engineering, a naturalism that invites poetry if it is allowed to 'soar'.

When we talk of symbiosis or of 'designing with nature', the architect who comes to mind most readily is the North American architect Frank Lloyd Wright. After all, it was he who wrote *The Natural House* (1954) and shares the copyright of Henry-Russell Hitchcock's *In the Nature of Materials* (1942), wherein 'natural' was used in relation to construction, materials, and harmony. It is not Wright who is of interest here, however, but an architect who for many would seem to be his complete antithesis, the Australian architect Harry Seidler. Seidler has achieved a symbiosis between natural forces and the systemics of building of the kind suggested above and, like his mentor Marcel Breuer, found not only a kindred spirit in engineer Pier Luigi Nervi, but precisely that mix of naive savant and alien prophet that provoked him to invention.

For Seidler, nature holds certain truths, as he says in the quotation above, respect for which if properly handled provides opportunities for 'richness', 'longevity', and 'validity' in buildings. So, too, do the processes of construction and the limitations of materials; and respecting them while at the same time mastering them provides an opportunity for the celebration of continuity within the particularity arising out of program and site. For an architect known to be combative about his own achievements and the environmental conditions around him, as so many architects are, Seidler's architecture is remarkably peaceful. What his later work evidences more and more is Seidler's naturalism, a naturalism grounded in equilibrium, *isostasy*, which occasioned Kenneth Frampton to label his architecture from the mid-1960s onward 'isostatic' and to describe his formal arrangements of plan and mass from that period 'isomorphic' (Frampton and Drew 1992:85–111). While it may seem a bizarre pairing, Seidler joins company with the North American architect and theorist Claude Bragdon, who wrote in *The Frozen Fountain* (1932) that "what happens in a fountain and in its every drop happens also in a building and in all its parts, where stress and strain, compression and tension, thrust and counter-thrust are ceaselessly operative" (10).

Architecture viewed as 'like' nature in that it is similar to a natural organism in its harmony, character, and unity, or because its shapes and structure are based in natural forms and blend with nature, or imitate natural processes or outcomes—especially the nature that organizes things, reacts to environmental forces, gravitational forces, undergoes the mysterious process called growth, flowering, and seeding, then eventually decays only to start all over again—has been labeled *organic* architecture (Hatje 1963:220–221). Starting in the nineteenth century, the organic movement reached its apogee with Frank Lloyd Wright, who was not altogether clear on what 'organic' meant; in a Princeton lecture in 1930, for instance, he gave it fifty-one definitions (Jencks 1973:125). At least fifteen years earlier in an essay "In the Cause of Architecture" (1914), he did say, "By organic architecture I mean an architecture that develops from within outward in harmony with the conditions of its being as distinguished from one that is applied from without" (cited in Collins 1965:152).

Broadly speaking, though, organic architecture comprises 'natural' forms, forms that seem to derive from circumstances and environments as if they might have been a by-product of nature's growth forces. Such forms seem natural too because human intervention appears to have been only minimally involved, the natural qualities and limitations of materials and forces doing most of the organizing, the role of human agency being merely that of catalyst or handmaiden. Seidler's architecture is not like this at all; it is defiant of nature, in the way one who practices a martial art is defiant of an opponent but uses the opponent's strength. By placing natural qualities at the heart of his architecture, Seidler is paying homage to the power and force of nature but daring them to beat him, all the while saying "I am in command here"; by doing so, Seidler acts out the challenge of naturalism.

FURTHER SOURCES   Antoniades 1990; Collins 1965; Sullivan 1918; van Leeuwen 1988.

4. Nature as Exemplar in Architecture

Alberti advocated the imitation of nature: buildings should compare with the corporeality of natural creations, and their builders should strive to understand and reflect the laws of nature (as *concinnitas*)—particularly, "ideal" human proportions. **Joseph Rykwert.** Rykwert, Leach, and Tavernor 1991:Glossary, 421–422.

Nature always means to produce excellence in its workings. **Giovanni Pietro Bellori.** 1672. *Lives of Modern Painters, Sculptors and Architects.*

Nature is but a name for an effect, whose cause is God. **William Cowper.** 1785. *The Task,* Book vi: "The Winter Walk at Noon," l.223.

Nature is only an idea. **Eugène Delacroix.** Cited in Wexner Center for the Arts, the Ohio State University, *About Landscape* Exhibition Catalog 1991.

. . . for whatever is in architecture fair or beautiful, is imitated from natural forms. **John Ruskin.** 1855. "The Lamp of Power":§2.

Don't take the example of others as your guide, but nature! **Ludwig Wittgenstein.** Cited in Bartley 1973:191.

The works of man are . . . microcosmic and mirror the laws of nature: but they do so to satisfy both maker and user; they do not follow natural laws as if in obedience to some blind necessity. These laws are the dispensation with and on which the *energiae* [activities] operate. They are the product of the collective, of society. . . . **Joseph Rykwert** on Gottfried Semper. 1982:129.

TRACE   The etymology of *nature* relates to birth as stated in the previous section, and standard definitions vary from the power that creates and regulates the world to the qualities of anything that make it what it is to inborn mind or character to a primitive undomesticated condition. In explaining the term, Antony Flew (1979) says "since, however, there seems to be nothing in the nature [!] of material particles as such to explain why their arrangements change at all, or change in accordance with laws, [certain] accounts of Nature had to treat its order as somehow imposed from without," hence the need of nature for a Mother or Creatrix Universalis.

Alberti used *natura* in his *De re aedificatoria;* Rykwert, Leach, and Tavernor (1990) translate this as 'nature' but qualify it in their glossary as probably meaning something closer to 'natural philosophy'. For Alberti, nature provided examples worth imitating, at least metaphorically. In the nineteenth century, Quatremère de Quincy sought a rationale for architecture based in imitation of nature, favoring *natura naturans,* indirect imitation of the 'spirit' and principles of nature rather than direct replication; the outcome being at best ambiguous (Lavin 1992). On the other hand, the North American architect Louis Sullivan discerned nature as transcendental in that natural creative processes, the 'radiant soul', produced the outward expression of all natural things. This all-pervasive quality was what gave each natural thing individuality; in its self-development Sullivan equated it with democracy. His architectural comprehension sought a similar 'radiant soul' or 'function' in the individual architectural task that it transcended to produce its outward expression, hence his maxim that 'form ever follows function' (Menocal 1981). The acknowledged manipulator of nature to building advantage was Frank Lloyd Wright, and from him comes the modern sense of using materials in their 'natural' state and in the arrangement of buildings to utilize the forces of nature such as water, wind, and sun.

COMMENTARY   Turning to nature as the exemplar for action and outcome has been a tactic of designers and architects for centuries. The forms of nature are such that "nature makes nothing incomplete, and nothing in vain," as Aristotle said, which ascribes to nature a perfect economy of means from which may be drawn a lesson and, for some, inspiration. Economy of means was to become a rallying cry of modernism, although it arose out of *minimalism* rather than naturalism. Trying to achieve the most with the least was developed to a state of high refinement and mythopoeic potential by Mies van der Rohe. While the idea of economy of means has had enormous appeal for architects in helping to focus the mind in refining detail and in taking materials to their visual limits, if not always to their structural limits as nature does, it is not the reduction of superfluity or the search for highly wrought solutions based in nature that is of interest here. More provocative for design and architecture is a notion Aristotle provided in one of his succinct formulations of the understanding of human actions and their relationship to nature, the notion of *completion:*

> Aristotle's most basic statement of what art is occurs in *Physics,* where he describes it as a purposive process that produces a final form out of preexisting matter (194b24 *ff.*). A man builds a house by following an orderly series of steps that are aimed at creating a specific product in the same way that nature follows an orderly process when it produces the leaves of a plant. Art thus "imitates nature" (in the sense that its processes are analogous to nature's), but it can also be said to complete nature (199a8 *ff.*) in that it brings about forms that are inherent in nature's materials but which nature itself does not produce. The artist differs from nature in that the materials he uses are not inherent in himself, and his products differ from nature's in that their form is not natural to their material. . . . (Pollitt 1974:36).

This sense of completion is demonstrated by our use of the phrases 'return to nature' and 'love of nature' in speaking of the rejuvenating effects of nature, without which we feel incomplete. This notion of completion embodies a return, closure, or fulfillment, and the role nature plays in our lives may be likened to the serpent swallowing its tail, the symbol of eternity; nature is the tangible eternal constant in the impermanence of existence.

Architects of a certain sensibility attempt to utilize the qualities of nature in buildings to instill a sense of duration both in the dynamics of diurnal and seasonal shifts and patterns, and in the near-constancy of substantial natural materials. Especially in houses, they employ particular elemental forms such as the hearth, the broad sheltering roof, sunken floors, or cave-like recesses in conjunction with elemental qualities of earth and water as inducements to giving oneself up or returning to nature. Some writers suggest that these belong among the archetypes of architecture (Thiis-Evensen 1987). Such atavistic concerns permeated the work of Frank Lloyd Wright, as Peter Blake (1960) explains: "For at the heart of every

Prairie house, there was a fireplace, often of rock, always broad and firmly anchored at the centre of the composition. From this hearth all spaces would extend, radiate into the landscape. This was the *source of all life* [emphasis added] within the house. Beyond that heart, there would be airy spaces, then, quite frequently, pools of water, and, finally, earth" (42). The bedrock floor of the living room in the exemplary Kaufmann retreat, Falling Water, at Bear Run, Pennsylvania, makes of the 'earth' connection a deeply personal and transitive communion.

Certainly, many architects in following Wright's lead have attempted to link their architecture with nature by direct connection to the ground and by using 'natural' materials, especially from a site itself, for the esthetic qualities of their acquisition—rough-sawn and unstained timber, stone rubble, untinted bricks, unglazed clay paving tiles, off-form concrete, even thatch in some cases. All these with a view to minimizing the taint of machine processes and artificial colorings and thereby gaining that elusive but morally correct alignment with nature, however much it might need to be contorted to fit.

The tactic of invoking architectural forms as if they were natural artifacts and inevitable in the sense of obeying natural law, either in operation or in growth, is also found quite often in architectural discourse, especially in the design studio. For example, Louis Kahn's appeal to letting a building (and material too) be 'what it wants to be' is wedded to the notion that there is an inherent quality in a building task that, given appropriate nurturance and the right sensibility by the designer, will emerge inevitably to inform that task, to breathe life into that task. Or at least that is what would happen in Kahn's view if the designer-ego were set aside or played down sufficiently to allow the laws *natural to the task* to work. In other words, Kahn believed and forcefully argued for an inexorability in designing as potent as the Platonic notion of Forms dictating physical manifestation, the inexorability of which nature is abundant evidence.

But more than anything else, the idea of 'letting be' is to do with Plato's concept of justice set forth in the *The Republic*, "in our state a man was to do one job, the job he was naturally suited for . . . [and] justice consists in minding your own business and not interfering with other people" (433). And a little further on, "Justice, therefore, we might say, is a principle of this kind [sticking to one's own business]; but its real concern is not with external actions, but with a man's inward self" (443). This is the Sanskrit *svadharma,* "one's own norm" corresponding with the Greek . . . *kata physis,* "doing of what is by nature one's own to do" (Coomaraswamy 1977, vol. 2:n150). Those architects who apply this 'letting be' to the materials and forms of architecture are acting out a judicial role; they administer justice as they see fit according as their view of the world is constructed. Some would say they are therefore *pre*judicial, in the sense that their attitude to the world is a *natural attitude,* as phenomenologist Edmund Husserl has said, borne of the trust they place in their construction of the world that surrounds them (Strasser 1963:198–200).

Finally, the appeal of extramural forces such as nature or spirit of the age at large in designing, and the desire to capture it, is primarily a modern sensibility to form-making (beginning in the nineteenth century) needing to bolster personal decision or esthetic preference, something believed difficult to justify without an authority greater than the individual. In practice, this apologetic fertilizes the 'mystery of design', which architects and designers promote as their *raison d'être,* their claim to professional domination, the thing that is their 'very own to do'. And it explains the deep sense of injustice they feel if others attempt to usurp or erode their relationship with nature, nature that is theirs alone to interpret and to complete.

FURTHER SOURCES   Antoniades 1990; Jarzombek 1989; Wright 1939, 1943, 1954, 1957.

B. The Totality of Architecture

1. The Whole as a Long-Standing Construct

And the very God of peace sanctify you wholly; and *I pray God* your whole spirit and soul and body be preserved blameless unto the coming of our Lord Jesus Christ. I. Thessalonians 5:23.

. . . in the members of a temple there ought to be the greatest harmony in the symmetrical relations of the different parts to the general magnitude of the whole. . . . **Vitruvius.** 1486:Book III.I.4.

. . . since nature has designed the human body so that its members are duly proportioned to the frame as a whole, . . . in perfect buildings the different members must be in exact symmetrical relations to the whole general scheme. **Vitruvius.** 1486:III.I.5.

It is the property and business of the design to appoint to the edifice and all its parts their proper places, determinate number, just proportion and beautiful order; so that the whole form of the structure be proportionable. **Leon Battista Alberti.** 1755a:1.1.

It is the function and duty of lineaments, then, to prescribe an appropriate place, exact numbers, a proper scale, and a graceful order for whole buildings and for each of their constituent parts, so that the whole form and appearance of the building may depend on the lineaments alone. **Leon Battista Alberti.** 1755b:1.1.

. . . not only is there but one way of *doing* things rightly, but there is only one way of *seeing* them, and that is, seeing the whole of them, without any choice, or more intense perception of one point than another, owing to our special idiosyncrasies. **John Ruskin.** 1859. *The Two Paths:*120.

Elimination of all *concept of form* in the sense of a *fixed type* is essential to the healthy development of architecture and art as a whole. . . . A block of houses is just as much a whole as the individual house. . . . Since the new architecture permits no images (such as painting or sculpture as separate elements) its purpose of creating a harmonious whole with all essential means is evident from the outset. **Theo van Doesburg.** 1924. In Conrads 1964:78, 80.

. . . architecture of complexity and contradiction has a special obligation toward the whole; its truth must be in its totality or its implications of totality. It must embody the difficult unity of inclusion rather than the easy unity of exclusion. More is not less. **Robert Venturi.** 1966:16.

We can 'dissect' a complex whole into its composite holons (whole/part) of the second and third order, and so on, but we cannot 'reduce' it to a sum of its parts, nor predict its properties from those of its parts. The hierarchy concept of 'levels of organisation' in itself implies a rejection of the reductionist view that all phenomena of life (consciousness included) can be reduced to or explained by physico-chemical laws. **Arthur Koestler.** 1967:54.

TRACE   The word 'whole' came into English usage from the Old Saxon *hal*, High German *heil*, Old Norse *heill*, and Gothic *hails, gahails*, all deriving from the Germanic. So, despite the rhetoric of Western philosophical speculation stemming from Greece, wholeness entered the English-speaking sensibility via the very different angle of the Nordic *heill* signifying 'hale and healthy', which Onians (1951) suggests can be interpreted "as originally connoting not just 'wholeness' or 'completeness' nor merely 'health' but the positive and desirable potency of life" which compares with "the strength, vitality, intrinsic in the concept of the *psyche* or *genius* . . . *valeo*, and the Swedish identification of the soul with 'the strength' " (477, n2).

In the art criticism of the ancient Greeks, wholeness does not appear to have been a *critical* concept, though it was certainly a quality tacitly held to prevail in a created work. Pollitt (1974) does not list *olon* (whole) at all, the nearest concept to wholeness being *eurhythmia*, which became important from the fourth century B.C. and basically means "the quality of being well shaped," both in reality and in appearance. Pollitt points to a fragment from an optics treatise of a late antique writer, Damianus, wherein "The goal of the architect, 'Damianus' says, is to make his work *eurhythmos*, and in order to produce this appearance he is obliged to make compensations for optical distortion, aiming at *eurhythmia* and equality (*isotetos*) not in reality (*kai aletheian*) but in appearance (*pros opsis*). The implication is that there is a real, measurable, *eurhythmia* and a *eurhythmia* that one sees or feels, and that an artist could strive for one or the other" (29). Wholeness as an architectural quality is indirectly discussed in most Renaissance treatises (for example, Alberti, *The Art of Building*, 9:6) but gained greater distinction in the nineteenth century in the face of stylistic eclecticism only to deflect with the onset of modernism. Wholeness is seeing a small resurgence as the twentieth century comes to an end.

COMMENTARY   It has long been and is still the conventional wisdom of architecture that it is holistic, that a completed building consists of parts arranged in symmetry with the whole, and that this whole is greater than the mere sum of its parts. Yet it remains largely unacknowledged that to agree with this is to subscribe to an idealist and, at its most forceful, totalitarian view of architecture. In the twentieth century, a totalizing spirit dominated the 1917 *De Stijl,* the 1918 *Novembergruppe,* the 1919 *Arbeitsrat für Kunst* (Work Council for Art) and the foundation of the Bauhaus, an attitude that Walter Gropius was to reiterate in *The Scope of Total Architecture* (1955) and a sensibility his pupils have continued, among them the notable Australian architect Harry Seidler. Despite a lifetime rightly decrying esthetic dictatorship by bureaucrats, Seidler berates much recent Western architecture as "re-heated, fake history" and "superficial images with hideous clichés," giving the work of Ricardo Bofill a special serve as "the kind of architecture that totalitarian regimes of both left and right have always favoured," urging instead "restraint and disdain for willful waste or physical or visual extravagance" as a more worthy creed for 'our time' (Seidler in Frampton and Drew 1992:380–382). While they may not subscribe to Seidler's strict view of contemporary architecture, many architects would still admit to seeing architecture as the rightful leader into the future.

On another tack, what most designers will admit to is that they comprehend wholes as they design, not visionary flashes of completed works, but veiled semblances that are only vaguely sensible yet whole nonetheless. The wholeness that designers perceive 'in the mind's eye', so to speak, usually involves a central idea that is catalytic though rarely capable of articulation in the early stages. Indeed, it may well be that it is the idea of the whole being sensed rather than the whole itself, if such a distinction be granted, but this advances the discussion before it has begun. Suffice for the moment to say this synthetic vision of the whole does not follow but accompanies any procedures or protocols adopted while designing.

Those devoted to finding and developing processes and methods instrumental to creative designing will agree that there are only a small number of methods that begin with wholes and progressively refine them, examples being the conjecture-refutation (generate and test) approach, and various techniques of successive approximation (see also chapter 6B). Most procedures of design are partial in that they conceive of the task as a 'problem' then tackle discrete parts of the problem piece by piece by means of analysis. Analysis is fundamental to the Cartesian, or so-called scientific, method, which has served human understanding so well for several centuries now, but it is primarily a method of explanation, not of generation. This is not to say that science cannot be generative; it can, hypothesis being but one example of a generative scientific formulation. The issue is rather that science is generative only by means of analytical method rather than by some other means.

Moreover, externalizing method as a description or formula, be it scientific or design, seems to actually distance or defer the holistic quality of whatever it is being tackled. It is as if method interferes with or impedes the emergence of the whole. If method is imagined as a 'louvered window' into the task, then its transparency and alignment are crucial. Any misalignment and the whole task may be missed, any opacity and only parts of the task will be discerned. Method, then, becomes a matter of selecting an appropriate window with which to 'capture' and view the specific task and thus it must embrace some conception of the whole task.

Realizing this alignment between our comprehension of something and the means by which we comprehend it prompted Christopher Alexander to more closely examine the unity he perceived in certain made objects, and to eventually discover the notion of hierarchical centers of focus that signified an all-pervasive 'One' and an attendant 'letting go' or submission to its effects that the designer must admit, a congruence and yet a freedom (Grabow 1983:chapter XIX). Alexander's discovery is not new; it has existed for centuries in a variety of expressions. But what Alexander has brought to the current age is a re-emphasis on the whole as a long-standing construct; he directs us to the means of achieving it, whereas Renaissance writers tended only to discuss the means because unity of the whole was already implicit in the classical canon. A question, however, remains: Are we all bound eventually to come to the same conclusion as Alexander, that centeredness and congruence aligning with a classical or traditional past is the core of architecture—dare I say *all* it is?

There are those who worry that concern for the whole has so declined over the past few decades that architecture is now in need of a fundamental injection. Pluralism and individuality are seen to have even further eroded what little remained of the superlative architectural quality of the whole. The quest for the renewed precedence of the whole over the partial underlies criticism of the fragmenting forces of postmodernism and deconstructivism. Just as society in some quarters is undergoing a fundamentalist religious revival, so architecture appears in some quarters to be in the grip of a reactionary fervor. Recent architectural experiments in formal dissolution are seen as a sickness that has been caused by this lack of wholeness, and one way to cure it is to pursue wholeness as if it were a religious value.

It is not hard to imagine how the line of reasoning behind this stance runs. If a building is observed to lack 'cohesion', to be assembled from a series of parts whose shapes are all disparate and apparently selected at random, this is evidence of a lack of wholeness. Most architects would probably agree that this is so, especially if it implies also a deficiency in evident 'design', because design is the act of bringing cohesion and parity to bear on assemblies. And if there were observed to be many such buildings, then presumably as a group they would be observed to lack cohesion and wholeness too (except, of course, *as* a group). And if there were observed to be a number of groups of such buildings, then lack of wholeness might be assumed to be reaching plague proportions and therefore be in need of 'cure'.

A conceptual difficulty with this line of argument is this: If wholeness is a quality that pertains to existent entities in order that they exist at all, and if this wholeness is necessarily greater than the sum of its parts, then it is difficult to know what is being observed by those who maintain there is a lack of wholeness, because any observed 'parts' must necessarily belong to a 'whole' to be parts of it. Or at least they would be seen to possess qualities suggesting they belonged to a whole, but because some essential bits were missing they therefore must be partial. If such parts were clearly distinct and separate entities they would, of course, be wholes unto themselves. So, wholeness appears to structure the relation between parts, and parts somehow carry with them a code indicating their position in this structure, a code that signifies they belong together as a 'family'; in other words, the coding somehow implicates one part with another.

If the implications of elements within an assembly are such that they appear not to belong together, then they must be parts and the assembly must be a partial one, not a whole. There cannot be partiality pure and simple. If some elements, but not others, are seen to belong together, then we would presumably have a partial whole or 'wholish parts', clearly unacceptable if expressed in the latter way. While it is usual to say, "Don't be so pedantic, we all know what is meant," I venture that we know precisely the opposite: nothing. I contend that this line of argument must be privileging either particular *degrees* of wholeness, which by definition cannot be because partial wholeness cannot be; or, it must be arguing for some other quality, the gist of which is what 'we all understand'.

In summary, it is deceptive to speak of wholes *a priori*, as if without such a conception nothing can eventuate or a result will be imperfect, because anything that comes into being, no matter by what route, will be holistic by definition. To argue that there are greater or lesser wholes is both pedantic and contradictory, even if by doing so the intention is to gain leverage on designing by insisting that greater clarity about the task at hand will be achieved by keeping one's attention on some presumed 'holistic essence' earlier, for longer, and with greater concentration.

FURTHER SOURCES   Alexander 1992; Berlin 1953; Kollar 1985; Snodgrass 1990.

2. The Part in Relation to the Whole

"[Connections], wholes and not wholes, convergent divergent, consonant dissonant, from all things one and from one thing all." This suggests that the world is both wholes and parts in a dynamic unity. **Paul F. Emmons** quoting Heraclitus. 1987:91.

Definition of good design: An object is well designed where the relationship of the part to the part and of the part to the whole shall appear to be inevitable. **Anon.** Knevitt 1986:#493.

Beauty will result from the form and correspondence of the whole, with respect to the several parts, of the parts with regard to each other, and of these again to the whole; that the structure may appear an entire and compleat body, wherein each member agrees with the other, and all necessary to compose what you intend to form. **Andrea Palladio.** 1570:Book 1, Chapter 1.

The principle determining the whole is . . . logically prior to every part and it is in the whole that the explanation (intelligibility) of the part must be sought. One cannot therefore begin from the parts that are structureless and hope to find the principle of construction by accumulating large numbers of them. **Errol Harris.** 1970:331.

I should like to convince everybody of a truth which I myself believe absolutely, namely that the parts of an architectural order are the parts of the building itself. They must therefore be applied so that they not only adorn but actually constitute the building. The existence of the building must depend so completely on the union of these parts that not a single one could be taken away without the whole building collapsing. **Abbé Laugier.** 1753. Quoted in Herrmann 1962:20.

If the business of getting the house to run well takes precedence over your artistic invention the result won't be architecture at all; merely an assemblage of useful parts. **Philip Johnson** in 1954. 1979:138.

. . . that a whole governs its parts, that an idea tends of itself to complete and enrich itself, that the forward movement of consciousness is not linear, like that which proceeds from cause to effect, but synthetic and multi-dimensional, since every idea retains within itself and assimilates to itself the totality of antecedent ideas, that the structure . . . is not the simple juxtaposition of invariable elements which might, if necessary, combine with other elements to produce other combinations, but rather an organization whose unity is such that its secondary structures cannot be considered apart from the whole without becoming "abstract" and losing their essential character. **Jean-Paul Sartre.** *Literary and Philosophical Essays.* Cited in Charmé 1984:37.

In a conventional approach, a building is considered a whole and the rooms or areas inside are its parts. [Frank] Gehry inverts this view by making programmatic parts into distinct wholes. **Paul F. Emmons.** 1987:91.

TRACE   A dictionary definition of part (Latin *pars,* share) offers nothing toward the understanding of it in saying it is portion of a whole, that which with another or others makes up a whole. This dialectical relation between antithetical notions is the stuff of philosophy and the frustration of architects. However, the Latin root is an extraordinarily generative one, which is ironic considering the architectural emphasis on wholeness as a desirable generative quality argued in 2B.1, Whole. One figure of speech with parallels in architecture is synecdoche, the substitution of a more complex term for a simpler term or *vice versa* wherein, say, a whole is used for a part or a part is used to describe the whole.

For some theorists, notions of parts versus whole and variety versus unity as they have occupied philosophers since the Enlightenment assume that "parts imply variety while the whole implies unity. This may be the result of the primacy of our scientific world view where parts are considered simple units, such as atoms. In this sense, parts have variety in their quantity and diverse natures. Wholes are complex entities resulting from the addition of parts" (Emmons 1987:93). The whole and the part often appear in the architectural literature but only ever as givens, their meaning and implications taken for granted. They are rarely examined in any depth.

COMMENTARY   The idea of the whole and the part is as ancient as civilization and exercised the minds of ancient philosophers like Plato and Aristotle as well as many since. Aristotle, for instance, remarks in *The Politics,* "the state is by nature clearly prior to the family and the individual, since the whole is of necessity prior to the part. . . . The proof that the state is a creation of nature and prior to the individual is that the individual, when isolated, is not self-sufficing; and therefore he is like a part in relation to the whole" (1253a). A little further on, in speaking of slaves, Aristotle comments, "a possession is spoken of as a part is spoken of; for the part is not only a part of something else, but wholly belongs to it; and this is also true of a possession. . . . The slave is not only the slave of his master, but wholly belongs to him" (1254a). Further on again, Aristotle makes the point of rulers and those ruled: ". . . for in all things which form a composite whole and which are made up of parts, whether continuous or discrete, a distinction between the ruling and the subject element comes to light. Such a duality exists in living creatures, originating from nature as a whole" (1254a). It is not difficult to see that this leads to the view that the whole is the ruler of the parts, and why the notion holds (still) great appeal for architects of a certain persuasion.

Moving forward one and a half millennia, Immanuel Kant in the *The Critique of Judgement* (1790) writes of the peculiarity of human conception to be discursive, of having the characteristic of moving from one subject to another without needing to unify anything. Kant argues that any totality the objects of our conception might have must belong 'outside' it, "for the particular is not determined by the universal of *our* (human) understanding" (Pt. II:§16). For Kant, since "our understanding is a faculty of conceptions," any universal belongs to the intuition, or nondiscursive understanding. Mediation between our discursive and intuitive understandings for Kant occurs through judgment, and any accordance we conceive among things through judgment "is only thinkable when ends are introduced as a middle term effecting the connection, as *necessary,*" whence comes his notion of teleological judgment. Put simply, our discursive understanding leads us to "regard a real whole in nature as the effect of the concurrent dynamical forces of the parts" whereas our intuitive understanding points us to the opposite conclusion. Judgment mediates between these seeming opposites.

So, what might the part be in relation to the whole? Of course it is the whole of it, but only insofar as it remains a-part. Such conundrums as those just described abound in philosophy and in the traditional cosmological literature. The separation of whole from part is critical to the understanding of the part, because in that conceptual distance lies the mechanism of the whole. In the preceding section the quality that implicates parts in being parts is what enables us to discern them as parts and makes them potentially wholeable. Because this quality is supplementary to the part, without committing to what precisely this quality might be, it appears there will always be a supplementarity or surplus among parts, which is the 'sum' by which the whole is greater. This supplemental quality is rooted in the *assignments* we give parts as entities.

By an assignment is meant the job we make parts do, and this varies with the context within which we construe them. In other words, it is impossible for us to stand outside of our assignment of roles to parts, we reserve unto parts the possibility of wholes until such time as they assemble either in *contradiction to, confirmation of,* or *intersection with* our assignments. Until then, parts remain parts, although in this fundamental sense it *is* possible to have 'wholish parts'.

Architecturally, assignments may be functional, formal, or descriptive. An example of a *functional* architectural assignment would be the collection of buildings constituting the homestead of a working farm that only come to a whole if seen in the longitudinal timeframe of a farming cycle. At any one moment, certain parts might be devoid of any actual function and at that moment are redundant; their momentary surplus, though, is what constitutes their potentiality as a whole farm. In fact, they may absent themselves until such time as they are needed, and still be considered parts of a whole farm. In other words, physical presence is not a requirement for a part still to be a part of a whole, and neither therefore is absence necessarily a sign of whole malformation.

An example of a *formal* architectural assignment is the usual unequal (sometimes hierarchical) weighting of parts in a composition or assembly, the privileging of one more than another (figure to ground, made more difficult through our natural perceptual apparatus), the layering of one over another (spatial precession and procession), the centrality of one more than another (alignments of all sorts and our natural inclination to *Gestalten*, roughly meaning our visual affinity toward creating wholes). More demanding, especially because of the bad press modern repetition has given to equality, is the privileging of parts *equally*, especially if they differ one from the other. This is the realm of architect Frank Gehry's work on which Emmons comments at length.

An example of *descriptive* architectural assignment is the inclination to classification and taxonomy, the structuring of any architectural task in order to understand, consume, and control it. By establishing descriptive structures that identify and isolate parts, just as this text is doing now, albeit temporarily, we forestall the whole until all bets are in. When the ballot closes, either there is a whole or there is not. Overseeing—and even that word is charged with wholeness—these assignments is each individual assigner, and it is to the assigner that the parts and the whole belong; the assigner is the surplus that makes of wholes a sum greater than their parts. Emmons likens the relationship to one of dynamic unity, but the dynamism and the unity reside in us.

Finally, few today would agree with Laugier about the primacy of parts being such that to take away even one would 'collapse' a building. What Laugier is suggesting has been the view of all idealists (holists) and was a fundamental tenet of modernist minimalism: that there is a degree of subdivision or multiplication, beyond which lies oblivion of the whole—too much evidence of parts will destroy the whole, too much elaboration of decoration will smother the whole. However, there is always redundancy in any designed artifact that makes it malleable and adaptable, from the moment the designer chooses one arrangement over another that is equally acceptable. The inclination today is to capitalize on the elaboration of meaning and expression rather than to minimalize.

In view of the explosion of potential in the wealth of historical understanding and in the dissembling of the Western philosophical base, while architects may be reveling in this freedom for its experimental opportunities, will the forces of intuition overtake that of our discursive understanding and once more seek to have the whole control the parts? Or will architecture continue to find even newer modes, wherein the relation between the whole and the parts will never arise as an issue again?

FURTHER SOURCES   Alexander 1992; Berlin 1953; Herrmann 1962; Kollar 1985; Snodgrass 1990.

3. Why Holism Is only Part of the Game

Every work of architecture may be considered as an organic whole made up of primary, secondary and contingent parts which stand in a specific volumetric relationship to one another. Where organic structures are concerned, this relationship is determined by nature itself in such a way as to meet the particular functional needs of individual structures. In respect of architectural structures it is determined by man. . . . The proportional relationships between the various parts, and between each individual part and the whole, is determined partly by considerations of stability, partly by the need for comfort and partly by the architect's desire to create a particular impression. **Alois Hirt.** 1809. Cited in Germann 1972:33, 34.

Wholeness of the design process and of the work is always in the process itself rather than a quality determined from outside, from the point of view of extraneous principles, and it is not represented in a closure of the resulting synthetic form. Wholeness is in the nature of the series of changes and in the intensity and quality of the differences that are lived and consummated. **John Knesl.** "Architecture and laughter." In Al-Sayed *et al.* 1988:n44.

A 'part' as we generally use the word, means something fragmentary and incomplete, which by itself would have no legitimate existence. On the other hand, a 'whole' is considered as something complete in itself which needs no further explanation. But 'wholes' and 'parts' in this absolute sense just do not exist anywhere, either in the domain of living organisms or of social organisations. What we find are intermediary structures on a series of levels in an ascending order of complexity: sub-wholes which display, according to the way we look at them, some of the characteristics commonly attributed to parts. **Arthur Koestler.** 1967:48.

TRACE Holism, from the Greek *olos*, whole, was coined by the South African statesman Jan Christiaan Smuts in his *Holism and Evolution* (1926), in which he promoted the view that historic evolution consisted in successively more comprehensive integrations, a notion exemplified politically by the British Empire and the growing world community that was to culminate afterward in the formation of the United Nations. Smuts's evolutionary view is based in the tendency observed in nature to produce wholes from the ordered grouping of units. However, while not labeled 'holism', the notion of the whole as a predominant quality wherein the whole is seen to be more than the sum of its parts, is at base a very ancient one that informs Plato's Theory of Forms.

COMMENTARY Far from being a universal process in nature, holism, in Smuts's sense of differentiated parts *actually* creating a whole by aggregation, is the exception found only in slime molds whereby cells stream toward centers of aggregation and change their shape from amoeboid to long thin vegetative forms (Moment and Habermann 1973:222). All other biological processes achieve wholes by the multiplication of cells through cell division, and are not strictly aggregative in the sense described. Yet it may rightly be claimed that the cells of all biological entities are, by being cells, differentiated and become organisms only as there are laws that pertain to their assembly. So, holism as the prescription of particular and distinct ends is a fundamental principle of nature, of life, a 'blueprint' that assigns the location and aggregation of cells their appropriate places—which, of course, is precisely what the genetic code is. And it is theological wisdom that God is the 'blueprint-maker' of life and of nature.

With the presupposition of God as Grand Architect of the Universe, the association of architecture as a creative activity with nature as God's creative activity was bound to happen sooner or later, particularly the observation that all created things, if they are to exist, must come under some guidance by rules allocating parts their appropriate places in the schema of the whole. While Vitruvius said as much in the principle of *symmetria*, the "relation between the different parts and the whole general scheme, in accordance with a certain part as accepted standard" (I.II.4), he emphasized the *relationship* rather than the whole, as did the Renaissance architects and theorists who mirrored him until the nineteenth century. It was with the rise of the 'organic' as an architectural concept that the whole was to receive renewed emphasis. For Germann (1972), it was Alois Hirt quoted above who applied the term 'organic' to architecture to describe the Vitruvian symmetry of part to whole but with the twist that purposiveness made it like nature, imitative of nature's orchestration of parts to the purpose of the whole; indeed, purpose was the surplus that made nature whole, just as human purpose was to make architecture whole.

It is purpose that makes the whole worthwhile, just as in a game. Entities in free play or free array make no sense until they purposely gather together, their assembly and future being constrained by rules of deployment and interchange. Designing as an active and vivifying process becomes a matter of reconciliation between compliant or competing forces and demands within rules. The game as a whole cannot exist without a purpose, and needs rules to organically sum its events in the playing. In football or baseball, for instance, no two games are ever the same and no one game can ever be said to constitute the whole of the game of football or baseball. It makes no sense to speak of an ideal game of football or baseball. Just as no two games are alike, no two design events are alike, and no two outcomes are, or need be, alike. The rules—for an architect, the attitudes, beliefs, and values—are the boundaries within which the design game is played; the relations between the parts, whether of process or of product, are the game plan, and the vector tracked as a result of their interaction is the game, the design.

Direct design experience confirms that designing is a holistic experience, one that fully implicates the conceptual frame of designers and their technique of designing. But it is only holistic in a partial sense, in the extent to which it is a sequence of events and circumstances—in effect as a game. There is no ideal design experience or ideal building task. This is a compelling challenge to those who are attempting to replicate designing in terms of routines and procedures, either when learning or teaching design or when assembling machine correlates of design. And it presents a significant obstacle: How do we step outside ourselves to comprehend our designings in order to establish more holistic procedures and, more pertinently, how are such procedures to be divested of their human frame in order to be implemented by machines, if that is indeed the agenda? Obviously we cannot step outside ourselves. Our designings are conceptually bound; they are interior, and artificial intelligence similarly needs to be made interior, to be conceptually bound to the designer, before it will have any chance of success.

Totalitarianism seems to lurk in the shadows of architecture, emerging with conceptions of architecture as a light leading society in social, economic, spiritual, or esthetic reform. Totalitarianism requires holism to best effect its agenda. As a theory, totalitarianism is "the doctrine that the State, or the nation, or the community is capable of a good different from that of individuals and not consisting of anything that individuals think or feel." So wrote Bertrand Russell (1952), who went on to explain that this doctrine was advocated especially by the philosopher G. W. F. Hegel, who sought it to be as 'organic', or natural, as possible. "In an organic community, he thought, excellence would reside in the whole. An individual is an organism, and we do not think that his separate parts have separate goods . . . in an organic society, good and evil will belong to the whole rather than the parts. This is the theoretical form of totalitarianism." For Russell the flaw in this theory was that "it extends illegitimately the analogy between a social organism and a single person as an organism. The government, as opposed to its individual members, is not sentient . . . whatever pain is to be felt must be felt by its members, not by it as a whole" (65).

The importance of this observation for architecture cannot be stressed too much for the conclusion that Russell draws from it: "The good of the multitude is a sum of the goods of the individuals composing it, *not a new and separate good* [emphasis added]. In concrete fact, when it is pretended that the State has a good different from that of the citizens, what is really meant is that the good of the government or the ruling class is more important than that of the people. Such a view can have no basis except in arbitrary power" (66). Russell's conclusion suggests that whenever holism is detected as a philosophical position among architects, we need only look to its purveyors to see the ruling class at work, or at play. There are other players in the game of architecture, and their play is as valid as that of the architect. What kind of game do architects wish to play?

FURTHER SOURCES   Berlin 1953; Emmons 1987; Kollar 1985.

4. Multiplicity and Unity, the Central Concerns of Architecture

. . . if you know whether a man is a decided monist or a decided pluralist, you perhaps know more about the rest of his opinions than if you give him any other name ending in *ist*. To believe in the one or in the many, that is the classification with the maximum number of consequences. **William James.** 1907:58.

Philosophy has often been defined as the quest or the vision of the world's unity. . . . But how about the *variety* in things? . . . What our intellect really aims at is neither variety nor unity taken singly, but *totality*. In this, acquaintance with reality's diversities is as important as understanding their connection. **William James.** 1907:58.

"The world is One," therefore, just so far as we experience it to be concatenated, One by as many definite conjunctions as appear. But then also *not* One by just as many definite *dis*-junctions as we find. The oneness and the manyness of it thus obtain in respects which can be separately named. It is neither a universe pure and simple nor a multiverse pure and simple. **William James.** 1907:66.

An organic-entity, this modern building as contrasted with that former insensate aggregation of parts. Surely we have here the higher ideal of unity as a more intimate working out of the expression of one's life in one's environment. One great thing instead of a quarreling collection of so many little things. **Frank Lloyd Wright.** 1910. *Organic Architecture.* In Conrads 1964:25.

Let us face it courageously and serenely: all is beginning, becoming, and returning; nothing endures unless it is reaffirmed again and again. The only way to affirm the unity of this universe is to affirm all multiplicity and plurality. This is so because a unity affirmed as such . . . [is]a unity secretly imposed on multiplicity. Such unity rots and thus betrays fear of the risk of becoming. **John Knesl.** "Architecture and laughter." In Al-Sayed *et al.* 1988:near n1.

The bird, which is almost completely spherical, is certainly the sublime and divine summit of living concentration. One can neither see, nor even imagine, a higher degree of unity. Excess of concentration, which constitutes the great personal force of the bird, but which implies its extreme individuality, its isolation, its social weakness. **Jules Michelet.** Cited in Bachelard 1964:237.

TRACE So as not to privilege unity and to assist the explication, the title of this section has placed multiplicity first; it is inevitable, though, that this ploy will fail. Multiplicity, from the Latin *multus,* much, + *plicare,* to fold, and hence 'many folds', points directly to *manifold,* which stems from the German *mannigfalt* and its variants. The clue to the dialectic of multiplicity with unity is that its 'many folding' only gives the impression of many, because in its 'extension', its unfolding, unity becomes clear.

Definitions of unity, from the Latin *unis,* one, are notoriously unable to give it sense without tautology. While not as regressive as trying to define 'meaning', to say that unity is oneness or singleness begs the '-ness', or to explain that it is 'the fact of forming or being *united* into one whole' or 'an undivided whole' is less than edifying. In everyday application, unity may be understood as the bringing together of many things into an arrangement that makes them appear as one, with all that so saying *implies* (here is folding again) for harmony, consonance, cohesion, accord, and so on. It is useful to think of unity as that state of 'unfoldedness' wherein the quality of a thing or concept is revealed, made plain, or brought out into the open, rather than as an abstract singularity.

COMMENTARY Unity is the core of metaphysical writings, and it is not possible here either to treat the concept comprehensively or to do justice to the literature. Discussion of a traditional concept like unity can quickly bog down unless kept moving by faith in and practice of those Eastern traditions in which it is alive. Architecture is not such a tradition in the West, although it frequently employs a concept like unity, often in ignorance of, or at least without full cognizance of, all that traditional Eastern thought brings to it. All that will be attempted here is to highlight two aspects of unity and multiplicity with implications for architecture.

First, the quest for unity is not dissimilar to that for the whole raised in 2B.1, Whole, and in 6A.1, Order, its main difference being that it is ruthless and uncompromising, likened by René Guénon to a war "to put a stop to disorder and to restore order . . . [and] concerned with the unification of multiplicity by means which belong to the world of multiplicity itself . . . a cosmic process whereby what is manifested is re-integrated into the principial unity" (1958:42). Unity is thus totalizing in its demand that multiplicity becomes subservient to the one, whereas wholeness offers the possibility for parts to maintain their autonomy because of their syncretic bond (see 6B.4, Analysis).

Wholeness may be considered a grass roots, ground-up process of accumulation by mutual agreement, whereas unity is a supremacist, top-down governance by sheer force of singularity. To discriminate between whole and unity in this way reflects everyday usage, which suggests a tolerance in the concept of wholeness that does not pertain for unity. Saying that something is 'multiply unified' is intolerable for most people in a way that saying that something is 'partially whole' is not.

Such unity as may be discerned among entities exists only insofar as each possesses that quality by which it partakes of unity; in other words, the 'bloodline' is evident, the family resemblance acute. This quality differs too from the surplus, by which parts relate to a whole, in that it is not possible to clarify unity by saying "unity is greater than the sum of its multiples." This narrowness suggests that unity may be inherent, "a wholly inward bond," as René Guénon (1958:x) puts it, whereas wholeness is not necessarily so. Guénon states that "order only appears when a standpoint is taken that is *above multiplicity* [emphasis added] and from which things are no longer seen in isolation and 'distinctively', but in their essential unity" (42). To even conceive of such a standpoint, 'above' is somehow to be 'outside' multiplicity and therefore unified, an impossibility, and one indication of the difficulties of language in trying to come to grips with metaphysical concepts. Targeting 'unity' in architecture raises formidable conceptual problems that need a comprehensive metaphysical doctrine for their full realization, and most architects are not equipped with such a doctrine.

Second, if a naturalistic basis for unity is sought to avoid the bind of traditional metaphysics, metaphysical difficulties arise. One potent argument has been that natural organisms possess nothing excess to requirements, nothing more than is necessary to their purposes, no redundancies, and are thus unified by purpose; therefore purpose will produce architectural unity. Hence the doctrine of functionalism in architecture that arose during the nineteenth century and dominated the early twentieth (see Collins 1965:Functionalism).

However, the quest for unity in architecture through purpose by way of analogy with natural organisms was fatally flawed from the start, because natural organisms are symbiotically embedded in the laws of growth and the impinging processes of environment, and as individual entities they are inherently nonspatial. Much as architects might wish to think of architecture as so embedded, its laws are partial and flawed, it is inherently spatial, and environmental processes impinge only as far as they are allowed. The closest natural spatial entities are the nest, hive, web, cocoon, and burrow, each of which is constructed by an agency that follows either genetically innate rules or learned behavior and reacts to material exigencies. These spatial entities, while not 'organisms', are possessed of unity of purpose and are not arbitrary or capricious.

On the other hand, architecture is a conscious act subject to the force and the caprice of human inclination for which there is no parallel in nature. The quest for naturelike unity in architecture may be seen as a seeking after lost innocence, an innocence that can never be regained by attempting to forget worldliness through a kind of rational empathizing with the state of natural organisms. Multiplicity in nature is subservient to its inherent unity in that all variation in nature complies with ordering rules that do not surprise even though they may differ within particular natural regimes. Multiplicity in humanity can be controlled only to the extent that rules and laws striving for unity make human manifestations appear unified. Unity as the resolution of multiplicity in architecture is a deception arising from perceiving unity as a 'thing' *a posteriori* and then seeking to implant it *a priori*.

Any unity that ultimately may be perceived in a work of architecture is a reflexive unity achieved as circumstances dictate while designing, as adjustments create new circumstances and new adjustments, a hermeneutic circularity of designing. The only unity of a designed outcome is one that embraces the conception, the process, and the formal manifestation, not just the formal manifestation alone. All completed buildings are what they are because of their *circumstances,* and to this extent they may be called unified in a natural sense.

However, contrary to natural organisms in which the intention or 'constitutive principle' dominates and is obvious in the formal manifestation, architecture for the most part has its intentions and principles obscured, and the unity of a completed building is less obvious. There are significant exceptions, though—buildings in which theological intention and symbolism dominate as in mosques, basilicas, and cathedrals. For most other buildings unity is rarely the most prominent quality, commercial architecture being most notable; or rather, the unity discernible is not fully accessible to scrutiny or understood through widely known values. Finally, a building is not indifferent to human attention, unlike natural organisms, which are supremely so. The indifference to human delectation of a flower or sunset or any 'beautiful' natural object or event is a shock when its implication is fully realized: that we count only for the harm we might do to nature and not for the joy and serenity we might experience in it. Whether the joy or serenity of architecture is to be found in the unity or in the multiplicity of a work depends on the judgment of the designer. John Knesl maintains that 'affirmation' is the key to serenity and says of its qualities: "It must affirm multiplicity and plurality, and not the One, in order to prevent the covert imposition of a unity that usurps the vital powers of multiplicity, of primitivist 'primordial' gestures. This affirmation of plurality will generate a kind of ever-absent but more 'real' unity of difference" (in Al-Sayed *et al.* 1988:near n35). Perhaps it is this "unity of difference" that theory must mediate in the practice of architecture.

FURTHER SOURCES   Berlin 1953; Coomaraswamy 1977.

CHAPTER

Power Structures and the Architect

Overview

*N*am et ipsa scientia potestas est. Knowledge itself is power. **Francis Bacon.** *Religious Meditations. Of Heresies.*

... whatever is in architecture fair or beautiful, is imitated from natural forms; and what is not so derived, but depends for its dignity upon arrangement and government received from human mind, becomes the expression of the power of that mind, and receives a sublimity high in proportion to the power expressed. All building, therefore, shows man either as gathering or governing; and the secrets of his success are his knowing what to gather, and how to rule. **John Ruskin.** 1855. "The Lamp of Power":s2.

It is the weak point of arbitrary power that in a short time it has to fall back upon those who have no settled conviction ... and who cannot therefore be reckoned upon at a critical moment. When that power becomes enfeebled, the servility which is called devotion, abandons, if it does not even turn against it. **Eugène-Emmanuel Viollet-le-Duc.** 1872:Lecture 20.

Pride, victory over weight and gravity, the will to power, seek to render themselves visible in a building; architecture is a kind of rhetoric of power. **Friedrich Nietzsche.** *Twilight of the Idols,* 1889.

Architecture. It is born of the most powerful thoughts ... Architecture is an embodiment of the power and longings of a few men. It is a brutal affair that has long since ceased to make use of art.

111

It has no consideration for stupidity and weakness. It never serves. It crushes those who cannot bear it. Architecture is the law of those who do not believe in the law but make it. It is a weapon. **Walter Pichler.** 1962. "Absolute Architecture." Cited in Conrads 1964:181.

What we now call 'monumental architecture' is first of all the expression of power, and that power exhibits itself in the assemblage of costly building materials and of all the resources of art, as well as in a command of all manner of sacred adjuncts, great lions and bulls and eagles, with whose mighty virtues the head of the state identifies his own frailer abilities. The purpose of this art was to produce respectful terror. **Lewis Mumford.** 1961:81.

In this paradise of the American, as well as elsewhere, experience has taught all beings that benignity is seldom found together with power. **Alexander von Humboldt.** Cited in Mumford 1970:15–16.

Design products, as pleasing objects, express the form of the new society of individual concentrations of power [when compared with preself-conscious societies of collective obedience to the 'divine model']. Design products are not any more means of communication of a cohesive community. They are signifiers of power grasped. Consequently, beautiful products are not valuable in what they are, but in what they represent. When man possesses them he grips neither the object nor the beauty of it. What is delicious for him is not the ornaments, the proportions, the materials. It is the power he holds to dominate other men. **Alexander Tzonis.** 1972:50.

Architecture is for Tafuri supreme among the arts simply because its other or exterior is coeval with history and society itself, and it is susceptible therefore to the most fundamental materialist or dialectical reversal of all. To put it most dramatically, if the outer limit of the individual building is the material city itself, with its opacity, complexity, and resistance, then the outer limit of some expanded conception of the architectural vocation as including urbanism and city planning is the economic itself, or capitalism in the most overt and naked expression of its implacable power. **Fredric Jameson.** 1985. In Ockman 1985:62.

Intellectuals ought to be struggling against the forms of power they are involved with: knowledge, truth, discourse. **José G. Merquior.** 1985:85.

Each of us in our several capacities is powerless ultimately to control our destinies. To generalize to the point of principle, there is an inexorability about the operation of 'the world', and an utter indifference of 'the world' to our inclinations to do whatever it is we choose to do when we choose to do it. We *do* make an impact, though frequently negative, as the chaos theorists argue about small events having large consequences, the so-called Butterfly Effect (Gleick 1989; see also 6A.3 Chaos). That dramatic effects may result from relatively minor events is shown by the careless handling of a candle that caused the near melt-down of the reactor at Wynscales, England; by the errors that led to a damaging nuclear leak at Three Mile Island, Pennsylvania; by the unauthorized testing that exploded the reactor at Chernobyl, Russia. The human and environmental disasters, in almost daily parade from the chemical soups we create, show how little control we actually exercise over our destiny. And this despite the achievers of life persuading the world of their successes only to wake at three in the morning in full sweat over the fear that they are impostors, that their victories have been merely illusory.

We continually seek the power structures to control because to give in would be to allow entropy to run its course and to deny our humanity. Depressing, you say? Read Lewis Mumford's *Pentagon of Power* (1970) and be more depressed. To have started this discourse on a positive note, though, would only have led quickly to cynical declarations of the oppressions that the abuse of power has assembled in the world; approaching it negatively leaves the text the possibility of somewhere hopeful to go.

Architects participate in various forms of power in their professional relationships, although they are largely subjugated by power structures that exceed their sphere of professional operation. Architects have only limited opportunities to participate in power structures in which they are equal or dominant players, notwithstanding Nietzsche's claim for architecture above as "a kind of rhetoric of power." Certainly the rhetoric has been important and still is, as will be discussed shortly, but it is of only marginal effect in those structures in which architects are secondary, and those are most of the structures that exist. The grand visionaries of social and urban reform—architectural utopists, futurists, modernists, postmodernists, and even deconstructivists—always begin by setting up confrontations with established ways in an attempt to establish structures of power in which they as architects can be the principal players. The visions either end in despondency and resignation or desperately cling to the promise of a new age to paper over the void that inevitably opens up as the world moves on.

It is on the eventual recognition of this inability to influence outcomes on any but a trivial scale that all notions of the architect's prestige, status, authority, and control, hinge. Architects invariably are obliged to recognize their almost total lack of domination in power structures, an incipient nihilism that is mostly repressed and rarely faced, and must adjust their sights to meet the nonarchitectural structures of power that override them, from which meeting they derive any and all their satisfactions and *raisons d'être*. This alliance always leaves architects open to attack over their values and loyalties, making them easy prey for ideologues of all persuasions, particularly those within their ranks who question their virtue.

The power people seek does not exist in some state independent of people or situations. Notwithstanding Lewis Mumford placing it among those 'archaic criteria' by which mankind assesses its own processes (in his case automation)—power, prestige, property, productivity, and profit—the Pentagon of Power (1970:240), power is not on a par with the other four; it is the very basis of the relationships that create them. When we speak of empowering, it is not to inject or invoke a quality or to tap into a reservoir of forces, although force is one of its manifestations; neither is it the near-physical force of fervent incantations against white dominance that rappers promoted in their call to 'Fight the Power', though the cabal such a call might solidify is nearer the mark. Power comes into effect through the structures of people and events, the relationships that obtain among people and between people and 'the world'. What makes governments strong is not the centralization of power but the power of centralization, the structure itself. The structures of power are necessarily oppositional because *power*, by definition, is the energy required to overcome its opposite, the void (*de-void* of power, powerless); power derives from the Latin *posse* (be able), which in turn is defined by its opposite, being unable or disabled.

Use of the word 'power' in English as meaning control over others can be traced at least to the thirteenth century according to SOED, but the concept is of more ancient origin. The Bible and other early writings give many examples: "Let every soul be subject unto the higher powers. For there is no power but of God: the powers that be are ordained of God" (Romans 13.1); "For this cause ought the woman to have power [of her husband] on *her* head because of the angels" (I Corinthians 11:10); "The society we have described can never grow into a reality . . . till those we now call kings and rulers really and truly become philosophers, and political power and philosophy thus come into the same hands" (Plato, *Republic*:7, §1). Science and nature give humans their cues: in physics, for instance, power is the relation between opposite poles; it comes into effect because opposing forces are capable of annihilating each other and so must be kept apart by structures maintaining a dynamic equilibrium. Power resides in the relation between doing and nondoing.

At the macro end of the scale there are the implacable power structures: the political decision structures of governments, institutions, and classes; the procedural under-government structures in laws, regulations, and rules; the management and efficiency structures of manufacturing and distribution; the economic structures adopted for the generation, allocation, and expenditure of capital; the numerical structures of unions controlling labor and skills; the communication structures of the media; and the information structures assembled by governments, institutions, and corporations. At the micro level there are the malleable powers: those that pertain in the relationship between individuals in all human affairs; the enhancements, suppressions, and repressions that obtain among individuals and social groups; the negotiation of advantage between competing human forces, means, and ends; the intercession of wider interests in the affairs of lesser interests and vice versa; the influence of charismatic people in convincing others about the choices they make; and the mechanism of default by which the macro and micro worlds meet to take decisions over choices not made. These structures and scales are not mutually exclusive; they interact at all times and in many ways. In all structures and at all scales there is one overriding quality that contributes to the definition and maintenance of power: the ability of any and every player to end their participation. Indeed, even the notion of the State as a 'megamachine' recognizes this: "Once a megamachine has been brought into existence, any criticism of its program, any departure from its principles, any detachment from its routines, any modifications to its structure through demands from below constitute a threat to the whole system" (Mumford 1970:241).

The power architects have in society is there only by virtue of what society has agreed to allow them. Within the architectural profession, the power of architects is only what its own structure allows them to have—any criticism, departure, detachment, or modifications *from below* are a threat to the whole. The power architects receive from the relationships with their 'clients' (see 3A.2, Client) and that they exercise over those with whom they negotiate to carry out their clients' intentions, is exactly the same. "The ultimate test of authority or influence in the design process is the capability to call an end to the entire project. Both architect and client hold this power. The situation in architecture is thus one of 'conditional viability', as defined by decision theorist Kenneth Boulding [1962], since each party has the ability to eliminate the other" (Cuff 1991:75). And in that ability lies the power each party achieves through the relationship; they do not 'hold' it so much as temporarily garner it by virtue of how much each is prepared to allow the other. And the power each has ends the moment the relationship ceases.

To be in a position to garner power from relationships, even though that power may be short-lived and not of much consequence when viewed in relation to the "broad scheme of things," is one source of satisfaction within the architectural profession. There are two concomitant aspects to power, namely, *authority* (and respect for authority) and *constraint* (the creation of rules and setting of limits), which must be agreed between the parties to any power structure before power can be effected. This agreement also includes which of the parties is to dominate and under what conditions. Aspects of these themes are discussed in part A of this chapter and concern the share architects have in the power of patronage, and some of the effects of this.

How power in whatever form is deployed and who benefits or loses from the exercise of that power is a matter of increasing concern in complex societies by which access to decision makers and the ability to influence the direction of one's life are less and less realizable without recourse to expertise, usually at a high price. Those disenfranchised by inequities in society have little or no say in their current or future circumstances; they are commonly thought to be powerless. To whom falls the responsibility for taking care of the rights of the disenfranchised, or those who are merely passengers on the social ride of life? Notwithstanding that the modernist zeal for an architecture-led future is now an illusion, one of the beliefs still animating architects is that it is they who should take this responsibility. And it is they who will make a difference through their intervention or intercession.

Architectural education emphasizes the responsibility a designer has to the anonymous others who will utilize their artifact or building. Architects N. John Habraken and Herman Hertzberger have turned this responsibility to advantage by making it a positive factor in their work, actively seeking ways for people to create their own niches, to personify and personalize and thereby become empowered, even if only to a limited extent, in otherwise corporate worlds. Advocacy is a role that many architects have taken up on behalf of disenfranchised others, as has already been discussed. Advocacy and just what direct or indirect effects architects can and do have on the people for whom they design is raised in part B of this chapter.

Another aspect of power is the way architects and others in the so-called 'rational' disciplines view 'pre-rational', or archaic, systems of design and organization. The theorist Alexander Tzonis wrote forcefully about this in *Towards a Non-Oppressive Environment* (1972), in which he makes clear that *power* through oppression is what designers exercise over societies and nature in order to still anxiety created by 'the unknown, the unexplained, the unstructured'. This oppression is seen to have existed in 'preselfconscious' cultures and still exists in backward or Third World cultures in the form of the 'divine model', which is emulated in every structure and relationship within such cultures, but collectively, thereby eliminating individual oppression (Tzonis 1972:34–37). The rationalistic thought of contemporary Western and technologically sophisticated cultures is seen also as power through oppression, but oppression by the privileged individual rather than by the 'benign' collective (this emphasis is because there are oppressive collectives). As Tzonis says, the basic force operating now is a kind of imperialism, "the desire to force people who function with a relative independence to submit to a different culture controlled by the power of the privileged of the western technological culture. It propagates the contemporary rationalistic approach as the only one in which designers possess objectives and in which they know what they are doing" (1972:15–17). Architects are part of this imperial force.

Finally, gender has been seen as a conceptual issue in architecture for only a relatively short period. Previously, gender was considered and discussed in historic terms, whether or not women were given access to opportunities in the profession, what differences there are or might be between ways of designing or the things designed, whether educational programs offer appropriate ranges of subject matter or experiences to satisfy gender differences, however they might be perceived, and so on. Gender studies are focusing on the power structures of society and the professions as never before. Because they are not confined solely to power but concern the attitudinal frame of architects, aspects of gender are examined more closely in 4A.5, Feminism.

A. Benefactors of Architecture

1. The Architect: Great Gift to Society

There is but one creator, and he is the artist; and the architect being an applied artist is as a demigod between heaven and earth, with his feet in the clay of his foundation trenches and his head amongst the stars. **Clough Williams-Ellis.** 1929:89.

Architecture is for everybody, hence the ideal architect is Everyman. **Mario G. Salvadori.** Foreword to Eugene Raskin, *Architecture and People* (1974).

Now into one of those aimless whirligigs where the old cultural tradition of high abstract ideals tugs against clumsy formulas for daily survival: Is the purpose of architecture to give architects something to do with their time on earth and the income to live well and raise a family, or is there some higher purpose? If no higher purpose, must one be invented? If so, who gets to invent it? One architect? A group of architects working together under a group name? An international convention of architects? Architectural journalists? Scientists? Politicians? Existentialists? And would the invention of a higher purpose produce the slightest effect on architecture?

Assurance for those troubled with such academic questions comes from all quarters, and in retrospect it becomes clear that, for at least the past century and a half, the single most important function of architecture has been to find a function for architecture in a world that has lost the ground of common ideological purpose which, long ago, charged buildings with the ritual energy of events. **Herbert Muschamp.** 1974:73–74.

Architects, perhaps more than other professionals, consciously or subconsciously harbor a desire for fame, for so much of their work is public—what we do shows. Perhaps we are in a kind of show business. Being famous may have its problems, but it is a form of public certification, a validation of success and a salvation from anonymity. **Roger K. Lewis.** 1985:8.

Architecture, like other arts, produces "culture capital" ... by which people display their upper-class status through their tastes and possessions. One can hardly consume more conspicuously than through architecture. **Dana Cuff.** 1991:32.

TRACE Three chapters in and 'architect' has been used many times without clarification, because many who are reading this either are aspiring to be or, like the writer, already are architects and need no definition. Originating in the Greek *architekton* (*archos*, chief, and *tecton*, builder, thus 'masterbuilder'), the word first entered the English language with a publication by John Shute in 1563 (see 1A.4, Language). Joseph Gwilt (1867:s319) claims 'architect' was rarely used in the Middle Ages and prompts that 'ingeniator' was its equivalent in the late twelfth century, and that 'supervisor', translated as 'surveyor' and 'overseer', was used frequently from the Norman Conquest. However, when Alberti goes against the popular etymology in saying "it is no carpenter that I would have you compare to the greatest exponents of other disciplines," it is because there *was* a medieval usage thought to derive from the Latin *archus* and *tectum* (roof) thereby associating an architect with a carpenter and builder of roofs (Rykwert, Leach, and Tavernor, 1991:366, n3).

There is little to add here except the definition that architects have given to themselves. Alberti announces in his prologue, "Him I consider the architect, who by sure and wonderful reason and method, knows both how to devise through his own mind and energy, and to realize by construction, whatever can be most beautifully fitted out for the noble needs of man, by the movement of weights and the joining and massing of bodies. To this he must have an understanding and knowledge of all the highest and most noble disciplines" (3). Near the end of the ninth of his ten books on the *Art of Building,* Alberti adds this prescription: "He must be of the greatest ability, the keenest enthusiasm, the highest learning, the widest experience, and, above all, serious, of sound judgment and counsel, who would presume to call himself an architect" (Rykwert, Leach, and Tavernor 1991:315).

COMMENTARY   The pejorative tone of the title of this section reflects a reaction to the fact that the still predominantly male-valued architectural profession combines naïveté with arrogance to assert that the world's or society's problems may be resolved by architectural solutions. Though this belief is less vehement now than it once was—even hidden in many cases—scratch the surface of an architect today and lurking just beneath is yesterday's reformer. A show of hands in a group of one hundred students in mid-course at my own school in 1993 showed the majority believe they are involved in social engineering of a sort, that they will effect changes in people's lives and perhaps even society by virtue of their work. They were a multicultural group, many of them from Malaysia, the majority of whom statistically will never end up in a practice of their own whereby they might have control over their own lives, let alone those of others. Curiously, fully half the students were women and the same proportion figured in the show of hands. I suspect there was a difference in motivation between them and their male colleagues, however, in why and how they might benefit society.

Le Corbusier no doubt expressed the feelings of most males of his generation when he remarked in 1925 of the traffic in Paris the previous October "Cars, cars, speed, speed! One is carried away, seized by enthusiasm, by joy . . . enthusiasm over the joy of power. The frank, ingenious enjoyment of being at the centre of power, of energy. We share in this power. We are part of this society whose dawn is breaking. We have confidence in this new society, confidence that it will find the magnificent expression of its energy. We believe in it" (cited in Conrads 1964:90). Nearly seventy years later, while the enthusiasm for traffic may have palled, the thrill of power and speed for many males and some females has not, as the road toll testifies. Neither has the thrill of power and speed receded for each, including architects, in the business world of today. True then and arguably truer today was Le Corbusier's remark in the same piece, "The city of speed is the city of success," although Los Angeles, of all North American cities, is perhaps the paradox with its contrasts of wealth and poverty, pace and breakdown.

In good times, architects feed off the frenzied activity of business, the power of wealth, and the speed of change occasioned by both with little talk of the side benefits of architecture. In not so good times or in times of pause, however, architects concentrate on what they can do to help society; they form committees, join committees, enter political skirmishes, act as advocates, and seek to spread their ideas by talking and teaching. When private practice is down, purportedly altruistic gestures always carry a sneaking suspicion of opportunism. It has been the story of the first half of the twentieth century that it was exactly this kind of egotism, combined with the ambition and arrogance (not to say desperation in economic bad times!) of its mostly male applauders, that encouraged the modernist agenda of reform by design to continue for as long as it did.

And it is not insignificant that the American Institute of Architects in its *Handbook* of 1972 could declare "No longer is the Architect committed solely to the interests of the client; he is as much concerned with the best interests of the community, the people and the land" (cited in Cuff 1991:106). Professional institutes in other countries usually adopt similar stances. Significant in the AIA statement, however, is the capitalizing of 'Architect' as against client, community, people and land, and the distinctly proprietorial tone of the architect's unsanctioned concern for the concerns of others. Architectural benefaction to society, the goodness an architect can bring, is the one quality professional institutes emphasize in marketing architects, as Cuff remarks of the AIA: "Part of the AIA's mandate is to convince the public that architecture's value is greater than has heretofore been realized, deserving more respect, compensation, and opportunity" (1991:106). Cuff does not derogate this mandate, but one interpretation of what she says is that unstinting public devotion by architects *in all fairness* deserves to be reciprocated! As a cynic might say, "In matters public, always back self-interest."

Of course there *are* architects who are public-serving without being self-seeking and who are sometimes rewarded in kind, as well as others who go on unrecognized, gaining rewards just from doing what they do. Indeed, it has been one of the nobler motivations of architecture as a profession that "architects view themselves as benefactors to society, as humanists and humanitarians," and in their work "feel an obligation to all who may use, occupy, or see the buildings they design, both in the present and the future—an obligation not only to provide shelter and accommodate activities but also to instruct and inspire" (R. Lewis 1985:10). It is likely, though, that this altruistic motivation is virtually an anachronism for almost a generation of architects trained in some schools that have de-emphasized functionalist concerns, user reactions, or social responsibility in their curricula in favor of high art (or rather high literature in the most Anglican sense of high) and élitist philosophical concerns. It would be interesting to forecast what the ideal of the profession might be if social benefaction ceased to be even the myth of the ideal professional that it now largely is.

Given the subtle and not-so-subtle discrimination women architects have endured in education and in practice, which is now being recognized, and given the noticeable differences in professional perception between women and men, the apparent drift away from the altruistic ideals of architecture, represented by the increasing obfuscation of recent theoretical concerns, may be short-lived. Despite some recent obscurantist writing coming from female theorists that reinforces the architect's élitism, the authority promulgated by male magician-architects is being countered by what is argued to be a peculiarly female trait in practice, namely, "a willingness to discuss the options, evaluate the choices, demystify the process, and share the decisions", a trait that at the same time unfortunately threatens to undercut the authority of the woman architect (Berkeley and McQuaid 1989:xxiii). Once the injustice against women in the profession is seen to be have been redressed, mediation of this kind may well be what architecture needs to progress beyond the theoretical discourse it is now being buried under.

FURTHER SOURCES   4A.5, Feminism.

2. The Client and the Patron

The position of an architect towards his client is not that of a mere executor of the ideas, fancies, and whims of the latter. He is also an adviser; and the talent he possesses should never be prostituted to the carrying out of an idea that is false, ridiculous, or injurious to the real interests of his clients. **Eugène-Emmanuel Viollet-le-Duc.** 1872. Lecture 17.

Architects like to do projects for institutional clients because in their view there is a much greater chance of producing memorable, newsworthy architecture. **Roger K. Lewis.** 1985:223.

The client always wants more than a well-crafted building, more than a space well-tailored to daily needs; the client wants "a bit of magic," says Goody, and "much of the magic is in the architect's presentation of himself as the magician. . . . The ability to express confidence, to carry others along on a magical trip, is critical." **Ellen Perry Berkeley.** Quoting the Boston architect Joan Goody. Berkeley and McQuaid 1989:xxiii.

Architecture's expensiveness inevitably binds it to the sources of finance and power, making it very difficult to achieve the autonomy from bourgeois standards that art had fought for since its emancipation from aristocratic patronage. Paraphrase of **Alan Colquhoun.** Cited by Margaret Crawford (Ghirardo 1991:30).

TRACE   There has been a curious reversal in the use of the terms 'client' and 'patron' in architecture over the centuries. *Patron* derives from the Greek and Latin *pater,* father, and *patronus,* protector of clients, advocate, defender. In ancient Rome, a patron was the former master of a freed slave over whom there were certain legal claims; in the Middle Ages it came to apply to a fatherly guardian or protector of a page at court. From the Renaissance *patronage* gained a philanthropic edge in actions supporting and encouraging a person, institution, work, or art, and it was not until the late eighteenth century that it assumed the commercial meaning of a supporter or regular customer. A *client* derives from the Latin *cliens* and *cluere*—hear, listen—and literally was someone at another's call. In ancient Rome, a client was a person under the protection of a patron, a plebeian under a patrician. In the Middle Ages it came to apply to the person for whom a lawyer acts and from the early seventeenth century assumed its current sense of a customer.

The curiosity lies in our understanding of the present-day architect-client relationship, in which the client is the customer of the architect, whereas it was several hundred years ago, and in certain respects still is, the other way around. The architect today is the 'listener' and is 'on call' in this relationship, a 'client' in the ancient sense; and the present-day client in fact, is a 'patron' in the sense of protecting, supporting, and encouraging the interests of another, namely, the architect. Architects are cautious about using the term *patron* today because of its implications of dependency, no matter how dependent an architect may be on a clientele; Dana Cuff (1991), for instance, lists "Patronage" in her index as "*see* Clients." So much has the matter been inverted that it is frequently the case now that the (celebrated) architect adopts an overbearing view of the client, in effect becoming the 'patron' of the 'client' in the ancient sense. A further curiosity is that architects mostly see the client as a customer for their services, while the clients frequently see the architect as a customer competing for their support.

Just when the shift occurred is difficult to say, but it appears to have consolidated with the advent of the Modern Movement.

COMMENTARY   Tom Wolfe writes in *From Bauhaus to Our House* (1981) of the difficulty North American architects have had in dealing with the question of corporate power and the rights of the corporate client in the face of the architectural ego. Wolfe recalls the panning Morris Lapidus received one evening in 1970 at the hands of the Architectural League of New York: "I kept trying to put in my two cents' worth about the general question of portraying American power, wealth, and exuberance in architectural form. I might as well have been talking about numerology in Yucatan" (94). Earlier, Wolfe relates the introduction to North America of *The International Style* via an exhibition of Gropius's work under that banner in 1932 at the Museum of Modern Art (MoMA) and of the impact its catalog was to have. Assembled by Henry-Russell Hitchcock and Philip Johnson (then twenty-six), Wolfe called the exhibit "one of the most dotty and influential documents in the entire history of the colonial complex" (37). This importation of the most recent European manner was not initiated by architects but by the corporate North Americans who had founded MoMA only three years earlier in a bid to match if not outdo their English counterparts and who wished "to carry the brave banner [of the avant-garde] forward and urge the practitioners to follow" (41).

MoMA's prestige via Philip Johnson mixed with cultural cringe and heavy pressure leading rapidly to closure within the architectural profession ensured rapid success for The International Style and its clones. It was what corporate North America was soon conditioned to receive and what it was invariably to be given. From then on, patronage in North America sought to portray an image of itself that even today, despite shifts in emphasis and fashion, dictates the acceptable face of contemporary architecture. Where else does one look to find what current architecture is about, if not the corporate building? And does such patronage make the commodification of architecture more or less palatable? Is there another architecture waiting in the wings, a 'truer' architecture, with the potential to displace this bastard, if only it had the power to implement itself? Is the licit compliance of corporate architecture to be countered only by the liberty of the individual house? Such questions dog the footsteps of the architect today trying to establish an approach that can hold its head high within the architectural community, yet appeals sufficiently to popular corporate taste to attract patronage.

There are two types of institution; each presents itself differently as a client and hence in its architectural relationships. First there is the *deconstructed institution,* which is largely deinstitutionalized in that it presents "a multi-faceted, fragmented image of establishment, inherently accessible, adjustable, changeable and an expression of many parts as opposed to one." In Australian terms its structure and management style are "overtly egalitarian and represents a prevailing political commitment among architects in Australia since the 1960s to provide open access to an apparently accessible power structure. . . . The deconstructed institution is now an accepted orthodoxy in Australian architecture. . . . " Then there is the *affirmed institution,* which is devoted to centralization and "desires clarity and a unitary image. Notions of civic dignity and clear legibility as a public building are paramount. Its aspirations may be said to be classical, affirming authority, order, and control. The resulting buildings are hermetic complexes, rarely additive or reductive. Designed in the name of both democracy and totalitarianism, the affirmed institution treads the fine line between political utopias of extreme opposites." (Phillip Goad in Beck and Turnbull 1988:ix).

The deconstructed and the affirmed institution each have their architectural expressions, although it would be too simplistic to divide them into romantic and classical sensibilities, respectively, for the classical is a quality of both in the sense of celebrating stability, continuity, and dependability. For instance, unless the ego of the founder is taken into account and overlaid upon the corporate image of the institution, the marvel of a New York skyscraper cannot be explained, as was the case with Frank W. Woolworth in 1913 (van Leeuwen 1988:60–68) or Gerry Hines, developer of the Transco Tower designed by Philip Johnson in Houston, Texas. Questioned about his relationship with Hines, Johnson replied "Patrons are more than half of architecture. Architecture is much too important to leave to the architect, because we get fantastic and silly ideas. . . . But if you have a patron, he'll stop you short and say you can't afford that, and you'll go home and cry" (Diamonstein 1985:156).

Herein lies one difference between a client and a patron—all architects have clients but few have patrons. The relationship between client and architect is such that either the client or the architect controls more and gains more depending on their relative strengths and weaknesses. In almost every instance of a corporate client, architects speak of efficient management, a clear chain of responsibility, and authoritative decision-making as essential in a good client. Perhaps typical of the 'architect-client relationship' as it is termed in professional parlance, is the way the North American architect Norman Pfeiffer describes it: ". . . it is the architect's responsibility to make clear to a client that there are certain points where decisions must be made and that turning back is not possible after that point. . . . The ideal client is also one who comes prepared, one who can match the architect's own organization. . . . It's an educational process that most clients are more than willing to go through. . . . It rarely is the case that a client is truly bad" (Diamonstein 1985:193).

Not even "bad," let alone "truly bad," could be used to describe the relationship between an architect and a patron, because patronage would usually have ceased long before reaching that stage. The relationship between patron and architect may at times be one of contest or of 'battle', but it is a battle between equals, which means that each gains no more or less than the other. Patronage is a form of empowerment for both the patron and the architect, and it is both adversarial and cooperative, born out of mutual respect for the caliber and talent of each. For example, a patron of Le Corbusier in this reciprocal sense was Henri Frugès, an altruistic and creative businessman, virtually a "Captain of Industry," who commissioned the experimental workers' housing at Pessac in 1925. Having been attracted by his writings, Frugès said to Le Corbusier "I am going to enable you to realize your theories in practice—right up to their most extreme consequences—Pessac should be a laboratory" (cited in Jencks 1975:72).

Another example of reciprocity was between Frank Lloyd Wright and Hilla von Rebay, Solomon R. Guggenheim's art adviser and founding curator of the Foundation's growing collection. There developed an ideal relationship of patron and architect in the design of the Guggenheim Museum in New York. Originally approached in 1943, over the next six years Wright enjoyed with von Rebay a friendly but combative relationship. By then the venerable master architect, Wright was condescending as always and at times projected himself as if he were von Rebay's patron. In architectural matters he was unforgiving and even intolerant, bringing to the relationship little of the instructional attitude of his early 'kindergarten' years at Oak Park (David van Zanten. In Berkeley and McQuaid 1989:55-61). But they were two charismatic individuals who, it has been said, challenged and amused each other. This *pari passu* was not to continue after Guggenheim's death in 1949, when von Rebay lost out to James Johnston Sweeney, the new director of the Foundation, who was to fight Wright on every point about the museum design. The transfer of power from von Rebay to Sweeney is a classic illustration of the shift from patron to client, not the ideal client but the bad.

And it is in the realm of the ideal client that this section ends, an 'other' than the actual purchaser of an architect's services. Margaret Crawford believes this ideal 'other' was identified at the World's Columbian Exposition of 1893 as "an ideological construct that allowed the profession to focus on the group the profession hoped to serve and that established the claims of ethical disinterest required for professional legitimization . . . the larger public as user of urban space" (in Ghirardo 1991:32). Crawford sees the future of the profession in a redefinition of the ideal client "not as the generic masses of modernism, but specific groups whose needs are not being served by the architectural marketplace" (44). Maybe Crawford is right, but not for the reasons she thinks; moving the ideal client to the specific will give architects someone to patronize.

FURTHER SOURCES   3A.5, Absent; 3B.2, Users; Hays 1987.

3. Elitism and Leadership: Rule by Rank Insiders

Architecture is not the satisfaction of the needs of the mediocre, is not an environment for the petty happiness of the masses. Architecture is made by those who stand at the highest level of culture and civilization, at the peak of their epoch's development. Architecture is an affair of the élite. **Hans Hollein.** 1962. "Absolute Architecture." Cited in Conrads 1964:181.

But who has the right to set himself up as judge of an established society, who other than the legally constituted agencies or agents, and the majority of the people? Other than these, it could only be a self-appointed élite, or leaders who would arrogate to themselves such judgement . . . democracy is preferable. However, this democracy does not exist . . . if the alternative is rule by an élite, it would only mean replacement of the present ruling élite by another; and if this should be the dreaded intellectual élite, it may not be less qualified and less threatening than the prevailing one. **Herbert Marcuse.** 1972:73–74.

Their inability to control their own professional marketplace left architects at the mercy of the larger market economy. As a result, architecture, a luxury rather than an indispensable service, remained within a premodern model of elite patronage, its provision of services primarily dictated by economic power. **Margaret Crawford.** In Ghirardo 1991:31.

Architects, to avoid the ever-present danger of incorporation into the dominant economic and political structure, created powerful myths that directly addressed the inherent dilemmas of professionalization; they structured these myths around the two main actors in the professional project, the architect and the client. **Margaret Crawford.** Ghirardo 1991:31.

TRACE   The term *élite* derives from the Latin *eligere,* elect, and came into English usage in the early nineteenth century. Related to eclectic and select, the term emphasizes being chosen by virtue of some special distinction, quality, education, or class, from among the ranks of society or a group. *Elitism* is belief in or consciousness of being élite or belief in government thereby and the necessary leadership this entails. Elites operate in and are made operational by 'rank' societies, those in which "positions of status are somehow limited so that not all of those of sufficient talent to occupy such statuses actually achieve them" (M. Fried. *The Evolution of Political Society.* New York, 1967:109. Cited in Harvey 1973:234).

In architecture, just as in science, the sign of élitism is an emphasis on the tacit and inarticulable in which the layperson can have little or no say or chance of judging "for the tacit dimension is shared and understood (*verstanden*) only by the élite. Only they can judge their own work. Thus in this tradition we have a combination of élitism and of a cult of the unarticulated . . ." (Lakatos 1978, vol. 2:227–228). The distribution of talent and opportunity within the architectural community is such that élites are formed which also emphasize the tacit and inarticulable and thereby operate by excluding the 'laity' of the bulk of architects.

COMMENTARY   It may be correct to say that élitism is not exclusive to architecture but is a characteristic of any profession requiring specialized education at high cost and offering expert service or knowledge to a fee-paying clientele. However, architects are perhaps seen as acquiescing in their élitism more willingly than other professionals and to support any system that privileges their view of the world and its problems and solutions. Robert Goodman, then professor of architecture at MIT, was highly critical of the élitist stances and ideas of architects and planners in his book *After the Planners* (1972), a criticism not uncommon in the heady days of building boom, drop-out communities, and futuristic ideas, a time when exuberance in the profession was running high. The criticism is still valid and will continue to be so, because élitism seems to be endemic to architectural thinking.

Elitism operates in a hierarchical fashion within any defined universe. In society at large architects constitute an élite; among architects there are élites, in some countries forming 'axes', for want of a better term; and within these axes there are élites, specific architects or groups of architects whose professed views or practices gather around them a coterie of devotees. It is important to stress the difference between the élite and the avant-garde, just as between the élite and particular stylists, because élitism so often crosses such boundaries. Elites may be established by virtue of their success and power within a community, they may have the tag applied to them by virtue of their associates or activities, or they may be an entirely self-appointed group around some issue on which they declare themselves to be the leaders.

Le Corbusier, for example, envisaged the structure of his *Ville Radieuse* as an 'anarcho-syndicalist' organization with one difference: it was to be led "if not controlled, by a small group of élite specialists: the great artist and statesman or the 'Captain of Industry', the enlightened businessman" (Jencks 1975:18). That Le Corbusier saw himself as one of the few, as a number of architects have done, who could lead society toward a better future by this and his many other inventive schemes made it inevitable that any form of government he imagined should also be élitist. Benevolent dictatorship has always been the alter ego of architects and planners bent on reforming society.

Elitism in the architectural profession shows up clearly in four ways: through education, practice, publication, and exhibition. Universities and other teaching institutions reinforce the élitist structure of the profession by generating or focusing on critical issues through faculty who themselves have critical views and have thereby gained leadership in those areas, and by attracting students who wish to be educated into that critical tradition, thereby reinforcing its primacy. In any country it is clear which schools of architecture are the élitist schools; they are those that market ideas, that are known for theory rather than technics, and that experiment in their design studios. Whether one can say that these institutions are educating tomorrow's 'power élite' in the profession is another matter, because the question is begged of whether an architectural élite can have any real power at all. Talk of élitism as a power play frequently runs the risk of becoming a conspiratorial theory in which success is seen as being hand in hand with big business and major political players.

In publication, all the signs are there that some recent architectural writers, especially those who have turned to certain obscurantist philosophical writings, have consciously striven for élitist status and have achieved some measure of this through what Imre Lakatos calls the Cunning of Reason (1978), certain 'theoreticians' being accorded privileges as have not been seen since the early days of modernism. Just as there are journals known for their avant-gardist edge, there are publishing houses regarded as the key to marketing critical theoretical writings that are essential to this process of leader-creation. Certainly monographs on individual architectural works or on individual architects have become both a major money-spinner for some publishers and, if popularity measured through sales is anything to go by, one way of gaining admission to the hallowed band of leaders nationally and internationally.

Then there are the architectural foundations and museums that encourage and in effect act as patrons for architectural ideas. Across the United States in 1984 there were almost thirty museums with important architectural collections of drawings and models (Gutman 1988:92). In some European countries the situation is similar. Some measure of the impact of exhibitions as purveyors of élitist values may be gained from the exhibition on *Deconstructivist Architecture* in 1988 at MoMA in New York (Johnson and Wigley 1988). This was not a display of avant-garde work, as the catalog makes clear, but of seven established architects. But they were virtually manufactured into an élite overnight by the exhibition, and now have a cult following as a result. Concomitant with exhibition in the creation of leadership is competition, and it is significant that of the seven deconstructivist projects exhibited at MoMA, four were competition winners.

In practice, the principle means of recognition is the awards system. Usually established by the professional institutions, and occasionally offered by architectural journals and civic authorities, awards bring recognition to works that might otherwise be noticed only by ad-hoc publication or through the concerted efforts of architects to publicize their work. The design awards system is also open to manipulation of direction by a jury pushing its particular agenda and in effect creating a 'leading edge' where perhaps none exists but that mostly represents the standards and values the profession hold out as constituting architectural worth. An architect who wins awards over several years is surely heading toward or perhaps has joined the bevy of worthies. At its most cynical, the awards system is just good business and many architects enter their work into competition because they cannot afford not to be seen.

Patronage aside, élitism mostly achieves its inside running by virtue of Lakatos's Cunning of Reason in science: "There is no predictable or ascertainable limitation on human imagination in inventing new, content-increasing theories or on the 'cunning of reason' (*List der Vernunft*) in rewarding them with some empirical success even if they are false or even if the new theory has less verisimilitude—in Popper's sense—than its predecessor" (1978, vol. 1:72). All who theorize about architecture rely on the Cunning of Reason (if not on logic) to persuade others to what they believe, or at least until they have achieved a credibility for themselves that assures them of serious attention. Once this happens they exit the realm of Good Argument and enter the realm of Worthy Arguers wherein *understanding* is the game and you are either an *insider* or not, an assessment, incidentally, that is only made by other insiders. Outsiders remain outside and continually misunderstand, and élitism reigns undisturbed in this rarefied realm, perpetuating itself (prompted by Lakatos 1978, vol. 2:227–243). Architects generally might say, along with Marcuse above, spare us the intellectual élite.

FURTHER SOURCES   Chapter 4A; Ghirardo 1991.

4. The Beastly Developer and the Architect

We are whores and want to be paid as highly as possible for doing what we do best. Therefore we do skyscrapers best—they're the most profitable. **Philip Johnson.** In Games 1985.

I'm very commercial myself and I find [commercial clients] just as intelligent. . . . The commercial people in this world—the really rich, the really successful and managerial types—have a justifiable sense of pride in their work, and majesty is what they need to celebrate it. But I would do it for Lenin too. I don't care. **Philip Johnson.** In Games 1985.

The architect looking for aesthetic patronage will usually not find happiness on the bottom line. **Roger K. Lewis.** 1985:218.

At a time when building is so expensive and will probably become even more so, there is a need for people whose profession it is to build for profit. They have replaced sponsors like the Medici or the popes. Developers are the Medici of today. They pick and choose architects, and there is a lot of competition to get selected. **Helmut Jahn.** c1984. In Diamonstein 1985:149.

What is so badly needed is for the architects, and developers who employ them, to be more sensitive to the deep-rooted feelings of 'ordinary' people and to find ways of integrating their opinions and their needs into the creative processes from which new buildings emerge. **Charles, Prince of Wales.** 1989:12.

In the climate of today, architecture's only substantial claim in New York is as a "Landmark." Indeed, the absence of sanction for any other constructive value has transformed the Municipal Landmarks Agency into a virtual rump planning department, the planners have relinquished authority to the developers. **Michael Sorkin.** 1991:364.

TRACE 'Develop' comes from the Old French, *desveloper* (disvelop), deriving from 'dis-' plus *volup-* or *velup-* as in the Old French *voloper,* envelop, and Italian *viluppare,* wrap up, although its origin is lost in antiquity. All such words derive from the Latin root *vel-, val-, ver-,* cover or guard, hence disvelop or develop meaning to uncover, unwrap, unfold more fully so as to reveal all that is contained, eventually leading to the idea of bringing forth from latent or elementary conditions—hence its adoption in photography—and to cause to grow or evolve from some germinating condition. Curiously, in relation to later discussion about the destructive aspects so often associated with the term 'developer', there is the second Latin root *vel-, vol-,* tear or pluck, as in 'vulture' and the obsolete 'vellicate'.

Whatever rapaciousness might have come to be associated with the term 'developer', the origin of the word lies in a benign gradation that seems almost soothing. Indeed, we use the term in any situation in which fuzziness becomes clear by the turn of events, in which chaos is turned into order, and in which from nothingness something emerges into its full glory. This is the scene at all building sites, as any sidewalk supervisor knows, and is arguably the source of greatest satisfaction for any designer or architect, to see a concept realized.

COMMENTARY In 1989, I asked more than a hundred architecture students midway through their undergraduate course at the University of New South Wales what they considered fundamental to architecture. They were prompted with a series of quotations from Philip Johnson taken from the chapter "The Best Hated Architect in the World" in Stephen Games's *Behind the Facade* (1985). Two of Johnson's more provocative pieces are quoted above.

Analysis of the essays showed a wide variety of sentiments and passions, as was expected, but one set of issues revolved around developers and development, the comments being mostly negative: developers are evil, they run the architectural profession, they (along with bankers) care only about short-term solutions, they are uninterested in architecture, if a building is a moneymaker it gets the go-ahead no matter what, architecture has fallen prey to the glass towers of the multinationals, skyscrapers destroy humanity, city towers and project homes just project image, not individuality. Students were also concerned about the profession's relation to developers and offered their own ethics: institutes of architects glorify the architect/developer and greed: the students intend to graduate and confront big business and money controlling design, but will stand by their principles in the face of greed, as fighters who will not sell out.

Where this antipathy to developers came from is unclear. When quizzed about this in an open forum afterward, the students stated that they were merely expressing what they thought to be a commonly held view, one not obtained formally from their course but apparently at large in the community. Obviously, their reaction is born of an idealism that students always have about architecture and about their future vision of themselves as architects. Not for them the compromise of principle, or the leveling of individualism through commodification, or the demeaning of artistry for money-making brutes, or the hoary (whorey!) iconoclasm of a Philip Johnson, but architecture as something beautiful and artful and untarnished. This view is not restricted to students, of course; architects express similar sentiments about developers (see Michael Sorkin above). Roger Lewis (1985) finds that many architects think developers "crass and shortsighted" and that "too many developers sacrifice human or cultural ideals to the so-called 'bottom line', rejecting any attempts by architects to design artfully" (217).

One attempt to reconcile the contradiction between the developer-client wanting value for money and the architect desiring money for value has been the move by architects to market their design talent as a product or commodity. Arguing that (presumably good) design sought in an open and competitive marketplace produces better quality, which in turn results in faster sales and better rentals and higher volumes of each (Lewis 1985:216), architects hope to convince developers to employ them in the belief that as a result they will claw back some of the edge lost to plan-drafting services and captive in-house designers. Of course there is no way to tell whether such claims are true because no system of assessment exists whereby designed (as against 'nondesigned') or good design (as against 'poor' design) may be objectively tested. So, such claims are really just a plea by architects for more consideration, relying in the end on the good-will and vanity of those in a position to commission them and on the architect's willingness to reduce fees. "Developers know they can get architectural work done quite cheaply because we're dying to build and would do it for nothing, as long as we could still eat," writes Philip Johnson (Diamonstein 1985:157).

Remove the subjective distaste of developers from the vision architects have of designing and the world seems a lot brighter. However, real moral dilemmas can surface in relation to the work of developers, especially in larger projects that can often involve historic buildings or those of substantial iconic value. Not that historical preservation issues are not also present in smaller work—they are—but the economic pressure in large-scale work is enormous, not only on architects but on all those involved in the decision-making processes, where public accountability is most evident. And for many architects there are some projects that are untouchable. For instance, Philip Johnson refused the commission to extend St. Bartholomew's in New York because he admired Bertram Goodhue as a great architect and thought the church contributed open space on Park Avenue. He also turned down building a tower over Grand Central Station, "my first statement of principle, because I felt it would have defaced Grand Central" (loc. cit.). Johnson was right in this case; the controversy that surrounded the Marcel Breuer–designed tower in 1968 ended up a decade later with the U.S. Supreme Court finding against it.

The soul-searching by architects involved in the design of new buildings, which often also means the demolition of existing historic buildings or buildings that have been just 'good citizens', can at times be daunting. The continuing presence of such buildings is the stuff of historic preservationist and urban estheticist arguments, whether as counterpoint to or as vital and contributory partners in new 'development', and remains one of the most vexing issues architects face today. Notwithstanding the vast literature on urban design, there are few guidelines for the resolution of such issues, no theory guiding practice.

It is a fact of professional life that most architectural commissions are commercial and involve developers whose ultimate intention is to gain a building as a commodity for trade. The moral dilemmas that students and others might perceive in a relationship in which architects are seen as in the pocket of developers are not so much matters for absolute determination, but need to be considered in the doing. A few cases are clear-cut and may be decided on principle. The rest are compounded into the matrix of professional life in which the actions of everyone contribute to and participate in mutual working out. Solutions are always a product of time and place settled by mediation between the developer, the public, and the architect.

FURTHER SOURCES   3B.2, Users; 7A.4, Context; Brolin 1980; Frampton and Drew 1992; Miller 1986; Sorkin 1991; van Leeuwen 1988.

5. The Absent Patron: Control of the Center

In the older church and palace there had been a permanent inhabitant whose actual or supposed relationship to the changing visitors was a fixed and lasting one. Now buildings become shells occasionally used by people who want to be restored to health, to bathe, learn, read, or buy. These buildings cannot be identified with one personality; they belong to everyone and therefore to no one. The absent patron is not replaced by the poetry in a theater, the science in a school, the hygiene in a public bath; even if, as is the rule, allegorical figures bring these general concepts to mind, these remain utilitarian buildings. **Paul Frankl.** 1914:182.

The worst crime of post-war London is not the new skyline or the destruction of Bloomsbury: it is the arid, under-used, man-hating spaces of the Hyde Park Corner underpass. That, and the attitude behind it, which still conceives of separate authorities with separate little power-empires. The city is one single organism, which at its best is literally super-human. **Ian Nairn.** Foreword to Ivor de Wofle 1971.

For some architects, teaming up with social scientists or using their "data" is seen as a way to resolve the contradiction of dealing with the building's financial developer, instead of the people who actually use the buildings. But the use of "data" is at best a way of ameliorating the contradiction rather than resolving it. At worst it can lead to some dangerous conclusions about how places should be designed. **Robert Goodman.** 1972:174.

The role of the architect today is not nearly as powerful as it used to be. I think that is primarily because we do not work for nobility, popes, the rich and famous. Their architects were able to transform whole cities. **Helmut Jahn.** In Diamonstein 1985:151.

TRACE   Patronage by the monarchy, church, and nobility was swamped by the rise of the merchant classes through the eighteenth century and by the consequent broadening of the wealth base. The industrial revolution saw the rise of manufacturing, and improvements in industrial technology generated new industries and created new building types; this resulted in a massive proliferation of buildings that brought with them dramatic shifts in scale and bulk. The built works of the traditional sources of patronage either receded into the greater mass of substantial buildings over the intervening two centuries or retreated to the unencumbered countryside and the margins of select society. Paul Frankl (1914) maintains that the decline of the individual patron followed the French Revolution, and sees the nineteenth century as the fourth phase of an architectural evolution in which patronage has become more and more impersonal.

So keenly has the loss of impact through patronage been felt that it prompted the Prince of Wales (Charles 1989), for instance, to offer his personal *vision* for Britain's built environment. Wistfully he mourns the swamping over the past thirty years of London's former "skyline inviolate," using Canaletto's painting of the Thames overlaid with a photograph (56–57) to show the visibility right up to 1960 of key symbols of Protestant patronage — St. Paul's Cathedral and Wren's church spires. His book is symptomatic of the diminished impact of the single patron and the need to control the center once again to counter the rise of the absent.

COMMENTARY   There is a profound sense that architecture today has ceased to be, ceased to have a presence revolving around a central concern emanating from the specifics of its situation and circumstance. This is primarily the result of the commodification of buildings wherein they strive for marketability by seeking a universality or commonality that appeals to certain features or qualities of Everyman or Everycorp rather than to Thisman or Thiscorp. Rather like a boxer who is afraid to hurt an opponent, architecture today is obliged to pull its punches according to the whims of all players in the building arena.

Financiers will only fund buildings they can resell in the event of default. Developers only build buildings for a known market. Building legislation and the approval processes are geared to having buildings conform to minimal and conventional standards. Building materials and construction systems rely on market acceptance for their continued existence, and therefore oblige a high degree of standardization and repetitiveness. High factors of safety in most structural and operational systems ensure a lack of precision in the relationship between physical forces and their materialization as built elements. All building endeavor may be gauged on a scale of specificity from the most generalized conception to the most specific fit, with the majority of buildings, whether designed by architects or not, nearest the general end.

Those architects who see themselves as service professionals favor the general end of the spectrum as they 'go with' client and market demands. Artist-architects are inclined to the other end of the spectrum because by definition they are in the signature business; individuality and invention are their hallmarks. There are many shades in between, with most architects content not to eke 'design' out of every situation but to remain within the bounds of material and constructional conventions. Those who do strive for invention or who 'stretch the limits' of convention are seen as achieving a purity or as coming closer to what architecture is *really* about, and are duly applauded and occasionally rewarded for their bravery or unwavering devotion to seeking the truth and for their unsullied genius. What underlies all their efforts, though, is a quest for the center. Whether the center is seen as "what the building wants to be"—in Louis Kahn's famous dictum—or whether it is blatantly ego-based, it is the placing of the architect at center-stage as seer or artist to overcome an absence of specificity.

Since 1914, when the historian Paul Frankl wrote of the *absent patron* in the above quotation, there has been an increasing feeling of absence in architecture that has needed to be replaced by seeking and expressing a specificity in every way possible. Frankl argues that during the nineteenth century (the fourth of his phases of history), as a result of the proliferation of building types to accommodate new uses, patronage was superseded by the buying power of the merchant classes, which resulted in buildings that "are spiritually empty until the moment when the public itself takes up the role of permanent possessor and autocratically permeates it [them?] with its collective demands." He maintains that the latest architecture (c1914) is characterized by the "assignment of responsibility to the public through its architects" (Frankl 1914:182), a characteristically reformist stance of the period presaging, though not admitting, a possible fifth phase (the twentieth century) in his taxonomy.

In many respects, however, Frankl's nineteenth-century fourth phase is still with us with a vengeance. The public *has* fulfilled the role of patron in one sense, namely, that the total of all demographic, behavioral, and user research to date, as well as standards, regulations, and legislation insisting on meeting human performance criteria, has obliged a high degree of professional concern for making buildings fit their purpose by architects as if being spoken to by a *patronus publico*. But the knowledge gained from this research is so diffuse that, rather than there being a *purposive intention* (Frankl's term) so forceful as to leave an indelible *individual* mark on architecture as a powerful patron might, there has emerged a gross and impersonal leveling that has only exacerbated the absence of a focused patron. The state and the marketplace are a barren substitute for an individual patron around whom a powerful and purposive architecture can be created.

Contrary to the belief that architecture begins where function ends, or that architecture is a product of excess or superfluity, contemporary architecture increasingly tries to re-establish purpose in the face of pervasive forces evacuating it—thus the *void* referred to by so many contemporary writers. Architecture 'wants to be' specific, not general; particular, not universal; it wants to be the tailor-made glove to fit the hand, not the one-size-fits-all rubber glove of production. Architecture wants to fill the lives of every person it involves with singular joys and nuances, not submit them to types, norms, and rote experiences. Architecture wants to possess, not to share. The greatest challenge for architecture both as a practicing profession and as a viable discipline has been to establish this center for itself, to recreate the patron. Despite Helmut Jahn's statement above, in contrast to one earlier in the same interview in which he says the developer is the modern Medici (see quotation in 3A.4, Developer), at the scale of the city, the developer *cannot* replace the patron; only the anonymous public can do that.

Not for some time has architecture been the mother and nurturer of the arts, because of the enormous scale shift of modern times, as a result of which architecture has been trying to act the father and aggressor in order to regain its place in the center, an analogy some will no doubt balk at for ideological reasons. The strategy, however, has not been a gender-divided one. Architects and theorists of all persuasions have attempted to concoct and disseminate mythic stories about architecture concerning its history and its future, about textuality and reading buildings, and about body relations and its physicality. It is hard to say how long it will take society to accept and begin to retell some of architecture's stories as part of conventional wisdom, to adopt modes of design-talk using the same language as architects and thereby to become the patron at the center, demanding these things because they are a pleasure. What a number of architects think needs to happen is not that human concerns once again become the center of architecture, but that architecture becomes the center of human concerns.

FURTHER SOURCES   3A.2, Client; 3B.6 Community; Hays 1987.

B. Beneficiaries of Architecture

1. Attending to the Public Interest

People like trees and water and human scale in public buildings, and they should have them ... theories at the what-people-want-level. Well, as one can imagine—how they sniggered at poor John Portman over that! **Tom Wolfe.** 1981:136.

We demand ... from property owners more consideration for the public interest, less self-interest, understanding and openness towards planning. From the exhibition *Heimat-Deine Häuser!,* Stuttgart, June 1963. Cited in Conrads 1964:185.

The lower one descends on the scale of social status, the less frequently one is likely to find people who are active in the user and consumer movements that relate to architecture. **Robert Gutman.** 1988:89.

The concept of the public as an intellectually active unity is, it is true, merely a hypostasis, which does not assert itself at all concretely and remains a fiction of a way of thinking which is reduced to a numerical category; nevertheless, there are groupings of the public according to the constitution of which the artistic experiences of individuals form or agree with one another. No matter how imprecise the concept of the "public" may be, the individual categories of the public are sharply differentiated. In historical times there was never a unified art, because there was never a unified public. . . . **Arnold Hauser.** 1974:448–449

. . . the whole tradition of planning is progressive in the sense that the planner's commitment to social harmony — unless it is perverted or corrupted in some way — always puts the planner in the role of "righter of wrongs," "corrector of imbalances," and "defender of the public interest." The limits of this progressive stance are clearly set, however, by the fact that the definitions of public interest, of imbalance, and of equity are set according to the requirements for the reproduction of the social order, which is, whether we like the term or not, a distinctively capitalistic social order. **David Harvey.** 1985:177.

TRACE   A beneficiary is someone who 'benefits' (*bene,* well, and *facere,* doing) or has been helped or received an advantage through the offerings of someone else. From an architectural point of view, a beneficiary is anyone who receives the benefit of an architect's services, design talent, or insight. The client is the most direct recipient of such benefits, followed by the client's employees (or the 'users' of a building for which the client is merely the market intermediary) and those involved in their customer/public interactions.

There is another level of beneficiary and an attendant responsibility architecture has with society, though it is beyond the immediate building client and user. This is encapsulated in the phrase 'the public interest', a cumulative benefit and demand that is the sum of all architectural advice and architect-designed works to any point in time. The conception of a unified 'public', however, is mistaken in that it does not recognize that there are 'groupings' of interest within it (of which the art historian Arnold Hauser speaks above).

COMMENTARY   It was the 'public interest' that modernist architects strove to address and to change with their agenda of reform-by-design and education-by-example. "The basis of the modern architecture . . . [is] the new mentality; . . . the view we take and the manner in which we judge our needs," wrote Marcel Breuer in 1937, " . . . we investigate, foster and utilize ['the new materials'] only if we can thereby achieve a genuine improvement, a greater degree of clarity, a greater ease, and *a truer exposition of living as a whole,* including aesthetics" [emphasis added]. The new mentality was of course intended to become a public one, as the editorial to *Circle* (Martin, Nicholson and Gabo, 1937), in which these remarks of Breuer's appear, makes clear: "The ideas represented by the work in this book have grown spontaneously in most countries of the world . . . they have, in the course of the last twenty years, become more crystallized, precise, and more and more allied to the various domains of social life, [which] indicates their organic growth *in the mind of society* and must prove that these creative activities cannot be considered as the temporary mood of an artistic sect, but are, on the contrary, *an essential part of the cultural development of our time*" [emphasis added].

The notion of public or community interest was then and remains today only loosely understood. The modernist presumption that society at large will ultimately benefit from design through a diffusion of designer artifacts, new construction techniques and materials, and an osmosis of designer ideas, thereby increasing esthetic appreciation, improving performance, and assuring the future of architects and designers, is still widely held among architects. Yet the cherished notion of public interest as a homogeneous and universal 'mind' capable of change in one direction only—toward 'improvement'—is contradictory if it does not also recognize fickleness and susceptibility to fashion.

For example, attempts at modern architecture in Australia in the forties resulted in 1948 in a famous court case over the refusal of a building permit for a flat-roofed house designed by the Australian-born architect Sydney Ancher, who was among the first in Australia to design houses in the Miesian manner of clean lines, open plans, and flat roofs. In 1950, the Viennese-born Harry Seidler, trained at Harvard under Walter Gropius and Marcel Breuer, thwarted a local council decision against his design for a house by having the then Minister for Housing sponsor it as a 'demonstration' home. Recalling the Ancher decision, Seidler said "[the judge] considered encouragement for *progressive architecture* to be in the *national interest,* which in his view must be put before parochial interest of the local community" (Frampton and Drew 1992:393).

Public interest in the immediate postwar period in Australia, as it may have been in other countries, was interpreted by the courts as allowing architects of repute to try out contemporary design ideas accepted overseas. Over the last twenty of the almost fifty ensuing years, public interest has been reinterpreted as favoring homogeneity of environments and precincts, continuity of streetscapes, similarity in scale and form, good esthetic manners, and respect for amenity. The shift to such matters being deemed as in the public interest over new architectural ideas has resulted from "the lack of public acceptance of the architectural offerings of the modern movement and the so-called International Style" (Cooke 1991).

Architectural institutes in their codes of conduct usually contain a statement to the effect that their members have a responsibility "to serve and promote the public interest," and go on to elaborate several rules to amplify what they mean. The RAIA, for instance, exhorts its members to "be of constructive service in civic affairs and apply their skill to the creative responsible and economic development of their community" (Directory 1988,

Code of Professional Conduct, Rule 1.2). Members are also to give to projects "full and proper consideration and evaluation including the public interest" (Rule 1.3). Notes supplementing the rules suggest that members should "create within the community an awareness and appreciation of the impact which architecture has on society" (§1.0.3). They are to "provide the community with *information which will assist it* in formulating policies and making decisions on matters affecting the built environment" (§1.0.4), as well as strive "to improve the built environment *and quality of life*" [emphasis added] (§1.0.5). But while the RAIA code enshrines attention to the public interest, as codes in other countries no doubt do, in one of its three principles, the code does not define what it means. Neither does the code define 'information', although it is construed to be a resource from which the community will gain benefit.

The implication for conventional architectural theory of such declarations is either to find a thoroughgoing way to reconcile architectural ego and design invention with a definition of the greater public good that is presumed to flow from design, or to eliminate from architectural discourse all references to the public interest, or any agenda that hints at it, until such time as there is such an understanding. The stance of this book is to suggest the latter because of the inability of theorists, architects, and their professional bodies to mouth anything other than platitudes about the public interest. In an admittedly angry frame of mind, Robert Goodman said in 1972: "The more architecture can be described in the morally neutral currency of 'aesthetics', devoid of political content for the people affected, the more elite and the more removed from the political review of ordinary people become the experts who use the currency" (153).

The plethora of fine art commissions, design review boards, citizen advisory committees, statutory impact procedures, and other techniques for public comment that have grown over the past two decades, have been an attempt to make architects accountable for their esthetic values. Presumably, the architect no longer needs to take into account the public interest because the public already has its attention focused on the business of architects. However, all that has happened is that Goodman's 'currency of aesthetics' has switched from the architect to these public bodies. The so-called public interest has become morally inured to the *real* public interest of ordinary people by its own vicariousness. Meanwhile, social unrest, social inequality, homelessness, lawlessness, and a myriad other issues continue to grow worse. The sad thing is that public interest in esthetics has *never* been an interest of any consequence by comparison with these other interests; it has merely been easier to attend to, and deflects attention from real public-interest issues. And politicians and architects know it.

If esthetic public interest is now the province of statutory bodies and the courts, then what is gained by architects espousing an interest over which they have no control? Instead, why not prepare student architects for the political complexity of negotiating these bodies, as Dana Cuff (1991) suggests? While there are no doubt many emotions and inspirations invested in the esthetic public interest, why not educate students to design values that, for instance, assist the homeless, the national obscenity of North America and many other countries? Architects should examine what they really mean by public interest.

FURTHER SOURCES   Brolin 1980; Goodman 1972.

2. Users, Anonymous Others, and Architectural Conscience

As an architect, if I had no economic or social limitations, I'd solve all my problems with one-storey buildings. Imagine how pleasant it would be to always work and plan in spaces overlooking lovely gardens filled with flowers. **Minoru Yamasaki** (an architect for the Pruitt-Igoe Public Housing Project, St. Louis). *AIA Journal,* August 1952:74.

A man in an apartment house must have the possibility of leaning out of his window and scraping off the masonry for as far as his hands reach. And he must be allowed to paint everything around pink as far as he can reach with a long brush, so that people can see from far away, from the street: a man lives there who differs from his neighbours. . . . And he must be able to saw up the walls and carry out all sorts of alterations. . . . and he must be able to fill his room with mud or plasticine. **Hundertwasser.** 1958. "Mould Manifesto against rationalism in architecture." Cited in Conrads 1964:157.

Architects grew in status with the growing separation between the users of buildings and the people who commissioned them. Renaissance princes generally lived in the buildings they commissioned. . . . The modern, bureaucratic, princes, in contrast, have opted for building committees, with architects often given a prominent place. . . [Speculative office blocks] were built according to general design considerations, with the voice of the architect becoming more important than the eventual users of the buildings. **John R. Short.** 1987:37.

[Modernism's] uniform geometries, rather than offering an egalitarian order, were seen as imposing an alienating social regimentation. This posited a modernist architect who was not only an elitist by birth and training but also an oppressor who forced an unwelcome vision of modern life on unwilling users. **Margaret Crawford.** In Ghirardo 1991:38.

TRACE   The building user has been the largely undeclared conscience of architects from the beginning of the Modern Movement. There always was a social agenda involving people and their betterment, from the earliest manifestos. "Think rationally, cultivate artistic sensibility!" cried Henry van de Velde in 1903. "Each one of us today can do this for himself; if only a large number of people do this a new social atmosphere will be brought about." And three years later Hans Poelzig declared, "Life in the modern era is dominated by economic questions; thus the participation of the people and the artists in architectural problems of this kind—from the private dwelling to town planning—is constantly grow-ing" (both from Conrads 1964:13, 14). But it took another forty years before ergonomic information was available in a form to assist furniture designers, and another decade before user surveys began to supply somewhat dubious information about buildings, mainly housing (Broadbent 1973:156–174).

Two decades further on we find the academic Margaret Crawford claiming that "In order to serve the cultural and social needs of society, radical architects [of the 1960s] proposed solutions ranging from participatory design to advocacy and self-help architecture. All of these strategies required a profound transformation of the nature of the professional structure, inverting the traditional relationship between architect and client to allow previously excluded users a democratic voice in the design process" (Ghirardo 1991:39). She argues that the move failed because 'the masses' for whom architects sought to design under their radical agenda were merely idealized clients in the sense that they were outside the power structures. "Thus, unwittingly, radical architects replaced modernism's welfare state with a marketplace, in which, unfortunately, their ideal client did not have the means to purchase architectural services" and therefore was unable to effect any substantive changes. Herein lies the dilemma of users and anonymous others: they may be the architect's conscience, but they are powerless to insist that the architect fulfill any perceived obligation.

COMMENTARY   As a step in instilling a sense of public conscience, the first design exercise I set for my students as a young academic newly arrived from practice in 1972 was to survey 'The Public Seat' in the Sydney Central Business District (CBD). The public seat comprised those places used by people to sit on or lean against, including places where they placed parcels or bags to change hands or retrieve a wallet. It emerged that there were steps, ledges, and sills used by people associated with the many nineteenth-century buildings that then comprised Sydney and some early twentieth century masonry buildings, but there were relatively few such places to be found in the more recent precast concrete and glass-walled commercial blocks. The lesson learned was that perhaps architects needed to consider providing these opportunities at street level, whatever else they might do above as a building reached for the sky. Unlike residential settings, in which nonresidents are discouraged from close contact with buildings for privacy, security, and control of vandal-ism (Marcus and Sarkissian 1986), the edge effect or provision of 'zones for staying' in city building design at the street face is essential to street vitality and convenience, as has been explored by several writers over recent years (Gehl 1987; Krier 1979; Trancik 1986) and occasionally addressed in strategic plans for city development.

A decade later I set another studio project for a major public housing scheme for two thousand people on a vast disused railway goods terminal adjacent the Sydney CBD and now redeveloped as the popular Darling Harbour urban recreation, retail, and exhibition area. During the final critique, I asked one student about a number of undesignated covered spaces at the ground floor of his development, which he said were deliberately set aside for occupation by the homeless and itinerants. His answer provoked a vehement debate among the other critics on his jury about whether it was valid to provide such spaces, how much an architect might 'design' such spaces, who would be responsible in law over their provision, whether the city council would allow such usage, whether marginal groups might not be better accommodated elsewhere, whether such spaces and usage would incite open conflict with residents, and whether they would demean the newly created housing.

What emerged from the debate were legitimate questions. For whom is the architect responsible in designing a publicly accessible building? How comprehensive should be the definition of building 'users'? What are the rights of anonymous others when designing? What exactly is the public amenity of a building? And do any of these questions constitute an architectural conscience? The issues raised highlight the influence of established power structures and the conventional wisdom of government bodies, clients, and occupants over disenfranchised individuals or groups, and involve questions of ethics over equity (see chapter 5B). From a theoretical point of view, how are we to accommodate such issues into a way of thinking and talking about architecture? Only one possibility will be touched on here, based on *A Theory of Justice* (1971) by the legal theorist John Rawls.

When applied to economic and social cooperation, one of the rationales for Rawls's analysis of justice pivots on the 'difference principle'; Rawls devotes chapter 2 of his *Theory* to the "Principles of Justice" one section of which (§13:75–83) deals with the difference principle—it is worth reading to gain a fuller understanding of the concept. The principle governs the distribution of the gains from economic and social cooperation, and Princeton academic Alan Ryan offers a succinct summary of it: "distribute the benefits of co-operation in such a way that the worst-off person does as well as possible. If nothing is gained from an unequal distribution, things should be equally distributed; but if an unequal distribution would make things better for the worse-off person . . . then an unequal distribution is better than an equal one, and among all the possible distributions the best is that which makes the worse-off person as well off as possible" (in Skinner 1985:110). To strive for a theory of architecture or design, or at least for a range of arguable positions concerning architecture or design, constrained within and sustained by a reasonably well-wrought system of justice at a philosophical if not a legislative level, is not as difficult as one might think. The Rawlsian fundamental that "nobody is merely a means to the ends of society at large" means that nobody should be made to give up their (even slender) hold on a situation for the so-called good of the whole.

Architects sometimes fall afoul of this way of thinking, that the good of the whole requires sacrifice by 'lesser' players, because architects convince themselves of the rightness of the task in which they are involved, especially in urban redevelopment. But there is no 'rightness' peculiar to a task independent of the rights of the various players. Engineers can develop the same mind-set, and politicians are particularly prone to it. One notorious and all too typical example is a new urban motorway through an existing residential area in which those residents close to the route may be expected to tolerate a greater loss of amenity than others in the neighborhood and noise and pollution levels higher than, say, World Health Organization standards, because the road is deemed necessary for 'the greater public good'. Residents in such situations may be ridden over roughshod by government agencies, or by corporations in the case of privately funded tollways, in their negotiations for fair compensation, in airing grievances during construction, or in seeking redress during later operation as real traffic conditions are experienced and change.

The challenge for politicians, agencies, designers, and contractors in these circumstances is *not to evade* the real issues of residents but to confront and resolve them equitably according to some system of fair play. The motorway example may be replaced by an airport or by almost any other substantial building project—such as an office tower, a school, a factory, a shopping center, or a sports facility—that will have an impact in terms of noise, traffic, nuisance, or intrusion on privacy. The greater public good, or the tyrannical 'price of progress' shrug-off are not valid arguments without some procedure for bettering the lot of those most affected by a proposal. That there are such compensatory processes in place in many parts of the world is commendable, but the issue is, how far down the line does this kind of thinking need to go? For architects it needs to be there at all levels of thinking and at all scales of project.

Confronted by the enormous range of players in even an average-sized building project and the potential, and in many cases realized, conflicts of interest involved, architects need some firm basis upon which to determine equity among the players. To allow for the rights of users and anonymous others who do not have direct input into the design process, or to embrace the effects a proposed building will have on a surrounding context that is not statutorily required to be considered, are matters of professional conscience. Something like John Rawls's theory of justice, an architectural bill of rights for the underrepresented, an ethics of design, needs to be developed to assist architects in their professional judgment. The codes of ethics of professional institutes merely sidestep the task.

FURTHER SOURCES   5B.1, Obligations; Benhabib 1992; Perin 1970; St. John Wilson 1992, Chapter 2.

3. Architectural Nobles and Public Acculturation

If he combines enthusiasm and diligence with a knowledge of these arts [discussed by Alberti], the architect will achieve favor, wealth, fame for posterity, and glory. **Leon Battista Alberti.** 1486b:9.10.

. . . if there be any one point insisted on throughout my works more frequently than another, that one point is the impossibility of Equality. My continual aim has been to show the eternal superiority of some men to others, sometimes even of one man to all others; and to show also the advisability of appointing such persons or person to guide, to lead, or on occasion even to compel and subdue, their inferiors according to their own better knowledge and wiser will. **John Ruskin.** 1862:§54, 102.

Painters, Architects, Sculptors, you whom the bourgeoisie pays with high rewards for your work—out of vanity, snobbery, and boredom—Hear! To this money there clings the sweat and blood and nervous energy of thousands of poor hounded human beings—Hear! It is an unclean profit . . . we must be true socialists—we must kindle the highest socialist virtue: the brotherhood of man. Extract from a manifesto of the *Novembergruppe.* 1918. Cited in Wolfe 1981:14–15.

There is no doubt, of course, that the mood has begun to change in the last few years. G.K. Chesterton once wrote, 'We are the people of England, that never have spoken yet.' Well, the people of Britain *have* now begun to speak about what kind of architecture they want. **Charles, Prince of Wales.** 1989:13.

I can assure you that I wouldn't be saying all this now if I felt I was alone in having these opinions. **Charles, Prince of Wales.** 1989:21.

TRACE   Social ordering has existed for thousands of years across many cultures, and Leon Battista Alberti (1755b:4.1) gives one account of the classification of citizens in ancient times. Prior to the 1780s English society was divided according to ranks and orders devised a century before, but with the revolution of industry this was quickly modified and greatly extended by stratification into classes, in line with newly created roles according to the division of labor. British society broadly consolidated into working, middle, and upper classes (although Matthew Arnold considered their equivalents to be Populace, Philistines, and Barbarians), but there always has been a division between nobility and commoners.

In North America the middle class rose to dominance during the nineteenth century, and became the chief beneficiary of America's rapid development in industry and dramatic urban growth. By the last quarter of the century the demand for professional services had grown dramatically, and architecture burgeoned from then on. But the middle class, "conscious of its power and numbers and rather too confident in its ability, was anxious to get hold of American society and remake it according to plan. All around were problems that needed solving. . . . " So the middle class set about solving them as a matter of civic duty, their motives "self-evidently virtuous." But "Behind the zeal of these technocrats lay an older tradition, betrayed in the word . . . [for] the philanthropic centres they established in the slums, 'settlements': to them the cities were wildernesses, the inhabitants alien savages and the new settlers were bringers both of superior techniques and superior ideas, like the settlers of old . . . " (Brogan 1985:460).

COMMENTARY   In the first section to this part (3B.1, Public), it was suggested that the 'public interest' was a fiction focusing interest in esthetics and thereby evading the real public interest and needs. Here I wish to focus on the 'public' as recipients of architectural skills and affections, assuming esthetic fascination and self-glorification are overcome. This is not an easy task, for a profession such as architecture largely comprises people of upper middle class background, and is unrepresentative of the population at large by virtue of privilege and education. Consequently, the profession is largely acculturated to middle class aspirations and ideals. So, if architects admit public concern in their work, they can neither define their target public nor speak for them, because on the whole they have no experience of what they presume to talk about.

North American architects shared the progressive middle class mentality and, if they did not succumb to conservatism and parochialism as much as their fellow middle class professionals, they did emerge from the ferment of the early twentieth century impressed by their own power to effect change in the most visible way, transforming the cities *by design*. Fueled further by the idea of architecture as an instrument of social reform emanating from Europe, and cemented by massive rebuilding after two World Wars, architects in America and across the world by the middle of the twentieth century were convinced of their supremacy in resolving by design all matters pertaining to life in the cities. The beneficiaries of their inventiveness were envisioned as the 'commoners', the counter to their 'nobility', the masses of people virtually everywhere in proportion to the scale of the work to be done. The only trouble was that as the population of the cities expanded and as architects' visions expanded to suit, at least in their eyes, the commoners did not homogenize into a solid mass. Instead they became increasingly differentiated by location, ethnicity, income, social opportunity, education, and turned into, not the 'public', but highly specific and localized communities of interest. And this is the way they remain today, overlaid with a heavy burden of issues relating to racial discrimination, drug currencies, illegal activities, and inequalities of all kinds.

So, if architects speak of designing with the 'public' in mind, assuming them not to be construing their response esthetically, they are really expressing either their own middle class values and predilections, or they are talking about acceding to a specific part of a community with whose interest they are fully acquainted. Since it is the exception rather than the rule that architects are acquainted intimately enough with any such public, particularly in the larger firms, they are therefore mainly reflecting their own values that, noble as they undoubtedly are, are of course not necessarily incorrect, just different from those of the masses. Thus the beneficiaries of architects' talents for the most part, while they may be a 'public' of the local kind one associates normally with sociometric studies, are actually a *professional* or *meta-professional* public like themselves that is selectively local, certainly at least regional, and, for many architects, international. What an architect offers in a work is the *release* of the common public (however defined) from their world and entry into the world of the architect, a vicarious process of acculturation deemed beneficial for the 'common good'.

This may account for the popularity reported by Dana Cuff (1991) of the San Juan Capistrano Library in California designed by architect Michael Graves, for instance, or any celebrated building by an architect for that matter. Graves had minimal contact with the locals to inform his designing, since the building was selected through competition in 1981. The client representatives with whom he and his staff negotiated until it opened in 1983 were professional people more at Graves's end of the social spectrum than not, and were enamored with the chance of participating further in the life of the architectural nobility, at least for a time. Michael Graves gave them a slice of Gravesian heaven, a building that had little to do with the world of San Juan Capistrano but transported them into a wonderful middle class fiction (and in this case, nonfiction). Indeed, it is possible but difficult to imagine what a wonderful building of working class fiction by an architect might be. In other words, architecturally, the trend by design and in design is always *upward* out of the mire of commonalty to the rarefaction of nobility.

Class distinction is not a topic usually found in the indexes of books on architecture; it became a taboo subject in the wake of modern egalitarianism and, because it was a sign of a gentleperson never to discuss social position (except in novels), it was never raised as a professional issue in the nineteenth century either. Therefore, class distinction was merely absorbed into the tacit understanding of architecture as a profession. However, the connection between class distinction and capitalist enterprise from the Industrial Revolution onward, especially the power and prestige that money brought to many without the privileges of birthright, has meant that class pervades architecture at all levels.

The choice of an architectural career for most students is made on the advice of family and friends, all of similar social position, and guidance from teachers and student counselors who mostly advocate middle-class aspirant values. These people, together with the media, all base their ideas around "strong social stereotypes of architects—stereotypes that are relatively ill-informed and go unexamined" according to Cuff (1991:117). As with any career path requiring university education, in most countries the cost of studying architecture is high and admission competitive, so only students from the relatively well-off families have the opportunity to gain the degree. This means that architects in the main are already steeped in middle and upper class beliefs and values. This is not to say, though, that there is a lack of social conscience among such students; there isn't. Or that there are no students from working class or low socioeconomic backgrounds who enter architecture courses and bring with them social values countering the middle class normalization; there are. The international draw of many universities ensures a racial and cultural mix that can precipitate a global concern for certain environmental and social issues that have profound architectural consequences, Third World poverty being but one example.

The Egyptian architect Hassan Fathy, even though of middle class background and primarily an esthetician, was a notable example of the rare individual whose social conscience remained uppermost and influenced his practice and educational agenda. Despite being thwarted in the execution of some of his low-cost housing projects using mud brick and rejuvenated traditional building techniques, Fathy throughout his life championed the cause of the poor, and his *Architecture for the Poor* (1973), originally published in 1969 as *Gourna: A Tale of Two Villages,* is considered to be a seminal handbook of such techniques. The appeal of Fathy was greater overseas than in Egypt, although his approach to building was to become an emblem for many who constantly talked of designing for the public but who, unlike Fathy, never went on to do much of consequence.

That the Prince of Wales should be championing the quality of life of the 'commoner', as he shows in the quotation above, smacks of another kind of unreality. Princes of high culture are driven by the same motives as capitalism—self-perpetuation—and Prince Charles's advocacy of a 'vision' for Britain seems nothing more than dilletantism, a gloss over the real issues confronting a substantial portion of the British population. Prince Charles appears to mistake the flattery of commoners and middle class supporters of his views, who have far more to gain from being associated with him than he with them, for genuine concern and progress.

Architects, too, often content themselves with flattery and adulation, thereby evading what they might do to help resolve the real issues confronting people. Thomas Jefferson's Monticello, seen by some as an architectural epiphany, may be extraordinary if not quite the purest example of 'contemporary' Classical architecture in the world. But, like Versailles, "each glory was made possible only by a deeply oppressive society which ruthlessly exploited the weak" (Brogan 1985:105). Might such a comment be made of any present-day buildings?

FURTHER SOURCES   Stern 1986.

4. Community, Advocacy, and Citizen Participation

95. Private interest will be subordinated to the collective interest. . . . Individual rights have nothing to do with vulgar private interest. The latter, which heaps wealth upon a minority while condemning the rest of the social mass to a mediocre life, merits severe restriction. It must everywhere be subordinated to the collective interest, every individual having access to the basic joys: the wellbeing of the home, the beauty of the city. **Congrès Internationale d'Architecture Moderne (CIAM) Charter of Athens: tenets.** 1933. Cited in Conrads 1964:145.

In a city, there is always the opportunity given money and property, to create your own society, to choose a locality and turn it into a village of friends. . . . But the serious point is that working class life itself has become much too expensive for the working class to live: all over London they are being ousted from their close-knit networks of terraced houses by well-heeled people who are buying neighbourliness as a part of the property. Community is becoming an increasingly expensive commodity. **Jonathon Raban.** 1974:89–90).

The community architecture movement . . . has steadily transformed the lives of what must by now be thousands of people who have taken an active role in the building of their own homes, the shaping of their own communities, and the creation of more congenial urban surroundings. **Charles, Prince of Wales.** 1989:13.

The right sort of surroundings can create a community spirit. . . . Good communities are usually small enough for people to get together to organise the things they want. . . . Pride in your community can only be generated if you have some say in how it looks or how it is managed . . . there is always local knowledge and that is where community starts. . . . **Charles, Prince of Wales.** 1989:96–97.

Community architecture is dead. It was not simply killed; it was overkilled. It was a PR exercise masquerading as a crusade, and what died was the idea that it was new. If community architecture had not existed, it would have been necessary to invent it. But it did exist, as it always has. . . .

The ideals of community architecture are eternal and unimpeachable. . . . It is time to regroup as an *architectural* community and time to drop the elitist notion that some of us are touched by a special gift. Community architecture is dead; long live architecture. **Maxwell Hutchinson.** 1989:145–146.

TRACE   Community was defined in 1B.5, Community, so suffice it to say here that community is a social concept and not a physical one. Community is a community of *mutual interest,* and forms as much around a threat to a group of people, such as the incursion of a land use considered deleterious or noxious, as in response to a need that might catalyze around, say, a specialized activity such as a sport (Harvey 1973). This is not to say that a community is not defined by physical or geographical limits, it often is; but such physical definition is incidental to the social definition of interest. The term 'advocate' has the same root as 'vocation', namely, the Latin *vocare* (to call), and to act as an advocate is to be called to assist someone or to represent his or her cause in some judicial situation, be it in a legal court or in the processes of government in the ordinary course of seeking building approval.

As early as 1812 "the principle of community" was advocated by the Reverend Thomas Chalmers in his *The Christian and Civil Economy of Large Towns* (Glasgow, 1821–26) as a means of seeking harmony between the classes through community pride, community improvement, community services, and community participation, thereby heading off potential social unrest and civil strife arising through the concentration of the working-class in urban Britain (Harvey 1985:179–180). In other words, community advocacy was recognized soon after the Industrial Revolution as a powerful method of social control, and for the planning profession today "the commitment to the ideology of harmony within the capitalist social order remains the still point upon which the gyrations of planning ideology turn" (Harvey 1985:184). In architecture there is a similar still point but with a major difference; advocacy remains the exception rather than the rule. Contrary to what many architects believe, any ideology of community in architecture remains loose until given purpose and direction by politicians or planners.

COMMENTARY   Most professionals are advocates, and architects especially so, in the ordinary relationship they have with a client because of the many everyday situations that require the putting of the client's 'case' in order to achieve decisions in relation to a building or some other project. But there is a politically and socially conscious side to advocacy, one that ties it into the welfare of a community, or attempts to make good an injustice or lack of probity that has affected or might affect a community, or empowers a minority group that otherwise has little or no leverage because of lack of information and sound technical advice. In this sense, an architect might become an advocate on behalf of a special interest group, as some have done for the underprivileged, ethnic groups, cooperatives, or the differently abled.

It is as a social or communal function, that advocacy is examined briefly here, the architect as community advocate, as carer for a specific community of interest. The term 'community architecture' embraces the idea of community self-help with professional architectural guidance. The concept gained wide currency in Great Britain where, from its lowly beginnings in the late-sixties, it reached the scale and impact of being labeled a 'movement' by the mid-eighties, as Prince Charles makes known in the quotation above. The Community Architecture Movement supposedly benefited people who would not otherwise have received financial support by house improvement grants, a people's movement communally engineered by the architect (or should that be *architected*?). For many architects it was just ordinary good practice in new drag, spurred on by royal condemnation of architects who did not practice with the community. In many other countries, community liaison by architects has been the core of practice for years. In Australia, the social planner Wendy Sarkissian has been active within many communities (as she has in North America), and the architects Colin James and Paul Memmott have worked extensively with aboriginal communities (see Judd and Bycroft 1989). In North America, many hundreds of architects have been actively engaged in community participation, among them Katrin Adam, Jacqueline Leavitt and Henry Sanoff, and the social planner Clare Cooper Marcus.

As was raised in 3B.1, Public, modern codes of professional conduct (CPC) and other architectural manifestos are usually silent about the architect's exact relation to people, preferring to couch it in terms of 'public interest'. Other than this, the concern of a CPC is primarily with intra-professional conduct and manifestos with environmental quality. For an expanded understanding of an architect's connection with and responsibility to people, one turns to the legal definition of *duty of care,* which shows clearly that architects have no more or less legal responsibility than anyone else, whatever argument might be made for their moral responsibility; and to areas such as housing in which there are proved and well-established routines for user participation and feedback, and where 'people concerns' are uppermost.

It is mainly public housing, or institutional estates such as retirement housing, that feature in the literature, because private housing developers are reluctant to make public any survey material that might jeopardize their image or sales, or give their competitors the marketing edge. So, perceptions of community and knowledge of community values gained from such material is necessarily biased in the direction of low-income or aged lifestyles, or is filtered through a corporate mouthpiece and therefore inflated or diluted depending whether responses are favorable or not. Other perceptions of community may be gained from sociological studies, but social surveys are notorious for their qualifications and for their propensity to reinvent the wheel with each new study rather than extrapolate. Notwithstanding these limitations, it is possible to make certain claims about community that are of architectural significance.

In the main, architects have a simplistic idea of what community is, a very crude idea of how it works, and an utterly idealized view of how they contribute to it. Architects are inclined to generalize community into some romantic idea of consensus without realizing that sheer size or generality is unworkable politically as a community concept. A large group needs representation at a small scale in order to negotiate its collective goods, and hence its representatives are more likely to favor their own self-interest over that of the larger group. Thus it is always the small-scale community of interest that bargains best, because it is cohesive enough to be consistently self-interested (Harvey 1973:71–79). Indeed, the very basis of early modernist dogma about community was flawed by thinking of it as an egalitarian model built around *reciprocity* or primitive communism that lacked social coercion. Consequently "it is accepted by most scholars that egalitarian societies are incapable of supporting urbanism. The typical symmetrical groupings do not permit the kind of concentration of social product necessary for urbanism" (Harvey 1973:209). For architects to presuppose an urbanism in which egalitarianism thrives and to which they could contribute, as Le Corbusier preached, was fundamentally untenable.

People generally have become more informed and consequently more voluble about architectural and planning matters than was the case, say, twenty years ago, partly because there is more information readily available, partly because negotiation procedures encouraging discussion are in place, and partly because there are more people educated in technical and building matters who are not necessarily professionals willing to act on behalf of communities of interest. Some local authorities in the major Australian cities, for instance, have formalized *precinct committees* of local residents arranged on a geographical basis whose task it is to adjudicate building applications in their precinct. Their comments, along with other departments of the authority, form the conditions of approval. Similar systems are no doubt in place in many other countries.

As a result of these trends, any building project today is likely to be subjected to intense scrutiny by communities of interest who will usually seek to negotiate some collective benefit from the project over and above anything already provided by the architect. For many architects this is a frustrating process, any benefit from community participation being outweighed for them by the undermining of their autonomy and control. The resentment of architects at what amounts to another tier in design approval process makes them ambivalent at best about citizen participation (Gutman 1988:91). Gutman also makes the point, though, that there are architects who are ideologically committed to participation, as well as clients "who are impressed by architects who demonstrate professional concern for the acceptability of a building to successive groups of tenants and users. These clients believe that buildings and spaces that users admire preserve their economic value longer" (Gutman 1988:91). Motivated by commercial sense rather than altruism, the effect is much the same, citizen participation becomes a game of political maneuvering and a matter of who can make the greater collective gain.

There are nevertheless architects and planners who are quite adamant that architects have a social responsibility to their respective communities in any project and that there are certain groups in society who are more deserving beneficiaries of architectural knowledge and skill than others (Cooper 1975; Marcus and Sarkissian 1986; Crawford in Ghirardo 1990; Johnson 1983a, 1983b, 1989). For these socially conscious researchers and critics there is one priority: architecture is fundamentally an instrument for adjusting and redeploying information as a communal resource, and therefore is a form of empowerment. They see architects as a kind of Robin Hood, taking advantage of their position in society to utilize the spin-off from wealth in which they share, namely knowledge gained from building projects and research, and applying it to the betterment, comfort, and well-being of communities, whatever their interest.

In the face of such uncompromising and ideologically sound social commitment, recent conventional (and not so conventional) architectural theory appears so self-indulgent that it is in danger of becoming too incestuous and losing the power it has to mediate social concerns. For the social crusader, lack of social justice or equity is not arguable, and professional conduct necessarily entails obligations to repay the community in kind for what it gains by way of opportunity and expertise. This is part of its social contract.

FURTHER SOURCES   Chapter 5; Goodman 1972; Hutchinson 1989; Sarkissian and Doherty 1987.

Professional Attitudes

Overview

Now, of all the acts the most complete is that of building. A work requires love, mediation, obedience to your finest thought, the invention of laws by your soul, and many other things you do not know you possess, but which the work miraculously draws out of you. The work derives from your innermost being, but is distinct from you. If it were endowed with thought it would sense your existence without ever managing to prove it or conceive it clearly. You would be like a God for it. . . . So let us consider this great act of building. Observe, Phaedrus, that the Demiurge, when he set about creating the world, attacked the Confusion of Chaos.

The process of building can be compared to the phenomenon of the creation of the Universe. **Paul Valéry.** c1921. "Eupalinos ou l'Architecte." *Oeuvres Complètes,* vol. II, Paris 1960. Cited in Borsi 1987:19.

He—the architect—is the divine jester—he may take liberties with reason and even with gravity—he may, within bounds, indulge his fancy and disregard facts—he may please himself and so please others and so perhaps please God. In short, he can and should have such a high old time that it will be reward enough in itself, with six per cent commission as a welcome gilding of the already refined gold. **Clough Williams-Ellis.** 1929:90.

The 'creator' in Platonic philosophy *(Timaeus),* the Demiurge (from the Greek *demiourgos,* craftsman or artisan), was less than a divine being. But, as the handicrafter of the physical world, the Platonic demiurge operated as if God was undertaking whatever action. In Gnostic theology, the demiurge was also subordinate to the Supreme Being, sometimes even the author of evil. But the Gnostics believed that a secret tradition revealed "that the one whom most Christians naïvely worship as creator, God, and Father is, in reality, only the image of the true God . . . a lesser divine being who serves as the instrument of the higher powers. It is not God . . . but the demiurge who reigns as king and lord. . . . " (Pagels 1979:62).

Initiation into this secret tradition enabled the Gnostic candidate to reject the authority and demands of the demiurge and via *gnosis* "to recognize the true source of divine power — namely, 'the depth' of all being," writes Pagels. "Whoever has come to know that source simultaneously comes to know himself and discovers his spiritual origin: he has come to know his true Father and Mother." With this knowledge a candidate receives a secret sacrament of redemption, *apolytrosis* (release), and is thereby able to transcend the demiurge and his/her agents and enter into an exclusive compact directly with the Mother/Father. Naturally enough, this Gnostic belief was threatening to the authority of the established church, which sought to expel Gnostics as heretics. Heresy encouraged insubordination, deviation from the one true faith, and the entertainment of doubts over the church's teachings and sacraments. Gnostic belief in individuality and equality mitigated against the hierarchical structure of the established church and the monarchic rule of the bishops.

This brief account of the demiurge shows just how like an architect (s)he is; the demiurge is the role model *par excellence* for the architect as creator, and is never far below the surface in the attitudes of many architects. I have known both academics and architects who were indeed like the demiurge in their teaching and practice and who, like the bishops, reacted against students or colleagues who seemed unimpressed by their monarchic authority; they considered their indifference a threat. Which leads to the question of how architects manage to acquire such an inflated view of themselves. The short answer is that architects are rarely brought to account, either as teachers or as practitioners; their opinions are what they are commissioned for and are what academic careers are built upon. But that is a hazard of the profession and one that most architects manage to control, if not avoid altogether.

It is little wonder that architects and designers develop such huge egos if a designer like Victor Papanek, in his book *Design for the Real World* (1972), can say in all seriousness in relation to industrial design, but couched intentionally in axiomatic terms, "The ultimate job of design is to transform man's environment and tools and, by extension, man himself." The bulk of manifestos written during the formative years of modernism sought to say much the same, and in some cases more. The demiurgic flavor of Le Corbusier advocating architecture over revolution is one of the more moderate statements made by a talented and heroic architect whose professional life, like those of his fellow architects then and since, depended upon convincing others that he was right and deserving of patronage. This is not to take anything away from Le Corbusier or any other architect or hero, for among them some truly deserving works were created and many truly memorable remarks made. Indeed, it was their very individuality of attitude and strength of conviction that made them remarkable, and these same qualities set apart those making an impact today. It is just such differences in attitude that in fact distinguish one architect from another, that make them the architects they are, and it is in the attitude of the designer that a definition of designing and of the designed lies.

One of the mysterious aspects of designing is just what the quality is that a designer brings to a project and what the best ways are to help elicit this quality. What is it "when we consider that the ubiquity of design threatens to blunt our understanding of the concept and its relationship to objects, without which we could not say that an artifact were 'designed'?" asks the industrial designer Volker Fischer (1989:10). Along with the inherent interiority of designing and faith in the worth of designing born of its incipient optimism comes one of its sustaining beliefs that is equally applicable in all design fields, namely, that intervention by designing will make a difference, that designing is always for the better, that designing is didactic, that designing indeed can be an agent of social and cultural change. Such notions represent a designing attitude, an attitude that guides designing at all stages, from the initial understanding of the task through the approach taken to problem solving to the final realization of the artifact, be it a tool or a temple. And what distinguishes a tool being simply 'to hand' from a tool as a designed artifact is precisely the consciousness of it as an object; and the same applies to a temple.

As Heidegger's analogy of the artisanal hammer illustrates, it is only after a hammer ceases to function *as a hammer* that we become conscious of it as a hammer; it becomes then an object, merely there, a mere thing. Heidegger writes of the 'mere' that it "means the removal of the character of usefulness and of being made. The mere thing is a sort of equipment, albeit equipment denuded of its equipmental being. Thing-being consists in what is then left over" (Heidegger 1978:160). In effect, this residue constitutes

> . . . a shift in standpoint: the hammer has been detached from the whole within which it was handled and conceived. . . . This shift in standpoint is neither the result of the fact that we have actually ceased to wield the hammer nor of the fact that we make an abstraction from such possible handling of it. These two aspects are left out of consideration in a purely negative way. The only important point is that we have adopted an entirely new attitude with regard to the hammer, in virtue of which we acquire an entirely new view of it. This viewpoint in turn leads to an entirely new type of understanding in which the hammer is regarded solely as a material thing that is 'simply there' (Kockelmans 1965:122–3).

Otherwise the hammer is collinear with us, it is our very artisanal affection, our means and our end. So too if any artifact ceases to be our affection it becomes autonomous, cast adrift in a world of its own. The desperate need of the artisan is to restore the hammer to its equipmentality, into that which it is: " 'that' it is made is a property also of all equipment that is available and in use. But this 'that' does not become prominent in the equipment; it *disappears in usefulness* [emphasis added]. The more handy a piece of equipment is, the more exclusively does the equipment keep itself in equipmentality" (Heidegger 1978:182). This *transitivity* of equipment is quite unlike the *intransitivity* of a work of art or architecture, the need of a 'work' being to obtrude (Heidegger 1978:178, 180). The contention here is that the notion of Heidegger's work and a designed artifact are alike; they each have their createdness obtrude. This obtrusiveness makes architecture what it is and, in the case of a so-called 'signature' building or a signature architect, is the signature. And that signature is the designing attitude.

By way of another example, consider the French sociologist and lexicologist Roland Barthes's analogy with the woodcutter who 'speaks the tree' rather than speaking 'about the tree' because of his working affinity with it. Putting himself in the role of the woodcutter, Barthes says:

> This means my language is operational, transitively linked to its object; between the tree and myself, there is nothing but my labour, that is to say, an action. This is a political language: it represents nature for me only inasmuch as I am going to transform it, it is a language thanks to which I *'act the object'*; the tree is not an image for me, it is simply the meaning of my action. But if I am not a woodcutter, I can no longer 'speak the tree', I can only speak *about* it, *on* it. My language is no longer the instrument of an 'acted-upon tree', it is the 'tree-celebrated' which becomes the instrument of my language. I no longer have anything more than an intransitive relationship with the tree; this tree is no longer the meaning of reality as a human action, it is an *image-at-one's-disposal.* Compared to the real language of the woodcutter, the language I create is a second-order language, a metalanguage in which I shall henceforth not 'act the things' but 'act their names', and which is to the primary language what the gesture is to the act (1957:158, 159).

Heidegger and Barthes approach the same issue from different directions, the subject-object paradox. Just as the artisan's hammer while usable corresponds to the available or ready-to-hand, presumably so too does the woodcutter's saw, obviously present but not mentioned in the preceding quotation. And just as the woodcutter's tree has a transitive relation with the sawyer, so too does the object of attention have with the artisan. Theirs is a language thanks to which the artisan and the woodcutter act the object. And, to follow through Barthes's analogy using Heidegger's artisan, presumably a nonartisan would no longer 'speak the object' but rather would speak 'about the object'. And, to take Heidegger's analogy further using Barthes's woodcutter, presumably once the saw ceased to act as a saw, the sawyer would then become conscious of it as an object, something to be contemplated in its own right.

So, the state of a situation prior to the moment of rupture or dissent is accompanied by an *expressive* component in having some purposefulness but is unself-conscious or transitive. After the moment of breakdown, or separation, the situation assumes a state wherein its description obliges a detachment in which particularity becomes prominent by being talked *about*. Designing is just such a state of intrusion, rupture, or dissent, an intransitive state and hence one in which the designed object dominates. This 'objectivity' of ideas that a designing attitude helps bring into being is fundamentally alienating, and enables an artifact to become a self-subsistent entity or, in other words, to become an object for contemplation and interpretation *by virtue of its separation from its creator*. It is also the trace of its designer's attitude, that particular way of construing that makes design what it is.

This chapter examines some aspects of designing attitudes, part A being devoted to the qualities professionals have over nonprofessionals and especially those that make an architect a professional. It explores the extent to which creativity belongs to the individual and to architects as a community of professionals, and looks at the basis for excellence and quality. Part B raises specific attitudes architects adopt in their professional life, notably their role or image as architects and then the fundamental division of architects into artists and scientists. The final section in part A examines gender issues in architecture and the impact of feminist attitudes on the existing and future operation of the profession. But there is a need to highlight the general matter of privileging before moving on.

With writings like Ann Bergren's "Architecture Gender Philosophy" (in Whiteman, Kipnis, and Burdett 1992:12–46), we start to see a realm in which gender operates in society as well as in architecture, but that has not hitherto been examined. Bergren co-opts from semiotics the terms 'marked' and 'unmarked' to nominate differences of privileging, or rather the privileging of differences in gender, racial, and role portrayals in society (12–13). Her piece must be read to properly appreciate what she is saying and the sources she uses, but the gist is that society (namely us) privileges certain aspects of every situation, either in the form of an antinomial or of a hierarchical qualification. The process of privileging is called *marking*. The 'marked' is considered the singular, particular, and distinguishable and, by default, it thereby differentiates the 'unmarked' or multiple, general, and indistinguishable. What is 'marked' is the privileged aspect.

Thus we see 'woman' (the marked and specific) distinguished from 'man' (the unmarked and general); 'skirt' (marked and specific) from 'trousers' (unmarked and general—although this is context specific as in 'man as the wearer of the pants', and in the cultural context of wearing the kilt); or 'tribal name' or qualification (unmarked and general) from 'non-tribal group' (marked and specific, as the term 'non-' signifies) from a tribal group perspective, which, of course, can reverse if the perspective outside the tribal group is adopted. There are many permutations in this process of differentiation, and the table on page 154 is one assembly utilizing this semiotic schema.

While the temptation is to read the terms in the 'marked' and 'unmarked' columns vertically as if they were concomitant, they are meant to be read only as antinomials and may change places according as differing contexts determine which term is privileged. It is revealing to determine which terms are marked and unmarked in the architectural discourse in which one is engaged.

Marked	Unmarked	Marked	Unmarked
woman	man	female	male
architecture	philosophy	architecture	building
interior	exterior	fixed	mobile
stasis	flux	theory	practice
practice	patronage	female practitioner	profession
parasite	host	truth	knowledge
figuration	truth	place (*chôra*)	space
task	situation	genus	species
manifestation	Form (Platonic)	order	chaos
technê	*mêtis*	artisan	citizen (*Timaeus*)
child	father	copy	paradigm
event	time	passive	active

Privileging differences based on 'marked' and 'unmarked' antinomial categories. (Using terminology by Bergren in Whiteman, Kipnis, and Burdett 1992.)

A. Investment in Know-How

1. Professional Expertise and Specialization

As a professional you have the obligation of learning your conduct in all relationships . . . in institutional relationships, and in your relationships with men who entrust you with work. In this regard, you must know the distinction between science and technology. The rules of aesthetics also constitute professional knowledge. **Louis Kahn.** 1964. "Talks with students." In Latour 1991:167.

A professional, as far as I can make out, is somebody who acts *pro bono publico* — in other words, who has social responsibility and is *not* a business man. **Serge Chermayeff.** In Whiffen 1965:24.

. . . professions characteristically justify their special status by claiming "cognitive exclusiveness," a unique access to some area of knowledge that is deemed crucial to the well-being of society. **Stanley Fish.** 1989:216.

Unless architects can establish or demonstrate a distinctive body of knowledge, their position [as a profession] is likely to become weaker. **Tom Heath.** 1991:54.

TRACE   To profess is to make a declaration, from the Latin *profiteri* (declare aloud publicly) and the root *fateri* (confess). As an entity, a profession is an occupation in which there is a public declaration of skill, learning, and expertise being offered to and involving the affairs of others. From the late sixteenth century it came to mean any 'calling'—hence vocation (*vocare,* call)—by which a person habitually earned their living, and stood for the body of such people. The notion of a calling is steeped in antiquity and to the eighteenth century was based on the 'station' in life given by birth, as in 1 Corinthians 7:20, "Let every man abide in the same calling wherein he was called." To be called is to adopt a life based on an inner conviction, or 'natural' inclination, heard as the voice of God and, as talent is thought divinely given, it is not to be squandered.

The word 'expert' is from the Latin *experiri* (try), and applies to someone who has gained authoritative knowledge or understanding through wide or special experience or training; 'expertise' is what this knowledge is, by virtue of which an expert makes judgments or forms estimates (opinions). 'Special' comes from the Latin *species,* appearance, form, or kind, which in turn derives from *specere,* look or behold. To be 'special' (apheti-cally from 'especial') is to exceed or excel, to be marked off from others in the same area by distinguishing qualities or features, or to have a particular devotion to a field of study or knowledge. It is in this latter sense that we use the term 'specialist', and it is the know-how of specialists that is their 'specialization'.

COMMENTARY   The term 'profession' has been used many times already in this book but is here addressed for the first time in a little detail. Since obligation and accountability are an inherent part of the definition of a profession, modern professions have each developed accountable structures and an ethics regarding public and intraprofessional responsibilities (see chapter 5). Architect and social scientist Dana Cuff (1991) considers professions to be "special occupations because they impart knowledge and skills related to tasks of high social value." The difference between a profession and an occupation, according to one definition cited by Cuff, is in terms of their operational characteristics: professions are full-time occupations; they have special schools and their own organization; they are legally licensed; they have a code of ethics; they are self-regulating. Cuff cites another study in which occupations are professional by virtue of their degree of pro-fessionalization, namely, the complexity of their relationships with people, their degree of organization, their length of training, their 'licensure status', and their prestige (23).

While such structuring ensures professional integrity and social accountability, in the case of architecture there is a curious relation between the profession and the marketplace. A dilemma is evident in that the *ideal* of professionalism serves to inspire architects in salaried employment who neither have the need to maintain their autonomy nor are accountable for their actions (Cuff 1991:24). They are acting according to ideals within a belief system in which they really have no tangible role and no power to challenge, until such time, that is, as they are able to set up practice for themselves. Parallel to and partly because of this internal dilemma, Gutman (1988) believes that the emphasis on marketing by firms and architectural institutes has undermined the *public* image of architects: "Users of buildings are very suspicious of architects' motives," he writes, "the profession is looked upon as venal and selfish. Architects are perceived as people who are mainly interested in advancing, often on the basis of spurious arguments, the economic interests of building owners and developers; and therefore, indirectly, the wealth of professionals themselves. The public's trust in the fidelity of the profession is being undermined" (21). In other words, unlike architect-employees who maintain the faith, the public seems less convinced by the ideals of the profession, at least as they are represented in practice.

The issue of public disillusionment with architects is too complex to deal with here but the expertise architects offer *qua* architecture as a specialized profession is a little easier. Expertise is the primary means an individual, group, or profession uses to distinguish their work or knowledge territory within society. In relation to a nonexpert, expertise is based on a core of shared knowledge and a periphery of esoteric knowledge, whereas, in relation to an expert area or profession, expertise is a specialization within it (Cuff 1991:36). On a day-to-day basis, the possession of expertise in an architectural office affords informal power, which influences decision-making through deference to those who possess it. Cuff maintains that there is a degree of ambiguity in the application of expertise within an architectural office in the necessary overlap between certain professional fields and that of the architect.

Among architectural practices, expertise frequently develops through an inadvertent opportunism. For instance, several commissions for a certain kind of building might precipitate others and thereby the firm rapidly assembles specialist skills in that area, hospitals and other institutional buildings being cases in point. It is rare that a firm will refuse work in which it has proficiency, so the professional system in fact works to create specialization. Among individual architects, expertise often comes about in the same way and may be consolidated by further education. It is a natural tendency for individuals to highlight strengths and downplay weaknesses, thereby giving themselves an emphasis that tends to become special.

The authority of expertise not only brings with it power but responsibility. In a formal situation such as the profession of architecture, there exists a social contract that obliges the profession to maintain its standards, competence, and knowledge base through professional and postprofessional education, in exchange for which architects receive certain remuneration, respect, and prestige. Without accountability, expertise can become tyrannical and oppressive as it does if imperviously hidden in government or industry. Expertise is open to political interference in the sense that expert opinion may be used to silence opposition. Expert knowledge has a tacit obligation to be open to challenge whereby its currency and legitimacy may be affirmed, to which end publication is the safeguard.

Herein lies one of the dilemmas of expertise: it is transient. As the expert knowledge base expands through dissemination of research and experience, so professional knowledge generally is increased and tends to dissipate the expertise that promoted it. The expert must therefore maintain not only an active awareness of current knowledge but, of necessity, must tend to specialize further as that knowledge is diffused. This creates the ever more discrete subdivision of a profession, and greater pressure is brought on the 'mother discipline' to justify its existence as an autonomous entity. Architecture has suffered this fracturing in the proliferation of subdisciplines that have emerged over the past century to the point where it arguably can exist only because of gateway legislation. In other words, architecture might well not survive if it was deregulated; it would proliferate into the architect-specialities that already tacitly exist, such as facade architecture, interior architecture, facility programming, post-occupancy evaluation, design review, and so on.

Cuff draws attention to this fracturing of the profession in a more tangible way by highlighting the generalist-specialist issue in the office and in education. In the office, whereas the generalist was once highly sought after, specialization leads to atomization as firms employ people for their differing skills in order to maintain the firm's generalizing capability. Within a firm, specialization leads to the dequalification of labor as tasks are broken down into smaller components. Stratification of labor increases and is arranged broadly into the rank and file of production, the administrative élite overseeing them, and the knowledge elite of academe and research. As a result, internal conflicts emerge around the differing priorities, standards, and career goals of specialists, and statuses tend to revolve around responsibility rather than design talent, leading to frustration, disappointment, and an undermining of the professional community (Cuff 1991:49–50).

Robert Gutman (1988) predicts that "some firms will continue to be more specialized and others will become more comprehensive," the implication being that 'general' and 'comprehensive' are no longer the same thing, comprehensivity is a density of skills which the 'general practitioner' can no longer match. All such arguments, of course, are meaningful only if buoyant economic conditions prevail; the specialist firm has little or no hedge against a sudden drop in the market for their services.

Turning to architectural education, the question of whether to provide a generalist or specialist training, or some combination of the two, remains a perennial issue. Architectural education is necessarily generalized, although postgraduate vocational courses layer this on to the specialized base degrees of its students. In relation to the generalist component, Cuff questions the value of the studio as the central integrative experience since building design has itself become a specialization. She suggests that emphasis shift to training in leadership and negotiation skills, and urban politics and economics. Cuff argues for educational programs as a shortcut to experience, and favors a mix of generalized plus continuing specialized education as and when the need arises.

But here we find yet another paradox: normal market demands in specialist education mitigate against extreme specialization in that low demand means that only those specialist courses that are sufficiently general to be appealing are financially viable. Yet the higher the demand, and the more it is serviced, the more 'specialization' is diluted and becomes part of the wider professional knowledge base because many people are receiving it. Such demand may be and generally is fine for educational institutions, but does not help specialist practice. In the case of medical specialists, this diffusion is counteracted by regulatory bodies that restrict intake to specialist subdisciplines in order to maintain their viability. In architecture such fine-grained regulation does not yet occur. Does it need to, or would this merely arouse further public suspicion of architects?

FURTHER SOURCES   Blau 1984; Heath 1991; Kostof 1977; Lewis 1985; Lipman 1971.

2. Wisdom: The Arbiter of Professional Know-How?

He is said to be wise in any order who considers the highest cause in that order. Thus in the order of building he who plans the form of the house is called wise and architect, in relation to the inferior laborers who trim the wood and make ready the stone: *As a wise architect I have laid foundations* [I Cor. 3:10]. **St. Thomas Aquinas.** 1265–1273. *Summa theologica*, Question 1, Article 6.

Wisdom is only a comparative quality, it will not bear a single definition. **Marquess of Halifax.** *Miscellaneous Thoughts and Reflections* (late 1600s).

Wisdom is the faculty which commands all the disciplines by which we acquire all the sciences and arts that make up humanity. Plato [in *Alcibiades I,* 124E *ff.*] defines wisdom as "the perfecter of man." Man, in his proper being as man, consists of mind and spirit, or, if we prefer, of intellect and will. It is the function of wisdom to fulfill both these parts in man, the second by way of the first, to the end that by a mind illuminated by knowledge of the highest institutions, the spirit may be led to choose the best. The highest institutions in this universe are those turned toward and conversant with God; the best are those which look to the good of all mankind. The former are called divine institutions, the latter human. True wisdom, then, should teach the knowledge of divine institutions in order to conduct human institutions to the highest good. **Giambattista Vico.** 1744:110.

Just as with space, whose separating of things seems exactly on a par with its uniting of them . . . so, in our general dealings with the world of influences, we now need conductors and now need non-conductors, and wisdom lies in knowing which is which at the appropriate moment. **William James.** 1907:62.

We do not receive wisdom, we must discover it for ourselves, after a journey through the wilderness which no-one else can make for us, which no-one else can spare for us, for our wisdom is the point of view from which we come at last to regard the world. **Marcel Proust.** 1919. "Within a budding grove." In Proust 1981, vol. 1.

In this series of lectures. . . . I appealed for wisdom: to attain the most with the least, the key to economy in general and the profoundest reason of the work of art. To economy, in its lofty sense. Thus one attains to dignity. **Le Corbusier.** Estuary of the Gironde. December 21, 1929. Le Corbusier 1930:231.

TRACE   Of Northern Germanic origin, the English word 'wisdom' describes the capacity to make right judgments in life or in conduct, or sound judgments in choices of means and ends, especially in the sense of practical affairs—hence the accrual of wisdom through experience and understanding. It is also applied to the having of deep or abstruse knowledge, learning and erudition, especially in early philosophy and science. In Greek, wisdom is *sophia, synesis, phronesis* (wisdom, good sense) and *phronimada* (wisdom, prudence, see also 5B.2, Duty). The old term 'sapience', now rarely used seriously, comes from the Latin, *sapientia* (derived from *sapere*) meaning wisdom or understanding as well as correct taste or judgment, a notion reflecting *sapere* in ancient usage signifying consciousness or intelligence and related "to the native juice in the chest, blood, and to the vapour exhaled from it, breath" (Onians 1951:61–63).

Knowledge derives from the Germanic languages based on *cnaen* and corresponding with the Indo-European *gno-,* the Greek *gnosis* and the Latin *gnoscere.* In the theory of knowledge there are seen to be two quite different kinds of knowledge: *espisteme,* or proven knowledge, and *doxa,* or opinion, and the dominance of the former is characterized by 'epistemology' being the word used for the theory of knowledge, the latter eventually being replaced by 'metaphysics' (Lakatos 1978, vol. 1). Design 'knowledge' tends to be of the metaphysical kind, what has been traditionally called *gnosis.* "But *gnosis* is not primarily rational knowledge. The Greek language distinguishes between scientific or reflective knowledge ('He knows mathematics') and knowing through observation or experience ('He knows me'), which is *gnosis.*" In Gnostic doctrine *gnosis* is insight, an intuitive knowing of oneself (Pagels 1979:18). Among the Hebrews, knowledge was divided into *law,* stating the obligation, *prophecy,* passing judgment upon those who have not accepted law, and *wisdom,* which seeks to find reasons; law and prophecy are of divine origin, while wisdom is human (Collins Gem *Dictionary of the Bible,* 1981). In our everyday terms we might say that practical knowledge is 'knowing how' and theoretical knowledge is 'knowing that'. Architecture utilizes both, the balance between them depending on the thrust of an architect's practice, from the more practical 'knowing how' to the more theoretical 'knowing that'.

COMMENTARY   Giambattista Vico (1744) ascribes Poetic Wisdom to the ancient poets and sages who were the founders of humanity (Gk. *poeisis,* making, creating). The translators of Vico write "To be good at making anything is doubtless in some sense to know how to make it, and the "know-how" is doubtless a sort of knowledge or wisdom. But what sense, and what sort? It was the discovery of the nature of this poetic or creative wisdom, the wisdom of the poets or makers of human institutions, that was the master key of the new science; a discovery which had cost Vico the research of a good twenty years [338]" (Vico, introduction K4). Vico ascribes to poetic politics the formation of cities, but makes no mention of buildings; he also gives a short history of the growth of wisdom.

"Take architecture," said Aristotle. "It is an art, that is a rational faculty exercised in making something. In fact there is no art which cannot be so described, nor is there any faculty of the kind that is not an art. It follows that an art is nothing more or less than a productive quality exercised in combination with true reason. The business of every art is to bring something into existence . . . since making is not the same as doing, it follows that art, being a kind of making, cannot be a kind of doing" (*Nicomachean Ethics*:6.5). Likewise, architecture can only be a form of making, not a form of doing. For Aristotle, *phronesis* as practical wisdom, a combination of prudence and wisdom, could apply only to the doing of something well because that is the very discernment it brings to action. Aristotle recognized excellence in art (and in architecture) but thought of it as 'wisdom' in the sense of principial understanding, not as *practical* wisdom, which was primarily human.

David Bell (1990) writes at length on Aristotle's use of *phronesis,* and disagrees with him over too rigid a distinction between making (production) and action. And once this distinction is relaxed a little, *phronesis* as the practical wisdom of "knowing how" becomes a useful concept for architecture. For inherent to the concept is the notion of mediation, or 'thought-in-action' as Bell calls it, a wisdom of practical consequence mediating between theory and practice. This idea resonates with the hermeneutical notions of Stanley Fish (1989) concerning the embeddedness of our understanding in any action and the necessary reciprocity between us and any situation. Reciprocity is also the key for David Bell: "The notion of *phronesis,* thought-in-action, a kind of reciprocity between theory and practice, has operative value for a world which is a stream of contingencies"; and contemporary architectural practice is, unlike art, nothing if not contingencies, which perhaps makes Aristotle over-simple in linking them.

What emerges from this return to one of the fathers of Western philosophy is that practical wisdom is thought-in-action mediating between theory and practice, a skill that only improves with experience in the *making* of architecture. Once architecture is accepted as not pure art but practical art requiring contingent thinking, thinking 'on the run', Aristotle's *phronesis* or practical wisdom is a precise description of the link between tacit knowledge and practical application. Tacit knowledge cannot be taught; it is "already known or dwelt in; it cannot be handed over in the form of rules or maxims and theories," according to Fish (1989:353). Tacit knowledge is a form of intuited craft knowledge in the sense that it is an article of faith and rather mysterious in its workings. Heath (1987) maintains that craft knowledge, or operative knowledge, is "knowing how, or 'know-how' rather than knowing what" and it is given vent by demonstration, not by explanation; in other words, it is already the thought-in-action of both doing and making that constitutes architecture.

In that, Heath is perhaps unknowingly in company with Stanley Fish, who writes "the trainee is not only possessed *of* but possessed *by* a knowledge of the ropes, by a tacit knowledge that tells him not so much what to do, but already has him doing it as a condition of perception and even of thought. . . . To be a judge or a basketball player is not to be able to consult the rules . . . but to have become an extension of the know-how that gives the rules . . . the meaning they will immediately and obviously have" (1989:127–128). Much the same applies in architecture, loosely structured craft knowledge is used (at times defensively and dogmatically) in practice precisely because it is a nonverbalized extension of a know-how that ordains certain rules (of thumb), and is *not* a thorough-going rationale. To repeat, the gaining and consolidating of *phronesis,* or practical wisdom arises in the process of mediation between nonverbal or tacit knowledge and the stream of contingencies that make up practical architectural application.

But so susceptible are tacit knowledge and know-how to criticism or the demand to explain themselves that it only takes someone like Jean-François Lyotard (1984b) to provocatively question the "legitimacy of knowledge, of the project, and of the project's know-how," and in so doing to throw parallel doubt upon professions whose claim to legitimacy is specialized know-how. It almost goes without saying that the design fields, depending upon such know-how for their very existence, are most vulnerable to these doubts. One answer offered by Lyotard, prompts Giovanna Borradori, lies in the function of postmodern knowledge, which is:

" . . . to refine our sense of difference and to strengthen our capacity to stand the incommensurable." To activate knowledge means activating 'differences,' discontinuities, the openness of the sense towards always new interpretations—for innovation always rises from dissent. Lyotard's formulation of the social, cognitive and aesthetic notion of an 'open system'—the anti-model of a stable system—is based on difference and discontinuity insofar as its role is in 'generating ideas.' To attempt mediation between indeterminacy and systematic control, and yet keep the notion of 'open system,' is a contradiction in terms. How is it possible to keep 'in control' the strategy of an indeterminate system, a system which is supposed to develop, organically, around dissent and the creative potential of difference? (Borradori 1988:13).

In short, if we do not accept the premise on which the demand to explain our professional knowledge is based but insist instead that difference, discontinuity, and dissent are quite acceptable, indeed vital to creative understanding, we can deflect the criticism. Tacit knowledge or professional know-how are not 'things' to be legitimated, they are processes of thought, they *are* what architects and designers *are,* and practical wisdom accumulated with experience is the controlling agent.

FURTHER SOURCES   6B.5, Anarchy; Antoniades 1990.

3. Talent: Individual or Communal Possession?

For *the kingdom of heaven is* as a man travelling into a far country, *who* called his own servants, and delivered unto them his goods.

And unto one he gave five talents, to another two, and to another one; to every man according to his several ability; and straightway took his journey. Matthew 25:14, 15.

The power of judgment rests on a potential agreement with others, and the thinking process which is active in judging something is not . . . a dialogue between me and myself, but finds itself always and primarily . . . in an anticipated communication with others whom I know I must finally come to some agreement. And this enlarged way of thinking . . . cannot function in strict isolation or solitude; it needs the presence of others "in whose place" it must think, whose perspective it must take into consideration, and without whom it never has the opportunity to operate at all. **Hannah Arendt.** 1961:220–221.

It is crucial to note that being intelligent is no guarantee of aptitude for architecture. A large dose of native talent must lie in the genes—talents can be brought forth and enhanced but not taught. **Roger K. Lewis.** 1985:33

. . . from the standpoint of justice our talents form part of a common social pool; it is the task of the theory of justice to discover what rights each of us should have over the results of using those talents . . . neither 'our' abilities nor what we can get for their exercise 'belongs' to us by natural right. **Alan Ryan** on John Rawls's theory of justice. In Skinner 1985:113.

TRACE   Talent is the regular descendant from the Latin *talentum,* in the Roman sense of an 'inclination of the mind, and from the Greek *talanton,* balance, weight, sum of money. Talent has the meaning today of a mental endowment, natural ability or aptitude, the word ability (Latin *habilitas*) deriving from *habere* (have) and relating to 'fitness', a 'capacity' in an agent, or bodily or mental 'power', thought to be divinely entrusted to a person—we say a person is 'endowed' or 'gifted'—for use and improvement.

The way in which 'talent' the weight has come to mean 'talent' the ability has its basis in the Greek Homeric tradition of the *talanta,* the scales of Zeus used to weigh the wool to be spun (the *pensum,* weight) in the metaphoric spinning of fate. Onians (1951) says "the original function of Zeus' *talanta* was the weighing of human fortunes. . . . Not only the unspun wool but the spun also or its dynamic agency, *ker,* could be weighed in the scales, that of one man, his fate, or of one host against that of another. Thus Zeus could demonstrate to others or remind himself to which he had assigned the heavier portion" (410). The *ker* was equivalent to the *psyche* appointed to each person at birth and to the *moira,* or thread of fate, spun at birth and bound to a person thereafter.

COMMENTARY   The biblical parable of the talents in the Gospel of St. Matthew, two opening verses of which are quoted above, goes on to relate how those servants who multiplied the talents distributed to them were rewarded and how the one servant who didn't was expelled 'into outer darkness' (Matthew 25:14–30). The moral of the tale is that whatever talents or abilities one has should be developed and employed to better one's situation, and it is in this sense that parents and teachers attempt to nurture or admonish their children or those under their tuition. But the dilemma of talent is that as a deeply personal possession, a quality unique to and one definition of an individual, it's nurturance aims at consolidating that individuality *qua* individuality, yet one is deemed to have no right to keep it private or to hide it, for that would be squandering.

The conventional wisdom is that we are only caretakers of whatever talents we have and that these must be 'aired' on behalf of humankind. To do otherwise is to flaunt the gift of the Grand Dispenser of Talents and to deny both one's humanity and one's social responsibility, for it is the sum of individual talents that makes a community or nation strong and productive. This attitude is part of a larger perspective that views individual differences not as competitive but as cooperative, 'brotherly dissimilitudes' according to Milton (cited by Fish 1989:410). Thus, the application of talent is one more means of realizing both a religious and a political agenda based in a well-meaning Christian ethic that prizes individual effort as a gift to humanity, "a gift that is returned to [the offerer] in the form of an enlargement of the self that [s]he has been willing to lend to a common project" (Fish 1989:411).

Years ago, what were called 'aptitude' tests attempted to measure the propensity a person had toward particular skills, and in turn the vocational possibilities for such a person, as well as the 'capacity' of the person to expand those skills. Capacity in this sense was used to describe the upper limit or maximum level to which a person might aspire, and continued the conception of human beings as empty vessels ('purses'?) awaiting the lodgment of talents, as in the biblical parable. To even conceive that persons might reach their capacity or 'fill up' with talents and abilities is to import the quantitative to something that is qualitative, and reflects the shift from a traditional to a scientific view of the world that began in the seventeenth century and dominates today. Yet the Parable of the Talents, while couched in material and sensible terms as all parables are, did not speak of 'limits' at all, but of unlimited expansion, of 'abundance'; indeed it shows the way to 'the kingdom of heaven'. If talent is the potential for such a wondrous achievement, how did we move from this inspiring prospect to the myopic severity of 'aptitude' testing?

The fact that such tests have not provided clear and unequivocal predictions to future career paths or assisted in education after several decades now is seen not as a failure of science, but as a *development* of science, explained by saying, "but at least some techniques and measuring instruments are now being applied in other areas that might never have been developed otherwise." The will-to-control now dominates science's, if not all scientists', professed will-to-truth. What science and scientists cannot face is that talent or ability or aptitude are diametrically opposed to the project of science because they are inherently nonmeasurable qualities; even the most talented and ingenious scientists cannot test their talent and ingenuity. What hope then hapless talented architects whose qualitative world steeped in will-to-truth is constantly beset by science-ordained demands to quantitatively explain and justify what they do?

Herein lies the difficulty for architects: if talent resides within the individual, whether believed to be God-given or some inherent biological predisposition, and for (potential) architects can be 'brought forth' and 'enhanced,' as Lewis declares above, and if its 'capacity' cannot be measured beforehand to any educational purpose, presumably when it does 'emerge' it can only be known by virtue of the actions or works it is evidenced in, by, or through. All architects hope for are sufficient opportunities to vent their talent; many never receive what they consider their full share of opportunities (R. Lewis 1985). All anyone could do who wished to gain some measure of architects' talent would be to throw more and more opportunities in their path hoping to trip them up, which, once it occurs, would then be a measure of their talent limit or capacity. Oh that there were more people wishing to find my limits in that way, many architects would say!

As a quality, talent is only possessed by an individual, whether alone or in a group; it does not transfer to the work of a talented individual in any common sense, it is only 'expressed'. The work is not 'talented'; it is only the result of talent. Therefore, talent is both a resident way of construing and, once activated, a dynamic and an insinuating force, by means of which a designer's signature is imprinted on a task or a work. It cannot therefore 'belong' to the community, except in the very restricted religious sense of being implanted in an eternally grateful recipient, although it may be seen as a factor in common among a community, as it is with any creative or peculiarly facilitative group. This innateness of talent can have bizarre ethical implications for the distribution of income and wealth, from some points of view. For instance, the ethical theory of the American philosopher John Rawls (*A Theory of Justice,* 1971) insists that, far from 'desert' being the central notion of justice, "People's successes and failures spring from characters and talents they have done nothing to deserve," and any entitlement they might have to recompense is only by virtue of the *rules* of appointment and performance in their position, not because they *deserve* to be rewarded. "Rawls's account of justice has no room for the thought that even if we do not *deserve* our talents, we still have a right to what we can get from exercising them simply because they are *ours*" (Ryan in Skinner 1985:113). In fact, Rawls is actually saying that, morally, talented individuals don't *deserve* to be rewarded just because they are talented. But in practice, they *are* rewarded for their talent.

Dana Cuff (1991) cites the favored relation between instructor and the most talented students that Michael Graves is presumed to have announced saying that it "reifies the belief that the talented . . . can claim special privileges in architecture. This talent is not taught; it is believed to be a natural gift bestowed upon the best designers" (122). Contrary to Rawls's view about the lack of proprietorship individuals have over their talent, the architectural profession promotes talent's anointed because, along with dedication, talent is believed a necessary ingredient for excellence in architecture. Cuff maintains that "individual talent, leadership, even genius are important to architecture when they exist in a social context that is conducive to such efforts—a context that consists of other demanding, talented individuals who operate as a team" (245), and in that sense the fostering of talent *is* a community responsibility with communal benefits. While it may be a desire of individual architects to express their talent, it is not within their power to foster it.

FURTHER SOURCES   Rawls 1971; H. Smith 1989.

4. The Basis of Architectural Quality and Excellence

. . . excellence in deliberation has nothing to do with opinion.

Seeing that a man who deliberates badly is in error, he who deliberates well is right, it is clear that excellence in deliberation is a form of rightness or correctness, though not in knowledge or belief. **Aristotle.** *Nicomachean Ethics:*VI.9.

In the whole picture, the shape of quality is not the shape of a particular but rather the essence of any thing which we may think of as excellent. This is true of all art—fine art, visual art, architecture, the making of artifacts, urban design. **Serge Chermayeff.** 1959. In Plunz 1982:171.

By comparing the individual work with the architectural system it belongs to, we may determine its *architectural quality.* **Christian Norberg-Schulz.** 1965:108.

. . . it is their qualitative components that make values, meanings, and purpose important. But qualities, being subjective, barely lend themselves to even the minimum requirements of science—objectivity—let alone submit to quantification. . . . Science's inability to deal with the qualitatively unmeasurable leaves it working with what Lewis Mumford called a "disqualified universe." **Huston Smith.** 1989:148.

Clients who participate in excellent projects . . . begin with an exacting attitude; what they exact is quality. . . . The excellent architects such clients choose . . . are principled individuals who remain flexible. . . . **Dana Cuff.** 1991:232–233.

TRACE   Quality has been used often throughout this book as being self-explanatory, but is now given some precision. Translated by Cicero from the Greek *poiotes* as 'qualitas', which derives from *qualis,* meaning how constituted, of what sort, nature, or kind, quality in relation to people is a variation of terms such as character, disposition, and nature; and in relation to things is an attribute, property, or special feature, or the degree of excellence possessed. From the Latin *cellere,* rise high or tower, to excel is to be superior to something or someone in certain, mostly good, respects, and 'excellence' is just such a state of superiority, merit, eminence, or dignity. Excellence is applied to those qualities or states that exceed the ordinary or usual standard.

In the chapter "Excellent practice: the origins of good building," Cuff (1991) sees excellence in building emerging from the evaluations of three interest groups: consumers/public, design participants, and the architectural profession. An excellent building is one agreed so by all three groups. Cuff's study shows that architectural excellence emerges from just this sort of congruence of circumstances arising out of the interaction of what she terms seven dialectical 'principles', namely, quality demands, simplicity within complexity, stereovision, open boundaries, flexibility with integrity, teamwork with independence, and exceeding the limits (245). From her examination of these principles Cuff concludes that excellence "comes not from a talented architect or exceptional client alone, but from an *emergent chemistry* [emphasis added] among principal participants. Thus, we cannot speak of excellent firms or excellent architects—only excellent projects."

COMMENTARY   Excellence is a term about which we think we know, but that we fall dismally short of being able to explain. It does not appear to be a God-given thing like a talent, yet the sense of reaching beyond the usual standards to achieve it has an air of obligation about it; in other words, it would be a personal failure not to at least try for it. Higher education is geared around notions of excellence, which is propped up with politically correct words to make it seem as though it is understood; but is only after the event that we know whether excellence has been achieved. This makes of excellence more a state of grace arising out of fortuitous congruence of circumstances, perhaps pushed along by well-meaning intentions, rather than an exquisite realm to be occupied by the select.

Design quality is an unexceptionable notion in architecture these days; quality assurance procedures are accepted for their ability to raise and maintain standards in the industry and there is a growing literature about quality in building (Preiser 1973, 1985, 1989; Preiser, Rabinowitz and White 1988; Preiser, Vischer, and White 1991). But the pursuit of excellence in reaching beyond accepted or usual standards is a far more demanding concept because there is no limit to what might be achieved or expected except insofar as a point is reached beyond which no one is available to undertake the work. Those who seek excellence or who think it should be sought seem unable to make clear their reasoning for doing so, except to say that it will result in some vaguely sensed gratification or betterment, as much in the doing as in the achievement.

Any attempt to question the ideal of pursuing excellence, though, is met with a disdainful retort of the "but why *wouldn't* you strive for excellence?" kind. Excellence has a revered status in human and especially academic pursuits or, rather, is a hallowed standard of human pursuit, but without the rigor of any means of testing either its standards or its achievement. I recall a visiting professor who, when presented with the grades of assessment of the school, which range in four steps from Pass (50 percent to 64 percent) to High Distinction (85 percent or greater), said "Oh, I never give more than 80 percent because it gives students something to strive for, it encourages excellence." Asked what for him would constitute an excellent student project in architecture—when in engineering and the sciences it was quite possible to achieve 100 percent in an assignment with a 'perfect' and 'correct' answer—he replied that the correctness of the answer was nothing to do with excellence, that it was all to do with the striving. Here, in a nutshell, I thought, is one source of torment in the architectural profession, a driving passion for an undefined excellence and perpetual dissatisfaction with never achieving it.

On the other hand, Dana Cuff's notion of excellence as an 'emergent chemistry' arising from the interaction of the principal participants is closer to what happens in the jury system of design adjudication in architectural education, and overcomes the bias and tyranny of the Lone Assessor. There are, however, many situations in design education where excellence in the striving can and does take precedence over the end result, in which case it is a matter of judgment as to whether some degree of excellence has been achieved. Indeed it may be argued that if a Pass grade is considered average, then each grade is a degree of excellence, of excelling the average, rather than some unattainable standard of near-perfection.

Turning to excellence in practice, the interactive chemistry of the jury or panel in annual design awards and in competitions is the means by which excellence is gauged, although on occasions an award is not made because the 'universe' of selection is too limited or the jury declares their standard of excellence not to have been achieved. More often than not, though, it is an awarded building (or person) that generates controversy, or at times worse; witness the many architectural awards over the years to buildings that have gone on to greater infamy (Pruitt Igoe being the classic case). In the ensuing furor over a nonaward or controversial award, excellence frequently becomes the (sometimes unstated) locus of the debate; witness the upset that Robert Venturi and Denise Scott Brown caused with their winning scheme for the National Gallery Extension competition in London (Prince Charles's 'monstrous carbuncle'). Similar controversies over building proposals rage around the world and will always do so; Michael Sorkin in 1985 railed against the Michael Graves extension to Breuer's Whitney Museum (the Breuer being 'magnificent' rather than excellent), and in 1986 against the Gwathmey Siegel and Associates extension to Frank Lloyd Wright's Guggenheim Museum in New York (1991:119–124, 148–154).

The great difficulty lies with excellence in the day-to-day adjudication of architectural quality, where it remains a silent sentinel to designing. There is no doubt that many architects constantly coax themselves into doing better while they are designing, all in the name of approaching excellence in the quality of their thinking and doing. But because excellence is so elusive and because it is generally seen to cost more, many products of architectural practice are of only mediocre quality. This is not to say that talent is lacking but, as Dana Cuff says, that 'exacting' is not at work and hence the chemistry cannot emerge. Certainly the major beneficiary of talented and excellent intervention is the community, just as the community is the loser if talent is wasted; but the community has a responsibility, too, to keep demanding it.

The pursuit of excellence is always a clarion call to both the community and the architectural profession to reconsider their attitudes about what they are doing and where they wish to go. No other issue can excite the community to respond qualitatively to buildings or natural environments as can a taste of excellence or a threat to it. Just as talent runs counter to the quantitative, excellence runs interference with the qualitative. There may not be fixed standards of excellence but debate about them just as surely helps focus the mind, and is decidedly healthier than lack of debate.

FURTHER SOURCES   Blau 1984; Charles 1989; Heath 1991.

5. Feminism: Shifting the Agenda

There won't be better parts for women until more women write the scripts. **Henry Root.** 1983. *Henry Root's World of Knowledge* (London, Futura).

BLD: How did you manage to escape the woman architect's ghetto of renovating kitchens? **JG:** Mostly because I don't cook and don't know much about kitchens. What you choose not to learn can be significant. I never learned to cook or to type, but I'm pretty good with a hammer. **Joan Goody.** c1984. In Diamonstein 1985:115.

It is not surprising that housing design and site planning frequently fail in their support of child rearing when the chief decision makers . . . are predominantly male and have little firsthand experience minding small children. It is ironic—and again not surprising—that many of the influential writers on the sociology of housing—how it really *works* for adults and children— have been women. **Clare Cooper Marcus.** Marcus and Sarkissian (1986):viii.

Two centuries after the American and French revolutions, the entry of women into the public sphere is far from complete, the gender division of labor in the family is still not the object of moral and political reflection, and women and their concerns are still invisible in contemporary theories of justice and community. **Seyla Benhabib.** 1992:13.

TRACE   Gender in architecture arose with Vitruvius's mythical account of the origin of the classical orders. The earliest, Doric, was masculine in proportion, appearance, and association, and the later Ionic, feminine; the ancient Greek temple builders "borrowed manly beauty, naked and unadorned, for the one, and for the other the delicacy, adornment, and proportions characteristic of women" (Vitruvius, Book 4.1.7). The third order, the Corinthian, "is an imitation of the slenderness of a maiden . . . [and admits] of prettier effects in the way of ornament" (4.1.8). However, the Greek names Vitruvius so faithfully transcribes are tropes for other ideas and sentiments to do with battle, capture, and violence, and from them we learn that neither masculine nor feminine associations are exclusive to any of the orders (Hersey 1988:53–67).

During the eighteenth century, Jacques-François Blondel encouraged his students to find the appropriate means of expression, the 'tone', for any building type by creating a list of genres similar to the traditional classical system of genres, among which were "included what he called 'male, or strong and virile', 'light, elegant, or delicate', 'rustic', 'naive', 'feminine', 'mysterious' "; they formed "the rudiments of a critical vocabulary" (Vidler 1990:20).

In the late-nineteenth century, Louis Sullivan was persuaded to views on masculinity and femininity in architecture by the writings of the eighteenth-century Swedish mystic Emanuel Swedenborg, who "believed that universal rationality, or wisdom, comes into harmony with the masculine principle of the cosmos, and emotion, or love, with the feminine." For Swedenborg the physical and spiritual were transcendent and "correspondences of wisdom-love, reason-emotion, and masculine-feminine existed between the two spheres" (Menocal 1981:25). Sullivan's latent transvestitism and that of his buildings, their masculine structure and virility eventually transmogrified by their feminine embellishment and saturation, is discussed in Twombly (1986:399–402).

COMMENTARY   Following on the binary oppositions he discerned in all spheres of life and thought, the German idealist philosopher G. W. F. Hegel assigned traditional gender roles to men and women and highlighted certain gender-specific differences as fundamental to their *Geist,* an animating spirit or mind, from which he developed his rational ontology. For Hegel, "women are viewed as representing the principles of particularity, immediacy, naturalness, and substantiality, while men stand for universality, mediacy, freedom, and subjectivity" (Benhabib 1992:245–246). Benhabib argues that the logic of such binaries is also a logic of 'subordination and domination', and that the invisibility of gender in contemporary thought is symptomatic of deep distortions and a primary skewing of theories of morality and public life. "The exclusion of women and their point of view," she maintains, "is not just a political omission and a moral blind spot but constitutes an epistemological deficit as well" (1992:13–14).

If we accept Benhabib's view that gender distortions pervade epistemology generally, then they certainly pervade architectural understanding. However, while examples of gender emphases, omissions, or differences are not difficult to find in the literature, just what the deficit is or how serious the skewing is not so readily discerned. Certainly it appears that masculine-feminine dialectic seems to have insinuated itself in various guises into modernist polemic so utterly that for much of the twentieth century it has been barely recognized, especially in architecture. Even as recently as mid-1991, "while the introduction of feminist forms and contents has been a major force for change in mainstream American art, the literature on women architects continues to avoid feminist issues and to emphasize professional advancement" (Susanna Torre. 1991:74).

Taking up the role and opportunity of women in architecture and design, from the 'pathetically scant literature', architecture is seen as a largely male vocation and, despite the substantial female intake of many courses of architecture and design (in excess of fifty percent over recent years), gender differences in ways of designing, the kinds of issues considered important in architecture, or the professional opportunities awaiting graduates remain largely unquestioned and unstudied. So prevalent is male dominance that it is still common to encounter female students using the masculine in philosophical, anthropomorphic, or cosmological discussion in relation to architecture, and most significantly those involving the architect 'himself' or the 'masters'. And this is despite the dramatic change in academic staffing profiles following the feminist advances since the sixties and explicit political moves recently to correct and re-educate public attitudes about the continuing inequality of women.

Of the gender studies undertaken, certain matters have attracted attention as primarily feminine concerns. In her "A feminist approach to architecture: acknowledging women's ways of knowing" (Berkeley and McQuaid 1989:201–216) Karen Franck discerns from recent feminist writings in other disciplines than architecture "seven qualities that characterize feminine or feminist ways of knowing or analyzing," 'knowing' for her being 'an act of creating'. The goals of her essay are to release these qualities and concerns suppressed among women in architecture, to celebrate them, and thereby to seek a profession more hospitable to women and, in turn, "more attuned to people's needs" (a hoary issue raised in chapter 3B). The qualities are, in summary: (1) connectedness, (2) inclusiveness, (3) an 'ethic of care', (4) everyday life and values, (5) subjectivity and feelings, (6) complexity, and (7) change and flexibility (203). Franck concludes that these qualities represent "only part of a fledgling effort to outline a feminist approach to architecture," and goes on to outline other qualities that might be explored to further advantage: "cooperation and collaboration, organic systems of spatial organization and form-making, and metaphors based on hearing and touching" (212).

These qualities seem to me to align with the female side of Hegel's gender-specific differences, and highlight Benhabib's observation that women's activities have largely remained in the private realm of children, human relationships, and traditions. The consequence of this feminine locus is that "the female experience has been more attuned to the 'narrative structure of action' and the 'standpoint of the concrete other'. Since they have had to deal with concrete individuals, with their needs, endowments, wants and abilities, dreams as well as failures, women in their capacities as primary caregivers have had to exercise insight into the claims of the particular" (Benhabib 1992:14). It is not inaccurate to say this view sums to: men universalize, women particularize. But are these broad qualities, or the seven qualities Franck highlights, necessarily so gender-specific? In her introduction, Ellen Perry Berkeley recounts the somewhat lighthearted claim of the architect Joan Goody about male architects that "most have played the female role in relation to their powerful patrons," and that they "have a fair number of the traditional female attributes (they are sensitive, artistically creative, and malleable) and the traditional female flaws (they are temperamental, spendthrift, and late)" (xxii). Without wishing to take away anything from the feminist debate in architecture so far, trying to argue differences in male and female attributes of architects as a basis for greater feminist leverage seems singularly unrewarding.

An apparent desire by male architects for an unassisted procreative role has been presented as one reason for the perseverance of nonparticipation by females in the profession, lest they upset Narcissus or interfere with 'pure paternity' (Bergren in Whiteman, Kipnis and Burdett 1992:21). Bergren gives the clue to such male dominance: "Here is the architect as figurative philosopher and the philosopher as figurative architect, building 'what he knows.' Like Zeus, this *demiourgos* is a god. . . . He, too, has 'swallowed' Metis. For he is a con-structor. . . . His construction is a harmony and a weaving. And he is a father . . . who 'marvels at the marvel he engendered' without female consort" (18). This seems like just a verbal play around the rather extreme notion that building creation by males is an hermaphroditic act that supplants the presence of the female. It seems a dubious line of exploration, notwithstanding that Louis Sullivan enacted such an idea in his works, and that Filarete adopted 'transsexual' building and city conceptions three centuries earlier (*Treatise on Architecture*, 1461–1463), prompting the notion of conception, birth, and nurture as male tasks, and thereby appearing to repress the female (Diana Agrest 1991:180–183. It is doubtful that Agrest sees these as 'innocent' actions). Whither the female in Bergren's classical scene?

Women *qua* women in architecture *are,* however, bringing insights into design via emphasis on particulars, and by other means, and in a manner that appears to be shifting the agenda rather than perpetuating the conventional Hegelian division. The dramatic increase in female writers on architecture, especially in history and criticism, has begun to stir the waters of detachment that at present suits the predominantly male architectural establishment. Feminism is effecting changes of emphasis in architectural theory and history toward the very qualities Franck has pointed to, and has created a veritable caravan of ideas that cannot help but intercept all designing. Whether there is a more deep-seated psychological obstruction among males in architecture that prevents the assimilation of women and therefore needs to be challenged, such as male 'creative birth' itself, is perhaps too difficult a task for pseudo-pyschoanalysts.

Finally, it is difficult not to construe as a conflict between feminine and masculine emphases in architecture the gap Heath observes between esthetic and functional orientations. He draws attention to "a continuing rift in the profession between the romantics and the rationalists, between the soft-hearted and the hard-headed, expressed, for example, in the repressed but never extinguished tradition of expressionism, in the division between 'organic architecture' and the influence of the Bauhaus in America, and more recently by the various proponents of autonomous housing, ecological architecture, participatory design, 'postmodernism', and so on as against 'big architecture'" (Heath 1984:73). Perhaps insisting that the rights of 'concrete others' be taken into account in any universalizing agenda by god-architect, be (s)he (fe)male or not, or at the very least obliging her/him not to ignore the detail and minutiae of life that make life meaningful to most people, will be a sufficiently radical act to realign the profession.

FURTHER SOURCES   Chapter 4, Overview; Kennedy 1981; Lorenz 1990; Torre 1977; Weisman 1992.

B. Positions Adopted by Architects

1. Roles Architects Play in Society and Practice

The demand that all buildings should become works of architecture . . . is strictly offensive to common sense. . . . One might possibly stipulate that architecture is a social institution related to building in much the same way that literature is to speech. **Colin Rowe** and **Fred Koetter.** 1978:101.

Many architects do live up to their image, exhibiting idiosyncrasies in the ways they dress, talk, and work, or in their beliefs. They strive to be individualistic and nonconformist, if not radical. **Roger K. Lewis.** 1985:17.

Having done away with the classical models of academic training, [Col. W. A. Starret] hailed the new generation of self-made *builders*—a new architectural breed, somewhere between engineer and architect. Preferably they were self-taught or at least had no brilliant academic career to boast of. The ideal must have come from the same material from which Ayn Rand had fabricated her unpleasant hero of *The Fountainhead:* strong, rugged, independent and sent away from school at least once. **Thomas A. P. van Leeuwen.** 1988:4.

In the lexicon of macroeconomic analysis, architectural practice is classified as a producer service business, since the bulk of practice today provides services to producers of commodities (manufacturers) and to other service businesses rather than to the final consumer. **Robert Gutman.** 1988:9.

TRACE   A *role* is the pattern of behavior a person elects to adopt or is expected to exhibit in a particular social position. Originating in the *roll* containing the script of an actor's part, it is used figuratively now to mean the 'part' a person 'plays' in society or life. As such, the term 'role' has overtones of being false or artificial, but role-playing and seeking suitable role models are quite normal human pursuits. Role and image, particularly self-image, are intimately related (Goffman 1959).

Many social roles have arisen out of the division of labor, and architects, no less than those in other professions, have had their social role formally prescribed by law and by institutionalized control of education and practice. But some social roles are informal, as with families, and are more or less understood rather than clearly defined. This tacit understanding is also part of certain phases of professional life, such as the mini-societies of architectural firms; it takes a while for newcomers to sense their 'place' and role (Cuff 1991). From an American point of view, Robert Gutman (1981) sees three competing role models and sets of ideals governing architects: architecture as a *profession,* architecture as a *service* business or industry, and architecture as an *art.* The English theorist Geoffrey Broadbent (1973:361–363) sees two: *management* and *design.*

COMMENTARY   We each perform daily in relation to others as we carefully manipulate what we say and do to convey certain impressions, and we try to organize the situations we find ourselves in to our favor as much as possible. For the professional it is extremely important to be taken seriously, and for this reason architects are seldom seen as lighthearted in their public demeanor, or if they are, great care is taken to also present an earnest side. This may seem a gross generalization, because there are cultures and communities in which it is acceptable to publicly display a less-than-serious aspect as a professional. But it is equally the case that to gain public approbation there must be a balance with conspicuously trustworthy attributes, such as integrity, sincerity, and dedication, for confidence to be established and maintained.

One area in which architects are granted liberties not readily available to other professions relates to their creativity. Society's attribution of creativity to architects, as well as to artists, designers, writers, poets, and others in so-called 'creative' walks of life, allows them considerable leeway in favor of unconventional dress, behavior, and lifestyle. Indeed, because architects and designers *are* nonconformist in many ways, there is every reason for them to 'trade' on this freedom by capitalizing on their lifestyle. This is not to imply that architects or designers are calculating about this pursuit, but offering friends and clients the chance to share in their creative, intellectual or idiosyncratic world is part of their appeal (Lewis 1985:17). But perhaps the more conventional side to the architect-lifestyle is literally visible success, and architects are used by advertisers to project that image of success, affluence, and confidence, not from creativity so much as from sheer tenacity and hard work. Some architects exploit their success by lending their names to product endorsements.

This, as it happens, also works the other way as a form of self-advertising, although whether it results in further commissions is unclear. Others unwittingly lend their names to commercial enterprises, as I once found Aldo Rossi did with a heavily thumbed copy of his book of works (among other architecture books) provided for customer browsing in a Structure men's wear store in Cincinnati. Of course I bought up big!

Professional images abound in the print media, and increasingly feature architects at work in the office or on the site, and occasionally at leisure. Industry journals are filled with such images, and the architect is usually a *man,* with drawings under his arm, or with mouse under his hand jousting a computer screen filled with pretend-architecture lines, the architect looking ever-so-slightly tousled. A recent article by Diane Favro on advertising imagery featuring women professionals (Berkeley and McQuaid 1989:187–200) reported that "in architecture today, 94 percent of the practitioners are male, but in the world of printed advertisements a disproportionate number are women"; from a survey of reading matter from 1980 and 1986 in general readership magazines, 40 percent of 'ad-architects' are women, and in women's magazines, 90 percent. Contrary to her expectations, though, Favro found that "ads emphasize the business acumen of female practitioners, not their creativity or social concerns . . . [her] suitlike attire . . . [and her] practicality and propriety rather than her style or flair. The message is clear. A female ad-architect is above all a professional" (188).

Favro finds that, whereas male ad-architects are shown actively at work designing, sleeves at half-mast, creative and self-assured individuals, female ad-architects in the office are inactive, cerebral, passive thinkers who are never harried; outside the office they are on the go, presenting to clients, authoritative. In summary, the stereotypes are the female professional and the male individualist. "All are white, Caucasian, and youthful," non-whites featuring in special interest magazines and in relation to ethnically associated products. The female-as-generic-professional thrust of such advertisements offers shock value, and is geared to appeal directly to women, who control most consumable spending, women architects portraying "the psychographic traits most admired in a career woman: efficiency, intelligence, self-assurance, creativity." Because such images contradict professional journals and real life, Favro argues they should be exploited, "architects can improve interaction both between themselves and the lay public and between professionals of different gender" (198).

Popular images of the architect in cinema and on television try to emphasize both the art and the technical sides of the architect, the most dramatically iconoclastic being the temperamental Howard Roark of *The Fountainhead,* portrayed by Gary Cooper in the movie, who became for some architects themselves a role model (Stanley Tigerman in Diamonstein 1985). More recently, media images of architects have shifted dramatically from Rand's rugged individualist to more moderate and conservative portrayals. They range from the besieged and exasperated father-and-architect in the Australian soap *Hey*

Dad to the sensitive lead in Spike Lee's *Jungle Fever* to the shy but hard-working and creative, if slightly irresponsible, character portrayed by Steve Martin in *Housesitter* (see Favro also for a summary of movies of the eighties that feature architects). The Martin character, however, did have a hustling, sycophantic and opportunistic cohort, and the partner of the firm was a blustery, crusty caricature of almost every corporate 'boss'. Such are some of the public images of architects that tend to confound the role architects are publicly expected to play.

Yet, for all their flair and creativity, architects on the whole are expected to be level-headed, dependable, and, above all, practical. Consequently, the role of architects has always been somewhat schizophrenic in combining the ascetic, esthete, and artist with the practical, hard-headed technocrat. The thrust of architectural education for more than a century has been to achieve a balance between these qualities. Historically, however, architects have suffered more than their fair share of identity crises because they "were unable to claim sole proprietorship over the technical aspects of building" as a result of engineers concerning themselves with heavier construction during the nineteenth century, thereby leaving architects to carry forward the Beaux Arts tradition of 'design-as-art'. But even in practicing their 'art', architects are given less room to move than artists, partly because they have to contend with a resistant marketplace conditioned by a public either indifferent or ambivalent to esthetics (Cuff 1991:31), and partly because the increasing number of bodies formally adjudicating esthetic matters are eating into this domain (see also 3B.1, Public and 3B.2, Users). Consequently, the art of architecture is being slowly displaced, or at least made more covert, by virtue of professional roles necessarily developing around other architectural skills or expertise in order to survive.

Charles Jencks (1980) saw the job of architecture as helping to "articulate daily life . . . the relations within a society and the relation of an individual to the rest of the world" and the turn to personal imagery as "scrupulously honest to the cultural *role* of architecture" (118), although if there is one role architects would commonly say they enact it is that of a provider of 'service' to a client. Certainly 'service' is the thrust of much vocational architectural education around the world, encouraged as it is by professional watchdogs visiting schools and certifying courses. But it is not the only commodified profession, as Gutman (1988) makes clear shortly after the extract quoted above: "Along with architecture, the professional producer services include accounting, engineering, law, management consulting, and scientific research" (9–10).

The trouble with this role for some theorists is that "there is something unattractive about the notion of architecture as a 'service'," as the architect and critic Tom Heath (1991) says. "The idea that an architect can be a servant, carrying out the wishes of the client in the same sense that a skilled craftsman or technician can carry out the wishes embodied in a drawing, is mistaken. It is based on false assumptions about the wishes, or 'needs', of the client: in particular, that they are simple, clear and *known to the client*. . . . To define architecture as a 'service' is to propose that it consists solely of transformation processes, that is, that it not be design at all. . . . 'Service' is not acceptable as a legitimation for architecture" (180–182). The role of the architectural theorist continues to be to find a more acceptable role for the architect.

FURTHER SOURCES   Johnson 1979; Lewis 1985.

2. Vision Quest: Architects and the Future

We call upon all those who believe in the future. All strong longing for the future is architecture in the making. One day there will be a world-view, and then there will also be its sign, its crystal—architecture. **Bruno Taut.** 1919. In Conrads 1964:47.

. . . what we need is the courage to accept inner experience, then suddenly a new path will open for the artist. . . . And this great total work of art [*Gesamtkunstwerk*], this cathedral of the future, will then shine with its abundance of light. . . . On the strength of his visual gifts, the artist reads the spiritual parallels of his time and represents them in pure form. . . . We artists therefore need the community of spirit of the entire people as much as we need bread. . . . **Walter Gropius.** July, 1919. *Address to the Bauhaus Students.* Cited in Benton, Benton and Sharp, 1975:80.

It is worthwhile speculating as to why the basic values and attitudes expressed in [architecture] school have transcended factionalism and fashion. It seems to me that those instincts that lead young men and women to pursue the study of architecture are based on an unshakable belief in the existence of a *better* future. The embryonic architect is both visionary and idealist. Students see themselves as translators of fantasies into realities. . . . **James Stewart Polshek.** Introduction to Oliver 1981.

The architectural critic has no business being an "ideologist," that is, a visionary proponent of architectural styles of the future, "revolutionary" architecture, and the like: her role must be resolutely negative, the vigilant denunciation of existent or historical ideologies. **Fredric Jameson** commenting on Manfredo Tafuri's 'working judgments' in his many writings. In Ockman 1985:53, 55.

It is strange that, even though the repositioning of the human subject has been *the* major concern in the evolution of modern critical thought, the problem of the human soul has rarely been explicit in architectural discourse. In its concerns for the problems of *order per se* . . . it can be said that architecture is some several centuries behind the times. **John Whiteman.** In Marvel 1986:13.

Magic is defined as the art of producing a desired result through the use of various processes assuring control of the supernatural and the mystical forces of nature. **Marc Angelil.** 1989:64.

TRACE   A ritual found throughout North American tribes is the *vision quest,* sometimes called 'crying for a vision', which "provides the average person, not just the medicine man, with access to the spiritual realms for help," and is usually sought by male tribal members (Guiley 1991). The ritual is thought to manifest a guardian spirit that accompanies and advises the individual for a specific task or period. In a lifetime there may be many such quests. The nearest Eastern equivalents are the systems of Shamanism and Yoga, while in Western thought there are only equivalents for the state of being possessed of a 'spirit guide' such as intuition, inspiration, creative visualization, positive thinking and, in certain respects, synchronicity. The notion of 'spirit', *genius* or *geist,* is discussed in 4B.3, Artist, chapter 7A, and 9B.5, Place.

Among architects there is belief that inspiration is a principal means of creative output, but just how it happens cannot be explained. It has been the task of all studies of creativity to try to understand inspiration and to determine conditions appropriate to its operation. Something like the tribal actions for 'vision quest' are said to accompany invention by architects and other creative people: retreat to a special ('sacred') place for days and nights, intense concentration ('meditation'), and imagination—sometimes induced ('hallucination').

COMMENTARY   For a profession so involved in prediction and invention, architects are notoriously short on evoking ideas or visions in the literature of late. The early years of the Modern Movement were filled with visionary manifestos and declarations about the future of architecture and of the world, be they nonsensical for the most part as we see with hindsight. There were also sketches and images of vast embrace showing wondrous ideas for hills crowned with glass (Bruno Taut), multi-layered ribbon buildings with motorways above stretching to the horizon (Le Corbusier), and endlessly repeating grids filled with playing fields, cultivated plots, and nodes of concentrated urban life (Frank Lloyd Wright). What has happened to the romance and adventure in architecture that we no longer produce such visions for the future? Spare us the histrionics, you might say, but has the calculating and rational and jaded so overtaken architects in the late twentieth century that the only experiments are private ones by artistic individuals who make them public for their own self-promotion rather than as communal dreams?

Admittedly there have been the delightful mega-eccentricities of the Architectural Association groupies, Paolo Soleri, Buckminster Fuller, and Marshall McLuhan during the sixties, and there have been occasional sorties by lone architects into imaginary settings since (Emilio Ambasz, John Hejduk). But there seems to have developed a level of cynicism among architectural writers that has all but killed off the joy and wonder of future possibilities. Why? Has magic now retired as the architect's assistant? Has the special-effects cinema now so overwhelmed the world, and computer animation so entranced youth that newer generations of architects no longer feel adequate to the task? I suspect this may be so. The multiple social disasters of disease, chronic unemployment, high death rates from motor vehicle accidents and homicides, nuclear accidents, assassinations of heroes, and large-scale media coverage of both local and global issues have made us sadder and presumably wiser today than a generation ago. We don't believe in the grand vision any more because we have seen that it will always be found wanting. We are convinced that we must content ourselves with small gains made piece by piece in among the disasters of life. If Charles Jencks could write of Le Corbusier's tragic view of architecture in 1973, such a book might be written in volumes today, only twenty years later, to embrace the tragic view of a newer and inured generation.

Yet, there was an architecture student conference held in April 1993 in Adelaide, Australia, titled "Alchemy." Perhaps all is not lost after all. Perhaps by returning to this ancient tradition of transmutation, a still very easily remembered element of recent Western history, something of the lost magic may be regained. A colleague from another (altered) state said to me on seeing the poster for the conference, "This is what's wrong with architects. There are still people who insist on such mystical notions. Is it any wonder we can't compete with other disciplines!" He most probably is right, but the feeling still nags that something is being lost by removing the whimsical, the imaginative, and the nonsensical that are the stuff of cloudy visions. More competitions just for the visions, not for choosing the right architect for the job.

The prominence given to historical writing is swamping architecture, especially what might be called the *adoration writings* of heroes and anti-heroes of architecture already gone. Theoretical concerns are left wallowing, trying to make sense of things past rather than assisting with projections of what might be. Notwithstanding the comments already made about theory not guiding practice, theory guiding futures is a different story. Architecture needs a fiction of the future to match the fictions it has already created and continues to create of its past. While there is a mass of such fiction in other disciplines, some of which is borrowed by architectural writers, there is a dearth of speculative theoretical writing within architecture.

Perhaps this deficiency reflects both the cynicism of the age and just how deep have been the inroads of scientific certainty and social uncertainty. Speculations do appear in practice though, constantly, as any sketch for a project shows and as the many competitions formally acknowledge. How else do projects come into being if they are not *projected,* or thrown into the future, as Martin Heidegger would say? Student architects are still being educated in ever greater numbers and still have hope enough to carry them past three in the morning. So, whatever 'guidance' there may be, theoretical or otherwise, appears to be alive and dwelling alongside every architect's drawing board, if not computer console (computer technology as mostly exists in offices is inimical to creativity, hence the drawing board). Undoubtedly Le Corbusier, had he lived, would not have agreed with the drawing board analogy for that would have been an admission of defeat. He would have persevered with installing the spirit in the console, probably seeing the computer as a 'machine for envisioning' the future, just as AI researchers around the world have been trying to do.

Friedensreich Hundertwasser recently remarked: "Every architect could do what I do, but they are afraid. They get their qualifications by becoming sterile. They say no to all dreams of romance and beauty. A trained architect is a qualified killer. He killed his own dreams, so then he is allowed to create buildings for mankind" (*Good Weekend: The Sydney Morning Herald Magazine,* September 19, 1992:64). Perhaps the principal role of the architect should be that of tragic hero, for this may be the only way to keep the vision quest alive.

FURTHER SOURCES   Colquhoun 1989; St. John Wilson 1992.

3. The Architect as Artist and Poet

Great art . . . is preeminently and finally the expression of the spirits of great men. **John Ruskin.** 1843–1860. *Modern Painters.*

. . . cast away as worthless the shopworn and empirical notion that an architect is an artist— whatever that funny word may mean . . . [the architect] is and imperatively shall be a poet, and an interpreter of the national life of his time. **Louis Sullivan.** Unpublished address to the Chicago Architectural Club, read at the Art Institute, Chicago, May 30, 1899. Burnham Library. Cited in Menocal 1981:194.

Only a very small part of architecture belongs to art: the tomb and the monument. Everything else, everything that serves a purpose, is excluded from the domain of art. **Adolf Loos.** 1910:55.

. . . true architecture is not, for all this, an arid combination of expediency and utility, but remains art—i.e. synthesis, expression. **Antonio Sant'Elia.** 1914. *The New City* in Benton, Benton, and Sharp 1975:72.

You yourselves will create, by yourselves, the true poetic vision of today that I shall show you. I shall talk "technique" and you, you will react "poetry." And I promise you a dazzling poem: the poem of the architecture of modern times. **Le Corbusier.** 1930:36.

The creative artist is by nature and by office the qualified leader in any society, natural, native interpreter of the invisible form of any social order in or under which we choose to live. **Frank Lloyd Wright.** 1935.

The idea, then, that architecture is somehow a "pure" art, one that is practiced by a dreamy-eyed charcoal-wielder in the solitude of his garret studio, is sheer nonsense. **Eugene Raskin.** 1974:20.

All I know is that when I hit a shape that pleases me, I can sing for the rest of the day, and if I'm working on a problem and it doesn't work, I just have to take too many drinks. It's so depressing,

I just don't want to face the world . . . to make beautiful shapes and if I can get them built, it's the greatest satisfaction an artist can have. **Philip Johnson.** Cited in Games 1985.

TRACE   Artistry is one term that is impossible to define, but some of its characteristics are easier. One is the concept of 'spirit' or *genius,* which has already been used freely in chapter 2A and as 'spirit guide' in 4B.2, Vision. It is commonly held, for instance, that "all art depends upon cutting off the practical responses to sensations of ordinary life, thereby setting free a pure and as it were disembodied functioning of the spirit" (Roger Fry (1961), in Frascina and Harrison 1982:91). The artist and original curator of the Solomon R. Guggenheim collection of nonobjective paintings, Hilla von Rebay, was convinced of this characteristic: "Beauty of appearance takes its way to the heart through the medium of intuitive intelligence called spirit. . . . Spirit begins where materialism ends. . . . The vocation of a born genius is to lead to new visions of beauty" (*op. cit.:*145–148).

It was Immanuel Kant's *Critique of Judgment* (1790) that made genius or spirit "the quintessential characteristic of the artist" (Harold Osborne [1970], in Brolin 1985:73, 83, n53). Genius was a quality that Kant saw as innate and not subject to reason or capable of development through 'hard work'. Its concomitant was 'originality', about which Kant says: "genius is a *talent* for producing that for which no definite rule can be given; it is not a mere aptitude for what can be learned by a rule. Hence *originality* must be its first property." (Brolin 1985:74).

And it is with Kant that the most orderly view of architecture as an art arises. Although Kant distinguished judgment of taste from that of purpose, he saw judgment as related to "three kinds of fine art: the art of *speech, formative* art, and the art of the *play of sensations* (as external sense impressions)." He presented formative art as comprised "either of *sensuous truth* or of *sensuous semblance.* The first is called *plastic* art, the second *painting.*" Architecture, along with sculpture, belonged to plastic art as "the art of presenting concepts of things which are possible *only through art,* and the determining of whose form is not nature but an arbitrary end. . . . In architecture the chief point is a certain *use* of the artistic object to which, as the condition, the aesthetic ideas are limited" (Kant 1785:II, §51).

COMMENTARY   The first inklings of architecture as an art start almost two millennia before Kant. Vitruvius was grateful to his parents for his training in architecture (" . . . for having taken care that I should be taught an art"). He saw in it a distinction from the 'impudent assurance' that characterizes businesspeople, and proudly proclaimed: "But for my part, Caesar, I have never been eager to make money from my art, but to have gone on the principle that slender means and a good reputation are preferable to wealth and disrepute." He plays down his own slight fame by hoping only that he "shall become known to posterity" and goes on to declare that it is the gentlemanly thing "to undertake a charge only after being asked," in comparison with those who 'petition' for business (Vitruvius 1960:Book VI, Introduction, 5). Vitruvius hereby put forward the basis for the view of the gentleman architect that emerged as the 'proper' model from the Renaissance, a notion that always had its mavericks, but was not to change substantially until the end of the nineteenth century.

In 1910, when Adolf Loos declared that the art of architecture was only to do with the tomb and the monument, that is, with death/memory where celebration by embellishment is tolerated, those who took notice of him or espoused similar sentiments virtually sealed modernism in a monumental tomb of their own creation. Loos's sentiment was entirely consistent with his stand against ornament, for he saw attempts at 'art' in architecture as *appliqué* rather than as intrinsic. This is precisely what artists say art is *not,* an addendum to an artifact or work, just as architects say that architecture is not something merely added to building. Without defining art, it is clear that there has been an interpretation among architects that the art of architecture is akin to "an art 'without purpose', Art-for-Art's sake ... " as opposed to the utilitarian in which art has no part, a distinction thought "too much in thrall to Kantian aesthetics" (St. John Wilson 1992:36–37).

This dilemma has daunted architects for more than two centuries, and St. John Wilson sees a potential answer to it in reinterpreting 'use' to become the bearer of meaning, so that "between the patient drawing out of the concealed agenda (what the Greeks called 'the hidden truth') and the discipline that will ensure relevance to the power of invention a certain alchemy is required to fuse the rigour of the one with the gift of 'play' of the other" (49). I don't know what else to call *a certain alchemy* other than art, the kind of elixir or 'hit' that makes Philip Johnson "sing for the rest of the day" (see quote above), and every architect the same. And with that we are simply (!) back to square one.

What has confounded the art of architecture is not whether it is an art—for art is there, as almost every architect will testify—but to find a way to let it reign *despite* the functions of architecture. The art of architecture emerges as the grip of function on it is loosened; only then can the *authority* of a situation pass to art. As Carlo Scarpa said in 1976 of his Beaux Arts education in a short paper ("Can architecture be poetry?"), "We had to struggle quite hard to free ourselves from our architectural training. An effort that one always has to make, in order to achieve that sense of moral authority that an individual has to acquire in order to call himself an artist. One always has to emerge from the material channel" (Dal Co and Mazzariol 1985:283). Likewise, function imposes strictures of a highly ordered material kind on architecture, and for architecture to achieve the moral authority to be called art it must struggle *against* functional demands; not to eliminate them, merely to dominate them.

If the art of architecture is authority over objective demands, it is therefore no more or less than a degree of subjective control by the architect, and there can be no art of architecture other than that brought to it by the architect. In this respect, art *is* the architect's signature (see 10B.5, Signature), and any discussion that ignores the living presence of the architect in designing just misses the point. Most icons of functionalism were not purely 'functional' at all, but were artfully chosen *personal* interpretations of utility or purpose. "Although architecture is, by definition, both the art *and* science of building," writes Christopher Alexander's biographer, Stephen Grabow (1983),

> the "science" side of the equation is usually interpreted to mean *applied* science — the realm of structure, materials, construction, and the technological hardware of building operations. . . . Nevertheless, the "art" side of the equation is usually reserved for the question of design — the realm of the synthesis and generation of architectural form. In terms of tradition then, the architect is fundamentally an artist, but one who *understands* science and can *apply* it to the problem of building. . . . (7).

This 'application' to which Grabow alludes is the very act of making decisions about which aspects of science, technology, or the hundred and one factual matters of building are to be given emphasis or priority. There is no *natural* placing of such things; there is no precise size or shape for anything in building; everything is a matter of judgment. Judgment involves esthetic decisions, and the *keenness* of such decisions (rather than their degree) constitutes the art of architecture. But art of a kind that gains critical peer support is not made all the time, neither can it be decided in advance by saying 'Now I will make art'. Paraphrasing what Carlo Scarpa went on to say of poetry: Art is born of the thing itself.

On the matter of *l'art pour l'art,* art for its own sake or as an end in itself, the art of architecture could never achieve total autonomy. Coined by the French eclectic philosopher and educator Victor Cousin, the idea was commonly used in art and architecture from the first half of the nineteenth century. It was to reach its apogee in the De Stijl movement and the art 'constructions' and declarations of Cornelis van Eesteren, Theo van Doesburg, and Piet Mondrian, and the designs and architecture of Gerrit Rietveld. But even these purists still recognized, albeit reluctantly, that the art of their architecture was limited by utilitarian concerns. Even the most extreme works of architects, such as those by Peter Eisenman and Bernard Tschumi, or any of the so-called New Spirit architects (Cook and Llewellyn-Jones 1991), are similarly constrained.

All attempts at artistic authenticity in architecture that rely on autonomy and independence from purpose are merely wishful thinking, because it never was and continues not to be possible to get 'outside' or beyond the utility of architecture in order to make of it an art in some sense separate or pure.

FURTHER SOURCES   Brolin 1985; Colquhoun 1981, 1989; Conrads 1964; Cuff 1991; Frampton 1980, 1982; Heidegger 1936; Jaffé 1967; Rasmussen 1959; Scruton 1979, 1983.

4. The Architect as Scientist and Technologist

Ars sine Scientia Nihil Est [art without science amounts to nothing]. **Jean Mignot.** c1391.

Architecture requires us continually to reinterpret and revalue technology in human and social terms. **Sir Phillip Dowson.** In Emanuel 1980:214.

Architects and scientists are alike in that their vision of the world depends as much upon what they are looking *at* as upon what their previous experiences have taught them to look *for.* During revolutions, however, scientists actually see new and different things when looking in familiar places. The question is whether architects do the same. **Stephen Grabow.** 1983:xiii.

What distinguishes science from the humane disciplines . . . is that in science there is a pattern of *discovery.* It was one of the early achievements of modern art history to reject the scientific and progressivist model of the evolution of art. . . . There is nothing *towards* which art moves (in the way science moves towards truth). **Roger Scruton.** 1983:172.

To recall Schopenhauer's distinction, the object of science is a description of the universal that contains many particulars; the object of art is the making of particulars that contain a universal. The distinction appears to be mainly between "describing" things and "making" them. **Stephen Grabow.** 1983:215.

The dogmatic belief that the scientific 'world-picture is at last commanding general recognition, independently of the good will of the individual researcher, independently of nationalities and of centuries—indeed independently of the human race itself' [M. Planck, 1908], is one of the greatest misconceptions of modern times. **Dalibor Vésely.** 1985:24.

Scientists are like architects who build buildings of different sizes and different shapes and who can be judged only *after* the event, i.e. only after they have finished their structure. It may stand up, it may fall down—nobody knows. **Paul Feyerabend.** 1988:2.

The scientific search for truthful and natural conditions . . . offered a meaningful base for the creation of man-made objects. This search contained an *a priori* stipulation of the essence of the object and therefore of objective truth. **Marc Angelil.** 1989:64.

Magical technique is based on imagination emphasizing mystical symbolism whereas material technique operates on rationality oriented towards technical "know-how. . . . " Magical and material technique evolved into science and technology. Material technique developed from craftsmanship and the experience of the artisan to mechanical art furthering discovery and invention. Magical technique developed into the natural sciences engaging in the explanation and study of natural phenomenon [sic]. **Marc Angelil.** 1989:64.

TRACE   Deriving from the Latin *scientia,* knowledge, science appeared to appropriate the world of factual things and leave the world of no-things (see introduction) to art, theology, and philosophy. But the 'facts' of science are at best ambiguous, as the history of science shows; some of the greatest breakthroughs occurred in contradiction to facts as they were then known. The quotation by Jean Mignot above comes from the minutes of architectural conferences in Milan held to determine progress on the construction of Milan Cathedral. It was a matter of distinct preference at that time to submit design to the rule of geometry, which was thought to ensure the proper marriage of esthetics and structure. "*Ars* here meant practical building knowhow; *scientia,* the rational theory of architecture based on geometry" (Kostof 1977:86).

Technology derives from the Greek *techne,* art or craft, and *technologia,* the systematic treatment of art or craft, with 'technic' (L. *technicus*) having the now-rare meaning of 'pertaining to an art'. The term technology today is a generalization, displacing the 'scientific' study of the so-called 'practical arts' by the whole apparatus of specialized production and methods, and their products. The history of science and technology is a history of technique, according to Marc Angelil (1989), whose writings are well worth reading, both for his broad understanding and his architectural insights.

In architecture, Vitruvius's *Ten Books* (1486) is a compendium of ancient technical know-how or technique for the architect. So too is Joseph Gwilt's massive *Encyclopedia* (1867), first published in 1842. In 1802, the French architect J. B. Rondelet wrote his *Theoretical and Practical Treatise on the Art of Building,* in which he claimed architecture was not an art but a science whose main aim was solid and comfortable construction (Collins 1965:204). Gwilt claimed that the ancient architect Pythius "considered it absolutely necessary for an architect to have as accurate a knowledge of all the arts and sciences as is rarely acquired even by a professor devoted to one." Gwilt's book enabled the gentleman architect "to merge the swiftly developing technology produced by the Industrial Revolution with more established and traditional concerns" writes architect Michael Mostoller in the foreword to the 1982 edition.

COMMENTARY   Given the above definitions and what has happened in architecture since the nineteenth century, the previous section could well have been titled *Architect as Artist and Technologist* and this *Architect as Scientist and Poet,* or perhaps artist with science and poet with technologist, so intertwined are the concepts even today. Beginning with the statement, "I do not assert that Architecture is an art derived from reason only, — a branch of pure science," Viollet-le-Duc (1872:Lecture 5, I.145) went on to say that the respective values of 'periods of Art' (styles, in fact) could be appreciated only through the method of "reasoning and analysis, — true science, which classes and selects after having compared. . . ." He thereby made science and scientific method the armature of artistic endeavor. And this was to remain the core of architectural thinking for another century, surviving even the momentous upheaval of the Modern Movement, despite the occasional severe oscillation toward Art more than Science.

Thus Hans Poelzig could say in 1906: "*Every real tectonic constructional form has an absolute nucleus,* to which the decorative embellishment . . . lends a varying charm. First, however, the absolute element has to be found . . . " (this and the following extracts are from Conrads 1964, *passim*). And in 1914 the conflict between art and science, broadly defined, could find expression in the Deutscher Werkbund; Hermann Muthesius and Henry van de Velde promoted opposing views over the emphasis on technique in craft of individual creative action (art-poetry) versus universal mass production (science-technology), which the formation of the Bauhaus in 1919 attempted to reconcile in the firm linking of art and craft. The 'science of materials' featured in the early Bauhaus curriculum as did art history as the study of 'historical working methods and techniques' and lectures 'in all areas of art and science', and by 1923 Oskar Schlemmer consolidated its median position in the manifesto for the first exhibition (pulped for declaring support for socialism) by declaring its ideal "of activity that embraces, penetrates, and unites art, science, and technology . . . [with which it] will construct the 'art-edifice' of Man, which is but an allegory of the cosmic system."

By 1926 the Bauhaus was changing under Gropius to a laboratory for experiment and production, and the shift in thinking generally was proceeding rapidly to mass production and the saving grace of mechanization (technology) in all spheres of life, including architecture. In 1928 Erich Mendelsohn cautioned: "Technology ends with man himself. For once technology becomes an end in itself mechanical theory leads to an over-evaluation of technical inventions and makes of technology an idol." In 1928, Hannes Meyer, by now director of the Bauhaus, presented a most succinct yet comprehensive summary of modern processes in building design as his educational program, under the title *bauen,* in which the architect was to be a specialist in organization and building "nothing but organization: social, technical, economic, psychological organization." Then came Richard Buckminster Fuller's near-incomprehensible prospectus of 1932 for a universal architecture combining art, science, and technology. In 1950 Ludwig Mies van der Rohe, by now at the Illinois Institute of Technology, preached an architecture of its time linked to technology, and in 1957 Conrad Wachsman returned to Germany and soon produced seven theses built around science and technology.

By the 1960s the science of architecture had gathered momentum and was becoming manifest as the *machine esthetic,* at first in the unbuilt experiments of Archigram—Plug-In City by Peter Cook in 1964, Fun Palace by Cedric Price, and Moving Cities by Rod Herron 1967—and then their real-life cousin, Centre Pompidou, Paris, won in an international competition in 1971 by Richard Rogers (a product of the Architectural Association) and Renzo Piano, and completed in 1977. Buckminster Fuller's dome experiments and patents resulted in his pavilion for the United States at Expo '67 in Montreal, but domes as a pseudo-technical dream world accrued an ever-growing following from the late-fifties, and peaked between ten and fifteen years later with their use by students and commune builders (Jencks and Chaitkin 1982). The technical mode continued throughout the seventies, beginning with Expo '70 in Osaka, followed by a wide range of 'slick-skin', high-tech, tubed, capsuled, atriumed, and column-free buildings with vast investments in services and climate control. There have been some quite exquisite works built in a highly wrought machine esthetic, not the least being Rogers and Partners' headquarters for Lloyd's Insurance, London, 1978 to 1986; the headquarters for Hongkong and Shanghai Bank, Hong Kong, by Foster Associates, 1980 to 1986; and the Institut du Monde Arabe, Paris, by Jean Nouvel, 1984 to 1987. But there has been a decline since the mid-eighties in this mode of expression (for reasons largely to do with fashion), if not in the science of architecture itself.

Some might think that linking technology and science in one section, and then lumping all these intentions, projects, and buildings together under the label 'science of architecture', too naive or too gross a generalization. Certainly "to think of science as motivated ultimately by practical goals, as judged or justified by bridges and bombs and the control of nature, is to confuse science with technology. Science seeks knowledge without regard to practical consequences, and is concerned with prediction not as a guide for behaviour but as a test of truth" (Nelson Goodman, 1972, in Frascina and Harrison 1982:191). But the science of architecture *does* seek the truths of scientific understanding in its research and development, and then it finds architectural applications for them, just as the results of pure science are utilized in applied science. To hold too steadfastly to such a hard definition as Goodman's suggests that there is something absolute called science; in fact there are many things called science. I am inclined to Paul Feyerabend's 'definition', that "science is what I am doing and what my colleagues are doing and what my and their peers and the public at large regard as 'scientific'. Given this situation it does not surprise us at all that there is 'scientific' wrestling and 'scientific' dogfood" (1988:257). Likewise, there is 'scientific' architecture.

So, armed with this soft definition of science, it is not difficult to see that much of the structure, fabric, and servicing of modern architecture (whether as the machine esthetic or not), both internally and externally, involves strict obedience to physical laws, and that it is impossible not to see it as science. The science of architecture has determined the truth of why foundations settle, membranes fail, artificial lighting affects colors, thermal comfort varies, corrosion among differing metals occurs, acoustic conditions aid or hinder speech, thermal fatigue fractures glass, friction coefficients are important in flooring, glare creates discomfort, refrigerants affect the ozone layer, plastic fabrics and coatings affect health, and on and on. As Alan Colquhoun remarked, "with the development of modern science, the word "art" was progressively restricted to the case of artefacts that did not depend on the general laws of physical science, but continued to be based on tradition and the ideal of the final form of the work as a fixed ideal" (1981:43). Nonetheless, art may still be the ideal and inspirational edge of architecture, but only science and its instrumental arm, technology, can keep it there. Moreover, without the science of architecture, design could only proceed by tradition, yet even this would not develop were there not some intrinsic fit, the *truth* of which is *proved* over time.

The issue for theory concerning the science of architecture is allied with what Paul Feyerabend says of the scientist: "The task of the scientist . . . is no longer 'to search for the truth', or 'to praise god', or 'to systematize observations', or 'to improve predictions'. These are but side effects of an activity to which his attention is now mainly directed and which is *to make the weaker case the stronger*' as the sophists said, *and thereby to sustain the motion of the whole*" (1988:21). If the architect is the scientist in the science of architecture, then it is also the task of the architect to make the weaker case the stronger and technology the means of mediation. It seems we have no other choice.

FURTHER SOURCES   Banham 1962, 1969; Collins 1971; Grabow 1983; Heidegger 1953; Kollar 1980.

5. Movements: Espoused Theory or Theory-in-Use?

A movement cannot subsist if its apostles denounce their followers as being formalistic imitators and snobs who have ignored their fundamental truths. Every movement needs its prophets; but if their good news is to be shared at any socially significant scale, there is also a need for priests who can institutionalize the message. **Juan Pablo Bonta.** 1979:49

Regionalism . . . is not so much a collective effort as it is the output of a talented individual working with a profound commitment to a particular local culture. Needless to say, the phenomenon is antipathetic to internationalism and to the cult of the 'star'. **Kenneth Frampton.** 1982:81.

TRACE   Of all the definitions of 'movement', the closest to that used by architect historians and writers is that of a divisioning of some fluid state. Hence, the series of actions and endeavors by a body of persons tending more or less continuously toward some end, or the way things are 'moving' at particular time or in a particular field. Both usages seem to have emerged during the first half of the nineteenth century.

In architecture the term seems to have been given life by Charles Jencks in *Architecture 2000* (1971): "If we consider the question of internal coherence in such a period [1920–1960] we can see that there is *a natural tendency for certain concepts and types of architecture to cluster together into a coherent whole.* This does not mean that all such clusters or traditions are monolithically consistent, but rather that they do tend to be relatively congruous" (36). Jencks calls this system (after Roland Barthes and Charles Osgood) a 'semantic space' or 'structure'. He goes into some simple analysis of several architectural 'traditions' and the ideas many held in common, saying, "If we analyse these ideas, as well as those of other extant *movements* [emphasis added], we will begin to see how they form self-consistent clusters that have a common core and that tend to be opposed to other clusters" (40). On the same page is a diagram of three antinomial pairs, labeled: *unselfconscious vs. self-conscious, intuitive vs. logical,* and *activist vs. idealist* (40). In its final form, Jencks creates an evolutionary diagram of the six traditions, with a viscous action-reaction swelling to 'blobs' representing intense activity and narrowing to febrile bands as interest wanes. The whole operates on a 25-year cycle in accordance with the ideas of Claude Lévi-Strauss's *The Scope of Anthropology* (1967). With this began a decade of feverish taxonomy by Jencks of *movements* within these six traditions.

COMMENTARY   Ritual and habit are acceded to and adopted on the assumption that they bring to the processes of living some sense and meaning, some structure, a way of engaging with events so that helplessness and lack of control do not seem so inevitable. So it is with architects who team up in practice or in theorists' categories as 'movements' or, to use Frampton's more guarded term, 'indicators of the ideological set'.

There is some recent experimental evidence that ritual may be congruent with fear and the need for affiliation, as the American social psychologist Stanley Schacter has reported: "Subjects with high fear were almost twice as likely to seek the company of others [that is, to affiliate] than were those with low fear" (Price *et al.* 1982:10–11, 306–307). One might wonder whether historians who seek company *for* others in affiliating architects into movements is a case of fear-abatement on the part of the historians; an attempt to forestall the chaos that for them would ensue without such orderliness. In Jencks's case, though, it was probably more that he saw a good thing and stuck to it; architecture movements were on the move.

The last chapter of Kenneth Frampton's *Modern Architecture a Critical History* (1980) entitled "Place, production and architecture: towards a critical theory of building" highlighted the frailty of many architectural ideas arising during the sixties. It also pointed up the ambivalence of the roles the architectural profession created for itself in the seventies, and issued a challenge for architecture to once more unite indivisibly the acts of building, dwelling, cultivating, and being; a desire in fact for a renewed state of grace. Frampton was to repeat this essay along with three others two years later in his *Modern Architecture and the Critical Present* (1982), and to include eight critiques of the earlier book, to which he then added a fifth essay as a response, "The isms of contemporary architecture" (60–83). Frampton's 'isms' were another attempt to classify architecture into movements, but he discerned only five: Neo-Productivism, Neo-Rationalism, Structuralism, Populism, and Regionalism.

Leaving aside Regionalism, which was geographical, Frampton saw four principles determining each of the other four categories: "*technical* (Productivism), *formal* (Rationalism), *anthropological* (Structuralism), and *contextual* (Populism)." He qualified his use of the term 'regionalism' in that "Regionalism intersects with the other *isms* of this 'taxonomy' so as to remain potentially open to all of them, but only on the condition that they are subordinate to the culture of the region itself. . . . If any Regionalist principle can be finally isolated, it is surely the commitment to *place* rather than *space;* or in Heideggerian terminology, to *Raum* rather than *spatium in extensio.* This stress on place may also be construed as affording the political *space of public appearance* as formulated by Hannah Arendt" (82).

The plethora of movements that arises from the Jencksian system covering 1920 to 1960 is bewildering: Functionalism, Heroic, Beaux-Arts, Utopian, Folk; Fascist, Revival, War Minimal; Parametric, Bureaucratic, Pop, Consumer Modern, Mobile; Megaform, Cybernetic, Neo-Fascist, Revolutionist, Adhocist; Space-Colonial, Semiological, Biomorphic, and Service-State Anonymous. Ten years after the first, Jencks developed another evolutionary tree, this time for his book *Post-Modern Architecture* (1977:80), and covering the period 1955 to 1980, but with six different traditions to those of 1977 and a host more movements. Then, three years later, he compared Modern (1920–1960), Late-Modern (1960–) and Post-Modern (1960–) in a detailed chart according to *thirty* variables, in order "to bring out the complexity of the situation." The chart was qualified with the comment that "if one tried to list all of these notions the list would become impossibly large—in fact a book," and is thereafter supported by a fifty-page pictorial essay littered with colorfully descriptive tags (1980:32). Two years later still, Jencks published *another* evolutionary tree covering 1960 to 1980, this time with yet another six 'traditions' in place of the original and a further batch of movements (1982:20). By now the complexity was more than apparent, and the number of pages devoted to it was rapidly approaching the number of individual works surveyed!

The taxonomic systems of style by Jencks or Frampton—or anyone else for that matter—raise questions about their eventual usefulness. I have not read a student essay in twenty years that has employed any of Jencks's categories. I have occasionally seen and heard certain terms coined by Jencks, but only as catch-all descriptions, no more and possibly less than terms purveyed by Reyner Banham or Peter Collins before him. As in many good architecture books, I suspect the parade of images and wit is appealing and convenient, but of more critical use to the author in his own writings than to others. Most architects, if tagged as belonging to such-and-such a movement, will resist such close categorization; like 'pointing the bone' in Australian aboriginal practice, being so tagged can apparently sap your strength and individuality. Which brings the discussion to the question of how such taxonomic assessments are made. On what basis are buildings assigned their categories? It is obviously a matter of judgment by the historian based on observing the signs that buildings and their attributes present. It is sometimes based on what architects say about their buildings. And it is sometimes a combination of both, in which case the historian has to decide which to favor. Those inclined to obnubilate will favor the most impressive (Heath 1991:170–172).

The signs, or visual cues, of a built work differ from the signs used by the designer to describe a work, and both differ from the signs used in designing the work. Dana Cuff (1991) maintains that when architects present justifications of their actions, they are stating their 'espoused theory', as against their 'theory-in-use', which is what they actually use in designing. If this view is modified to accommodate what has already been said about theory not actually guiding practice, it is more accurate to say that architects espouse two versions of the same conventional theory: one public and homogenized for the telling; the other private and the very mediation of designing itself, and quite ad-hoc. Jon Lang (1987) makes precisely the same distinction in remarking that "the professed normative position of a designer often differs from its behavioral correlate—practice." This words versus deeds stance of Cuff, Lang, and others, is not a dialectic but a monologue in two time frames: either the position professed first and the practice following, or the practice first and the professed position following.

When the historian categorizes works, it is the espoused theory that a designer's words or buildings signify and it is the espoused theory of the historian that regurgitates them as *movements*. So, movements are at least three removes from the motivations of designers. To tag a designer as belonging to a movement and thereby to imply a way of designing is at least four removes from the reality. Such shifts, or 'removes', are precisely what Roland Barthes shows in the 'semiological chain' he uses to explain his mythification system in *Mythologies* (1957:119–126). Creating 'movements' is a form of *language-robbery*, to use Barthes's term, and is descriptive of a mythic mode of understanding, a perhaps-useful fiction, rather than a mode of realistic description. Just as theory does not guide practice, so movements do not reflect practice. Neither do they predict future practices, as Jencks implies with his *evolutionary* trees. There is no evolution in a quasi-biological sense going on at all, and discussions of post-this and post-that are merely strategic conveniences.

What architectural theory—as against architectural history—needs to do is to find ways to employ language for criticism that do not take for granted the historicist impulse. The mediation of theory-talk would then be directly transitive, rather than retrospective or prospective, a form of practice. Does such a language exist?

FURTHER SOURCES   Chapter 7A; Johnson 1991.

CHAPTER

Ethics and Architecture

Overview

The sense of propriety dictates the following rule, that every building ought to have an expression corresponding to its destination. A palace ought to be sumptuous and grand; a private dwelling, neat and modest; a play-house, gay and splendid; and a monument, gloomy and melancholy. . . . **Lord Kames.** 1762. *Elements of Criticism.* Cited in Archer 1987:71.

The validity of ethics in general—of any ethics—presumes that there is some answer to this kind of question ["How do you know that what this principle dictates is imperative to do?"]. And it is unclarity about this matter of the foundation on which moral principles rest which leaves all questions of morals open to the skeptical doubt and to the cynical attack. Strictly, this topic does not belong to ethics itself, and discussions of it have been variously labeled metaphysics of ethics, ethical theory, moral philosophy, and—currently—metaethics. **Clarence I. Lewis** 1969:15.

We must guard against the accusation of naturalism at every step by insisting that the moral world and all that is in it is 'non-natural'. This will remind us that moral qualities are not ordinary qualities, moral judgements not ordinary statements and moral insight not eyesight. **P. H. Nowell-Smith.** 1954:48–49.

A book on the ethics of architecture would be about the architect's responsibilities in practice: responsibilities to society and to his fellow architects. To design well is one of those responsibilities. **Bruce Allsopp.** 1977:11.

191

It could be said, quite truly, that the social value of a building, of a school as compared with a casino, for example, is an important consideration. It is; but it is not an architectural consideration. **Bruce Allsopp.** 1977:11.

Every ugly or senseless building is an insult to the man passing in front of it. Every building should be embellishing and adding to its culture. **Hassan Fathy.** Quoted in Charles 1989:11.

Aristotle stated in the *Nicomachean Ethics* that moral goodness "is the child of habit, from which it has got its very name, ethics being derived from *ethos*, 'habit', by a slight alteration in the quantity of the *e*. This is an indication that none of the moral virtues is implanted in us by nature, since nothing that nature creates can be taught by habit to change the direction of its development" (Book 2:I). Ethics is the world of obligation in which human discretion plays a part, the world of 'ought' and 'should'. At its most emphatic it is the world of 'must', of dictates of behavior by which discretion is nearly eliminated. Most people associate ethics with a set of standards by which people or groups moderate their behavior or adjudicate what is correct or legitimate in their personal, business, political, or social pursuits.

The plural of *ethos*, habits or 'manners', ties it to the prevailing sentiment of a people or community, system or institution, and thereby embraces not only the science of morals but human duty in its widest extent, including law. Morality and ethics are thus etymologically and functionally connected with accepted social behavior. But, whereas morality concerns those aspects of ethics that can be formalized into obligations, by virtue of which it creates explicit boundaries and standards of behavior, "the notion of what is ethical at any moment is vague and not often explicit" (Bell 1990:23). As a philosophical term, ethics is the study of fundamental principles and concepts found or considered desirable in any field of human endeavor, and is necessarily a theoretical study, differing from the popular notion of it as a practical guide to living primarily in the way it treats its subject matter. It is well not to overemphasize the distinction between the theoretical and the popular, though, for, as Flew remarks, "in so far as the man in the street thinks about his own moral views or those of others, or ponders on their justification, or compares them with rival attitudes, to that extent he is a moral philosopher" (Flew 1979, 'ethics'). And insofar as 'architects in the street' do the same, so are they moral philosophers.

Curiously though, in his *Morality and Architecture* of 1977, the historian David Watkin does not make clear what morality in architecture is; neither does he clarify what those he writes about think morality is. Nonetheless, Watson implies that morality in architecture is to do with attitudes about the 'rightness of things'. He traces moral thinking in architecture as an almost unbroken line of development, starting with the writings of the English Gothic Revival architect and theorist Augustus Welby Northmore Pugin in the nineteenth century, through to those of the historian Nikolaus Pevsner in the twentieth.

For Watkin, there are three persistent explanations for architecture: the English view of it in terms of religion, sociology, or politics; the German view of it as representing the spirit of the age; and the French view of a rational or technological justification (3). The first, or English, view sees architecture "as an instrument for the attainment of social policy employed to achieve supposedly 'moral' ends," and also as something truthful, from which it follows that "it must be immoral for it to tell a lie" (4). The German, or zeitgeist, view is that architecture is an expression either of a temporal 'collective (un)consciousness' or of a 'will' that exists independent of the individual designer, and therefore regards morality as pertaining to collective rather than individual endeavor; hence it favors the classical vision of types, standardization, and mass production (5–8). The third, or French, view sees architecture as a dutiful and sincere expression of purpose (program) and structure, "the natural outcome of a rational intellectual discipline," the most ardent advocate of which was architect Eugène-Emmanuel Viollet-le-Duc (8). But history does not provide sufficiently precise guidance for moral thinking in architecture today, so we must return to conceptual modes of thinking.

Aside from their colorless grammatical use as auxiliaries, the nuances of meaning attached to 'should' and 'ought' arise from a sense of *duty*, whereas those of 'must', 'will', or 'shall' arise from a *resolve* or determination to effect some state or stance, and are usually accompanied by the power to carry out that resolve. An 'ought' carries an imperative, a plea to act in the best interests of whoever or whatever is its focus, but any force it has is rhetorical rather than mandatory, unlike a 'will' or a 'shall', backed up as they usually are by law in one form or another. Ethics thus resists all claims to naturalism or inevitability; it is a world entirely constructed from human intelligence through human interpretation for human application.

Philosophically there are three areas of concern in ethics. First, those everyday *principles*, virtues, and attitudes that guide our actions and are analyzed in an attempt to explain their basic tenets. Second, the necessary *conditions* for the sustained operation of any discipline, that give it purpose or meaning and justify its existence such that any moral principle or virtue may be assessed for the contribution it makes to that end. These are both *normative* concerns. Third, there are moral questions related not to content but to the *logic* by which judgments are made or beliefs held; this is the realm of *meta-ethics*, which in many respects precedes and conditions the normative (Flew 1979).

There are also three broad camps in moral philosophy, each with a set of principles to which adherents are committed (after Stone 1987). All three are labeled by Christopher D. Stone as Moral Monists in that they aim "to produce, and to defend against all rivals, a single coherent and complete set of principles capable of governing all moral quandaries," and "to yield for each quandary one right answer" (116). First, there are those who focus their morality on the outcomes or consequences of an action and belong to various schools going under the label *utilitarian*, possibly the most famous normative ethical doctrine in English-speaking moral philosophy, the three prime exponents of which are Jeremy Bentham, John Stuart Mill, and Henry Sidgwick. This has also been called the *consequentialist* position. Conseqentialists generally submit that an act is good if it brings about some improvement to a state of affairs over which they have influence and if the 'betterment' so gained is usually related to pleasure or welfare (often construed as the greatest happiness for the greatest number). Within this camp most discussion revolves around what are good acts and how various welfares are to be compared.

Those in the second camp are committed to ideals or duties that deal with what a situation 'ought' to be, or what one 'ought' to do in particular circumstances through being morally bound to do so, irrespective (or nearly so) of consequences. Within this camp discussion centers on the origin of duties, their province, and how principles arising from these duties determine what ought to happen in specific circumstances regardless of the consequences. This can be labeled the *deontologist* position (Gk. *deon, deont-,* that which is binding); typical of this approach are Immanuel Kant and the various neo-Kantian schools. Deontologists might argue for the deterrent value or incentive value in their ethical position, but would say that no such value was *necessarily* a principal force in their ethical formulation.

The third camp is of a contractual kind; moral limitations are imposed according to rules agreed to operate in a hypothetical original position, and rehearsals of sorts take place in imagining how one might act in concrete situations. Underlying this is some notion of social justice based upon agreement between individuals or a governing power in which certain liberties are freely offered in exchange for advantages gained from social organization or proper government. This usually entails ensuring the rights of the least-advantaged group in any situation. Exponents of this view are Hobbes, Rousseau, and John Rawls. This can be called the *contractarian* position (Stone 1987).

A great flaw of the orthodox monist view is that no one overriding principle can embrace every circumstance in which we ethically operate. Ethics involves a number of activities, notably in the areas of taste, preference, and conduct, in which choice is paramount. Stone's answer to the delusive single-schema ambitions of moral monism is what Stone labels Moral Pluralism, which is "a conception of the moral realm as consisting in several different schemata, side by side" (1987:132), although he cautions that it not be confused with moral relativism, which seeks to confine moral judgment to a specific group or place, be it a minority or majority. Instead, Stone's form of pluralism "conceives the realm of morals to be partitioned into several planes . . . intellectual frameworks that support the analysis and solution of particular moral problems . . . [each plane] composed of two fundamental elements . . . an ontological commitment, that is to say, a foundational judgment as to which things are to be recognized and dealt with . . . [and] its governance— essentially the rules that apply . . . the body of rules, principles, and so on, to which that version of the world is subject" (133–134). The ethical world of architecture is most like that of Stone's moral pluralism, a variety of intellectual frameworks consisting of sets of beliefs and judgments about the world and a body of rules or guidelines for administering them.

Stone's advocacy of pluralism over monism is the basis of his environmental ethics relating to nonhumans, wherein the stance is "that (animal) life does count, but that not all life counts equally, or comes under the same rules or considerations" (Stone 1987:137). His answer to moral issues is to equate pluralism's domains of interest with 'maps', each presenting a discrete domain of information, and to consider their governance as being leavened by the information available in the differing 'moral fabrics' of those domains. This leads him to project differing governances across different domains based on principles for those domains arising from their 'logical texture'. This is a concept he relates to the degrees of precision with which concepts can be discussed within a domain, or the standards of meaningfulness or rules of procedure they might possess.

Architectural ethics turns on identifying the limits of each of its domains, determining the principles that might be applied in any analysis, but primarily on isolating its 'textural variables', those factors and their conditions of governance peculiar to architecture as a discipline. Stone's position is perhaps most valuable for architecture because his approach is one of the very few, which deals with the rights of nonhumans—animals and natural objects such as trees. The step to buildings is not difficult to imagine, although it will not be attempted here. His thesis offers a way of thinking about the built environment and about the relationship between architects and buildings that is worth considering, and it underscores aspects of the topics raised in this chapter.

What, then, are the *oughts* and *ought nots* of architecture? In which directions should architecture be heading or be encouraged, and why? What imperatives are there in architecture that *ought* to be acceded to lest the profession fall into disrepute or irrelevance? The territory of these questions is the subject of this section.

As a further lead in to the philosophical implications of ethics in architecture, it is worth making a precis of an account Stone relates about a bison struggling to escape its plunge into an ice-covered river, taken from the magazine *Natural History.* The tale recounts the drama that ensued as the bison tried to extricate itself: the indifference of amateur photographers capturing its struggle on film, the "let nature take its course" attitude of the park ranger that placed it in the wider context of natural events, the intervention and attempted rescue by a snowmobile team ("friends of the bison," in effect) and their "at least put it out of its misery" attitude after they failed, and the haranguing over cruelty dished out to the Park Service by a radio commentator who declared the question of whether or not to intervene a moral one and that the Service was at fault for not doing so (Stone 1987:155–156). The difficulty is to decide who was right, because there are no universally agreed moral principles governing such circumstances and, therefore, each player was 'right' in his or her own terms.

By way of an architectural example paralleling that of Stone's bison, the following scenario is one that has no doubt been enacted many times over in cities all around the world. A building project is proposed in an older precinct of a city that contains buildings over a hundred years old. Amalgamation of smaller land holdings is considered essential to the viability of the project, but involves the incorporation and possible demolition of several buildings of heritage significance. The development is presently construed as a six-storey podium with twin thirty-storey towers in what would be best described esthetically as 'mainstream developer's modern'. The existing precinct is largely three to eight storeys in height. The critical issue turns on whether to preserve the older buildings and the precinct intact, incorporate them in some way into the new development, or demolish the lot and build anew. What is the correct stance to be adopted? Are there moral issues involved?

Paraphrasing Stone's struggling bison, one stance, favored by the "friends of the historic buildings," the preservationists, is to focus on the heritage buildings themselves and their specific singular attributes, individual history, ornamentation, detail, and workmanship. This stance argues their retention as gems. Another stance by an overarching heritage body places the particular buildings into the wider context of heritage buildings and looks at their merit relative to similar buildings among the stock of heritage items, comparing their uniqueness or representativeness, worth on a relative scale, and special significance in the broad historical spectrum. This view accepts that their demolition will not greatly diminish the supply of examples of the period—the equivalent of letting nature take its course. Another stance by professional institutes considers the esthetic quality of the individual buildings in their precinct, examines their townscape contribution, continuity, ambience, scale, and character, and argues for their retention in conjunction with reducing the scale and changing the detail of the new buildings, making the development a model of "sensitive" urban design. Each stance has its own set of concepts and values, and describes its concerns accordingly, each presenting in Stone's terms some valid "editorial viewpoint" (Stone 1987:155–157). Yet, at this stage of their description, these stances cannot be adjudicated; they need principles from which certain criteria might be developed and against which they may be compared.

Consequentialist principles might eliminate all three because of the greater benefit to be had from the new project. Deontological principles might favor the second or third viewpoint because of certain ideas about what constitutes "goodness" in urban design. Contractarian principles might embrace any or none of the three views according to how social or cultural benefit were construed (there might be a compensation or trade-off in monetary terms, for example). Such would be the monistic approaches. The pluralist approach, on the other hand, might accommodate all three viewpoints by advocating incorporating parts or all of the old buildings in a revised and sympathetic new development, or it might introduce other arguments altogether as workable rationales for what to do. The moral pluralist would argue that some combination of these views is adequate under the circumstances, rather than being doctrinaire about any one of them. And the pluralist would negotiate, using theory as a means to mediate a solution acceptable to the important parties.

Part A of this chapter examines a range of foundational moral issues that are important to theoretical stances concerning architecture. Part B looks at certain aspects of the application of moral principles and judgments as they might be applied in architecture.

A. Ethical Foundations in Architecture

1. The Basis of Architectural Ethics

... what we want of practical reasoning (as preachers and art critics are aware) is more often to identify and eliminate the bad and the ugly, an endeavor that does not require, and may not even be advanced by, a full-blown theory of the Good or the Beautiful. Indeed, I doubt that the typical knot in our moral lives comes in the form of deciding which of two alternatives is morally mandatory. Practically speaking, the issue is more likely to be, which of several alternatives is morally impermissible? ... What we want, in order to identify the boundaries of our permissible—and praiseworthy—conduct, is something much like a map of the moral terrain. **Christopher Stone.** 1987:139.

Ethics deals with means, ends, and their relationships. **David Bell** 1990:25.

There is one imperative [a self-governing creature] cannot heed—the imperative to heed no imperatives. **Clarence I. Lewis.** 1969:73.

You are free, therefore choose—that is to say, invent. No rule of general morality can show you what you ought to do. **Jean-Paul Sartre.** *Existentialism As a Humanism.* Cited in Solomon 1977:490.

No one can tell what the painting of tomorrow will be like; one cannot judge a painting until it is done. What has that to do with morality? We are in the same creative situation. We can never speak of a work of art as irresponsible; when we are discussing a canvas by Picasso, we understand very well that the composition became what it is at the same time when he was painting it, and that his works are part and parcel of his entire life.

It is the same upon the plane of morality. There is this in common between art and morality, that in both we have to do with creation and invention. We cannot decide *a priori* what it is that should be done. **Jean-Paul Sartre.** *Existentialism As a Humanism.* Cited in Solomon 1977:491.

The idea of reconstruction—as opposed to mere urban renewal—points, therefore, to a practical-moral project. For there exists a different relation between means and ends in reconstruction than in urban renewal. The aim of reconstruction, unlike that of urban renewal, is *the ethical rectitude of a community* [emphasis added] and not a particular end-product. **Demetri Porphyrios.** "Cities of Stone." In Porphyrios 1984:19.

Whenever you propose to do anything, you should stop and ask yourself—'If everyone did this, what would the world be like?' You will soon discover the right answer. **Nicholas Monsarrat.**

TRACE   As the overview makes clear, 'ethics' comes from the Greek *ethikos — ethos* meaning 'habit, custom, character', and is the science of morals, that branch of philosophy concerned with human character and conduct. It is also a *system* of morals, covering rules of behavior; and it may also be a treatise on morals as elaborate as a philosophical text or as brief as a professional code of conduct. Moral philosophy began in earnest with Kant, whose views were subsequently criticized by his much younger contemporary, Hegel, and later by a new breed of Aristotelians, like Hans-Georg Gadamer, Alasdair MacIntyre, and Charles Taylor, as well as other moral theorists.

Moral judgments were brought to architecture during the nineteenth century by architect-theorists such as Augustus Welby Northmore Pugin and John Ruskin in Great Britain, and Eugène-Emmanuel Viollet-le-Duc in France. They put forward rationales for the development of a modern style reflecting what they saw as the spirit of a changing age and technological necessity, or as a force for social good, as if an utterly natural relationship existed between these and architecture. They did not critically examine the terms or concepts they espoused. As the discipline evolved from a 'gentleman's calling' to a corporate profession with formal education, notions prevalent since the Renaissance of what was good and bad, or right and wrong, remained undifferentiated between societal norms and artistic criticism. The morality that did develop in architecture stemmed largely from esthetic judgments made from within a religious ethics advocating one or another version of the good life, exemplified by Pugin's belief in the primary connection between truth in architecture and truth in religion, which was the main argument in his *Contrasts* of 1836 (Watkin 1977). Or it solidified into the uncritical codification of matters of competency and practice based upon a utilitarian view of peaceful coexistence regarding conflicting interests, unfair competition, and professional conduct.

COMMENTARY   Throughout the *Critique of Practical Reason* (1787), which deals with the moral law and moral action in accordance with that law, Kant elaborates upon the *imperative* as the operative force on the will. The notion of the imperative appears in the earlier *Grundelgung zur Metaphysik der Sitten* (Groundwork [or Foundation] of the Metaphysic of Morals, 1785):

> The conception of an objective principle, so far as it constrains a will, is a command (of reason), and the formula of this command is called an *imperative*.
>
> All imperatives are expressed by an "ought" and thereby indicate the relation of an objective law of reason to a will which is not in its subjective constitution necessarily determined by this law. This relation is that of constraint. Imperatives say that it would be good to do or to refrain from doing something, but they say it to a will which does not always do something simply because it is presented as a good thing to do. . . .
>
> All imperatives command either hypothetically or categorically (Kant 1785:30, 31).

A *hypothetical imperative* counsels us to some line of action with some particular goal in mind, though we may choose not to act if we so desire, and is based on our experience of ways of achieving certain ends. Its reasoning adopts the form, "If you wish to achieve such and such, you ought to do so and so." In other words, the content of a hypothetical imperative is not known until the condition (the 'if-statement') under which it becomes an imperative is stated. As an obligation, it is not mandatory.

A *categorical imperative* is an unconditional moral obligation, and commands by force of pure reason independent of our experience, thereby making our action mandatory as a universal moral law valid for all rational people. Kant maintained that there was primarily one categorical imperative, namely, "Act only according to that maxim by which you can at the same time will that it should become a universal law" (Kant 1785:39). Monsarrat's comment above is exactly the same. By satisfying this requirement a maxim becomes 'law', and to act morally is to act out of respect for the law, in other words for the sake of 'duty', regardless of our capricious inclinations. Even after offering some extreme examples, Kant admits that if looked at in the light of common experience, "we cannot cite a single sure example of the disposition to act from pure duty." The consequence of this remark for architects and the definition and role of duty in architecture are raised in 5B.2, Duty.

Kant notes that many philosophers addressing moral issues remark on "the frailty and corruption of human nature, which is noble enough to take as its precept an idea so worthy of respect but which at the same time is too weak to follow it" (Kant 1785). Moreover, says Kant, because our acting morally is subject to the will and because any actual results or consequences may be affected by other extraneous forces, only *anticipated consequences* are a valid basis for assessing the worth of such actions. Philip Johnson said the same of the Portland Municipal Building in Oregon by Michael Graves: "It would be more fair to Graves to judge the building by looking at his sketches." Graves, he said, did 'pretty well' considering he was "up against an impossible situation" in being given "a squat, cubic building with much too much to go in it, and a budget with which no one could build a building" (Diamonstein 1985:154). Johnson is here aligned with Kant's view that morality is located squarely in the act and in the intentions that inform the act (including any anticipated outcomes), rather than in the tangible consequences of the act. In fact, of the many approaches to moral philosophy, most accord with Kant that morality is to do with human conduct rather than with the outcomes of that conduct.

Within absolute Kantian terms, then, an actual building can in no way be implicated in the morality of the intentions or actions of its designer because of the influence on it of extraneous forces and, likewise, to assign moral values to an actual building with the aim of further inducing the morality of the designer's intentions or actions would be incorrect. Yet there are senses in which we ascribe moral values to outcomes, especially in architecture, usually in an attempt to point out some evil that we believe has ensued from certain actions that in themselves might not necessarily have been bad, and sometimes also to implicate those actions.

For example, during an end-of-year review of student projects at UNSW, one highly awarded design for a municipal library was singled out for discussion. The scheme challenged and in most cases inverted the traditional functional arrangements of a medium-sized library in what was obviously a mini-psychodrama seeking attention. A reading room was omitted on the basis that it was primarily a borrowing library; instead, study carrels as cantilevered pods with gull-wing hatches for light and air were arrayed in a separate multi-level gantry. A single-storeyed tapered wing housed book storage, book-handling, administration, and public interface. The two elements comprised all manner of movable parts, knife-edged layers, terminations, and protrusions, and mechanistic paraphernalia. An exasperated colleague was prompted to ask rhetorically, "Don't you think this is a dangerous solution?" He meant it the same way that Carrie Nation meant it of the saloons she trashed; it was bad of itself, it would be a corrupting influence on other students if we endorsed it—even as a stage set for the heavy metal band AC/DC (which it resembled), he thought it was of dubious value. Its architectonics, which he admitted were *well-handled and very competently modeled,* he thought trendy and pseudo-sophisticated, ignoring most of the normal rules of architecture, showing a lack of concern for human comfort, and flaunting the largely domestic context with a red superstructure and a silver "prow."

No doubt this kind of scenario has been enacted in schools of architecture throughout the world time and again. Is the moral danger detected in this case soundly based? Or is it merely an esthetic opinion totally misconstrued as a moral issue? What of the apparent threat to formative minds still in the process of being 'properly' habituated? Is the danger really a misplaced fear of being overruled or undermined by another doctrine? How are we to decide such moral questions, or even if they are moral questions? Is it the designer, the designing, or the designed that is 'wrong' and in need of correction?

Such dilemmas arise daily in architectural education and in practice but, one way and another, are merely swept aside in the rush for completion. They are rarely discussed or resolved, and there is little contemporary moral philosophical writing to which one might refer for advice. Some philosophical positions offering leverage on moral questions will arise in the following sections.

We are imprecise in judging the results of our actions, be they buildings or business decisions, and tend to use terms like 'good' or 'wrong' in ways that imply an ethics either when there is no morality involved or when it is only of a weak kind. The rhetoric of architecture is peppered with 'weak ethics' or, rather, with statements frequently couched as though they have universal assent but are no more than morally flavored individual opinion. Architects tend to use good/bad or right/wrong in a descriptive way, as if they are natural characteristics of whatever is under discussion. When we read about or hear of 'good' architects with 'good' intentions using 'good' techniques and producing 'good' buildings, or any variation thereof, or when we make such declarations ourselves, rather than hearing or making such statements as moral assertions, we are offering opinions about certain qualities in an act of suasion.

There are few maxims with the force of 'moral law' in architecture that categorically require obedience. Those that have become law were accepted only for a time as the core of everyday design parlance in the studio, atelier, or office. 'Form follows function' and Mies's 'less is more' are two dictums that were to rise and then fall from favor. When people say "That is good" the *good* referred to is often thought to be a quality belonging to the situation, just as *yellow* is in the sentence "That is yellow." Architects are no different; they too impute qualities to situations where none can logically exist. The reason is this kind of statement "functions 'to express or to stimulate certain kinds of emotion.' 'Good' does not describe whatever 'this' is; it functions to express the emotion of the speaker or to evoke a like emotion in the person addressed. 'This is good' is not descriptive; it is expressive or evocative. The name 'emotivism' has been given to this doctrine of the function of moral utterances" (after philosopher C. D. Broad, cited in Vesey 1974:44). Architectural discourse operates very much in emotive mode.

FURTHER SOURCES   5B.4, Decorum.

2. Normative Architectural Ethics

. . . as soon as architects became aware of architectural history . . . as soon as they became uncertain as to which of a wide variety of tectonic elements they might appropriately use; they were obliged to make basic decisions involving moral judgements, and to discuss fundamental problems which their forbears had disregarded because in their ignorance of history, and the security of their traditions, they did not know that these fundamental problems existed, and hence were blissfully unaware that there were any ethical decisions to make. **Peter Collins** 1965:40–41.

Like individualism, pluralism applied to the arts is strongly antagonistic to the setting of any general norms or standards. . . .

If we attempt to maintain either individualism or pluralism at all consistently, it is difficult to see how public art, such as architecture, is possible. The range of possible forms for any given building is, today, very great. . . .

One way out of these dilemmas and a typically modern one is to count heads. . . . [The opinion polling] process is non-coercive in the sense that no-one is required to like the result, though they may have to live with it. It is normative, but the norms are educed rather than imposed. . . . The real difficulty and danger lies in the linking of such statistical norms to the process of design. **Tom Heath.** 1991:130–131.

The concept of the ethical . . . is not that of the censor but of a creative force directing the agencies at work to their proper end, and drawing upon whatever is essentially their intrinsic good to make possible a form of life that is wanted. In the field of architecture its task is to foster the transformation by which the appetite, once identified, is translated into building forms. Propriety is its cutting edge. **Colin St. John Wilson.** 1992:46.

As modern designers we can only develop our faculties of luring, adumbrating, and forming wills, powers, and values so that they may illuminate themselves in their differences between one another and between themselves and the power that looks at them, that lives its life over against them and 'us'. Any other approach would require a return to normative evaluative scales which in turn would have to be founded on metaphysical meanings and values, that is, on God. **John Knesl.** In Al-Sayed *et al.* 1988:n44.

TRACE   Normative comes from the Latin *norma*, carpenter's square, pattern, or rule, whence its common meaning as establishing a norm or standard, a norm also being the ordinary or most frequent value or state of something. The word, though, begs its own definition because normalization, one process whereby a norm comes into being, presupposes some way of achieving agreement or consensus. A normative ethics would thus be evaluative of circumstances rather than descriptive, and would *prescribe* rules to dictate morally correct conduct under those circumstances. A normative architectural ethics, then, would be one that by common agreement guides architects in the morally correct conduct of their profession.

In his *Dictionary of Philosophy*, while he sees a clear connection between them, Antony Flew distinguishes the layperson's view of ethics as the set of standards regulating a group's behavior, or the acceptability (or not) of pursuing its aims, from the philosopher's view of ethics as the theoretical study of fundamental principles and basic concepts in a given field of human thought and activity. He also discerns three ethical 'roads' along which philosophers travel: the critique of tenets (content), the justification of stances (application), and the internal logic of morality (reasoning). Flew holds that content and justification are *normative* ethical matters, by which he means an "investigation into the content of moral principles and virtues, and their justification in terms of the human condition." He considers reasoning a *meta-ethical* concern that is "in a logical sense prior to those of normative ethics" (Flew 1979).

COMMENTARY   Normative theory, for Kevin Lynch in *Good City Form*, "deals with the generalizable connections between human values and settlement form, or how to know a good city when you see one" (1984:37), but runs dangerously close to the 'naturalistic fallacy'—the mistake of deducing conclusions about what ought to be from premises that state only what *is*, or without at least examining any such statement to see if its premises are valid—in seeing normative theory as an evaluative device prompting what might prevail.

Jon Lang (1987) also sees 'normative theory' as a "prescription for action," but in the form of principles, standards, and manifestos guiding action. Both approaches—and they are not so different because Lang admits to agreeing with Lynch—see 'normative' as concerned with finding and enabling *goodness* in one way or another. The topic of goodness will be addressed in 5A.4, Absolutism, so the present discussion will focus on what constitutes a normative architectural ethics.

Unlike the normative theory of Lynch or Lang, the normative of ethics consists in morally correct conduct that may reflect established principles, standards, *or practices,* in the sense that what is good for the greater number is good to continue doing, or may be 'tried on' at the moment of action, thereby giving the semblance of something consensually sanctioned that, if successful, eventually becomes so. In other words, so-called ethical standards or principles might be tentative at first, but become entrenched with repeated success. So, the question of how the standards, principles, or norms are acquired in the first place revolves around who has the imagination or flair to try out an ethical maxim, and what strategies are needed to ensure its adequacy so that affirmation might follow. At its most cynical, this is a political question, one involving the professional power play at any point in time, which today usually means those professionals who command print space in the architectural media. What is deemed good to do is what the most domineering minds in the business say they are doing, say to do in print, or tell their students to do (for many of these people also have academic postings—Le Corbusier having been an exception).

While moral philosophy might seek to avoid the naturalistic fallacy, architectural thought has been projecting worlds of what ought to be from what is (or is not), frequently invalidly, since the late eighteenth century. The shift from the 'ought' of principle to the 'is' of practice can occur through consensus, but the shift from the practical 'is' to the principial 'ought' of a moral maxim on its way to becoming a norm can occur only through rational thought (but see 5A.5, Relativism, on the question of choice). And rational thought begins and ends with the individual, whether alone or as part of a group, and if cogently put and sufficiently apposite, may eventually become a norm.

What are we to understand as normative, then, especially if it is taken in its second sense of a statistical concept measuring the central tendency in a distribution within a universe? What is the universe of design represented by a norm? Because design is a productive activity and not merely a static reproduction, Heath (1991) suggests that popular taste is the basis for a norm, expressed through the display of people's preferences via either competition, in that a jury or at least a member of a jury acts as the people's voice, or participatory design through which people inject into designing their preferences directly. If popular taste is taken to include (exclusively?) the small universe of architects, then architectural taste becomes the innermost of a nest of circles, or the smallest of a carillon (to tease a metaphor out of the normal or 'bell' curve of statistics). From this quasi-statistical standpoint, a normative architectural ethics would be a measure of popular architectural taste assembled through professional spokespersons, jurors, and critics in the form of concepts, themes, and practices issuing from the architectural media.

But a norm based on quantity still begs the question as to *how* it comes to be known as a norm. Who arbitrates the consensus, or rather, who makes the census and then broadcasts the results? Obviously no one person or group can or does, so the answer must lie in the means of normalization, or in finding a means that involves census-taking. In the theory of architecture as discursive practice, the theory-talk of this book, morally descriptive utterances, if they occur at all, attempt to situate the discourse; that is, to set its limits by suggesting 'givens', and morally emotive utterances serve to affirm or to deny by evoking emotional reaction. Neither kind is a critical discourse. Hence, descriptivism and emotivism each disable theory as talk because they discourage introspection and prevent any contribution to understanding. Further, moral utterances are made mainly by charismatic or authoritative individuals trying to persuade individuals in inferior positions to a particular view, and are exactly like affirmative or refuting exchanges between parent and child, or master and pupil.

An alternative to the descriptive-emotive opposition is 'prescriptivism', "the doctrine that 'This is good' functions to prescribe or prohibit certain kinds of action" (after Broad in Vesey 1974:45). Prescriptivism is the stance of the Oxford moral philosopher R. M. Hare, who considers moral problems as always of an extremely practical kind revolving around 'ought', which has two properties that together make up its meaning. Writes Hare:

> . . . for any 'ought'-statement there's something that counts as acting in accordance with it, and that if you don't so act, when the occasion arises, you can't really and sincerely subscribe to it. . . . The second logical property that 'ought'-statements have is what has been called their universalizability. By this I mean that if I say that someone ought to do something, it has to be because of something about him and his situation, and that if this something were to be true of any other person and any other situation, I couldn't without inconsistency deny that the person in that other situation ought to do the same (R. M. Hare in Vesey 1974:46–47).

Hare's stance, however, is still like Kant's in that it requires an individual to make the decision about the universalizability of any action on the basis of established moral principles. Still, the question remains, How are the adjudicating moral principles established in the first place?

One way around this dilemma, and one useful to architecture, is to remove the categorical imperative from its individually universalizable frame and to rephrase it in a way that favors mediative discourse among contending maxims and demands, thereby allowing the participating individuals to be the census-takers. Fortunately, such a reformulation exists in the recent field of *communicative,* or *discourse,* ethics where, instead of applying Kant's categorical imperative as an individual and silent 'thought-experiment', we ask as a matter of argumentative procedure, "What principles of action can we [as a community of architects in the present case] all recognize or agree to as being valid if we engage in practical discourse or a mutual search for justification?" (Benhabib 1992:28). Upon closer examination, Benhabib maintains that for this discourse to happen there must also be 'mutual respect' and an 'egalitarian reciprocity' among the parties in order to engage in discussion of any worth, a willingness to engage as equals and to entertain other opinions. This means the experienced practitioner, the academic theorist, and the fledgling student would all be of equal status. These two requirements lessen the aspect of rational agreement and favor "sustaining those normative practices and moral relationships within which reasoned agreement *as a way of life* can flourish and continue" (Benhabib 1992:38), with the normative revealing itself in the discourse.

So, rather than trying for some fixity of normative architectural ethics, the moral philosophical basis of architecture may be brought to light by maintaining discourse so that contending parties strive to persuade others to their point of view and any and all views are encouraged to participate as part of an ongoing procedure. For some this may be equivocating, and may only frustrate the desire for certainty in which most practitioners take pride, making decisions and crashing through; arguably this is one of the major points of difference from an academic sensibility, thriving as it does on argumentation. But it accords well with the view of theory-talk, not theory driving practice, but theory as continuous discourse mediating practice or, better still, theory as the practice of mediating discourse.

FURTHER SOURCES   Lang 1987; Rowe 1987.

3. Ethics and Truth in Architecture

But the moment that the conditions of weight are comprehended, both truth and feeling require that the conditions of support should also be comprehended. **John Ruskin.** 1855. "The Lamp of Truth":VII.

But the moment that the iron to the least degree takes the place of stone . . . that instant the building ceases, so far as such applications of metal extend, to be true architecture. **John Ruskin.** 1855. "The Lamp of Truth":X.

. . . it does not matter one marble splinter whether we have an old or new architecture, but it matters everything whether we have an architecture truly so called or not; that is, whether we have an architecture whose laws might be taught at our schools from Cornwall to Northumberland, as we teach English spelling and English grammar. **John Ruskin.** 1855. "The Lamp of Obedience":IV.

"Grant an idea or belief to be true . . . what concrete difference will its being true make in any one's actual life? . . . " The moment pragmatism asks this question, it sees the answer: *true ideas are those that we can assimilate, validate, corroborate and verify. False ideas are those that we can not. . . . The* truth of an idea is not a stagnant property inherent in it. Truth *happens* to an idea. It *becomes* true, is *made* true by events. **William James.** 1907:88–89.

Perhaps the most influential aspect of Gothic Rationalism was its ethical message expressed in terms of its emphasis on 'truth' . . . in an age which professed itself tired of shams, the call for truthful expression had an irresistible appeal. **Peter Collins** 1965:216.

At this summit of architecture where the word "Palace" becomes honest again, a spirit dominates that I call the *spirit of truth.* The spirit of truth is a rigid measure diving to the very foundation of a work, crossing it, feeding it, carrying it without weakness all the way to its appearance, which wears the quiet smile given by the assurance of being true and the satisfaction of having overcome difficulties. **Le Corbusier.** 1930:161.

Truth is closely bound up with time, its faithful accomplice. Like the latter, it glides away and never surrenders itself. Its manifestations cannot be foreseen, it should never be awaited, for the expectation is bound to be disappointed. This is a profoundly Jansenistic attitude. **Roger McKeon.** Preface to Jean-François Lyotard 1984:5–6.

. . . the traditional attempt to discern the *essence* of truth—to analyse that special quality which all truths supposedly have in common—is just a pseudo-problem based on syntactic overgeneralization. Unlike most other properties, *being true* is insusceptible to conceptual or scientific analysis. No wonder that its 'underlying nature' has so stubbornly resisted philosophical elaboration; for there is no such thing. **Paul Horwich.** 1990:6.

TRACE   We think we understand the word 'true' but if asked to explain it, we quickly become confounded. From the Old English *ge triewe, treowe,* which corresponds with the Old High German *gi triuwi* and the Old Norse *trygoir,* meaning 'plighted faith', truth was applied initially to the steadfastness of adherence or allegiance of persons *to* a friend, leader, principle, cause, promise, or faith. It has since come to apply to the integrity, reliability, or constancy *of* things, to the agreement *with* a standard, pattern, or rule, and, in relation to statements or beliefs, to the consistency or agreement with fact and reality. The meaning of truth seems to revolve around the precision of the relationship between the things or matters being compared, and implies an integrity, an unimpaired unity or purity, in the state of that relationship.

    For the ancient Greeks and for idealists in the Platonic tradition there is a realm beyond our daily reality that is the realm of 'truth', as Plato showed in his analogy of the cave, a realm captured in the term *alethia* and frequently translated in Latin as *veritas. Alethia* also embraces the idea of 'bringing forth', of revelation, and the sense of truth laying 'at the bottom' of things, *en butho,* in the depths of the water or 'in a well', to be 'draughted' or excavated (Onians 1951:67). For the ancients, *alethia* had four meanings in relation to the arts: the real experience of seeing a work; reality as opposed to imitation; accurate optical representation; and the reality of a thing, in which state reality is measurable and calculable (Pollitt 1974:138). James Joyce employs the terms *entelechy*, used by Aristotle to mean the condition in which a potentiality becomes an actual perfection of form, an *epiphany* or manifestation, described by St. John Wilson (1992) as "those moments of *showing forth*, in which a remark or gesture becomes a sudden revelation in depth of a state of affairs hitherto concealed" (136).

There have emerged certain theories or properties of truth focused around four philosophical positions: *correspondence* with reality based on notions of fact or structure, or reference and predicate-satisfaction; *coherence* and consistency within a harmonious system of beliefs, which is primarily idealist and has difficulty admitting a difference between what *is* true and what is *believed* to be true; *pragmatic* in seeking utility through assumptions that work best and achieve desirable results; and *primitive*, wherein truth is an unanalyzable quality that some propositions have and others lack, and that therefore evokes a primitively mysterious response (Horwich 1990).

COMMENTARY   Truth in everyday life is of the first kind mentioned above, a form of correspondence with 'facts' or 'reality'. It is largely an article of faith in architecture that truth of this kind holds in day-to-day practice, especially in 'functional' matters. But the facticity of truth by correspondence is said to be "little more than a vague, guiding intuition" (Horwich 1990:1), mainly because it is inherently circular; one must assume the truth of the facts in order to accept correspondence with those facts. So, our ordinary use of the word 'truth' thus "straddles the world of fact and the world of value, and is made up of elements of both." This dual character inhabits the word across languages (Carr 1961:131). The historian Edward H. Carr points to the German *Wahrheit* and the Russian *pravda*, in which a distinction between fact and value is made. In the Russian case there is a further subtlety "since there is another old Russian word for truth, *istina*. But the distinction is not between truth as fact and truth as value; *pravda* is human truth in both aspects, *istina* means divine truth in both aspects—truth about God and truth as revealed by God."

Likewise, two kinds of truth are discerned in a legal context, one that stands in judgment of human achievement and one that is human achievement. The court favors the first kind because only it "will assure order that is *principled*, based not on the accidents of history and culture, but on the essence of enduring values" (Fish 1989:4). On the strength of these statements we may have no choice but to agree with Nietzsche: "What therefore is truth? A mobile army of metaphors, metonymies, anthropomorphisms: in short a sum of human relations which became poetically and rhetorically intensified, metamorphosed, adorned, and after long usage seem to a nation fixed, canonic and binding; truths are illusions of which one has forgotten that they *are* illusions; worn-out metaphors which have become powerless to affect the senses" (Nietzsche 1870:180).

While correspondence with facts is a widely held view of truth in architecture, all four definitional positions may be found (mostly in combination), although there has been a strong thrust by those architectural theorists of an idealist persuasion toward the *istinaean* kind of truth, an absolute truth, existing independently of design endeavor and adjudicating it. As seekers of truth, idealist architects are inclined to a metaphysical, mystical, or religious stance that leads them to yearn for and to construe qualities in programs, settings, and relationships that have eluded discovery up until the moment of their comprehension by that architect and their subsequent elucidation via design. One profound difficulty facing the idealist architect is what constitutes truth or falsehood in architecture, and by what rules they are determined. When everything is presumed false until worked on by such an architect to elucidate the truth, a maddening masochistic fervor is induced to do better that is only ever truncated by intellectual exhaustion or compromise by circumstances deemed beyond the architect's control (deadline, budget, regulation).

From a more pragmatic perspective, the truth of architecture relates to certain warrants brought to it by the inferences, assumptions, beliefs, and principles that underlie its rhetoric and practice. The guarantee of architecture's worth, quality, security, and continuity has been thought by architects since the nineteenth century to reside in their focusing on and embodying in buildings such desirable qualities as integrity, sincerity, and purity. From the time of Ruskin, the evocation of these qualities has been presumed to depend mainly on seeking and capturing the 'truth' of a building's relationships to its program, setting, and milieu, or of a building's deployment of materials, structure, and systems. The way the designer has achieved this until recently has been to inculcate appropriate habits of mind and to arrange circumstances conducive to allowing the 'truth' of any architectural task or situation to readily emerge. That this search for truth is not being made by a significant number of architects today, that truth-claims of this kind can fall out of favor, is an indication of just how elusive an architectural ethics is that ties itself to their exposition.

There are those who, in urging quality or excellence in architecture or art—as writers and critics sometimes mean to do when they draw a distinction between 'architecture' and 'true architecture' or 'art' and 'true art'—are merely adopting a semantic habit extolling certain virtues they believe architecture has, or should have. But the implication is often that something more adheres to architecture or art if it is 'true' than if it is otherwise, as Ruskin seems to say in the above quotations from "The Lamp of Truth"; truth then is firmly related to a perfection beyond excellence. In this conception, truth is intuited to exist outside the everyday bounds of architecture or art in a rarefied state from which emanates some supra-architectural or supra-artistic quality that infuses common verbal definitions and meanings and esthetic expressions. It is a sure sign of the idealist at work if 'true' is used as an adjective.

In the Western idealist and certain Eastern metaphysical traditions, any comprehension we have and any physical manifestations surrounding us are said to be but glimpses of a profound 'reality' to which we may aspire but can never reach. Plato developed his Theory of Forms to illustrate these separate realms, the pure or universal realm being that of the Forms wherein perfection, the 'itself' of any concept, resides, the gross or corporeal realm being that of everyday existence. Just how the Forms feature in architecture is the subject of 8B.2, Idea. For the moment, suffice it to say that the ethical task of the Platonic idealist designer is to determine and comply with rules that will guarantee the 'form' that best manifests the Form by seeking the truth or essence of particular circumstances. Knowledge of the Forms is an article of faith, and their operation is apprehended through intuition.

Until now I have referred to intuition only in passing. What do we mean by it? Stone (1987) sees intuitions as "the raw data of morals; the intuitionist believes that these hard-to-trace emotions stand to moral judgment in a relation exactly analogous to the relation between perceptual experience and scientific judgment" (243). Flew (1979) likens intuition to "a form of uninferred or immediate knowledge" (that is, about the truth of something), and puts forward two philosophical uses of it: "first, uninferred knowledge of the truth of a proposition; second, immediate knowledge of [the truth of] a nonpropositional object." There are four kinds of nonpropositional object that it has been claimed are intuitable: universals, concepts, sensible objects, and ineffable objects. Designing relies extensively on intuiting such nonpropositional objects despite claims for knowledge as the basis for design. Which brings us to the question of how we might theorize about truth and how truth is brought to bear in the mediation of architecture.

If architecture is to be believed in, if it is to be genuine, authoritative, entitled to respect, if it is to be considered real and actual, then it seems that truth needs to be somewhere involved. But all these desires and qualities are actually the definition of *authentic* (CTCD), and the question becomes, rather, can there be an authentic architecture that is not truthful? Since for a number of writers today there is no authentic architecture, at least not one that has the meaning of 'standing for' timeless values, there can be no truth over and against which architecture might be placed. Thus, any authenticity architecture might have, by which can be meant only credibility, must be gained through its political validity, by its time-dependent purposes and reactions. Theory, therefore, cannot adjudicate the truthfulness of architecture; it can only elucidate its social and cultural worth.

FURTHER SOURCES   5B.3, Moral.

4. Ethical Absolutism or G(o)od Rules.

Is holiness loved by the gods because it is holy, or is it holy because it is loved by the gods? **Socrates.** In Plato, *Euthyphro,* XII.

. . . if there be some one thing which is the end of all things consciously done, this will be the doable good; or, if there be more than one end, then it will be all of these. **Aristotle.** *Ethics,* 1:7.

Nothing in the world—indeed nothing even beyond the world—can possibly be conceived without qualification except a *good will*. . . . The good will is not good because of what it effects or accomplishes or because of its adequacy to achieve some proposed end; it is good only because of its willing, i.e., it is good of itself. **Immanuel Kant.** 1785:10.

. . . the concept of a will which is to be esteemed as good of itself without regard to anything else . . . dwells already in the natural sound understanding and does not need so much to be taught as only to be brought to light. In the estimation of the total worth of our actions it always takes first place and is the condition of everything else. **Immanuel Kant.** 1785:13.

. . . good architecture is inseparable from reasoning **J. F. Blondel.** Cited in Collins 1965:200.

Before God there are no good or bad architects. **Adolf Loos.** 1910:49.

The morally right is what is best in that manner of value-assessment which is to be accepted as taking precedence, in the case in hand, over any other mode of assessing values which are involved. **Clarence I. Lewis** 1969:102.

If it isn't worth doing, it isn't worth doing well. **Louis Kahn.** Remembered by Hugh Jacobsen. In Diamonstein 1985:135.

TRACE   For an ethical absolutist, only one correct morality exists, usually expressed in the form "Thou shalt/Thou shalt not." Absolutist reasoning is that what is good for an individual to do is overridden by what is good for society to do, which in turn is overridden by what is good for God to do. Hence the divine will is the Supreme Good as in Christian theology and most other religions, and absolute rules and laws are seen to issue from God. A pagan version was first formulated by Plato, who argued for universal good as the eternal Idea or Form of the Good, raised in the previous section.

Aristotle was critical of Plato's conception of an eternal good, and in a famous argument said, "A thing may be called good in three ways: in itself, in some quality it has, or in some relation it bears to something else" but concluded that "the essence of a thing— what it is in itself—is by its very nature prior to any relation it may have. . . . Therefore there cannot be one form embracing *both* the absolutely *and* the relatively good." Because he found that 'good' embraced six categories (substance, quality, quantity, relation, time, and space), Aristotle discerned two kinds of good: "things good in themselves and things good as means to these" (*Ethics:*1.6).

COMMENTARY   Reliance on some 'external' conception of the good, of a universal and objective standard, rules the thought of most people. This is especially so in relation to the everyday distinction between good and evil operating in the law and through religious understanding and observance, the most common arbiters of ethical standards. Popular moral essays are limited, though; as Kant says, "sometimes perfection, and sometimes happiness, here moral feeling, there fear of God, a little of this and a little of that in a marvelous mixture. However, it never occurs to the authors to ask whether the principles of morality are, after all, to be sought anywhere in knowledge of human nature (which we can only derive from experience)" (1785:second section). For Kant, moral laws were to be derived independently of experience.

In philosophy generally, it is Plato's concept of the universal good as the highest ethical good that has dominated thought; but this has been sufficiently discussed in 5A.3, Truth. Aristotle too, while disagreeing with Plato in key respects, maintained that goodness was a natural quality associated with the doing of things, namely, an 'end'. "Assuming then that there is some one thing which alone is an end beyond which there are no further ends, we may call *that* the good of which we are in search. If there be more than one such final end, the good will be that end which has the highest degree of finality" (*Ethics*:1.7). He concluded that something chosen for its own sake and not for the sake of something else is a supreme end, which he determined as *eudaimonia,* or 'happiness', though the abundance of 'felicity' (Onians 1951) is more evocative. Aristotle also concluded that the singular function of humans is to reason, and that the supreme 'doable good' of humans is to reason well.

Harking back to both Plato and Aristotle, Kant offered the concept of the 'good will' as the indispensable condition for determining the good in any action. He insisted that such a will is absolute, good 'of itself', and natural, as the above quotations show, and is the precondition for any moral act. It is out of this concept of the will, that he developed his notion of the *imperative* as a constraint upon the will and hence his famous distinction between the technical imperative (of skill), the hypothetical imperative (of means or prudence), and the categorical imperative (of morality), each dealing with goodness of differing kinds (Kant 1785).

From an Aristotelian perspective we may choose to apply 'good' or 'bad' in judging a thing or an outcome otherwise excluded under the categorical imperative, because the end toward which a set of actions is geared becomes its good, its *summum bonum,* as the above quotation from Aristotle tells us. The actualization of the best potentiality of something is the same as that which is aimed at—what it is to be a good person equates with the good sought by a person or, using Aristotle's building example, "it is the relation of actually building to what is suitable for building" (*Metaphysics*:1048a31–1048b7). Unlike Kant, who discriminated finely between means and ends, Aristotle saw the goodness (or badness) of an end as encapsulating the intentions that led to its present state, thereby unwittingly committing the 'naturalistic fallacy', coined by G. E. Moore and now known as Hume's law, of using an *is* to determine an *ought* (see 5A.2, Normative).

Relating this directly to architecture, the quest for the 'perfect' architectural solution (the good to which a building aims) by both the experienced practitioner and the flailing student, persists as a working agenda, even though it is unattainable by definition. Inasmuch as well-designing approaches Aristotle's supreme human doable good, this is unexceptionable. However, for many a perfectionist architect, well-designing becomes an exercise in pessimistic self-denial, because the equivalent of the 'fall from grace'—that is, imperfection—stares back from any resolution. Perfectionist architects, modernists by another name, are particularly prone to masochism concerning the inadequacies of their buildings, even after a lifetime of success and acclaim. Harry Seidler is said to have lately remarked about his work that his achievements are as nothing compared to what he still needs to do or could do; no doubt many other architects believe the same. Striving for the unattainable seems to be the only way these architects can achieve anything approaching a higher morality.

In summary, the Platonic and Kantian visions of what it is morally correct to do induce anxiety for a designer because they are absolutely demanding of goodness while at the same time acknowledging the frailty of resolve of humankind. While Plato's Forms may be hard to grasp—let alone apply—Aristotle's vision too fails to address how to determine what it is good to do, what end is most worthy to pursue, in the first place; a vital step for a designer. However, there are ways around the anxiety and obfuscation of these stances that assist in assembling an architectural ethics. One may be found in existentialism, the subject of the next section, and the other in pragmatism, which will be treated in 5B.3, Moral.

FURTHER SOURCES   Benhabib 1992.

5. Ethical Relativism and Existential 'Chosens'

. . . of all the actions a man may take in order to create himself as he wills to be, there is not one which is not creative, at the same time, of an image of man such as he believes he ought to be. To choose between this or that is at the same time to affirm the value of that which is chosen; for we are unable ever to choose the worse. What we choose is always the better; and nothing can be better for us unless it is better for all. **Jean-Paul Sartre.** *Existentialism As a Humanism.* Cited in Solomon 1977:488.

If I regard a certain course of action as good, it is only I who choose to say that it is good and not bad . . . nevertheless I am also obliged at every instant to perform actions which are examples. Everything happens to every man as though the whole human race had its eyes fixed upon what he is doing and regulated its conduct accordingly. **Jean-Paul Sartre.** *Existentialism As a Humanism.* Cited in Solomon 1977:489.

It is through my actions that I commit myself to values, not through principles I accept *a priori* or rules that are imposed upon me from God or society. If you accept the voice of some authority, you have chosen to accept that authority rather than some other. **Robert Solomon.** 1977:491.

TRACE   Antony Flew (1979) makes things clear, as usual: "To be a relativist about value is to maintain that there are no universal standards of good and bad, right and wrong." There are basically two relativist views: *cultural relativism,* in which different societies claim to have different moralities, and *ethical relativism,* in which different moralities are not only accepted but are seen as equally valid (Solomon 1977). The Anglo-American philosopher Walter Stace wrote in *The Concept of Morals* (1937): "Any ethical position which denies there is a single moral standard which is equally applicable to all men at all times may fairly be called a species of ethical relativity. There is not, the relativist asserts, merely one moral law, one code, one standard. There are many moral laws, codes, standards. What morality ordains in one place or age may be quite different from . . . another place or age. . . . Any morality, therefore, is relative to the age, the place, and the circumstances in which it is found." The best way to understand the ethical relativist position is that it is the opposite of the ethical absolutist position; whatever the absolutist asserts, the relativist denies.

For an absolutist, moral obligations are given, whereas for a relativist they cannot be, so they must be chosen in one way or another. In the existential philosophy of Jean-Paul Sartre and its ethical prescriptions, choice is all there is: "To say that it does not matter what you choose is not correct. In one sense choice is possible, but what is not possible is not to choose. I can always choose, but I must know that if I do not choose, that is still a choice" (Sartre 1949. Cited in Solomon 1977:490). Aristotle used the word *proairesis,* which was translated in medieval Latin as *electio,* to express the choice both of the ends and the means to an end.

COMMENTARY   If moral principles are universal, applicable across all times, societies, and universes, then determining an ethical philosophy for architects would be a matter of simply (or not so simply) transferring laws across disciplines; yet it is not that easy, as the preceding sections show. What it is good for a cleric, painter, or geneticist to do does not readily transfer to what it is good for an architect to do; it is at least difficult, and probably impossible, to discern which cross-disciplinary moral principles might apply to architecture. While it is accepted that well-doing in any discipline is the ultimate good, this is at the same time both too general and too trivial to be of any tangible use to that discipline other than as an exhortation to do well, architecture included. Ethical principles pertinent to the rationale of particular disciplines are needed, and once we say that, we enter the world of relativism. In other words, if there are no moral principles that may be applied categorically to architecture, then judgments of architectural morality can only be relative to the laws, codes, and standards of architecture.

A standard has two different meanings ethically: what people *think* to be good or right, and what *is* good or right. Both the absolutist and the relativist mean by 'standard' what *is* right, though only the absolutist accepts these two senses of the word. "For the relativist no such distinction can be made," writes Walter Stace. "There is only one meaning of the word standard, namely, that which refers to local and variable sets of moral ideas. Or if it is insisted that the word must be allowed two meanings, then the relativist will say that there is at any rate no actual example of a standard in the absolute sense, and that the word as thus used is an empty name to which nothing in reality corresponds; so that the distinction between the two meanings becomes empty and useless" (Stace 1937). An ethical relativist view of architecture, then, would seek goodness relative to some standard assumed *for the time being* and *within the ambit of* a particular architectural culture, whether defined geographically by a city, region, state, or country; limited geographically by climate, materials, or techniques; or constrained ideologically by concepts, themes, or movements; or some combination of these.

The moment relativism is raised, people duck for cover, because it smacks of arbitrary decisions of the will that allow people to do as they please, and is therefore thought to be bad or wrong of itself. But far from fear of being flung into a maelstrom of unbridled behavior, relativism is better feared because it is a lonely and precarious stance that places extraordinary demands on the individual professing it. A cautious architectural relativist would speak of gradations, intensities, and degrees of betterment; not of 'good' or 'bad' but of 'more or less goodness', not of 'right' or 'wrong' but of 'more or less correctness', not of 'perfect' or 'imperfect' but of 'more or less precision' or 'more or less attainment', all according to the prevailing standards of the particular architectural culture. Goodness, correctness, precision, and attainment would thus not be absolute architectural values, but states whose purity is conceivable but whose polarities are not necessary to their definition. It is certainly arguable that an architectural culture may be compared to a mini-universe and that by adopting a standard assumed to prevail for the good of all in that mini-universe, the culture assumes the status of an absolute for that universe. Would not the relativist then be a mini-absolutist, and thus no different from the absolutist in the larger universe?

Such a claim is countered once the derivation of a standard is considered. For the only way a standard can come to acceptance is through mutual selection and agreement, and mutuality involves discussion and choice. Inevitably, standards of goodness, correctness, precision, and attainment will obtain only through rationalization and the quality of that rationalization. Indeed, the rationalization is only as good (well-thought) as those rationalizing are capable of; there may be others who will rationalize better or differently, and as a result change the standard. Where then does the absolute standard lie? It is no use saying *at the end of such a process,* because, although an end is conceivable, the process is never-ending. And what of the decisions made along the way according to the standards taken as absolute and later superseded? They are no longer absolute and so must have been relative all along (to the time and the circumstance). Polarities, opposites and dualities become under relativism collateral rather than collinear entities.

What world view is capable of accepting an ethical relativism of the kind just outlined in which humanity is utterly bound up in its subjectivity and morality, supposedly fit for all humankind, is a matter of individual agreement? It certainly cannot be one that insists absolutely. Coming to a morality by agreement presupposes that existence precedes essence. Morality in architecture thus becomes what architects choose it to be rather than what it is willed to be as an absolute duty. Because of Kant's own admission that he cannot find one single example of a pure action from duty, the 'categorical' of the Kantian imperative that eliminates choice immediately obliges a choice, the imperative being that one cannot *not* make a choice. And the obliging of choice is existentialism and Jean-Paul Sartre.

From an existentialist perspective, Sartre's conception of morality as choice is partly Kantian in maintaining that we choose as if for all humankind, but at the same time, it avoids Kant's unattainable absolutism. Sartre also sees choice as an affirmation of the individual and the inevitable outcome of the individuality-anonymity dialectic that underlies existentialism, thereby ensuring accountability beyond mere self-gratification. The implication for architectural ethics of an existentialist stance is that making moral judgments while designing, the selection of 'good' over 'bad', is a choice made on behalf of all humankind, seen from within the architectural mini-universe. Architectural ethics is not a 'given', but a 'chosen' commitment to certain values by individual architects who believe such values would be chosen by others similarly placed. While this may not present a difficulty for those in the architectural profession wherein all architects are 'similarly placed'—hence professional codes of ethics—it is much more difficult to choose values relating to nonarchitects. Contrary to what many of them believe and declare, architects are not in a position to discern the 'similarities' among others for whom they are designing and, thus, how they might be 'placed' (see Benhabib 1992). More of this in chapter 5B.

FURTHER SOURCES   4A.3, Talent.

B. Ethics Applied in Architecture

1. What Architectural Obligations Are There?

As a citizen an architect may (perhaps should, but that is a matter for his own conscience), refuse to be involved in an activity of which he morally disapproves, but this ethical problem must lie outside the scope of our present enquiry into the theory of architecture as such. **Bruce Allsopp.** 1977:11.

As long as we fail to make a rigorous distinction between *Is* and the categorical *Ought,* as long as we fail to realise that all attempts to ground architecture and urbanism on experimentalism and opportunism cannot possibly succeed, we are doomed to failure. In that sense, the primary aim of Leon Krier's *Critiques* has been to demonstrate that there is a rational certainty that informs both architecture and the city. **Demetri Porphyrios.** "Cities of Stone." In Porphyrios 1984:16.

To my own moral sense, especially before I threw it all over and became a success boy, it did seem that the only important project for an architect was to house the people of the United States. **Philip Johnson.** c1984. In Diamonstein 1985:160.

Architecture awakens sentiments in man. It is therefore the task of the architect to define exactly the sentiment. The room must evoke a warm feeling (*gemütlich*), the house must be pleasant to live in. The Judicial building must appear as a threatening gesture to secret vice. The bank must say: here your money is secured and well-protected by honest people. **Adolf Loos.** Cited in Archer 1987:70.

One of the City's main functions is to create wealth, but surely there should also be an obligation to spend some of that money on buildings that are beautiful, that are a pleasure to look at—and to work in. We should have architecture that celebrates London's mercantile success, and then *humanises* it. **Charles, Prince of Wales.** 1989:63.

TRACE   Obligation stems from the Latin *obligare,* bind around or up, bind by oath or other tie; pledge, impede, restrain. It shares with *nexus* the limiting of a sphere of operation. While the notion of constraint is common to all interpretations of obligation, in the strongest sense, obligation implies an ongoing, even perpetual, constant attention to some course of action because one is morally bound to continue with it. The weaker sense of the term implies a termination, some point in time or in a relationship, a point at which the obligation is deemed to have been met. Attending to an obligation is, in this latter respect, seeking release from it, being 'loosed' from the binding, so that the obligation ceases to be effective. Popular usage of 'obligation' favors this weaker sense, as politicians do in speaking of electoral obligations, or as architects do in referring to obligations toward their clients. Occasionally people recognize the limits of this weaker temporary character of obligation as needing more substantial support; they use qualifiers such as 'longstanding', or 'long term' —they are reluctant, it seems, to believe that the term, unqualified, has sufficient power. A continuous or perpetual obligation is seen as somehow unnecessary, if not unreasonable. If an obligation is of long duration, it is invoked only under certain circumstances, after which it returns to dormancy or latency. This latency of obligation underlies the professions and comes to the foreground because they are frequently confronted by situations that demand of them an ethical stand.

Architects and theorists throughout the twentieth century have recognized that they primarily have a social responsibility to those for whom they design, to those who build or use their buildings, and even to those who are only incidentally involved. This has led architects to make some extraordinary claims for their responsibilities, obligations, and abilities. The foundation of the Congrès International d'Architecture Moderne (CIAM), at the Château Sarraz in Switzerland in 1928, produced the first of a succession of declarations by international architects (meaning a select group of twenty-four Europeans) about their "professional obligations toward society." The Sarraz Declaration was doctrinaire, as were CIAM's many later declarations. The Congress was to pass through three stages before its last meeting in 1956 in Dubrovnik: the period from 1928 to 1933 emphasized minimum living standards, rationalization and efficiency; the second, from 1933 to 1947, was dominated by Le Corbusier and emphasized town planning (the Athens Charter emerged from CIAM IV in 1933); the third, from 1947 to 1956, brought a more liberal idealism based in people needs rather the materialism of the earlier phases and resulted in the succession of Team X to 1964 (for a summary, see Frampton 1980:269–279).

COMMENTARY   The kinds of principles with which architecture starts are 'moral principles', principles that set in train a collection of beliefs about life and people. The principle of equality among people would suggest an architectural belief of the kind that would promote community architecture. The principle of fairness would promote an architecture in which equity in whatever conditions were thought desirable for all to have was uppermost, or would produce a building that did not overshadow or obstruct key views in fairness to others having an equity in those things. Architects go about their daily professional life making decisions based on such principles as they have acquired individually and supplemented, changed, or adjusted during their professional education. Under certain circumstances, an architect might choose to go against a principle in undertaking some action, though this is not to say that the principle has been abandoned as a consequence. If quizzed, most architects would admit as a moral consideration that the principle would be upheld in most circumstances within which they anticipate operating. But it is the architect's choice whether to maintain principles or not and under what circumstances. The same applies to other principles architects adopt in their designing.

In 1959 the Liaison Committee of Architects of United Europe was founded to implement the general policies and objectives of the Treaty of Rome as they affect architects, and to promote high standards of practice for architects in the European Community. There have been three principles agreed on for professional conduct (*Vademecum of the Architectural Profession*. 1984. Delft, Delft University Press):

1. An architect shall faithfully carry out the duties which he undertakes and shall have proper regard *for the material and human interests* both of those who commission and *those who may be expected to use or enjoy* the product of his work [emphasis added].
2. An architect shall avoid actions and situations inconsistent with his professional obligations . . . or likely to raise doubt about his integrity.
3. An architect shall rely only on ability and achievement for his advancement, without soliciting, undercutting or supplanting.

The *vade mecum* mentions 'professional obligations', and goes on to list under a separate heading the two primary obligations, which insist that architects working in another country abide by the code of conduct of the profession in that country and that they work in conjunction with host country architects. In other words, the obligations are couched in the terms of most institutional codes of conduct. But there are wider obligations architects have that convey the sense of submitting to principles of more far-reaching importance or effect, something more than abstract architectural principle. Obligation not only involves considering the demands of others, but may even bind the architect into a contractual responsibility to those others. This is not to say that principles are less important than obligations, only that obligations often involve reciprocity, whether real or imagined. The obligations of architects are closer to those listed in the *vade mecum* under principles; they are to do with the material and human interests of those likely to use or enjoy their creations.

There are many matters architects may feel obligated about in their day-to-day practice. They may feel obliged to be straightforward with their clients, to be honest in their dealings with all parties involved in a project, to maintain impartiality in adjudicating builders' cost claims, to consider the welfare of anonymous others who will use their buildings, to insist on certain quality standards, to ensure that rainforest timbers are not depleted, to bring some 'magic' quality to their design, to ensure a steady stream of work for their employees, to maintain a lifestyle for themselves, to speak out on urban issues affecting their home city, to participate in their professional institute, and so forth. But how many of these matters involve duty, matters that they must do absolutely, or about which they believe they have no choice? Very few, because for any obligation to be so binding as to override individual preference would require widespread consensus, and there are few, if any, matters commonly agreed among a sufficient number of architects for them to be deemed 'universal'.

Those obligations that seem to be agreed by architects of late—and that is all that may be said of them, *seem* to be agreed—are so general that they are barely of assistance to daily practice, and there is no way in which they may be applied in the teaching of architects. Just how knowledge of any consensus, or indeed the consensus itself, is gained is a problem because of the diffusion of issues throughout the architectural media. The only unanimity is that which commentators perceive as coming from small groups forming some nascent movement, from groups professing particular standpoints at conferences or colloquia, from editorial comment and selection of what is acceptable for publication, or from educational emphases. Any such 'consensus' is a political attempt at cornering the market. The debate in the British architectural press over the advent of 'The New Spirit' (*The Architectural Review*, August 1986, and subsequent correspondence) and the book of the same name that emerged five years later (Cook and Llewellyn-Jones 1991) is a case in point. More generally, consensus may emerge from the considerations and choices of individuals based on what they read and hear or how they act over time, but is a historical interpretation rather than a conscious contemporaneous structuring.

Thus, the only practical basis architects have for determining the obligations attaching to their actions is whether they can foresee the obligation coming to an *end* rather than continuing. For example, to make an obligation of not using rainforest timbers is to do so *until such time* as rainforest timbers are no longer threatened *by you*. Logging of rainforests in South America or Northern Australia for veneers or woodchips may still continue, and you might extend your obligation into another sphere, but architecturally there is no further obligation until you are again faced with a choice about whether to use rainforest timbers. To feel obliged to participate in a professional institute is to do so *until such time* as *your* contribution is of no further use. To make an obligation of considering the welfare of anonymous others using a building is to consider them throughout the design and operation of the building *until such time* as the horizon of potential problems to others *and to you* disappears, even for those design matters deemed to continue in perpetuity. The architect's obligation to others in providing handrails to the external podium steps of the Sydney Opera House ceased when government decreed they were not required, even though the issue has arisen a number of times since as the result of accidents.

In other words, if it is not possible to know the consensus of the architectural profession over its obligations at any one moment, it falls to the individual to decide what is or is not an obligation. Obligations generally are a matter of both professional and personal history, personal selections from an historical array of matters communally agreed by virtue of actions and stances already taken. But specific obligations at any moment are adduced from among whatever matters, from the past to that moment, have not been superseded or removed from your province (that is, by law or industry standard). Hence, obligations are as numerous as human ingenuity may wish to conjure, and as human conscience may wish to bear.

FURTHER SOURCES   8A.2, Principles; Conrads 1964; Team 10 1962.

2. Duty and Prudence

A sagacious man is supposed to be characterized by his ability to reach sound conclusions in his deliberations about what is good for himself and advantageous to him. . . . We also speak of a man as sagacious or prudent in a particular way when he calculates well for the attainment of a particular end of a fine sort . . . the man who is sagacious in every department of life will be one who deliberates in general to good purpose. **Aristotle.** *Ethics:*6.5.

In the estimation of the total worth of our actions it [a will that is good of itself] always takes first place and is the condition of everything else. In order to show this, we shall take the concept of duty. It contains that of a good will, though with certain subjective restrictions and hindrances; but these are far from concealing it and making it unrecognizable, for they rather bring it out by contrast and make it shine forth all the brighter. **Immanuel Kant.** 1785:First Section.

For what is prudence but the skill to use free men and even the natural dispositions and inclinations of oneself for one's own designs? **Immanuel Kant.** 1785:Second Section.

...to us clarity means the definite expression of the purpose of a building and the sincere expression of its structure. One can regard this sincerity as a sort of moral duty. **Marcel Breuer.** 1934. *Marcel Breuer, Buildings and Projects, 1921–1961.* 1962:261 (cited in Watkin 1977:13).

To Aristotle both *Tekne* and 'prudence' are ways of arriving at truth; and the Greek perception of truth is of something concealed that has to be brought into the light. The philosopher Heidegger has very convincingly related this perception to the origin of the work of art. **Colin St. John Wilson.** 1992:32.

TRACE   The 'science' of duty or moral obligation is *deontology,* from the Greek *deon, deont-,* 'that which is binding, duty'. Duty has already been alluded to in chapter 5A as the *modus operandi* in Kant's moral or categorical imperative. It is also superordinate to the good will, as one Kant quotation, above, shows. Kant's definition of duty is "the necessity of an action executed from respect for law" (Kant 1785). Whether duty is exercised through conduct, according what is due to a superior, or out of homage, reverence, or respect or, more commonly, whether it is done under legal obligation or absolutely as a moral charge, in its purest sense it is exercised selflessly. Like obligation, duty is occasioned through time and circumstance, but unlike obligation, it continues beyond both and cannot be eradicated even though the threat of legal sanction may cease after a statutory period.

   Prudence, on the other hand, relates to the Kantian hypothetical imperative, and therefore involves self-interest, as Kant shows above. What the ancients referred to as *prothein,* forethought or foresight, we call today *prudence,* sound judgment in practical affairs, wisdom and discretion in conduct, or the ability to choose the most suitable course of action, sagacity and discretion, or, more simply, caution or restraint, particularly in relation to one's own welfare. Fundamentally, though, prudence as foresight incorporates *providence,* pro-vision, preparation beforehand. "To decide according to the value of the experience as immediate, and immediately felt, will be, in general, to follow the dictate of our inclinations; to decide according to the contributory value of the experience will be to follow the dictate of prudence," wrote the American philosopher Clarence Lewis (1969:50–51).

COMMENTARY   While the word 'obligation' is frequently interchanged with 'duty', duty is strictly beyond an individual's power to decide. For Kant, duty rests in principles that are universal in their application. The great difficulty is to determine what such universally applicable principles are that so predicate duty for it to be unimpeachable. For example, the claim of confidentiality by the priest needs to be unimpeachable if the hearing of confession is to continue as a legitimate religious activity; confidentiality becomes a duty of the priest. The claim by the journalist to protect sources needs to be unimpeachable if investigative journalism as a legitimate activity is to continue; protecting sources becomes a duty of the crusading journalist. In both cases, of course, there have been legal challenges that have set limits to these duties by way of extent and circumstance, which rather proscribes their effectiveness as duties.

Under Kant's definition, duty as such "wholly excludes the influence of inclination and therewith every object of the will, nothing remains which can determine the will objectively except the law, and nothing subjectively except pure respect for this practical law. This subjective element is the maxim that I ought to follow such a law even if it thwarts all my inclinations" (Kant 1785:First Section). And a very noble basis for a conception of duty it is. But Kant admitted that in everyday terms he could find no pure example of anyone acting in accordance with this conception of duty. So, are all attempts to formulate concepts of duty in everyday human terms doomed? Not if duty is considered in concert with the actions it is likely to enjoin and not as a 'thing' unto itself; not if it is kept within the bounds of practical reason. What, then, might be practically reasonable duties in the professions, especially in architecture?

In daily practice, apart from respect for and attention to the law, which is a duty of all citizens, there seem to be only three professional duties architects are expected to exercise routinely: *care, integrity,* and *conscientiousness.* While there are variations from country to country, the duty of care is widely recognized legally in tort (the breach of a duty imposed by law whereby someone has the right of action for damages) as an explicit duty of anyone dealing with, providing services or advice for, or acting on behalf of the public. Integrity is indirectly legislated in that dishonesty, fraud, embezzlement, and misrepresentation are actionable. Conscientiousness comes into play under the laws of agency, and in considerations of professional negligence. There may be circumstances in which care, integrity, or conscientiousness are exercised more for the sake of personal interest (prudence), than because they *ought* to be for their own sake (duty), but they are primarily moral issues within the mini-universes of professions. Indeed, they may well be candidates for wider application, in which case they would constitute duties in a universal moral philosophy.

Certainly, some will argue that architecturally, concern for people, pursuing truth, being honest, respecting the zeitgeist, or conveying meaning have been and are still the stuff of maxims courting duty, but the challenge has been to achieve universal assent for any of them over a period prolonged enough to confirm their universalizability. In other words, duties are precisely what we would not haggle over, and would therefore need to be both as inclusive as the three duties already defined, *and as benign,* in the sense of being uncontroversial. Since no further issues can be discerned that can be generalized to the same extent, it is reasonable to assume that any other matters either come under these three headings, or are obligations in the sense outlined previously.

Moving to the issue of prudence, in discussing happiness as the one purpose to which all humankind is naturally disposed and the practical necessity of action for its achievement, Kant offers that "Skill in the choice of means to one's own highest welfare can be called prudence in the narrowest sense. Thus the imperative which refers to the choice of means to one's own happiness, i.e., the precept of prudence, is still only hypothetical; the action is not absolutely commanded but commanded as a means to another end" (Kant 1785:Second Section). A footnote explains two senses of the word 'prudence', one public and the other private. The public sense accounts for the skill in influencing others that results in their being used for an individual's own purpose. The private sense is the ability to bring together all such purposes for lasting individual advantage.

But a more useful formulation of prudence is that of Lewis, following the extract used in the trace above, where he says: "If you wish to know *what* it will be prudent to do, the answer to *that* question is to be found by assessing the value of experiences consequent upon any choice of doing to be decided—assessing them according to their contributory value. . . . You know what is prudentially right to do by knowing what choice of action will result in experiences having the greatest contributory value" (*loc. cit.*). For architects, the prudentially right thing to do is always a matter for judgment under *particular* circumstances. It remains of course to decide to what or to whom the 'greatest contribution' will be made (for you under those circumstances), which for dutiful reasons is assumed to be to some recipient other than you as architect or your client. If there is likely to be some greater social benefit or broader environmental gain by virtue of a decision, then this would be a prudent action.

It is the task of mediation always to seek the prudent path to resolution, one that provides all parties in a conflict with the greatest contribution to each that it is possible to have under the circumstances. It is the practice of architectural theory to explicate the context for mediation, to set up the forum as it were, within which the architect might make such prudent judgments in practical matters as are necessary to achieve the greatest contribution under the circumstances.

FURTHER SOURCES   4A.2, Wisdom; Aristotle *Ethics*:6.5.

3. Moral Architecture Is in the Making

By morality the individual is taught to become a function of the herd, and to ascribe to himself value only as a function. . . . Morality is the herd-instinct in the individual. **Friedrich Nietzsche.** *The Joyful Wisdom.* Cited in Solomon 1977:484.

Technology is morally, socially and politically neutral, though its exploitation may require adjustments of social and political structures, and its consequences may call moral attitudes in question. **Reyner Banham.** 1962. "Towards a Pop Architecture." In Banham 1981:61.

An architect does not arrive at his finished product solely by a sequence of rationalizations, like a scientist, or through the workings of the *Zeitgeist*. . . . He thinks of forms intuitively, and then tries to justify them rationally; a dialectical process governed by what we may call his theory of architecture, which can only be studied in philosophical and ethical terms. **Peter Collins.** 1965:16.

I use the word "ethic" rather than "aesthetic" because Mies's belief system had—or at least we interpreted it as having—a very significant moral dimension. This was both its strength and its limitation. Within this belief system, there was a right and a wrong way of making things, and that notion of right and wrong permeated the entire enterprise of architecture, from its broadest conception at the scale of urban planning to its ultimate materialization in the smallest detail. In retrospect, it seems an irony that this rigorously moral attitude toward architecture should have been adopted by so many American architects as the lodestone for practice in an era now viewed as having been pragmatic to the point of expediency. **Henry Cobb.** In Diamonstein 1985:36.

The ethical question arises in architecture because the production of architecture is thought-in-action taking place in the world. It is always within history, no matter how it is expressed or its purposes directed. **David Bell** 1990:25.

TRACE   Morality has been discussed at length in chapter 5A, so its etymology will be raised only briefly here. As an adjective, moral stems from the Latin *moralis,* an ancient rendering of the Greek *ethikos,* and relates to *mores,* customs, manners, character. It is to do with discriminating between right and wrong, or good and evil, in actions, although it is also applied to character. It is its active sense that is being examined here. Making derives from the Germanic *machen,* while the Sanskrit *kr* and the Latin *cer, cre,* to do or make, are the roots for our 'creation'. Coomaraswamy writes that "in Christian doctrine, the moral virtues do not belong to the contemplative life essentially, but only dipositively, while they do belong to the active life essentially" (1977:II.269).

Albert Hofstadter (1965) remarks on creative art as being "art that brings forth a vision, producing it where it did not exist before; and, on the other hand, the coming into being of vision, i.e. intuition, is art that creates and does not merely copy a preexistent model" (34). Likewise, architecture is the bringing into being what did not exist before by means of intuition. Hofstadter again: "We have an intimation, or an anticipation, which tells us, like a monitoring conscience, when we are on the right path and when on the wrong—and it itself may be wrong; *the result is the test*" [emphasis added]. The choice of path is at base a moral action, and the chooser is the moral agent; hence the morality of outcome is in the making, not in the made.

COMMENTARY   Much of the 'critical' literature on architecture and design and advice in architectural education is preoccupied with choice of action, the rightness or otherwise of what to do or to have done in a specific situation; in other words, prescription. Often, prescriptions for right action also involve exemplification, acting as particular persons might act or have acted, working 'in the manner of', and so on. Indeed, exemplification abounds in architecture—from indentureship through to master studios as pedagogical stances, to mimesis, inspiration, alignment, and consensus in whatever degree using other buildings or architects as guides to individual action. Exemplification brings with it notions of character-building as much as of creating good habits or good works. But the focus of attention in teaching is not to make someone into a good person but to inculcate ways of doing the right thing.

Dilemmas can arise in relation to a single ethical view about the rights or wrongs of a work, or about ways of designing, if confronted with multiple values or other interpretations. An architect can ill-afford to insist on a doctrinaire functionalist approach to designing or understanding in the face of the task to design, say, a spiritual work such as a mosque. This may be an obvious example, but architects have sometimes fallen afoul of a single, or doctrinaire, view that is unable to cope with a tangential situation. What do they do under these circumstances? They must either reject the situation out of hand, or they adjust. The difficulty in adjusting is that by abandoning the safety of their single view, architects more than likely leave themselves with no basis for decisions at all. The rights and wrongs of any new situation must now either be judged anew with terms of reference quickly learned, or the architect must fall back on more primitive personal mores. "Once we abandon a single maximand, there may be no rule to give guidance in a situation in which we can feel the moral perplexity" (Stone 1987:169). A moral system may be silent on a particular issue or may not help because of some defect in its logic.

Stone cites the quandary of Orestes in Greek tragedy who slew his mother to avenge his father's death at her hands, and thereby went against the principle 'protect thy mother'. The question this example presents "is whether a system of moral governance that lacks the capacity to eliminate such quandaries should be regarded as fatally defective, so that the entire system has to be amended or withdrawn . . . [whether it is] a requirement of every moral viewpoint that it yield one and one only right prescription for every dilemma it recognizes?" (170). What might be the equivalent of Orestes's quandary in architecture? One common case is the saving of a historic building at the expense of completely gutting it so that it can be incorporated into a new development, resulting in a repatriated façade or a few lonely remnants of the original. "We intended to renovate much more of the building, but there was so much restoration to be done and the brief changed and. . . . At least we were able to salvage this much" is a line of argument heard quite often. Should the result be judged for what it is or in relation to the good intentions and their working out of the dilemma? Is the single view of historic preservation able to accommodate such drastic shifts?

As was shown in chapter 5A, an anticipated outcome is the only basis Kant would admit moral judgments to be made about the results of action; otherwise it is the actions of the actor that are subject to moral judgment. It is slightly different for Hofstadter; the *result* is the basis for testing whether right decisions were made, but the result itself is not subject to assessment for its rightness or wrongness. So, for the one the goodness or badness of a work of art or of architecture cannot be judged except in the light of its intentions, while for the other the work becomes the standard by which to measure the rightness of the actions leading to it, its judgment of worth presumably not being a moral judgment but an esthetic one. There are few critiques of buildings that take only the intentions of designing into account, and almost none that use the building to assess the correctness or otherwise of the decisions made in getting there (except in architectural education, where this happens regularly, if less than consistently). Yet pronouncements upon buildings are made all the time. If they purport to be other than esthetic judgments on matters of taste, and especially if they make claims about rightness or wrongness, are they valid judgments at all?

For Collins (above), the forms an architect intuits are near the horizon of truth and are the best that can be mustered under the conditions at the time; they may be bettered with knowledge and rationalization, but their realization comes through intuition. Ethical intuition is a particular kind of emotion engendering feelings about a situation unrelated to any particular principle or idea. If we commonly report having a "gut reaction" to someone, or if we speak of a "bad feeling" about something, we are not necessarily relating a truth. The 'good' or 'bad' intuited in such instances functions "to express or stimulate certain kinds of emotion, or to command or forbid certain kinds of action, and not to state certain kinds of fact" (Broad 1942:58). The evocative function of moral utterances has been labeled *emotivist*, and the mandatory function *prescriptivist*.

Emotional responses influence more than our moral judgment; they affect our esthetic judgment too and guide the decisions we make while designing. If you say to yourself while designing, "that's good" or "that's the right way" or "there's something wrong here" but are unable to rationalize the feeling further, you are affirming or denying the stance adopted rather than stating a truth about the matter. Continued work on the task is the only path to resolution, all the while guided by similar feelings, until a point of calm is reached and disconcerting worries diminish. The vagueness of the feelings we commonly experience needs to be better understood if we are to separate our moral from our esthetic feelings and thereby maintain consistency in the judgments we make, because we so often fail to recognize that our assignments of good/bad or right/wrong may be misplaced or may be bringing an illogic to bear upon a particular situation.

Despite morality being absent from architecture, in any absolute sense of truth correspondence, design studio tutors and critics continually make truth-claims by assigning good/bad and right/wrong in giving advice to students. While these may be attempts to persuade students to improve habits or ways of thinking in the emotional sense just outlined, they often are intended as loose moral injunctions. Because they are moral claims, students have freedom of choice about whether to follow the advice (Kant's hypothetical imperative), because every act, as outlined above, is essentially the making of a choice. But, more pertinently, it is mistaken to think that the truth-claims tutors who have imputed moral outcomes will, of themselves, induce right habits and right solutions in students merely from their cognizance; one person's truth-seeming has never been much of an inducement against another's willfulness. It is this prompting of certain actions and the linking of them to the goodness or badness, rightness or wrongness, of the ensuing buildings that has confounded architects for more than a century, and has led to the making of moral issues out of matters that are essentially amoral. Architecture appears to be almost totally bankrupt when it comes to a moral philosophy of its own, despite certain appearances to the contrary.

FURTHER SOURCES   Chapter 5A; H. Martin in Langdon *et al* 1984; Watkin 1977; Zambonini 1989.

4. Decorum and the Public Good of Architecture

Bienséance demands that a building is neither more nor less magnificent than is appropriate to its purpose. **Marc-Antoine Laugier.** 1753:III.3.

For both the English and the Americans demand of an individual that he be well dressed. . . . But what does it mean to be dressed well? It means to be dressed correctly. It is a question of being dressed *in such a way that one stands out the least.* **Adolf Loos.** 1902. Cited by Colomina in Al-Sayed, *et al,* 1988.

A public building is one which is supposed to be for "us" but really belongs to "them"; therefore, to regard it with a tinge of hostility is almost in the nature of a civic obligation. **Eugene Raskin.** 1974:68.

Buildings should be good neighbours. **Paul Thiry.** 1980. In Emanuel 1986.

The building's contribution to the context is that it is an entity unto itself; it has an architectural identity that doesn't result from borrowing reflections from the sky or from appealing too much to memory. **Emilio Ambasz** on the Museum of American Folk Art, New York. In Diamonstein 1985:23.

. . . a building should relate to its existing context and be respectful of that context: it should not make the adjacent buildings look ridiculous; it should not cast other buildings in its shadow. But it should also make a positive contribution, not only by its function, but by being something special on the street. **William J. Conklin.** In Diamonstein 1985:47.

TRACE   *Decorum* is that which is proper, suitable, or seemly, and it also relates to fitness, propriety, and congruity leading to appropriateness. Its etymology also ties to decoration, with which it is intimately related by degree, decorum being more toward the simple and solemn end of the spectrum. "The term derives from the rules of rhetoric in antiquity which demanded that the choice of words should always fit the occasion" (Gombrich 1979:229). Its moral overtones appear with the use of 'should' in relation to anything to do with the fitness or aptness of something, as shown in the Thiry and Conklin quotations above. This reciprocity between a person or thing and the context in which they operate, is the equation decorum seeks, a giving back by not taking away.

Vitruvius uses the term *decor,* or 'propriety', for one of his six architectural principles. "*Decor* is connected with *decet* in the basic sense of 'it is seemly, fitting, or proper'. Along with another variant, *decorum,* the term implies the quality of a thing's 'being as it should be', hence 'appropriateness' or 'propriety'. *Decorum* more often implies propriety in an ethical sense, *decor* in an aesthetic sense . . . the essential idea behind *decor* is appropriateness—the form given to a building must be appropriate to the building's meaning." The linking of *decor* with *oeconomia,* and the latter in turn with appropriateness, is confined to Vitruvius, who associated it with the Greek *oikeios,* 'pertaining to the house', through a chain of associations coming to mean 'proper to oneself' and ultimately fitting or suitable (Pollitt 1974:343–347).

The *bienséance,* or decorum, of Laugier's *An Essay on Architecture* (above) was ill-defined, despite the praise given to the book's clarity, decorum being a decorative quality more or less equated with the lavishness of a building's function: a church to have splendor; a palace to have magnificence; buildings for the poor, like a hospital, to "retain something of poverty." For Laugier decorum was tied to status; a building had to be "commensurate with the rank and wealth of the owners," and he advised that architects "must only propose what is fitting," because a beautiful building is one that "has all the beauty that is befitting and nothing beyond" (98–99). It is the ethical meaning of decorum as 'fittingness' that is pursued here, the appropriateness of buildings in public settings and the obligations they have to present themselves in a 'proper' manner.

COMMENTARY   One of the more perplexing issues in designing any building, especially a public building or a building having a distinctly public prominence in, say, a central city location, is to reconcile one's private esthetic desires with the demands of the setting and obligations to the so-called public good. The desire for businesses and public institutions to maintain a 'good front' is an anthropomorphism of great potency, a point that will be discussed shortly. In a very real sense, the maintenance of 'front'—the façade, and the way the building connects with the street—and deciding what constitutes proper civic manners are moral issues. Esthetic presentation in a public location is not a matter of willful imposition of individual taste but of decorum, of manners, of civic-mindedness. The principal issues in urban design are to do with what today is called *fit* in terms of scale, color, materials, detail, and proportion.

The idea of decorum initially was of refined control and restraint, a certain reserve in presenting an appropriate front in 'addressing' the public realm either in speech or in person, as outlined above. It occurred at all levels of social life—in modes of behavior as social etiquette, as well as in buildings. Decorum favored simplicity over elaboration, restraint over ostentation, and quickly became allied with the minimum necessary to achieve the required yet proper effect. Within the critical conscience of the classical tradition, the doctrine of decorum, stemming as it does from Cicero, "lays down the conditions under which display is admissible and even necessary, while appealing to good taste to set it limits and to be aware of its pitfalls" (Gombrich 1979:19). Cicero's description of Attic oratory as "restrained and plain, imitating common usage," a plainness of style that "seems easy to imitate" yet, once tried, "nothing less is so" (cited by Gombrich), was a commendation to classic simplicity that has never lost its power in rhetoric, and influences architecture to the present day. Moreover, Gombrich says that "the absence of artifice could be a special merit" and that in the canonic passage from Cicero, "aesthetic and moral issues are hard to separate."

Turning to the personal sense of decorum, there is a remarkable correlation between the way people conduct themselves—the mostly unwritten rules of behavior they establish—and the procedures they adopt in order to respect those rules or standards in the name of propriety. There are two groups of requirements in personal decorum, moral and instrumental. "Moral requirements are ends in themselves and presumably refer to rules regarding non-interference and non-molestation of others, rules regarding sexual propriety, rules regarding respect of sacred places, etc.," writes Erving Goffman. "Instrumental requirements are not ends in themselves and presumably refer to duties such as an employer might demand of his employees—care of property, maintenance of work levels, etc." (1959:110). While some might feel, says Goffman, that decorum should cover only moral standards and that a different term should be adopted for the instrumental, most social standards do not differentiate between them. "Provided the standard is maintained by sanctions and by a sanctioner of some kind, it will often be of small moment to the performer whether the standard is justified chiefly on instrumental grounds or moral ones, and whether or not he is asked to incorporate the standard" (110–111).

Building and planning controls, supposedly for the public good in insisting on certain standards of 'performance', operate in a similar way. Once in place they are acceded to, and their justification matters little until a 'performer', in Goffman's terms, defies them or is prepared to legally contest them. Goffman goes on to align 'manner' with politeness and 'appearance' with decorum, saying that while decorum entails respect for a "region and setting," its motivation may be for reasons other than respect, such as impressiveness or merely compliance for smooth progress. He also notes that "the requirements of decorum are more pervasive ecologically than are the requirements of politeness," because the public front is always under inspection, whereas politeness entails some degree of choice. The equivalent of these ideas architecturally is that appearance and decorum are a matter of buildings en masse 'behaving morally', while manner and politeness are to do with how an individual building engages at the local level with, say, the street or its neighbor.

The implications of decorum in design are manifold, from the primary separation of front-of-house from back-of-house and the careful management of the interface between them so important in theaters, hotels, shopping centers, hospitals, and many other building types, to the more subtle aspects of seemliness and maintenance of appearances in terms of corporate and institutional imagery, to the orchestrated but eventually self-sustaining maintenance of the qualitative ambience of places and cities. So we begin to see that decorum in architectural terms is a matter of reflexive performance, part of a chorus line of values, as it were, geared to maintaining the momentum of the whole yet allowing some independence of character to emerge at the same time. Decorum has been proposed as just this ability to fine-tune contextual relationships.

Yet decorum and the 'whole' that it presupposes are products of ancient traditions and wisdoms of a scale other than that of modern cities, and of social mores that belong to another time. Decorum and holism lose their potency the moment they are removed from the coherent contexts of historical centers, or central business districts, into the seamless individuality of modern sub-urbanism, where bravura and conservatism co-exist, a realm that is largely dismissed by architects and self-styled urbanists as without grace, where decorum would be an impossible task. Precisely because decorum may be so easily dissolved suggests something about its efficacy as a concept and about urbanism as a realm of action. The importation of decorum into presentday urbanism, and its consequent demands on architects, has indeed caused some theorists to have serious doubts about urbanism as a discipline, about conceptions of the future city that this discipline supposes, and about the perceived moral consequences of compliance or lack of compliance with the rules of urban decorum (Macarthur 1991).

What might be done to reduce the arbitrariness of architecture if the rules of decorum supporting notions of an urban, if not suburban, public good are taken away?

FURTHER SOURCES   Brolin 1980; Lynch 1984; Rowe and Koetter 1978; Rossi 1982; Tafuri 1976b; Tzonis and Lefaivre 1986.

CHAPTER

Ordering Architecture

Overview

I cannot think that the world . . . is the result of chance; yet I cannot look at each separate thing as a result of Design. I am, and shall ever remain, in a hopeless muddle. **Charles Darwin.** Cited in F. Darwin. 1888. *The Life and Letters of Charles Darwin* (London: John Murray). Vol. 2:353–354.

Knowledge which is derived from wonder is unhappy unless it relates itself to other knowledge. And this relation of knowledge to knowledge is what you might call a sense of order; a sense of the position of this knowledge in relation to other things around. When we get a sense of order—not just knowledge or information—then we are very happy. We wink at wonder and say, "How am I doing wonder?" Because wonder is activated by this knowledge, and better still, by this sense of order. **Louis Kahn.** 1962. "A Statement." In Latour 1991:146.

The stupendous fact is that all the evidence accumulated by science indicates a rational world . . . the faith of our time is that the world, the whole cosmos . . . is designed in an orderly rational way. This was believed by the Greeks of ancient times and by Alberti. It was, and perhaps still is, a reasonable assumption that architecture should conform to the order of the universe, not contradict it. **Bruce Allsopp.** 1977:18.

Philosophically, there is no foundation for the claim that our system of reasonable behaviour is the definitive expression of sanity and reason in human affairs. **Roy Boyne.** 1990:32.

What might be offered here about the world and our comprehension of it that is profound and insightful and that has not been said more eloquently by others? Nothing, I suspect. Yet, the dilemma of chance versus design that Darwin remarks upon above continues to irritate the modern conscience, especially concerning the individual creativity of our intervention in and interpretation of the world. Christopher Marlowe's view of nature as the 'wondrous Architecture of the world' (*Conquests of Tamburlaine*, Part 1) remains the marvel it ever was, but his use of 'architecture' suggests a pre-eminence for the divinely structured that has infected thought since the earliest times.

It is difficult to imagine the world without human agency at work, and impossible to know what kind of world that world would be. Trying to comprehend a world free of human comprehension would surely be an act of supreme human arrogance, the kind of supremacy that only gods are supposed to command. And such a comprehension would be beset by all the same difficulties philosophers and theologians have struggled with for more than two millennia in relation to the Grand Architect knowing the world yet not intervening in it.

To persevere with the speculation about a world free of human agency for a moment, assuming the laws of nature as we now understand them prevail, individual circumstances and events taking place within the world would be utterly indifferent to one another except insofar as, say, Darwin's 'survival of the fittest' in conjunction with random mutation would still be primary determinants of biological processes. Environmental phases would come and go as the world changed according to the laws of dynamics, equilibrium, thermodynamics, and so on, dictated by accidents within and random incursions from without (space). Ecologies would complexify in some places, simplify in others, and evolution as well as extinction would occur in all forms of life as the world advanced in whatever directions and toward whatever ends it might.

For what are laws, or the fittest, or phases, or changes, or advances, or directions, or ends, and especially Marlowe's *a priori* 'architecture', if not human concepts and constructs already devised by us and layered over the world as a means of giving it order and making it comprehensible? All that astronomers, cosmologists, and science fiction writers can do in their attempts to describe other worlds, futures for this world, or our hypothetical non-human world, is to reflect the human image.

It is difficult to go beyond this simple prognosis because already language is interfering and obscuring what has been and might be said about this nonhuman world. Of human preoccupations, perhaps nomination is the most potent ordering device imposed upon the world because it fixes time as well as things. Naming both affects and reflects our perception and placement of whatever is named in the constellation of other named things—our *classification* of things. So central is naming to our ordering of the world that exploration and geography have been possible only because of the ability to name, not just in creating markers of journeying but in giving dimension to space (Carter 1987). A parallel may be drawn with our spatial understanding and description as anthropocentrically based—front/back, left/right, up/down, inside/outside, here/there.

These sorts of observations lead to the thought that the world does not exist except through our conception and comprehension of it, and is a notion that has intrigued certain philosophers. Is it possible that all notions of order, all ideas of structure, are but human impositions intended to facilitate further ordering and structuring, and to facilitate communication between humans. In other words, might the world not inherently possess such orders and structures, or even laws? All we can say is that the world *appears* to be ordered, for that is the way we begin to comprehend it and to anticipate our further actions within it; and perhaps that is all that matters. If there were no human desire to reach for the stars, to build and work against gravity, or to delve into the primaries of matter, the laws of physics would cease to be facts *for us,* if not to be facts. This evidential paradox lies at the heart of all human endeavor and is of special importance to architecture because of the singular role ordering plays in how and what designers design.

It follows, therefore, that if the architecture of the world precedes the world, as Marlowe and others suggest, and if architectonic words precede their use in architectural language, then the *architecture* of architecture is the conceptual *structuring* of architecture so that it can be imaged and discussed. From this viewpoint, the ordering of architecture is not intrinsic but extrinsic, brought—as with all things and no-things (see introduction) of the world—by the human need for comprehension. So, if architects speak of order, hierarchy, chaos, simplicity, complexity, and the impact of time, they are speaking about themselves and their own needs.

Part A of this chapter explores those notions of order relevant to architecture and that architects either talk about or adopt implicitly. The investment in bringing order out of the 'chaos' of multifarious requirements in a building program is one long-standing construct of designing subscribed to by architects, as is the corresponding idea of making a simple resolution out of complexity. Part B examines the implementation of these notions and of a designing attitude raised in chapter 4A. It is argued that only with a great deal of qualification can what is commonly called 'method' be considered conducive to this attitude or to architectural notions of order. For the most part, transcendence of order and attitude remains a mystery that even the inculcation of students into the secret ways and traditions of architecture and design fails to elucidate. But, as discussed in chapter 4, just as the Gnostic initiate bypasses the demiurge, so designers and architects somehow circumvent all methods and rules and deal directly with being and becoming.

A. Order By Imposition

1. Order, the Imposition of Human Constructs

. . . it is often stated that the beauty of classic architecture resides in Order. And Order, upon analysis, is found to consist in correspondence, iteration, and the presence of fixed ratios between the parts. Ratio, identity, and correspondence form part of the necessary web and fabric of our thought . . . . Order is a desire of the mind . . . . What more natural, then, than to say that architectural beauty—the beauty of classic architecture, at any rate—consists in Order? . . . . It should at once be apparent that Order in design is totally distinct from Beauty. Many of the ugliest patterns and most joyless buildings . . . possess Order in a high degree; they exhibit fixed and evident ratios of design . . . . Here is Order, and no beauty, but, on the contrary, ugliness. **Geoffrey Scott.** 1924:205–206.

Each generation feels a new dissatisfaction, and conceives of a new idea of order. This is architecture. **Alison** and **Peter Smithson of Team 10.** *Architectural Design.* June 1955.

> *Order is*
> *Design* is form-making in order . . .
> In *order* is creative force . . .
> Thru the *order*—what . . .
> The same *order* created the elephant and created man . . .
> *Order does not imply Beauty* . . .
> *Order is intangible* . . .
> *Order supports integration* . . .
> **Louis Kahn.** 1955. "Order Is." In Latour 1991:58–59.

Design demands that one understand the *order*. When you are dealing, or designing in brick, you must ask brick what it wants, or what it can do . . . . If you're dealing with concrete, you must know the order of nature, you must know the nature of concrete, what concrete really strives to do. **Louis Kahn.** 1972. "I Love Beginnings." In Latour 1991:288.

From birth we struggle to establish a fragment of *order* in the infinite variety of our environment. The order we attain is . . . a result of collaboration and the transmission of information. The achieved order is defended against all charges; the need for order makes man at the same time creative and conservative. A *common order* is called *culture*. **Christian Norberg-Schulz.** 1965:79.

Design is the conscious effort to impose meaningful order. **Victor Papanek.** 1977:17.

I have come to believe that the problem of physical order—the kind of order which creates quality in architecture . . . is of so great a stature, that we shall have to modify our picture of the whole physical universe in order to see it clearly. **Christopher Alexander.** Foreword to Games 1985.

TRACE   The term 'order' derives from the Latin *ordo* and *ordin-*, row, series, rank, class, or degree, and is also related to *ordiri*, begin, and *ornare*, adorn. Some *ordinary* thing or event is one in accordance with the established or common order or arrangement, an *ordinance* is a municipal rule or law, while to *ordain* is to put in order or to prepare something (or someone) for a purpose. There are two Greek terms used to mean order—one is *kosmos* (Sanskrit *rta*), "whether with reference to the due order of or arrangement of things, or to the world order" (Coomaraswamy 1977, I:249). *Kosmos* also means ornament adorning animals, humans, and speech, *kosmeo,* to order or arrange; *kosmetikos* means skilled in ordering, *kosmema* is an ornament or decoration, and *kosmetike* is the art of dress and ornament, hence *kosmetike,* cosmetic (Coomaraswamy, *loc. cit.*). The other is *taxis,* the orderly arrangement of parts (Aristotle, *Poetics,* VII:§35), with *poiesis* as the making of something by bringing order to it.

To the ancient Greeks, architecture consisted of *taxis* or *ordinatio* in Latin, and *diathesis,* arrangement—*dispositio* in Latin. Arrangement not only involved the placing of parts in relation to one another, but elegance of composition. There were also considered to be subcategories of arrangement, called *ideai* in Greek, which for architecture were the ground plan, elevation, and perspective (Pollitt 1974:160). Vitruvius (1486) says that order "gives due measure to the members of a work considered separately, and symmetrical agreement to the proportions of the whole." (Book I:II, 2). Tzonis and Lefaivre (1986:18) quote the 1931 MIT Press translation of the same part as saying order is "balanced adjustment of the details of a work separately, and, as to the whole, the arrangement of the proportion with a view to a symmetrical result" remarking, however, that this is 'not very clear' compared with Aristotle.

COMMENTARY   When Victor Papanek wrote the above quotation in *Design for the Real World* (1972), he articulated the three central concerns of design as a universal preoccupation: that it is a *conscious* act, that it seeks to elucidate *meaning,* and that it *imposes* order upon an otherwise less-than-orderly world. The preamble to this chapter explores the imposition of order as a means of comprehending the world, and puts forward the view that order in architecture as a tangible design goal is an artificial construct. If this notion is extended to include those sources to which architects occasionally turn for inspiration— namely, nature and natural objects—then architecture may be seen to be an edifice unto itself, a self-fulfilling prophecy. The right or wrong of architecture can relate only to those constructions of it used to assess its correctness, of which traditional Eastern ideas and classical canons are only two, though longstanding, versions. Hence the almost infinite variety of architecture across ages and cultures.

In ancient Greek culture and in traditional cosmology, the archetypal universe (*kosmos*) was an ordered, harmonious system having two modes: the *mikros kosmos,* or microcosm, the 'little world' of humankind, was the epitome of the 'great world' or *makros kosmos,* macrocosm. This mirroring of the great by the little was the 'order' in which architecture, too, participated, and in which those who are traditionally inclined believe it still participates. The ancient classical 'orders' derive from the Greek *kosmopoiesis,* architectural ornament, and carry the sense of decorum, without which a building is not properly 'dressed'. Thus, the perfection of Shaker furniture accords with a tradition in which everything is to be made following the order of the Master Craftsman of the Universe because "order is the creation of beauty. It is heaven's first law [cf, Gk. *kosmos,* Skr. *rta*] and the protection of souls. . . . Beauty rests on utility" (Coomaraswamy 1977, I:257). Of course, the exposition of just what the cosmological schema is then becomes a total way of seeing the world in which architectural order is merely one of many orders that exist in a total unified understanding—something far beyond the scope of this limited essay. Suffice it to say that this is the 'order' to which Louis Kahn and Christopher Alexander refer above.

As against the archetypal order, the prototypical and stereotypical orders (for explanations of terms, see 7A.5, Archetype) have been the classical canon and its products. This canonic system consists of three levels of formal devices: *taxis,* the division into parts; *genera,* the individuated elements; and *symmetry,* the relations between part and part and between part and whole (Tzonis and Lefaivre 1986). Symmetry was raised in passing in chapter 2B, and is dealt with in more detail in chapters 9A and 10A, so it will not be touched on here except to say that as an ordering device, bilateral symmetry is still a potent architectural force today. Junior students find it the most comforting device of ordering while designing, and are initially reluctant to break away from it until they come to understand other possibilities of arrangement and composition. Many natural objects are near-symmetrical about an axis, so are most everyday household items and implements involving human contact, physical balance, and nonhandedness. So, it is natural for students to think of symmetry first while designing buildings, and difficult for them to understand that differences in built relationships and scales do not also necessitate bilateral symmetry. What *will* be discussed here is *taxis,* not only as a classical system but as a general ordering system.

Under a classical canon in which the whole predominates, *taxis* "divides a building into parts and fits into the resulting partitions the architectural elements, producing a coherent work" (Tzonis and Lefaivre 1986:9). It thereby constrains these elements according to some logical procedure. The two basic 'schemata' of *taxis,* according to Tzonis and Lefaivre, are the grid and tripartition. The grid schema may be either rectangular (or more correctly, quadrangular) or polar (radial-concentric), and the tripartition schema organizes the inside and outside of an arrangement, the border elements, and the enclosed element.

Thus there is lateral tripartition, edge-center-edge, which is mostly bilaterally symmetrical, and vertical tripartition, bottom-middle-top, which is not. And, since these schemata may be applied to the whole building and to the parts at various 'levels' of scale down to the smallest, they are hierarchical in their application, scale implying the notion of a *module* as the unit of measure (see 9A.4, Scaling). Classical ordering thus is "inconceivable without a conception of its essential characteristic—measure, which involves both definition (marking the boundaries of things) and analysis of the interrelationships of discrete forms" (Pollitt 1974:15). Further, "all classical works, whether in words, sounds or shapes, are identifiable by their strict adherence to the schema that demarcates a realm of departure, a central realm, and a realm of arrival. It comes under many names: opening, continuation, completion; introduction, main part, conclusion; exposition, development, recapitulation" (Tzonis and Lefaivre 1986:27).

Turning to modern conceptions of order, in many ways classical *taxis* prevails too, except not in strict accordance with a canon. Many buildings today commonly use lateral tripartition (frequently bilaterally symmetrical or near-symmetrical) and vertical tripartition (some division into a base element, an intermediate element, and a skyline element). They also use the grid as a structural and façade-ordering system, often with a regular A-A-A . . . repetition rather than variable A-B-A-C-A . . . repetition or similar. Most multistorey buildings and many smaller buildings use tripartition and the grid as their ordering schemata, and may therefore be classified as classical. Le Corbusier adopted what was largely a variation on a classical canon in using the grid—"regulating lines," in his terms—and vertical tripartition, although he generally 'worked against' lateral tripartition in avoiding or playing down bilateral symmetry (except, curiously, in certain of his town plans, such a *La Ville Radieuse* of 1933, where such symmetry is strongly evident).

Other ordering notions developed by the early modernists to counter the classical resulted in moving away from the cosmic order presumed to govern manifestation to a human order that was presumed inherent in the particularities of the project and in individual discrimination. Modern architectural order accepted that external dictates might govern where context is dominant, as in concentrated urban settings, but otherwise related to internal dictates of the designer's own making. The implication of this has been that the order for any design task exists in the mediation between the designer and that task, and that it develops as an understanding of the task and the self develops. Adjustments made to whatever ordering constructs are applied to a task throughout the designing *create* the order of the outcome.

However, since the fifties, both classical and self-ordering as continuities between things have been increasingly questioned, and the *discontinuities* among things increasingly favored, as Michel Foucault suggests in *The Order of Things* (1966). A simple example would be to ask of a work of architecture what constitutes its order, and then to ask what does not fit this order. Is what does not fit the orderly schema *disorder,* or something else? The only answer must be 'something else', because it was placed there by the designer even though it may appear 'discontinuous'. Thus we are faced with the architectural equivalent of what Jean-Paul Sartre calls man, the *universal singulier* or *individual generality,* general in all that connects, singular in all that does not (Ormiston and Schrift 1990:166–170). The only order for architecture, then, appears to be arbitrary aggregation. What does this say for the concept of order?

FURTHER SOURCES   Alexander 1992; Ardrey 1970; Arnheim 1966, 1982; Colquhoun 1989; Critchlow 1969; Dewey 1934; Kollar 1985, 1987; Merquior 1985; Porphyrios 1978; Tyng 1975.

2. Hierarchy: A Special Case of Order?

A formal structure generally consists of *primary* and *secondary* elements, or exhibits a still more complicated hierarchy. The primary elements are by definition basic to the structure; if they are taken away the composition disintegrates . . . . The secondary ones, instead, may be treated with a relatively high degree of freedom, though care must be taken that they do not interfere with the primary elements. **Christian Norberg-Schulz.** 1965:149–150.

Self-similarity is symmetry across scale. It implies recursion, pattern inside of pattern. **James Gleick.** 1987:103.

Order implies making distinctions; when creating order the first task is to distinguish and classify; order involves separation. By contrast, the avant-garde movements had sought connection, osmosis, liaison . . . .

The validity of the classifications denied by Croce's aesthetics emerged in a form of 'hierarchy'— a concept beloved of the fascists—of qualities. **Franco Borsi.** 1987:12–13.

There are two kinds of hierarchy . . . . One is the size of buildings in relation to their public importance. The other is the relative significance of the different elements which make up a building—so that we know, for instance, where the front door is! . . . . Only in recent large buildings have we lost this sense of hierarchy. **Charles, Prince of Wales.** 1989:80–81.

TRACE   Hierarchy comes from the medieval Latin *(h)ierarchia* stemming from the earlier Greek *ierarches* (*ieros,* sacred + *-arches*), high priest. The term relates to priestly rule, and in everyday usage means 'a body of persons or things ranked in grades, orders, or classes, one above another' especially in natural science and logic from the mid-seventeenth century. Its foremost quality is that of a whole assembly (body of persons, priests, angels, and so on) that is internally arranged in an order of precedence, a not quite perfect hierarchy being the levels of organization in biology wherein subatomic particles, chemical elements, molecules, cells, multicellular organisms, and populations are related. One way to clarify hierarchy as a single entity having successively subordinated grades or layers is to conceive of it as a 'nested' set, as with concentric spheres, wherein the larger entity contains the smaller but diminishes proportionally in intensity. In other words, the smallest entity is most concentrated or most powerful, and its intensity permeates the whole.

The term 'classical' reflects the hierarchical social ordering of ancient Roman society, from the *classici* to the *proletarii,* and the ordering of classical architecture of the West consists equally in the placement of parts in a system of rank ordering. The same applies to buildings in which there is geometrical and spatial interrelation based on some central, dominant element, as occurs in much religious architecture of the East and West. Indeed, any building that may be described or understood in terms of the greater and lesser structuring of its parts would be hierarchical, which embraces all but some recent architecture.

COMMENTARY   The reason the title to this section is stated as a question is to oppose ordering systems based in intervals, in subtraction and addition between parts, with ordering systems based in hierarchy, those that remain connected with the whole by relying on multiplication and subdivision between parts. In chaos theory, the notion of self-replication stated by James Gleick above is arguably the perfect example of hierarchy. All dependent chains of the kind found in biology, such as the food chain, are hierarchies. Another term describing hierarchy is 'levels', favored by planners and architects for their nested embrace. "On one level, the design for this situation concerns the condition of life of the individuals in this place, but on another level it is representative of the living conditions of all who live in this climate, while on yet another level it participates in the living qualities of humankind, in what it means to *dwell*." This hypothetical statement is the sort of hierarchical structure one comes across quite regularly in commentaries by architects and critics.

For example, for Christopher Alexander, the essence of community is made clear using a similar kind of statement concerning the 'overlapping, interconnected structure': "the most fundamental issue in politics has to do with the size of groups and the hierarchy of groups . . . each person inside the house has a room of his own, and then each member has some communal space . . . each house has its own territory . . . [and with] a dozen other houses . . . [forms] a house cluster . . . [then] say there are ten clusters which make up an identifiable 'neighborhood' of about five hundred people . . . and then you have a community of approximately five to ten thousand people and perhaps a dozen or twenty neighborhoods" and so on (Grabow 1983:154). Such tree-like structures are prevalent particularly in town-planning, in that pre-eminence establishes priorities that are seen as fundamental to implementation. This is arguably why town planning is so readily bureaucratized; hierarchy necessarily attends certain tasks because of their sheer size, and the will-to-power over such tasks warrants command structures in which responsibility devolves to finer and finer levels. Indeed, the very notion of 'levels' is a certain indication of hierarchical structure.

The point of the hierarchy is that any instance of it implies all other instances of it; it bears much the same relationship to any affiliated concept contained by it as it does to its own overarching concept. When terms such as *primary* and *secondary* are adopted, as in Norberg-Schulz above, hierarchy is signaled. The *primary* quality of, say, a spatial order usually refers to its most holistic spatio-geometrical structure, while its *secondary* qualities relate to the primary in certain spatial and geometric ways, but are of subsidiary importance and are frequently of lesser volume. There might a *tertiary* spatial or geometric order attaching to the secondary system in equivalent ways. Such a hierarchical spatial comprehension of architecture is found in the system developed by the historian Paul Frankl (1914), who elaborates categories of *spatial form* in which he discerns eleven distinct but interrelated spatial sets, by means of which he analyzes ecclesiastical buildings.

At the risk of some crudity in generalization, traditional and Renaissance classical architectures have privileged holistic order and geometric proportioning, which were hierarchical, with some notable exceptions like the villa plans of Palladio (March and Steadman 1971:224). Later, Beaux Arts education and examination *en charrette* insisted on the *parti,* the composition being conceived as a whole, with the detail being filled in later; it thus also favored hierarchic proportioning, in this case 'downward' from the whole. Modern architecture of the early twentieth century, reacting as it did so vehemently to Beaux Arts conceptions and methods, employed different educational techniques that went against the parti; they tended toward cumulative assembly and hence an additive order in which autonomy of parts prevailed, again with a few notable exceptions like Le Corbusier.

Judging by its rare appearance as a discrete topic in the architectural literature of the past decade, after a bit of a run during the seventies, hierarchical ordering seems now to be a topic of curiosity rather than a living issue, or features only in the fringe literature by metaphysician-architects (Critchlow 1969, 1976). Order in architecture is undoubtedly considered by many architects to be too well-known to excite interest now, or else the fall from favor of traditional and classical hierarchical ordering brought about by the rise of modernism is seen as more than adequately compensated by the freedom offered designers. Yet, hierarchical ordering of some kind is perpetually in demand by architects, and is frequently a major item of discussion with students in the design studio. In the face of the rising interest in Islamic architecture and the advocacy of traditional values by an *agent provocateur* as influential as the Prince of Wales, we may well be witnessing a renewal of interest in classical ordering again, a 'return to order'.

But remove the classical notion of the whole or the need for control that the will-to-power demands, and problems with hierarchy emerge. As Kevin Lynch (1984) remarks, despite *seeming* to be a natural and inevitable way of ordering complexity, "it is not a grand rule of nature" and, while it may be a common social, corporate, and political pattern, "informal social networks often develop to subvert it. It is a way of imaging convenient to our minds." In relation to Lynch's topic, the form of cities, "it is difficult to maintain hierarchy in very complex organizations such as cities. It is harmful to the easy flow of human interactions, wherever it is forcibly imposed . . . hierarchy is laborious . . . . Hierarchy is primarily useful for indexing and cataloguing . . . . At the city scale, hierarchy keeps relapsing into disorder, or a different order" (96). What Lynch says about hierarchy in relation to cities is evident in complex architectural situations in which evenness of aggregation and distribution may be just as workable, as housing estates (contrary to Alexander above) and many process-based buildings (factories, schools, hospitals, universities) attest. At the same time, this equality of placement points up the artificiality of hierarchy in less complex circumstances. To repeat the question at the end of 6A.1, Order, "What does [the only order being arbitrary aggregation] say for the concept of order?"

If theory does not control practice, as is argued throughout this book, insisting on hierarchy in any form as a theoretical construct is only a power play, and power plays inhibit theory's mediation.

FURTHER SOURCES   Chapter 2B; Alexander 1992; Heath 1984, Chapter 6; von Meiss 1986; Snodgrass 1990.

3. The Investment in Chaos versus Order

A "chaos," once so named, has as much unity of discourse as a cosmos. It is an odd fact that many monists consider a great victory scored for their side when pluralists say "the universe is many." " 'The Universe'! " they chuckle—"his speech bewrayeth him. He stands confessed of monism out of his own mouth." Well, let things be one in so far forth! You can fling such a word as universe at the whole collection of them, but what matters it? It still remains to be ascertained whether they are one in any further or more valuable sense. **William James.** 1907:60.

Observe, Phaedrus, that the Demiurge, when he set about creating the world, attacked the Confusion of Chaos . . . . But the builder I now show you finds before him, in place of chaos and primary matter, precisely the worldly order that the Demiurge drew from disorder in the beginning. **Paul Valéry.** c1921. "Eupalinos ou l'Architecte." *Oeuvres Complètes.* Vol. II, Paris 1960. Cited in Borsi (1987):19–20.

Turbulence is history's vocation, and organized man burdened with his so-called knowledge, will never learn, to judge by his persistence in deluding himself, that he always arrives too late to train it. **Roger McKeon.** Preface to Lyotard 1984a:4.

A system in which the final results can be very different, even though the initial conditions are nearly the same, is said to be "chaotic." The connection between nonlinear systems and chaotic systems is far from simple. All chaotic systems are nonlinear, but there are many nonlinear systems that are not chaotic . . . a system operating with the implication that two points close together at the start will not be close together at the finish is a system taken to represent "chaos." **James Trefil.** 1986:203

How could it be that ever since Herakleitos we have repressed the challenge and risk of becoming and have gone instead for representational systems designed to erect, classify, and represent hierarchical stabilities and redundancies in order to allay the fright of facing Chaos? **John Knesl.** In Al-Sayed *et al,* 1988.

Chaos may be a little overfamiliar nowadays, especially in its studied inscription in architecture. **Michael Sorkin.** 1991:347.

TRACE   From the Latin *chaos* in turn adapted from the Greek, vast chasm or void, chaos is based in the ancient Greek creation myth wherein *Chaos* and *Choma* (Earth) are the first beings. *Chaos* created and mated with the goddess *Nyx* or *Nox,* Night, out of which union eventually came all gods and men. "A universe created from Chaos was in perfect keeping with the Greek belief in an unpredictable Nature run by capricious gods," writes Carl Sagan (1981:175). Late in the sixteenth century chaos came to mean figuratively "a confused mass" and, in the seventeenth century, "a state of utter confusion and disorder" (SOED). A traditional term for a state of chaos is the *undifferentiated,* about which it has been said, "We may conceive the undifferentiated as a sort of extension without variation or discontinuity: but it does not follow from this that it possesses unity" (Vivante 1955:11). Chaos came to be thought of as the shape of matter before it was reduced to order, the state of disorder and shapelessness, and hence the state to which any 'world' would return if order were removed.

Chaos theory of recent times, though, proffers chaos as the new cosmos, the ultimate order of the universe, and differs dramatically from the classical version. "Where chaos begins, classical science stops" writes James Gleick (1987:3). Chaos theory was formulated in the 1970s, yet only a decade later it was a booming business. "Chaos [theory] breaks across the lines that separate scientific disciplines. Because it is a science of the global nature of systems" (5). Theorists of the picturesque in the eighteenth and nineteenth centuries thought chaos could be tamed. The French architect Marc-Antoine Laugier, writing in 1753, thought that, esthetically, towns should be places "where there is order but nonetheless a great confusion . . . from the multitude of regular parts, there results in the whole a certain idea of irregularity and chaos" (Colquhoun 1989:107). While really a critique of classical order, Laugier presents a quality that architects have absorbed and pursued in towns ever since, lacking, however, a theory to mediate it. Hillier and Hanson (1984) offered one possibility in their studies of the ordering systems of villages; 'chaos theory' possibly offers another in the way it uses simple rules to generate regular patterns at different scales.

COMMENTARY   Chaos, or at least chaotic systems matching Trefil's description above and defying prediction, abounds in nature and in our everyday world. The weather is one notable example, as is all turbulence, including the mountain stream and boiling water; populations of many kinds, especially insects; and pedestrian behavior in public plazas, which defies prediction despite certain discrete patterns being discernible. The presence of a chaos 'theory' in physics today is comforting; chaos may be tamable, it is certainly beautiful, and it no longer intimidates us with formlessness. Threats of chaos lurking just beyond complexity are nowhere near as daunting or damning as they used to be, because chaos theory offers a counter to scientific determinism—linearity, reductivism, and the definitive solution—as another way through.

Inherent in the architectural understanding of chaos as an absence of either order (dis-), structure (un-), or shape (-less) has always been one major difficulty—that it may be defined only by inverting knowable concepts. For precisely this reason, chaos in the classical sense has been inherently unknowable, even unimaginable, no matter how we tried. In other words, *chaos has been a nameless dread* used to prop up the classical system of ordering. But rather than chaos itself, what is feared is the *absence* of order, shape, or structure. If we have had an image of chaos, it has been of a random and diffuse distribution with no tangible ordering cues, nothing out of which a pattern or arrangement might be created. Yet there is really no difference between this image of chaos and that of an extensive forest, except that a forest is not labeled chaotic, presumably because we give a name to it. In fact a forest is something many find solace in, which prompts some intriguing questions. Is this solace achieved because individual elements (trees, leaves, rocks) may be discerned in a forest, or because we know it *is* a forest (as against other, non-forested, regions) and it has finite limits? Is a kind of order, structure, and shape therefore created for a forest by virtue of its 'parts' being discerned, or by knowing it *is* a forest of limited extent (a whole, with parts)? If the answer is "yes" to any or all of these, what might be the equivalent of chaos in a forest—being lost? If being lost in a forest is the inability to discern its structure (its 'direction', its extent, its limits), is the forest then equivalent to chaos? And is being lost, being in chaos, a property of the forest or of the participant?

At its most chaotic, this classical image of chaos might be considered 'perfectly' random or diffuse, betraying the paucity of English adjectives to qualify it. That a state of chaos might be conceivable in which randomness reigns to such an extent that any sample of it is like any other sample, implies a homogeneity that is at the outset denied by the classical image of chaos. But modern chaos theory claims precisely this. In other words, a perfection of chaos is presumed to exist in which a unity reigns; a Platonist would be hard-pressed not to label this the Form of Chaos. But in this we strike a paradox, for Plato's Form is unable to deal with perfect disorder or 'formlessness', or especially accumulations of accretive substances like dirt, hair, excrement, and so on (Hollier 1989:98–102). The only way in which a Platonist deals with chaotic situations is by applying an extrinsic descriptor but contriving its agglomeration or arrangement as formal, that is, as some physical shape, such as a pile, heap, or tangle. And herein has always lain the promise of classical chaos as an architectural concept upon which chaos theory seems to capitalize.

Absence of structure is akin to Diana Agrest's notion of *nondesign,* vis-a-vis *design,* which for her "describes the way in which different cultural systems interrelate and *give form to* [emphasis mine] the built world; it is not a direct product of any institutionalized design practice but rather the result of a general process of culture" (Agrest 1991:32). So, if the architect as demiurge argues for the closed world of design as the solution to the 'chaos' of the city, suburb, street, slum, wasteland, dockland, or whatever, it is not Chaos (the big C of architecture!) that is threatening—for that can never be—but a state at some remove, a degree of order that is perhaps so loose as to be barely discernible, and with which the architect is not aligned or does not agree, the open world and cultural order of Agrest's 'nondesign'.

Because classical chaos has been described only as an *absence* of the order being designed into some situation, the argument for it as a threat is circular. However, in classical terms it is arguable that there can be no 'perfect' chaos, just as there can be no perfect whole. If there can be only an imperfect chaos, then, in a classical sense, there must be some structure to chaos, but a structure that is not discernible. Hence the appeal of chaos theory—it says just that. The thrust of arguments against complexity and for simplicity has been that descent into chaos (as imperfect order, not as a *real* possibility) was otherwise always imminent. This threat brought the imperative to classical order. What has not been recognized is that this threat has always been a political act, and therefore has been a matter of negotiation and mediation. What modern chaos theory offers is a way around the conglomerate arguments of classical ideas and traditional cosmology. Recent trends in architecture that emphasize difference parallel the rise of chaos theory that looks at turbulence.

Chaos theory undoubtedly has seductive appeal for those architectural theorists who have argued from a classical holistic viewpoint all along and see it as an affirmation. They probably rejoice to read that "believers in chaos," as Gleick calls them, "feel they are turning back a trend in science toward reductionism . . . . They believe that they are looking for the whole" (Gleick 1987:5). The mistake of architects has been to interpret chaos notions that explain *natural* phenomena as if they relate to architecture, which is artificial. Architects have known for almost a century that natural systems do not apply to architecture. Whatever its intellectual appeal, the application of chaos theory to architecture might only be yet another notion from a discipline outside architecture to be exploited by piracy through analogy.

Chaos theory has already impacted upon architecture in one respect, that of the 'Butterfly Effect', a term explained by Gleick: "Tiny differences in input could quickly become overwhelming differences in output—a phenomenon given the name 'sensitive dependence on initial conditions'. In weather, for example, this translates into what is only half-jokingly known as the Butterfly Effect—the notion that a butterfly stirring the air today in Peking can transform storm systems next month in New York" (1987:8). How far architects have gone already in marauding chaos theory is shown by Coop Himmelblau's insistence on maintaining complexity and resisting reductive simplicity by enshrining in its work the Butterfly Effect so beloved of chaos theorists, the 'sensitive dependence on initial conditions' (Sorkin 1991:347), both literally and figuratively. Literally by building every line of initial sketches (or so these architects have said), figuratively by transmogrifying Cartesian linearity and straight buildings into architectural insectivores parasitizing rooftops.

The Creature of Chaos may be on the wing but for the ardent Platonist every bite of chaos theory merely feeds the god of Perfect Wholeness. However, if modern chaos theory is making classical chaos knowable, then what is to replace classical chaos? What will be the new equivalent of the threat of disorder if not chaos? In the Platonic system there needs to be an antithesis for a thesis to make sense, and the effect of modern chaos theory is to *threaten* the very notion of order as a dialectical term. The potential for chaos theory in architecture is to clarify what this order might be so that even Agrest's 'nondesign' might have a name. But because architecture is the last stronghold of Platonism and because it is unable to handle the precision of chaos theory, architects will continue to believe that they have known it all along, or chaos will be commodified on other rooftops. Either way, its disruptive power will be dissipated.

FURTHER SOURCES   Chapter 2A; Eliade 1954; Marvel 1986.

4. Simplicity Is Not Made to Order

Simplicity (artless finality) is, as it were, the style adopted by nature in the sublime. It is also that of morality. **Immanuel Kant.** 1790:I.II.§29.

No architecture is so haughty as that which is simple. **John Ruskin.** 1851–1853. *The Stones of Venice.*

The truth is rarely pure, and never simple. **Oscar Wilde.** 1891. *The Importance of Being Earnest,* Act I.

Much of the best architecture has resulted from the adoption of a simple and limiting format. Many architects make things much more difficult for themselves than is necessary. There is no virtue in virtuosity deployed in the solution of problems which need never have arisen! **Bruce Allsopp.** 1977:89.

TRACE   From the Latin *simplicitas* or *simplex,* simplicity is the form, state, or condition of being composed of a single portion or structure and an absence of complexity, intricacy, or adornment. Perceptual studies have shown that parts are perceived in relation to conceptual wholes, whether of context or of imposition, and unmediated perception favors organization into simple whole figures (*Gestalten*) as a way to make sense of any given pattern or array of elements. This has led art theorists and estheticians to propose that in esthetic judgment "moderate simplicity is necessary if we are to intuit relations and shapes at all, instead of a great blur of confused masses and lines, and moderate complexity, if the object in its spatial character is to interest us" (Prall 1929:122).

Simplicity has been a pursuit of architects at least since Vitruvius prompted that the Doric Order was male-based and that 'male simplicity' and severity were aligned with 'republican simplicity' and exterior modesty, to be combined in the Greek Revival (more accurately, the Doric Revival) and prized in the United States from the eighteenth century (Collins 1965:90). Simplicity was to receive another boost with the onset of the Modern Movement from the early twentieth century; "it was an attempt to purify architecture, to remove the accretions of style, to get back to simple and direct building so as to form a fresh starting-point for the architectural expression of the spiritual, social and economic life of the time" (Whittick 1974:48).

COMMENTARY   So often the architectural studio or office is filled with mutterings that an evolving project is 'too complex' or that an emerging solution could be 'simplified' or made more 'elegant'. Just what is being sought in these brain-wracking demands that designers and architects make on themselves? Is simplicity a quality that can be defined in a building in such a way that it may be targeted while designing? Is it a state of mind that enables the paring away of the extraneous to reveal the essential? Or is simplicity something that attends the best architecture as a result of 'a simple and limiting format' suggested by Allsopp above, the natural outcome of a process appropriate to the task at hand viewed with the outcome in mind? Most architects would probably say that achieving simplicity is just sheer hard work, a detail that looks simple, for example, often taking an inordinate amount of time to resolve.

Simplicity does not imply a simple process, though it may be the result of one that progressively and efficiently simplifies the task. The process followed by experienced designers, what Rowe (1987) calls their 'protocol', at times seems to lead so inexorably to a solution that it seems inevitable when viewed retrospectively. On other occasions a design problem presents no end of trouble in its resolution usually because it is 'wicked' from the outset by being ill-defined, and simplicity remains as elusive in resolution as it was from the start.

From case studies and other accounts of designing, Rowe observes that the 'style' of the completed project is the result of two factors; first, "the sustained influence of initial design ideas in the form of organizing principles, rules and references" and, second, the influence "of the particular structure of the problem-solving process itself," in which regard "the sequence in which design principles were applied seems to have mattered the most" (37). It is reasonable to suppose, therefore, that outcomes agreed to be simple and elegant must follow similar protocols that lead to their simplicity, protocols that do away with all superfluity as part of their ordering.

Some people also seem to have a simple, ascetic, and perhaps even naive view of life that manifests in how they live, how they think, and the things they say. People of greatness are said to possess simplicity, as the poet Alfred, Lord Tennyson, said of the Duke of Wellington, "Rich in saving common-sense, / And, as the great only are, / In his simplicity sublime." Having a simple view of life certainly helps relieve the burden of complexity, witness the wishful "Oh for a simple life," that we tend to plea for under the pressure of work or complex circumstances. Architects known for the simplicity of their buildings appear to bring a clarity of thinking to bear on the task that somehow eliminates confusion and unnecessary aspects, thereby allowing only the essential to hold sway. Certainly the quest for unity, truth, and purity in designing is usually linked with the achievement of simplicity in an artifact.

Together with the tendency of many architects of the Modern Movement toward simplicity went a uniformity that Demetri Porphyrios (1978) terms *homotopia,* a quality he defines as "the necessity for homogeneity, a necessity the character of which is both constructional and ethical, defining the ordering sensibility of Modernism . . . the kingdom of sameness; the region where the landscape is similar; the site where differences are put aside and expansive unities are established." Simplicity and homogeneity were concomitants of a rationalism that sought architectural purity through the clarity of function, honesty of materials, transparency of production, and the consistent application of analytical methods. Porphyrios describes the effect of the new ordering sensibility thus: "Homotopias afford consolation; they favour continuity, familiarity and recurrence, becoming the untroubled regions where the mind can stroll freely, always discovering little clues alluding to the sameness of the universe" (9).

The homotopic sensibility has its adherents in classical and traditional architectural thinking, as well as in the modern, and has led to some quite formidable declarations about the order of things. For example, unity and simplicity have been equated in the underlying order to the so-called Platonic solids, the five regular polyhedra, laid down by Pythagoras and reiterated by Plato. The tetrahedron, as the 'simplest' solid, has been pivotal in the Platonic lambda for more than two millennia, with the octahedron and icosahedron on one arm and the cube and dodecahedron on the other. From this elemental arrangement has flowed a multitude of cosmological and metaphysical constructions over the centuries and a rich mythology that has informed much that we still take as the core of traditional science and lore.

But the work of a New Zealander, Robert C. Meurant, looks set to overturn all that has gone before because of what he maintains was a mistake in the ordering of the perfect solids by ancient geometers. Meurant suggests instead that five regular polyhedra be arranged in three pairs (one pair being identical tetrahedra in opposite orientations), which gives the same definite sequence from simplicity to complexity as the Platonic lambda but, unlike it, no one solid is the perfect center. "The perfect forms are therefore *extremes,*" writes Meurant. "They are perfect forms only in the realm of duality. This suggests that the quasi-regular polyhedra—the tetratetrahedron (i.e. octahedron), cuboctahedron, and icosidodecahedron are the *perfectly balanced* centers. They precisely mediate and harmonize the polar extremes. They can be considered to give birth to, to give rise to all of the regular and semi-regular polyhedra of their respective class" (Meurant 1992). If Meurant is 'correct'—and in this area correctness is a matter of acceptance by those who are adherents—then *all* ancient and current cosmological and metaphysical speculation built on the Platonic solids will need to be recast!

That simplicity may not be quite the basis of truth in tradition as has been thought, but rather a degree of complexity, contains a lesson for modern thinking. Alignment with simplicity has given it the status of an ideal, a measure of the perfect solution. Since simplicity is not a state that can be unequivocally identified beforehand but is more readily recognized only if it has been achieved, the desire for simplicity remains a virtue, a moral matter linked with integrity and thoughtfulness. But simplicity will also remain the mark of originality in the working out.

FURTHER SOURCES   Collins 1965; Pollitt 1974 (*aplotes*); von Meiss 1986.

5. Complexity Can Be Quite Orderly

I like complexity and contradiction. **Robert Venturi.** 1966:16.

If modern architecture tended toward a distilled simplicity where many requirements were purified towards simple, regular shapes, then Late-Modernism, keeping this overall simplicity, allows it to become irregular and complex. The mixture 'complex simplicity' is itself a form of oxymoron.

Complex simplicity is a series of 'yes, but' statements. **Charles Jencks.** 1980:50.

. . . Ashby's Law of Requisite Variety: the complexity of the controlling agency must equal the complexity of the thing controlled. **Tom Heath.** 1984:191.

What I was trying to say in these books is that in our time architects should acknowledge complexity, contradiction, and ambiguity more than simplicity, unity, and clarity. The word "accommodation" describes this approach in a nutshell. Another way to put it is that I was advocating mannerism in architecture. **Robert Venturi.** In Diamonstein 1985:231.

TRACE   A transformation of the Latin *complexus* and its stem *complectere, complecti*— encompass, embrace, comprehend, comprise, and sometimes analyzed as *com-*, together, + *plexus*, woven—the adjective 'complex' describes an assembly that is involved or intricate. Complexity, then, is this intricate quality or condition, and in everyday use, the sense of an assembly being complicated is frequently given the moral overtone of being unnecessarily so.

Architecturally, complexity is mostly seen as a quality in need of control, of order. In line with Cartesian rationalism, which has dominated modern scientific thought, architects have attempted to evolve design methods that aim at reducing complexity on the assumption that architecture too may become rational and scientific, and also because designing is considered easier by doing so. Just to confound matters, Charles Jencks (1980) introduced the notion of 'complex simplicity', quoted above.

COMMENTARY   Designing is a complex matter, and for certain sorts of complicated buildings it sometimes makes sense for the process of designing to become an analog of the management and operational process of the building. This necessitates 'inventing the client', as the architect and theorist Tom Heath (1984) puts it, in accordance with Ashby's Law quoted above, so that information may be garnered and decisions taken that approximate the organization being dealt with; hospitals are a notable example. The normal conceptual frames and systems of architects are otherwise unable to cope with the complexity of such situations.

Moreover, architects have a vested interest in maintaining that designing is a complex matter, or rather that designing is the resolution of complex matters, because this goes some way to ensuring that there will always be an opportunity for architects to utilize their skills. That designing is a complex matter and that it seeks to resolve complex matters is a fact of professional life. This is now being realized by computer scientists, many of whom working in the design field are also architects, who have been insisting that design can be simplified into computerized routines (for the same reason that architects have insisted that it is complex; namely, cynics would suggest, continued funding and employment). This realization may lead to some reconciliation between the complexification of architects and the simplification of computer scientists at some time in the future, but it looks to be a long way off.

In *The Order of Things* (1966), Michel Foucault refers to a 'certain Chinese encyclopaedia' cited by the Argentinean writer Jorges L. Borges, in which animals are categorized by dividing them into these groupings: "a) belonging to the Emperor, b) embalmed, c) tame, d) suckling pigs, e) sirens, f) fabulous, g) stray dogs, h) included in the present classification, i) frenzied, j) innumerable, k) drawn with a very fine camelhair brush, l) *et cetera,* m) having just broken the water pitcher, n) that from a long way off look like flies" (Foreword). This most ludicrous list defies any rational comprehension, and Foucault uses it as the springboard for *Order* to explore the cultural codes we impose on experience to order it, and the limits or borders of that ordering. Dismaying as the Chinese classification may be, to arrange matters alphabetically in an encyclopedia is just as arbitrary if one is trying to build a comprehensive understanding of a subject, and any taxonomist faces the same difficulty in structuring a subject—witness Charles Jencks's many attempts at bringing order to the flux of architectural ideas in the naming of movements (for which see chapter 4B).

One way of understanding architectural complexity is Porphyrios's application of the notion of *heterotopia* to the work of Alvar Aalto. Heterotopia is the opposite of *homotopia* outlined in the previous section, a sensibility that "distributes the multiplicity of existing things into categories that the orthodox glance of Modernism would be incapable of naming, speaking or thinking . . . that peculiar sense of order in which fragments of a number of possible coherences glitter separately without a unifying common law. That order, which western rationalism mistrusted and has derogatorily labeled disorder . . . the state of things laid, placed, assigned sites so very different from one another that it is impossible to define a common locus beneath them all" (Porphyrios 1978:9). The focus of Porphyrios's article is to re-situate Aalto from Giedion's myth of him as an 'irrational-organic' architect to being an architect of heterotopic sensibility, for whom planning is consciously based in defaults and ad-hoc spatial adjacencies.

Porphyrios uses Aalto's Cultural Center at Wolfsburg as a paradigmatic example of his heterotopic sensibility, seeing it as a series of "autonomous syntactic fragments . . . cohering merely through spatial adjacency." Undoubtedly, Aalto's work *looks* complex and defies easy analysis of the kind that Clark and Pause (1985) do, which is probably what prompted Porphyrios to explore the heterotopic as a possible rationale (he did so before these authors did their analysis). But if the building is analyzed spatially into a series of rotational plays, as the architect John Gamble at the School of Architecture, UNSW, has done, it is possible to place Aalto firmly, though unconventionally, back within the modern homotopic sensibility, contradicting Porphyrios's claiming of him as a heterotope, thereby leaving complexity without a champion. However, if the point of Porphyrios's analysis is taken as demonstrating that complexity can be handled by a modern architect like Aalto, irrespective of whether he expresses a heterotopic sensibility, then an architecture of complexity is possible and may even be at least as desirable as, if not more desirable, than an architecture of simplicity. An architecture that is somewhat gritty and lumpy, a tangle of impressions and associations, is undoubtedly closer to the reality of the issues it purports to resolve or to provide for, and may be the better for that.

Rather than seeking a theoretical approach that clears an instrumental path of all or most obstacles, an architecture of complexity would demand a 'complex and open format', to counter Allsopp quoted in 6A.4, Simplicity, one that entails a variety of critical, evaluative, and purposive mechanisms that take more rather than less complexity into account. The results have to be less prone to the simplistics of dogma, be richer in their potential for interpretation, and be more adaptable to change, both during and after their creation.

FURTHER SOURCES   Bennington 1987; Kroll 1986; Venturi 1966; von Meiss 1986.

B. The Rationale of Method

1. Method: A Knee-Jerk of Belated Modernism

In every investigation the best possible method must be employed. Now this method consists in studying the parts of a science in their necessary order. **Roger Bacon.** 1268. *Opus tertium.*

Every transitional period however must have a limit; it must tend towards an aim of which we get a glimpse only when, weary of searching through a chaos of ideas and materials brought from every quarter, we set to work to disentangle certain principles from this disorderly mass — to develop and apply them by the help of a determinate method. **Eugène-Emmanuel Viollet-le-Duc.** 1872:Lecture 10.

Without method, you have no soup, my dear boy. Well, whatever one does in life, if he wishes it to succeed, must be done with method. **Eugène-Emmanuel Viollet-le-Duc** as engineer Majorin to his protégé Jean. 1881. *Learning to Draw, or the story of a Young Designer.*

They all wanted a complete recipe. . . . There was one student who came to us from Argentina 'When' he said 'Chris, are we going to get the Grand Panoram?' And this grand panoram didn't exist as far as I knew, but he expected a complete ideology worked out and fully finished. **J. Christopher Jones.** 1977. In Cross 1984:331.

. . . the idea of a fixed method, or of a fixed theory of rationality, rests on too naive a view of man and his social surroundings. To those who look at the rich material provided by history, and who are not intent on impoverishing it in order to please their lower instincts, their craving for intellectual security in the form of clarity, precision, 'objectivity', 'truth', it will become clear that there is only *one* principle that can be defended under *all* circumstances and in *all* stages of human development. It is the principle: *anything goes.* **Paul Feyerabend.** 1988:19.

His [Louis Kahn's] Sufi-sounding proposition of asking a brick, or a room, or any other architectural element "what it wants to be" is a denial of the creator's dominion as the privileged subject. **Richard Ingersoll.** "Louis I. Kahn: The Last Master." *Design Book Review.* Issue 21, Summer 1991:7–8.

TRACE   Method, from the Greek *methodos,* pursuit of knowledge or mode of investigation (*meta,* with or sharing + *odos,* way), is commonly used for any means of accomplishing an end in a regular manner, an orderly procedure, or systematic arrangement of matters. As 'way-sharing' or 'having ways' of doing things, the basis of method lies in bringing replicable order or classification to bear on a task, the better to comprehend and manipulate it. The term *methodology* is of more recent origin, being derived from the modern Latin *methodologia* in 1727, and is the 'science' or study of the reasoning structures of method, or the study and evaluation of methods.

The French philosopher and mathematician René Descartes (1596–1650) founded methodology with *Discourse on Method,* in which he outlined four procedural rules: accept as true nothing that is not known to be evidently so; divide each difficulty into as many parts as are required to solve it; think in an orderly fashion from what is simplest and easiest to what is most complex; and completely enumerate links in an argument and thoroughly review them so that nothing is missed (Descartes 1637:Part 2).

Design method in architecture, on the other hand, came to be refined through advances in modeling as a conceptual tool of the designer both graphically, through the use of the grid and of analogy (or the homomorph), and physically, via models and perspective (Heath 1984:7, 12). When design and construction were conventionalized, as they were to the end of the eighteenth century, representational modeling of buildings was sufficient to convey what was intended or required. With the advent of new materials and building types in the nineteenth century, these old ways became inadequate, and it was Viollet-le-Duc (1872), quoted above who first formulated what we today call method. The method Viollet advocated as the panacea for then-current ills was to deliver up a bright new age, and came straight from Descartes.

COMMENTARY   More than a century later, the face of architecture has dramatically changed from the world Viollet-le-Duc knew, although it is arguable whether this change has been for the reasons he was pushing. His advocacy of method as the route to a new and truthful architecture, an architecture expressing its own time, has seemed for twenty years now to have fallen far short of the glory that it was assumed would accompany it. Indeed, it is fascinating that just on the eve of modernism failing, just when it seemed as if Viollet-le-

Duc was to be revisited, in a sudden burst of enthusiasm methodology was touted as the source of a reinvigorated architecture of the age.

The initial flush of manifesto modernism in Europe was deflected for a time by World War I, then consolidated during the twenties only to be threatened by an obviously decorative, and for many therefore decadent, modernism. What remained of heroic modernism was exiled by World War II, principally to America. In the flush of victory that followed the defeat of the Germans in Europe, British stoicism, pragmatism, and empiricism were to emerge triumphant, and as an outgrowth of this hard-won triumph, once austerity had passed away, the design methods push emerged from among the ranks of a younger generation of architects and planners bent on creating a better world.

Expertise in management, strategic planning, problem solving, and production and delivery systems, many of them invented and honed throughout the war, became Britain's major new export to the world. For a decade, beginning in the late-fifties, Britain cornered for herself the architectural market in design methods in an attempt to wrench yet another victory from the ashes of Europe. That many architects and theorists around the world locked themselves into their methodology attests to the efficacy of British propaganda and the power of technocracy. All the while, and in the grand espionage tradition, the Architectural Association (AA) was chipping away at the establishment, as was to become more and more its wont, in refusing to countenance such rationalism or technocratic determinism. The AA turned out knights errant in search of battle, which took the form of inventing their own romantic technologies and playing them as popular tunes.

There was a fundamental flaw, though, in methodological thinking that was eventually to undermine the whole endeavor. The AA breakaway unwittingly epitomized this flaw, best identified by the American philosopher Paul Feyerabend, writing of science in his *Against Method* (1988):

> The idea of a method that contains firm, unchanging, and absolutely binding principles for conducting the business of science meets considerable difficulty when confronted with the results of historical research. We find, then, that there is not a single rule, however plausible, and however firmly grounded in epistemology, that is not violated at some time or other. It becomes evident that such violations are not accidental events, they are not results of insufficient knowledge or of inattention which might have been avoided. On the contrary, we see that they are necessary for progress . . . [scientific events and developments] occurred only because some thinkers either *decided* not to be bound by certain 'obvious' methodological rules, or because they *unwittingly broke* them. . . . There are even circumstances . . . when *argument* loses its forward-looking aspect and becomes a hindrance to progress. Nobody would claim that the teaching of *small children* is exclusively a matter of argument . . . and almost everyone now agrees that what looks like a result of reason . . . is due partly to indoctrination and partly to a process of *growth* that proceeds with the force of natural law. And where arguments *do* seem to have an effect, this is more often due to their *physical repetition* than to their *semantic content* (14).

Feyerabend's argument here and that *anything goes* above is a principle that may be explored only by *counterrules* that proceed *counterinductively* in two ways, i.e. by developing hypotheses inconsistent with accepted and highly confirmed *theories,* and by developing hypotheses inconsistent with well-established *facts.* In other words, scientific methods (of which analysis is one—see 6B.4, Analysis) not only hinder progress, they inhibit invention, and for architecture this can be death. Feyerabend advocates a pluralistic approach that is singularly appropriate in architecture, one that admits its own assumptions, together with those of other constructions, and does *not* discard anything that fails to fit some configuration of (scientific) fact. Rather, he argues for an approach that is inclined to make the weaker, not the stronger, case stronger, and in this respect is much like John Rawls, who advocates in his *A Theory of Justice* (1971) an equity based in bettering the outcome for the most seriously affected in any situation (see chapter 5A).

Feyerabend's approach is the antithesis of design methods that seek techniques appropriate to the task at hand, admitting marginal behavior or aberrant thinking only in 'strictly' creative techniques such as brainstorming. In other words, for the design methods theorist, appropriateness is the measure of model structures that parallel real-life settings on the basis that such simulations will elicit results most closely approximating actual performance once built (Heath 1984). However, the British philosopher and esthetician Roger Scruton notes that "The greater part of our aims cannot be stated in advance of their realization, and the attempt to find a 'solution', in terms of means to end, will usually involve the arbitrary limitation of the problem it is proposed to solve. This must be so in those activities which reflect the 'aesthetics of everyday life', activities like tailoring, decorating and building, which—because we have to live in the most intimate contact with their products—cannot be separated from the *Weltanschauungen* [philosophy of life] of those who engage with them" (Scruton 1979:228). Scruton is actually offering a hermeneutic interpretation, saying that unless we take into account our own embeddedness, design methods are of little or no use because the 'detachment' they impose on a task is completely fictitious.

This situatedness prompts a number of questions. On what basis do we seek method? Why do we apparently need to structure our approach to designing? What authority does 'having method'—as against not having method—bring to problem-solving or designing? Are the results 'better'; if so, better than what? It seems that being rational and methodical is an attempt to demonstrate being 'scientific' and therefore rational and methodical—curiously circular. Seeking and adopting method is somewhat like a ringmaster arranging the performance or, more cynically, a politico-judicial process that tries to make the designer into prosecutor, defender, judge, and jury all in one. Just as theory as an attempt at a conjunction between ideas and practice does not have theoretical consequences of the kind it supposes, method as a search for an authoritative way of synthesizing does not achieve the synthetic consequences it supposes. It does have consequences, though, the most potent being that through it reassurance is gained that an outcome is likely to be more easily achieved and possibly more 'correct' than without it. Method is a way to talk ourselves into designing.

FURTHER SOURCES   Alexander 1992; Broadbent 1973; Broadbent and Ward 1969; Cross 1984.

2. Method: Telling Tales and Naming Places

I fell into these thoughts; of which there were two ways to be delivered; the one historical, by description of the principal works . . . the other logical, by casting the rules and cautions of this art into some comportable method: whereof I have made choice; not only as the shortest and most elemental, but indeed as the soundest. **Sir Henry Wotton.** 1624. *The Elements of Architecture.* Cited in Mitchell 1990.

. . . for the most banal event to become an adventure, you must (and this is enough) begin to recount it. This is what fools people: a man is always a teller of tales, he lives surrounded by his stories and the stories of others, he sees everything that happens to him through them; and he tries to live as if he were telling a story. But you have to choose: live or tell. **Jean-Paul Sartre.** *Nausea.* Cited in Charmé 1984:10–11.

If you call it, "It's a Good Idea To Do," I like it very much; if you call it "method", I like it but I'm beginning to get turned off; if you call it a "Methodology," I just don't want to talk about it. **Christopher Alexander.** 1971. "The state of the art in design methods." *DMG Newsletter,* 5 (3):3–7.

I felt that it was towards the week that would begin on Monday . . . that they were hastening to absorb themselves, on emerging from that ideal Time in which they do not yet exist—those two queens of cities [Venice and Florence] of which I was soon to be able, by the most thrilling kind of geometry, to inscribe the domes and towers on a page of my own life. **Marcel Proust.** 1981:426.

. . . a person trying to solve a problem whether in science or elsewhere *must be given complete freedom* and cannot be restricted by any demands, norms, however plausible they may seem to the logician or the philosopher who has thought them out in the privacy of his study. Norms and demands must be checked by research, not by appeal to theories of rationality. **Paul Feyerabend.** 1988:283.

TRACE   Method is an attempt to distill rationality from unique design events presumed to contain universalizable qualities, and to create a universal narration out of the distillate. Narration derives from the Latin *gnarus,* knowing, and is the *action* of relating or recounting a factual story or account; it is also used for that which is narrated, the narrative. For present purposes it is useful to call the action of relating *narration,* and the account related *narrative.* Design narration is thus method, the action of bringing into factual account, the design narrative would be the factual account. Narration, as it is used here, concerns production rather than experience (for which see P-A. Croset "The narration of architecture," in Colomina 1988:201–211), although it is later argued that there is little difference between them.

Methodology, the Alexander quotation above notwithstanding, is the study of method and the telling of stories about it. It acquired an importance for architects with the *Conference on Design Methods* at Imperial College, London, in 1962 (Jones and Thornley 1963). This led to the formation in 1966 of the DRS (Design Research Society) in England and shortly after of EDRA (Environmental Design Research Association) and DMG (Design Methods Group) in America. The twenty years to the Design Policy Conference held in London in 1982 (Langdon *et al.* 1984) saw a succession of conferences on design methods, the growth of a wide-ranging literature on methodology, and, somewhat belatedly, the establishment of the journal *Design Studies* in 1979. Since then design methods have lost their appeal, although a fair amount of research is still being produced. A mid-term review of design methodology is Broadbent (1973), a later-term review is Heath (1984), while Cross (1984) provides a good selection of key writings.

COMMENTARY   If there is a pattern at all to designing, of which method is purportedly the tool, it has to be the imagining process about which Proust writes in *Swann's Way,* the evocations and emotions that place-names conjure for him. An architect indulges in reveries of the place-name kind while designing, remembering existing places or those that exist inasmuch as they can be remembered, and inventing places that do not yet exist. Designing is an engagement with a design task in the most personal and intimate way and with its attendant reality as yet only imagined, just as Proust engages intimately with Venice and Florence as a reality that was, in the novel, then only imagined, notwithstanding the photographs and paintings his character had seen. The architect's inventions are, to invert Proust, projections of conceptual domes and towers on the pages of other people's imagined lives. The mental processes architects use to invent places is the thrust of research into creativity, while the 'channels' and contexts conducive to such mental processes are the subject of methods research.

Proust describes this mental inscription of Italy as being gained "by the most thrilling kind of geometry" and, if geometry is considered a coalescence of parts into a possessive alignment with ordering principles, for the architect there is a kind of geometry in designing too that 'thrills'. Seeking ways that allow this mental alignment to happen is the challenge of method, not its application as a rationale bringing order to a task, but its *mapping* of the task on to the designing psyche. Method, if it is anything at all, is the invention of a topographic representation of the facts of a particular task of a scale and format suited to a particular designer. In this regard, method is a universalized procedure only insofar as it makes use of certain mapping conventions.

Design method as the sequences or 'plays' adopted by a designer is more like the action of a game, the rules or conventions of which countermand the action now and then, always mediate, yet are occasionally deferred or deformed to allow flexibility in play to keep the game alive. And with this latency of rules method faces its first major difficulty: if only portions of the game of method are *in fact* strict applications of rules and the rest of the game is discretionary (can it be imagined that choice is not open to the designer?), method is not 'methodical' in any universalized sense. Method is tailor-made every time, the 'trace' of the game played, not its armature.

If method is the path followed in designing, the locus or trace of steps taken, choices made and decisions agreed, then regard to completed actions is an historical review. Just as in history, there is an inexorable facticity about the outcome, the fact that an outcome is the way it is and can only have been the way it is because of the decisions made. Had other choices been made, the outcome would have been different, even if only slightly or trivially. The conceptual difficulty for methodologists is to distinguish the structures that assisted in the actual choices and decisions, and to discern the commonality, if there is any, among a range of discrete design events.

Another difficulty appears in trying to 'apply' method to designing, because method, conceived as routines to be applied, is the collection of recurring actions from existing 'narratives', deemed by their recurrence to be 'universal', into varieties of 'narrations', or routines to be triggered by rules of the 'if this circumstance arises, do that' variety. But the narratives from which the narrations are derived are themselves *ex post facto* accounts of design events, and are already cleaned up in comparison with the actual events. So-called methods derived from such accounts are therefore already at one remove from reality; they are at best only meta-narrations.

Educator Donald Schon (1979), while discussing the use of metaphor in designing, not method, illustrates the problem using the example of a research and development team trying to develop a new paintbrush with synthetic bristles. Schon's example appealed to Fish (1989) who discusses it at some length. Fish highlights the conceptual breakthrough that arose as someone prompted that "a paintbrush is a kind of a pump," whereupon attention switched from the bristles to the spaces between being considered as hydraulic channels. With this was born the 'theory of pumpoids', and with it a methodical story that was nothing like "the fumbling, groping process" of discovery. The model-cum-theory came *after* the fact and to read it as guiding the process would be to engage in what Schon called 'historical revisionism'. The research team's account of the event, as Fish remarks, "followed in response to whatever pressures prompted them to present their achievement in terms more orderly and rule-governed than their actual experience of it" (Fish 1989:374–376).

Likewise, a designer's account of designing is tidied up to make a more cogent story, and design methodologists have largely had only these stories from which to distill methods. As a consequence, order has been the order of the day. Even the few 'live' accounts of designing (Rowe 1987) are either made tidier in their recounting because of the difficulty in talking about designing while doing it, or, if there is no direct interaction with the designer, suffer the interpretive difficulties that accompany all passive observation techniques. There is a parallel between the stories of designing and those of self-understanding presented by Sartre in *Nausea,* which shows narratives bring structure and pattern to life's episodes, as the above quotation emphasizes. Charmé (1984:12) makes some interesting observations about this inclination toward tidy sequence:

> According to Sartre, as we actually live through projects and actions minute by minute, they are uncertain and risky. Their final meaning is inescapably opaque, since we must always wait for future results and the perspective of the larger whole in order to judge present endeavors. When *telling* a story, however, we can examine an event and its meaning in every temporal direction. We are not constrained by the irreversibility of lived time. We can clarify the past by what came later, evaluate enterprises by their results, or judge the sincerity of intentions by the consequences. We inevitably interpret events and experiences by taking into account results which were not foreseeable at the time the events occurred. We produce a sense of retrospective destiny. . . . Each event within our story receives a meaning by providing a step leading to the conclusion. We look back from the present and see causes for it inscribed in every moment of the past. . . . Since we cannot use the future to illuminate an event when it first occurs, a story that presupposes the future end to give meaning to the events along the way is dishonest in a certain sense. . . . The only reliable "predictions" we make are about what has already happened.

Finally, returning to the notion of naming, if an architect is asked about his or her current project and the reply is, say, "I am designing an art museum," what is being designed—one more species in a genus of art museums, or a special place for art? If the architect is quizzed more closely about how this art museum is being designed and responds about museum types, the special qualities and problems of this museum, the stages the project has gone through, the key that precipitated the current solution, and so on giving as full a *description* of the place as it is possible to give, so that we feel closely enough aligned with the project that it lives for us, has a method been described or only a place? What is the difference between an elaborate description of an art museum and a description of how it was achieved, its so-called method? The answer is probably "Nothing!" because to anyone other than the designer it has the same effect of aligning attention to the task at hand, as best it can.

Describing a project's past, what a designer has experienced and been influenced by, what has sparked this or that idea, a project's current status and where it is going, *is* all there is. In other words, naming to all intents and purposes *is* method; it is a conversation about designing. Similarly, mapping is a recording of names that mark out the spatial *and* the conceptual territory of explorers (Carter 1987), and design method can be construed as the mapping of a designer's mental geography. The claim that naming is designing is premised on personal experience and confirmed partly by some novel research into naming as a design activity wherein words are both influenced by the task at hand and are influential in comprehending the task (Thomas and Carroll 1979). This applies only insofar as designing can be named or talked about, for there are some who argue that designing is not amenable to verbalization at all (Daley 1982). Despite the disillusionment with design methods and the rise of subjectivity in design, the certainty of some kind of design method is still sought by many students of architecture.

FURTHER SOURCES   6B.4, Analysis; Cross 1984; Heath 1984.

3. Model Methods for Model Designers

There were black box methods like synectics which worked well but nobody knew why and glass box methods, like decision theory, which were logically clear but which didn't work. **J. Christopher Jones.** 1977. In Cross 1984:331.

In the seventies I reacted against design methods. I dislike the machine language, the behaviourism, the continual attempt to fix the whole of life into a logical framework. . . . I realize now that rational and scientific knowledge is essential for discovering the bodily limits and abilities we all share but that mental process, the mind, is destroyed if it is encased in a fixed frame of reference. **J. Christopher Jones.** 1977. In Cross 1984:333.

There are many reasons for the apparent failure of modern architecture, and a complete analysis of paradigm collapse has yet to be made; but it is clear that the constellation of shared values, facts, beliefs, and methods which have their origin in early 20th century architectural thought can no longer be relied upon solely to solve the variety of aesthetic, functional, or technical problems with which it is today confronted. **Stephen Grabow.** 1983:xv.

Are we really to believe that the naive and simple-minded rules which methodologists take as their guide are capable of accounting for such a 'maze of interactions' [referring to history]? And is it not clear that successful *participation* in a process of this kind is possible only for a ruthless opportunist who is not tied to any particular philosophy and who adopts whatever procedure seems to fit the occasion? **Paul Feyerabend.** 1988:9.

TRACE   Stanley Fish (1989) defines foundationalism as "any attempt to ground inquiry and communication in something more firm and stable than mere belief or unexamined practice" (342). Further on he says "the successful foundational project will have provided us with a "method," a recipe with premeasured ingredients which when ordered and combined according to absolutely explicit instructions . . . will *produce,* all by itself, the correct result" (343). Fish could well be describing the study of method as a foundational project in architecture.

On the other hand, anti-foundationalism "teaches that questions of fact, truth, correctness, validity, and clarity can neither be posed nor answered in reference to some extracontextual, ahistorical, nonsituational reality, or rule, or law, or value; rather, anti-foundationalism asserts, all of these matters are intelligible and debatable only within the precincts of the contexts or situations or paradigms or communities that give them their local and change-able shape" (344). This is the current state of mind of many progressive architectural educators, although not perhaps of most of their students, for whom self-reliance and poetic license do not come easily.

The methods project has been to find suitable models that approximate actual designing and derive suitable techniques for problem-solving or puzzle-solving. Another word for model is 'paradigm', the ancient Greek word *paradeigma* meaning a physical 'model' or 'pattern' of any sort made by an artist or architect, though it could refer to those from nature as well as intellectual or spiritual models. When an intellectual model was meant it was either a 'poetic image' or some tangible ideal of beauty using perfect proportions and forms. When a spiritual meaning was invoked it conjured an intelligible ideal akin to Plato's Forms. Paradigm in ancient usage therefore had a number of shades of meaning (Pollitt 1974:211–214).

COMMENTARY   The history of methodology has shown that designers, teachers, and researchers privilege certain 'theories of design' or philosophies of method to predicate particular models of the design process, and that these in turn lead to specific methods for designing; so it is worth reviewing briefly some of these theories and models. There are four primary philosophies of method. Of these, three purport to be 'scientific', and one takes a more circumspect view of the relation between so-called scientific thinking and method—even to the point of questioning whether 'method' in design itself is capable of rational explanation. Two of the three scientific approaches and the ideas upon which the last, or non-scientific, is based, may be found in Cross 1984:chapter 4:

1. That designing is a matter of arraying the *parameters* of the design task such that, with proper understanding, a solution may be found within those parameters.
2. That designers have cognitive schemas or *prestructures* that they bring to their designing (Hillier, Musgrove, and O'Sullivan 1972); and that design is a question of value, not of fact and logic, and that rational thought flows from this distinction by virtue of an initially creative hypothesis or *speculation* (March 1976).
3. That designing is a normative science with a predictive base in that it consists of *paradigms* that operate consistently until they undergo a change or shift by virtue of arguments and evidence that attack the pseudonymous aspects of paradigms (Broadbent 1979; Kuhn 1970; Lang 1987).
4. That designing is utterly embedded in the way we structure our view of the world and may be inherently incommunicable in words; that design is not susceptible to

objectification of the kind supposed by more 'scientific' approaches (Coyne *et al.* 1991; Daley 1982; Snodgrass and Coyne 1992).

The first, or parametric, philosophy of method raised above is the most frequently encountered modern approach to designing, and produces an *analysis-synthesis* model, perhaps with a phase in between allowing for possibilities flowing from a rational analysis to be presented from which a selection is made and synthesis follows. This is discussed separately in 6B.4, Analysis.

The second, or prestructural *cum* speculative, philosophy of method produces a *conjecture-refutation* model of design stemming from a view of science prompted by thinkers such as Karl Popper, Thomas Kuhn, and Imre Lakatos. In such a model, designers offer up tentative solutions based in 'type solutions' and 'instrumental sets'. In this model, the truth or falsity of the types or sets within which architectural notions are derived is not at issue; they are accepted for the moment—their value is only in the aid they provide in establishing the rules by which to proceed. For instance, Imre Lakatos (1978) presents a rule from the ancient Greek heuristic method of analysis and synthesis: "Draw conclusions from your conjecture, one after the other, assuming that it is true. If you reach a false conclusion, then your conjecture was false. If you reach an indubitably true conclusion, your conjecture may have been true. In this case reverse the process, work backward, and try to deduce your original conjecture. If you succeed, you have proved your conjecture" (Vol. 2:71–72). The analysis-synthesis reversal offered here may not strictly accord with the way architects think (for which see 6B.4, Analysis), but if synthesis is considered a conjecture that guides analysis, then it accurately maps what actually happens in a conjectural prove-or-refute model of designing.

Further, recognizing that designing is a temporal sequence, Cross suggests that "conjectures must necessarily come early in the design process, to enable the designer to structure an understanding of the problem and because a vast range of design decisions cannot be taken before a solution in principle is known" (Cross 1984:238). Cross's prompting of such prestructures suggests the conjecture-refutation model might better be called a *prestructures-conjecture-refutation* model. A variation on this model is Jane Darke's 'generator-conjecture-analysis' model which, she argues, more closely fits the way architects work as determined from case studies she has investigated (Darke 1979).

The speculative variant of the conjecture-refutation model put forward by Lionel March makes use of what Charles Sanders Peirce called *abduction,* a mode of reasoning that enables something original to come into being (see also 9A.3, Geometry). This kind of reasoning is speculative, although March prefers to call it *productive*. It generates a rationale for designing called the PDI, or *production-deduction-induction* model of design, or, to align it with its cousin by Hillier, Musgrove, and O'Sullivan, the *presuppositions-conjecture-analysis-evaluation* model, coined by Cross (1984:240) to show an evaluation component—one that arises out of refutation and helps arrive at a synthesis by reduction.

The third, or paradigmatic, philosophy of method produces a socio-professsional stance that may incorporate any of the above methods, depending on the level of their acceptance within the profession and in education at a given time. The approach of designers from a paradigmatic perspective is primarily expedient and exploitative in that current ideas or 'theories' are used to gain leverage, if not on solving problems, then on selling their solutions. To say this is 'scientific' is only to show that scientists, too, indulge in similar mind-sets and 'changes of mind' occasioned by newly acquired convictions resulting from other people's arguments.

The fourth philosophy of method arises from those who recognize that the designer does not stand in relation to method as driver to vehicle, separable yet combined, but that designing is entirely the designer's conception of it, as is whatever is designed, and that any 'method' flows only from that. At the risk of doing injustice to the growing hermeneutical philosophy of design by rashly over-simplifying it, and of perhaps thoroughly confusing the issue of method, I will call this the *hermeneutical* model. While Daley (1982) does not call the perspective she presents 'hermeneutic' and, in fact, makes no mention of hermeneutics at all, she is counted here because of her recognition that "we must portray the designer not as an intellect executing decisions but as a human being whose entire mental life is immersed in the parameters and priorities of his existence as a social being . . . This is the true province of design, which is not a meta-language, nor a set of deductions, but a systematization of our experience of the physical world" (300–301). With this emphasis, Daley rightly may be grouped with those design theorists and others who are today querying the basis of human understanding (Fish 1989; Coyne *et al.* 1991; Coyne and Snodgrass 1991; Snodgrass and Coyne 1990).

The three so-called 'scientific' models (parametric, conjecture-refutation, and paradigmatic) each presume designers who act strictly as the methodologists see them—namely by adopting behavior suited to the model of method they have created—model designers. This calls to mind what the father of methodology, J. Christopher Jones, had to say about both design problems and systematic methods. Design problems become increasingly unstable as they are widened to embrace more of life, and this tendency is neither liked by rationalist thinkers nor dealt with by them. Systematic methods need to *anticipate* human side-effects, not ignore them, which was one principal agenda Jones set himself as he began investigating making a public process of design. But such side-effects and the idiosyncrasy of human choice and action in design still have not been dealt with sufficiently for design methods to persuade their efficacy. Shock waves were sent through the methodological community by Blake (1977), Brolin (1976) and other writers and theorists declaring the breakdown of the modernist paradigm, although, like modernism itself, faith in the logic of method is hard to kill, and it has undergone a revival as artificial intelligence (AI) in design began to develop in the eighties. However, criticism is being leveled at the philosophical basis of AI, and its future may be under a cloud (Coyne and Snodgrass 1992).

Conceptually, the so-called scientific models of method, even the analysis-synthesis model, which is touted for its objectivity but has never fully convinced architects and designers, all depend on some construct of the outcome, principally that the solution will be a building and not management restructuring or some other alternative. As with a novel, the story (designed object) "has already been carefully 'plotted'; it has been 'set in order, pruned, and clarified' by the reflections of the narrator. The reader does not so much reexperience real events as remember them with an omniscient narrator who knows past and future simultaneously" (Charmé 1984:14). In architectural education, these models of design method are presented by the teacher as omniscient narrator and remembered by students during the course of their own narrations, a voice over the shoulder so to speak. Even at the most elementary level of method, the cryptic statement or aphorism, the master is remembered—witness the many architects who pay tribute to their teachers for years afterward (Diamonstein 1985; Tigerman 1987).

It has been those institutions maintaining that architectural education is primarily a vocational enterprise that have most embraced methodology. While paying lip service to individuality and creativity, they are merely tolerated within an educational agenda that has as its bottom line the making of model professional citizens—model designers who will interpret correctly, perform correctly and on time, and produce the right outcome. The great countervailing force is architectural free will, which is intractable and resists such demands, if quietly and privately, and thereby deflects again and again one all too common form of tyranny, the surgical strike.

FURTHER SOURCES   Billings and Akkach 1992; Scruton 1979.

4. Rational Analysis and Mystifying Synthesis

To arrive at synthesis we must necessarily pass through analysis. **Eugène-Emmanuel Viollet-le-Duc.** 1872:Lecture 10.

The creative moment demands not the transparent will, not the beautiful surface, not construction but synthesis. And this synthesis is not the sum of petty and doubtful details, but the outcome of an intuitive frenzy. **Bernard Hoetger.** 1928. In Conrads 1964:108.

Architecture is a series of successive events going from an analysis to a synthesis, events that the spirit tries to transmute by the creation of relations so precise and so overwhelming that deep physiological sensations result from them, that a real spiritual delectation is felt at reading the solution, that a perception of harmony comes to us from the clear-cut mathematical quality uniting each element of the work to the others and the whole to that other entity which is the environment, the site.

It is then that everything that serves, everything that is useful is transcended. An overwhelming event: creation. A phenomenon of poetry and wisdom that is called beauty. **Le Corbusier.** 1930:160.

Synthesis . . . is carried out essentially from within; by this we mean that it properly consists in envisaging things in the unity of their principle, in seeing how they are derived from and dependent on that principle, and thus uniting them, or becoming aware of their real unity, by virtue of a wholly inward bond, inherent in what is most profound in their nature. **René Guénon.** 1958:Preface.

. . . analysis and synthesis in proper thinking and investigation form a pair of concepts which are dialectically inseparable . . . they develop *pari passu* and are interdependent at every stage of development. . . . A fruitful analysis can be accomplished only in the framework of an anticipated synthesis. **Arnold Hauser.** 1974:367.

Synthesis has, more than any other single factor, mystified the practice of architecture and encouraged imprecise thinking. It has vitiated the study of the opposing conditions that are present in each and every building and project. Whereas law and medicine engage in precision and succinctness, architecture masks these qualities, avoiding demystification—all the while extolling the general values of transformation and synthesis. **Stanley Tigerman.** 1982:11

Before analysis, everything exists "without shading, without relief, without connections . . . not that these shades, these values, these reliefs exist somewhere and are hidden from it, but rather because they must be established by another human attitude and because they can exist only *by means of* and *for* knowledge." Analysis isolates, condenses, and conceptualizes the sense of life as a whole. It provides reflective knowledge of what was lived or understood in a state of prereflective consciousness. **Stuart Charmé** quoting Jean-Paul Sartre. Charmé 1984:40.

TRACE Analysis comes to the English language via medieval Latin from the Greek *analyein,* unloose (*ana,* up, back + *lyein,* to loose); in ancient Greek *lyein* or *lysis* were 'loosenings' of the bonds of indebtedness or other 'fetters' or constrictions imposed by a person, fate, or society. More clearly, loosing was release from entanglement (Onians 1951). In logic, analysis is the tracing of things to their sources, or the discovery of general principles underlying phenomena. The modern sense of analysis resolving something complex into its simple elements or component parts has lost this notion of loosening a tangle or knot that, for architecture, is far more provocative.

Synthesis also comes to English via medieval Latin and the Greek *synthesis,* composition or formation (*syn,* with, together + *thesis,* a placing), deriving in turn from *syntithenai,* composed of, put, or placed together. As the assembling of parts into a complex whole, a procedure that for many architects means applying principles to produce consequences, it is the opposite of analysis. But synthesis has no meaning equivalent to the antithesis of loosing; for this we must turn to the ancient Greek *syntalysais,* not re-entanglement or twisting like a rope, but 'closer weaving' (Onians 1951).

COMMENTARY   Traditional philosophy employs the symbolism of weaving, to which *syntalysais* refers, in this way: "the warp may be said to represent the principles that bind together all the worlds or all the states, each of its threads forming the connection between corresponding points in the different states; and the weft, the chains of events that are produced in each of the worlds, each thread being thus, the development of events in a given world" (Guénon 1958:chapter 14). This is the 'world fabric' of traditional doctrine, and each intersection of warp and weft threads is an individual manifestation. The world fabric as a synthesis is already and always complete, whole, or One in traditional terms, and from this view the task of analysis (not, note, a traditional procedure) would be merely to 'loosen' the weave in order to understand it, not to take it apart as in the modern sense. The traditional notion of a holistic fabric was not overturned by modern analytical thought after Descartes, but there was great difficulty in comprehending the 'linkage' or synthesis, especially where it involved the creation of something anew.

Of course, not only for traditional science, but for modern science, analysis is unexceptionable since the synthesis of whatever is analyzed has already taken place and remains intact during and after analysis; all analysis does is force apart the continuous and ongoing fabric, so to speak. But for creative disciplines like art and architecture, analysis applies to an entity that is only *imminent,* only a potentiality—yet to be realized in synthesis or *syntalysais* —although from a traditional *a priori* holistic view synthesis is merely a matter of keeping the lamp of unity firmly on the task, as Guénon noted earlier. Arnold Hauser also incorporates analysis into a traditional view by maintaining that the analysis-synthesis dialectic is dominated by synthesis.

But for those who do not subscribe to traditional doctrine, synthesis presents real difficulties, to which Stanley Tigerman only vaguely alludes above in complaining of the 'mystification' still surrounding it in architecture. It has been the self-styled task of methodologists since the sixties to try to demystify synthesis and to persuade would-be designers, and lately artificial intelligence purveyors, that design synthesis is a rational, explicable, and replicable process. Despite all efforts, so far design researchers have failed in the first and second, replication occurring regardless. What this suggests is that design synthesis *is* mystifying and will continue to be so, because it is not a process at all but an attitude that informs decision making, something that arises and remains within the individual and is knowable only in the doing. Arnold Hauser is perhaps closest; analysis and synthesis are reflexive but not dialectic, because the designer's attitude always and already frames the analysis toward a synthesis, the more so with experience—what Peter Rowe terms "the *enabling prejudices* that designers bring to bear on the situation" (1987:37).

In short, while analysis may be capable of separation and explication, it is the servant of synthesis. Synthesis is not dialectic with analysis but with the task at hand, it is the very dialogic procedure of designing, predetermined in its direction but dynamic and open to its outcome. In this respect, synthesis is not predictive in any scientifically accessible way or from any examination of past actions or from analysis as its antecedent. In fact, Sigmund Freud highlights how little we are able to offer a genuine predictive synthesis by constructing retrospective interpretations:

> So long as we trace the development from its final stage backwards, the connection appears continuous, and we feel we have gained an insight which is completely satisfactory or even exhaustive. But if we proceed the reverse way, if we start from the premises inferred from the analysis and try to follow these up to the final result, then we no longer get the impression of an inevitable sequence of events which could not be otherwise determined. We notice at once that there might have been another result, and that we might have been just as well able to understand and explain the latter. The synthesis is thus not so satisfactory as the analysis; in other words, from a knowledge of the premises we could not have foretold the nature of the result. (Sigmund Freud, 1963. Cited in Charmé 1984:12–13.)

The best that can be hoped for in learning design synthesis is to be involved somehow in what is happening while it is happening. This has led to the 'reflective practicum' of the educator Donald Schon (1983, 1985, 1987), and to the publishing of design teaching experiments in which the theories, prompts, and critiques of the professor are reacted to by students and those observing or tutoring (Marvel 1986; Beck and Turnbull 1987, 1988; Turnbull 1989). Next to direct experience in either the design studio or the office, such academic accounts are probably the closest to mediating theory that one can get; except maybe for the interactive possibilities of virtual reality as design simulation.

Further to the trace above, the neologism 'syntalysis' might be a useful addition to architectural discourse to suggest the closer weaving of *syntalysais,* as opposed to the 'looser weaving' of analysis, and to counter the state of complete disengagement upon which synthesis is assumed to operate in such a mysterious way. Such a word could possibly unite traditional thought concerning universal *a priori* structures that are said to govern manifestation, and the 'enabling prejudices' that Rowe believes frame both analysis and synthesis, as appears to happen in practice.

FURTHER SOURCES　　6B.3, Model; Alexander 1992; Cross 1984; Heath 1991; Kleinsasser, in Gilland and Woodcock 1984; Lakatos 1978, vol. 2; Lawson 1980.

5. Is There Room for Anarchy?

Anarchy, or random noise, I hope for as a new vital energy for city and architecture. **Kazuo Shinohara.** Cited in Cook and Llewellyn-Jones 1991.

There is no need to fear that the diminished concern for law and order in science and society that characterizes an anarchism of this kind [previously outlined by Feyerabend] will lead to chaos. The human nervous system is too well organized for that. **Paul Feyerabend.** 1988:13.

We took our scorn for conventions to the limit, with no other object in view than that of being negative: the 'right to do anything' knew no bounds. It was the excess of this anarchy which brought about, as a reaction, the desire for system and the taste for theories. **Maurice Denis.** 1909. "From Gauguin and Van Gogh to Classicism." In Frascina and Harrison 1982:52.

In contrast to the presence of the past in postmodern architecture, Lévinas' nonoriginal anarche cannot be re-presented. . . . Immemorial, unrepresentable, and invisible, this elusive anarche can never be captured in the prison house of language. **Mark C. Taylor.** 1988:25.

TRACE   Anarchy derives from the Greek *anarchos,* meaning 'without a leader' (*an,* not or without + *archos,* leader), and is used to describe any state of lawlessness perceived from within an established order or authority because it is a direct threat to that order or authority. Curiously, an 'anarch' is an author of anarchy or a leader of a revolt, so anarchy is not entirely leaderless. Architecture—as the combination of the Greek *archi,* master or chief, and *tecton,* builder—is rooted in the same word.

   Anarchy is not a quality that readily springs to mind in architecture, so it is impossible to conceive of *anarchytecture* as nonmasterly building, unless of course it is the vernacular. Certainly anarchy has arisen in architecture during times of major ideological conflict, an essential phase, according to Thomas Kuhn (1970), in which 'paradigm shift' occurs in the sciences, and a characteristic, it seems, of any authoritative discipline.

COMMENTARY   In an essay that is at best a dense read and at least an even denser read, Mark C. Taylor's "Deadlines approaching anarchetecture" (1988) teases out of the word *arche* (origin), and Emmanuel Lévinas's use of *anarchie* (from *Otherwise than Being or Beyond Essence,* Boston, Martinius Nijhoff:1981) referring to "an irreducible past that was never present," the notion of a nonorigin (*anarche*) and from this a nonoriginating architecture (*anarchetecture*). The notion of 'anarchetecture' is especially provocative in view of the modernist project to create an architecture of its time, a 'now' architecture, situated in a present so derided by Derrida! Postmodern architecture and New Classicism tried to revivify elements and values from a past that is inherently *passed* and beyond resumption. It is perhaps the deepest of architectural paradoxes that architecture, in the most exemplary sense, is always anarchic—it is inessential; it does not originate, replicate, or anticipate—it reaches beyond such terms as Taylor suggests above. It is just possible, then, despite the trace above, to conceive of *anarchytecture,* in the hardest sense of anarchy, although nobody will ever use the term.

   Adopting a less radical sense of anarchy, it is possible to conceive of design generally as disturbing an existing situation, as intervening into some already-functioning constitution in which certain rules prevail; therefore it is possible to conceive of designing as disruptive, anarchic. A situation in which existing rules are adjusted, whether by intentional replacement or supplementation, or by the intrusion of contingent circumstances, is akin to Feyerabend's 'anarchy' (Feyerabend 1988) or, more conservatively, to the contemporary pragmatist Quine's 're-evaluations' (Quine 1961) or, more radically, to the notion of 'dissent' adopted by Lyotard (1984b), wherein intervention triggers what in design thinking are considered *creative* changes. What the creative dissenter-architect obliges in an existing constitution is a variation. It is the collusion between the existing and the intrusive that generates a new constitution and from which new outcomes may emerge. This collusion is a communicative act involving the dissenter as the willing and daring individual intruder on the one hand, and the existing constitution as the receptive and tolerant collective *status quo* on the other.

This equation prompts the question: where does the designer or architect as a creative anarchist dwell? Architecture is a conservative discipline in offering its 'services' to the community. But architects are also considered generally more creative than many others in society and a degree of tolerance is extended them for that. For this reason architects are often considered 'marginal' in their role in and impact on society; just as comedians are marginal in the tolerance extended them to make extreme comments on people or society, so architects can operate (if they so choose) at the creative margins of society, if not with quite the freedom of comedians or artists; this is part of the architect's social contract. Within the relatively conservative ranks of the architectural profession, design architects are frequently accorded a privileged status and those who pretend to the avant-garde see themselves as operating at the margins rather than at the center of the profession. In other words, the creative and inventive edge of the profession is just that, an edge; it operates marginally.

In this toleration and marginality of architects, a comparison may be made with the cultural critic and anthropologist Victor Turner's studies of ritual in early Western and tribal cultures and the role of the 'liminal' or 'transitional' as the place in which change and revolution occur. Turner's descriptions of liminality are repeated by Doty: "Liminality is the realm of primitive hypothesis, where there is a certain freedom to juggle with the factors of existence . . . the domain of the 'interesting', or of 'uncommon sense' . . . [it offers] a limitless freedom, a symbolic freedom of action which is denied the norm-bound incumbent of a status in a social structure. . . . Liminality is pure potency, where anything can happen . . . where the elements of culture and society are released from their customary configurations and recombined in bizarre and terrifying images" (Doty 1986:91–92). Turner prefers the term *liminoid* in relation to our less highly structured contemporary culture because liminoid activities are "more characteristically individual activities taking place at the margins and interstices of the main cultural processes; they "are plural, fragmentary, and experimental in character", and they are closer to individual than to collective concerns" (Doty 1986:93).

Of particular interest in the present argument is Turner's notion of the *trickster* as the principal 'player' in the liminal areas of society:

> Turner notes the kinship between trickster figures, neophytes in the liminal phase of rituals, and court jesters, dwarfs and clowns. All these figures appear in a status of marginality: they "(1) fall in the interstices of social structure, (2) are on its margins, or (3) occupy its lowest rungs". . . . Medieval jesters or jokers, for instance, represented the poor or deformed classes and had a "structurally inferior or 'marginal' " position; they symbolized what David Hume termed the "sentiment of humanity." In a highly stratified society jesters were marked as the inferior group. . . . In opposition to the authorities and power of controlled consensus in the social *structure,* these figures represent for Turner the ideal pattern of social interaction he calls *communitas.*
>
> Communitas constantly is sidetracked by the growth of social structures, and its reappearance may so threaten the social structure that a revolutionary movement comes about. . . . And in rigidly structured societies, it is primarily advocated or evoked during liminal phases or by persons such as clowns or tricksters whose social status is likewise marginal. (Doty 1986:91–92)

While it may seem insulting to think of architects and designers as clowns and jesters, Turner stresses the creativity of tricksters and their ability, in their privileged position, to go against formal structures and ways of thinking. Indeed, in many respects architects and designers are *expected* by society to be different, and it is important that architects do not miss the opportunities that affords them.

FURTHER SOURCES   Conrads 1964; Marshall 1992; Tafuri 1976b; Voyce 1949.

CHAPTER

Authority in Architecture

Overview

The legitimate authority of the professional as representative of a discipline and tradition of knowledge is too often replaced by the authoritarianism of the individual; particularly, of the *insecure* individual. **Tom Heath.** 1991:178–179.

We shape our buildings, thereafter they shape us. **Winston Churchill.** In *Time* magazine (1960).

If we believe that the quality of our lives is shaped by the quality of the buildings that surround us we are naive, but if we do not believe at all, there is no reason to stay in business. **Paul Goldberger.** 1983:3.

The word 'authority' comes from the Old French *autorité,* which in turn derives from the Latin *auctoritas.* The root 'author' is from the Latin *auctor,* itself a derivative of *augere,* meaning 'increase, promote, originate'. Thus 'author', 'august', and 'auction' are from the same root, and an *auctor* was someone who had the power to bring something into being and to maintain it (Pollitt 1974:315). Apart from the power to sanction that having 'authority' entails, and the consequent importance, prestige, and influence the wielder attains, there is the quality of soundness and worthiness, as contained in the notion of 'good authority', and the power so wielded may well be commanding and impressive.

Authority in architecture today turns on who has the most influential say, which translates to who gets the best, if not the most, press. Newly completed work in the regular professional and industry journals gives average Joe Architects a chance to show the kind of work they are doing and keep the office open, while getting up in the annual, and especially the national, architecture awards is a sure way to accumulate respectable credits and gain quality commissions. Competitions both at home and abroad are another, and for some a more desirable, way to gain a reputation, especially if one scores a place. The next step, or at least a sideways step, is the exhibition—not the retrospective but the prospective—preferably as part of a limited group, the number 'five' being magical. And projects are eminently suitable for taking moral stands about what architecture should be because, as Kant makes clear, it is the intention that has the moral power and is thus worthy of critical debate (see chapter 5). Projects are fresher than built works and more portable too, as students and young aspiring architects attest by quickly becoming rapt with the latest graphic and model-building techniques—for half the battle is fought and won in 'picturing architecture' (see Luscombe and Peden 1992).

In the United States, support from the *New York Times* critic Paul Goldberger may seem high praise indeed for some, yet *not* getting slammed by the former critic Michael Sorkin is better. Indeed, Sorkin (1991) sees favorable press from Goldberger as tantamount to being low on the evolutionary tree. A Rizzoli monograph, or an *Architectural Design (AD) Profile* or *GA Architect* special edition is a sure-fire way to show you have reached the core of the architectural reactor, though you may have spent at least forty years in refinement to get there, by which time it would be a mere bonus. Combine theoretical projects with writing about them, build an occasional rarefied building, and mix with a French philosopher or two, and you may well achieve meltdown. But the fail-safe mechanisms are so well-entrenched, the filters so carefully managed to separate the heavy water from the drizzle, that only the very exquisite manage this breakthrough.

The plethora of architecture publications means that the question is no longer how to get published but where. The choice is wide and becoming wider. Discrimination runs high among architecture people, since an architectural reputation depends as much, and perhaps more, on the publisher's reputation and the caliber of the commentator as on the quality of the work. The will to publish so endemic to the academic system, combined with a powerful marketing mentality, probably accounts for the dominance of North American publishing houses as authoritative sources of opinion. That, high volume production and low retail prices, and the stability of the U.S. dollar combine to enable architecture publications to travel more cheaply than those of many countries, especially from the European Economic Community.

For example, architecture books from Great Britain and Europe, even in soft cover, are now quite expensive in Australasia compared with those from North America, and students can rarely afford them. Academic reading lists need to take this into account so, more often than not, British architectural writings tend to become reference works accessed through libraries rather than course texts. The British journal *AD* is a major source of Anglo-European design ideas and thought and, while it is heavily utilized in libraries, thematic issues languish on the shelves of bookshops because of its high cost. This means that over the past decade in Australasia, texts of authority *for architecture students*—and this includes especially those purchased of their own volition—have shifted rather dramatically toward those from North America. The domino effect is that those international architects and writers favored by American academics and theorists have come to dominate the discourse of countries like Australia and New Zealand.

Inasmuch as these forces shape the architects who design buildings, they shape the buildings, and they 'shape' or, more accurately, impinge on the people for whom they are designed. Users do not shape buildings as directly as some might wish to have them do (see chapter 3B); the shapemakers and tastemakers are the makers of architecture. The impact of fashionable trends and ideas is at least as deterministic and predictable in its outcomes as any expressly declared and sincerely held behaviorist or functionalist approach to architecture might be; some would say even more so. It can be guaranteed that someone somewhere will be willing to wear an architect's personal inventiveness or experimentation, or to act as a promoter for the avant-garde, in other words, to indulge in the art of architecture for art's sake without an attendant meaningful social agenda. To the extent that such ventures are rewarded by publication and awards, they and their designers become and remain authoritative. By the same token, because the vagaries of fashion so permeate architectural culture, many architects seek something more substantial to hold on to as their authority; they seek an architecture based in context, history, tradition, or other abstracted or long-lasting qualities. And it is these issues that are the subject of this chapter.

It is frequently the case in architectural and philosophical discourse that ancient usage is brought to a word as the authority to persuade people of its proper meaning and effective application. In architecture the use of authoritative devices based on past usage is often encountered, be they words, geometries, or architectural elements and buildings, in an attempt to persuade a reader, critic, designer, or amateur enthusiast that the current or intended use of some architectural geometry, figure, or motif is worthwhile. For example, the measurement and analysis of nature, music, art, sculpture, ancient architecture, and certain modern artifacts discussed by György Doczi in *The Power of Limits: Proportional Harmonies in Nature, Art and Architecture* (1981) is intended to persuade a return to natural proportions and patterns in modern artifacts in order to effect realignment with a cosmic harmony ('the power of limits') he believes has been lost. The assumption here is that, because some continuity has been observed in retrospect, continuity should inform the present and the future. The two major authoritarian concepts of continuity in architecture to be discussed in this chapter are *historicism* and *determinism*.

Historicism is included under part A, External Assuagers, because of the inclination of designers on occasion to assent to or to seek reasons for what they are doing 'outside' themselves, as in attempts to understand the 'spirit of the age' to better focus their attempts at designing for the present, or when tradition is looked to as a guide, or when typology becomes a force in design. There is also an inclination to be subjected to certain pressures 'from without', such as being required to fit the context, or to comply with certain esthetic rules. The reason context became important to architects is explained by one urban theorist in this way: "The need for an authoritative basis for design . . . arose out of the belief that the Modern Movement's insistence on the programme as the source of design integrity could no longer be sustained. For if the internal logic of the problem could not provide sufficient reason for action, some other generator must be found, and where better to look than to the context in which such action should occur" (Barry Maitland. "The uses of history," *AD Profile: Urbanism,* 51, 1984:4–7).

Determinism is included under part B as an internal persuader because of the conviction with which designers adopt certain stances in dealing with tasks, with the processes of design, and with the habituated routines they go through as they design, for the force of the program in design and the privileging of function, all of which may be construed as 'inside' the task at hand. Of course historicism is deterministic and determinism can be historicist, the one no more 'outside' than the other is 'inside', because both are stances freely, though perhaps unwittingly, adopted by the players. The topics that follow represent a range of attitudes leading to self-warranting by architects, to their belief in what they do, and their desire for habit and method, although detailed discussion of specific methods and their consequences is to be found in chapter 6.

A. External Assuagers

1. Historicism

Nothing in history is inevitable, except in the formal sense that, for it to have happened otherwise, the antecedent causes would have had to be different. As a historian, I am perfectly prepared to do without 'inevitable', 'unavoidable', 'inescapable', and even 'ineluctable'. Life will be drabber. But let us leave them to poets and metaphysicians. **Edward H. Carr.** 1961:96.

Historicism has no real method whereby to associate the works of a given period with its ruling spirit. All it can do is to reflect on their association *after* the event, and try to derive, from a critical understanding of individual buildings, a suitable formula with which to summarize their worth. It follows that it can say nothing in advance of observation, and can set no dogmatic limit either to the architect's choice of style or to his expressive aim. There is something truly absurd about the attempt to command obedience to a rule which can be formulated only when it is already obeyed. **Roger Scruton.** 1979:55–56.

Historicism is the belief in the power of history to such a degree as to choke original action and replace it by action which is inspired by period precedent. . . . That this kind of architecture was the almost universal trend in architecture [in the nineteenth century] I need not emphasise. **Nikolaus Pevsner.** 1961. Cited in Watkin 1977:108.

TRACE   Historicism has a number of meanings. Dictionary definitions give only a hint of its usage in historical discourse and not a sign of the controversy it has generated. For instance, historicism as a theory that all sociological phenomena are historically determined, or as a strong or excessive concern with and respect for the institutions of the past, says nothing about the assumption of, inevitability of, or lack of attention to chance in history. For historian Edward H. Carr, historicism is both a "savoury red herring" in historical inquiry and an imprecise term whose meaning was emptied by the philosopher of natural and social science Sir Karl Popper in *The Poverty of Historicism* (1957), where he uses it "as a catch-all for any opinion about history he dislikes," particularly those of Hegel and Marx (Carr 1961:91–92).

Alan Colquhoun (1989:3–19) discerns three main kinds of historicism: historical determinism combined with relative truth, interest in past traditions and institutions, and the adoption of historical forms. Most pertinent here is the doctrine and prevailing popular view that there are laws or principles of historical development, which Popper condemns for its attempts at historical prediction. Within such a frame of predictability there are two seemingly distinct emphases, one seeking a future based in continuity from the past, the other seeking a present based in discontinuity from the past. What we will focus on here is the inclination to that inevitability that seeks to assume events as inevitable *before* they happen, as against the practical historical view of events as inevitable *because* they happened.

COMMENTARY   The first kind of historicism is exemplified by Popper in *Conjectures and Refutations* (1963) as "the view that the story of mankind has a plot, and that if we can succeed in unraveling this plot, we shall hold the key to the future" (cited in Watkin 1977:6). This is a variation on another metaphor he used almost twenty years earlier in *The Open Society and its Enemies* (1945), where historicism is a quest "to find The Path on which mankind is destined to walk: it is to discover The Clue to History" (cited in Watkin 1977:53–54). This view of history is unitary and holds that there are lessons to be learned from history of the kind that will facilitate smooth transition into and implementation of the future. The future becomes a matter of guardianship by those in positions of influence or power, monitoring and nursing the present in relation to the near past much as a flux enables solder to meld to metal.

The other kind of historicism is also "the view that the principal aim of the social sciences should be historical prediction, along the lines developed so successfully by the physical sciences," but with one major difference: that it may be achieved "by discovering the trends that underlie the evolution of history, by laying bare the 'spirit of the times' "

(Macrae-Gibson 1985:xii). In this view, history is seen as a succession of discrete periods, and therefore obeying general laws (the oscillation of birth, maturation, peak, decline, death), but each with its own distinctive qualities reflecting a *Zeitgeist* or 'spirit of the age'.

The modern movement was founded on overturning the power of history by making it anew, but merely replaced one mode of historicist thought with another. However, respect for continuity was to resurface following the devastation of the blitz in Great Britain and Europe in the 1940s, and slowly clawed its way back to a position of influence in architecture by the late 1980s. Much to the dismay of modernist architects, this resurgence has taken the form of historical imitation, which they have vehemently decried. Those modernist architects who recognize context and tradition (such as Richard Rogers) grapple with continuity through form, bulk, and scale rather than historical motifs, reflecting current social needs, and seeking to maintain integrity by using current materials and technology.

In a commissioned critique in 1980, Charles Jencks criticized David Watkin's book *The Morality of Architecture* (1977) for once more "killing off the *Zeitgeist,*" the historicist view that Jencks maintained having already been killed by "other knights, indeed veritable battalions" over the preceding fifteen years (Jencks 1980:Chapter 4.1). Yet, two years later, in his *Current Architecture* (with William Chaitkin), Jencks is nothing if not historicist by virtue of his valorization of 'current' architecture, the zeitgeist in less obvious drag. According to his introduction, works were selected for the book "on the basis of their *relevance to the current architectural discourse* [emphasis added]." The current discourse was presumably indicative of the theory and architecture of the time, the why and how of the here and now (or there and then). The corollary, of course, is that those works not selected, or at least the bulk of them, were *irrelevant* to current discourse; either they were not current or they were relevant to some previous or other discourse. What is at issue here is not whether historicism is alive or dead, but how it continues to be deployed.

As a very recent example, in 1991 Peter Cook and Rosie Lllewellyn-Jones wrote the *New Spirit in Architecture,* the New Spirit being found among lesser-known architects "near the cutting edge of ideas" whose architecture "uses form, placement, and aesthetics in a *more thrusting, forward-looking way* [emphasis added] than the work of other practitioners, which tends to be calm, contemplative, even cautious." Theirs is a vantage point from which as authors they have chosen to isolate "the new explosive architecture," which they view as having "the condition of coercion, or catalysis, that occurs in a *certain place at a certain time*" (9) [emphasis added]. They question whether there is "a genuinely new spirit being expressed" in countries like Holland and Spain (18), and they conclude their review of the world with a declaration that "Anything is now possible . . . *as never before*" (19) [emphasis added]. This might not at first seem a historicist view, but its emphasis on the difference between then and now makes it so. As Jencks so cynically remarked in 1980, historicism in the form of the zeitgeist "has an awful habit of surviving lethal attacks" (174).

Notwithstanding Jencks's comments, David Watkin is vehemently critical of a historian like Nikolaus Pevsner, who sees only a stylistic historicism and fails to recognize the colonizing power of a historicist attitude and his own participation in it, "The view that the ideas and forms of past periods are continually being rendered obsolete and out of date by the new 'essences' of new ages is precisely that which Popper had in mind when he wrote in *The Poverty of Historicism:* 'Every version of historicism expresses the feeling of being swept into a new future by irresistible forces', and 'historicism claims that nothing is of greater moment than the emergence of a really new period' . . . " (Watkin 1977:110). Historicism of the mimetic Pevsnerian kind prevailed in the eclectic borrowings of everything the term *postmodernism* in architecture covered. It was evident too in the hankering after the figures of Russian Constructivism as the stylistic prescience of Deconstructivism in the late-eighties, just as it will no doubt continue to pervade any new movement.

We might expect someone writing in the turmoil of the mid-seventies to not be quite clear about the direction of events. Yet the claim by Macrae-Gibson (1985) to now being in a period of 'lyric modernism', which he opposes to the utopian modernism earlier in the century and sees as posthistoricist, is faulty. His definition of lyric modernism as "a condition of mythological investigation through architectural form of the fact of life, sense of threat, and possibility of action that are the principal themes of life in industrial society as the century draws to a close" (xiv) is just as much a historicist notion as anything Pevsner or Jencks has said! It makes no difference that he tries to make his definition of the lyric phase retreat from "the view that there is a single legitimate sensibility by which the uniqueness of our time can be revealed," and embrace instead one that "makes the mysterious, complex means by which types have been transformed into artifacts accessible *for the expression of contemporary culture* [emphasis added]." Macrae-Gibson's lyric modernism is inherently no different from his utopian modernism; both are historicist, both emphasize some singularity that marks the difference between one period and the next, and both point to some future state of architecture.

There are many recent examples that give the lie to historicism by showing how events have occurred or means have become available to achieve things not considered possible initially, or by showing that the success of such events and means and the changes flowing from that success were completely unpredictable. For instance, the impact of iron and steel technology on building has gone way beyond what John Ruskin forecast when, in concluding his first Edinburgh lecture in 1853, he spoke about the unlikely impact of iron and glass in the future: "The force of the image of the Corner Stone, as used throughout Scripture, would completely be lost, if the Christian and civilised world were ever extensively to employ any other material than earth and rock in their domestic buildings: I firmly believe that they never will; but that as the laws of beauty are more perfectly established, we shall be content still to build as our forefathers built, and still to receive the same great lessons which such building is calculated to convey; of which one is indeed never to be forgotten" (Ruskin 1854. Lecture 1:s28).

History as a source of reference for architectural expression is still a major issue today: Can one, should one, or how can one not, draw inspiration from and make reference to past styles, modes, and forms, and to what degree? Does one start from some set of 'basic principles' and thereby seek originality in any new design as a way to avoid the historicism of believing in a zeitgeist? And if so, on what basis are such 'principles' discernible if they reside in a universal realm that is itself unknowable by definition, or if they are not the result of some history of use, or if they do not arise out of certain unique conditions of the day?

Any attitude obsessed with the uniqueness of a period and the spirit of its time, and that denies artistic tradition or individual imagination and creativity, is historicist. Historicism underlies the current push in architectural writing that denies the worth of positivistic ideas in its emphasis on intersubjectivity and the textuality of architecture, as against other ways of comprehending architecture. In other words, historicism infests all current talk about architecture, in which ideas are couched as being postmodern or poststructuralist, and denies or ignores other views not seen as 'current'. All so-called avant-gardist positions are historicist. It is impossible for architecture not to be utterly bound by historicist notions. Better to ignore the word altogether and let historicism take us where it will.

FURTHER SOURCES   Berlin 1953; Colquhoun 1981; Eliade 1954; van Pelt and Westfall 1991; Vidler 1992.

2. Progress Is Inevitable, Isn't It?

. . . it is again no question of expediency or feeling whether we shall preserve the buildings of past times or not. *We have no right whatever to touch them.* They are not ours. They belong partly to those who built them, and partly to all the generations of mankind who are to follow us. The dead have still their right in them . . . we have no right to obliterate. **John Ruskin.** 1855. "The Lamp of Memory":XX.

The clearest advantage we have today is the experience of yesterday. **R. Buckminster Fuller.**

There are differing views of the past and different weighting given to what remains, but the only genuinely uncreative interpretation is that which argues that the collective memory needs to be erased in order to progress—to recommend denial is, as even Hollywood cowboys remind us, 'running away from oneself'. **Terry Farrell.** 1984. *British Architecture After Modernism.*

The history of science was regarded by Bacon as progress, an accumulation of valuable experience derived from the past for the future development of society. **Marc Angelil.** 1989:69.

The idea is that change is intolerable unless it is perceived as progress and that the sense of progress must be underwritten by a belief in the achievability of some desired end . . . [that it refers] not to an ultimate state of rest or closure but to a time when things will be better. **Stanley Fish.** 1989:159.

TRACE   Progress stems from the Latin *progredi,* go forward, which in turn is comprised of *pro + gradi,* step, walk, or go. Locomotion along a path is the usual metaphor of progress as the quotations from Popper in the overview show. Relative position along the path is the measure of progress, though the path and its direction are matters of judgment and values. In 1605 Francis Bacon advised in the *Advancement of Learning* that progress was to do with goals as well as techniques, though his counsel "did not have much influence until recently because motion rather than direction has been the chief concern of those responsible for economic and technological development" (Dubos 1981:243).

Progress in science is thought of as burgeoning knowledge, and in technology as greater power to do things in more compact bundles; both also reflect humankind's quest for greater control. Progress in society is associated with increased material wealth, physical and mental health, and personal happiness. The English statesman and essayist Thomas B. Macaulay considered progress the ebbing and flowing of a great flood that was always advancing and never receding. "History is full of signs of this natural progress of society. We see in almost every part of the annals of mankind how the industry of individuals, struggling up against wars, taxes, famines, conflagrations, mischievous prohibitions and more mischievous protections, creates faster than governments can squander, and repairs whatever invaders can destroy. We see the wealth of nations increasing, and all the arts of life approaching nearer and nearer perfection." (Cited in Cannon 1980:59). Notwithstanding Viollet-le-Duc in *The Habitations of Man in All Ages* (1875) attributing to Epergos, his fictitious spirit of progress (as against Doxius, the conservative spirit opposed to change), the way to make the first hut and thereby setting in motion progress in architecture (Hearn 1990:18, 24–27; Oliver 1969:7), architectural progress is mostly esthetic, the outward and visible signs of technological advance and social benefit in various combinations.

COMMENTARY   The present is seen to be progressive by those who view life as dynamic, always new and 'making progress', and unprogressive by traditionalists who view life as cyclical and principial. Both viewpoints are historicist. The former reflects the Promethean myth (in which Prometheus gave fire to humankind, thereby enabling civilization to advance) of continuous change toward an omega point, a new state different from the past; the latter reflects the 'myth of eternal return', wherein change takes place within an eternal stability (Dubos 1981:243).

While the early modernists attempted to cut themselves off from history, historians of the Modern Movement have tried to give modern architecture a respectable genealogy. "In doing this they have been reinforcing the positivist notion that history is a continuous, coherent, and, on the whole, beneficial progression. It is true that the idea of progress that this historicist view propagates necessarily includes the idea of 'newness'. But it also implies that the present has grown out of the past on the analogy of biological evolution, and any reasonable interpretation of this idea must imply that the architecture of the present contains evidence of inherited characteristics . . . " (St. John Wilson 1992:viii).

While Charles Jencks (1980) may have pronounced the first kind of historicism dead, both kinds are still alive and well in architectural education in the 1990s. The first is most noticeable if students are asked to consider designing something that is not current, not 'of today'. And the second kind is undergoing a resurgence, to a greater extent than Jencks probably imagined when he pointed it out in 1980, in the reaffirmation of traditional values in architecture. Despite more than a half century of being dumped on, historicism is still a vital force among architects and architectural writers. Indeed, the very demise of modernist ideology that Jencks sheets home to Jane Jacobs's *The Life and Death of American Cities* (1961) attests to the perpetuation of the historicist cyclic view of progress.

For architecture, historicist laws translate to 'progress' and to the mistaken view, like the popular conception of natural evolution, that architecture at any moment is in transition from a less developed to a more developed state, and that it achieves this by gradual (but stepwise) refinement rather than random mutation. History as a string of phase-beads and transition-beads enables the present (any present) to be viewed as unitary and therefore capable and worthy of its own separate expression through difference, although constrained and carried along into the future by inexorable forces beyond the control of any one person or action.

It was Popper who mounted the most potent criticisms against the logic of historical progress in social and political philosophy in *The Poverty of Historicism* (1957) by arguing that human society is not amenable to this kind of historical projection or prediction because all choice and responsibility we have is ours individually and is not necessarily binding on society (Flew 1979). Architects have always had a vested interest in molding society to some vision of the future through their works, and so have simply ignored this and similar arguments. Historicism continues unabated in the guise of a respect for continuity of the kind architects mean if they promote 'fit', 'context', and 'harmony' as the ground for their vision, and in a disdain for continuity if it interferes with the proper emergence of 'an architecture of our time' as the ground for their vision.

At the end of *The Structure of Scientific Revolutions* (1970), Thomas Kuhn asks, "Why is progress a perquisite reserved almost exclusively for the activities we call science?" He immediately points out that the question is in part semantic because 'science' is reserved "for fields that do progress in obvious ways," as is shown in recurrent debates about whether certain disciplines are indeed science. Essential to an answer is not precision of definition but some concept of a discipline being *cumulative,* progress being a measure of or measured (marked) by the stage of accumulation. What is accumulated is a matter of how focused the discipline, how narrow the endeavor, and how unified the community is about the goals they are pursuing. "Viewed from within any single community," writes Kuhn, "the result of creative work *is* progress. . . . No creative school recognizes a category of work that is, on the one hand, a creative success, but is not, on the other, an addition to the collective achievement of the group." But he adds an important qualification, "If we doubt, as many do, that non-scientific fields make progress, that cannot be because individual schools make none . . . [but] because there are always competing schools, each of which constantly questions the very foundations of the others" (162–163). Kuhn goes on to suggest that the acceptance of a common paradigm within a discipline makes progress easier to see and that not needing to re-examine first principles means ever finer discrimination and adjudication within its own field; science has these qualities.

Does architecture conform with Kuhn's prescription? Not much, it would appear, though it does in parts, namely those that are more 'scientific' and technical. From Kuhn's analysis, architecture is making the least progress (or none at all) in the areas it is least unified (or most diverse), namely esthetically. Yet this is not what architects believe in using the term *progressive,* a word applied mostly to the esthetic avant-garde; or the term *progress,* which is seen mainly in the succession of styles or movements. How can this be? If Kuhn's suggestion about science's insularity from social concerns may be paraphrased, architecture's very connection with society provides a clue (164–165). Architectural education, like that of the arts and humanities at large, believes in exposing students to the works of its own (architects), both earlier and contemporary, and in using textbooks secondarily, mainly to point to the range, not the core, of concepts, themes, and practices. Students thereby become aware of the immense variety of problems that architects have, in the course of time, attempted to solve, and constantly have before them "a number of competing and incommensurable solutions to these problems," solutions that students must ultimately evaluate for themselves.

This situation may be contrasted with science students who are given textbook summaries of the discipline until the very last stages of their education so that the paradigms of science become firmly entrenched. Consequently, even at the risk of rigidity, science maps out a path that inexorably leads onward from its past achievements, with only the direction taken (being the site of paradigm shift at the hands of creative individuals when it occurs) changing. "In its normal state, then, a scientific community is an immensely efficient instrument for solving the problems or puzzles its paradigms define . . . the result [of which] must inevitably be progress" (166). This is not the case with architecture; there is no cumulative knowledge base that so informs protocols that only the direction and not the techniques change. Even in what Kuhn terms 'extraordinary science', revolution overturns and renounces an oppositional stance such that the victors claim progress, following a line straight to their present (see 7B.2, Direction). In architecture, while it may be wished and is certainly argued that modernism is now 'post-' and even postmodernism has been superseded, this is not accepted by everyone; there is no agreed victor or new paradigm as yet.

Admittedly, Kuhn was writing more than a generation ago, and it is unscientific to now hold up his relatively ancient analysis as truth; unscientific, perhaps, but not unarchitectural, judging by how often Kuhn is cited in the architectural literature, and by how often architects go back over 'old ground' to resurrect ideas or architectures cast aside but thought in retrospect to be valuable. It seems that architects are, by inclination, archaeologists, and that the modern movement may have been an aberration.

On a slightly different tack, Colquhoun (1989) talks of modern architecture in relation to the existence of a 'master narrative' providing it with a purpose and a social context, its loss being "the most striking feature" of modernism's decline (viii). This master narrative is Kuhn's 'common paradigm', defining a scientific community in another guise, and in this respect architecture may be said to have been, over the period of modernism, scientific. Colquhoun remarks that the present pluralism of architecture "cannot in itself sustain a coherent architectural discourse, and it becomes increasingly difficult to *measure particular developments against a common standard of architectural values*" [emphasis added]; this reads like a (closet architectural) scientist yearning for a setting for progress, a return to the certainty of authority and prediction.

That various (and much less forceful and ubiquitous) paradigms have arisen to displace the modern narrative, and not another single forceful paradigm has been agreed by all, however, suggests that architecture may not be like a science at all. More important, progress may not be inevitable in architecture. That Colquhoun's collection of essays is offered "as a contribution toward the development of such a [coherent] discourse" (xi) seems to be coaxing architecture into being something it can never be; though what it might rightly be, only talk will tell.

FURTHER SOURCES   Becherer 1984; Colquhoun 1989; Eliade 1954; Feyerabend 1988; Vidler 1992.

3. The Force of Continuity and Tradition

Are there moments when Straight Revivalism is appropriate? . . . The argument here might be that Georgian or Edwardian terraces work better than modern estates, because a tradition— whichever one it is as long as it is unbroken—contains more values, and well-balanced ones, than a modern architect can invent or design. **Charles Jencks.** 1977:93.

. . . the architect has no general theory of codes, how they are built up through usage and feedback and how they differ according to class and background. **Charles Jencks.** 1977:91–92.

. . . the elite movements in our century have merely thrown up the new stylistic options. They have never led society at large, nor captured its imagination. And it's probably in the nature of a mass consumer society that traditional elites no longer have the power to lead, at least in cultural fields. **Charles Jencks.** 1980:180.

Tradition brings past and present into immediate visual relation, and can be understood only by someone with a trained and sensitive eye. . . . A tradition is a *spirit,* and its youth is changed by the retrospective vision of maturity. . . a tradition is something that is made anew by anyone who elects to join it, provided he can succeed in doing so . . . tradition always makes its object present. It aligns itself with a past only to redeem that past for our present feelings. **Roger Scruton.** 1983:23–24.

The greatness of an artist is more in the faith of his tradition than in the arrogance of his revolt. **Abdel Wahed El-Wakil.** c1990.

It is . . . *possible* to create a tradition that is held together by strict rules, and that is also successful to some extent. But is it *desirable* to support such a tradition to the exclusion of everything else? Should we transfer to it the sole rights for dealing in knowledge, so that any result that has been obtained by other methods is at once ruled out of court? . . .

The attempt to increase liberty, to lead a full and rewarding life, and the corresponding attempt to discover the secrets of nature and of man entails . . . the rejection of all universal standards and of all rigid traditions. **Paul Feyerabend.** 1988:12.

The enterprise of the law . . . is by definition committed to the ahistoricity of its basic principles. . . . That is why a judge will do almost anything to avoid overturning a precedent . . . the very point of the legal enterprise requires that its practitioners see continuity where others, with less of a stake in the enterprise, might feel free to see change. The scientific community has an even greater stake in its own continuity. **Stanley Fish.** 1989:157.

TRACE   Tradition is the handing over (Latin *tradere,* hand over, deliver) of knowledge in the form of facts, beliefs, sayings, rules, and customs over time that are affirmed as unchanging by their reiteration and wide dispersal. Tradition for most people is what is habitually said or done because it has 'always' been said or done without question, as testified by the manifold sayings and doings by everyone from families through corporations to nations, though 'always' may be only a few iterations. The power of tradition lies in its self-reinforcement, and is such that there is never any shortage of advice or pressure to maintain it. The anchor of tradition is frequently a core of essential knowledge held by a 'master', or encapsulated in the sacred writings of religions, the canons of the sciences, arts and crafts, the interpretations of law, and the etiquettes of social intercourse.

Tradition in all cultures is intimately tied to the calendar as the cycles of day/night, week, month, season, year, decade, century, and millennium create the rhythms so necessary to its perpetuation. But tradition in the sense of knowledge handed on is temporally based only in generational terms, whether familial or educational. Tradition as the handing on of so-called 'unchanging' beliefs and practices is a dynamic force in Eastern architecture, Eastern being a generic for those cultures in which Judaeo-Christian religion is not dominant. In Western architecture, tradition has come to embrace a broad range of beliefs and practices, "the recognition, often retrospective, of a kinship of ideas and assumptions" largely based in humanism. Western tradition is construed as "a broad tendency, a dimension of thought and belief, a continuing debate within which at any one time there will be found very different—at times opposed—views, held together not by a unified structure but by certain shared assumptions and a preoccupation with certain characteristic problems and topics, which change from one period to the next . . . the humanist tradition" (Bullock 1985:9).

COMMENTARY   At the broadest level, tradition in architecture informs the commitment to design having an impact on people by uplifting them, and this impact is not only physical and esthetic but spiritual. The shift to then saying that architecture is designed for people is relatively easy, but it has produced different emphases in the East and the West. While clarifying 'for people' as meaning for their spiritual, mental, and physical well-being aligns Western tradition with Eastern tradition, a profound difference in priority separates them. Western architects have been inclined to emphasize the physical over the mental and to nearly exclude the spiritual since the Renaissance, especially over the past century, making their claim of 'designing for people' a glib though cherished humanist belief. Eastern architects continue to give prime emphasis to the spiritual, claiming 'design for people' to be a matter of alignment with universal spiritual forces first and foremost, although they have found increasing difficulty in the face of Western economic and technological imperialism.

To step away from such broad generalizations and say precisely what else presently exists in Western architecture as received wisdom from previous generations is difficult. It appears that many architects still have a strong belief that function drives architecture, albeit in a more lyrical way now than was the case with the puritans of earlier in this century, and that material and technological change affects the appearance of a building to the extent that they are largely what make an architecture 'of our time'. There is also a belief in the primacy of circulation as a major generator of plans and, for some architects, of form. There continues to be faith in methodical procedure, particularly analysis as a prelude to synthesis. And there is certainty that people's needs and behaviors will continue to be more or less universally predictable, which brings discussion around to the ritualistic and habitual in architecture.

Spiro Kostof subtitled his 1985 *A History of Architecture* "Settings and Rituals" with the express intention of conveying the repetition of human engagement with architecture across times and cultures. Kostof defines ritual as "the poetry of function: insofar as a building is shaped by ritual it does not simply house function, it comments on it" (19). But he cautions that to say as a consequence that buildings are images of society's values and aspirations—while it is a fundamental challenge—is deceptive because we can no more know with certainty what is embedded in the architecture, and we can know such things only in the light of our present preoccupations. What might be said with some certainty is that there are certain recurrent aspects in architecture that reflect the rituals and habits of lifetimes, and that some of these take place in the same sorts of settings over centuries. Indeed, ritual behavior and its effect of creating fixity of settings is a superordinate and instrumental force for some architectural theorists, one being Christopher Alexander, who has taken it so seriously as to build a methodological edifice of substantial weight in his work with 'pattern language'.

The philosopher of science Paul Feyerabend (1988:Part 17) sees a fundamental difference in attitude about questions in science between those who see themselves as observers and those who are participants: "Observers want to know what is going on, participants what to do. An observer describes a life he does not lead (except accidentally), a participant wants to arrange his own life and asks himself what attitude to take toward the things that may influence it" (234). As a result, Feyerabend sees participants as opportunists who follow a line of research for where it leads, their attitude being necessarily pragmatic. "A pragmatic philosophy can flourish only if the traditions to be judged and the developments to be influenced are seen as temporary makeshifts and not as lasting constituents of thoughts and action" (234–235). Architecture is a pragmatic enterprise just as science is, but many architects, unlike scientists, attempt to claim what traditions it has (and however they may be defined) as universal and unchanging. Yet architecture is also whimsical, and consequently has more choice in its directions than science, which presents a dilemma for the authority and fixity of tradition. It is salutary to consider some of Feyerabend's theses about tradition (243–247):

1. *"Traditions are neither good nor bad, they simply are"* [emphasis here and later is Feyerabend's]. The corollary to this is that "rationality is not an arbiter of traditions, it is itself a tradition or an aspect of a tradition. It is therefore neither good nor bad, it simply is."
2. *"A tradition assumes desirable or undesirable properties only when compared with some tradition."* For this reason, projections from within a tradition only appear to be objective, when in fact they are subjective because the tradition is tacitly accepted.
3. *"[Theses 1 and 2] imply a relativism of precisely the kind that seems to have been defended by Protagoras."* Protagoras's subjectivist thesis that 'man is the measure of all things' and his skepticism "is reasonable because it pays attention to the pluralism of traditions and values."
4. *"Every tradition has special ways of gaining followers,"* some are reflective and changeable, others unitary with argument either supportive or dismissive accordingly.
5. *"Judging a historical process one may use an as yet unspecified and unspecifiable practice,"* judgment and its standards being contingent upon ones's interaction with circumstances as they arise.

Continuity, on the other hand, has two distinct modes: either a profession is continuous or the objects of its concern are continuous. Feyerabend (1988) uses the history of philosophy as an example, although it could apply equally to architectural history. "If someone with that idea [of having tapped into a fundamental stratum] sets out to write the history of philosophy, he will already have ruled out the possibility that what he will be writing is a history of changes" (157–158). This produces a story "that is a cyclical rather than a progressive one" compared with the 'new historiography' of Michel Foucault and others, wherein the persistence of genres and themes is a fiction, discontinuity is rampant, and change is inevitable because its assumptions preclude rigid and rational patterns. In this context, discontinuity is linked with 'progressive', and may be compared with Darwinian evolution in that mutation is a discontinuity that aids progress, progress being a stage of betterment suggested by Fish as quoted in 7A.2, Progress.

Architects can be similarly divided for this discussion into two groups. First, there are those who believe they have tapped into universal principles and historical constants and who would write a history in that vein, talk of architecture as cyclical, and try to persuade (educate) others to see the architectural profession, its practice, and its outcomes as unitary. Second, there are those who are changelings, who adjust principles and are prepared to modify historical precedents, who would write a history of changes, talk of architecture as directional, and try to persuade others to a plurality of views about architects and architecture. In my view, the first group is idealist and reactionary, the second, pragmatic and progressive. Continuity in architecture, therefore, is itself a matter of which tradition one subscribes to and is not an entity independent of either architectural culture or personality.

FURTHER SOURCES   Colquhoun 1989; Eliade 1954; Fish 1989; Kolb 1990; Papageorgiou 1971; Vidler 1992.

4. Context and Contextualism

. . . I cannot properly enjoy an individual building unless it has what I consider a suitable setting, it must not be jostled by unworthy neighbours, it must be part of a coherent picture. . . . I am decidedly inclined to seek intimacy with competent obscurities rather than with the acknowledged masterpieces when these are dishonoured by uncivilised surroundings. . . . I have, I must confess, but little enthusiasm for isolated masterpieces of any sort thus detached from their settings, the poignancy of the contrast between them and what adjoins is too liable to produce a depression that the grandest sight cannot utterly dispel. . . . I would rather a land in which there were no masterpieces and yet nothing mean . . . a desire for a higher average rather than for exceptional and dazzling altitudes. **Clough Williams-Ellis.** 1929:160–162.

While modernists have shown little interest in relating their work to older contexts, they have been less obstinate about it when the context is modern. **Brent Brolin.** 1980:38.

Buildings are often criticized because they do not blend with their immediate and visual context. But why should they? Buildings must relate not to their neighbours in the street but to the broader context of images and ideas that constitute culture. **Juan Pablo Bonta.** 1979.

Always design a thing by considering it in its larger context: a chair in a room, a room in a house, a house in an environment, an environment in a city plan. **Eero Saarinen.** In *Time* magazine (1956).

. . . contextualism has been used as an excuse for mediocrity, for a dumb servility to the familiar. **Philip Johnson** and **Wigley.** 1988:17.

To context is opposed the idea of the monument. **Aldo Rossi.** 1982:126.

TRACE   From the Latin *contexere,* weaving together, 'context' in modern usage is the setting of an event, composition, or text, in the sense of describing the spatio-temporal parts immediately preceding or following that determine its meaning. The now obsolete 'contexture' is probably more explicit for architectural use—a mass of things interwoven, the weaving together of words and sentences, or the structure of a composition. While *contextual* may be the adjective now used instead of 'contextural', in architecture *textural* (as against 'textual', which, while perhaps a very significant term in current theory-talk, carries a quite different meaning) is evocative of the very stuff of architecture, the mix of elements, the tactility of surface, the perceptibility of material property, the cue to scale, the sign of handiwork.

In its modern architectural usage, however, *context* refers to either the physical built fabric within which a project is situated, the 'ground' in a figure-ground perception, or the 'milieu' (French for 'middle place'; also environment, surroundings) within which an architect or group of architects, a work or body of work is culturally and historically placed, or in relation to which they may be understood and assessed in particular aspects. In either case, context implies a saturation of mutually influential qualities.

COMMENTARY   Joining the élite company of weaving analogies in architecture, 'context' has generated a vast literature through its subdisciplines, civic design and urban design. Context is historicist in that it has authority by virtue of its precedence over anything newly conceived (whether original or rejuvenated) that is desired to be placed within it. In this regard, context becomes 'the context' in its public demand for respect and conformity (what Johnson and Wigley refer to above as servility), and has a tangible and defensible public presence that sets standards, proffers rules, and promotes appearances that can be captured and documented. The force of its authority is largely a matter of its degree of consistency, whether of homogeneity or of variegation. Mostly it is a formal matter of scale, bulk, outline, and color rather than a detail matter of fenestration, ornament, materials, or construction. In a highly variegated context almost anything goes; in a homogeneous context almost everything stays.

Built contexts are always larger than the item under design (see Saarinen above) and always older. A contextualist is someone who advocates the authority of context because of extent and age. At best, contexts are seamless and consistent so that the obligation rests with buildings being introduced to show that, once present, they will be contiguous, that they will "blend with their immediate . . . context," as Bonta remarks. Continuity is, of course, what *'scaping* is all about—landscape, townscape, streetscape, roofscape, floorscape—provided one is selective about which scape is meant. It is not the cry of a snipe as it is flushed (though sniping may attend it), not an escapade or a transgression or a slip (precisely what is *not* wanted), and certainly not a bare peduncle or column-like shaft (which Hellman so aptly showed as not at all apt in a cartoon of a high-rise tower looming over a street of ornate low-rise houses and shops).

When a maverick modernist (to a contextualist, that is) like Bonta asks 'Why should I conform?' the question may well be moral as well as esthetic, but it is primarily political (What of artistic freedom? What of the autonomy of the architect? What of individual rights?). All architects have faced and will continue to face this kind of question: do I fit in or do I go my own way with this project? There is no correct theoretical position on the issue, although an idealist will argue that 'fit' even over an esthetic matter is a duty, not a choice, except that in esthetic matters choice is always an option. For example, there is the urban myth of the architect who carefully designed a sensitively scaled and detailed building into a cared for and sensitively scaled neighborhood only to have the neighborhood demolished a year or two later by a landowner who was not so sensitive. On a larger scale, there is the real-life example of Ralph Erskine's continuous multistoreyed building (called the 'wall') at Byker, Newcastle-upon-Tyne, which was carefully designed to *resist* its intended context (and in this way was totally 'contextual') in that the site was to be rimmed by a proposed multi-lane motorway. Erskine proposed to block noise by creating a multistoreyed ribbon of flats having very few windows toward the motorway (to minimize intrusion to the flats) in order to block noise completely from the low-rise density houses within the site. The authorities abandoned the motorway soon after Byker was completed but, in the mid-eighties, built a rapid transit link along the motorway easement and a much smaller bypass road several years later. Is the Byker wall now an over-reaction to its present context or, alternatively, given the present circumstances, would Erskine consider the same approach justifiable?

Context is a slippery concept to theorize, though, because the one thing essential to its definition is continuity, a quality usually changing in modern settings, a state of perpetual transition, and therefore always in doubt. There are rare exceptions that appear to be intact because of a historical and constructional consistency, such as parts of the delightful Greek island towns of Mikonos or Santorini. While change has occurred in such places, it has done so within the tight constraints that vernacular building, strict building regulation, or historical preservation orders decree, at best a 'living' tradition of compliance for the good of some perceived goal. And this is the clue to the dilemma facing us in our less-constrained modern situation. Any context assembled over the past fifty to one hundred years, especially in Western countries, consists of buildings of differing arrangements, materials, construction, details, and qualities. To discern a 'living tradition' among such variegation that might speak of continuity in a way that might assist architects to design 'in context', in the vernacular sense, is almost impossible. Tradition can be applied only to those aspects such buildings share in common, and any commonality is not of the vernacular kind—the handing down from one generation to the next of constructional knowledge being one of the more forceful constants. It appears that the 'tradition' of modern buildings and places does not consist in the obvious detail, as it might in a vernacular setting, but in tacit or explicit limits and boundaries to development, such as shape, street frontage, height maxima used to control light and shadow, equity in views, conditions imposed by site, and certain limitations imposed by materials and construction practices (although these last are less pronounced now because technical ingenuity has helped overcome many former limitations).

Finally, overriding all that has just been said, context as the repository for traditions and meanings, 'things' to be inferred and then impressed in new buildings, poses a challenge that is usually passed over to avoid destroying one's case. For, as Stanley Fish (1989:22) points out in relation to discourse generally, there is no meaning distinct and separate from its context, only differing contexts from which interpretations of meaning ensue. The physical context with which architects deal has no intrinsic qualities independent of any interpretation of them. There are conceptual contexts, within which physical contexts are construed, that are always and already binding. A physical (urban, suburban, rural), social, or cultural setting has whatever qualities and values it has *only through an interpretation ascribing them to it,* and hence, the meaning of a setting and of anything placed or to be placed within it is also an ascription. The fact that a range of settings may concur with the inscripted qualities does not make them intrinsic, it merely demonstrates the extent of the context within which they arise.

Any so-called 'context' in the architectural literature is thus itself already contextual in having an ideological basis from which it is construed, which in turn has implications for how it is to be treated or discussed. So, it is the interaction of contexts, one context viewed from another context, that is evidenced in any debate about context, and Bonta (above) is quite entitled to make a claim for 'the broader context of images and ideas that constitute culture' if it suits him, just as Brolin (above) notes the modernist favoring of modern contexts over old. Whether they or anyone else can achieve what they want is political, persuasion by argument and/or numbers in the end. Drawing on the authority of continuity and tradition or design principles may well be a part of the argument, but these too are contextual matters. Once this is realized, all that remains is to talk about them.

FURTHER SOURCES   Bonta 1979; Brolin 1980; Colquhoun 1981, 1989; Kolb 1991; Papageorgiou 1971; Rudofsky 1977.

5. Type, Archetype, and Typology

. . . all inventions, notwithstanding subsequent changes, always retain their elementary principle in a way that is clear and manifest to the senses and to reason. It is similar to a kind of nucleus around which the developments and variations of forms to which the object was susceptible gather and mesh. Therefore a thousand things of every kind have come down to us, and one of the principal tasks of science and philosophy is to seek their origins and primary causes so as to grasp their purposes. Here is what must be called *type* in architecture, as in every other branch of human inventions and institutions. **Antoine Chrysostôme Quatremère de Quincy.** 1832. *Dictionnaire historique,* vol. 2. Cited in Rossi 1982:40.

This is the paradox: how to become modern and return to sources; how to revive an old, dormant civilization and take part in universal civilization. **Paul Ricoeur.** 1961:276.

Ultimately, we can say that type is the very idea of architecture, that which is closest to its essence. In spite of changes, it has always imposed itself on the "feelings and reason" as the principle of architecture and of the city. **Aldo Rossi.** 1982:41.

TRACE English usage of 'type' derives either from the French *type* or Latin *typus,* which in turn comes from the Greek *typos* meaning a blow, impression, image, or figure in the sense of being struck or beaten. The term is broadly used to describe the general form, structure, or character distinguishing a particular class of beings or objects, and from the mid-nineteenth century came also to mean the pattern or model after which something is made. It was also applied to a person or thing that exhibits the characteristic qualities of a class, and specifically to a person or thing that exemplifies the ideal qualities or characteristics of a kind or order and a perfect example or specimen of something.

Pollitt (1974) provides by far the largest number of citations—(98)—for type and its derivatives in his review of terms used in ancient Greek art and art-related literature, even though it "is not, strictly speaking, a critical term." In ancient usage, *typos* meant a range of things, "but it does seem that the preponderance of the evidence is *against* the interpretation of *typos* as 'model'. The two really clear-cut meanings of the term when applied to the visual arts are 'mold' and 'relief'. . . . There admittedly exists, however, a residue of passages in which *typos* does seem to have been used to refer to a mold-made image or perhaps any sort of statue that resembled a mold-made image" (291).

Vitruvius is not cited by Pollitt as an example of architectural use of the term *type,* but by the 1780s it was commonplace, "derived from a more or less logical combination of the idea of origins, as enunciated by Laugier and epitomized in the primitive hut as a paradigm of structure, and the notion of characteristic form, as both embedded in the classical tradition and newly adopted in the terminology of the natural sciences . . . [type was] a term whose peculiar etymology and history of use lent itself especially well to an idea that was vague and precise at the same time: vague in its general reference to a world of ideal forms and metaphysical beauties, precise in its application to the expressive qualities of different building types" (Vidler 1987:147).

COMMENTARY   The notion of something made as an impression from an original, whether a mold or not, is certainly contained within the many modern uses of *type*. In architecture, type has been written about so extensively that all that will be attempted here is some clarification. Type was differentiated from the model by the nineteenth-century French theorist Quatremère de Quincy as "not so much the image of a thing to copy or perfectly imitate as the idea of an element that must itself serve as a rule for the model . . . when a fragment, a sketch, the thought of a master, a more or less vague description, has given birth to a work of art in the imagination of the artist, one will say that the type has been furnished for him by such and such an idea, motive, or intention. . . . All is precise and given in the model; all is more or less vague in the type" (extracted from Vidler 1987:152 and Rossi 1982:40).

In everyday practice and conversation, though, type is used uncritically by architects, who usually do not discriminate between its three key derivatives, prototype, stereotype, and typological (rather then 'typal'). Type has its correlates *archetype, prototype,* and *stereotype,* although the first and second are used indifferently in architectural discourse.

Adopted from the Latin *archetypum* and its Greek equivalent, 'archetype' is the original pattern from which copies are made, confoundingly also called a prototype in some dictionaries, with the emphasis being on the originary (arche-) rather than the general. In Platonic philosophy, 'archetypal' was applied to the idea or form as it appeared to the divine mind prior to creation, and as it is presumed by some to be apprehended by the intellect now, independent of the 'ectypal' object, which is a copy like that made by the impression of a seal, something embossed, or an object in relief. Archetype is found in the writings of Philo Judaeus, Irenaeus, and Dionysius the Areopagite, and the concept, though not the word, in those of St. Augustine (Guiley 1991:30–31), long before Jung's psychoanalytic.

On the other hand, 'prototype' is the first or primary type of anything, a pattern or model, and is not altogether distinguishable from archetype. However, the emphasis here is on it being the first, or chief, or superior (proto-) conceptual re-presentation of the archetype, rather than on something originary in the Platonic sense, if such fine precedence is allowed.

With 'stereotype' the meaning shifts to something permanent and reproducible, a threedimensional, conventional re-presentation in solid (stereo-) form of some already created or acknowledged prototype or, more generally, type. Unfortunately, it is now commonly used as a pejorative.

To help reduce the confusion it is useful to construe an order of precedence here: archetype—the abstracted image of a grouping; prototype—the 'first-formed' of the archetype from which a thing is (deemed) to be copied; stereotype—the replication; and type—the generalization or portmanteau term. Without favoring or prejudicing the Platonic notion, it would greatly enhance architectural discourse if it were agreed that, say, archetype was reserved for the Form or the ephemeral and ideational attributes of something, type was the general class to which something belonged, prototype was the first attempt at something in physical form (model, mock-up), and stereotype was its solid (and/or continuing) reproduction. A fond wish, but no doubt doomed.

By way of example, Allsopp (1977) discerns four 'architectonic archetypes': the standing stone, the trilithon, the mound, and the *aedicule* (57) that seem to be based on the time-honored Pythagorean point, line, plane, and volume. From the suggested ordering, these 'archetypes' would be 'prototypes' and everything reiterating them would be 'stereotypes'. *Archetypes* would apply only to the loosely comprehended abstracted images of, say, 'centrality' (the standing stone marking position, or point), 'territory' (the mound marking occupation by something, or plane), 'boundary' (the trilithon marking a threshold, or line) and 'shelter' (the aedicule delimiting space, or volume). Another very recent example is Thomas Thiis-Evensen's book *Archetypes in Architecture* (1987); archetypes are used here to describe the 'first forms' or 'original models' as a formal basis for architecture, a fundamental 'grammar' of images relating to form, function, and technology. In my view, Thiis-Evensen is dealing with prototype and stereotype, not with archetype at all, and the book would be better called *Fundamental Forms in Architecture* or some such, though no doubt a neo-Platonist would be upset by that.

The art historian Rudolf Arnheim (1966) discusses archetypes and quotes from Jung's *Die Welt der Psyche* (Zurich, Rascher, 1954) their principal traits: "chaotic complexity and order, duality, the opposition of light and darkness, above and below, right and left, the unification of opposites in the third, the quaternary (square, cross), the rotation (circle, sphere), and, finally, centricity and radial arrangements organized, as a rule, according to a quaternary system." Certainly it is a common experience of architectural teaching that much of the output of student designers tends to replicate these very traits as the basis for two-dimensional ordering and spatial organization. To the extent that these traits emerge 'raw', as it were, are modified only through extensive tutoring of other possibilities, and recede with maturity and experience suggests that it might be worth systematically investigating the archetypal images of student architects. This could be helpful to those educators who work with and build upon a student's existing conceptions, as many do, to do so in a more directed rather than a confrontational way (it seems mostly confronting to students to have their orderings criticized, even if a tutor is careful not to be harsh).

However that may be, Arnheim sees two implications in Jung's claim that the disposition toward certain types of shape is inherited and that he counts his archetypes among that inheritance: "First, it assumes the existence of specific hereditary mechanisms geared to furnishing the organism with the pertinent archetypal disposition for, say, the production of centric 'mandala' figures. Secondly, the theory need not assume that the organism producing archetypal figures be aware of their symbolic significance, any more than the bird knows why it is building a nest. Hereditary activities do not require understanding."

Jung believed that archetypes and their symbolic meanings intersect, and that their survival depends on their being directly perceived and aligned with human existence. But Arnheim concludes from this that "what he does not seem to realize is that once he admits the perceptual self-evidence of such symbolism there is no need to enlist the services of hypothetical hereditary mechanisms at all . . . no genetics is required to explain why these shapes turn up independently in many cases." (Arnheim 1966:222–223).

To further confound matters, 'typology' is frequently misapplied to situations in which 'type' is meant, as is its adjective 'typological' for 'typal'. Strictly, 'typology' is the knowledge (-logy, Greek *logos*) and study of types, their succession and their meaning or symbolism, the systemics of types, or the categorical overview of types. Aldo Rossi (1982) says it this way: "Typology presents itself as the study of types of elements that cannot be further reduced, elements of a city as of an architecture. . . . The process of reduction is a necessary, logical operation, and it is impossible to talk about problems of form without this presupposition. In this sense all architectural theories are also theories of typology, and in an actual design it is difficult to distinguish the two moments." (41).

To say, for example, that the temple is a 'typology' if what is meant is that it is one type of shrine, or to use 'typological' as the adjectival form instead of 'typical' or 'typal', merely confuses. To call a collection of temple forms or a body of built works exemplifying a type 'a typology' in discussing such matters taxonomically, for me is more correct. Many will disagree, perhaps including Alan Colquhoun, one of the current generation to interrogate the topic in 1967 (Colquhoun 1981) and a number of times subsequently (Colquhoun 1989), and Anthony Vidler, who wrote about type a decade after Colquhoun (Vidler 1977), reified typology in "The Third Typology" the following year (AAM 1978), and has tended to use type and typology interchangeably ever since (Vidler 1990, 1992).

Equating architectural theory with typology, Rossi parallels Colquhoun (1989); he exculpates type from a retrograde historicism by seeing it as a structuralist translation that has enabled modern functionalist and historically determinist (futurist and utopist) notions to be circumvented. As he explains, "Just as language always preexists a group or individual speaker, the system of architecture preexists a particular period or architect. It is precisely through the persistence of earlier forms that the system can convey meaning. These forms, or *types,* interact with the tasks presented to architecture, in any moment in history, to form the entire system" (248). Typology, for him, is reinvesting architecture with associations and meaning. Type is the clue to postmodernist preoccupations with historical reference; it is the vehicle for collective memory rather than mere revivalism, and it brings a new imperative: "It sets limits to the fancy of the architect and binds him to something analogous to the concept of *langue* in Saussure—a received structure and a collective possession that must be presupposed before any significance can be attributed to the *parole* of the individual speaker" (248–249).

There is, however, a basic issue that still remains unclear in the recognition and application of type, the question of what in practice constitutes type, archetype, prototype, or stereotype, and how these are defined as part of some collective system of articulation. What is it that sets apart one from another or makes something belong to one or another type? And among whom and by what means is agreement reached on what the type is? This is particularly pertinent for those archetypes Jung declared the basis for the recurring human themes and predispositions he discerned in his cross-cultural studies of myth and religion. Application of the term in architecture does not conjure all the complexities and antitheses with which Jung imbued his conception of archetype. Indeed, since Jung's psychoanalytic has situated archetypes firmly within the psyche, any conception of them 'outside' his frame may well be problematic. Are Allsopp's four archetypes, or Thiis-Evensen's three, or those of anyone else for that matter, actually collective human possessions at all, as Jung's archetypes are proposed to be? And, if so, in what way do they inform human existence, let alone architectural manifestation? Or are they merely a strategy, names invented to make tangible certain categories of coherence and degrees of difference perceived in physical forms, to maintain focus and authority and thereby help perpetuate architecture, just as the judge does the law?

FURTHER SOURCES AAM 1978; Coomaraswamy 1977, vols. 1 and 2; Eliade 1954; Frampton 1982; Krier 1979, 1983, 1984; Gosling and Maitland 1984; Rossi 1982; Vidler 1977.

B. Internal Persuaders

1. Determinism

That universal reason, practical or ethical, that determinism, those categories that explain everything are enough to make a decent man laugh. **Albert Camus.** 1955:25.

. . . let us first dismiss the idea that we can ever design an environment which will be in any significant way "therapeutic," nor should we claim that the users of a design are "happier," "get along better," or "are better adjusted," *because of design.* There is nothing we can say about someone's internal state of satisfaction or health which can be causally related to his interaction with the physical environment. **Charles W. Rusch.** In Moore 1970:280.

The designer's responsibility must go far beyond these [marketplace] considerations. His social and moral judgment must be brought into play long *before* he begins to design, since he has to make a judgment, an *a priori* judgment at that, as to whether the products he is asked to design or redesign merit his attention at all. In other words, will his design be on the side of the social good or not. **Victor Papanek.** 1972:53.

There is little feeling these days that environment determines what people do, whether they want to or not. The perspective is very much more one of opportunity, rather than determinism. Is the wide range of possible movements and activities permitted by the environment those which were desired to occur? Or, on the other hand, does the design really make them more difficult or even impossible? **William Michelson.** 1975:5.

TRACE   Turning to the second of the two authoritative modes, determinism—from the Latin verb *determinare,* bound, limit, fix—is the doctrine that everything that happens is the result of a necessary causal chain, the general belief that an event has its sufficient natural cause arising from its antecedent conditions, and that the relation between these conditions is sufficiently stable as to make an event predictable if we know them (Solomon 1977:403). The historian Edward H. Carr (1961:93) defines determinism as "the belief that everything that happens has a cause or causes, and could not have happened differently unless something in the cause or causes had also been different." Carr also comments that "Determinism is a problem, not of history, but of all human behaviour. The human being whose actions have no cause is as much an abstraction as the individual outside society."

In architecture, the term is used to impute to certain (usually physical) circumstances, actions, or events a causality or inevitability of architectural outcome, as functionalists attempted to do from the nineteenth century onward, and as behaviorists still claim in varying degrees today (see chapter 1B). The belief that buildings can and should control behavior arose in architecture during the early Modern Movement, but was not labeled 'architectural determinism' until Broady (1966) defined and attacked it. Some social research, notably the 'Hawthorne experiments' by Mayo of Harvard University in 1927, showed no direct correlation between work output and work environment, which "has been a disappointment ever since to those who believe in architectural determinism" (see Broadbent 1973:158–159), if not a deterrent to the recurrence of the belief. Determinism had a brief but powerful run among architects following World War II, and was supposedly put to rest by Janet Daley in 1969 (Broadbent and Ward 1969:71–75).

COMMENTARY   At its most general, architectural determinism revolves around the belief that adherence to a prescription assumed to be authoritative will guarantee a certain outcome. In looking back over the literature, it is curious to note how *aggressive* the anti-determinism reaction of the late sixties was. With hindsight it is possible to say that this was probably an overreaction, caught up with the antimodernist feelings aroused over the emerging failure of social reform by design. The number of apologies being offered by architects, theorists, and researchers as they were nonetheless espousing some form of social determinism for architecture is noteworthy. What was being said, of course, was that they were against the idea of environment actually *controlling* behavior—a hard architectural determinism—but were accepting (and asking for acceptance) of a softer version couched in terms of 'influence', 'limits', or 'opportunity' instead of 'control'. Oscar Newman, for example, qualified his notions of *Defensible Space* (1972) in his summary by insisting that architecture "can create a setting conducive to realizing the *potential* of mutual concern . . . [and that it] allows mutually benefiting attitudes to surface" (207).

Hard determinism used to be the driving force behind design methods because they too promised success. It now seems no coincidence that design methodology fell out of favor during the same period as did determinism; they were obviously linked. The adoption of any method, whether highly wrought and explicated and therefore public, or unarticulated and merely private, predetermines the outcome in the sense that the choice of certain procedures of searching and culling will privilege some possibilities as solutions and ignore others altogether. This is a subtler though no less powerful form of determinism, and one in which all designers are involved, because they cannot escape their own predilections; this is the hermeneutic circle referred to elsewhere in this book, and it needs to be recognized and encouraged for the force that it is, especially in students. So, determinism in one form or another is an authority trap that designers find difficult to avoid.

In short, architects are unable to simply shrug off their designing as not affecting people in some way or another. To do so would be to admit to a *fatalism* that is as aggressively and negatively deterministic as hard determinism, in so many respects, is positive. Common sense shows that where responsibility exists or is assumed, so there must be determinism of a sort; otherwise how is responsibility assigned? If there were no possibility of *causing* harm by design, or by neglect of design, there would be no need for responsibility existing in law regarding the design professions. Whereas architects are no doubt relieved not to have to admit to a direct connection between environment and behavior, for all that such an admission would mean in terms of their responsibility and potential litigation, the corollary of determinism is a moral and ethical responsibility and a duty of care that they have never been able to avoid (see chapter 5).

There is, though, the softer form of determinism referred to above; it 'seeps in' and can become at times quite emphatic, if not hard in the sense of unavoidable. This is the soft determinism that informs conventional wisdom and that most architects believe in and offer up in the form of *aphorisms*. The popularity of dictums, maxims, and aphorisms in architecture encapsulating prescriptions that lead to actions and solutions, and the predilection of architects to formulate them, appear to be unbounded. There are the famous and in many ways notorious aphorisms of recent history, such as 'form follows function', 'less is more', and 'less is a bore' and this book is filled with many more. The tendency to aphorize seems to arise in part as a device by practicing architects to efficiently convey their intentions to their staff, a habit that in time spreads into their writings and teachings. It is also a self-affirmation, a way of insisting an approach upon an unwilling task to make it comply, and is highly marked in signature designers (see chapter 10B).

One more concept that is authoritative in an internal determinist more than an external historicist sense is the continued presence of older ways of thinking or doing, the kind of thinking represented by function, for example, when function is no longer a conscious part of current concerns. The printing through of things past may be likened to a palimpsest, a manuscript in which old writing has been rubbed out to make room for the new (or, perhaps, a monument's brass that has been turned over for a new inscription). Deriving from the Greek *palin,* again, and *psestos,* rub smooth, palimpsest involves the notion of something that once existed that has been erased and used again but with traces of the former image or use still evident. It has much to do with ritual and habituated modes that have undergone change but maintain a connection with the original. The rebuilding of towns or cities on the sites of former towns over time, with evidence of previous use affecting their form, and the continual modification of existing towns or cities *in line with* what has gone before, are examples of palimpsest.

There are traces of older ways in designers too, and more the older they get; repeated patterns of thought that may emerge as aphorisms but most certainly emerge as themes in their corpora. Such themes and habituated modes become a designer's theory, perhaps not highly wrought but influential nonetheless, and these form the context within which design decisions are made. They do not guide practice; they are the personal context of practice, the place of mediation.

FURTHER SOURCES   Bailey 1975; Broady 1968; Gutman 1972; Steadman 1979.

2. Direction and What Is Pointing the Way

The true genius is a mind of large general powers, accidentally determined to some particular direction. **Samuel Johnson** on the poet Cowley. 1905. *Lives of the English Poets.*

If we look at any current history writing or criticism we'll find [an] ideological direction, or else presumed direction, and this entails that the critic act, from a moral point of view, rather like a conscientious traffic cop. . . . He tries to steer the flow *towards* something. He may have no clear idea of what this something is . . . but he usually has a very good notion of the direction to take. **Charles Jencks.** 1980:180.

. . . the critics' moral role should be directional among elites, and for these reasons I have supported the participatory architecture of those such as Ralph Erskine and Lucien Kroll. But, let me reiterate, not because it is great architecture, but rather because it points the direction towards which architecture should go; from *my* perspective. **Charles Jencks.** 1980:180.

There is a discernible visual direction in our time. It permeates the work of many painters and sculptors and is manifested in our immediate history . . . [the] credo of getting the most aesthetically and physically for the least in effort and material. . . . To do the minimal *only* leads to dullness, stagnation and rejection, but to do little in such a way that riches result, both visibly and tangibly—that is where our direction lies. **Harry Seidler.** In Frampton and Drew 1992:382.

TRACE   To direct is to put or keep straight or in right order, to cause something or someone to move or point straight *to* or *toward* a place, to regulate the course of something or to guide the conduct of someone, and to command or appoint someone *to do* something. Deriving from the Latin *dirigere* (di- + *regere*, put straight or rule), the term 'direction' is used for situations in which control, constraint, order, regularity, and efficiency are needed. Direction implies a target, an aim, a purpose, without which nothing can be achieved. Direction is intimately involved in *doing*, because *to*, emphasized above, as with all prepositions, is a spatial term that itself is directional and thereby defines a relationship or connection that can be understood only by experiencing it.

In architecture, teleology is the mode of direction, the 'end' dragging a work into existence. The dictum that 'form follows function' is a prime example of the teleological mode, function as an end having an inexorability about it. Kant's *The Critique of Judgement* (1790) deals fully with this notion, but few architectural writers cover it. Those who do, relate it to a 'means–end' equation of some kind in which the end is at once the end and the means to it; utility is such an end, and architecture cannot be thought of without reference to it or without some sense of 'need' (see Scruton 1979).

COMMENTARY   Direction is an ordering device that confers certain privileges and thereby authority. 'Ascent' is always for the better (climbing the ladder of success), 'descent' always for the worse (falling into disrepute or chaos). On a map north is always 'up' and south is always 'down', a perceptually natural ordering (looking "up" and "down") that transferred easily to cartography, or so it has been for most maps over the past four centuries of mapmaking. But a curiosity arises if someone who lives east, west, or north of a location comes 'up' to that location, and if they come back 'down' to the point of departure. Such an orientation appears to involve accepting and then privileging the dominance of a town or city over the rural areas surrounding it, or in relation to other towns or cities, by virtue of its size or importance (being the state capital, for instance). Such usage is not, of course, universal; it is culturally conditioned. A Britisher or Australian will often say that they are coming "up to town"—coming "up to London" from the counties, or "up to Sydney (Melbourne, Adelaide)" from the country or regional cities—whereas an American will usually say they are coming "in to town" or just "to town." While New Yorkers might travel "upstate" to Syracuse or to the capital, Albany, New York State people would not say they are traveling "up to the Big Apple" in deference to its size and intensity—although New Yorkers no doubt believe they should! It is mainly within corporate (ladder) structures that people speak of traveling 'up' to head office (often located, incidentally, in a major city). For those cultures in which phraseologies privileging dominance are used, such inflections agree with the age-old convention of importance being 'above' or 'over' or 'up' relative to the plane of normal events or everyday existence.

Similarly, if someone directs, they cannot avoid privileging one route over another. Leaders are followed for the direction they favor, for the goals they have, and for the expectations of achievement they create. And this is the clue; artistically there is no path that is not already clear to those who wish to pursue it, as Jencks (above) notes about himself; it is just that some people, like Janus, are better at controlling the gate.

Direction is also a conventional cultural sign in the sense that some of its symbolic content needs to be learned, but it is also an indexical sign in its uttering and in not requiring to be learned, merely followed. The difficulty for architects is to know which is being signified in discerning a direction in current events, a 'trend', in marketing jargon; is it a direction merely to be followed, or does it comprise a symbolism to be learned? When students emulate Norman Foster, Morphosis, Coop Himmelblau, Team Zoo, Aldo Rossi, or Daniel Libeskind by utilizing their motifs or compositional strategies in a studio design program, are they learning to symbolize or are they following directions?

If direction requires both a point of origin and a clearly positioned destination, positioned in the spatio-temporal sense of having been fixed by coordinates and defined as to its ultimate form, what remains for the designer but to follow blindly some predetermined route toward its resolution? If the destination is so clear then obviously bright illumination is all that is required, making of it a beacon amidst the *stürm und drang* of architectural fashion. No orders or heroes, just advance toward the light. A familiar ring? Salvation! Accounts of near-death experiences are filled with directional light offering relief and reward and peace. Plato's cave was blindingly biased toward its mouth once the shackles of bondage to shadows were released. King Lear was offered salvation by the Fool but refused it, to his eternal undoing.

Direction also has implications for method and protocols, for ways of thinking and construing the task right from the start. All very comfortable if faced with its presumed opposite—chaos and aimlessness, like the *flaneur,* the pedestrian dawdler, who so irritates the traffic planner and crowd controller. Is the eminent person leading the way, merely giving direction, like Jencks's cop critic on point duty? Or the leader of a conga line at a party? Architecture without direction seems inconceivable. Without a game plan, what is there for architecture to *do*? How will the game proceed? And yet there are Bernard Tschumi's pavilions in Le Parc de la Villette, red-faced architecture—from exertion, not from blushing; no functions, no *raison d'être* except as events unto themselves, *folies bijou, folies bergère,* enticing the sheep to follow as Mary did the cattle, "across the sands of De-." Determination feeds determinism, de-termination—make no ends, deter-minism—make no small plans, de-constructivism—make no plans for building the future. *Que sera, sera.*

FURTHER SOURCES   7B.5, Function; 8A.4, Needs; Eliade 1954; Rowe 1987.

3. Faith, the Absurd, the Universal, and Experience

On this the knight of faith is just as clear: all that can save him is the absurd; and this he grasps by faith. Accordingly he admits the impossibility and at the same time believes the absurd. **Søren Kierkegaard.** 1843:75–76.

The absurd is precisely by its objective repulsion the measure of intensity of faith in inwardness. Suppose a man who wishes to acquire faith; let the comedy begin . . . the absurd is the object of faith, and the only object that can be achieved. **Søren Kierkegaard.** 1846. *Concluding Unscientific Postscript to the Philosophical Fragments.*

Of whom and of what can I say: 'I know that !' This heart within me I can feel, and I judge that it exists. This world I can touch, and likewise I judge that it exists. There ends all my knowledge, and the rest is construction. **Albert Camus.** 1955:24.

The absurd is born of this confrontation between the human need and the unreasonable silence of the world. This must not be forgotten. This must be clung to because the whole consequence of a life can depend on it. The irrational, the human nostalgia, and the absurd that is born of their encounter—these are the three characters in the drama that must necessarily end with all the logic of which an existence is capable. **Albert Camus.** 1955:32.

A child's experience is much more individual than the grey uniformity of adult experience. Because there is so much less in it all the things stand out in their difference instead of sinking into some sort of average. **Edward de Bono.** 1971:119.

Current philosophy is dominated by a humanism which is hopeful in spite of all hopelessness, a critical rationalism, and a dialectical historicism, all of which lighten up the shadows of existentialism. This is in contrast to literature, in which everything which was not saturated with the senselessness of existence seemed pointless. Absurdity became the leitmotif of authentic literary works, since the whole relationship of people to the world seemed absurd . . . but especially absurd was the fact that they were not identical with the things that surrounded them and that these remained inaccessible. **Arnold Hauser.** 1974:744.

TRACE   Faith derives from the Latin *fidere,* trust, but is a term that defies explanation and definition; to say, as the dictionary does, that it means having trust, confidence, belief, reliance in, or being assured about something or someone is to say no more than any one of these. To have spiritual apprehension of divine truths is to say a lot more than is meant by the everyday use of the word. In his index, Feyerabend (1988) says of faith "see religion; separability assumption." The Danish philosopher Søren Kierkegaard pioneered the phrase 'the leap of faith' across the borders of rationality and thought. Rather than objectivity being the path to truth, he supposed that subjectivity was primary and that faith resided there, in the absurd, as the above quotations show.

The universal has been touched upon in several chapters, and in chapter 8B it is raised in relation to the architectural idea construed as a Platonic state beyond everyday reality (although for the Platonist, it *is* reality). The question of universals is one of the fundamentals of philosophy, and may be explored in any standard text. It is also impossible of definition, for it seems that indefinable faith is required for the support and continuation of the universal, a uniquely binding couplet.

Experience, on the other hand, is what we all have and know; we talk about it, share it, and exchange it, yet it is one of the most highly contentious issues in philosophy, and it, too, requires faith. Faith, by means of which we live all the time but know nothing about, excites little curiosity; experience, the life we live all the time and know most about, excites vast tomes geared to showing how little we can know of it.

COMMENTARY   As with all creative endeavor, the practice of architecture involves a commitment that on many occasions goes beyond the rational and the logical because architects do not know at the start whether the task they are faced with is soluble. To be sure, there are many tried and true ways of doing architecture, from concepts through planning and shape-making to detailing. But every day there are challenges to the orthodox that require inventiveness, a certain daring, and an unfailing acceptance that solutions can and will be found. While many of the tasks architects confront are not absurd in the commonly accepted sense of logically irrational, in the more human sense of architects arguing in the face of the impossible that something *is* possible, there is absurdity in abundance. From the shortest deadlines that must be met to the 'wickedest' problem that is eventually solved, architects rely on what can only be called *faith* to get them through. Curiously, faith and trust do not appear in the indexes of most design and architecture books, even though these disciplines depend on them perpetually. Why?

The Old Testament allegory of Abraham, 'the father of faith', bringing Isaac to the brink of sacrifice is the armature of Kierkegaard's *Fear and Trembling* (1843), though the story itself is not the subject; rather, it becomes the vehicle for discussing the conceptual basis for esthetics, the ethical life, and the relation between the particular and the universal. "The aesthetic life is a life dedicated to what Kierkegaard calls 'immediacy'," writes translator Alastair Hannay in the introduction. "The word is taken from Hegel, for whom it means unreflective knowledge, in which . . . he includes faith." But instead of viewing faith from the privileged position of the Absolute Rational Mind that Hegel postulates as reality, Kierkegaard, through his pseudonymous author, maintains that "faith begins precisely where thinking leaves off," effectively marking the boundary of thought and prohibiting faith itself from being understood by being talked about at all, though its effects (upon Abraham) can be and are discussed at length (9–13). Notwithstanding Kierkegaard's highly wrought notion of faith as devotion to God, the gist is that faith enables the rational to be circumvented and, if devotion to Design is the god of designers, offers a crucial edge on designing.

For Kant, faith is a 'Postulate of Reason'; for Kierkegaard it is 'the strength of the absurd' that sets faith apart from other forms of conviction because it defies the rational in its subjectivity in accepting that a paradox can be resolved. "The absurd is not one distinction among many others embraced by understanding. It is not the same as the improbable, the unexpected, the unforeseen." The absurd is that instant of recognition of the impossible with its opposite, the acceptance of incongruity as at the same time congruous. "Faith is therefore no aesthetic emotion, but something far higher, exactly because it presupposes resignation; it is not the immediate inclination of the heart but the paradox of existence" (Kierkegaard 1843:76). It is precisely this intersection of the impossible with the 'deemed' possible that makes much of the world of designing absurd—only faith can ensure an outcome.

But what Kierkegaard shows by so closely interrogating the allegory of Abraham is something far more profound than the strength of the absurd as the catalyst of faith, and its implications for designing are staggering. He declares that Abraham's actions show, among other things, that by 'suspending the ethical', the universal good of not killing Isaac, he thereby places himself 'above the law', as it were. The law is assumed to have universal validity and to apply to all situations equally, its corollary being the orthodox epistemological tradition in which the only valid knowledge is that of unchanging laws and principles. The opposite of universal law is the anarchy of the particular, so conventional wisdom tells us. But for Kierkegaard, the particular may precede and pre-empt the universal, as the example of Abraham shows (30–31); this contention was later to become one of the foundations of existentialism. For designing, this means that particular and individual expressions of faith, the irrational, and the absurdity of paradoxes may have validity as much as the authority of rationalism and subjugation to the universal have had and continue to have, especially as reinforced by science.

The commitment designers necessarily and frequently make to an ongoing expectation of resolution in the face of circumstances and events stacked against them, cannot be explained rationally; it is 'an article of faith'. That gifted designers have the ability to conjure solutions in this way is well-known and is a clue to their magical allure, their charisma, a much sought-after quality that defies logical explanation. It may well be possible at some future time to give public expression, contrary to Kierkegaard's claim to the contrary, to just what this designers' faith consists of and how to publicly inculcate it as an educational agenda, for therein lies the essence of creativity as the ability to rescue from the irrational, the paradoxical, and the absurd, new realities that otherwise would not exist at all.

By virtue of its linking of knowledge and principle, universality is a powerful authoritative force in those cultures in which cosmology relies on tradition. Architecture is a culture that relies on tradition, or at least on arguments that are premised on the existence of traditions, for much of its discourse and application (see 7A.3, Continuity). But the appeal of an all-pervading universality constantly bumps up against the expression of originality and the particular. Designing may be conceived as a limitless sea of universality *within* which originality and particulars are buoys or pylons. Or, to invert the metaphor with great difficulty, designing may be considered a sea of universality *marked out* by buoys of originality and pylons of the particular. This is once again the primordial question of whether essence precedes existence or existence precedes essence. Either way, the dialectic remains, a paradox that only faith can transcend. The authoritative base for architecture shifts according to where your faith lies.

FURTHER SOURCES   Coomaraswamy 1977; Guénon 1942; Snodgrass 1990.

4. Customs and Architectural Habits Die Hard

. . . construction, apart from certain branches of scientific and practical knowledge, which you will be able to study at leisure, is nothing but a method—a habit of reasoning—a compliance with the rules of common sense. **Eugène-Emmanuel Viollet-le-Duc.** 1874. *How to Build a House.* Cited in Hearn 1990:123.

History begins with the handing down of tradition; and tradition means the carrying of the habits and lessons of the past into the future. **Edward H. Carr.** 1961:108.

There are those who believe that experience is carefully put together by the mind to create ideas. It seems more likely, however, that separate experiences come together of their own accord, one latching on to another to give a train of thought. It is only later that this train of thought is improved by ritual examination. **Edward de Bono.** 1971:11.

TRACE   Custom stems from the Latin *consuescere,* accustom, and to accustom refers to making familiar through habitual or usual practice. Habit in turn stems from the Latin *habere,* to have or hold, and is a settled disposition to act in a certain way, especially one acquired by frequent repetition of the same act. The Greek for habit or custom, *synetheia* (*syn,* together + *ethos,* habit, character) unites the habitual characters or dispositions of an individual, group, or race over time in that 'together' is not a spatial but a temporal accumulation.

As spoken of in architecture, custom behooves regularity of action, which implies procedure and proven ways of thinking and doing. In education this amounts to 'exercising' design skills, inculcating good and efficient habits to take care of routine tasks, those that follow a regular course or pattern. Custom also relates to the patterns discerned in human behavior, particularly in the constancies of human settings that Christopher Alexander has explored and distilled so thoroughly in his books applying his 'pattern language' (Alexander 1977, 1979).

COMMENTARY   It is the custom of designing, as it is with music, that it must be practiced to gain proficiency and practiced extensively to be mastered. This leads to routine ways of thinking, organizing, and doing, that by their habituation bring control and tend toward predictable results. It is the accepted wisdom of designing that human activities and settings can be comprehended as customary, habitual, and ritualized, and that once understood they may be cataloged as spatio-temporal maps, patterns of static use, human interaction, and desire lines. This leads to replicability, systematization and typing of solutions that gives ample scope for variation. Both the practice and the comprehension may be combined with formal compositional rules to produce buildings that are within the norms of performance and appearance.

But there are always the mavericks, rogue variables out to upset routine and predictability. These invariably are matters of individual taste, action, or belief, and the architectural challenge is to find either the most resistant or the most adaptable solution that can absorb or tolerate the effects of the aberrant individual element without disabling the whole. This disinfection applies at the level of an individual building as much as to the profession collectively. For this reason, architecture as a profession is always erring on the side of conservatism and convention; it always works toward maintaining its customs and reinforcing its habits; otherwise it ceases to be a profession. Tantalizing though new trends and experiments in design may be, they are always filtered through the social and political apparatus of the business of architecture, an intricate web of professional and commercial mechanisms that ensure due process and thereby continuity.

The power of architecture as a commercial enterprise to consume or defuse itinerant behavior is so assertive that the avant-garde, for instance, is inevitably either overrun or ignored, and hence its ideas and ideals are never immortalized in pure form but are doomed to become rearguard the moment they arise. This appropriation has led to the view that the avant-garde, certainly as the handmaiden of 'progress', can only ever be a myth. This appropriation parallels the way in which society transmutes the subjective originality of architecture, because of its intimacy with the 'life-world', into a cultural discourse and a 'frame for life', unlike art, where it "seeks to preserve the intrinsic, inalienable essence of the artwork in its mint condition" (Kenneth Frampton. In Ghirardo 1991:18–19). The authority that custom and habit wield is enough to ensure that dire predictions of the end of architecture as a profession will continue to be wide of the mark, especially wherein some *other* view of architecture is promoted as more deserving than conventional practice. Trauma that changes architectural thought and practice is a normal process of rejuvenation, like a snake shedding surplus skin, though the reptilian allusion points to other qualities that are not so benign but will not be raised here.

Customs external to the practices of architecture itself necessarily involve an encounter with social norms and rituals, but these will not be discussed at length here except to mention the six categories of custom isolated by Antoniades (1990:Chapter 5) that may influence designing in varying degrees. *Sacrificial* customs are now of historical interest only, but were intended to ensure the life of a building by substitution of another through animal sacrifice (and human sacrifice in earlier times). *Exorcism* in its undramatic form is a propitiatory custom intended to ward off evil spirits, one example being Chinese *feng-shui* whereby proper siting, orientation, and alignment of buildings is thought to ensure health and prosperity. The custom of making *offerings* at significant stages of construction (for example, ground-breaking, foundation stone, first slab) is practiced in all cultures. *Warnings and good deeds* are customary in traditional and tribal cultures in which superstition is a living force, and are used to ensure continued safety and habitability. *Celebration* occurs when construction is finished and/or occupation begins (topping off, dedication, open house, house warming). Finally, there are *social and regional* customs that exist in all cultures and in the main need to be provided for through suitable urban public spaces, although the numerous and subtle needs for privacy are probably more directly influential in designing.

A more profound aspect of the persistence of custom and architectural habit is their privileging of the formal over the circumstantial, the rules over the action. In this respect, custom, habit, and tradition are the enemy of hermeneutics rather than of the positivism of science and Cartesian thought or method. The existential interpretive dialogue between building and participant, and before that between program and designer, is the dynamic of architectural hermeneutics, a dynamic in which a totality is vivified by the participant or designer in action. While the immediacy of interpretation and 'free play' takes place in and is informed by memory, precedent, and knowledge, it is fixated by custom, habit, and tradition, which mitigate against creative idiosyncrasy. The challenge for hermeneutics is to overcome the conceptual difficulty it has in addressing customary arrangements and forms, their predetermination of the rules under which they operate, and the obstacle to invention they present. The challenge for architectural theory is to overcome the conceptual bind that custom and convention impose while at the same time allowing free reign to interpretive discourse.

FURTHER SOURCES   Chapter 6B; chapter 10B; Eliade 1959; Fathy 1973; Quantrill 1974; Rykwert 1972.

5. Function and the Formal Demands of Architecture

It seems to me then, that you do not speak of [a breastplate] well shaped in an absolute sense, but only in regard to its function. **Socrates.** In Xenophon. *Recollections of Socrates and Socrates' Defense Before the Jury.* Translated by Anna S. Benjamin. Indianapolis: Bobbs-Merrill, 1965.

In architecture only that shall show that has a definite function, and which derives from the strictest necessity. **Carlo Lodoli.** Cited in Kaufman 1955:96.

The first thing to be required of a building—not, observe, the *highest* thing, but the first thing—is that it shall answer its purposes completely, permanently, and at the smallest expense. . . . It indeed will generally be found that the edifice designed with this masculine reference to utility, will have a charm about it, otherwise unattainable, just as a ship, constructed with simple reference to its service against powers of wind and wave, turns out to be one of the loveliest things that human hands produce. **John Ruskin.** 1854. Addenda:s59, 60.

It is the pervading law of all things organic, and inorganic, of all things physical and metaphysical . . . that the life is recognizable in its expression, that form ever follows function. This is the law. **Louis Sullivan.** "The Tall Office Building Artistically Considered." *Lippincott's* 57, March 1896:403-409.

Function and environment determine form. **Dankmar Adler.** "Influence of steel construction and of plate glass upon the development of Modern style." *Inland Architect* 28, November 1896:34-37.

The pressure we call Function; the resultant, Form. **Louis Sullivan.** 1918:48.

Architecture and design for the masses must be functional, in the sense that they must be acceptable to all and that their well-functioning is the primary necessity. **Nikolaus Pevsner.** 1968:9.

The twentieth century has had to rediscover what the nineteenth century learned so painfully: eclecticism is the vernacular of sophisticated societies; architecture begins where function ends. **J. Mordaunt Crook.** 1987:Preface, 11.

The modernists argued that form follows function, and that functionally efficient forms necessarily had a pure geometry. But their streamlined aesthetic disregarded the untidy reality of actual functional requirements. In deconstructivist architecture, however, the disruption of pure form provides a dynamic complexity of local conditions that is more congruent with functional complexity. Moreover, forms are disturbed and only then given a functional program. Instead of form following function, function follows deformation. **Philip Johnson** and **Mark Wigley.** 1988:19.

To claim that form follows function is to claim that some formal feature or quality of an object is necessary for functional adequacy: if the feature or quality is not present, then the object cannot perform the function we have in mind. **William Mitchell.** 1990:212.

TRACE   First used in English in 1533, *function* derives from the Latin *functio,* which is in turn a stem of *fungi,* perform, although the extract from Socrates above indicates long use of the term. 'Perform' here means to fully and completely furnish an action, process, or work, so function embodies completeness and due action, which leads to its modern use as that special kind of activity proper to anything or the mode of action by which it fulfills its purpose. Function thus signifies an active rather than a passive or inherent quality in something. In architecture it has come to refer not to the activity so much as the *static* *reflection of activity* relating to a building's purpose, although 'functions' certainly conveys the idea of a building's action and use.

In architecture, functional notions have been current from the eighteenth century. The Franciscan friar Carlo Lodoli (1690–1761) coined the expression *organic architecture* and elaborated upon the idea of function in his teachings. It was from Lodoli that the American sculptor and theorist Horatio Greenough (1805–1852) garnered his functional ideas for architecture "and the whole doctrine of necessity as the true source of ornament and of beauty. And from Greenough the tag that form follows function passed to Sullivan, to Wright and into the common-place of architectural talk" (Rykwert 1982:115–121). Greenough was to express his first ideas on function in an essay "American Architecture" (1843) and more clearly in another, "Aesthetics at Washington" (1851), saying that to organize buildings was to "model their shapes for their functions" and to arrange for "the external expression of the inward functions" (Small 1947:21). The architect Gottfried Semper made a connection between function and form in an essay on a comparative system of styles written in 1853 and following on the natural history ideas of the French naturalist Georges Cuvier utilizing a taxonomy equivalent to that Alexander von Humboldt developed for the universe in *Der Kosmos* (see Semper entry in Placzek 1982).

COMMENTARY   Congruence between function and form has been an authority for architecture for well over a century, and most powerfully for half that, although you would be hard-pressed to find a reference to function in the index (if there is one!) of a book on architecture published since 1987.

Just how function assumed the authority it did in giving birth to a new style has been questioned by Demetri Porphyrios (1978), among others. He concluded that coherences perceived in the plans, spaces, and iconography of buildings were connected with the functions of the building as a consequence of wanting to make form analyzable. "In effect, function is to the object one looks at what cause is to the representation it effects. The Modernist pathos for establishing zones or functions in the plan, for frantically articulating stairs from corridors, columns from non-structural members, or general spaces from specialised ones, has its roots in this alliance between function (utility) and representation; that is, in the obsession of expressing the 'utilisable' with the 'identifiable' " (13).

Functional justification, therefore, has been the publicly acceptable face of architectural form, making it publicly comprehensible and capable of being utilized in popular discourse. Architects generally have desired the transferability of architectural concepts, despite being accused of insularity, because it assists communication and affirms their continued public worth. In short, if form was not analyzable through its relation with function, there could have been no architecture industry, no critical apparatus, no basis for design education, no theoretical discourse; in fact, no creation. Formal analysis with functional justification has been essential because it has given architects political leverage in synthesis, the means to convince others that a solution is appropriate and worth supporting; not because it assists in synthesis as a design process necessarily, although it obviously plays a part. In the absence of a suitable substitute, function is likely to continue as an important preoccupation of architecture even if form does not now follow it or fixity of use within form is no longer insisted on.

The advertisement and investment of modernism was that function needed appropriate form, that it was a natural relationship, and that architects were most suited to catalyzing it. Remove the necessity of this relation and architects merely join the throng of individual tastes and opinions; this is why function has not been lightly set aside. To expect the average person to adjudicate or the average client to seek, let alone the average architect to be able to offer, refinement of taste alone (or something equally rarefied) as the basis for their existence and on their say-so is a dramatic mistake. The retreat to the conservatism of historical reference, neo-vernacular and the whole community architecture push (a push that has always been there, by the way) is a response to the underlying consternation that another movement as powerful as modernism (in its imperial ambitions) has not yet arisen. This will not change until something emerges to replace function as the *new* substantiation for architecture and that at the same time ensures a natural place for architects in its working out. This is why signature architecture and the idiosyncratic concerns of architectural theorists are misleading as models for the future of the profession—students, take note.

Just how embedded function still is in the professional psyche may be judged by choosing any current mainstream architectural journal at random; in it there will be references to function, both obvious and camouflaged. One example of the obvious from *Architecture Australia,* January/February, 1993, is the Information Technology Building at Queensland University of Technology by John Simpson and Associates, reviewed by Susan Savage (24–27). Savage refers directly to the lower four floors ("the base") clad in brick-work and white concrete screening, which "also [to which add "are seen to"] accommodate building functions least likely to change"; that is, fixity of use matches solidity of appearance. Other parts of the building are generated by 'need'; lecture theaters and fire stairs "refer to the building's functions," and the structural grid is, as it has been for ages, associated with "flexibility." There are many such descriptions to be found in other national journals.

When the cause-effect relation of function and form was shown to be untenable, architecture was thrown into disarray not because a truth was suddenly revealed, but because what had been an asset soon became a liability. Architects have not been dissuaded from championing a cause for their formal concerns; they have merely cast around for different cause-effect relations. For example: replication or reference on the strength of historical precedence (the simplest mode while awaiting new ideas); emphasis on bodily spatial connection, empathetic comprehension, and doctoring (gender pundits and apologists seeking validation and direction); reading, interpretation, narration, and all manner of literary allusion (ways of finding intellectual support for emotional inventions); straight contradiction of modern compositional tenets (neo-constructivism and the little deconstruction there is). Always, the formal is justified in terms of a cause producing it, functional concerns being merely sidelined rather than eliminated and remaining useful fall-back positions in case all else fails. It is also a fact of life in early undergraduate teaching that functional matters are the starting point for most students in grappling with a design task, and only after assuring themselves that the practical can be met do they experiment in their formal pursuits.

From a different angle, and one that is representative of a substantial focus of effort in 'design science', that netherworld of computerized aids to designing, William Mitchell (1990) reinforces the functional as a substantial basis for form in talking of language and its application:

> . . . an architectural language establishes a repertoire of forms (the vocabulary) that an architect can use, and the synthetic rules of that language specify possible contexts of use. An architect needs to understand the useful roles of vocabulary elements in their possible contexts. . . . For each vocabulary element, possible context, and role in that context, there are conditions of functional adequacy that can be expressed as constraints on the values of form variables. Thus full characterization of a vocabulary element requires specification not only of essential formal properties, but also of possible contexts of use, roles in those contexts, and conditions of functional adequacy that must be satisfied (217).

For archi-linguists, then, forms are 'useful' as architectural repertoire, repertoire situated in 'contexts of use' which are political in that 'roles' are demanded and, instead of generating, function now 'constrains' repertoire's formal elements. This is not gobbledygook; it is the real thing, and needs to be taken seriously because design science of the computerized kind is one area of architecture that is commanding a great deal of research and development funding and is producing an enormous literature. The fact that architectural theorists inclined to history and literature make almost no reference to function at all in any contemporary sense, suggests that its demise may have been their plot all along, which is why for the bulk of the profession it has survived mostly unscathed.

FURTHER SOURCES   10B.4, Metaphor; Benton, Benton and Sharp 1975; Small 1947; Van Leeuwen 1988; Voyce 1949.

CHAPTER

Governing Concepts of Architects

Overview

Instead of receiving long, related 'strings' of ideas, organized or synthesized for us, we are increasingly exposed to short, modular blips of information—ads, commands, theories, shreds of news, truncated bits and blobs that refuse to fit neatly into our pre-existing mental files. ... Assailed by what they perceive as the bedlam of blip culture, Second Wave people feel a suppressed rage at the media.

Third Wave people, by contrast, are more at ease in the midst of this bombardment of blips. ... But they also keep an eye out for those new concepts or metaphors that sum up or organize blips into larger wholes. ...

Instead of merely receiving our mental model of reality, we are now compelled to invent it and continually to reinvent it. This places an enormous burden on us. **Alvin Toffler.** 1980. *The Third Wave*:177–178.

It may seem contradictory to include 'governing' in the heading of this chapter when so much effort has been expended in the introduction and earlier chapters to show that the relation between theory and practice is not one of governance but of mediation between competing concepts, themes, and practices. This is not to say that in the process of mediative discourse governance does not emerge either directly, as in the rules of debate ensuring fairness and coverage, or indirectly through ways of organizing thoughts, structuring arguments, interpreting facts, comprehending situations or simulating futures. Of course, governance does appear in all these ways, if only to act as a constraint upon discourse, for that is the way we are as humans. Whether it is because we are Third Wave people or not, we are always inclined "to keep an eye out," to organize, invent, and reinvent, as Alvin Toffler remarks.

This chapter is not about what the concepts of architects might be for the future in Toffler's sense, but about what the beliefs and concepts *are* that architects bring to their present discourse and practices. It raises questions about how architects and designers now go about what they do and how they compare with the way those in other fields approach what they do, not in terms of method but in the ideas they hold dear and believe necessary to achieve successful outcomes in their endeavors. That there is and must continue to be faith that an outcome will be achieved while designing lest the designing never get started is a truism in architecture and is probably true for other fields. It is no doubt as impossible to make headway in other design fields as it seems to be in architecture if you are pessimistic about the possibilities of what is being attempted. What beliefs are most productive in architecture or facilitate a presence of mind that allows free reign to creativity? What makes some beliefs or concepts long-lasting and others, equally evocative, not? What illusions do we labor under in what we do as designers, and does it do anyone good to disturb these?

The literary theorist Stanley Fish would no doubt answer 'yes' to the last question because beliefs are not static and shifts in belief are inevitable anyway, requiring no specifically interrogative or declarative situation to precipitate them. He argues that beliefs interact with one another, though they are never held at the same 'level' or operate at the same time; they are 'nested'. For him the mind is not a static structure but an assemblage of beliefs that are 'an engine of change', constrained yet capable of continual adjustment (Fish 1989:146). On this basis, any fixity of belief or concept can only be provisional, and the governance it offers only transitory. What, then, of the architectural quest for unchanging principles to inform designing, the relation of these principles to changing individual beliefs, and the propensity architects have for uttering and mouthing reductive maxims, particularly as they gain age and stature?

The prospect of a path to the future paved with 'one-liners' has an immense appeal for architects, perhaps because the maxim is itself architectonic in being definitive, essential, to the point, or authoritative, as was suggested in the overview to chapter 7. Or perhaps because it aligns with that other inclination architects have always had—handbooks, the shortcut to practice. However, there is at times a cynical, ironic, or paradoxical edge to architectural maxims that makes them aphoristic, idiosyncratic, and subversive though nonetheless universal, Robert Venturi's 'less is a bore' or Peter Blake's 'form follows fiasco' being two that come to mind. The fashion of aphoristic writing in architecture was pioneered by the French engineer Auguste Choisy, according to Robin Middleton (1982), the economy yet clarity of which also imbued the axonometric drawings in Choisy's *Histoire de l'Architecture* (1899) and endeared them to the Modern Movement pioneers

(Frampton 1980). Being singular, universal, and yet competitive probably makes the aphorism *the* architectural one-liner *par excellence,* verbal ground-zero, joining type and trope as concept-building techniques, or building concepts pure and simple.

The ideas that seem most to influence designing must be optimistic in that they offer positive encouragement by way of useful axioms and ways of thinking about a design task preparatory to and while undertaking its resolution. These are matters of governance, boundaries, and limits, permissible extensions and liberties, devices controlling and channeling effort to facilitate process and production. They are applied right from the start of designing and even before. Much of what was outlined in earlier chapters comes to bear in forming an attitude in a designer such that a task may be comprehended only through a sieve of predilections, prejudices, prejudgments, and even premonitions. Such issues regarding the beliefs architects need and use to sustain their designing (including 'need' itself) are the subject of part A of this chapter.

Abstraction as it appears in axonometry is a skill architects have developed with great facility in many aspects of their conception, writing, drawing, and practice, although it tends to narrow communication to those who fully understand its alien reductiveness. In this narrowing is both a definition and a defense of architects, just as it is with artists. Abstraction sets architects apart, preserves their domain, and offers a measure of control over their destiny. But it is not the only or the most prominent quality possessed by architects; there are a number of conceptual skills vital to formal invention and manipulation, problem-solving and practical implementation, not least among them being versatility, the ability to switch and adapt one mode to another. Only four are examined in part B of this chapter—abstraction, metaphor as the portmanteau concept *extraordinaire,* idea as a core conceptualizing force, and the novel concept of *meme* as the hair-trigger of creativity.

A. Architectural Belief Systems

1. The Illusory Face of Beliefs

Custom is a Connection which the Mind makes of two Things of a different Nature, for by this Connection, it comes to pass, that the Esteem, wherewith the Mind is prepossessed for some things whose Value it knows, insinuates an Esteem, also for others, whose Worth it knows not, and insensibly engages it to respect them alike. This principle is the natural Foundation of Belief, which is nothing else but an Effect of that Prepossession, by which the Knowledge and good Opinion we have of him who assures us of anything, whose Truth we are ignorant of, disposes us to make no Doubt of it. **Claude Perrault.** Cited in Tzonis 1972:54–55.

We plunge forward into the field of fresh experience with the beliefs our ancestors and we have made already; these determine what we notice; what we notice determines what we do; what we do again determines what we experience; so from one thing to another, altho the stubborn fact remains that there *is* a sensible flux, what is *true of it* seems from first to last to be largely a matter of our own creation. **William James.** 1907:112.

. . . in the best of Mies's work we are brought up to the question of belief, because, depending on our own beliefs in the existence of a transcendental world, we will experience this work as an adequate symbol of that world or, alternatively, as just a very exquisite farce. **Charles Jencks.** 1973:105.

But as E. M. Forster remarks, "The man who believes a thing because he feels it in his bones is not far from the man who believes in the authority of a policeman's truncheon," since neither belief has a basis in intellectual scrutiny and conviction. **Berthold Lubetkin.** Royal Gold Medal Address. In Murray 1982:45–49.

. . . any practice one engages in is conceivable only in relation to some belief or set of beliefs— but . . . beliefs are not theories. A theory is a special achievement of consciousness; a belief is a prerequisite for being conscious at all. Beliefs are not what you think *about* but what you think *with,* and it is within the space provided by their articulations that mental activity—including the activity of theorizing—goes on. Theories are something you can have—you can wield them and hold them at a distance; beliefs have *you,* in the sense that there can be no distance between them and the acts they enable. **Stanley Fish.** 1989:326.

You don't know what the building is, really, unless you have a belief behind the building, a belief in its identity in the way of life of man. Every architect's first act is that of either revitalizing a prevailing belief or finding a new belief which is just in the air somehow. **Louis Kahn.** 1965. "Remarks." In Latour 1991:194.

TRACE   Deriving by substitution of prefix from the Germanic meaning 'to hold dear, cherish, trust in', of which later renditions are the Gothic *galaubjan,* the German *glauben,* and the Dutch *gelooven,* to believe and *belief* are assents given or withheld about propositions that are founded partly in trust and partly in truth. "Clearly related to knowledge, belief may be characterized as stronger than mere ungrounded opinion but weaker than full knowledge" (Flew 1979). Beliefs, as the things believed, may also be based in opinion or intuition; that is, in nonevidential understanding.

Architectural beliefs, in the sense of assents given to propositions about what in architecture is based on introspection, or how architectural designing operates based on behavior or performance, have formed the core of architectural theory since Roman times (via Vitruvius). Unlike the philosophical inclination to doubt following Descartes, architects have not developed any systematic strategy for questioning beliefs, relying instead on exhortation, earnest admonition, or laudatory urging, to persuade or to cajole into leaving well enough alone.

COMMENTARY   The relation between beliefs and a belief system is straightforwardly described in a historical study of 'the common people' by an English history professor, J. F. C. Harrison (1984:155), who sees the focus as our philosophy of life, "a bundle of attitudes, beliefs and values with which we navigate our way through the pleasures and perils of everyday living." This navigation is largely unreasoned, instinctive, and automatic, except on those occasions when people differ with us and we are suddenly obliged to confront what we do and do not believe. Harrison argues that our beliefs are clustered, structured into a system with behavioral consequences, though they are not all held equally strongly, being arranged more or less concentrically. Central beliefs about our own existence and the world are so basic that "to question them would be to cause a serious disruption in our lives" while others are more peripheral and flexible, "beliefs derived from the authority of family, class or religious group, and we recognize differences of opinion about them." Another layer of beliefs has to do with taste and opinion, which "are inconsequential in their relation to our central or primary beliefs," and therefore expendable. There is no reason to suppose that architectural beliefs or belief systems are any different.

It seems hardly necessary, then, to say that the core beliefs that architects and designers hold regarding design and how it is best achieved are crucial to their designing. It does not matter whether these beliefs are 'true' or 'factual'; truth and facticity are difficult if not impossible to authenticate even if designers *can* explicate their beliefs. What architects genuinely accept is that their beliefs are authentic (Cuff 1991:20–21), and they see them as establishing a position in relation to the profession and as facilitating thinking and action. To say that their facticity or truth does not matter, though, places those who wish to convince others, especially educators, in a difficult position because they must present their beliefs to students *as if they are factual and truthful* for them to be worthy of emulation. Architectural educators, and many architects too because they teach, tend to couch their beliefs as positive maxims, a form highly suited to persuasion because it is easily memorized and readily repeated; in this they have the characteristics of memes (see 8B.3, Meme).

Dana Cuff (1991) devotes a chapter to reporting beliefs in practice encountered in her studies and highlights certain core beliefs among architects. Architects act and believe as they do within the context of a professional ethos: "The context set by the profession promotes and discourages certain ways of rationalizing practice's daily events" (20), and it is rarely challenged. One core belief is that design is a 'master value' of the profession that produces a consequent distaste for management. Another is the primacy of the studio as both a teaching setting and a model for practice, the small group with discursive decision-making. A third is that talent warrants the bestowal of special privileges, among which is an allowance that excuses errant behavior. Allied with this is the primacy of creative individuality over productive collectivity. Yet another belief is the image of the architect as a generalist as against the specialist reality of the competitive marketplace. Such beliefs and their oppositions are the basis for a number of changes Cuff recommends for the profession involving the three main institutions of architecture that "together form the wellspring of beliefs within the culture of practice, maintaining professional unity around those core beliefs"; namely, the schools, professional organizations, and the press.

Skepticism often accompanies the politics of architectural practice, and is exhibited by pragmatist-architects in their reaction against sweeping metaphysical claims. It is evident too at the outer edges of architectural writing, either in avant-gardist counterclaims to conventional thought or in the oppositional writings to established movements, of which antimodernism has by far the largest stake (for an overview see Jencks 1980:175). At this margin, cynicism can haughtily about-face, as Robert Venturi's *Complexity and Contradiction* did in 1966; it can 'outrage', as did Peter Blake's criticisms of the folly of modern architecture in an article of the same name in *The Atlantic* (Blake 1974) and subsequently (Blake 1977), and as Charles Jencks (1977) did with his declaration for postmodernism; or it can fracture and displace, as the MoMA exhibition on Deconstructivist Architecture was intended to do and did in 1988 (Betsky 1990; Johnson and Wigley 1988).

On a different tack, considering the positivist legacy of modernism and given the amount of poetic license with which a substantial number of individual architects indulge themselves, skepticism that obliges justification is a quality rarely found in the intermediate levels of writing, that myriad range of monographs on individual architects and buildings, although it exists on an interpersonal level in peer critique and plain old malice. This public reticence may be a fear of legal retribution, but is more probably because few writers want to be offside with either the establishment or the heroes; constant negativity makes for poor sales. By the same token, it does not do for a designer to openly say that inspiration or actions come from dreams or visions. Such an admission is unlikely to improve credibility or to gain admission to schools of architecture as a legitimate instructional device, however much it might be so for that particular designer. Even the most extreme designers still want to maintain some credibility.

For example, early in the twentieth century, Frederick Bligh Bond, an eccentric English archaeologist, psychic researcher, writer, editor, and ecclesiastical architect, discovered the buried remains of parts of Glastonbury Abbey, particularly the Edgar and Loretto chapels. He maintained that he made these discoveries based on his geometric and architectural knowledge, and also on revelations provided him through automatic writings from the discarnate "Brotherhood of Watchers." This was an admission he was to keep to himself for a decade until he wrote about the archaeological discoveries in his *Gates of Remembrance* (1918), in case ridicule prevented him from completing his research. While he never swayed from his belief in such powers, evidenced by the remarkable finds he made, he was to receive almost universal condemnation from the religious and architectural communities. As Bond's biographer states, "It is never easy for a biographer to reconstruct the inwardness of any man" (Kenawell 1965), and it is symptomatic of all biography and of architectural thinking generally that the private world of beliefs, no matter how publicly they may be professed, is always incomplete and may even be illusory. How many latter-day architects like Bond are there?

As for the would-be architect, it is the recognition of the essentially personal, individual, and highly selective and idiosyncratic nature of our beliefs and belief systems, and the need to array them for analysis and criticism in the firming up of an ideology of architecture, that is at the heart of architectural education and is perhaps the most confronting aspect for many students. Such outpouring is especially hard for students from cultures in which personal confession, criticism, and/or affirmation are not encouraged because of social etiquette or fear of reprisal in one form or another. The mind games that architectural educators play with students, even with the best of intentions, can amount to an infringement of personal liberties, or overstep the bounds of educational expertise into that of counselors. The fact that educators are constantly dancing along the edge of playing amateur psychologist, as the quotations from James and Fish show, suggests that there may be more gained from psychology than from philosophy in understanding how beliefs and values are acquired; common sense, too, favors psychology. Studies of the psychology of bias, for example, are potentially significant to architectural education. *The Journal of Architectural Education (JAE)* and *Design Studies* are important outlets for such psychological studies as have been done relating to beliefs and values in architecture.

FURTHER SOURCES   Clarke 1984; Cuff 1991; Hejduk 1985; P. Rowe 1987; Schon 1983, 1987.

2. Principles — Validation and Suspension

Architecture aims at Eternity; and therefore is the only thing incapable of modes and fashions in its principles. **Sir Christopher Wren.** *Parentalia.* Knevitt 1986:#386.

"Principles in art, are no other than the trains of ideas which arise in the mind of the artist out of a just and adequate consideration of all those local, temporary, or accidental circumstances upon which their propriety or impropriety, their congruity or incongruity, wholly depend." Payne Knight, cited in **Joseph Gwilt.** 1867:§2494.

To treat abstract principles as finalities, before which our intellects may come to rest in a state of admiring contemplation, is the great rationalist failing. **William James.** 1907:43.

. . . the law of correspondence . . . is the very foundation of all symbolism. By virtue of this law, each thing, proceeding as it does from a metaphysical principle from which it derives all its reality, translates or expresses that principle in its own fashion and in accordance with its own order of existence, so that from one order to another all things are linked together and correspond in such a way as to contribute to the universal and total harmony, which, in the multiplicity of manifestation, can be likened to a reflection of the principial unity itself. **René Guénon.** 1958:Preface, xii.

There is one principle no self-governing creature can adopt—the principle of having no principles. **Clarence Irving Lewis.** 1969:73.

I don't believe in principles. **Philip Johnson.** Cited in Games 1985: "The Best Hated Architect in the World."

A theory of judgement as *Mittelglied* must be constructed. But there will be "great difficulties" in finding for judgement *a priori* principles which are proper to it and which would protect the theory from empiricism. One can find *a priori* concepts only in the understanding. The faculty of judgement uses them, it applies them, but it does not have at its disposal any concepts which belong to it or are specifically reserved for it. **Jacques Derrida.** 1987:41.

Not with high principles nor buried in the details does one start, but as Heisenberg once suggested, "somewhere in the middle," or "in the concrete" as Adorno stipulated. **John Knesl.** In Al-Sayed *et al.* 1988:text near n44.

TRACE   The term 'principle' was adapted from the Latin *principium,* beginning or source, and in the plural, foundations or elements; it is often used for emphasis with the modifier 'first'. Of its several meanings, its general sense of a fundamental source, a primary element, force, or law that produces or determines particular results, the ultimate basis or cause of the existence of something, may be applied to architecture. So too might its meaning as a fundamental truth or proposition on which many others depend, a fundamental assumption forming the basis of a chain of reasoning.

Principle is used in architecture mostly in the sense of a general law or rule as a guide to action, a fundamental motive or reason of action, especially one consciously recognized and followed, which from 1653 was applied absolutely to 'moral principles'. Even so, architectural principles are not like philosophical principles such as those of the identity of indiscernibles (Leibniz), indeterminacy, individuation, induction, plenitude (Lovejoy), sufficient reason (Leibniz), universal causation, utility, and verification (Flew 1971, 1979; Solomon 1977). Neither are they like the 114 principles or axioms governing the world put forward by Giambattista Vico in Book 1 of his *New Science* (1744), although Vico's ideas have received the attention of the theorist and historian Joseph Rykwert (1972, 1982).

Vitruvius, in *De architectura* (1486:Chapter 2), outlined the principles of architecture as Order, Arrangement, Eurythmy, Symmetry, Propriety, and Economy. They were to be applied "with due reference to *durability, convenience, and beauty*," the source of the famous

Vitruvian triad of *firmitas, utilitas, venustas,* repeated by Alberti and Palladio but made famous among English-speaking architects by Sir Henry Wotton in 1624 as *firmeness, commoditie, delight.* The six Vitruvian principles were not contested or replaced by Gropius, but he did adapt the triad to which they applied to *technics, function, expression.* Neither did Christian Norberg-Shulz (1965) offer any alternative to the six principles, instead revamping the Vitruvian triad to *technics, building task, form.*

COMMENTARY   Traditional notions of principle in architecture are predicated on what is thought to be historically substantiated usage, but they have little authenticity in fact and no universality of agreement. This is indicated by the diversity shown in what constitutes a principle. Any consensus that might be discerned between them is minor. There is no guarantee that principles operate in a universal or unassailable sense; rather, principles in architecture seem to be time- and culture-dependent. Another consideration is their intractability because, unlike the principles of *inertia, entropy,* or *conservation of energy* in science, which have demonstrable application across a range of situations, so-called principles of architecture, however defined, do not have effective potential, let alone anything approaching a rule or law. They are static statements. In the following discussion, 'principle' is used in its everyday, uncritical, conversational sense.

Because Vitruvian principles do not take the human being into account in any but a passive sense, attempts have been made to develop more actively human-based principles. The environmental psychology literature from the sixties, for instance, generalized from the studies of self-actualized individuals and of the psychology literature by the existentialist psychologist Abraham Maslow, who construed human needs as a hierarchical set. The accompanying human principles of Maslow's hierarchy may be broadly construed as having architectural implications (see 8A.4, Needs). The Californian architect Charles Moore has developed five humanistic principles that are more directly architectural in that they demand that buildings be worthy; free to speak; inhabitable by bodies, minds, and memories; anthropocentric; and connective through space and time (Moore, Allen, and Lyndon 1974).

For principles concerned with esthetics and composition we must return to the Ecole des Beaux Arts, where planning was of major importance and entailed adherence to certain organizational principles accrued over many years and delivered in the atelier, largely unwritten, but captured by the historian George R. Gromort in his *Histoire générale de l'art français de la Révolution à nos jours* (Paris 1922, vol. 2:14), where he lists them as:

- assure unity by making the principal element clearly dominate;
- sacrifice as many secondary elements as possible to reduce the plan to its most simple expression;

- avoid equalities between elements that are not identical;
- allow no building or street that is not well lit; let light and air penetrate throughout, and make courtyards ample;
- orient whenever possible the entire composition toward the most extended horizon, opening out the body of the building more and more in that direction (Cited in Kostof 1977:225)

The Modern Movement never established a consistent set of design principles, seemingly because it was never one consistent ideology, even though in its formative decades it comprised no more than three dozen people. During the 1920s hardly a mention was made of continental, particularly French or German, architecture or ideas in the English architectural press. Even though a number of key manifestos by a pioneering few had been published by 1920 and the Bauhaus was under way, it was not until the following decade that modernist ideas were to achieve wider currency in Great Britain and the British Empire. While there was broad agreement on the general thrust of modernism, individuals differed markedly in their detailed concerns, many of which they expressed as 'reservations'.

Because of its belated arrival on the modern architectural scene, the British experience provides an interesting case study and is symptomatic of the spread of modernist notions to other isolated parts of the world. Formed as an English chapter of CIAM (Congrès Internationale d'Architecture Moderne) in 1932 by the Canadian émigré Wells Coates, the Modern Architectural Research Society (MARS) became the focus of modernist architectural thinking and comprised "a group of people with a sense of mission, a common cause: to create a new architecture . . . [although] the cause was never very clearly defined" according to Ove Arup (1979), who joined the society shortly after. Despite its enthusiasm, activities, and rhetoric, it soon became clear that MARS was basically out to promote the International Style.

Principles of sorts there were, though, which may be gleaned from a report cited by Arup of the MARS exhibition committee of 1935 to the executive committee, which he calls the 'Modern Style' document (it was ultimately rejected by the executive committee). The exhibition committee wrote of "certain considerations or principles which guide [the designer] in the realm of pure design after the needs of function and structure have been fulfilled" as useful for arranging the exhibition then being contemplated, "and for explaining those values which are beyond pure structure or pure functionalism." There follows under four headings—characteristics, principles, negative principles, and considerations—a formidable summary of thoughts in which Arup found "much to baulk at," primarily because "it wasn't functionalism at all." The fourteen guiding 'principles' were as follows: functionalism is health; the wall is an enclosing shell; 'surface tension' is essential to such a wall; architecture is volume, not mass; clearly articulated form and function; maximize simplicity; make buildings light ('floating') and effortless; create a classic repose; use flat roofs for lightness and clean geometry; achieve regularity by repetition and standardization; use new materials honestly; avoid 'weighty' ashlar materials; adopt a scientific and sociological approach to problems; and use white or light tones to create the effect of weightlessness and to maximize light (1979:317, 319).

The negative 'principles' were only four: one should avoid the conscious symbolism of function; avoid axial symmetry; avoid applied ornament in favor of a 'natural' kind growing "probably out of gadgets"; and avoid 'movement' not derived honestly from structure (319). The later MARS exhibition of 1938, for which the group became famed, rejected any hint of a stylistic approach and firmly focused on modern architecture being instead "an affair of infinite adjustment, [in which] unity can only be achieved by sure intuitive judgement," as the catalog says. Arup, however, still thought there was something 'phoney' in their stance because the founders of MARS, rather than being scientists, engineers, and manufacturers who knew all about the new materials and methods, were "visionaries, artists, social reformers who had never calculated or constructed anything, and the followers who were enraptured by the vision." Arup accuses modern architects then and since of avoiding the main issues of the materiality of building: "They do not face facts, they fake facts" (320).

It has been important to highlight the ineffectiveness of modernist design principles in Great Britain at some length because the situation has not changed, no matter where one looks around the world. For example, Egon Schirmbeck reviews the design approaches of nine well-known architects, an international cross-section, in a detailed analysis of certain of their works in *Idea, Form and Architecture: Design Principles in Contemporary Architecture* (1983). In seeking 'design principles', Schirmbeck is propounding a rationalist and idealist cause, unwittingly or not, one that harks back to Plato and his conception of a 'real' world of truths, forms, and principles (see 8B.2, Idea). The fundamental difficulty with Schirmbeck's thesis is that principles from a Platonic viewpoint are necessarily irreducible and, because the principles he finds are deduced from maxims and diagrams used by the selected architects, which are themselves based in experience, they *cannot be universal and principial.* From an idealist view, the task of architectural and design theory is to direct and align thought in ways that favor the revelatory power of truths in the pure realm to infuse the corporeal realm via the subtle or mental realm, so that physical outcomes might approximate the real. It is this reality that is lost sight of or its approximation diminished without due adherence to principles. When Schirmbeck's principles are examined closely, they are not like this; they are as multifarious and as arbitrary as those of the MARS document cited above. And a look at almost any other architecture book that features design principles will reveal exactly the same confusion and variegation.

Herein lies the central dilemma of architectural principles. If principles are to guide action, they can never be made concrete enough to do so in the form of *in situation X, take action Y.* And they can never be elaborate enough to fully describe either the situation at hand or the action recommended because of the infinity of them. Prioritizing certain of them as 'first' principles only complicates the matter further. Conversely, if principles are to be universal and act as design beacons, emblematic exhortations to the good or to betterment, in the way that the idealist view would have it, they would necessarily be phrased as to stand alone, in which case they would need elaboration before they could apply to any specific case. But there is no known way to engage them with the world of specifics of designing; they remain enigmatic and aloof. Even if there were a way, they would no longer be principles but something else—rules or guidelines or suggestions or whatever. If principles are to be helpful at all in either thinking or doing, there must be something in them that helps to focus the mind in the way, say, desperation to meet a deadline does. Merely mouthing so-called principles as if they are mottoes only trivializes them, which is what the history of architecture unfortunately shows has happened. Architecture does not have and never will have unanimously agreed and long-standing design principles; all it has is talk, wonderful, provocative, and inspiring talk.

FURTHER SOURCES   9A.3, Geometry; Feyerabend 1988; Kollar 1983; Lang 1987; Marquard 1981; Snodgrass 1990; Tyng 1975.

3. Dictums as the Denial of Unease

Architecture in general is frozen music. **Friedrich von Schelling.** 1775-1854. *Philosophie der Kunst.*

. . . commoditie, firmnesse and delight. **Sir Henry Wotton.** *The Elements of Architecture.* 1624. Describing the Vitruvian triad in English.

The maximum effect with the minimum expenditure of means. **Ludwig Mies van der Rohe.** 1923. First issue of G.

Less is more. **Ludwig Mies van der Rohe.** c1923.

A house has to fulfill two purposes. First it is a *machine for living in.* **Le Corbusier.** 1924. *The New Spirit in Architecture.* Cited in Benson, Benson and Sharp, 1975:133.

Architecture is the masterly, correct and magnificent play of masses brought together in light. Our eyes are made to see forms in light; light and shade reveal these forms: cubes, cones, spheres, cylinders or pyramids are the great primary forms. **Le Corbusier.** 1923:7.

Consider well that a house is a machine in which to live but architecture begins where that concept of the house ends. **Frank Lloyd Wright.** 1932. "Young Architecture." In Conrads 1964.

Less is a bore. **Robert Venturi.** 1966.

Architecture is inhabited sculpture. **Constantin Brancusi.** Quoted in Igor Stravinsky's "Themes and Episodes" (1966). Knevitt 1986:#25.

Architecture is a machine for the production of meaning. **Arata Isozaki.** Cited in Emanuel 1980:385.

What makes eclecticism most appealing right now is that it is an architecture without dogma—an architecture without a rigid ideology to foist upon the world. The International Style was a kind of missionary architecture. **Paul Goldberger.** 1983:27.

TRACE   Dictum is the past participle noun of the Latin *dicere,* say, the source of many words in English—dictate, diction, addict, contradict, benediction, edict, predict, jurisdiction. The way it is used in architecture is as an authoritative saying, adage, axiom, maxim, aphorism, or precept. An aphorism is a definitional statement of principle, an axiom is a self-evident, well-established, or universally conceded principle, and a maxim is either an axiom or an aphoristic proposition expressing some general truth of science or experience or some principle of conduct; but a dictum is 'merely' a saying, and is preferred in light of the section 8A.2, Principles.

Just as a slogan originated as a clan war-cry, a dictum may also call up support of a feverishly loyal kind and, along with aphorisms, axioms, and maxims, may lean toward *dogma,* a philosophical tenet, stemming from the Greek, *dokein,* to seem, seem good, or to think (at the time!). Dogma is an opinion, belief, tenet, or doctrine that is sometimes expressed as an arrogant declaration, arrogance being a quality not unknown to architects and one reason why fully-fledged doctrinal systems are rarely agreed on by architects, although individual dogmas abound.

COMMENTARY   A selection of dictums on what architecture is are given above. The issue is also addressed in chapter 2A, regarding the essence and nature of architecture, and in chapter 4B, concerning the attitudes of architects to how they understand themselves and what they do. The architect as artist sees architecture as art, the architect as technical facilitator sees architecture as technocracy; the architect-scientist sees it as a science. Yet still architecture remains elusive. Why this should be so when philosophers see philosophy as architectonic in having foundations, constructions, and edifices, or when computer scientists devise whole systems of structure and operations which they call 'architecture' without even blinking, remains a mystery. Jacques Derrida, for instance, has spent much of his life deconstructing the edifices of Western philosophy, and Stanley Fish much of his pushing people back 'inside' the literary and legal understandings they thought they had built from the 'outside'.

In the ubiquitous spirit of seeking clarity from outside, statements by architects about architecture are frequently couched as dictums in terms of other disciplines, although it is a source of wonderment what benefit might have been had from reversals of some of the more famous sayings quoted above. 'Music is liquid architecture' is a good deal more provocative and poetic than its original, to an architect though maybe not to a musician;

'A machine is a house for living in' raises prospects that might have changed history; and 'Sculpture is uninhabited architecture' makes better sense of the photographs with which architects illustrate their work. Facetiousness aside, the inclination to draw parallels between architecture and other disciplines does architecture little good if it denies the unease of not knowing itself and if even *less* sense of itself is the result of *more* words, also not understood and gathered from alien territory. The application of tropes architecture is touched on in chapter 1B2: social comprehension.

The dogmatic edge of a dictum occurs after condensation and repetition has insinuated it into conventional wisdom and the context of its invention has dissolved away. For example, most people have at one time either heard or used the saying that what is good is 'the greatest happiness of the greatest number', and would consider it a truism or, if pressed, would relate it vaguely to politics or to the law. Many would know this to be the so-called greatest happiness principle of Utilitarianism, though they may not necessarily be recalling or invoking Utilitarian ideals when they hear it or say it. Some would know that it was the London-born philosopher and legal reformer Jeremy Bentham who made the notion famous in his *Introduction to the Principles of Morals and Legislation* (1789). But few would know enough about Bentham's works to fix the saying to his commonplace book of sayings, where it was garnered from the British moral philosopher Francis Hutcheson's *Inquiry into the Original of our Ideas of Beauty and Virtue* (1725), and that it was related to the idea of a 'moral sense' that instinctively judges the good. In short, while the dictum has lived far beyond either its origins or its later applications, its *scope* has diminished to virtually nothing.

Some of the longest-serving and most celebrated dictums in architecture are similar; they are all that remains of substantial theoretical positions of notable architects. Their continued assertion in the absence of the deeply held convictions that generated them is the blunting of the edge of dogma that dictums achieve with time. So much was this the case following World War II that a younger generation of architects emerged, victims of "a vacuum at the heart of contemporary practice" created by poor contemporary history teaching and an equally desultory architectural press. The result was "architects brought up on 'Functionalism' who had barely read a page of Le Corbusier, Stam, Meyer or Lubetkin [and who] were bound to fall easy prey to the first challenge" to what they had been taught to believe, according to Tim Benton in the November 1979 editorial to the *Architectural Review.*

Aphorisms, dictums, and maxims continue to be successful because architects are increasingly besieged by advertising, and any philosophical position intent on propagandizing must be cast as a 'quick grab'. With the power of a headline, the architectural dictum becomes implanted in the way it always has, through glib repetition in practice and education. However, even the shrewdest assessment of the power of the slogan in the first quarter of the century could not anticipate the simultaneous inurement and amnesia of so many aspects of modern life today. The propensity in architecture for dictums such as those above and many others besides, or the portentous word (variously 'organic', 'functional', 'space-time', 'postmodern', 'deconstructive') is now propelled by marketing techniques. These ensure that the level of popular awareness of a slogan far exceeds that of the object being marketed simply because it exploits the rhythms of modern life and media, the commercial break, the saturation payola of popular music, and the ubiquity of the silk screen on billions of T-shirts. The need for simplicity demands that architectural dictums contain only the most reduced and potent message, which would be unexceptionable were it not that expansion of its content needs a fuller education in history and theory.

Ironically, while education has changed substantially and continues to do just that, it is the quality and relevance of current dictums that are under fire in many quarters of the profession! The Australian academic and critic Tom Heath warns that definitive assertions of the form 'architecture is . . .' can be a trap, even though he says that von Schelling's dictum quoted above "is such patent nonsense that it does little harm." He also warns against the fine poetic phrase as a self-evident truth. In recognition of the dictum as a source of weakness in architecture, Heath makes a plea for someone to "write a history of architecture devoted to the buildings and careers wrecked on the *obiter dicta* of great, not so great, and even downright bad architects: " 'Make it as simple as possible—no matter how much it costs', 'What the building wants to be'; 'Main Street is almost right'." (Heath 1991:24). Many architects no doubt share Heath's concerns. For them many current dictums are about as enticing as the traditional chant in a street-march: "What do we want? Name your fancy! When do we want it? Now!" Despite any distress or unease architects might feel about current trends, they will be the first to be suckered in by a 'substantial' new dictum, one that offers a message of deliverance to the difficult task or 'wicked problem', or that points the way out of this period of unease and to a brighter future.

FURTHER SOURCES   Chapter 2; Conrads 1964; Kipnis 1990a; Le Corbusier 1923; Sorkin 1991; Wolfe 1982.

4. *The Needs of (Ir)rational Beings*

Nothing is really beautiful unless it is useless; everything useful is ugly, for it expresses a need, and the needs of man are ignoble and disgusting, like his poor weak nature. **Théophile Gautier.** 1835. *Madamoiselle de Maupin.* Translated by Joanna Richardson. Baltimore, Penguin Books, 1981:39. Cited in Brolin 1985:n49, 83.

The idea that a city is in essence a rational structure, and that evidence of irrationality is a sign of decadent deviation from its intrinsic cityness is entirely comprehensible; it is even perhaps administratively and psychologically necessary. But it seems intuitively wrong . . . reading Mumford, Howard, Geddes, Corbusier, Park, Weber, I can never manage to believe in their cities or their citizens . . . they seem to belong to an entirely different culture from mine. **Jonathon Raban.** 1974:Chapter 7.

It is, however, hard to say, in the present state of the art, which is the more obstructive to progress in architecture: rationalism, which provides a veneer of observation and careful thinking on bases which are profoundly irrational; or the belief in inspired conceptual design, basing itself on knowledge revealed to genius and superior to ordinary processes of investigation. **Tom Heath.** 1984:36.

Le Corbusier and his followers have provided an agreeable rhetoric . . . which reduces the human being to manageable proportions, which construes him as a collection of more or less quantifiable 'needs'. For example, the human being has a need for air, light, open space, movement, everything, in fact, that is *not* architecture. All the architect has to do is to ensure a man's ready access to those simple and quantifiable commodities. The concept of a need is well suited to the justification of that *'machine a vivre'* which Le Corbusier has recommended to us. It has an admirable hygienic quality, and suggests a straightforward biological idea of human fulfillment. The satisfaction of a need is a matter of degree: it can therefore be effectively quantified. The difficulty in arriving at a truly human architecture becomes a purely mathematical one. **Roger Scruton.** 1983:185.

Originally the cavemen would decorate their caves before furnishing them. . . . In those first marks gropingly traced in the dark, we see two features: the irrational, spontaneous, instinctive, barbaric gesture, devoid of technique, and then, almost immediately afterwards, an appearance of rationality in the diagonal marks, in the circles containing squares, instinctive marks but traced by an ordering mind. **Carlo Scarpa.** 1964. "Furnishings." In Dal Co and Mazzariol 1985:282.

We're developing a direct discourse about the connection (or disconnection) between use and form, which questions both the priority of function within the design process and the assumption that the satisfaction of our needs is the most important goal. **Thom Mayne** and **Michael Rotondi.** Foreword to Cook and Rand 1989.

TRACE   A need is an absence of something signaled by an imperative call to presence or attention, a necessity arising from circumstances or facts requiring action. A more technical definition of need, according to Bronislaw Malinowski, is a "system of conditions in the human organism, in the cultural setting, and in the relation of both to the natural environment, which are sufficient and necessary for the survival of group and organism" (*A Scientific Theory of Culture,* 1960:90). As a psychological concept, the existence of needs was inferred from studies of behavior by Henry A. Murray (*Explorations in Personality* 1938), in which he discerned twenty human needs and from which he developed his needs theory of personality. Later studies by Abraham Maslow (*Motivation and Personality* 1954, *Toward a Psychology of Being* 1963) organized needs into a five-level hierarchy—physiological (survival), safety (security), belongingness and love (affiliation), esteem (learning), and self-actualization (esthetics).

In architecture, concern for certain human needs was part of the utopic egalitarianism of the early Modern Movement. The importance of personal needs became a focus for architects following World War II, and with the rise of design methods research, eventually became a distinct field of study dominating certain architectural processes and outcomes, especially in mass housing. User consultation or participation and the evaluation of buildings after occupation, wherein the needs of people are expressed or assessed, continues to occupy a substantial place in the architecture-for-people view of the profession, and constitutes one of two major research bases for human values in architecture, the other being esthetics.

COMMENTARY   Since the fifties the concept of needs has appeared regularly in those writings dealing with the 'human sciences' (mainly behavioral) end of the architectural spectrum, the practical and the rational part of architecture capable of modeling and testing—at least that is how researchers in those areas like to think of their fields. But the classic studies of needs in psychology have featured very little in this work because, like so many sociology studies that have also been examined, they are incapable of ready adaption to architecture. It was only Maslow's hierarchy of needs that assumed an importance for architectural writers, and even that was way beyond its potential contribution to architectural understanding, no doubt because it appealed as a structured array to the almost natural sense of *hierarchy* of most architects, especially with physiological needs as foundation and esthetics as peak. The base accorded with what most architects were best at dealing with anyway, and the peak matched a 1961 study of the creativity they all aspired to (Heath 1984:70–73).

The discovery of Maslow by architectural researchers during the early sixties and his citation in research, no matter how superficially, served to legitimize what was to become a rush of investigations into physical standards, community attitudes, and esthetic judgment in relation to the environment during the seventies in a fledgling discipline desperately looking for a theoretical core—environmental psychology and the whole gamut of 'man-environment' studies. There appears to have been little research, however, in levels two and four of Maslow's hierarchy, safety and esteem needs, respectively, although Oscar Newman's *Defensible Space* (1972), though it does not refer to Maslow, covered all that was needed on environmental safety for many years afterward. Let it be clear though that in 1962, user needs were low in the pecking order for making architectural awards and, despite all that has been researched and written about users and their needs since, still are. That this was so after the British profession showed 'an overwhelming concern' for user needs in two studies by Alan Lipman in 1970 and 1976 (Heath 1984:71–72) says a lot about the user priorities of architectural institutions.

Perhaps one reason for this is the fundamental difficulty that arises immediately when one attempts to clarify exactly what user needs *are* from any theoretical perspective—nothing in particular emerges as primarily architectural. The need for shelter may be satisfied by a vast array of natural and certainly nonarchitectural means. The need for privacy is not homogeneous across cultures, and again may be met by any number of natural or created means not requiring intervention by an architect. The need for safety is largely a matter of administration, surveillance, and policing, admittedly helped along by planners and architects not inadvertently creating dead zones, hardly a glorious architectural attribute. The need for self-actualization of those unable to achieve it for themselves (notwithstanding that it may be attained at varying esthetic levels) is certainly able to be satisfied architecturally; artistic patronage of notable architects of the past and present suggests this to be a discernible need. But this last is seen to be marginal and élitist and therefore not worthy of the name, harking back to the modernist egalitarian ideal. Needs be 'needs' must embrace a far wider cross-section of people than high-art patrons for them to be 'needs' at all in the universal sense.

Raising the prospect of high art patronage presents yet another of the many dilemmas facing architects: if architecture is to be art, indeed spatial art in its perfection, then what need is there to satisfy 'common needs' at all? What imperative is there for a house to be habitable if art can demand that it need not be, or for a thousand and one students not to ape Marcel Duchamp's *Large Glass* to the exclusion of human concerns in their current project? How is the happy marriage to be made between user or people needs and the thousands of unbuilt and built spatial and metaphorical experiments architects have undertaken in the name of advancing the cause of architecture? Of course the answer is that for the most part they cannot be reconciled, at least not in one and the same place; art is one thing and practical concerns are another. They each have their place in the greater scheme of things.

The belief that the needs of people may be satisfied by design, especially by an architect, is so firmly entrenched, however, that it will not go away. As one of the profession's motivational beliefs, hung over from functionalism or not, it is the one constant in the flux of twentieth-century stylistic movements. As an illustration, take the attitude toward 'wants'. It has been a custom of functionalist architectural thinking to differentiate between needs and wants, the implication being that wants are unnecessary—merely self-indulgence, caprice, extravagance, or at the extreme, delinquency—with all the overtones of moral condemnation that 'wantonness' conveys. Needs, in this view, are the opposite—essential, true, honest, sincere—and therefore worthy of serious consideration. The authority for their opposition arises not from any substantive difference between needs and wants but from the morality play upon which the Modern Movement was premised, a legacy that persists today in condemning postmodernism, neo-constructivism, and other experiments for their self-indulgence and capriciousness in prospect of there being something purer, another brand of functionalist honesty and frugality perhaps, just around the corner.

Reyner Banham (1976) probably had it right when he said "The architect can only aim at generalised satisfaction of averaged social needs, and that may satisfy nothing." And, after commenting on the then-emerging crisis of confidence in modern architecture (the book was written in 1962, then revised), he followed this up a few paragraphs later with: "The profession clearly no longer feels that it is uniquely qualified to interpret and then serve the functional needs of others, and this greater humility before the problem of function may yet prove to be one of the great divides between the modern architecture that was and the modern architecture to come" (27).

There has accrued to date a wealth of user information about housing following the many minor successes and the few experimental disasters of the seventies and about the gains and losses in many other building types gathered from POEs. Veritable warehouses are filled with government-funded reports and private studies into the interaction of buildings and people, enough knowledge to at last get it right. Given all this and the further inroads being made into the profession's monopoly on design by the creation of new specializations (POE, quality assurance, building diagnostics, design review) during the almost twenty years since Banham (re)wrote the book, the profession appears to be presenting with a severely advanced case of selective amnesia. Beginning in the spirit of Hans Hollein saying in 1962: "Architecture is not the satisfaction of the needs of the mediocre, is not an environment for the petty happiness of the masses. . . . Architecture is an affair of the élite" (Conrads 1964:181), avant-garde architects are promoting an individualism equal in fervor to the collectivism of their modernist predecessors. Attempts to satisfy people needs by typal design are branded re(ar)visionist, and new spirit designs are pointed out as the equivalent of the *Twilight Zone* 'creature on the wing' by reactionary modernists, whose only shift has been from raw concrete to raw steel.

FURTHER SOURCES   Broadbent 1973; Lang 1987; Perin 1970; Rapoport 1969; Saarinen 1976;

5. Personal Volition as the Maverick

By his innermost essence the artist is a burning idealist, a free spontaneous creator. Of his own free will he will never subordinate himself to a discipline that imposes upon him a type, a canon. Instinctively he distrusts everything that might sterilize his actions, and everyone who preaches a rule that might prevent him from thinking his thoughts through to their own free end, or that attempts to drive him virtually into a universally valid form. **Henry van de Velde.** 1914. In Conrads 1964.

There is an old and a new consciousness of the age. The old one is directed towards the individual. The new one is directed towards the universal. . . . Tradition, dogmas and the predominance of the individual stand in the way. . . . The artists of today, all over the world, impelled by one and the same consciousness, have taken part on the spiritual plane in the world war against the domination of individualism, of arbitrariness. **'De Stijl' Manifesto I.** 1918. In Conrads 1964.

All predetermined purpose falls like a heavy, inhibiting hand upon the motive force of a divinely free, pure will. Forget that you exist, create vast divine vessels. **Herman Finsterlin.** 1924. In Conrads 1964.

Wise insight and the needs of artistic creation will break through all restrictions imposed by recipes and principles. . . . We want the individual room, not the factory-made product; we want personality, not norm, not schema, not series, not type. We want no violation of our creative feeling, not even by architecture, we want to live our life. **Bernhard Hoetger.** 1928. In Conrads 1964.

All 'individuals' . . . are an obstacle in the path of development, and in fact progress takes place in spite of them. But nor does progress take place without them, without individuals, artists and strong personalities. **Hugo Häring.** 1932. In Conrads 1964.

Form in architecture is determined by the individual, is built form. **Hans Hollein.** 1960.

At this moment in history we are supposed to be wary of the role of the avant-garde . . . perhaps because it threatens the neat structure of architectural categorizations by its maverick patterns of play. **Peter Cook.** In Cook and Rand 1989.

TRACE   Free will and determinism are two opposing concepts in philosophy, their equivalents in architecture being individuality and conformity, or personal volition as the maverick to canonic design. Volition, from the Latin *volo*, I wish or will, has two edges, one of choice after due consideration or deliberation, the other of *merely* willing or resolving to act in some way; the one careful, the other willful. Individual volition, of course, prompts again the issue of genius raised in 4B.3, Artist. Genius is now understood as that character attending individuals that makes them individual, equivalent to the Greek *psyche,* as opposed to the *animus* or consciousness of an individual, in ancient thought *genius* being the masculine and *iuno* the feminine (Onians 1951). One etymology has genius stemming from *gignesthai,* to be born or to come into being, hence its connection with individual creativity.

   In architecture, individual volition or genius versus conformity or standardization are the fundamental terms of reference for all debate and in negotiations beyond the profession. Whether the debate is between romantics and rationalists, Henry van de Velde and Hermann Muthesius, Richard Rogers and the Prince of Wales, or Joe Architect and any government authority, it is frequently a matter of creative and individual genius versus compliant and common practice.

COMMENTARY   The above quotations are an uneven chronicle of the shift in emphasis over the role of the individual in architecture for seventy years, beginning with the early outpourings of the Modern Movement. The Modern Movement was certainly very selective in its condemnation of individuality in favor of collective action, gradually reaching a point of refined ambivalence. The individual was to become more favored after World War II, but has never completely supplanted the collective and idealist aspirations of the profession, although there has always been a sneaking suspicion lurking just below the surface that individuality was all there was to creative progress. "Rulers do not dance," wrote phenomenologist Irwin Strauss, meaning that to be caught up in a mass movement is to surrender oneself to the environment and to destiny (see Cook and Rand 1989:18).

But the history of science shows that humanity has been lost to the environment, or rather that it has never been part of the environment, more a grand accident quite extraneous to nature's plan. In one sense, rationalist science has alienated humankind from any role in the cosmic dance, thereby reinforcing us as rulers of our own individual kingdoms, as if nature and the cosmos were quite indifferent to our presence. Conversely, recent ecological science (of which the Butterfly Effect of chaos theory is one instance) is showing that human existence does have biological effects. And the downside of chemical engineering combined with the unknowns of genetic engineering are signaling human intervention as a major factor in the future of life on the planet.

Søren Kierkegaard's attack on Christianity as he saw it emphasized that to *become* Christian was a matter of individual choice of a very strict kind and not a matter of birth, convention, or habit. In this view, Christianity is a radical religion, one that is first and foremost a continual affirmation of one's individuality in always being able to choose *not* to be Christian, to lapse from faith. Notwithstanding the apparent collectivity that attends all Christian religions, their strength is as an assembly of individuals who believe they have fallen from grace and have individually chosen the personal salvation Christianity offers. As a profession, the structure of architecture is similar to that of Christianity; at any moment its collectivity is the sum of the individuality of its practitioners and practices, and its creativity is the sum of its individual creativities. The difference between architecture and Christianity lies in the concept of God in the one and not in the other, a superadded realm that is aspired to by Christians. That architects too may aspire to something superadded does not make the discipline of architecture a religion, even though it may at times have many of the attributes of one.

Remove idealist concepts like the Platonic Idea, spirit (especially the Hegelian *Geist*), truth, essence, the precedence of whole over part, and similar *a priori* claims, and many would argue that nothing remains of architecture. Others might be assured by the universal of rationalism left over. Still others might say that rationalism of itself can only be accompanied by maverick individualism as an arbitrary collection of appetites making arbitrary rational decisions under arbitrary particular circumstances, and that nothing remains of architecture. The denial of essences is the classic liberal doctrine that argues that we are unable to infer essences from particular instances or to project any overall view of the world. However, as Stanley Fish maintains in his summation of this argument in Roberto

Unger's *Knowledge and Politics* (1975), "even as modern man is committed by his denial of intelligible essences to this landscape [of particulars], he is also committed to escaping it, because his practices depend for their justification on the abstract universality he elsewhere denies" (Fish 1989:404). So, both the conceptual extremes of architecture above are correct because, as it is presently and as it will continue to be thought of and practiced, architecture is always a combination of the ideal and the individual. The ideal and the individual are not always or necessarily in opposition, though, they can be and mostly are combined in a cooperative, collective venture that benefits the individual architect and the collective discipline.

Two examples of contemporary architecture in which maverick individuality predominates but that nonetheless still reconcile the universal will suffice. According to the English architect and academic Peter Cook, Thom Mayne "has described the goal of Morphosis as 'searching for the ability to absorb the idiosyncratic' [and] although he was talking about a particular building, the Sixth Street House, the phrase is applicable to much of the work the firm has done" (Cook and Llewellyn-Jones 1991:24). The 'ability' of which Mayne speaks combines the formal repertoire of Morphosis, one that engages the highly individuated aspects of contexts, of people, of materials, and of geometries in a symbiosis with universal aspects of architecture such as "an everpresent search for *order*," with a concern for the indeterminacy that characterizes much of the world, "the unfinished nature of things." What is created in turn by this marriage are the highly individual works for which Morphosis is noted but that nevertheless at the conceptual level share values in common with other architectural works and are thereby collinear with the profession.

In *Architecture Must Blaze* (1980), Coop Himmelblau declare their lack of conformity with the norms of architecture. "We are tired of seeing Palladio and other historical masks, because we don't want architecture to exclude everything that is disquieting [maverick]. We want architecture to have more: we want architecture that bleeds, that exhausts, that revolves, and even breaks; architecture that burns, that stings, that rips, that tears under stress. Architecture should be cavernous, fiery, smooth, hard, angular, brutal, round, delicate, colorful, obscene, voluptuous, dreamy, alluring, wet, dry, throbbing. Alive or dead. Cold: then cold as a block of ice. Hot: then hot as a blazing wing" (cited in Cook and Llewellyn-Jones 1991). By propounding their architecture as a thesaurus, a *copia verborum*, and declaring this the 'having more', Coop Himmelblau then set about creating its visual equivalent, investing their works with multitudinous spatio-visual qualities that virtually guarantee idiosyncrasy rather than absorb it. Yet in their insistence on perpetuating the moment of conception caught in the sketch, the flash of inspiration, the fire of enthusiasm, the pitch of battle, the blaze of glory, the moment of separation of the blazing wing, they reiterate the ancient concept of *genius* (Onians 1951), and thereby engage the creativity that marks the architectural profession as a whole.

FURTHER SOURCES   Antoniades 1986, 1990; Guénon 1958; Hejduk 1985; Heath 1984.

B. How Architects Conceptualize

1. Abstraction in Architectural Thought

It is quite possible to project whole forms in the mind without any recourse to the material, by designating and determining a fixed orientation and conjunction for the various lines and angles. **Leon Battista Alberti.** 1755b:1.1.

Is it not a hard thing to imagine that a couple of children cannot prate together of their sugar plums and rattles and the rest of their little trinkets, till they have first tacked together numberless inconsistencies, and so framed in their minds abstract general ideas, and annexed them to every common name they make use of? **George Berkeley.** *The Principles of Human Knowledge:*§14.

The art of reasoning consists in getting hold of the subject at the right end, of seizing on the few general ideas that illuminate the whole, and of persistently organizing the facts around them. **Alfred North Whitehead.** 1914. *Presidential address to the London Branch of the Mathematical Association.* Cited in Lawson 1980:94.

. . . without abstraction there is nothing of any sort that thinking can seize upon and manipulate. **David W. Prall.** 1936:146.

My particular interest is in using familiar pieces, mostly cheap pieces, putting them together in ways that have never been before, so as to get something that's strange and revolutionary and mindboggling and often uncomfortable, but only using the ordinary pieces. I think that's a better way of making a revolution than just inventing a whole new crazy set of shapes. **Charles Moore.** In Cook and Klotz, 1973:235.

Of course, abstraction always was and presumably always will be an indispensable component of artistic form. Even in the most extreme naturalistic art, it is not entirely lacking and is among the constitutive factors of aesthetic objectivity. Abstract and concrete are not only conceptually but also practically indivisible. They belong to the antinomies to whose dialectic art owes its existence. Abstraction certainly appears, like its opposite pole, to a different degree in different historical situations, social orders, and stylistic movements. **Arnold Hauser.** 1974:691.

While construction as a technological process is prosaic . . .architecture is poetic, necessarily an abstract order but in itself a metaphor emerging from a vision of the world and Being. **Alberto Pérez-Gómez.** 1984:226

TRACE Abstraction is not a term easily defined by looking it up in a dictionary, although its etymology from the Latin *ab-*, off, away, from + *trahere,* draw, and therefore literally 'draw off', 'draw away (from)', gives its broad sense. What is drawn off is the essence, the relevant distinguishing features, of a class or universe of things or no-things (see introduction), what David Prall (1936) calls "the non-separable but distinguishable aspects of objects [of attention]" (35). And what is drawn away *from* is concrete, complex, variegated, full-color actuality. Abstraction is achieved by leaving out of consideration or ignoring what is apparently irrelevant; hence all classification requires abstraction to some degree. In philosophy, abstraction (as opposed to actuality) is equated with 'subsistence', "a monochrome and insubstantial analogue possessed by universals, numbers, and the difference between red and green. [Some] would allow subsistence to the fictional and the imaginary also" (Flew 1979).

In architecture, 'abstraction' in all its guises of classical modernism, 'bare necessities', International Style, laboratory style, and doctrinaire functionalism (all from Klotz 1984) came to be the *cause celebre* of modernism in their simple arrangement, primary forms, pure geometry, lightness, and transparency. The emphasis given here to 'abstraction' highlights that it was only the 'image of abstraction', what abstraction looked like when universals were attempted to be given particular form. Which is why the Modern Movement got it wrong, although its elementary *formal* qualities were ultimately to be the major target of criticism against modernism, not abstraction *per se*. "Though at first modernism staked everything on purified primary forms, it ended up in abstract compositions serving the total disintegration of meaning" (Klotz 1984:36). Since the demise of modernism, images of abstraction have come to be associated with the Italian rationalists Aldo Rossi, Georgio Grassi, and Carlo Aymonino. Avoiding abstraction has been the thrust of the topological movement since the 1960s in the creation of 'place' and a human 'concrete' architecture.

COMMENTARY   Abstraction was addressed briefly in the overview, where it was suggested that it functioned to control admission to the architectural world, shaped its presence and reserved its future. But before considering its architectural aspects in any detail, we must explore abstraction further to clarify the sense in which it will be used in discussing architecture. David Prall's succinct declaration above was preceded by his earlier observation that "to prefer the pattern to the concrete object of intuition . . . is the old mistake . . . of identifying the abstraction with the concrete whole from which it is drawn" (Prall 1929:141–142).

Abstraction is a primary human process, one that enables reality or actuality to be codified in a manner independent of its particularity and therefore aids the communication of concepts. But abstraction needs to be reinhabited in any new location in order to be actualized again. As the fundamental human reasoning process, it can never be denied or circumvented; only utilized in different ways. Abstraction involves all the classical problems of philosophy, universals and particulars, the representation of words, conceptualization, symbolization, and classification. Primary to them all is the portability that abstraction offers, the occasions to trade it encourages, and the currency by means of which one negotiates. It is within this combination of abstraction's distance from the particular and its portability that current architecture may be reconsidered.

Abstraction in the form of abstract art had a positive function, as opposed to a revolutionary one, which Herbert Read prompted while discussing revolutionary art in 1935 and which is relevant to architecture. Abstract art, he argued, "keeps inviolate, until such time as society will once more be ready to make use of them, the universal qualities of art—those elements which survive all changes and revolutions. It may be said that as such it is merely art in pickle—an activity divorced from reality, of no immediate interest to the revolutionary . . . [though] in architecture and to some extent in industrial arts, it is already in social action. There we find the essential link between the abstract movement in modern painting and the most advanced movement in modern architecture. It is not merely a similarity of form and intention, but an actual and intimate association of personalities." (In Frascina and Harrison, 1982:126). Notwithstanding Read's connection of abstraction to architecture and the subsequent history of that marriage that is contemporary architecture's legacy, I want to return to his first observation of one of abstraction's uses in art.

This extract prompts the thought that abstraction in architecture may be construed as 'keeping inviolate' the universal qualities of architecture until such time as they might be made use of again. In other words, abstraction is both a process and a *code* that acts as a repository, an archive, of architecture and offers a way to overcome the effects of time and place. The much-berated *formal* expression of abstraction in modernism is not a criticism of abstraction *per se* as a means of keeping architecture's future alive; abstraction is a code for the architect to utilize at any time—if not just when society is ready. Inasmuch as theory is the reservoir of practice, abstraction is the object of architectural theory, dealing as it does with principles, rules, patterns, typology, interpretation, language, and meaning.

It is certain that the abstract formal code of architecture is not simply the Platonic solids or Le Corbusier's five primary shapes. It involves these and at least John Hejduk's formulation of 'elements': grid, frame, post, beam, panel, center, periphery, field, edge, line, plane, volume, extension, compression, tension, shear and the ubiquitous 'etc.' (Hejduk 1985:Frame 2). And it at least involves the anthropocentric antimonies: front/back, left/right, up/down, inside/outside, here/there, which situate architecture firmly in human consciousness. The withdrawal characterized by abstraction, however, keeps these elements and antinomies at a distance and makes their union a matter of disinterest. The Japanese architect Tadao Ando, on the other hand, interpolates the code by means of *shintai,* which for him is the union of spirit and flesh that enables the concretization of architecture. "Architecture is the art of articulating the world through geometry . . . not abstractly, but as concrete places *(topi).* . . . A 'place' is not the absolute space of Newtonian physics, that is, a universal space, but a space with meaningful directionality and a heterogeneous density that is born of a relationship to what I choose to call *shintai.* . . . The problem with modern architecture lies in the abstract and homogeneous character of its spaces. Such spaces and the *shintai* simply do not blend" (Tadao Ando. 1986. "Shintai and space." In Al-Sayed, *et al.* 1988).

Inasmuch as it has been dormant since the street attacks on modernism obliged its shuttering, formal abstraction in Western architecture has begun to re-emerge in the recent compositional experiments of Neo-constructivism (also known as Deconstructivism) and the works of so-called 'New Spirit' architects (Cook and Llewelyn-Jones 1991). There are portents of another formal 'revolution' on the horizon, though whether it will be as pervasive as modernism will no doubt depend on whether it will be able to re-establish the equivalent of Ando's blending through *shintai*. Certainly a number of architects have been working toward an architecture of context and 'sensorial' quality, notably some in Latin America (Sylvia Arango. c1986. "Sensorial architecture and contextuality." In Al-Sayed *et al.* 1988).

In speaking of revolution, Charles Moore above refers to making the familiar strange as a necessary step, although for him revolution is more a backyard affair than one to be enacted on the boulevards of capitals (though ironically, Moore or Gehry on the Mall in Washington would be a revolution!). In the sense that abstraction estranges the familiar in order to redirect the creative understanding toward new departures, it is revolutionary—if by that is meant an engine of change. But abstraction as codifying keeps elemental qualities intact, so revolution as far as it can be recognized through formal qualities in architecture (and, rhetoric aside, that is the principal way it would be known) lies in the deployment and in the elaboration of the code, not in its abstraction. In other words, abstraction as code has been and remains a constant in architecture, and there is no question of it being overturned; it is more a question of the extent to which the code is made evident as against being merely implicit. When Le Corbusier declared "Architecture or Revolution. Revolution can be avoided" in *Vers une Architecture* (1923), he served up a formally abstracted architecture so bare that revolution turned on architecture instead of on the social and industrial conditions where it rightly should have been. One can only wonder where architecture might be now if instead he had said ". . . Architecture can be avoided."

Finally, Descartes's uncompleted *Rules for the Direction of the Mind*, composed during the 1620s and published posthumously in 1701, compared thought to vision—one *looked* at notions with a steadfast mental *gaze* under one's mental *illumination*. Improving abstract reasoning was thought merely a matter of increasing the 'inner vision'; the brighter the illumination, the clearer the understanding. While this analogy no longer has currency, a legacy remains in admissions of 'seeing' after finally comprehending a difficult concept, or of 'looking into' a problem, and in the figurative definition of 'see' as to *perceive* mentally with metaphorical light or eyes (after Hacking 1975:31–32).

There is certainly the opinion among many architects that something like inner vision enables creativity and design conceptualization, often called 'visualization'. No doubt this is reinforced by the visual modes architects use to record their thoughts; drawings as external aids to conceptualization have long been considered essential to efficient production (Lawson 1980; Heath 1984). Despite notions of 'black box' design and 'conceptual architecture', wherein concepts emerge 'in a flash', having been decried as incorrect and as only obfuscating the understanding of design processes (Heath 1984), architects continue to think of some version of abstracted 'insight' as the procedure and setting for design. "Whatever the initial catalyst," writes John Hejduk, "let us assume that an architect has an architectural image inside his mind's eye . . . like a single still-frame." (from introduction to *Five Architects* by Judith Turner. Hejduk 1985:Frame 4).

And with mention of the 'mind's eye' we go full revolution to Plato's *Republic* and the education of the philosopher in dialectic, "When the eye of the mind gets really bogged down in a morass of ignorance, dialectic gently pulls it out and leads it up." (*Republic:*533), resulting in the true philosopher, whose "eyes are turned to contemplate fixed and immutable realities, a realm where there is no injustice but all is reason and order, and which is the model which he imitates" (*Republic:*500). The idea illuminates this realm, just as the mathematician-philosopher Alfred North Whitehead affirms above, and as every architect knows—don't they?

FURTHER SOURCES   Chapter 6B; 8B.2, Idea; Frascina and Harrison 1982; Hofstadter and Dennett 1981; Scruton 1979.

2. The Central Idea: Informing the Act or Enacting the Form?

I see a horse; horsiness I do not see. **Antisthenes.** Cited in Onians 1951:464.

. . . the form or idea—"*Idea* enim graece, latine forma dicitur" (For the Greek word *Idea* is in Latin *forma*)—is the goal of all generation—"In all things not generated by chance, the form must be the end of any generation"—which implies that the agent of this generation already has in itself some analogy or resemblance ("similitudo") with this form . . . "and thus the likeness of a house pre-exists in the mind of the builder. And this may be called the idea of the house, since the builder intends to build his house like to the form conceived in his mind." (Question 15, Article 1.) Consequently, the architect himself is caught up in the Thomist argument, where he occupies the position of the clearest analogy one can offer men of what God is. **Denis Hollier** 1989:44, citing and commenting on St. Thomas Aquinas.

These two, I say, *viz.* external material things, as the objects of sensation; and the operations of our own minds within, as the objects of reflection; are to me the only originals from whence all our ideas take their beginnings. **John Locke.** *Essay Concerning Human Understanding.* Cited in Jacobus 1986:528.

. . . words like 'intention' and 'idea', with their mentalistic, subjective, artist-oriented implications, are far from being forced on us as necessary instruments in the critical descriptions of architecture. **Roger Scruton.** 1979:58.

Form is not shape. Shape is a design affair, but form is a realization of inseparable components. Design calls into being what realization—form—tells us. You could also say that form can be detected as the nature of something and design strives at a precise moment to employ the laws of nature in putting that into being, by allowing light to come into play. **Louis Kahn.** "I Love Beginnings." In Latour 1991:288.

True ideas are those that we can assimilate, validate, corroborate and verify. False ideas are those that we can not. **William James.** 1907. *Pragmatism.*

First, we have an idea, or a problem, *then* we act, i.e. either speak, or build, or destroy. Yet this is certainly not the way in which small children develop. . . . Creation of a *thing,* and creation plus full understanding of a *correct idea* of the thing, *are very often parts of one and the same indivisible process* and cannot be separated without bringing the process to a stop. **Paul Feyerabend.** 1988:17.

TRACE Idea is adopted from the Latin *idea* in the Platonic sense and adapted from the same in Greek, look, semblance, form, kind, nature, ideal form, or model. For Plato, *idea* (or Idea, capitalized to identify the Platonic version) is equivalent to *eidos,* Form, both of which are connected with the Greek *idein,* to see, such that an Idea "is something that is seen—but seen by a kind of intellectual vision" (Flew 1979; *cf.* also 8B.1, Abstraction). Plato argues that Ideas belong in Reality as a state beyond everyday reality and partake of some objective standard independent of what is thought. Descartes used Plato's sense of Idea being an idea of something, but considered it to be whatever was directly perceived by the mind, and thereby indefeasible.

While the Greek equivalent of idea in Latin is *forma* (see Hollier above), unlike our current 'form', it was only of minor importance in ancient criticism of the visual arts. The Greek *rythmos* was mostly used in art criticism, usually translated as *numerus.* Of the four meanings of *forma*—form or figure, beauty, mould, and plan—the first is unambiguous and links with the Greek *eidos* as 'visible form', making it similar to the obsolete meaning of the Latin *species* as outward appearance or image (Pollitt 1974:376).

Idea is most frequently encountered in architecture as the *central idea* that 'illuminates' a design task and thereby provides the armature, without which a work of architecture would either not exist or would not be *architecture.* Kollar (1983) defines idea as the Platonic Idea, an "intelligible principle determining its sensible embodiment" and recognizes three phases in the application of Idea to designing: the conception of pure Idea, the formulation of an architectural idea, and the embodiment of the architectural idea in sensible form.

COMMENTARY In 8B.1 Abstraction, Alfred North Whitehead was quoted as saying that ideas "illuminate the whole." It is in this sense of an illumination, which brings clarity to what is being 'seen' by the 'mind's eye', that this discussion will focus upon concerning architecture. All great architecture—indeed, all architecture that deserves the name—is said to be guided by a central idea of illuminating power, although on close examination such pronouncements are based on postrationalizations. It is rare to find the central idea admitted by an architect as guiding a work *during* the act of designing or, if it is admitted, it is said to accompany the working out rather than preceding and determining the work. Architects will admit to many ideas in designing and to some sorting out or reduction, by means of which one better solution more or less clearly identifies itself from amid a number of possibilities.

That there appears to be a catalyst for a solution and that it may be labeled a central idea is not at issue because narrative accounts of designing are evidence enough for a widely held belief that there is such a presence. What is questioned here is the claim that such a catalyst is evidence of or emanates from another realm, or that it actually 'guides' designing at all in any *a priori* sense, 'actually' being a key word, as will become clear. What is proposed quite simply is that the belief in a central idea is an emotional one grounded in an entirely human process of prioritizing, and is in no need of further justification. That we may choose to further justify the feeling of purpose in design is an outcome of a deep history of Western thought that began with the concrete preceding the abstract in language and was eventually turned about.

For example, the Homeric Greek terms *peirar* and *peiraino,* originally meant rope, cord, knot, band or bond, but came to be used metaphorically or abstractly as end or limit (Onians 1951:Part 3, Chapter 2). When the problem of universals was confronted, and before Plato's Theory of Forms evolved, the Homeric terms for bonds or 'bindings' became concretizations of the universal, and *apeiron,* the unbounded, unlimited, or infinite, was the recipient. "A mere determination, qualification of something else, which has no visible form apart from that which it affects or qualifies, is given substantial existence and shape as a thing *per se,* as something superadded, wrapped around the other thing, as a *peirar,*" writes Richard Onians (1951:464); hence the quotation from Antisthenes above. In short, the concrete informed the universal, and Plato grounded his theory in *this* mythic past, then conjured the reverse:

> "Plato's *eide* satisfied the mind's demand for substantive reality in the objects of thought and gave to qualities, etc. *a separate substantive existence* [emphasis added] in the region of the gods above. Of one or another of them the individual partook . . . as long before he had his share (*moira*) of this or that *peirar* in the jars of Zeus. In the earlier solution of this problem there are already distinguished the formal cause, the *peirar,* and the efficient cause, dynamic agent, god, even as for Plato there are *eidos* and *theos.* Homer is on the way to a single efficient cause, *theos,* the god Zeus. . . . It is striking how close is the function of his eternal *Eros, Hypnos, Charis,* etc., each respectively with an unfailing supply of *eros, hypnos, charis,* etc. for transient individuals, to that of Plato's *theos* and *eide* also eternal and unfailing" (Onians 1951:465–466).

Plato's Theory of Forms is the most powerful and certainly one of the longest-standing philosophical notions ever conceived and, within Platonic philosophy, Idea is the generative link between the universal Form and any human concept; it is what is 'grasped' by the mind. Necessarily, Form and Idea presuppose manifestation, which is, also necessarily, a pale version of the Real. The central idea in architecture has been co-opted to the service of a partisan idealist and largely Hegelian view of the world as the Central Idea (Kollar 1983; Tawa 1991). This view of ancient immutability was to revive with academic classicism from the eighteenth century, and sustained modern classicism a century and a half later in the seeking and imitating of a standard of perfection. It may be that the Central Idea is intentionally being used to install in architecture its dependence on emanation from another realm of the kind Plato posited so long ago. Using it casually as 'central idea' or its equivalent the 'parti' (one of a number of Beaux-Arts terms undergoing a revival in current architectural discourse), whereby some superordinal human system is admitted to designing, can unwittingly implicate the user in the same plan. So it is important to be clear about what is being invoked *in extenso* about architecture if a central idea is posited.

However, judging by the rarity in recent architectural writing of admissions of the impact of a central idea, it would seem that the Platonic notion of the Idea as the conduit from the universal realm of pure Forms is no longer acceded to by Western architects. In Eastern architecture, the 'realm of ideas' still has currency, although it is as much ignored by younger architects as it is accepted by their elders. By way of example, of the ten presentations by architects in Abby Suckle's *By Their Own Design* (1980), half talk about a governing idea in one way or another: Arthur Erickson refers in passing to the 'formal idea'; Cesar Pelli advocates technological expression as the 'idea of the present'; Kisho Kurokawa distances himself from faithful adherence to a formative idea in favor of aggregation; Herman Hertzberger talks of 'an underlying objective structure of forms' he calls 'arch-forms'; John Johanson talks of 'organizing ideas' but denies any formal compositional emphasis; Fumihiko Maki refers to a 'germinal idea'; Gerald McCue bases his designing on models; Richard Rogers seeks a 'universal' rule-based approach; Harry Seidler advocates systematization; and Norman Foster proffers a celebratory optimization.

In contrast, the notion of a unitary central idea is nowhere near as prominent among the twenty-seven American architects interviewed half a decade later by Barbaralee Diamonstein (1985). They almost all admit to being subservient to society in some way and to coming to grips with the multiplicity of societal demands. They recognize that their buildings are "an element of a larger encompassing architectural fabric," and that they themselves are "part of a larger, encompassing social fabric." In creating a 'serviceable' architecture they are mostly united but differ in the way they do it, "yet, in responding to current social imperatives and environmental realities, they have in common a perspective devoid of the often self-righteous ideals and principles that inspired and bound their modernist teachers" (14). Neither is 'idea' used other than as a normal conversational term by most of the twenty three architects who each presented one project for critique in Chicago in 1986 (Tigerman 1987), although several did try to focus discussion with partial notions of idea, except for Stanley Tigerman, who elaborated upon the conceptual basis of 'exile' for his synagogue without actually calling it his central idea. In recent architecture journals, 'central idea' in any all-embracing generative sense is never mentioned by architects and, if quizzed, they will say they do not discern a single, comprehensive notion central to their way of working; or they will defer to critics any determination of what the central idea of their work might be. So much the worse for architecture, an idealist might declare!

As far as architectural theory is concerned, to be able to give clear expression about what is believed to be the principal issue or issues of a design task is no doubt useful in communication and as a discipline for thinking about the task, a centering device that helps concentration. Otherwise it appears to have only marginal intrinsic worth. Perhaps its greatest demerit is that it encourages the vested interest a designer has to make life simpler or less demanding, to willingly participate in a deceit rather than admit a conceit. In this respect, Brian Elkner (1970) comes close to an accurate summation when he says: "'a clear idea', [Edmund] Burke tells us, 'is . . . another name for a little idea', and the tangle of impressions and associations is a far more powerful mainspring for the aesthetic emotion than any logical functioning of the mental process" (153). This resonates with the desire of many architects today to embrace multiplicity full on without the impediment of "a simplistic and reductive idea, intended to impose completion and order, [that] limits the potential expression of a multiplicity of desires. The imperative of the supposed 'Big Idea' attempts to ensure complete subordination of the parts to the elusive 'meaning' of the whole" (Center, Hart and Knecht 1984:137). The impediment is made all the more limiting because "Despite the necessity, whether real or imagined, to emphasize one style more than another in a particular place and time, the system remains impervious, the authority unchallenged, the language anything but universal" (loc. cit.). The idea might inform the act actually, but whether it enacts the Form of the act must ever be in doubt.

FURTHER SOURCES   6A.3, Chaos; Coomaraswamy 1977; Kollar 1983; Schirmbeck 1983; Tawa 1982.

3. Meme: The Creative Parasite of Architects

A memory is what is left behind when something happens and does not completely unhappen. **Edward de Bono.** 1969:41.

It [recent architectural history writing] is a catalogue history, devoid of narration, in which the phenomenal past is digested to a set of timeless motifs on which the designer can call to deck out his project in a garb which will produce, so it is generally thought, the right kind of denotative response in the public. **Joseph Rykwert.** 1976:Preface.

If a scientist hears, or reads about, a good idea, he passes it on to his colleagues and students. He mentions it in his articles and his lectures. If the idea catches on, it can be said to propagate itself, spreading from brain to brain. **Richard Dawkins.** 1989:192.

Stylistic analysis has too often become a self-fulfilling system in which it was assumed that change always followed an orderly progression, and that chronology could be based [on] this order. Once established in all its rationality and propounded to generations of scholars it has become engrained in most teaching methods. This meme of artistic progress assumes that art has evolved progressively towards some definable aim, and not by leaps and bounds nor with revolutionary concepts being used concurrently with very old-fashioned ones nor with periods of back-sliding. **John James.** 1989:92.

TRACE   The term *meme* will not be found in dictionaries older than 1988 because it is a neologism, a reduction of 'mimeme' (rooted in *mimesis,* memory) and concocted in the early eighties by the zoologist Richard Dawkins (1989) for what he calls a replicator of culture, a 'gene-of-memory'. Memes are "tunes, ideas, catch-phrases, clothes fashions, ways of making pots or of building arches" according to Dawkins, and, quoting a colleague's idea of such a replicator, may be summarized thus: "Memes should be regarded as living structures, not just metaphorically but technically. When you plant a fertile meme in my mind, you literally parasitize my brain, turning it into a vehicle for the meme's propagation in just the way that a virus may parasitize the genetic mechanism of a host cell" (192).

The notion was imported to architecture by John James (1989:4), who paraphrases Dawkins's use of the term. The meme has physical consequences in that it structures the nervous system and manifests in the world as a notion that leaves a memorable trace after death. "In short, the meme is any idea which has ceased to be open to reflection and has been accepted to the point that it directs our thoughts and actions. It is therefore invasive and concealed, parasitic and often limiting." (James 1989:4). Etymologically at least, *meme* gathers around it a credibility more acceptable than that of 'engramming', the neurological procedure supposed to establish the permanent trace of long-term memory described first in 1921 and resurrected by Peter Smith (1974) as a simplistic model of the way the external world is captured by memory and coopted by him in the service of urban design.

COMMENTARY   Within Gothic cathedral building, James discerns a series of art-historical assumptions and memes, some of which are common to historical inquiry generally. An assumption becomes a meme when "it has formed part of the belief-system of more than a generation of scholars and for which there is insufficient evidence" (1989:5). He instances the beliefs that: Gothic invention spread out from the cathedral workshops (the dominance of greater over smaller); whole buildings were conceived *in toto* from the ground up; stylistic advance or retardation establishes the chronology (and progress) of a building; clergy rather than builders were the innovators; and medieval sensibilities should be like our own classically developed notions, especially in matters of unity, order, and symmetry. James concludes *Template-makers* on the note that while it is difficult not to construe the many great Gothic cathedrals and churches as the work of one mind and a consistent theory, the fact is that they were produced by a number of minds working quite separately over time with the inescapable potential for cessation at any moment. That the

Gothic had any formal consistency was at best a fluke rather than a relentless unraveling of progress.

James's studies show the meme to be an idiosyncratic concrete manifestation of an idea that develops universal consequences, whether by accident or from pretensions. Propagated through repetition and unquestioning acceptance, a meme colonizes just as ancient Greek ideas promoted as concrete images in time prompted their universal abstract equivalents (see 8B.2, Idea). So, a meme can be either a static or a dynamic concept. As James prompts above, a meme is the least complicated way for ideas to propagate among architects, not as fully fledged and highly wrought workings out of complex philosophical notions, but as simple and personally appealing concepts that either attract further adherents or wither on the vine. As a working practice, though, the meme adopted by architects is mainly a visual rather than a verbal device, and its power lies in its viability as a ready-made currency for comprehension and application.

Architectural education and theory-talk promulgate the verbal meme in their personal maxims and rules-of-thumb; witness the many architects who recall with affection the sayings of their teachers, or pick up pet themes of peers or historical figures (Diamonstein 1985; Tigerman 1987). Architectural education and practice promulgate the visual meme through vicarious plundering and imitation—not in a strict archaeological sense but loosely and experimentally. For instance, if architects or students cruise books, journals, or actual buildings in search of design ideas or elements that appeal to them, they are looking to appropriate visual memes, atoms of visual currency that they might exploit from within the theme of the targeted work or architect, or within their own themes. Visual memes spread rapidly once they achieve currency status, and in this way become the fashion or mode among a collaborative group.

In architectural education the idiosyncrasy and autonomy of memes explains the rapidity with which visual themes come and go, and their apparent superficiality. Fads of design motifs, presentation techniques, design jargon, right reading, and 'happening' persons continually proliferate among groups of students in schools of architecture, sometimes to the consternation of academics concerned at their sheer transience, at the apparent erosion of values, or at the lack of direction. The reason for their fleeting appearance, however, is not a lack of substance; it is that visual memes never commence as anything more than a single, maybe trivial, idea, and therefore remain disconnected, rarely developing further unless as part of a coordinated schema based in a recognizable movement or a particular architect's work or teaching, or as evidencing a maturing personal approach to design.

The occasional meme that does precipitate a movement or enjoy prolonged success does so purely because it captures the imagination and sustains scrutiny, not because it is good or true necessarily, but because it fills a need. Stripped of its foundational circumstances and rhetoric, 'functionalism' offers nothing by way of a formal vocabulary. Recalling his early practice, the engineer Ove Arup remarks, "I don't think much of those who say that I should decide on an appropriate structure for the job and they will fit their architecture to it, and I have met a few of those, especially in the early days of functionalism, when the functionally 'right' thing was supposed to produce the right architecture. It doesn't, it produces no architecture at all" (Arup 1979). Ironically, the long life that functionalism has enjoyed revolves around propping up architects of all calibers, especially those Arup condemns. 'Form follows function' is, after all, no more than a slogan that can be as portentous as you want it to be and is capable of the most banal as well as the most uplifting visual interpretation. At the risk of stretching an already overworked phrase, the imperial action of meme suggests that form follows faction. Until another equally charged word or phrase grabs wide architectural attention, today's pluralism will prevail. Not that the wait is a bad thing; the present mix is the architectural equivalent of a primordial soup and the cooking can be at least as enjoyable as the broth.

Extending the concept to include *memory* as a design technique (not the mental power but the event remembered) or as an attribute of a building may circumscribe certain profound difficulties if memory is considered a thread of memes. For an individual, a memory is a singular recollection or a series of such recollections that forms a threadlike narrative; across individuals, single recollections remain isolated and the narratives perhaps form a web, provided there is some way to assemble them from individual accounts (the so-called collective conscious or collective memory). However the memory structures of the brain and memories themselves are construed, they are dynamic, three-dimensional, and holistic, and may be triggered spontaneously or by external things or events (Rose 1992).

That objects, whether created or natural, prompt memories goes without saying, for it is common experience that this happens. The notion of objects deliberately arranged to convey, let alone prompt, memories is a romantic fiction that has been entertained by architects for several centuries, and at no time more than the late twentieth century. This is the thrust of Joseph Rykwert's condemnation above of the use to which history writing is put in architecture. The most that may be expected through design is that signs and symbols deposited in a work *might* prompt certain memories, although there is no guarantee that they will or surety as to their predictability, accuracy, or extent. Turning to buildings as repositories of memories, for secular buildings there may be threads assembled in the minds of the designer or the participant linking separate single visual memes in a building. Only in religious or quasi-religious buildings with high ritualistic content might memories be assisted in their accumulation through built concatenations. Even the house is not ritualized enough as a building to assist in assembling memories, despite the ingenious attempts by Anthony Vidler (1992) to do this from among the haunts of literature and via the 'theatre of memory'. Moreover, one has to work extremely hard at both implanting and extracting in order to recapture even a semblance of a narrative from the memes of buildings, even those assisted by ritual.

All that has been said adds up to the view that evocations of vernacular, locational, formal, historical, or spatial memories are extraordinarily difficult to achieve in any comprehensive way in newly created works. There is no 'vocabulary' of sufficiently proven memes that can be placed in a building to evoke specific isolated memories, let alone memory narratives that in any way equate with the richness of human recollection. All the designer has is the meme, a personally invented singularity of theme that has limited reach and short life expectancy. Even if several memes in a work trigger emotionally satisfying or intellectually stimulating memories in one or another person, it is impossible to know how many memories might be common and it is fruitless to speculate. So, all historical reference and all esthetic cross-reference in a building (and even in a city, contrary to Rossi 1986) reduces to what individuals understand *individually;* the only architectural collective unconscious, conscious, or memory, is the score of those who run while the ball is in the air, not the metaphysical pitch. And who is keeping score?

FURTHER SOURCES   Dawkins 1989; James 1989; Pepchinski 1991; Rossi 1981, 1982; Yates 1966.

4. Allowing for Change and Contingency

Designing within a truly free structure which outflanks hierarchically structured signifying codes and systems does not mean that any wild-looking network goes. One starts with the ordinary, the program, and with radical openings that allow chance to enter, affirm everything and anything. **John Knesl.** In Al-Sayed *et al.* 1988:text near n44.

It is the ability to draw it and in the drawing to see how the building will look, that makes an architect a virtuoso on-the-spot experimenter. This is what I mean by the architect's reflection in action. **Donald Schön.** *The Reflective Practitioner* 1983.

Since a subjectivist sees things as they appear to the senses and not as they are, he is incapable of rational appraisal, and is led to ignore the basic function of architecture, which according to Professor Worringer is "to wrest it from temporality, confusion and obscurity, and raise it from contingency into the realms of necessity." **Berthold Lubetkin.** *Royal Gold Medal Address.* In Murray 1982:45–49.

TRACE   *Contingency* is the anticipation of uncertainty, the chance that something might or might not happen, the possibility of an accident or unforeseen event or circumstance; we say, for example, "we must be prepared for any contingency." In medieval Latin it meant 'circumstance', the context which surrounds an event and, like context, makes contact with it, hence its etymology from *tangere,* to touch, such that to be *contingent* is to depend upon. Its opposition with uncertainty seems to be reconciled by the tangent, the fleeting touch of one upon another, accidental or incidental yet consequential.

Technological change and its concomitant, progress, were part of the sweeping vision of the Modern Movement with the consequence that "a new conventional wisdom was established: building technology is changing at a frightening rate and architects have a duty to act as midwives of this change. Technical innovation became a mark of professional responsibility" (Heath 1991:44). Flexibility to accommodate functional change has been a byword of architects for almost a century. More demanding than either of these, though, has been change that occurs during designing. Contingencies infect every design task and make designing both exciting and frustrating. Well-known models of design developed during the sixties (see chapter 6B) do not handle change or contingency well, and hermeneutics is seen by some as a conceptual basis more suitable for developing design models.

COMMENTARY   Though technology is declared to be a powerful agent of change in architecture, "the building industry does not change very rapidly, for good reasons. Building materials are used in very large quantities and must, in general, be very cheap and reliable. This means that they are usually the products of mature, if not actually obsolescent, industries; old technology, not new technology. There is change, but not enough to justify a constant pre-occupation with technical innovation" (Heath 1991:44). This preoccupation has always been there in the use of the 'latest' technical devices and mechanisms for moving people and goods through and around buildings and in servicing their personal needs of comfort, control, and cleanliness. For years now, doors have opened unattended, stairs and footways have moved, louvers have turned against the sun, and temperature and humidity have changed to suit internal conditions, and remote sensing for lighting, security, entertainment, and operations is now commonplace.

Apart from these devices, few other avenues for the expression of technological change are available. Certainly there have been changes in materials technology that have resulted in membrane structures and cladding materials, and changes in structural materials have enabled some adventurous gymnastics in steel, cable, and concrete. But overall, it has been difficult to signify change in architecture because of the mainly conventional means of construction at its disposal, and because much of the really advanced innovation was miniaturized and hidden as service and control systems. So, architects resorted to *images* of technological change to convey the impression of being in step with the age. Just a few of the more obvious examples from the seventies and eighties are the Centre Pompidou, Paris, by Rogers and Piano; the Lloyd's Insurance headquarters building, London, by Richard Rogers and Partners; the Medical Faculty at Aachen, Germany, by Weber Brand and Partner; and the Institut du Monde Arabe, Paris, by Jean Nouvel. All except the last, however, rely on an image of old technology—exposed tubes, slats, wires, struts; and, like many other buildings, have their most advanced technology concealed. The point of raising this issue is that in education, the preoccupation of students is often with the expressive potential of new technology, frequently more imagined than real because of ignorance about its actual impact, but the results are the same—tubes, slats, wires, or struts.

The other and even less tangible aspect is designing for the accommodation of change by means of 'flexible' buildings. In this there are three approaches: undifferentiated sheds capable of almost any internal configuration; investment in some kind of modular system allowing remanipulation of any configuration within minutes; or various species of additive arrangement wherein other built elements may be adjoined without disturbing the existing arrangement. The architectural challenges are: in the first case, to embrace one of the many clear-span structures, which then becomes the esthetic; in the second, to determine an 'appropriate' module, which is then reiterated and becomes the esthetic; and in the third, to place self-contained units in such a way that further elements can be added such that each or any stage may be construed as a whole, the esthetic being its particle-like aggregation. In most cases the investment of thought and cost in systematizing is wasted because change rarely occurs at a scale commensurate with that anticipated. Or, if it does, it may not be for a decade or more, by which time an already committed system may have become a potential liability because building advances may have superseded it, and/or technology may have shifted in emphasis such that building demands previously resolved by a particular system might be interpreted and satisfied in an altogether different way. In almost all instances, the response of architects has been to *confine* change for esthetic reasons rather than allow it free reign and accept whatever that may imply.

Turning to the more persistent day-to-day matter of change and contingency, chances are that the average designer won't take chances because uncertainty is inimical to efficient production and to surety of purpose, or so it would appear. Because architects live with change and contingency in practice, their natural instinct for self-preservation inclines them to prefer certainty and to seek design methods that sort through complexity but that, in doing so, often fail the test of meeting changing conditions or parameters. It is for this reason that the design methods movement peaked and then died as it was realized that nothing could replace the sheer slog of working through a design task. There were no quick fixes and none quick enough to also accommodate change without internal hemorrhage. The teleological structure of design processes is determined to reach an end, and by definition must ultimately be intolerant of uncertainty, conflict, instability, or contingency.

Yet all designing thrives on unknowns, divergencies, challenges, spontaneities and intuitions internal to its own operations, while at the same time absorbing unexpected pressures and changes of desire or intention outside its control. How, then, *do* designers cope with the intrusion of extraneous factors or unpredictability? One explanation is given by the educator Donald Schön (1983): "We have a kind of knowledge in the action, we know more than we can say . . . something in the action which is frequently the opposite of what we say. We have an intuitive capacity for understanding in action which is incongruent with our espoused theories of what we do." This knowledge in action is the one ability architects and designers have that artificial intelligence will probably never achieve: the capacity to both change minds and to accommodate the mind changes of others, or changes obliged by shifting circumstances, and to then intuit the right path in the midst of wrong clues.

Schön argues for architectural designing being a practical intuition, one that reflects on action as it happens and symbiotically experiments with the situation and adjusts received theory and counteraction to achieve an outcome. The practical application of reflection in action is called *competence,* and its theoretical frame is philosophical hermeneutics, the interpretive context within which we are all embedded. Some theorists are now arguing against the algorithmic model of designing derived from language theory, a world of 'truth-functional semantics' involving notions of graphic tokens and rules to assemble them as shape grammars and the like (Mitchell 1990; Oxman, Radford and Oxman 1987), and for a human and hermeneutic model in which designing is holistic and operates in dialogic fashion (Snodgrass and Coyne 1990). The strength of this model and of the hermeneutic stance generally is that it handles the contingencies of designing without inherent dilemmas, although this is not to say that designing is thereby made easier. The challenge for the future is still to show how we actually do it and to demonstrate that a critical hermeneutics will produce equally critical and responsive buildings.

FURTHER SOURCES   Colquhoun 1981; Jones 1984; Papageorgiou 1971; Steadman 1979.

CHAPTER

Relationships in Architecture

Overview

Today I am considered a revolutionary. I shall confess to you that I have had only one teacher: the past; only one education: the study of the past. Everything, for a long time, and still today. . . .

It is in the past that I found the lessons of history, of the reasons for being of things. Every event and every object is "in relationship to. . . ." **Le Corbusier.** 1930:33.

Technically function is a relation, not a quality. **Tom Heath.** 1991:25

To imagine that anything can be defined or *constituted* by its relations is the fundamental relativist mistake. Architecture and architects cannot be explained solely by reference to *something else,* but only in terms of their own characteristics. **Tom Heath.** 1991:183.

Interaction among the parts of anything involves some kind or degree of association, some way of bringing them together, connecting them, or maintaining their separation in such a manner that they still cohere or by which they may be compared, or which by their difference they may contrast. Even to say 'parts of' is to express some connection with a whole, and implicates a system of ordering that assists first in conceiving and then in arranging things. So, relationship is first to do with the identifying characteristics of elements by which they are recognized as belonging or not belonging to some family of

347

elements. And, second, relationship is to do with the distance between the elements, be it abstract, conceptual, mathematical, semantic, or physical (Euclidean) distance.

However, using these terms tries to force a separation in what is a compound distinction because the terms just mentioned are often interactive, abstract, and mathematical or conceptual and semantic, for instance, although most relations may be subsumed under the semantic. Though there are purely mathematical relationships, a notion like hierarchy or succession has mathematical instances but is primarily a semantic quality, although it is only capable of being understood spatially. For the origin of language lies in spatial comprehension and expression.

The mechanisms of relationship are transitive in that they embody some 'passing over' or movement *from* one thing *to* another, just as prepositions themselves do, and there is reciprocation between the elements of a relationship. Sometimes the relationship involves an ordering concept for it to take effect, as, for instance, in saying that three or more elements are related and hierarchical, or that one element is subordinate to another. In fact, scaling uses ordering to effect its relationship, and might have been included in chapter 6A, Order by Imposition, as well as here. Indeed, many of the concepts gathered in this chapter are so fundamental to architecture that the whole book might have been, and in certain respects is, devoted to their explication as relationships. Turning to Roget's Thesaurus, which influenced the structuring of this book, it is illuminating to find that the concepts under just two relational classes, Abstract Relations and Space, embrace slightly more than 30 percent of all the concepts covered by Roget. Little wonder, then, that architecture as *the* concrete spatial art (and science), should consist primarily in relationships.

At a conceptual level there are held to be two sorts of relation, *internal* and *external.* An internal relation is one in which the property by which the relation exists is *necessarily* a property of the thing to which it relates. For example, the relation of being married is internal to the term 'wife' or 'husband'. An external relation is one in which the property by which the relation exists is *not necessarily* a property of the thing to which it relates. For example, the relation of a wife being taller than her husband is ordinarily external to the terms 'wife' or 'husband' (Flew 1979). Another example would be religious belief, wherein, if 'purity' of religion is part of the orthodoxy of marriage, then similarity of religion would also be internal to being a wife or husband.

Architectural equivalents to internal and external relations are to be found in the 'lawful' distribution of elements according to compositional rules, no matter whether they are usual or arbitrary. For example, *cluster* as a proximity relation has the internal property of several elements being close to each other, whereas similarity of shape would normally be an external relation. On the other hand, an overlapping or interpenetrating set of clusters or *pattern* as a proximity relation requires both closeness and similarity as internal properties (wherein a *Gestalten,* the tendency to holistic closure, is what discriminates the pattern), though similarity of shape may be internal and color external, or vice versa (after Norberg-Schulz 1965:140–146).

Internal and external relations have also existed throughout the history of styles in architecture, where stylistic purity is identified by the consistency of its multiple internal relationships and impurity by the degree to which external relationships interfere with them. For instance, rules of proportion accepted as fixed for the three classical orders are part of the stylistic definition of Classical Revival styles, but when distortion appears by increasing height of columns or pilasters or by dramatic shifts in size, the stylistic purity is said to be affected. The same applies to details and motifs, shifts from accepted relationships being labeled Mannerist.

Once removed from the recognizably set-piece situations that classical buildings provide, the distinction between internal and external relations quickly becomes too difficult to discriminate and the notion is of limited application. Hence it is not possible to offer a general framework for architectural relationships within which discussion might proceed. However, for the purposes of this chapter there is one commonality in certain relationships whereby they may be discussed, namely, that of a comparison with some standard, such as measure, scale, or the human body (anthropocentrism), as well as those relationships involving a pure and simple precision such as number and geometry (symmetry, though, is discussed in passing in chapter 10A, for its impact in architecture is esthetic rather than systemic). These are the subject of part A, on the measurement of architecture.

Then there are relationships of extension on a surface and in space, which involves comparisons that are normally 'subjectively' experienced more than 'objectively' measured, even though they may in fact be measurable. Within this group falls the compositional and the locational, which act together, in many respects, and reflect certain conceptual frames of designers. Apart from the fundamental aspects of 'addition' and 'division' in the spatial composition of buildings, for instance, Paul Frankl discerned 'interpenetration' and three additive aspects—series, open grouping and closed grouping—as compositional modes (Norberg-Schulz 1965:Fig. 20; Frankl 1982:chapter 1). This structuring is not unlike that for rooms devised by Moore, Allen, and Lyndon (1974:147–175), namely rooms linked, bunched, cored, and enfronted, and the prominence of a room within or encompassing. These are common spatial and relational experiences in architecture, which many houses and museums use as their spatial order. As with surfaces, solids and spaces of these kinds cannot exist in isolation; they meet, and the connection between them, the links, thresholds, openings, narrowings, and widenings, becomes the means by which they are comprehended and therefore important locations of architectural endeavor.

A necessary ingredient of spatial experience is time, and time was to become a leitmotif for many early modern architects. From its rarefied beginnings as the mysterious fourth dimension of architecture, time was to have a long and varied career as an essential component of architectural understanding. It was eventually to become absorbed into a broad experiential and qualitative view of architecture that led to notions such as 'serial vision', the core of the urban and townscape ideas of Gordon Cullen (1961). While temporal and spatial seriation has been a pervasive notion in architecture, centrality has been a longer-standing and more important one, together with its antithesis, marginality or boundary. It would be no exaggeration to say that centrality has in fact been *the* 'central' concept of architecture, as earlier chapters have indicated.

The center of things is what architecture has sought for so long in its language, a language bristling with the terminology of centricity and marginality, much of which has been used throughout this text: heart, core, point, place, essence, spirit, idea, focus, intersection, conjunction, and confluence all speak of center, and periphery, edge, interstice, boundary, margin, and wall all speak of marginality. These are some of the topics of part B.

A. Measuring Architecture

1. Measure as the Fundamental Engagement

Measure and commensurability, as it turns out, are everywhere identifiable with beauty and excellence. **Plato.** *Philebus*:64E.

To measure signifies to know and scrutinise the quality of a thing or state. **Emanuel Swedenborg.** c1780. *Apocalypse Revealed*:n486.

The moderns, generally speaking, cannot conceive of any other science except that which deals with things that can be measured, counted or weighed . . . the stage has been reached even of supposing that there can be no science at all . . . except where it is possible to introduce measurement . . . they end by ceasing to understand that the possibility of measurement rests solely upon a property inherent in matter, namely its indefinite divisibility. **René Guénon.** 1942:82–83.

TRACE   Measure is one of the foundational concepts of human understanding. Deriving from the Latin *mens-,* past participle of *metiri,* measure, and equivalent in the Greek to *metron,* measure is also etymologically related to the Germanic *nama,* the 'name' of an individual manifestation—the Sanscrit root *na-* is the unmanifest principle and *-ma* is the measured manifestation (Tawa 1991:60). Measure is the core of all words containing -mens- or -metr-, such as geometry, symmetry, meter, diameter, dimension, mensuration, and immensity.

The importance of measure in ancient thought is explained by Pollitt (1974:15): "The urge to discover or construct an order behind the flux of experience in the world is as inherent in the Greek mind as is, for example, the urge for identification with an incorporeal, transcendental existence in Hindu thought. Order is inconceivable without a conception of its essential characteristic—measure, which involves both definition (marking the boundary of things) and analysis of the interrelationship of discrete forms." For Plato, measure had moral connotations, as shown above, and an absolute existence in that it was not just the relative degrees between opposites but, as the *mean* (neither excess nor deficiency) pursued by the arts, was essential to their existence and that of the good and the beautiful (*Politicus*:283E–284B from Pollitt 16–17). Aristotle too developed a concept of excellence based in the mean, "every form, then, of applied knowledge, when it performs its function well, looks to the mean and works to the standard set by that . . . goodness is the quality that hits the mean" (*Ethics*:II.6; see also II.7–9). And as the spatial art, the measure of architecture is deeply implicated in the pursuit of the good and the beautiful.

COMMENTARY   To discuss measure is to enter the world of traditional science and the so-called natural order in all its extensions because of its unitary premises and understanding. Nowhere is this better exemplified than in the primacy and indivisibility of the number one in traditional thought and the pivotal position of zero and the use of negative numbers in western thought and mathematics (Guénon 1958:75–79; Lawlor 1982). Traditional science and mysticism maintain what Christianity and Western thought since the Renaissance have confounded and confused, a belief in the essential unity of the unmanifest and the manifest. This is not the place to review natural order, traditional science, or even the role of measure in tradition, save for recognizing the archaeology of language (prompted a little in the *trace* above) that perpetuates in everyday terms their megalithic and traditional origins. The words 'origin' and 'orient' are but one example of how deeply language is embedded in natural events, stemming from the Latin *orior,* rise, and the natural alignment of life with the cosmic cycles. What we will focus on here are certain architectural qualities of relevance to everyday Western thinking and practice.

In the cyclical nature of natural events was the basic measure of life through which all manner of manifestation came to be divisible by humankind, and succession came to consciousness. Temporal division into increasingly smaller components of seasons, night/day, months, hours, and minutes are now too remote to be of other than academic interest, except to say that intervals marked out by cycles were complemented by the rhythms of human movement and activity to create measures of spatial extension. For instance, song, dance, and music represented cycles and set limits and boundaries, while the human pace reiterated succession and determined extent, separation, and distance. This distinction is not absolute, though, as evidenced by the association of ritual and music involving spatial transit (marching, procession, and so on), or by the long trumpet players of Islam taking 'possession' of space by turning successively to the cardinal directions, or the use of song and rhythm accompanying work of all kinds, whether spatially static, as in weaving, or extended, as in tilling and harvesting (Larousse 1971:17, 18). In relation to tilling, one direct connection between cosmic cycles and measurement is land measure, for instance, the *morgen* (morning) enshrined as the area of land that can be plowed in a morning.

It is significant that Le Corbusier begins his *Modulor* by pointing to the destruction of the perfect continuity of human sound through notation, the human need to codify sound, "breaking up a continuous whole in accordance with a certain [artificial] convention," as means of perpetuating it other than through the oral tradition (Le Corbusier 1954:15). He then proposes his modular system as "a tool of linear or optical measures, similar to musical script" whose intended effect is "to unite, co-ordinate, bring into harmony the work which is at present divided and disjointed," namely the imperial and metric measurement systems. What Le Corbusier went on to elaborate was something far grander, a system that sought to re-establish a unity of measurement in the modern era equivalent to that of ancient lore, something that had resurfaced in the Renaissance but had gradually been lost, one that united humanity and architecture in a scheme of cosmic significance. But more of the *modulor* in section 9A.2, Anthropos.

The reinvention and application of systems of measure was one aspect of Renaissance classical architecture that made it such a powerful and influential force, not just because such systems accorded with 'correct' ancient exemplars in their quantitative perfection as they did early on, but for the additional value that was assigned to the parts as superior or inferior that emerged with the baroque period. "Such differentiation would have been strange to antiquity ... but postmedieval composition which emphasized the different values of the parts made of the whole hierarchy of well-disciplined elements. The means ... were concatenation, integration, and gradation" (Kaufmann 1955:79). Decisive classical *canons* of measure and proportion appealed to and aligned with natural human inclinations to order, architects being no less human than ordinary mortals in this regard. But the baroque hierarchy was the touch of supremacy and mastery, and architects gathered eagerly to drink at this fount. That canonical systems were couched not only in terms of musical and cosmic harmonies but eventually portrayed beauty and perfection as systemic meant that architects and artists always ignored them at their peril; these systems of measure were political and artistic *currency*, and were not to be trifled with. Indeed, the challenge was to better any accepted system, and the history of architectural theory after the rediscovery of Vitruvius is of purportedly ever-better measures, as systems, of beauty and perfection.

Dramatic shifts of emphasis concerning hierarchical structure and the subservience of parts to the whole occurred from the eighteenth century with the redefinition of what should constitute the whole. The nineteenth century's emerging focus on structure as primary and on the innate quality of materials was to reverse the baroque denial of these, but it was not until the twentieth that they were to conceptually dominate architectural thinking to the extent that any ordering system was relinquished. Only Le Corbusier was to carry on anything like the classical systemic, with his 'five points' of architecture, his *tracés regulateurs* or regulating lines developed from Auguste Choisy, and his *Modulor* proportional system, Alan Colquhoun (1989:Part II) claiming that the first of these merely reversed the five-point classical canon. In terms of beauty and perfection, Le Corbusier rather coyly claimed that if harmony should result from his system, so be it.

On the other hand, Plato's insistence in the *Philebus* on the mean as absolute and as being the key to order and beauty and therefore the good has some fascinating implications for architecture. For all practical purposes, when faced with an indefinite variety of manifestation or possibilities, as a designer is while designing, it is necessary to impose some limit to bring precision to the mixture of opposing qualities, to bring order to the 'chaos'. Imposing a limit on this mix of qualities is the way of making them, in Plato's terms, "commensurable, harmonious, and instilling number into them" (by means of the unit, the odd or the even), which is achieved by employing measure (*metron*) and proportion (*symmetria*) (after Pollitt 1974:16). Alberti was to comment of the mean: "But it is clear that in everything Nature thrives on moderation; and what is good health but a moderation composed of a fabric of different extremes? The mean is always pleasing" (Alberti 1755b:5.8 and p425). Measure is not simply a relative comparison of pairs, but is absolute in the sense that the mean represents the *best possible resolution under all the circumstances* and, if this is so, the mean must represent the highest good, the highest Platonic good presumably being the Form of the Mean.

Cast in this way, Plato's 'mean' (and presumably Aristotle's 'mean' as well) is quite a radical claim because it emphasizes the central tendency that is recognized today, some 'measure' of each, rather than one or the other extreme in pairs of antinomial qualities so often construed as a linear relationship in Western thought. It should be emphasized, though, that this conception is not a matter of merely reconstruing antinomials as concentric with the most desirable quality in the center. What is most radical about what Plato says is that the mean is just that mixture that is neither too much of one nor too little of the other—the ultimate compromise, if you like.

Applying this to, say, the design of a table, the best table under a set of circumstances is that which does what it has to do without going to extremes, that table that 'best fits', or befits, the circumstances. Given a certain mixture of culture, climate, materials, skills, spatial setting, cost, and so on, the best table is that which takes into account all these circumstances. The Idea of the table, therefore, is not some ideal Form of Table, but is tied to circumstances as the ideal Form of Mean Table, and is in the most radical way *ultimately contingent.* Even for a Platonic idealist, the Mean rather than the Good becomes the measure of manifestation, the nexus between concept and application. Is this what Plato meant? If so, it would be a plus for architecture.

FURTHER SOURCES   Le Corbusier 1954, 1958; Padovan 1986.

2. Apropos Anthropos

Man is the measure of all things, of the things that are that they are, and of the things that are not that they are not. **Protagoras.** Quoted in Plato, *Theatetus*:152a.

Architecture . . . must be a thing of the body, a thing of substance as well as of the spirit and of the brain. **Le Corbusier.** 1954:60–61.

What are the consequences for architecture of the 'death of Man,' the revered subject of humanism? . . . an important topic for an architectural discourse whose very foundations, we have been taught to believe, rest on its relation to the human figure. Once 'man' has gone, and presumably taken his body along with him, what are architects left with? Who do we serve? Where do we look for our formal models? **Robert McAnulty.** "Body Troubles," in Whiteman, Kipnis, and Burdett 1992:181.

TRACE   There is not much to say etymologically about the prefix anthropo-, from the Greek *anthropos,* human being or man, except that its combination with the suffixes -centric, -geny, -glot, -graphy, -metry, -morphous, -pathy, -phagy, -phobia, -phugy, -sophy, and -tomy, along with anthropurgic (from *theoyrgos,* operating as man), covers every aspect of human operation. Humanism, broadly conceived, is the devotion to human affairs, even though 'humanism' was not a term known to the ancients or used during the Renaissance. Humanism was coined in the German *Humanismus* in 1808 and first applied to the Renaissance in George Voigt's *The Revival of Classical Antiquity or the First Century of Humanism* (1859), according to Bullock (1985), although *umanista* was Italian slang applied in the late fifteenth century to a teacher of classical languages and literature and *studia humanitatis,* our humanities, was what was taught. The Latin *humanitas* was a Roman version of an older Greek idea of education, *paideia* (from *pais, paides,* boy or child), already in use before the fifth century B.C., the core of being uniquely human depending on a 'well-rounded' education, *enkyklia paedeia,* which Cicero equated with *humanitas* (11–12).

   Architecturally, *anthropos* featured physically in ancient measure as the terms *digit, palm, foot, cubit* (see the Vitruvius quotation in 9A.5, Number), and their dimensional variations across time and culture show; physically and metaphorically in the sacrificial terminology and meaning of classical architecture (Vitruvius 1486; Hersey 1988); in Medieval and Renaissance physical and symbolic embodiment of human form in built form through proportion (Wittkower 1973); in the empathy of human sensation and feeling with constructional forces during the nineteenth century (Viollet-le-Duc 1872); in the proportioning systems of certain modern architects (Le Corbusier 1958; Padovan 1986); in the sociospatial constructs of behavioral studies (especially Alexander *et al.* 1977); and metaphorically in recent preoccupations with the body and gender (t)issues (Agrest 1991; Al-Sayed *et al.* 1988; Frascari 1991; A. Kahn 1991; Whiteman, Kipnis, and Burdett 1992).

COMMENTARY   For all that has been pointed to above, however, there is little that has a tangible or enduring impact on the architect in current practice. Certainly there are exceptions, architects whose buildings are carefully thought through theoretically and highly wrought dimensionally and spatially. Though proportioning of a systematic and coordinated kind like the Modulor may be periodically applied today, for the most part, architects just muddle through, relying on site constrictions, the structural module, standard floor-to-floor or floor-to-ceiling dimensions, or the economics of constructional modules to set the proportions of a building. In architecture and planning it would be rare to find anyone who regularly applies Christopher Alexander's 'pattern language' in a rigorous way, although a number of architects might admit to having studied it or to thinking of human activities as patterns of a loosely ordered kind while they are designing.

Certainly one could hazard a guess that much of what is being raised on the conceptual and metaphoric relation of the body to architecture is of far greater interest to theorists and occasionally to students than it is to most architects in practice. So myopically focused and densely written are many of these concerns that, far from presenting either a threat or a promise of revolution or significant change in the profession, they are consigned by the bulk of architects to the margins of art, philosophy, and theory as indulgent effusions by the few. If pressed, most architects would admit architecture as concerned with people, but as part of a broad-brush humanism based in their ad-hoc assimilation of social and behavioral research findings and their own experience rather than as the core of a finely tuned and critical humanism based in poststructuralist philosophy, cultural theory, or comparative literature. For most architects, architecture remains a pragmatic affair that still combines aspects of art and science ('artful science') in the service of 'the people' who become, however ill-defined, the measure of the success or failure of what they do.

This commentary on architects may seem somewhat glum, and a few celebrities may be moved to respond with cries of "Jeremiah," but the bottom line is that for many architects, architecture is being increasingly marginalized and they are fearful of letting go the human concerns that some might label 'primitive' (but that for them are fundamental) until they can see the profession once more affirmed as important to society and culture. The point at issue is whether attention to *anthropos* of the kind with which current theoretical writing is fascinated will reposition the discipline or is way off. It just may be that there is another equally enthralling humanist agenda, one more widely accessible to both the profession and the public, that can reinculcate an architecture of deep public engagement.

This quest is one message of the collection of essays in *Out of Site: A Social Criticism of Architecture* (Ghirardo 1991) and of the blurbs on its rear cover, which speak of current writing as "the thick cocoon of self-referential discourse that has made architecture little more than a private advertisement for itself" (Ed Soja) instead of exploring "that which has been so neglected in contemporary architectural culture—the *social*" (Mary McLeod). It also seems to be the message of many feminist architectural writers once the grievance element, at present necessary to redress past injustices, is removed. It may take another generation for this to become clear, at least in the sense that, as studies appear to be showing, feminine inclination would appear to be toward cooperative effort, whereas competition usually dominates masculine affiliations or movements.

The questions Robert McAnulty raises above are highly pertinent, because the issues they tap have been obscured by recent discourse. The archaeology of some current writing that rakes over past humanistic attitudes for things missed or overlooked, or questions assumptions that have been made, particularly in gender-related issues, suggests that *anthropos* is not being ignored but is undergoing a revival. We have not yet lost human affairs as the standard of architecture, but may be seeing instead a renewal of human considerations, with a different emphasis. Marco Frascari (1991) is certainly projecting such a scenario; he writes of a potentially new 'corporeality' of architecture as the "metonymic relations between built and human bodies" and as "the reconciliation between the art of living well and the art of constructing well" (4). Obviously he does not mean seventies comfort and fit revisited, but something more deeply subjective, something that unites the visceral with "the objects proper to architecture resulting from a knowledge internal to architecture concerning human nature and its way of organizing time, space, and artifacts in a place" (5).

There is another form of relation between self and architecture involving the autonomy of human conceptions of the self and the necessary role of architecture as a human prop characterized by Jacques Lacan and discussed by Ingraham (1991). This view is that from the time a child experiences and recognizes his or her image in a mirror, that event "returns the image of the self to the self as image," and the separation and alienation of that event continues to consolidate a relationship between the self and the world in which the world (architecture) shapes the self as image rather than the self filtering and controlling the world. In this application of Lacan, the transaction between space (architecture) and self is one of image-in-space rather than body-in-space or, more complexly, of space modifying the image of our bodies in space. In this psychoanalytic sense, Winston Churchill was right in saying that our buildings 'shape us' (chapter 7).

Faced with a Lacanian mirror-space theory requiring architectural props or with Frascari's new corporeality, what human measures might be applied to architecture? Centricity will no doubt still be prominent. But are we likely to witness an anthroposophical emphasis on individual spiritual growth through sensory connection, imagination, inspiration, and intuition, replacing the mere shift to a feminine anthropocentrism contemplated at present? If such an anthroposophical shift were to be confirmed, it would seem that individual spiritual growth might mean judging architecture against agreed but revitalized human standards. Or perhaps a radical spiritual individualism might emerge, embracing the paradox that this entails, which accepted the autonomy of individual architectural expression and experiment without the imperative to justify or the pressure to conform. What, then, of the critical reading of architecture and the discourse that ensues—can it be any more than bonus mileage?

FURTHER SOURCES   Broadbent 1973; Chermayeff and Alexander 1963; Guénon 1953; James 1981; Lawlor 1982; Papanek 1972.

3. Geometry: Lord of the Invisible

. . . it must, I think, be admitted that the objects of that [geometric] knowledge are eternal and not liable to change and decay. **Plato.** *The Republic*:527.

. . . Plato put above the entrance to his Academy a sign that Mies might have placed above all his entrances: 'Nobody Untrained in Geometry May Enter My House'. **Charles Jencks.** 1973:105.

Space is a necessary apriori representation, which underlies all outer intuitions. . . . The apodeictic certainty of all geometric propositions, and the possibility of their apriori construction, is grounded in this apriori necessity of space. **Immanuel Kant.** *A Critique of Pure Reason.* Cited in Flew 1971:424.

Geometry is a science which determines the properties of space synthetically, and yet apriori. **Immanuel Kant.** *A Critique of Pure Reason.* Cited in Flew 1971:422.

[After the Renaissance] the role of geometry in the design process is gradually transformed from that of mirroring the secret map of the "Celestial City" to that of creating the concrete reality of a "Pleasing Object." **Alexander Tzonis** 1972:49 paraphrasing Robert Morris's *Lecture in Architecture.*

Geometry is the foundation. . . . It is also the material basis on which we build those symbols which represent to us perfection and the divine. **Le Corbusier.** 1929. *The City of Tomorrow.* English translation by Etchells of *Urbanisme,* 1925. Cited in Agrest 1991:64.

. . . geometry is a realm of eternal (everlasting) truths, contrasting most favourably with the merely ephemeral truths of everyday life and science. **Anthony Flew.** 1971:249.

TRACE   Stemming from the Greek *geometres,* geometrician, surveyor and literally 'earth measurer', the term 'geometry' is of great antiquity and is used to describe any proportional system or positional manipulation on a surface or in space. Beginning as an empirical skill, the Greeks systematized this *demonstrative* geometry and Pythagoras developed axioms as the basis for geometric logic and conclusions eventually summarized by Euclid. Conics and various curved figures were subsequently investigated but there were no great advances until the seventeenth century, when René Descartes combined geometry with algebra to produce *analytic* geometry. Non-Euclidean or Riemannean geometry overturned certain key geometric axioms and showed them as arbitrary conveniences (thereby paving the way for Einstein to formulate his Theory of Relativity), although it differs significantly from Euclidean geometry only at vast scales. Recently, *fractal* geometry, wherein the degree of irregularity of natural patterns remains constant over differing scales, has been hailed as the key to creating semblances of complex wholes, which some traditional Eastern geometers find unsurprising.

Stereometry, or solid geometry, and *stereotomy,* the sectioning of solids, are of most direct concern to architects. However, most architects have only a rudimentary understanding of geometry and design using more or less straightforward permutations on regular polygons and the circle, or occasionally more complex curves such as the ellipse, parabola, catenary, and spiral. At the risk of over-simplification, for more than two millennia basilica, domed and vaulted structures, have been generated principally by the projection or rotation of three primary planar figures—circle, rectangle, triangle—although boat builders have used more complicated curved geometries that have influenced vernacular roof structures. Membrane and cable forms have existed since antiquity and were used to shade (*velaria*) and roof Roman amphitheaters and theaters, but their mathematics was largely heuristic until the nineteenth century, when surface geometry was investigated and understood. This, combined with advances in material science and technology, has enabled the shell, geodetic, and membrane structures familiar today. The two great medieval planar geometric systems were *ad triangulum*, based on the equilateral triangle, and *ad quadratum*, based on the square. Among architectural writers, Joseph Gwilt (1867) defined geometry as "that science which treats of the relations and properties of the boundaries of either body or space" (§874).

COMMENTARY   Geometry has traditionally been a matter of finding the *unchanging* quality of a spatial relationship, the rule under which it operates. The mathematician Hermann Weyl (1952:130) calls geometry "the science dealing with the relation of congruence between spatial figures" and later says, paraphrasing the German mathematician Felix Klein, "A geometry . . . is defined by a group of transformations, and investigates everything that is invariant under the transformations of this given group" (133). While geometry remains an empirical science in architecture, assisting the resolution of space, isolation of the invariant is the interpretive aspect of the order geometry brings to bear on spatial relationships.

For example, the geometry of a triangle is not the specific triangle being considered, or so it would be argued by a Platonic idealist, but is the geometry of the *triangle of triangles,* the 'triangularity' in which all triangles participate, the rules or axioms of triangles. This supposed universal invariance of the triangle is its order as a symbol, and as a structuring device, the quality that makes triangularity or orthogonality the basis for a grid or system of proportion. The precision of geometry was only a relative fact in the practical world, though, for the medieval mason presumed it to reflect the truths of the 'invisible college'. "The most compelling reason for the use of geometry, particularly in sacred structures, was nowhere mentioned by Euclid. It was to give the structure significance," writes John James of Chartres Cathedral (1981:549), each master having his own private system and refusing to alter it even in the light of other masters. "It is as if there was no final arbiter or ultimate root from which the geometry sprang, but as if each master had evolved his own from his private communion with the Almighty."

The invariance of geometry has been utilized, along with number, since antiquity by all cultures in the service of cosmology, philosophy, and architecture to denote truths about the universe, the three principal symmetrical figures of circle, square, and equilateral triangle being most frequently employed. It is significant that, of these three primary planar figures, the Pythagoreans "always considered the equilateral triangle as the basic design of all created matter" (Doxiadis 1972:16), and the medieval masons considered it the basis of the more spiritual parts of cathedrals. It is noteworthy, too, that triangulation is the principal method of precise navigation and surveying. Also, the fascination for triads in religion and philosophy has been so long-standing and tyrannical a pursuit that it still inhabits much modern-day thinking and occasionally haunts the very text you are now reading.

However, the metaphoric processes of assigning truth-statements to geometrical figures and relationships by the ancients are principally *abductive*—a term coined by the American semiotician and linguist (and one-time surveyor) Charles Sanders Peirce for the human logical process of hunches, guesses, and creative formulation (see also 6B.3, Method), and a form of syllogistic reasoning in which the middle term does not warrant the third (Eco and Sebeok 1983)—and are inherently imprecise. Of course, the precision of deductive reasoning and geometric axioms has so colored our thinking that the *-ularity* of the triangle or any other geometric figure is equated with the *-ness* of other notions in what are seemingly natural synonymous relationships. Yet because of their abductive reasoning, the suffixes lack precision (as do all metaphysical notions) by their lack of extension (that is, spatially), and they are hypothetical and imprecise by their very intension (that is, comprehension—see Flew 1979; Arnauld 1964).

The equation of geometrical with architectural figures, too, is only what we choose to make of it, which means that analyses like that of Clark and Pause (1985) need to be treated with some care, as they are not categorical. A designer might admit to a geometrical underpinning in a design, but will also say that the outcome is as much a product of deviations from it as of compliance with it. In the absence of a highly wrought cosmological geometric tradition in almost all Western architecture, analyses ascribing precise geometries have no way of determining the invariant other than by appearances; precision *per se* is not enough, no matter how satisfying it may be to the analyst. For instance, merely showing the full circle, square, and diamond of John Hejduk's *1/2 House* (Clark and Pause 1985:191) without also showing that the three shapes are dimensionally equal or explaining how the halves are related in the plan, or showing the Sydney Opera House as a collection of shells based in circles and not as they actually were, based in spheres (191, 210), is only a very elementary description, not an explanation, of their geometry (compare Hejduk 1985:Frame 4; and M. Smith 1984).

Thus, there cannot be declarations of, say, universal principles of triangularity capable of the precision of geometric axioms, because triangularity is a quality guessed (abducted) about triangles. Axioms apply *only* to classes (and even then with considerable difficulty), and not to finer discriminations between things. So the question remains as to what the undisputed truth might be that makes a doberman a doberman (doberman-ness) and not a Pekingese, while both are admitted to be dogs. A show judge would say the distinction is obvious (self-evident, axiomatic) and would further maintain that there are dobermans and dobermans. A prizewinning doberman is one that more closely aligns with the 'true doberman', and selecting the champion of champions requires ever finer discriminations among prizewinning dobermans.

The apparent linearity (extension) of such a discriminating process is directly attributable to both deductive and axiomatic geometric thought in that 'at the end' lies (or sits) the perfect, unchangeable, and androgynous doberman, as would the ideal anything at the end of any similar line of reasoning. Another view is that there is no end, merely an indefinite extrapolation of refinements that are brought to an 'end' only because to continue serves no practical purpose. It would seem either that axioms apply across all levels of discrimination and are therefore indefinite in number, such that ultimately the axiomatic truth of anything becomes what discriminates, *not* what unites; or that there are no axioms at all, which seems untenable, for there *must* be some certainty to axioms for them to have survived as axioms. One way around this dilemma is to say that the truth of anything is in its very existence, or to say that axioms as self-evident truths are *for the moment* true, but may change later.

The indefinite regress of discriminating axioms is one burden of the persistence and elusive precision of geometry in discourse that underlies all notions of origin or precedence, so much so that it is too much of a load for any originary argument to bear. Which is the point of Jacques Derrida's criticisms of Western philosophy—that it is 'always already' in whatever state it seeks to rationalize—and the thrust of the introduction to his 1989 edition of Edmund Husserl's *Origin of Geometry* (Lincoln, University of Nebraska Press) in which Derrida attempts to show that Husserl cannot escape the already existing 'geometry' of the origin he seeks. The pursuit of geometric ideals through 'lines' of reasoning, of 'extensions' of discrimination, and of 'rules' that mete out and demand alignment, together with the very ephemerality of the line in architectural representation and geometry, is also what Catherine Ingraham calls 'the burden of linearity' dogging the footsteps of architecture (Ingraham 1991).

Since geometry is the means by which architects bring their concepts into being, it is as well to understand that in architecture there are two aspects that need further clarification: the *corpus,* or *sui generis* (self-regulating qualities of the work or task), and the *modus* (mode), or *technic* (the way in which the corpus is expressed in relational terms). If students or architects say they are 'playing with geometry' in designing a building, they usually mean they are manipulating known geometrical shapes (mostly the circle or the regular polygons), and are talking about the modus, often without having fully understood or considered the corpus. In other words, they are superimposing on the work or task at hand, predetermined patterns or shapes that are fictitious, that may have nothing to do with the inherent qualities and demands of the work or task. What needs to be made absolutely clear is that *the manipulation of regular geometric figures for their own sake has nothing to do with geometry as a controlling device in architecture.* In other words, it is not a question of which geometric shape or shapes are best for fitting a building program into, but which shape or shapes best fit the geometry of that particular building program. That geometry will ideally be axiomatic. Welcome to the invisible college.

FURTHER SOURCES   Blackwell 1984; Etlin 1991, chapter 14; Guénon 1953,1958; Lawlor 1982; March and Steadman 1971; Pennick 1980; Snodgrass 1990.

4. *Scaling Architectural Mountains*

It may be a matter of encouragement . . . , though one also of regret, to observe how much oftener man destroys natural sublimity, than nature crushes human power. It does not need much to humiliate a mountain. A hut will sometimes do it. . . . A single villa will often mar a whole landscape, and dethrone a dynasty of hills. **John Ruskin.** 1855. "The Lamp of Power":IV.

. . . it is not to be supposed that mere size will ennoble a mean design, yet every increase of magnitude will bestow upon it a certain degree of nobleness: so that it is well to determine at first, whether the building is to be markedly beautiful, or markedly sublime; and if the latter, not to be withheld by respect to smaller parts from reaching largeness of scale; provided only that it be evidently in the architect's power to reach that degree of magnitude which is the lowest at which sublimity begins, rudely definable as that which will make a living figure look less than life beside it. **John Ruskin.** 1855. "The Lamp of Power":V.

Generally good scale in a building means a consistent relationship to the human figure through-out the design, but relationship to the environment is also important and in moving from inside to outside a subtle transition of scale has to be made. A 'great' architect reveals his quality in his handling of architectural scale. **Bruce Allsopp.** 1977:25.

TRACE   Latin *scala* (ladder), Greek the same and *klimax*, English *scale*, a graduated series or order, a graduated measure, a system or scheme of relative values or correspondences, ratio of representation to object, or relative extent. Rooted in the metaphor of a ladder and in the ancient use of 'scaling machines' (Vitruvius: *epibathra*, over + stepping) in siege, a scale in music 'ascends' or 'descends', while a scale for measurement repeats the look of a ladder in the repetition of a *radix*, or module.

The modern architectural term 'scale' as the quality of fitting to a setting is largely what the analysis of ancient Greek stereotomy and spatial arrangement by Doxiadis (1972) is concerned about, although he does not use the term. Neither is scale used in Vitruvius's *Ten Books*, although something like the notion is conveyed in his discussion of symmetry in relation to sites: "After the standard of symmetry has been determined, and the proportion-ate dimensions adjusted by calculations, it is next the part of wisdom to consider the nature of the site, or questions of use or beauty, *and modify the plan by diminutions or additions* [emphasis added] in such a manner that these diminutions or additions in the symmetrical relations may be seen to be made on correct principles, and without detracting at all from the effect" (6.2.1 and 6.3 on the cavaedium or atrium house). This rescaling of the whole or respacing of the parts for esthetic purposes was also done by the Greeks. The use of the term 'scale' in later architectural treatises has depended upon the translation of cognate terms. Alberti's use of *modus,* for instance, has been translated variously as size, disposition, and most recently as 'scale' by Rykwert, Leach, and Tavernor: "It is the function and duty of lineaments, then, to prescribe an appropriate place, exact numbers [*certum numerum*], a proper scale [*modum*], and a graceful order for whole buildings and for each of their constituent parts" (1.1), and ". . . although it is wrong to make either the width or the height of a wall greater or less than reason and scale [*modus*] demand." (1.10)." (Alberti 1755b).

COMMENTARY   It is obvious to say that scaling is the basis for proportion, just as it is obvious that scaling was employed in ancient times in the adjustment of the whole to the module or standard adopted for any building. The Greek for symmetry, according to Vitruvius, is *analogia,* the equality of ratios, and our use of analogy in turn reflects a geometric relationship between conceptual notions. Yet the notion of scale as an abstract and autonomous quality governing the size and placement of a building in its setting is not analogous; it is quite different from proportion or symmetry as they have ordinarily been used.

Doxiadis (1972) grounds his thesis in the pursuit of a 'traditional system' (vis-à-vis "the modern fashion which Hippodamus introduced") of site planning, to which Aristotle alludes in *The Politics* (7.11.1330b) as "the antiquated mode of building, which made it difficult for strangers to get out of a town and for assailants to find their way in." While Aristotle here emphasizes its defensive and strategic quality, he also implies that the 'antiquated mode' was arranged irregularly ("as farmers plant their vines in what are called 'clumps'") and related to beauty, hence Doxiadis's study. Doxiadis believes the traditional system to have been a radial positioning of buildings from a fixed point using ten-part (thirty-six degrees) or twelve-part (thirty degrees) divisioning of a circle, a system of massing that placed buildings and other urban artifacts so that they could be fully seen without interfering with one another; in other words an esthetic system wherein buildings as masses were *scaled* relative to one another and to the surrounding landform. The system was human, both in the position of the viewing point and in the *effect the composition had on the observer.* Such an approach to composition did not reappear until the picturesque landscape and painting movement of the eighteenth century and its descendent, the concern for townscape in the middle of the twentieth (Cullen 1961).

The human basis for measure in architecture was raised in 9A.1, Measure, and it is by the normal perceptual device of scaling that we relate to architecture. As a participant or observer, we comprehend the scale of a building by imagining being inside it or by comparing it with another person positioned in relation to the building. Constancy is the basis of all perceptions of distance and size, as any basic text on psychology will show, and is fundamental to our comprehension of architecture. If people exclaim that a high-rise building or a stadium is 'out of scale', they usually mean they are overwhelmed by it, a natural reaction if it is realized that each is geared secondarily to human scale and primarily to the scale of hundreds, or thousands of people. The recognition that scale is also a hierarchical concept is one reason for the incredible recessional portals and other compositional devices of the Gothic cathedral façades needed to map the nearly human-sized doors to the vast bulk of the building, and why the classical portico is needed to mediate an otherwise insignificant human entrance to a large building.

The key to the architectural meaning of scale takes the idea of a ladder or stair from which the term derives, and uses it to 'reach someplace' from the human being. This analogy adopts the perceptual rationale of utilizing elements familiar (and constant) to human use, such as windows and doors, as 'steps' to effect the connection between person and building, thereby enabling the building to be 'conquered' (Antoniades 1986:53). In this view, scale always depends on the human being as the standard. "In contrast to 'proportion', which designates the interrelations of physical dimensions, 'scale' designates the 'real' size. The real size obviously has to be measured relative to a dimension of comparison, such as the meter or the human figure. 'Scale', therefore, is usually employed to designate the relationship of the sizes of a building to man himself. As buildings serve human actions, any building task will prescribe a particular scale." (Norberg-Schulz 1965:103)

Crucial though the human perception issue might be, it is the 'symmetry' of a building with its setting that is at the heart of *fit* in modern planning and architecture—the recognition of a hierarchy of scales and the placement of a building within that hierarchy. Whereas the Vitruvian notion of symmetry stemming from a module dictates the overall composition of a building, the modern notion of fit is a challenge to distill the appropriate module or standard from the whole and then incorporate it into the architecture. The hierarchy of an urban setting, though, is nowhere near the orderly affair of a classical canon. It is crude by comparison and quite variable, not to say subjective. The zone of major contention is always the point at which the skyscraper meets older buildings near the ground. The only way to reconcile a mass of Victorian buildings (such as terrace houses) with a modern setback tower is either with a podium or by ignoring the conflict. Another zone of contention is the point at which a major site consolidation with its efficiencies and concentration of entrance meets small land holdings with their multiple street crossing and entrances. Yet another zone is commercial development meeting residential, or medium-rise meeting low-rise residential in either urban or suburban settings.

Moore and Allen (1976:17–24) discern four main possibilities as the basic measure for scale: relation to the whole, to other parts, to usual size, and to human size. They also point out that scale has important conditional aspects such as expected or familiar use, proximity of the compared objects, and shape factors, and suggest that scale is mostly a complex choreography of these possibilities that enables both order and surprise to intersect and engages the observer in a dialogue. The choice of relativities may be resolved, they suggest, by asking "What relationships do you care to call attention to?" But they address these concerns mainly to single buildings, not to settings.

Scale can have emotional and perhaps even 'spiritual' connotations. Reactions may be evoked through the conscious manipulation of scalar effects inducing sublimity, humility, modesty, arrogance, "et cetera," paraphrasing Antoniades (1986). It is not clear just what the *et cetera* is, except that it heads in a direction opposite to that of human scale; sheer size is the core of the romantic preoccupation with the sublime, whether in nature or in built form, the suppression of life to insignificance by magnitude. Magnitude is the principal element of the monumental architecture of politically dominant regimes as much as it is the domination by commercial enterprise represented in unbuilt and built skyscraper projects from the 1930s onward (see Van Leeuwen 1988). The main and not surprising ingredients of monumentality are "spatial amplitude and grand dimensions," employed as measures of the prestige, dignity, power, or authority of empires. But the most potent is height: "Verticalism, symbolising the ambition to conquer static compatibilities, is a factor in monumentality because it dehumanises proportions, breaking the anthropomorphic equilibrium of Renaissance Classicism. . . . 'Never too high' is an assertion of violence, a reconquest of freedom, an ambition to exceed a subconscious limit . . . an affirmation of the 'modern' as an open work, breaking away from historical equilibrium" (Borsi 1987:91).

But breaking away architecturally comes at a cost, for it knows no language, even fifty years later. In his magnificent drawn projects, the eighteenth century French architect Etienne-Louis Boullée showed a monumentality that has been matched in real life only a few times before and since. The lesson of Boullée's inventions is that they showed that a hierarchy of scale and a symmetry between the parts and the whole and with the human figure was neither strict nor necessary, and that a rather Gothic approach to scale can work. Boullée foreshadowed the architectural issues of composition in the skyscraper and other modern day vastnesses, if not the more fine-grained issues of the shifts of scale within a setting.

Shifts of scale bring with them problems of their own, though, as Heath (1991:49) has noted: "proportions, textures, and colours, relationships of all kinds, which will work at one size and distance, will not work at a significantly different size and distance, a fact pointed out at some length by Vitruvius." Heath notes especially that "the key modern aesthetic invention of 'elementarism', the conception of buildings as arrangements of elements in space, cannot be made to work above certain quite modest dimensions; large buildings are essentially solid, not spatial, though they may contain such arrangements." And it remains a perennial challenge for architects to devise ways to successfully reconcile the shifts of scale in form and space; just as it remains a challenge to perhaps pursue the potential that the Gothic tradition offers for ad-hoc scaling, so thoroughly overlooked in the plethora of literature on rational classicism, both Renaissance and modern. The hills are alive with the sound of Ruskin!

FURTHER SOURCES   Allsopp 1977; Brolin 1980; de Ménil 1968; Tyng 1975.

5. Number as an Absolute Quality

. . . those who are to hold positions of responsibility in our state . . . [are] to pursue [arithmetic] till they come to understand, by pure thought, the nature of numbers—they aren't concerned with its usefulness for mere commercial calculation, but for war and for the easier conversion of the soul from the world of becoming to that of reality and truth. **Plato.** *The Republic*:525.

. . . it was from the members of the body that they derived the fundamental ideas of the measures which are obviously necessary in all works, as the finger, palm, foot, and cubit. These they apportioned so as to form the "perfect number," called in Greek *teleion,* and as the perfect number the ancients fixed upon ten. For it is from the number of the fingers of the hand that the palm is found, and the foot from the palm. Again, while ten is naturally perfect, as being made up by the fingers of the two palms, Plato also held that this number was perfect because ten is composed of individual units, called by the Greeks *monades.* **Vitruvius.** 1486:3.1.5.

One must study the activities and essence of Number in accordance with the power existing in the Decad; for it is great, complete, all-achieving, and the origin of divine and human life and its Leader; it shares . . . the power also of the Decad. Without this, all things are unlimited, obscure and indiscernible. **Philolaos.** Cited in Doxiadis 1972:17–18.

As with form, so with number: we have lost much of our sensitivity to the meanings of numbers because our education accustoms us to regard number as simply an expression of relative quantity. Yet the meanings for the first four numbers represent truths so profound that there is not a culture or tribe that has not understood them in a similar way. **John James.** 1987:55.

TRACE   Pollitt (1974) discusses the Latin *numerosus, numerus* as having two basic meanings: literally "manifold, numerous, prolific," and stylistically "rhythmical, measured." He connects the Latin to the Greek terms *arithmos* ('number' or 'quantity') and *rythmos* ('form', 'shape', or 'pattern') which act as delimiters; that is, "*rythmos* limited space so as to produce form, while *arithmos* limited infinity so as to produce specific quantity. . . . All the arts were limited in this way. . . . In the visual arts *rythmoi* were shapes. These shapes were related to numbers in that they were characterized by a particular number of bounding points [and] . . . were also characterized by proportions . . . which were in turn expressible by number."

In Pythagorean doctrine numbers are both qualitative (formal and principial) and quantitative (corporeal expressions of form and principle). Traditionally also, there are three categories of number (four, if we include the ineffable monad, but see below)—pure or *divine,* concerning the metaphysical; *epistemological,* concerning the ontological; and *quantitative,* concerning the existential degrees of Being. Unity (Latin *unus,* one) as the principle of all numbers and the reconciliation of all differentiation is not considered a number, so the duad is unmanifest substance and the triad unmanifest essence, their combination accounting for all manifestation. In this schema there are only four generative numbers. One represents point (Being, intellect, *nous,* arithmetic), and the remaining numbers represent the various stages of Becoming: two represents line (archetype, science, *episteme,* music), three represents plane (prototype, opinion, *doxa,* geometry), and four represents volume (stereotype, sensation, *aesthesis,* astronomy) (Tawa 1991:63ff).

These four numbers, if added, form the decad to which Vitruvius and Philolaos refer. When arranged as points in numerical order they form the sacred triangular *tetractys,* an emblem of "the orderly genesis and divine pattern of the universe" (Pollitt 1974:18). Pollitt suggests that Vitruvius's term 'perfect number' (Latin *perfectum numerum*), in the quotation above, "is perhaps best understood not only as an abstract numerical quantity but also as a shape, a *rythmos* . . . [and that] possibly all *rythmoi* had similar numerical counterparts" (19; see also 411–415). A mystical Hebrew scriptural exegetical system, *gematria,* in which letters may be substituted for numbers, is said to hold the key to so-called 'ancient wisdom' (Bond and Lea 1917; Stirling 1897). Gematria was used in laying out Gothic cathedrals (James *et al.* 1987:71) as well as early Australian towns (Johnson 1990). In architecture, number symbolism emanated from the group of artists around the American photographer Alfred Stieglitz, who founded the Photo Secession in 1902 and whose gallery '291' in New York became a center for avant-garde artists just after the turn of the twentieth century.

COMMENTARY   Review the history of architecture, and number features prominently, especially in the proliferation of classical canons that sought to instill number as the key to the lock of manifestation in the door to the universe. This fixity of number belongs to what is called the *coherence theory* of truth so beloved by idealists, for whom the whole dominates and all numbers are considered for the way they inform the holistic view. As was made clear in chapter 2B, the whole, and its concomitants of idea and form, are concepts favored by architects, although for some people they are remnants of a now-discredited Platonic idealism (Whiteman in Marvel 1986; see 4B.2, Vision).

Auspices and augers were important to ancient cultures and were part of architectural and town-planning lore (Rykwert 1976). They are very much a part of certain traditional societies and spiritual communities today, a matter that comes to the fore if long-held cultural beliefs and mores confront the rational and 'scientific' forces of the world, which treat them as mere superstition. The acute political conflicts that arose in recent years over Native Australian land rights in relation to claims by both government and private enterprise for mineral leases revolved around misunderstandings of the cosmological and spiritual significance of sacred sites to tribal aborigines; the experience was similar for

Native Americans. Though we may not now employ the *haruspex,* or liver-diviner, to inspect the entrails of animal sacrifices as was the ancient Roman practice, we still enjoy certain 'superstitions', many of which involve numbers. Witness the faith ordinary people across many modern cultures place in the propitiatory power of numbers, or equally the fear that certain numbers engender.

The numerical prophecies of Nostradamus, the daily astrology columns, the fascination with the coming millennium; the numerical symbolism interpreted in vehicle license plates, telephone numbers, house numbers, and building floors; the superstition about 13, and Friday the 13th; fear of 666 (Beast of the Apocalypse); and the psychical investment in 'good luck' numbers or in systems of numeration in gambling, all testify to the prominent place numbers occupy in the minds of many today. Given this widespread popular interest and other circumstantial evidence of more esoteric significance attaching to number such as scriptural exegesis by gematria—26 (JHVH, Jahweh or Jehovah), 153 (Icthys, the fish, a longstanding Christian symbol), 284 (Theos), 600 (Kosmos), 729 (Kephas, the name given by Christ to Peter, and 9 cubed), 841 (AMΩ, the beginning, middle, and end of Creation), 888 (Jesus), 150 (Phos or Light), and so on (Bond and Lea 1917)—and the simple monad, duad, and triad and their extensions significant in traditional science, one may be reasonably certain that there are architects too who perceive certain qualities in number and see benefit in incorporating such symbolism in their architecture. For instance, in Chartres Cathedral, the numbers 241 (*Beata Virgo Maria Assumpta,* and also the dedication of the cathedral) and 354 (*Regina Coelis,* the Queen of the Sky) form the basis for the geometry of the cathedral's layout, and position the labyrinth and the center of the apse (James 1987:70–71).

The living Chinese geomantic tradition of *feng shui* holds that certain numbers are inviolate and essential to the well-being of the inhabitants of a building or city. Temples are measured and built strictly according to the number calculations of geomancers. The numbers 1 and 9, beginning and 'fullness', are the most auspicious numbers for the Chinese, strings of numbers, dates and so on being totaled to see if they sum to nine for 'long life'. Homonyms add a special significance to numbers, those ending in four being reacted against because in Cantonese four sounds like 'die'; Chinese buyers especially avoid 424 because it sounds like 'die and die again' (Rossbach 1983:Appendix 3). As a homonym for 'rich', eight and its multiples signify wealth to the Chinese also, as the million-dollar cost of a license plate having the number 8888 in Singapore testifies. There are also good and bad dimensions based on certain ranges determined by the eight divisions of the geomancer's rule and additions of multiples of its forty-three centimeter length, by which the dimensions of a building may be checked in *feng shui* divination (Lip 1979:38–39).

The American architect, theosophist, and writer Claude Bragdon (1866–1946) promoted the symbolism of number. Bragdon was a great admirer and friend of Louis Sullivan (Twombly 1986). He began his lecturing career in 1901 with an address to the Architectural League of America entitled "Mysticism and Architecture," and wrote sixteen books on architecture, theosophy, and ornament (Placzek 1982). "Although architecture is based primarily on geometry," he wrote in *The Beautiful Necessity* in 1910, "it is possible to express all spatial relations numerically: for arithmetic, not geometry, is the universal science of quantity." Bragdon presents a more or less traditional Pythagorean interpretation of the symbolism of the monad, duad, and triad, their human and geometric connotations, as well as the mystical number seven ('man's sevenfold nature' and 'a number of singular beauty and perfection'), his book being divided into seven chapters. In chapter 6 he discusses what he calls 'numerical conjunctions', the import of certain number multiples (such as 12) for the series they entail, really no more than a straightforward factorial exercise, although he insists that to think of these conjunctions in this way "is to miss a sense of the wonder, beauty and rhythm of it all ... number concrete in time and space." He argues for a certain naturalness of number in architecture by attempting to show the recurrence of such conjunctions through a highly selective series of façade illustrations that largely prove whatever you want them to.

While it may be accurate to say that architects in the later twentieth century no longer place much store by the mystical or symbolic qualities of number—at least not in traditional terms and not publicly—it is possible that numerical symbolism is still incorporated in certain works. This is difficult to demonstrate because there is rarely any obvious indication in drawing or text that numbers are playing any formal part in a design. There are, however, occasions on which certain buildings lend themselves to such symbolism; Australia's Parliament House in Canberra by architects Mitchell/Giurgola and Thorp, appears to be a case in point. Walter Burley Griffin based his design for Canberra on the triangle because it symbolized for him the three principles of democracy—Liberty, Fraternity, and Equality—apart from other connections that the triangle enabled for this particular site (Muller 1976). Griffin was an anthroposophist and can be at least ideologically aligned with some of the views expressed by Bragdon.

Romaldo Giurgola said in an interview once that he believed a building should have a resonance with the past, that it should establish a continuity not only with its architectural past but with the history of the city and with both the urban and natural orders. "The city develops an order of its own . . . ," declared Giurgola to Barbaralee Diamonstein, "it's difficult to disrupt that order; it can only evolve and change. When you build, you have to be very concerned with this urban order and at the same time concerned with the natural, geological order, the configuration of the land" (Diamonstein 1985:106). Of Mitchell/Giurgola and Thorp's winning competition design for Australia's Parliament House, he remarked, "It's a place of work and debate for the whole nation. In that, it's a pure architectural problem. . . . In principle we followed that plan [Griffin's] very closely and the form itself resolved a certain condition of the geometry of the city. It's a project that completes, three-dimensionally, certain ideas that were set in the original plan for Canberra—the axis of the land and the lake and, finally, the culmination of a triangle at that particular point" (109).

In the arrangement of Australia's Parliament House it is possible to interpret Pythagorean number symbolism of the kind Bragdon maintains in many places: the unity (point) of the flag and pyramidal flagstaff as the *axis mundi* dominating the whole; the duality (line) of debate in the opposing 'views' of the two curved walls and the bicameral system of government in the Senate and House chambers (not in itself unique, for it applied also to the American Capitol and the British Houses of Parliament); the triplicity (plane) of the embrace with Griffin's triangular axes and democratic principles, the planimetric public sequence from Portico to Foyer to Great Hall, the planimetric parliamentary sequence of Senate and House to Members' Hall, the double three-way planimetric spatial sequences of these as 'rooms', the three transitions between Portico and Members' Hall, and the compositional triplets that abound in many detailed aspects; and the fourfold (volume) division of the building into quadrants, the fourfold people-gathering spaces, the quadrilateral 'grid' of subsidiary circulation, the quadrangular internal spaces, the cubic Members' Hall; and, finally, the return to unity in the pyramid of the flagstaff (for explanatory diagrams of Parliament House, see Beck 1988). While unconfirmed, given Romaldo Giurgola's own architectural inclinations and his respect for the order of Griffin's plan, it comes as no surprise that number symbolism of the kind suggested appears to underlay the design.

The question is whether such number symbolism makes any difference, whether an architecture resulting from this conceptual integration is more 'architecture' than one without. There is a lot to be gained from interrogating a building such as Australia's Parliament House, and apparent metaphoric numerical relationships are intellectually satisfying, but is the architecture better for that? If it is, does architecture comprise the 'surpluses' that this building has over others or, from the traditional perspective, must all architecture have this quality as its conceptual base to be architecture at all? What of those buildings that do not have the potential for this kind of number symbolism, or for any symbolism inherently? Or is this a non sequitur because buildings always have this potential and architecture is a matter of mind over matter?

FURTHER SOURCES   Ashe 1977; Beck 1988; Etlin 1991, chapter 14; James 1987; Snodgrass 1990.

6. *Proportion and Its Well-Shaped Bases*

There is nothing to which an architect should devote more thought than to the exact proportions of his building with reference to a certain part selected as the standard. **Vitruvius.** 1486:6.2.1.

However free the composition of a façade may be, its proportions are never arbitrary. Of all variations possible for an elevation there is only one which is right for a given length. **Marc-Antoine Laugier.** 1753:62.

Just as in music, where deep voices answer high ones, and intermediate ones are pitched between them, so they ring out in harmony, a wonderfully sonorous balance of proportions results . . . so it happens in everything else that serves to enchant and move the mind. **Leon Battista Alberti.** 1755b:1.9.

Proportion is a principle, not of architecture, but of existence. It is by the laws of proportion that stars shine, that mountains stand, and rivers flow . . . the assertion that "architecture is *par excellence* the art of proportion," could never be made except by persons who know nothing of art in general; and, in fact, never *is* made except by those architects, who, not being artists, fancy that the one poor aesthetic principle of which they *are* cognizant is the whole of the art. **John Ruskin.** 1854. Addenda:s63.

Scale is a "dialogue" between human and object, while *proportions* denotes only a dry concept of physical relationships between the parts of a building. In a strictly architectural sense, the concepts of proportions represents a geometric concept that results from the comparison of physical (linear) dimensions. **Anthony C. Antoniades.** 1986:62.

What we have noticed is that the rules of proportion are *a posteriori:* they derive, not from the meaning of the term, but from some discovered criterion for its application. They do not tell us what proportion essentially *is,* but only give laws for its production, laws which hold at best only approximately and from certain points of view. **Roger Scruton.** 1979:66.

TRACE   Appearing in English from the fourteenth century, the word is adopted from the Latin *proportio,* analogy. The Greek *ana logia* was translated by Cicero to the Latin *pro portione,* hence linking proportion and analogue, analogy, similarity, resemblance, and agreement. Used as the relation existing between things or magnitudes as to the size, quantity, or number, it is the quantitative that is uppermost (but see below). The idea of *due* proportion is associated with the application of rule, especially if harmony or some kind of appropriateness is seen as a result of the relation.

In architecture, proportion is "a correspondence among the measures of the members of an entire work, and of the whole to a certain part selected as standard" (Vitruvius 1486:3.1.1). A more succinct definition is hard to find, though the fundamental principle for Vitruvius was *eurythmia,* eurythmy being "beauty and fitness in the adjustments of its members" (1.2.3), or the quality of being 'well-shaped', that is, intervention by alteration and adjustment to rhythm to subjectively satisfy eurythmy (Pollitt 1974:180). This subjective correspondence was given a special name by Alberti: "proportion comes from *concinnitas:* that is, the successful combination of number, measure, and form (*numerus, finitio,* and *collocatio*)" and for Alberti the task of *concinnitas* is "to compose parts that are quite separate from each other by their nature, according to some precise rule, so that they correspond to one another in appearance" Rykwert, Leach, and Tavernor (1991). Starting with neo-Platonic philosophy and its flowering at Chartres during the Middle Ages and continuing throughout the Renaissance, proportion was thought to participate in the realm of the divine if, as a mathematical system, it was observed in nature and in the human body.

COMMENTARY   Remove proportion from architectural consideration and what remains? Traditional architectural thinking would have it that harmony is lost and replaced by a disharmony akin to chaos, and that consequently beauty is an impossibility. Proportion has been entrenched in architecture for so long that it has come as a shock to find that if proportionate ratios of the traditional kind are ignored, nothing nasty happens. A composition in which free reign is given to the meshing of parts, especially in the ad-hoc way that characterizes the work of Frank Gehry, the completed work still has esthetic appeal. It would seem that proportion, while related to the quality Alberti called *concinnitas,* the "spouse of the soul and of reason" and what we might call elegance, accord, polish, is not *necessarily* an essential ingredient for a quality architecture. In other words, proportion is but one means of achieving a convincing elegance and accord between elements; we recognize other ways and through their acknowledgement we embrace works that might otherwise be discounted. Far from being precise and predictable, as Alberti would have us believe in describing it as "the absolute and fundamental rule in Nature," *concinnitas* is difficult to pin down, admits of no discernible rule or law, and yet we know it when we see it. Which is why Rykwert, Leach, and Tavernor wisely give it Latin autonomy in their translation.

One explanation for its elusiveness is that *concinnitas* is used in a moral connotation of right behavior that Scruton (1979:230) thinks derives from Cicero's *Orator,* "where it denotes a kind of sweetness and persuasiveness of sound, and used it in several early [literary] works, in particular in the *Della Famiglia,* to refer to the harmony and grace intrinsic to civilized behaviour. It is this moral significance that Alberti sought to transfer to the aesthetic sphere." For Scruton the Albertian origin relates to what is 'due' in 'due proportion', a quality that speaks of the value of proportion and of the effects it engenders, but not of proportion *per se*. Indeed, Scruton deliberately avoids attempting to define words such as 'proportion' and 'beauty', preferring instead to try "to dispense with the notion of an 'aesthetic' term, and to expound aesthetic judgement by exploring the state of mind, and the mode of reasoning, in which it is based." He issues a warning "to beware of providing definitions and analyses, when the form of judgement with which we are dealing has as its aim not theoretical knowledge but the transformation of experience" (234). The section on proportion in Scruton (58–70) is essential reading for his demonstration that any mathematical conception of proportion is unrelated to what proportion is, as his above comment about rules shows.

So, proportion is only one means to an esthetic end, and is not what it appears in its mathematical-geometrical expression; it is the feelings of rightness it engenders combined with an intellectual satisfaction arising from knowing that parts are consonant with one another and with the whole. Take away the knowing and it is arguable how or whether one would comprehend proportion or feel any of the effects it is supposed to induce. Take away knowledge of the mathematical limits to growth that analysts like Doczi (1981) and Thompson (1968) see operating in nature and it is arguable how or whether one would comprehend proportion or notice its effects in nature at all. Once it was assumed there were laws and rules of nature and the quest was made to understand them, it became impossible to dissociate the rules and laws from perceptions of proportion, accord and harmony in nature; proportion became tied to the knowing—indeed, it *was* and *is* the knowing. But it was and is a knowing of a highly selective kind based on the *well shaped man* (Vitruvius 1486:3.1.1).

The science of proportion arose through observing nature, according to Alberti, assignments of value to number in particular coming "from those objects in which Nature displayed some evident and noble quality." In his view, "our ancestors learned through observation," and having observed, they then declared that "Nature, as the perfect generator of forms, should be their model." But their observations, while convincing enough to make nature their model, were not sufficient because "with the utmost industry, they searched out the rules that she employed . . . and translated them into methods of building." They also studied "the patterns both for whole bodies and for their individual parts," and found "that at their very origins bodies do not consist of equal portions" (1755b:9.5).

To show the difficulty of ascertaining precisely what is beautiful in nature, Alberti chooses the example of men preferring various female 'proportions' (either slender, plump, buxom), noting "that we observe them to be infused with a quality through which, *however dissimilar they are* [emphasis added], we consider them equally graceful." However, he shirks from confronting the dissimilarities, saying "what it is that causes us to prefer one above all the others, I shall not inquire." So, while admitting a pervasive graceful quality that cuts across differences and informs preference but is too difficult to discuss, Alberti has no trouble in insisting that there are 'excellences' in Nature that are primarily proportional (which is why he advocates imitating nature) and that are capable of observation and measurement. The question is immediately begged as to how the particular proportions of male and female forms that were selected by the ancients as the basis for their classical proportions in columns, and so on, so excelled if their differences did not, of themselves, constitute sufficient reason to deny gracefulness. Obviously, there was no direct correlation with human forms; the proportions were totally arbitrary in their connection with nature and were, thus, purely metaphoric.

I am reminded of a colleague who taught architectural history and who spent every spare hour over many months searching the suburbs of Sydney to photograph a 'typical' Australian Federation Bungalow, one that exemplified the desirable attributes of that manner of building. He at last found one having enough of the qualities he was looking for and sufficiently excellent to serve as his example of the typical. No doubt many architectural historians have done the same, tried to obtain just the right photograph to illustrate similar exemplary qualities in whatever it is they are concerned with. Proportion is much the same; you may sort through and dismiss many examples before you find one that triggers just the right emotional and intellectual response, one that 'feels good'.

Moreover, Alberti's ineffable and invisible 'quality' that infuses dissimilarities is just such goodness of proportion, if proportional goodness is anything at all. The voluminous writings on the Golden Section, Proportion, Ratio, Mean, for example, show that it does not exist as a precise ratio in nature but is only an *approximation*. György Doczi (1981), for all his calculations, misses the point that ratios between numbers or linear dimensions are not the same as ratios between surface areas and volumes, that natural elements are three-dimensional not two, and that they do not begin as points and end in indefinitude but as smaller and larger finite and complete entities. Hence, there is a mismatch between what he draws and what he shows in photographs; the florets of the sunflower, for example, do not increase significantly in size from the center to the edge, even if their number and spacing does. The sunflower is an example of positioning with separation, not of incremental growth through contact, as human artifacts are. All the growth sequences Doczi shows are diagrammatic simplifications only; models and hypotheses, not actualities. He chooses to assimilate differences to his thesis as 'tendencies toward' the proportional systems he illustrates, not as meaningful 'differences from' them.

This criticism of natural proportioning systems throws into doubt all architectural proportioning that suggests it is something divine or natural; proportioning is no more than a human preoccupation, and to think of it as systemic avoids the crucial issues of beginning, end, and fracture. Natural systems of the kind Doczi explores or D'Arcy Thompson writes about in *On Growth and Form* (1968) are useless as a means for understanding proportion because their appeal is precise, rational, and explanatory rather than loose, experiential, and affective. Systemics may fit our sense of order and our intellectual sense of nicety, but in no way explain actual phenomena. Unhappily, architecture must be content, as it is in so many other ways, with geometric systems that merely *look like* the real thing, that merely seem natural but are not; because architecture is not, has never been, and never will be a natural system. Proportion will always remain a matter of choice between analogies, mostly of a highly ramified kind. The challenge in moving to analogies that have no classical, traditional, or natural equivalents just makes dimensioning more difficult to rationalize. Any proportioning that helps in more efficient decision-making about dimensions is worthwhile, even if as a private matter it remains inaccessible: the 'architecture' will take care of itself.

FURTHER SOURCES   Critchlow 1969, 1976; Etlin 1991, chapter 14; Lawlor 1982; Le Corbusier 1954,1958; Mitchell 1990; Padovan 1986; Snodgrass 1990; Tyng 1975.

B. Position and Distance

1. Relation and (De)position

Arrangement concerns the site and position of the parts . . .

Even when the smallest parts of a building are set in their proper place, they add charm; but when positioned somewhere strange, ignoble, or inappropriate, they will be devalued if elegant, ruined if they are anything else. Look at Nature's own works: for if a puppy had an ass's ear on its forehead . . . [it] would look deformed. **Leon Battista Alberti.** 1755b:9.7.

Outside and inside form a dialectic of division, the obvious geometry of which blinds us as soon as we bring it into play in metaphorical domains. **Gaston Bachelard.** 1964:211.

. . . the sense of "whereness" may well be no more than a convenient habit. As far as we have any way of knowing, three-dimensional space does not exist outside our minds, and the feelings of height and width and depth . . . are not objective realities. **Charles Moore** and **Gerald Allen.** 1976:4.

One of the limitations I perceive in classical architecture is the fact that gravity forces one into orthogonal systems and that anything not in an orthogonal system is seen as expressionistic, romantic and non-rational. I'm not convinced that such is the case. I believe we can have a rationale, in the sense that there is some systematic attitude outside of an orthogonal condition. **Anon.** Extract from discussion in Eisenman/Kipnis studio. In Marvel 1986:57

TRACE   It almost goes without saying that 'position' is a point occupied by someone or something in relation to someone or something else. From the Latin *pono,* to put down, set down, put, place, fix, lay, or deposit, the term relies on spatial comprehension. In its literary translation as 'thesis' (Gk. *thesis*) or 'theme' (Gk. *thema*) the position of the thesis or theme in relation to other situations or themes is what matters, not the thesis or theme itself. A *deposition* is a laying or putting down or aside from office or place or authority, a dethroning, the taking down of Christ from the cross, and a testimony under oath taken down in writing to be read as a substitute for personal appearance by a witness.

Turning to architecture, position is the operative spatial aspect of the science or art of architecture, the placement of elements in space or on a surface and the concomitant partitioning of that space or surface by those elements. "Position, as the location of an idea or architectural construction, affirmatively asserts the connection between place and ideology" (Carol Burns in A. Kahn 1991:165). Deposition is the opposite of position, the inoperative, the taking down (in writing?) or laying aside (for future use?) of elements in space or on surfaces, the uncoupling of place and ideology.

COMMENTARY   The term 'relation' has already been used many times in other chapters and of course in this, for that is its title. An idea of the 'reach' of relationships was given in the overview, and in the discussion on the human basis of measure in chapter 9A, the bodily relations were outlined, namely, up/down, front/back, left/right, inside/outside. In coming to *position,* the same terms are implicated although they are not used in connection with the central 'I', but in the connection (or not) elements have with one another. The Czech-born historian Paul Frankl (1914) attempted to create a stereometric language using terms like 'spatial group' (*Raumzellen*) and 'mass-forms' (*Körperformen*) as quantitative concepts, appropriated terms from Gestalt psychology, and employed *addition* and *division* as his two primary organizational modes (Norberg-Schulz 1965; see also 9B.2, Connection). More recently, a perceptually based system of proportioning space has been attempted (Padovan 1986). But neither these or any other self-contained system has claimed architectural patronage.

In the absence of an agreed spatial vocabulary, we have adapted anthropocentric notions and apply them in relative terms by speaking of above/below (over/under, high/low, tall/short) front/back (in front of/behind, figure/ground), inside/outside (between/beyond), and adjacent (beside, against) instead of right/left, as describing the relations among elements, the parenthetical terms being frequently recurring equivalents (after Mitchell 1990:18–21). And we also speak of the relative sizes of elements (large/small) while trying not to relate them to a particular fixed standard or module such as human size or dimensions, although a standard is always inferred (if only as the opposite of that privileged—'large' is large compared to smaller items of whatever is being discussed, and vice versa).

Of all the relational qualities just outlined, inside/outside is enjoying a privilege in the literature as never before, prompted by hermeneutical questioning over the supposed ability to stand outside a discourse and from there subject it to scrutiny. It is argued that the division of which Bachelard speaks (above) is artificial and there is no dialectic between outside and inside, even in the common spatial parlance that is their source, a point that Bachelard goes on to make. But as with all antinomials, the moment either term is interrogated, the division becomes elusive and further layers of the nominated concept appear. Instead of a clear distinction emerging between inside and outside, we find that they are 'nested' concepts; there are always more insides inside and more outsides outside. And the moment this happens, the 'between' is invoked, the one term above that is not dialectical; there is no reciprocity 'among' the 'betweens', which is significant because between is therefore a purely relational term. Perhaps there is a potential relativist architectural vocabulary waiting in the wings here.

Another privileging of long standing is that of placement above or below a plane of general reference or occupation, the shift up always being toward the divine and the universal and down always toward humankind and the manifest elements. This shift is played out by Frank Lloyd Wright in the Kaufmann House, Falling Water, at Bear Run,

Pennsylvania, where there are many shifts from ground to sky, from earth to space, and most dramatically from the bedrock of the Living Room floor via suspended steps down to the surface of the water below, "the lowest point of the existential level," and symbolic also of the waters under the earth, that elemental relationship so much part of traditional Japanese symbolism (Thiis-Evensen 1987:73, 79).

Vertical displacement need not be dramatic to have effect, though—witness the 'high table' of a ceremonial banquet placed only a matter of inches above the main floor—although verticality for its own sake has become the conventional wisdom in commerce. Raising a building on high has always been a mark of privilege and command and ascending stairs to an entrance has traditionally been a sign of importance. Vitruvius remarked about siting temples on high ground that those for protector gods like Jupiter, Juno, and Minerva "should be on the very highest point commanding a view of the greater part of the city" (1486:1.7.1); their later Christian counterparts were similarly placed or used their spires to metaphorically place them so. A near-contemporary example of the power of positioning on high is the placement of Le Corbusier's pilgrimage chapel of Notre-Dame-du-Haut at Ronchamp, France, replacing one bombed during World War II; anyone who has experienced the climb and the transition to the interior knows how profound the effects can be. Similar experiences are to be had in many sacred buildings around the world.

Adjacency is another positional description frequently encountered in the literature regarding the placement of rooms or spaces, an 'adjacency diagram' being a chart or matrix showing the degree of connection between rooms or spaces and used in the early stages of design analysis to gain an understanding of the programmatic structure of a task. It has also been used to describe the lack of order that 'mere' adjacency of spaces represents. Or at least a certain kind of order in the hands of a master that Demetri Porphyrios (1978) discerns in the 'heterotopic sensibility' of Alvar Aalto, the kind of spatial ordering "with the curious privilege of discriminating independent coherences, while sustaining a cohesion between the parts only by default and through spatial adjacency."

Changes in level of floor and ceiling combined with the placement of walls or vertical elements to create complex and subtle spatial successions and relations is the mark of the architect who has understood and exploits the spatial power of architecture. This totalizing skill characterizes the work of the hero architects and is a skill we might all experience at someone else's hand if not at our own, for we are no more or less than creatures of our own extension. The traditional currency of architectural discourse and theory has been to expound these sorts of notions in a way that makes them manipulable by students and architects and, to the extent that we share a visual and linguistic terminology that enables us to communicate fairly accurately what we mean, theory has been successful. It is a success that comes at the price of pseudo-detachment, a seeming ability to talk about architectural matters by standing 'outside' them, yet all the while knowing that we are not—and here with typical traditional closure we return to the first opposition raised above.

To render spatial position objectifiable, to describe it without reference to human experience, is extremely difficult, though the constant in the elemental relationships or in their enunciation *is* human experience, where left or right handedness, for example, cannot easily be wished away (Thiis-Evenson 1987:125–127). This affinity with humanity is reassuring for most architects, and it makes almost all architectural studies of position (composition, disposition, opposition) classical and traditional. The oppositions above are classical; they are humanist oppositions inherent to the classical way of thinking. The thrust of certain architectural experiments of late, such as the work of Peter Eisenman, Zaha Hadid, and Daniel Libeskind *et al.* (Johnson and Wigley 1988), has been to try to break away from, or at least to break down, human constancies to reveal subterranean ('repressed' is the vogue term) orders with a view to eking from them new compositional possibilities. Cues taken from Russian Contructivism have provided enough leverage to show that relations need not reiterate classical arrangements or oppositions; the question is, where to go from there?

To get at whatever nonclassical structures there are assumed to be among elements, Deconstructivism seeks out the flaws in traditional structuring by metaphorically applying either an architectural poultice or 'violent torture' so that "impurity is drawn to the surface." Deconstructivism "gains all its force by challenging the very values of harmony, unity, and stability, and proposing instead a different view of structure: the view that the flaws are intrinsic to the structure" (Johnson and Wigley 1988:11). This position of the 'deconstructive' architect as a modern day Xipetotec, flaying traditional architectural values for new blood, may suit certain theorists and those architects comfortable with the label, but it sits uneasily with most practitioners as a potential future. There has been a fondness for theorists to draw upon Thomas Kuhn (1970) during the reaction against Deconstructivism and to proclaim "paradigm shift is occurring"; sheer (or, more appropriately, *shear*) terror has been the reaction of those architects prompted to speak out at the instability of it all. Hard-bitten architects, on the other hand, see no need to change paradigms. All that is at stake for them is merely another style in a succession of styles; the Modern Movement at least showed that.

If there is to be a substantial change to the way architects think about composition, if that is the underlying premise of moves away from modernist and classicist closure—assuming this to be desirable—it will be necessary to declassify existing compositional elements as elemental entities. Walls, floors, and roofs will need to cease being walls, floors, and roofs; geometrical relationships will need to be completely rewritten; and all traditional historical and symbolic reference will need to be divested of its formal, compositional, and geometric components. That is certainly a tall order and would be a radical agenda in the fullest sense. But why undertake it? What promise is there that the outcome of what would be mind-wrenching agony will be worth it? While applauding attempts by Peter Eisenman to refute the classical and traditional constructions with which architecture is presently bound, as these were addressed in the three-year experimental design studios conducted at

Harvard University's Graduate School of Design during 1983, 1984 and 1985, John Whiteman admits being "at the limit of my imagination" over how far to go with Eisenman's "critical architecture of negation" (Marvel 1986:10).

Without fully understanding the implications of what I am about to say, instead of being utterly negative about or fearful of 'Tradition'—and its companion, the 'Flight from Architecture' (as was the case in Eisenman's 1985 Harvard Graduate School of Design studio project, for which see Marvel 1986:42–47)—traditional architectural installations might be successively declassified and depositioned rather than annihilated by war. This is neither the fractal re-scaling attempted by Eisenman at GSD, nor the flood of information following declassification, nor the symbolism of substitution by deposition, but the laying aside and covering over of successive layerings—an elimination not a complexification. Successive stages of such a procedure might be layered (deposited) to show transferable positives and negatives, not as a geometric exercise but as a predictive process in time-reversal of the archaeological understanding we now adopt and having its base in present revitalization, subsequent erasure, anticipated development, and future origin, each layer needing assumptions. I have no idea of the spatial or surface terminology for such a procedure—except that portent, omen, and harbinger might figure somewhere—but our present historical procedures use terms such as 'apparition' and 'aroma' for residual effects in space, 'pentimento' and 'palimpsest' in surfaces, and 'anaphora' and 'ellipsis' in text.

The 'points' emerging from an architectural task predicted in this way would form the locus of an incidental geometry and the 'ground' would form the space and surfaces for new positionings. Already there have been shifts in geometrical thinking in architecture as dramatic as the shift from radiality to orthogonality was for the ancient Greeks (Doxiadis 1972); declassifying and depositioning might enable one to reach beyond the orthogonal while still allowing a grasp on present conceptual skills. Maybe it is already happening despite the experiments of generals and heroes.

FURTHER SOURCES   9B.5, Place; Bachelard 1964; Tawa 1991.

2. Connection, Division, and Monstrous Fracture

. . . compartition alone divides up the whole building into the parts by which it is articulated, and integrates its every part by composing all the line and angles into a single, harmonious work that respects utility, dignity, and delight. **Leon Battista Alberti.** 1755b:1.9.

. . . the supreme principle [is] pure *spatial addition*. . . . No matter how rich or complicated a whole space thus governed by spatial addition might become, each of its members is, for the observer, a detachable, clearly defined entity, an addend. . . . It also follows that the individual members of differing shape must be subordinate to a higher community of spaces—a community that they freely create without losing their own identities. Rhythm, which even the series possesses, is the result of addition. **Paul Frankl.** 1914:29–30.

. . . the opposite of spatial addition [is] *spatial division.* The components of spatial form are no longer complete, isolated addends, but fractions of a pre-existent whole. The space does not consist of many units; it is *one* unit divided into parts or fractions. These parts are incapable of independent existence. They are fractional interior forms suspended or floating within the total space. The clarity of the bounding surfaces of these fragmentary spatial parts is also diminished. **Paul Frankl.** 1914:57, 60.

TRACE   Connection, or connexion, stems from the Latin *connectere,* to bind or fasten, and is the bringing together of separate things or ideas, not by way of fusion but via some form of wrap, joint, fastening, or link. Its assembly from *nectere* and its root in *nec-* (hence nexus), ties (!) it to necessity. Divide, devise, and device stem from the Latin *dividere,* part or force asunder, the root of which (*vid-*) relates to the Greek *eidon,* see, as in the opening of the eye. Fracture and fraction stem from the Latin *frangere,* break, the Christian variant of which is *fractio,* the breaking of bread. The root is *frag-,* as in fragile and fragment.

Architecturally, because of the long-standing emphasis on holism, division (of a whole) took precedence over connection (aggregation to a whole) until the nineteenth century when the rush of stylistic revivals brought with it a host of compositional variations based in aggregation. Frankl (1914) attempted to systematize spatial terms and concepts, defining *addition* and *division* as the two primary ways to organize both space and forms. Throughout the twentieth century, both holism (division) and aggregation (addition or connection) have existed in inverse relation, the earlier part of the century being devoted to holism and the later years to aggregation. To confuse matters, though, criticism of these shifting modes of architecture over the century has used the terms in reverse, holism being accused of demanding too severe and restrictive a connection among the parts, and aggregation being criticized for its divisive and *ad hoc* inclinations. The two relational aspects of composition, connection and division, will be discussed here, while esthetic and conceptual implications are to be found in 10A.5, Composition.

COMMENTARY   Regarding the fundamental strategies of connection (Frankl's 'addition') and division, the architectural question has traditionally focused on division, how and where it occurs and how far it can go before fracture sets in, whereby the whole is irreparably altered and the parts take on independent life (usually construed as other wholes)? A holist sees the question as rhetorical because the whole is sacrosanct and division is regarded as a necessary but potentially monstrous procedure. Connection and division are thus in a dialectical relationship and the art of architectural composition has traditionally been to arrange connection without undue interference from division.

In philosophy, while the term 'composition' and its opposite, 'division', are used differently, composition nevertheless applies to a whole considered collectively and division to a whole considered as individual parts; but significantly, each is recognized as giving rise to a fallacy. The *fallacy of composition* argues that what is true of the parts is also true of the whole, while the *fallacy of division* argues that something true of the whole is also true of the parts (Flew 1979). There has been a long-held belief that architectural composition is whole-making, that the whole is greater than the sum of its parts, that what is true of the parts will be true of the whole in greater measure, and what is true of the whole will have a trickle-down effect on the parts (see chapter 2B). Could it be that architecture subscribes to a double compositional fallacy?

Consider for a moment that architecturally this 'greater than' and the reciprocal truth-relations between parts and whole is a fallacy, that the whole is one thing and the parts are quite separate things, and that any consonance between them is contrived to suit our own sense of order. What would be different about an architecture so conceived? I venture that nothing would differ; architecture would still be what it is and be seen for what it is. This suggests that architecture is what we contrive, whereupon it becomes a matter of preference and taste, the *monster of discretion!* When Bernard Tschumi superimposed the grid of points, lines, and surfaces in the Parc de la Villette and used the cube as the basis for the follies, he first of all *chose* certain traditional ordering geometries, which he then *chose* to fracture by various divisional (per)mutations to create his architecture. Connections are as plentiful as divisions, and the architecture relies for its potency on the dialectic between them.

In other words, it is equally plausible that architecture is not 'greater than' the parts but is the 'dialogue among' the parts, whether one chooses to approach designing from a conception of the whole and use division, or from a conception of parts and use connection. The etymology above suggests that division is primary, and experience in architectural design certainly confirms that division is not a dastardly beast. Indeed, architectural experimentation with urban and architectural structuring over the past decade has shown that ad hoc connection is a powerful way to generate architecture, and that division as fracture offers creative possibilities rather than irresolvable contamination.

Further, it is impossible to prevent the particulate qualities of the elements of a building being always in evidence, even though certain seminal modernist buildings attempted to do so by making the joints in materials secondary to continuity of surface and space. For centuries the practical architectural issue of connections has been a matter of degree — how much the separation between *spaces, elements,* or *surfaces* is expressed or suppressed. Arguably, the widespread popularity of vernacular buildings has been due in no small part to their use of materials such as adobe or whitewash to make them appear seamless. In elemental connection generally, seamlessness is attempted by de-emphasizing the joint, as, for instance, in a Gothic cathedral interior where it is common to imagine the forces of the vaults 'flowing' down sinewy ribs to the floor because the alignments and jointing of the stonework make them look as though they are acting that way, when in fact they are distributed unnoticed through the whole mass of masonry (James 1989:Chapter 6).

In spatial connection, providing an opening in a minimum thickness wall to mark a threshold between successive spaces is less satisfying experientially and visually than contriving a transition zone of spatial significance itself, one that by its difference enhances the separation between adjoining spaces. Removing transitions to achieve a continuous 'wraith-like flow' of space by positioning overlapping planes, as Mies van der Rohe did in the Barcelona Pavilion, was the principal contribution of modernist thinking to the issue of connection. But it was achievable only through making walls into particulate elements and in the process drawing attention to the particulate qualities of the materials with which the walls were clad. These instances of connection show that parts of any architectural assembly always remain independent by virtue of differences in material, changes of direction or plane or size, junctions between the parts, and the names used for them; we choose whether to emphasize or de-emphasize their particulate qualities, surfaces being by far the easiest to manipulate, although we can never eliminate them.

Connection unites parts by contact, association, adjacency, or fusion (primarily in building by bonding in brick or stone, although render, steel, and concrete can be made to look like fusion) to create the impression of continuity, but the parts will always at some point reveal their additive quality and remain separate. Indeed, it is the subtle and not so subtle discontinuities of construction that John James turned into a science, toichological analysis (Gk. *toichos,* wall), and used to discriminate the work of one master mason from another in his remarkable studies of Chartres Cathedral and his survey of other French Gothic cathedrals. As he remarks, in Gothic work, "junctions were an opportunity to modify" and were never hidden, their presence and the changes they signify being the primary explanation for "one of the most puzzling characteristics of medieval building . . . the lack of unity" (James 1989:Chapter 2).

The fracturing that was such an intrinsic part of the dynamic of medieval building has become, in the light of Renaissance classical holism and later modern classicism, the major site of the *monsters* of architecture: "Monsters are always located in the joint between architectural elements," says Marco Frascari of the carvings in the portal margins and keystones of many older buildings; they "set the enigma of the construction of a transition . . . the enigma of past and future architectural artifacts" (Frascari 1991:18). Along with the *architettura di spoglio,* the architecture of fragments taken from older architectures and used in vernacular and medieval architecture, which metaphorically dominates current architecture, the joint as the location of division and fracture is one of Frascari's monsters.

In surface and solid connections, the meeting of different materials, different styles, or different stages in a cumulative work (cathedral, house, streetscape) is often handled simply by juxtaposition or by separation and either a recessed or protruding link. Although he did not give it this tag, the *monster of fracture* in the guise of the link was aired thoroughly (if that is what one does with monsters) by Brent Brolin (1980) who cites many examples of it as a popular device used to connect old with new, popular because it allows us "to pretend that the old is no longer there . . . [and] ignore whatever is on the other side." Its ubiquity was criticized by Brolin as a sign that we have lost the skill to join, his remedy being "to exorcise this link from our architectural vocabulary [and to] solve the purely visual problem of relating *directly* to what is there" (Brolin 1980:143).

All very fine, except there would be no more connections like the hundreds of thousands of such articulations between old and new, or between the various elements within almost any architectural assembly, anywhere around the world. Rapid growth of concern in writing and projects about the monstrous or dark side of architecture since the seventies, variously labeled 'the void', 'the other', and 'the absence', is offering little at the finest grain of tectonic. Will the monster continue to inhabit the joint in the articulation, misalignments, and obsessive mechanismo preoccupation with lapping, plating, washering, knuckling, crotcheting, interlocking, sleeving, grometting, ratcheting, levers, sprockets, and spindles?

FURTHER SOURCES   Marvel 1986; Moore, Allen and Lyndon 1974; Norberg-Schulz 1965; Oxman, Radford and Oxman 1987; Pollitt 1974.

3. Space and Time and Hocus-Pocus

There are architects who do things differently. Their imaginations create not spaces but sections of wall. That which is left over around the walls then forms the rooms. **Adolf Loos.** 1898. "The principle of cladding." In Risselada 1989:135–137. See also Loos (1921).

What distinguishes architecture from painting and sculpture is its spatial quality. . . . Thus the history of architecture is primarily a history of man shaping space, and the historian must keep spatial problems always in the foreground. **Nikolaus Pevsner.** 1963:Introduction.

Time is the substance I am made of. Time is the river which sweeps me along, but I am the river; it is a tiger which destroys me, but I am the tiger; it is a fire which consumes me, but I am the fire. The world, unfortunately, is real; I, unfortunately, am Borges. **Jorge Luis Borges.** "A new refutation of time." 1970:269.

The doctrine of 'space' can often simplify the description of architectural experience to a point of near vacuity, and that of *Kunstgeschichte* [art history] lends itself to the facile manufacture of significance. The critic can therefore use them to advance directly from description of an experience to a description of its meaning without any serious understanding of the building which he purports to describe. This, in a nutshell, is the critical method of Giedion and his followers [of which Pevsner is prime]. **Roger Scruton.** 1979:56–57.

Space and time are thus vehicles of continuity by which the world's parts hang together. **William James.** 1907:60.

We cannot both experience and think that we experience. 'The concept of dog does not bark'; the concept of space is not in space. **Bernard Tschumi.** 1975. In Tschumi 1990:27.

TRACE   Space is a term that has only a concrete etymology in that the Latin *spatium,* extent or room, and the Greek *topos* or *choros,* place or location, are expressions of spread across a surface more than the fully three-dimensional quality we ascribe to the term. The Greek *ogkos,* bulk, volume, mass (and the basis for English terms like *oncology* with its modern meaning of the study of tumors), is closer to the spatial notions of architecture, as is *oikos,* room. This is not to say that the abstract sense of spatial extension, interval, or separation is not also meant, though in Greek interval is *diastema* or is to do with the density of placement, *araiono,* hence *araeostyle* describing the wide spacing of columns and *pycnostyle,* the close (dense) spacing of columns. In other words, the word *space* was originally firmly anchored to and interchangeable with existential surface. Time was inextricably linked with spatial extension as an *experiential* quality, just as it was to its cosmological understanding. For a comprehensive account of traditional and cross-cultural notions of space and time see Tawa (1991).

In the Western architectural tradition, there are no references to ancient site-planning traditions; the spatial relations between buildings and evidence for them needs to be gleaned from nonarchitectural sources (Doxiadis 1972:15). Vitruvius does mention *diathesis* (arrangement) "the putting of things in their places and the elegance of effect" (Vitruvius 1486:1.2.2). In the Renaissance, Alberti employed *compartition* for "the process of dividing up the site into yet smaller units, so that the building may be considered as being made up of close-fitting smaller buildings, joined together like members of the whole body" (Rykwert, Leach, and Tavernor 1991:Glossary). Space was not a term used descriptively in architectural treatises until the mid-eighteenth century, and not in the modern sense of a direct connection and evaluation with architecture until the late nineteenth and early twentieth centuries via the Swiss art historian Heinrich Wölfflin and the Czechborn Paul Frankl. From the beginning of the twentieth century, space was to become increasingly the preoccupation of architectural theorists and historians notably Bragdon (1910, 1913, 1916), Frankl (1914), Giedion (1941), Zevi (1948), and Langer (1953). The concept of space-time belongs to Giedion and Zevi.

COMMENTARY   As architectural concepts, space and space-time are notoriously difficult to explain or discuss for the reason that Tschumi states above; we cannot (easily, or at all?) experience space and time and also think that we experience them. So, how are we to understand them? It seems that all we can do is participate in their partitioning, unfolding, and layering. This experience equates with the definition of *volume* as the Greek *tomos* or tome, slice, piece, roll, which is sliced into segments or sections and bound together. The placement or separation of elements within some spatial or temporal continuum prompts relations between elements of which repetition is but one manifestation and *rhythm* the measure of its degree of regularity. To the ancient Greeks, *rythmos* meant a variety of things, from disposition and temper, to shape and form, to time and order in dancing, this last coming closest to our modern-day usage.

Sequence and hierarchy in space and time are the 'flow' of rhythm, and each element is the 'pause', "the steady limitation of movement," producing the sequences and hierarchies, as, for example, windows occur in a façade or vaults in an arcade. Scholarly debate over the etymology of the word is divided between the 'flow' camp (hence repetition) and the 'draw' camp (in the sense of delineation, delimitation, composition, and pattern). From the eighteenth century, rhythm was used for the perceived regularities in shape or line, something even measurable, thereby precipitating our most common modern meaning of it and a host of affirmative terminology (Pollitt 1974:221). However, irregularity in space and time have no equivalent terminology, except by way of absence (ir-, non-, a-, in-, dis-, un-) and a bunch of pejoratives, which is why irregularity is so elusive a concept in latter-day architectural work and writing.

On the wondrous hocus-pocus of space-time, Peter Collins devotes the last chapter of *Changing Ideals in Modern Architecture* (1965) to five conceptions of it he discerns in the writing of Siegfried Giedion—Einstein's relativity, avant-garde (Cubist) art, non-Euclidean, four-dimensional, and Zen Buddhist—with a view to seeing if it means anything at all. He dismisses the non-Euclidean connection and the Einsteinian, but points to Einstein's comment on the conceptual link between space and place as "a small portion of the earth's surface identifiable by a name. . . a sort of order of material objects and nothing else," which accords with that outlined in the trace above. Collins remarks of this comment: "This is precisely the kind of space involved in architectural design . . . a 'place' (plaza, piazza) is the largest space that an architect is able to deal with as a unified work of art" (289). On the Cubist connection he has little to say, brushing it aside in a sentence or two. Of the fourth-dimension, he understands movement to be all that is needed to fully experience and appreciate the spatial interconnection of modern architecture, and that the transparency of glass assists in allowing visual 'movement' through a building; while movement is nothing new in architecture, he concludes that it and space-time "are nothing more or less than modern developments of the exploitation of effects of parallax" (292). Finally, he sees the reference to Zen Buddhism as merely an example of the modern "appetite for pseudo-scientific mumbo-jumbo." Writings on space subsequent to Collins have improved only marginally, with one or two exceptions.

In one of the exceptions, Bernard Tschumi, in the same essay just cited, elaborates upon the sixties, which saw street, square, and arcade become the currency of urban and civic design. With the rise of these terms came the semiotic notion of there being a language of space and the question of a possible "dialectic between social praxis and spatial forms."

Concomitant with these concerns, architecture began to dematerialize into sets of concepts and empty signs; space began to lose its primacy for a while, but has since reinstalled itself with renewed interest in the relation between the body and architecture. The re-embedding of the body in space is what Tschumi likens to the *labyrinth* "where no overview is present to provide a clue about where to get out" (1990:23), but where nonetheless subjectivity is uppermost (29). The fact that most architects still think of space as a material to be modeled is enough to make Tschumi (1981; 1987; 1990) essential reading; since 1975, when his first 'questions of space' were raised, he has been saying that space is the common denominator of architecture.

Of course Tschumi's questions come late in the history of modern space. The German concepts of *Raum,* space or room, and *Raumempfindung,* or 'felt volume', were well in place by 1915, and "by 1923 the idea of felt space had merged with the idea of composition to become a three-dimensional continuum, capable of metrical subdivision that could be related to academic rules. From then on, architectural space was consistently seen as a uniformly extended material to be modeled in various ways" (Tschumi 1990:14) and even Cubist obsessions with multiple imagery did little to alter the conception of space from "a simplistic, amorphous matter to be defined by its physical boundaries." The term *Raumplan* was used only in connection with the work of the Viennese architect Adolf Loos, according to one of his pupils, Heinrich Kulka (*Adolf Loos.* Vienna, 1931:14), and is 'a container concept' that translates as 'space plan' and needs to be understood in association with two affiliated concepts, 'living plan' and 'material plan' (see Johan van de Beek. In Risselada 1988:27). But even as for Loos, space is not a concept capable of easy discussion. It remained elusive throughout and since the Modern Movement, despite the enormous amount written about it and the universal agreement among architects that space is what they deal with best, even though it is ineffable.

It is worth quoting what Martin Heidegger says of *Raum* in *Building, Dwelling and Thinking* (1954):

> What the word for space, *raum,* designates is said by its ancient meaning. *Raum* means a place cleared or freed for settlement and lodging. A space is something that has been made room for, something that is cleared and free, namely within a boundary, Greek *peras.* A boundary is not that at which something stops but, as the Greeks recognised, the boundary is that from which something *begins its presencing.* That is why the concept is that of *horismos,* that is, the horizon, the boundary. Space is in essence that for which room has been made, that which is let into its bounds. That for which room is made is always granted and hence is joined, that is gathered, by virtue of a location, that is by such a thing as a bridge. *Accordingly spaces receive their being from locations and not from space.* (Cited in Frampton 1982:29).

This extract picks up certain issues already discussed in early sections of this chapter, and anticipates others to be raised in the next two sections; it is pertinent here for the act of *clearing* it offers and for the boundary as the start for *presencing* it introduces; for an architecture of space as the containment of something negative is nowhere near as charged a concept as a space endowed with positive *Prägnanz* (expectation or potential), to use a term beloved of Gestalt psychology.

I wish to end by working through something Stanley Fish (1989) remarks upon concerning certain principles of the new criticism in poetry, 'the doctrine of organic unity', which he describes in this way: "All the parts of a long poem are unified in their relation to a single theme or vision which informs them and of which they are the (repeated) expression. Consequently, sequence is once again legitimated, not, however, as the generator of meaning (as it is in the logic of narrative) but as a succession of spaces in which the same meaning is endlessly and variously displayed" (268). Fish does not make a connection with architecture, but a connection is undeniable since organic unity *belongs* to Frank Lloyd Wright and his house constructions of space and mass are Froebel blocks 'endlessly and variously displayed'. The notion of organic unity is evident more generally too in the endless reiteration of tradition, patterns, and typology employed to effect lasting architectural relationships.

Taken to illogical extreme, an architecture subscribing to a doctrine of organic poetic unity in which all the parts are unified by a single theme or vision can only comprise a succession of spaces in which the same meaning is endlessly and variously displayed. There can be no more apt description of the New Classicism now infecting architecture; typal reiterations, the capturing of timeless patterns, and 'a timeless way of building' (Alexander 1977, 1979; R. Krier 1979, 1988; Porphyrios 1982). If historical time is frozen, only experiential time remains; architecture becomes a video pause that describes a momentary space, a gesture caught in the act, or a *miracle,* in Jarzombek's terms (1989:188). Bound by timeless architecture, the poetry of living is acted out in front of a blue screen and matted to an oneiric miracle-world of your choosing, Zelig with Xanthippe, a shunting of time and space to be readily had by cruising Bannister Fletcher or *Country Life* (nineteenth-century revivals were almost right!). As the conveyor of unitary meaning, space also becomes unitary; the same spatial array endlessly and variously displayed, the same scenario as the obsessive fractal rescaling of Eisenman raised in 9B.1, Relation, above. Despite their apparent inventiveness, in this poetic sense the repetitions of Wright and Eisenman make their works compliant and classical. Is there another angle that can explore three-dimensionality without losing the richness of experiencing it and without making it unnecessarily complex? After all, some of the most profound spatial experiences, like vastness, are stationary and simple.

FURTHER SOURCES   Antoniades 1992; Bachelard 1964; Eliade 1959; Guénon 1975; Hays and Burns 1990; Henderson 1983; Norberg-Schulz 1971; Trancik 1986; Zevi 1948, 1978.

4. Central Tendencies and Boundary Disputes

A boundary is not that at which something stops but, as the Greeks recognized, the boundary is that from which something begins its presencing. **Martin Heidegger.** *Poetry, Language, Thought* (1954).

. . . boundaries of species are as men, not as nature, made them. **John Locke.** Cited in Mitchell 1990:94.

There are many routes to the understanding of complex ideas. . . . We take the unorthodox route of regarding a 'point' as physically real; its relative size being dependent on human experience. The point then, can be handled, visualized and seen to occupy a position in space . . . what physical form can be given most appropriately to the 'point'. . . ? Any form, however random, if completely rotated on its centre of gravity eventually describes a sphere at its extremities, hence the sphere is the most economical form that is non-exclusive. The sphere thus seems the most suitable form to give to the 'point' as it has complete rotational symmetry and is least 'biased'. **Keith Critchlow.** 1969:4.

. . . in space considered in its existing reality, and not as a symbol of the total being, no point is or can be the centre; all points equally belong to the domain of manifestation, by the very fact of belonging to space. Space is one of the possibilities whose realization falls within that domain, which, in its entirety, constitutes no more than the circumference of the "wheel of things," or what might be called the outwardness of universal Existence. **René Guénon.** 1975:128.

Margins imply closeness to limits, outside edges, and boundaries along which what is "inside" becomes "outside." The word "margin" has directionality built into its meaning: the direction to the center or central region. Margins are close to thresholds (which have the related directionality of crossing), but are themselves not the thresholds. Margins have an area, and adjoin and include the inside border of the border.

Centers, in complement, imply the notions of depth and heart, the place of concentrated meaning and "gravity," the points at which action originates from within and the destination at which it finally arrives from without. Centers are also defined by their embeddedness, their insideness, or their remoteness from the outside in every direction. If outside there is danger, then in the marginal zone there is precaution, and at the center, security. **Michael Benedikt.** 1991:29.

TRACE   The quotation from Guénon gives the traditional sense of center as the universal essence of any manifestation that is everywhere and belongs to no *particular* location. Such a clear yet diffuse concept only confounds the modern sensibility, which is so accustomed to geometry controlling manifestation that it always seeks a center as a fixity, a source of origin, in everything it deals with. Center is sourced in the Latin *centrum* and the Greek *kentron*, goad, peg, or stationary point of a pair of compasses (and stemming from *kentrein,* prick); center in everyday terms is presumed as fixed and stable, not diffuse. A center-seeking tendency is *centripetal,* and a center-fleeing tendency is *centrifugal,* the boundary being the limit of flights between adjoining realms with centripetal and centrifugal tendencies.

In architecture, centralization has always been a centripetal process, one of drawing elements together around a core of some kind, and centralized forms dominate the history of institutional and religious architecture especially, whether around a point (circular and polygonal shapes) or an axis (directional shapes and arrangements, bilateral symmetry). The center and axis are the core of a city's 'persistence', whether as monuments or as streets (Rossi 1982). Metaphorically, the center is secure and permanent and the boundary is precarious and transitory, as Benedikt remarks above. For Marco Frascari, though, margins "determine the phenomenon of the spatial environment, and they are the locus where the transformation of space takes place"; and margins are where the transformation of meaning from looseness into fixity occurs (1992:21–22). For a detailed account of the complex ritualistic and symbolic aspects of center and boundary, *mundus* and *terminus,* in ancient Roman lore see Rykwert 1976:chapter 4.

COMMENTARY   Prompted by Edgar Allan Poe's remark that "nonsense is the essential sense of marginal notes" taken from his "Marginalia, November 1844" (in Poe 1844:1309–1330), in his own marginalia Marco Frascari makes less use of its potential (1991:111–121) than he does in his main text, while as a text among the architectural genre it is undoubtedly quite marginal in Poe's sense. This is in line with the work of cultural anthropologist Victor Turner, for whom the margin — in his terms the *limen* — is an important site for "ambiguity, even paradox, outside or mediating between customary categories" and most significantly from an architectural point of view, "a 'realm of possibility' where new combinations of cultural givens could be playfully tested" (Ashley 1990:xviii). The disputatious realm of liminality is the natural place for daring and creativity, for wayward discourse and for audacious experiment; that is why the clown, the insane, the avant-garde, the poet, and the researcher are always found there.

The boundary is also traditionally a permanent and in certain respects sacred realm, revered by ancient Roman planners, by land-owners from time immemorial, and by the professions whose areas of expertise are protected from erosion by other disciplines. The ancient Roman custom was to delimit the boundary by an initial furrow, the *sulcus primigenius* within which was established the *pomoerium,* a strip of land around the town within which defensive walls were built. The furrow was the symbolic marriage of sky with earth, the ploughshare being considered the male counterpart to female earth, tilling being the first stage in yielding fertility from the soil. The ditch (without the symbolism) has continued to be one means of marking a boundary. But ditches are rarely practical, and boundaries as lines are marked by stones. For the ancient Romans, the god Terminus resided in the boundary stone that, in keeping with the solemnity of the ritual of its installation, was shrouded in fatal curses to ensure its permanence (Rykwert 1976). The marriage with sky still exists today in that property and national boundaries extend vertically indefinitely, leading to airspace being claimed as a sovereign right. But boundaries today sustain only for as long as the parties on both sides agree, the often calamitous disputations that have arisen between states and nations around the world attesting to their impermanence.

In architecture, the boundary or margin is metaphorically the location of competition; spheres of creative influence meet, clash, and are adjudicated there. Conceived in the margin of competition, Stirling and Wilford's Neue Staatsgallerie extension at Stuttgart experimented audaciously and won. They did it with the sense of play, fun, and ridicule that characterizes the court jester, able to insult without offending, able to offend without insulting, and embodied the spirit of competing as a marginal activity in their solution. The gallery as the container of creativity inhabits a boundary of its own creation, in the center it places permanence and tradition, a rotunda, the circle of the cosmos. Marco Frascari reiterates the critics' comments about the Staatsgallerie, emphasizing its monstrous ingenuity, admitting that "impossible things have been unified in a whole" and marveling at its ability to evoke so many associations (1991:78–82), but relishing its de*monstra*tions rather than its cosmological resonances.

The secure rotunda is accessible only from within, via a door permanently marked with foundational architectural icons—trabeation and a pair of Doric columns and symbolically the duad of all creation. Being an outdoor space and subject to the ravages of the elements, the only opportunity for artistic display is sculpture—enduring pieces, nothing ephemeral or transitory. The 'public' remain permanently outside, reminded and obliged by geometry to walk *around* the center, sticking to the circumference that tantalizes them into thinking they are seeing a center. The boundary of exhibition galleries is itself bounded by the immediate urban setting, and by other cultural entities further afield. Reversing the order, the Staatsgallerie design became a center of world attention, a center of intense criticism, and a center of the city's art, and the rotunda became a center for the 'select' to reach after a rite of creative passage only to find that there is no singularity there. The gridded pavement of the rotunda and scattered fragments of culture dissemble to make the 'point' that there is no point, as Guénon says, that art is manifest everywhere around them and in no one particular place. The question is immediately prompted, if the gallery had a center, what piece from the collection would take pride of place at its center?

The Neue Staatsgallerie is in a formal sense atypical of architecture, because most buildings *do* have centers, as do groups of buildings, suburbs, towns, and regions, and they manifest more directly the interplay between boundary and center. Indeed, one of the key debates in town-planning for years has been how far a city can expand before the centrifugal tendency creates satellites, before the center no longer acts as a meaningful 'presence' for far-flung suburbs. The architectural counter to the centrifugal is an insistence on cohesion and unity in design, the 'central idea' (see 8B.2, Idea), universal principles, the re-establishment of human values as central, and so on to the hundred and one other centralizing tendencies considered desirable. "It could be shown that all the names related to fundamentals, to principles, or to the center" writes Jacques Derrida, "have always designated an invariable presence—*eidos, arche, telos, energeia, ousia* (essence, existence, substance, subject) *alethia*, transcendentality, consciousness, God, man, and so forth" (1978:279–280). And it is this desire for the presence of certain qualities that has been paradoxically *at the heart* of Jacques Derrida's philosophical speculations about the structures we give to things:

> Structure . . . has always been neutralized or reduced, and this by a process of giving it a center or of referring it to a point of presence, a fixed origin. The function of this center was not only to orient, balance, and organize the structure—one cannot in fact conceive of an unorganized structure—but above all to make sure the organizing principle of the structure would limit what we might call the *play* of the structure. By orienting and organizing the coherence of the system, the center of a structure permits play inside the total form. And even today the notion of a structure lacking any center represents the unthinkable itself. (Derrida 1978:278–279).

Why else would Los Angeles prescribe for itself a downtown a generation ago if not to try to neutralize its incessant perpetuation, to have a center to anchor it, to give it the semblance of permanence? Of downtown Los Angeles Reyner Banham wrote in 1970: "In terms of the real life of the seventy-mile-square metropolis today, most of [downtown] could disappear overnight and the bulk of the citizenry would never even notice" (1971:208). And it has changed little since, despite some celebrated architecture the city is still struggling to affirm its center, like so many American cities. Australia too is experiencing a retreat from its city centers. Sydney is looking to reverse a perceivable drift away from the central business district (CBD) by injecting more people into its heart through commercial rezoning, which will, it is hoped, also rejuvenate building sites abandoned by economic recession.

But as Guénon, Derrida, and Banham make clear, the center is everywhere, it governs structure but is not itself structural. The moment that centers are structurally considered constitutes a fundamental rupture, according to Derrida. Attempts to resuscitate an urban center in Los Angeles or Cincinnati are tangible examples of Derrida's unthinkable "that there was no center, that the center could not be thought in the form of a present-being, that the center had no natural site, that it was not a fixed locus but a function, a sort of nonlocus in which an infinite number of sign-substitutions came into play. This was the moment when language invaded the universal problematic, the moment when, in the absence of a center or origin, everything became discourse . . . that is to say, a system in which the central signified, the original or transcendental signified, is never absolutely present outside a system of differences" (Derrida 1978:280). Such is the structure of architectural theory: no center, just the play in between, just discourse.

FURTHER SOURCES   9A.1, Measure; Arnheim 1982; Davis 1991.

5. *Place as* Genius Loci

The room is the beginning of architecture. It is the place of the mind. **Louis Kahn.** 1971. "The room, the street, and human agreement." In Latour 1991:263–269.

I would say that the desire to be, to express, exists in the flowers, in the tree, in the microbe, in the crocodile, in man. **Louis Kahn.** 1969. In Latour 1991:235.

One of my feet stepped on a flagstone lower than the ones next to it . . . and then, all at once, I recognised that Venice which my descriptive efforts and pretended snapshots of had failed to recall; the sensation I had once felt on two uneven slats in the Baptistry of St. Mark had given back to me and was linked with all the other sensations of that and other days which had lingered expectant in their place among the series of forgotten years from which a sudden change had imperiously called them forth. **Marcel Proust.** 1957. *Time Regained* (London, Chatto and Windus):210–211. Cited in Canter 1977:9.

. . . we have not fully identified the place until we know *a* what behaviour is associated with, or it is anticipated will be housed in, a given locus, *b* what the physical parameters of that setting are, and *c* the descriptions, or conception, which people have of that behaviour in that physical environment. **David Canter.** 1977:158-9.

The basic property of man-made places is therefore concentration and enclosure. They are "insides" in a full sense, which means that they "gather" what is known. To fulfill this function they have openings which relate to the outside. **Christian Norberg-Schulz.** 1980:10.

In a vast number of [urban] areas throughout Hong Kong, much of the identity of 'place' is generated from [illegal] activity which has no space allocated to it. . . . In spite of its essential invisibility, it has an immense effect on the 'design' and appearance of the city, taking a multitude of forms from illegal factories in people's houses, vegetable markets, cooked food stalls, and the totality of 'hawking' as a way of life. **Alexander Cuthbert.** 1985:84.

. . . material profit devoid of responsibility for the 'genius loci' debases both the individual and society alike. **Alexander Cuthbert.** 1985:86.

TRACE   Whereas position is a point in space without, necessarily, physical dimension (although it invariably does have physical dimensions in an everyday sense), place is extensive, a possession of space, a definite part of space. Resonating with both position and place, 'location' stems from the Latin *locus,* place or spot, as does 'local' and 'loculus', a small chamber or cell in an ancient tomb for corpses or urns. In Greek the term for place is *topos,* which is the base for the English topic, toparchy, topography, topology, toponymy, and topophilia. In mathematics, *locus* is the set of all points satisfying an equation of relation or generated by a point, line, or plane moving in accordance with certain stated conditions.

The notion that a place is inhabited perhaps by a guardian spirit that is its life 'breath' has led to the 'spirit of place' or *genius loci*. According to Christian Norberg-Schulz, "*Genius loci* is a Roman concept. According to ancient Roman belief every 'independent' being has its *genius*, its guardian spirit. This spirit gives life to people and places, accompanies them from birth to death, and determines their character or essence. . . . The *genius* thus denotes what a thing *is*, or what it 'wants to be', to use a word of Louis Kahn" (1980:18).

As architectural concepts, place, sense of place, and spirit of place are relatively recent. In 1960 Kevin Lynch wrote of the city as potentially a "sense of place [which] in itself enhances every human activity that occurs there, and encourages the deposit of a memory trace" (1960:119). Aldo van Eyck wrote on 'Place and Occasion' (*Progressive Architecture*) in September 1962 and the same year Donlyn Lyndon, Charles Moore, Patrick Quinn, and Sim van der Ryn wrote "Toward Making Places" (*Landscape,* vol. 12, no. 1, Autumn) and place as an experiential concept clearly had overtones of Kevin Lynch's notions of edge, path, node, district, and landmark (Lynch 1960). Bloomer and Moore (1977) declared that "Architecture, the making of places, is . . . a matter of extending the inner landscapes of human beings into the world in ways that are comprehensible, experiential, and inhabitable," which summed up an agenda that architects were to pursue for another decade. The so-called 'place movement' has several seminal texts, one being *Place and Placelessness* by Edward Relph (1976), another *Genius Loci* (1980) by Christian Norberg-Schulz, while the proceedings from the People and Physical Environment Research (PAPER) conference *Place and Placemaking* (Dovey, Downton, and Missingham 1985) represent a good cross-section of place theory and the literature, even if somewhat equivocating.

COMMENTARY   It was the 1958 *La poétique de l'espace (The Poetics of Space)* by the French phenomenologist Gaston Bachelard (1964) in which place as an art *cum* science of studying place in literature, particularly poetry, was introduced as 'topo-analysis' combining "descriptive psychology, depth psychology, psychoanalysis and phenomenology" (xxiv, xxxii). Bachelard suggested that his spatial orientation might be called *topophilia* in seeking "to determine the human value of the sorts of space that may be grasped, that may be defended against adverse forces, the space we love" (xxxi). He introduced 'soul' and thus 'spirit' into the equation when he said "Our soul is an abode. And by remembering 'houses' and 'rooms', we learn to 'abide' within ourselves. Now everything becomes clear, the house images move in both directions: they are in us as much as we are in them" (xxxiii). Bachelard has become a standard reference in the topophilic literature.

The architectural conception of place differs from the rather matter-of-fact definitions above, and consolidates that of Bachelard's topophilia by introducing the idea that place is special, a space of particular qualities and impact informed by some perceivable difference from another place, hence a 'sense of place', and by implicating design as either somehow sharing in place or as the instrument for achieving it. The feeling, or sense, of a place is either the direct expression of the 'spirit of place' immanent in a physical setting or is its residue, and it is through the ritual of designing that it is invoked. "Inspiration is the feeling of beginning at the threshold," writes Louis Kahn, "where Silence and Light meet: Silence, with its desire to be, and Light, the giver of all presences. This, I believe, is in all living things; in the tree, in the rose, in the microbe. To live is to express. All inspirations serve it." (Latour 1991:224). Louis Kahn's 'desire to be' and 'inspiration' say the same thing, that a spirit or *genius* is awaiting manifestation, awaiting the charm of the magician's wand.

The magician-architect is like the poet, inhabiting the margins of sense and rationality and at liberty to weave spells of the most wondrous and evocative kind; and Louis Kahn was a master sorcerer. Kahn conjures a university for his apprentices, not by being given a program, but by suggesting they "think in terms of a university as though it never happened, as though it isn't here. You have nothing to refer to, just the sense of a place of learning, an undeniable need; *an undeniable desire on the part of all of us that a place be for learning*" (Latour 1991:236). He prompts a sense of place that of necessity has a spirit as its consort, and then proceeds to woo. He sprinkles some 'golden dust', invokes the spirit through 'inspiration' and from the Silence. . . . Poof! . . . a sanctuary, an acropolis even, comes to Light. Now, there is nothing wrong in this—indeed, it makes for wonderful reading and memorable teaching. While for many architects such an approach is madly frustrating, for others it is rewarding for the promise it holds, much as geomancy or *feng shui* (Rossbach 1984) is to the Chinese. Cynics might say both are just shrewd mystifications of commonsense understanding, but the more charitable will admit each as the rightful province of the inventive and mysterious mind.

Either way, one would be hard-pressed to find any reference to 'sense of place' or *genius loci* in the architectural literature of the 1990s, a strange fact after three decades of favor that suggested there was enough content and interest in place to constitute a new paradigm (Dovey, Downton, and Missingham 1985). The place paradigm has been largely consumed by landscape architects and urban designers, and is now part of their conventional wisdom, although its residual effects are still noticed in certain architectural writings, especially of the down-to-earth and homely kind (Marcus and Sarkissian 1986; Rowe 1991) and some-times of the mystical and unhomely kind (Vidler 1992), that emphasize the reciprocity between use of buildings and meaning.

The most vexing question, however, remains: Can place can be designed? Can there be a calculated act called placemaking? A sense of place originates in at least the following: fields of care, in which we invest much effort and harbor memories; place ballets, the observed routine daily activities; public ritual, the special occasions or major celebrations; pivotal events, unique and memorable occasions; geographic events, characteristics of landform that are interesting or noteworthy; functional sites, buildings with distinctive uses, content, or arrangement; and landmarks and monuments, noticeable or significant built artifacts or natural events that aid orientation or position (Dovey, Downton, and Missingham 1985). In summary, 'place' is particular, is shared, and is memorable. But the upshot is that architects have little control over whether a place becomes a 'place', although

Missingham believes they can assist it by seeking and providing enduring spatial and built forms, patterns, geometries, and 'archetypes'.

Unlike Missingham, Peter Downton (Dovey, Downton, and Missingham 1985) stresses that "places are not entities; places are processes"—processes of imagination, intention, potentiality, living, bordering, remembrance, and of dying—although he recognizes that "changing what architects provide may be easier than the ways in which they provide it." Kim Dovey puts forward his *Ten propositions for an ecology of place (loc. cit.)* as a way of providing "healthy places," but his propositions are descriptive rather than prescriptive; they do not help the designer. Because architects often project a 'false consciousness' about the correctness of what they design, mostly without external verification, place cannot be tested for its appeal without first being built, despite the many simulation techniques available. Indeed, the concept of place may forever elude architects as a predictable field because, like much design feedback, its recognition is always too late, and architects already teeter on the edge of the 'naturalistic fallacy' of projecting what ought to be from what is (see chapter 5). All they can do is hope that the *genius* will guide them or, if that is unacceptable, that their own magic will overcome.

FURTHER SOURCES   9B.1, Relation; Agrest 1991; Bachelard 1958; Canter 1977; Kolb 1990; Krier 1979; Kunze 1987; Pérez-Gómez 1985; Proust 1981; Trancik 1986; Tuan 1974, 1977.

Architecture Expression

Overview

Form . . . is not simply the physical facilitation of function. Rather, it *translates* an object's function into the language of perceptual expression. **Rudolf Arnheim.** 1977:263. Cited in Heath 1991:72.

For Hegel . . . architecture was a medium only half articulate, unable to give full expression to the Idea, and hence relegated to the level of pure symbolism, from which it must be redeemed by statuary and ornament. **Roger Scruton.** 1979:5.

. . . expressionism is widespread, shifting attention from the quality of the product to the character of the producer, and thereby encouraging the romantic preoccupation with personality that is so prevalent in, if not an expression of, our culture. **William W. Bartley III.** 1973:172.

Coherence is the root of expression; symbolism is its fruition. **Tom Heath.** 1991:72.

In day to day discussion in the design studio one often hears the phrase 'architectural expression' used in relation to a student's scheme or to architecture generally, just as one might hear its equivalent in other creative fields such as art, music, poetry, or literature. The phrase is a commonplace of architectural education, a portmanteau term, like so many in architectural discourse, that lacks precision but has enough meaningful charge to carry a conversation, in this case on esthetics and communication. In parallel with its formation as a word (from verb to noun), 'express' has the curious ability to actively engage some particular architectural quality or qualities in the act of outpouring or evidencing themselves, yet, with the addition of the suffix '-ion', manages to reify these qualities as though they are both intrinsic to architecture and the effect of the action.

Vitruvius used the term *expression* in his *Ten Books* to advise that the size of columns in the higher tiers around forums be diminished to match the reducing building loads in imitation of the way natural growth reflects how forces diminish with height (5.1.3). Nature, for Vitruvius, is the exemplar for architecture. He also talks of certain qualities he observes in the way uninterrupted columns supporting roof beams directly add 'an air of sumptuousness and dignity' (5.1.10), how columns for temples have a 'dignity', and how columns in colonnades and public works achieve 'elegance' (5.9.3).

Vitruvius's physiognomic approach is precisely what the father of modern art history, Johann J. Winckelmann, advanced in 1764 in his *Geschichte der Kunst des Alterhums* (translated by G. H. Lodge as *The History of Ancient Art*, Boston, 1880) in which he "regarded the impassive marble fronts of classical statues as an expression of the 'noble simplicity and quiet grandeur' of the Greek soul" (Bartley 1973:172). Winckelmann's *History* also established the idea of art as reflecting the soul or spirit of the age or zeitgeist (Watkin 1980).

But it was Kant who took the giant step in formulating a philosophy of esthetics with *The Critique of Judgement* (1790). Among many things, Kant proposed that the *geist,* or soul, esthetically "signifies the animating principle in the mind," and that this principle "is the faculty of presenting *aesthetical ideas.*" For Kant an esthetic idea is "a representation of the imagination, annexed to a given concept" and, since imagination constrained by understanding can combine in a certain way to constitute *genius,* he argued that "genius properly consists in the happy relation, which science cannot teach nor industry learn, enabling one to find out ideas for a given concept, and, besides, to hit upon the *expression* for them—the expression by means of which the subjective mental condition induced by the ideas as the concomitant of a concept may be communicated to others" (§49). In this one formulation may be found the thrust of this chapter: architecture as the 'hitting upon' of *esthetic* ideas and their *expression* as a means of *communication.* Further, the transaction between the engaging subject and the immanent esthetic idea has two components according to Kant, *manner* and *method.* Method was the concern of both chapter six and nine, manner is the concern of this chapter.

Part A focuses on esthetic immanence in the architectural object and on the manner in which it is recognized and reflected upon. One of a number of esthetic matters that concerned Kant was beauty, which he maintained "may in general be termed the *expression* of aesthetic ideas. But . . . with beauty of art this idea must be excited through the medium of a concept of the Object, whereas with beauty of nature the bare reflection upon a given intuition . . . is sufficient for awakening and communicating the idea of which that object is regarded as the *expression*" (Kant 1790:§50). The Kantian differentiation between the basis of expression via an intermediate object in art as against its direct apprehension in nature was to be dissolved in architecture when romantic organicism took hold during the nineteenth century. Esthetic discourse in architecture since then has been largely about whether or not they should be separated again.

Considering the prominence given to esthetic ideas in the Kantian schema and the precedence of the symbolic idea as the first stage in Hegel's conception of art, which has also strongly influenced architectural thought, it is little wonder that students and architects tend to be carried away by the term 'expression' and adopt it willingly and lovingly, for it embodies everything to which they aspire in their work, not just *an* architectural expression but Architectural Expression. It is as if Architecture is a kind of precious efflux dormant within the matrix of built form that under the right conditions issues through the interstices; the latent life in an outwardly barren desert needing only the rains of creative exertion to activate it.

On the other hand, the notion of architecture as communication adopted for part B of this chapter is not to do with graphic technique or visual presentation of the sort one finds in design drawings, perspectives, or working drawings, although these are mentioned in some of the commentary. It is to do with the conception of architecture as expressing certain messages, the kinds of message, and the manner in which these are transmitted. Architecture as a language was raised in the introduction, and the topic has been reviewed by structuralist writers on architecture such as Norberg-Schulz (1965) and Bonta (1979) both of whom offer sign systems and their modes of operation and interrelation. "Communication . . . is based upon common symbol-systems which are attached to common behavioural patterns or 'forms of life'," writes Norberg-Schulz, and we are brought to "understand that a meaningful message presupposes the use of symbol-systems which are connected with systems of expectations, and that the message has to contain a certain moment of surprise, without breaking completely with the expectation" (Norberg-Schulz 1965:60). It is the conventions adopted in such symbol systems that are examined here.

Norberg-Schulz argues that if our expectations are fully satisfied, the resulting communication is banal, and that if a sign's appearance is beyond our expectations of order and coherence, then the message is meaningless. But it is almost impossible to conceive of a condition in which an order of some kind cannot be recognized, so the latter case never happens, the recognition and assimilation of novelty being a case in point. So exactly how does architecture communicate; what expectations do we have regarding the communicative power of architecture? What might be the grammar, the system rules, of architecture in this case? In fact, what makes for a *communicative architecture*? The prevalent notion of recent times that architecture is a text that can be read raises issues about how it is read and what is being read. The paraphernalia for such linguistry is to be found in recent semiotic literature, and for architecture particularly in the writings of Charles Jencks, who has fully endorsed architecture as a language. For example, in section two of his *Language of Post-Modern Architecture* (1977) under the heading "Modes of Architectural Communication," he includes four subsections labeled *metaphor, words, syntax,* and *semantics,* and in the index there are many more linguistic terms. More on this in 10A.2, Beauty.

Finally, there is the matter of expressionism. If expression is the reification of architecture's intrinsic and extrinsic esthetic ideas, expressionism is its institutionalization. W. W. Bartley maintains, admittedly with a focus on the place of expression in the work of Wittgenstein, that uncritical acceptance of expressionism is logically in error, his reason being that human communication is basically unfathomable and carries with it unwanted and even unimaginable content in its transactions. His comment about literary ideas is remarkably like the transmutation that occurs when architectural ideas are made public; indeed, architectural ideas are precisely the same too if they are written down, as mostly they are:

> When one produces an idea—whether about oneself, about the nature of the world, about human society, or language, or whatever—this idea, being formed in descriptive language, takes an objective life of its own, and particularly so when written down and published and thus made available to others. It has unexplored and sometimes *unwanted* potential transcending what could possibly have been intended, or expressed, in the moment of its utterance. . . . This web of ideas is autonomous in the sense that it generates its own problems and that its content is largely independent of our wishes, existing independently of being realized in the subjective consciousness of any individual. (Bartley 1973:181)

The important question to ask is how do we differentiate the 'web of ideas' from the author's persona from the unwanted content, if expression is to be a worthwhile concept? In a word, we can't. And *expressionism* of the kind that abounds in the 'readings' of architecture purportedly carrying meanings, be they personal ones by the designer or encapsulating the spirit of the age or institution or client, is therefore fallacious. In order that ideas attain an 'objective life', no matter whether in literature, art, design, or architecture, and that in informing a designed artifact they remain equally indeterminate in their impact by attracting unwanted and unintended reactions through the interpretations that are brought to bear by critics, observers, and participants, we cannot get at them to know they are independent. They are always and already lost in the interpretation we bring to comprehending them. If 'expression', in the sense of a transfer of a state of mind or a personality or a spirit in a designed work, is not actually capable of being so expressed, then what *do* we recognize when we say it is 'designed'? One answer is offered in the last section.

A. Esthetics in Architecture

1. Esthetics: An Architectural Speak-Easy

There has lately grown into use in the arts a silly pedantic term under the name of Aesthetics . . . said to be the science whereby the first principles in all the arts are derived . . . it is, however, one of the metaphysical and useless additions to nomenclature in the arts . . . and its application to architecture of least value; because in that art form is from construction so limited by necessity, that sentiment can scarcely be said to be further connected. **Joseph Gwilt.** 1867:§2493.

The scientific method is intellectually and practically useful, but the naive, the anthropomorphic way which humanises the world and interprets it by analogy with our own bodies and our own wills, is still the aesthetic way; it is the basis of poetry, and it is the foundation of architecture. **Geoffrey Scott.** 1924:218.

Our minds are on the one hand, superb devices for . . . the construction of a world; and on the other hand they are bundles of activities, curiosities, ongoing involvements with specifics, events, states of affairs, the surprising and the novel. The two aspects are always conjoined. . . . When we specifically pay attention to this conjunction, as Kant realised, we engage in aesthetic contemplation. . . . In studying aesthetics therefore we study the very stuff of mind, the most central subject of psychology, including aesthetic psychology. But first of all we must be brave enough to say 'aesthetics' in front of the children. **Tom Heath.** 1974:183.

It was an aesthetic impulse that led to the development of a language of architecture, with its own particular visual vernacular. **Roger Scruton.** 1983:187.

TRACE   The term 'esthetic' comes from the Greek *aistheta,* meaning things perceivable by the senses; it may be opposed with *noeta,* those things thinkable or known intellectually or immaterially. Esthetics as the Greek *aisthetiki* can also be linked tenuously with *aisthanome,* meaning 'to feel', which in a wider sense connects with the pursuit of 'what is good' (Gk. *kalologia*) in art and social life, according to Anthony Antoniades (1986), wherein lies one of its greatest obfuscations.

Esthetics gained an élitist edge through its misapplication in German to the 'criticism of taste' formulated by the philosopher Alexander Gottlieb Baumgarten in his unfinished treatise *Aesthetica* (1750–1758) and has been used that way in English since the early nineteenth century. Among the principles of architecture Vitruvious outlined, there are two that involve esthetics: Arrangement *(diathesis),* "the putting of things in their proper places and *elegance of effect*" [emphasis added]; and Eurythmy, "beauty and fitness." Under

Arrangement, Vitruvius lists two departments: Reflection, which is "careful and laborious thought, and *watchful intention directed to the agreeable effect* of one's plan" [emphasis added]; and Invention, which is self-explanatory (Vitruvius 1486:1.2). Esthetics is the realm of elegant and agreeable effect.

COMMENTARY In prospect of visiting Venice, Florence, and Pisa, a visit that was to be ironically thwarted by a fever brought on by 'a sort of ecstasy' into which he had worked himself, Marcel Proust in *Remembrance of Things Past* reflects on the emotions he was experiencing leading up to his departure and declares "the motive force of my exaltation was a longing for aesthetic enjoyments, the guide-books ministered even more to it than books on aesthetics, and, more again than the guide-books, the railway timetables" (vol. 1, 1981:424). Haven't we all been affected by 'longings' while traveling for pleasure in anticipation of arrival and had progressively more intense feelings once the train or flight timetables were perused and after the tickets were in hand? But few of us would call such longings esthetic, we tend to label such feelings excitement or emotion or desire, real 'aesthetic enjoyments' being what Proust points to, no matter how intense our feelings might be.

What exactly were the esthetic enjoyments Proust was anticipating? They were related to the 'domes and towers' of Venice, Florence, and Pisa, the explicit materiality and spatiality of the architecture, the sheer volumetric exuberance and richness of surface already hinted at in the guide books, which he allowed his imagination to multiply. The esthetic experience for Proust was already under way, but it needed the actual moments of raw and untrammeled contact to be complete, something that was to elude him on this occasion, as it turned out.

There were at least three factors bound up in Proust's longings—sensitization to the potential for esthetic enjoyment, immediate and first-hand experience to realize the potential, and the feeling of completeness once the potential had been fulfilled, a pleasure that could be appreciated for its own sake. For Proust in this instance esthetic enjoyment was a calculated *and* passionate affair, not accidental or spontaneous, because he already knew from experience that there were certain pleasures or delights to be had from architecture and he was looking forward to experiencing exactly those qualities in Italy *for what they would give him.* His was a fully conscious, highly rationalized, emotionally supercharged esthetic enjoyment that would be completed by the fine discriminations and nuances of immediate experience.

Most people are not equipped for esthetic enjoyments of the Proustian kind, because he was an *aficionado,* not to say a connoisseur. Esthetic enjoyment is not just the province of those educated to it, though, so refined that it is beyond the brutish masses; esthetic experience is enjoyed by everyone exactly to the extent that they are able to comprehend it, there is as much of it to be had in a football game as in a work of art, and enough in each to fill a person's capacity for it; no more, no less. A question arises here over whether there can be esthetic autonomy, esthetics attaching to an object independent of any intention or interpretation of it. Stanley Fish (1989) points out in relation to 'artistic' texts that esthetic autonomy is a positivist assumption, and that "neither artists nor anyone else can produce texts capable of being detached from intention" (118). Similarly, architectural creations cannot be detached from intention either in their creation or their interpretation, "since intention is an interpretive fact," according to Fish. Esthetic autonomy is therefore a myth.

Thus, esthetics as an umbrella term is used for qualities possessed by an artifact or building after it has been *designed*—it is not an autonomous quality but an intention that designers and architects bring to designing; it is their stock in trade. For one critic, a crisis began in architecture more than two centuries ago when certain purveyors of taste, notably the picturesque theorists Uvedale Price, Payne Knight and J. C. Loudon, applied 'esthetics' to architecture and drove a wedge between form and use, a distinction that was to oblige architecture and building to commence separate lives (St. John Wilson 1992:viii). Almost overnight, architecture became a matter of securing refinement in the face of a ravaging materiality and destructive natural forces, an us-and-them attitude that coincided with the consolidation of architecture as a nascent profession offering design as discernment. From the mid-nineteenth century, esthetics came to mean anything pertaining to the appreciation or criticism of the beautiful, or displaying refined taste, or things done in accordance with 'good taste'. Thus, the philosophy of taste or the beautiful was 'esthetics', and this became one way in which the term was used in architecture, the other being as a descriptive and uncritical catch-all, as in 'a building's esthetics', that bundle of concerns involving composition, shaping, colors, textures, and proportions, or the 'goal' or critical pursuit of these.

From the 1920s the numerous attempts to understand esthetics by trying to quantify it through psychological studies or so-called 'experimental esthetics' (Arnheim 1954, 1966; Birkhoff 1933; Heath 1971) cooperated with the growth of 'psychophysics', which involved quite elaborate studies of 'affectivity', esthetic impact in relation to appearance, mood, character, meaning, and other abstracted qualities (Heath 1974; Prak 1968; Preiser 1989; Thorne and Arden 1980) to constitute a nascent 'science' of esthetics. At the same time, there has been some particularly hardnosed writing about the myths, faults, and absurdities concerning esthetic appreciation and understanding, notably by Nelson Goodman in 1972 (Frascina and Harrison 1982:191–201). Goodman's brief insights into the connection between art and science, his positing a necessary link between emotion and cognition in relation to esthetic experience, and his proffering of a basis for esthetics grounded in a cognitive symbol system, some of the features of which are syntactic density, semantic density, exemplification, and 'relative syntactic repleteness', are still beacons of clarity compared with the semiotic obscurantism of some recent writings about sign, syntax, and code as surrogate esthetic topics in architecture (Jencks 1977, 1980; Broadbent, Bunt, and Jencks 1980).

However, the quest for clarity and the attempt to make of esthetics a science, have conspired to remove esthetics from the province of intention and interpretation and locate it in the object, to give it an autonomy that was shown above to be problematical. Most recently, computer researchers in architecture have taken the so-called science of esthetics a step further by attempting to develop syntactical rules and semantic codes for a language of architecture (Oxman, Radford and Oxman 1987), as well as algorithms of design that try to assimilate design with artificial intelligence systems (Stiny and Gipps 1978; Mitchell 1990). Concurrent with this liberally funded scientific push toward the Cartesian project of 'a language' has been a noticeable drift in the opposite direction in the critical architectural literature, one embracing free interpretation, reflexivity, and an unavoidable intersubjectivity both textually and graphically; the outcome for esthetics is two entirely counterposed agendas that are unlikely to reconcile despite the role computer-aided drafting (CAD) technology already has in practice.

The worry is that informed discussion of esthetics as an interpretive issue is now almost absent from professional architectural journals and from open public debate, even though it is warranted as a public concern of the highest order among architects, planners, fine arts commissions, and design review boards. Architects seem to believe either that esthetic matters such as beauty, style, composition, harmony, character, and taste are now so understood that they may be codified and loosened from human involvement, or that they are so little understood that it is best not to talk about them at all. Architects mostly offer esthetic opinions by way of advice in situations where they will not be challenged or where they can trade on and be accepted for their artfulness. They avoid open discussion of esthetics because it would show how fragile their grasp of such notions actually is, as court appearances by architects under cross-examination can show. Esthetics has been so corralled that it has been forced underground to be uneasily spoken about privately and in hushed tones, as though waiting for Prohibition to be lifted.

FURTHER SOURCES   Ashihara 1983; Banham 1962; Birkhoff 1933; Dewey 1934; Heath 1971, 1974; Prall 1929, 1936; Rasmussen 1959; Santayana 1896; Sartre 1963; Scruton 1979; Stiny and Gipps 1978.

2. Beauty: The Ken of Designer and Architect

To put it shortly, the house in which the owner can find a pleasant retreat at all seasons is presumably at once the pleasantest and most beautiful. **Socrates.** In *Xenophon.* Cited in Mitchell 1990:204.

Beauty is that reasoned harmony of all the parts within a body, so that nothing may be added, taken away, or altered, but for the worse. It is a great and holy matter . . . beauty is some inherent property, to be found suffused all through the body of that which may be called beautiful. **Leon Battista Alberti.** 1755b:6.2.

What we feel as 'beauty' in architecture is not a matter for logical demonstration. It is experienced, consciously, as a direct and simple intuition, which has its ground in that subconscious region where our physical memories are stored, and depends partly on these, and partly on the greater ease imparted to certain visual and motor impulses. **Geoffrey Scott.** 1924:261.

Beauty has been defined by some as fitness for purpose. It is a good slogan . . . but it is quite untrue. It is blatantly untrue in its extreme form: fitness equals beauty, and it is not even correct in the more moderate form: no beauty without fitness. **Nikolaus Pevsner.** 1946. *Visual Pleasures From Everyday Things*:12. Cited in Crook 1987:307.

The capacity for wonder is a primitive instinct: with no knowledge, no study, by wonder alone one can get really close to beauty which is total harmony. . . . We know in a spontaneous and innate fashion when things are beautiful. **Louis Kahn.** 1974. "Harmony between man and architecture." In Latour 1991.

[Hegel] posited that a philosophical work devoted to aesthetics, the philosophy or science of the beautiful, must exclude natural beauty. It is in everyday life that one speaks of a beautiful sky. But there is no natural beauty. More precisely, artistic beauty is superior to natural beauty, as the mind that produces it is superior to nature. One must therefore say that absolute beauty, the *telos* or final essence of the beautiful, appears in art and not in nature as such. **Jacques Derrida.** 1987:25.

TRACE   The ancient Greek term *kallos* or *kallone,* beauty, and *to kalon,* the beautiful, is the basis for calligraphy, calisthenics, kaleidoscope, and kaleidophone in English. Its Latin equivalent in an abstract sense (see below) is *pulchritudo,* beauty, excellence or attractiveness, which gains nothing by its English use as 'pulchritude'. Another term used by Homer for beauty is *charis* (Onians 1951), which allied with the pursuit of esthetic good and had two meanings: objectively it described the outward grace or beauty of something; subjectively it meant 'favor', whether given or received or possessed by something, hence *charisma.* The term has been mostly translated as 'grace' or 'charm', and its Latin equivalents are *venustas* and *gratia,* according to Pollitt (1974:298–299) who also writes:

> *Pulchritudo* seems distinguishable from *venustas,* as *kallos* is from *charis,* in that *charis-venustas* expresses a graceful appearance or effect which is essentially a matter of simple sense experience, while *kallos-pulchritudo* can sometimes express a beauty which is understood as an abstract quality or idea. The latter shade of meaning undoubtedly explains the frequency with which *pulchritudo* occurs in connection with *phantasia* theory as preserved by Cicero and Quintilian (425–426).

Venustas brings us directly to the three qualities Vitruvius deemed fundamental to architecture, *firmitas, utilitas, venustas*—firmness, usefulness and delight, or technology, function, and form according to St. John Wilson (1992:38)—delight being transport of beauty. Alberti formulated a theory of beauty on the basis of his 'reasoned harmony', which he summarizes thus: "Beauty is a form of sympathy and consonance of the parts within a body, according to definite number, outline, and position, as dictated by *concinnitas,* the absolute and fundamental rule in Nature. This is the main object of the art of building, and the source of her dignity, charm, authority, and worth" (Alberti 1755b:9.5). Overshadowing these foundational writers in architecture and those who were to follow in the nineteenth century, however, looms the towering intellect of Kant, whose *Critique of Judgement* of 1790 was to permanently alter the conception of beauty.

COMMENTARY   Setting aside Kant's thesis for a moment, the 'reasoned harmony' to which Alberti refers would appeal to those who believe that beauty is still a major pursuit of architecture. This rare and quietly spoken breed, like Alberti, would also abjure 'mere fancy' on the part of individual judgment in maintaining that beauty is both "a reasoning faculty that is inborn" and a quality resident in a building which is "some natural excellence and perfection that excites the mind and is immediately recognized by it." The conclusion Alberti reaches, which is summarized in the trace above, introduces the elusive notion of *concinnitas,* "in which all beauty shines full face," a term that, as 'concinnity' in rhetoric, means a symmetry of style, finish, or elegance, a skillful fitting together of parts. Most architects would admit of some quality like concinnity guiding designing, but would probably call it artfulness or talent; certainly they would see it as an insightfulness accompanying designing that eludes nonarchitects and that has degrees distinguishing the better architects from their contemporaries.

Returning to Kant, a number of definitions of the beautiful were presented throughout the *Critique of Judgement,* although Kant is careful to say that "there can be no objective rule of taste by which what is beautiful may be defined by means of concepts" (§17). With this qualification, he maintained that the beautiful is the disinterested object of delight in something discerned by taste (§5); that which, apart from a concept, pleases universally (§9); the form of finality in an object, apart from its end or purpose (§19); and that which pleases necessarily (§22). Kant summarized beauty thus: "Beauty (whether of nature or of art) may in general be termed the *expression* of aesthetic ideas" (§51), with the proviso that art needs "the medium of a concept of the Object," whereas nature does not. He positions architecture as a *plastic* formative fine art, along with sculpture, but differentiates it from sculpture as it:

> is the art of presenting concepts of things which are possible *only through art,* and the determining ground of whose form is not nature but an arbitrary end—and of presenting them both with a view to this purpose and yet, at the same time, with aesthetic finality. In architecture the chief point is a certain *use* of the artistic object to which, as the condition, the aesthetic ideas are limited. In sculpture the mere *expression* of aesthetic ideas is the main intention . . . adaptation of the product to a particular use is the essential element in a *work of architecture* (§51).

What Kant tries to say with all this is, basically, that beauty is not a feature of any object to which it applies, but is the core of the delight we experience arising from that object's esthetic finality or 'closure'. Herein lies a quandary, because in his argumentation Kant differentiates two kinds of beauty: free beauty *(pulchritudo vaga)* and dependent beauty *(pulchritudo adherens),* of which "the first presupposes no concept of what the object should be [while] the second does presuppose such a concept and, with it, an answering perfection of the object" (§16). He gives examples of what he means, saying of the second "the beauty of man . . . , the beauty of a horse, or of a building . . . presupposes a concept of the end that defines what the thing has to be, and consequently a concept of its perfection; and is therefore merely appendant beauty." Thus architecture does not fit Kant's scheme neatly as an art of pure contemplation, but like an errant child draws attention to its misfit behavior, awkward and ungainly in an otherwise refined system, obliging Kant to compromise not his *Critique* but architecture, by calling its beauty 'mere' and 'appendant'. Architecture reeled away dazed and confused.

For almost two hundred years since Kant, architecture has been haunted by the specter of beauty being mere appendage, confusingly moralized by the lamplight of John Ruskin, criminalized in the form of ornament by Adolf Loos, insanely certified in glass by Paul Scheerbart, spiritualized and idealized if not decriminalized by Gropius, Mies, and Corbusier, then suffocated by Krier and the Prince of Wales, so terrorizing the natives that they now discuss beauty furtively, if at all. So convincing has the marginalization of beauty been that Roger Scruton (1979) refuses to offer a definition, preferring instead to explore "the state of mind, and the mode of reasoning" while hinting at some possible definition in the future but content to remain in the realm of process. "It seems to me that we should do better to forget about all that," writes Scruton. "To accord to beauty its traditional emphasis is not only to elevate it above a cluster of aesthetic terms, all of which deserve equal prominence; it is also to suggest that our problem is one of meaning, rather than one of the philosophy of mind" (235). Apart from the odd eccentric or professedly poetic architect like Carlo Scarpa or Louis Kahn promoting it, the beautiful has been shamed by all this into being so mere and so appended that it is just used blandly as an adjective by popular critics mostly in relation to drawings or photographs (Sorkin 1991).

While the 'suffusion' of beauty Alberti writes about as occurring throughout anything described as beautiful does not now excite much attention, it nonetheless still inhabits the texts of architecture if for beauty one substitutes *esthetic.* Because of the renewed interpretative role all observers and participants (collectively 'players') are now thought to have in relation to art, architecture, or the appreciation of design, beauty has lately figured as one value transferred in the quest for meaning if not as an end in itself; which raises a question about how the transfer occurs. For this it is useful to mix a little from Alberti with the phenomenology of Christian Norberg-Schulz (1965). The engagement of the artist, designer, or architect in the act of designing, that concinnity brought to a work, is re-cognized by the players through *cathexis,* a charge or mental energy interpreted as attaching to a work, a term Norberg-Schulz (1965) appropriates from psychology in relation to art. Concinnity-cathexis as a way of actively engaging the esthetic emotion with architecture, concinnity at the conceptual end of the process and cathexis at the interpretive end, ensures that beauty still has channels through which it can migrate.

Indeed, the Spanish-American philosopher and poet George Santayana's exposition in *The Sense of Beauty* (1896) is still valid. Beauty is still the cooperative venture it was then, an act of mediation ('fusion') between and among values and things, resident totally neither in us nor in things, although his *affection* for Platonism inclined him to make esthetic qualities free and independent agencies. Santayana construed beauty in both the values brought to and the qualities assumed in the object of contemplation. "Beauty is pleasure regarded as the quality of a thing" offers Santayana as his most succinct definition, although by way of qualification he says "Beauty is a value, that is, not a perception of a matter of fact or of a relation: it is an emotion, an affection of our volitional and appreciative nature." Of course, one difficulty is in applying his definition to a designed object that is yet to be built. If the 'thing' to which beauty is assigned via pleasure is only a drawn concept and has no independent built existence, because it emanates just from the designer, unless another (ethereal) agency such as Platonic Form is invoked, beauty cannot be other than resident in the designer. Or can it?

As a final word, it is amusing to read the work of the Australian architect and critic Robin Boyd, writing more than three decades ago. For Boyd (1961), beauty was 'a theocratic term'. Referring to the late fifties, he saw architecture as "moving towards theism, without concern for a moral code but sustained by a blinding faith in the unerring rightness and self-justification of one god: Beauty" (158). Boyd declared against Beauty because he saw its pursuit as the cause for him of one of the worst excesses of architects, 'featurism'. Beauty was "too full of mysteries" and was merely "a private understanding between an observer and an object." He sought to substitute for it another term, appropriateness, which many architects have tried to seek but failed (see 10A.4, Character). The trouble is that appropriateness is just as theocratic, and the beast beauty has not been roped; it just needs someone game enough to talk about it again, other than historically.

FURTHER SOURCES   Bonta 1979; Collins 1965; Colquhoun 1989; Dewey 1934; Hays and Burns 1990; Prall 1929, 1936; Rowe 1987.

3. Style and Mundane Life

Style is a unity of principle animating all the work of an epoch, the result of a state of mind which has its own special character. **Le Corbusier.** 1920. In Conrads 1964:60.

In spite of a century of speculation, we are no nearer to having formulated a theory of style adequate to the psychological and historical problems it involves. **Joseph Rykwert.** 1982:130.

Precisely because style deals in surface impressions, it is difficult to concretize, to discern its definitions. It forms a chimerical, yet highly visible corridor between the world of things and human consciousness. Yet investing profane things with sacred meanings is an ancient activity, a universal preoccupation. This, in and of itself, does not define style; nor does it situate style within the particular conditions and contradictions of contemporary life. **Stuart Ewen.** 1984:125–126.

Relations of power in society are transformed, by style, into things of beauty. . . . The deflection of social concerns through the channels of style has become an earmark of the culture within which we live. **Stuart Ewen.** 1984:130.

The hermeneutical 'why?' [of meaning] has many varieties. Two in particular deserve mention at this juncture: the 'why?' of intention [or reasons], and the 'why?' of style. [The second] refers, not to reasons, but to the greater or lesser degree of coherence, or 'significant relation', between the action explained and those which surround it. 'That was the appropriate thing'; 'It was his way'; 'It was a fitting response'—all such. . . . I shall call answers to the 'why?' of style. **Roger Scruton.** 1983:170–171.

Style in architecture is a way of building codified in imagistic form. **J. Mordaunt Crook.** 1987:11.

. . . the fundamental terms for any profound and broadly outlined theory of architecture must be a rational objectivity, historical continuity, social idealism, and a universality of primary ideas. Formal styles should not be the primary object of comprehensive theoretical thought. Styles are the outcome, not the initiators, of fundamental ideas. **Lesnikowski** and **Spheeris.** 1987:38.

There is a word we should refrain from using to describe contemporary architecture—'style'. The moment we fence architecture within a notion of 'style', we open the door to a formalistic approach. The contemporary movement is not a 'style' in the nineteenth-century meaning of form characterization. It is an approach to the life that slumbers unconsciously within all of us. **Nikolaus Pevsner.** 1949. *Pioneers of the Modern Movement*:204 (later called *Pioneers of Modern Design*. Penguin 1960, 1975).

TRACE   In English the word 'style' is adapted via the Old French from the Latin *stilus*, although the spelling with *y* has been associated with the spelling of the Greek *stylos,* for column. From its origin as the stylus, pen or engraving tool, style came to mean writing, particularly the *manner* of writing, and during the sixteenth century that manner characteristic of a particular writer, group, or period. From the beginning of the eighteenth century style referred to a mode of skilled construction, execution, or production. Later in the century and into the nineteenth, style came to refer specifically to the special characteristics or ornamentation of architecture by which differences were distinguished, known for a century as 'taste', and by extension the distinction among aspects of the architecture of any one age, period, region, or person.

Since style arose from habitual tricks a person used in forming individual letters in handwriting, any distinguishing characteristics relating to works of literature came to be known among sixteenth-century Italian critics as *maniera*. "This goes beyond mere habit and includes the artist's way of drawing from memory, not detailed solutions, but ways of solving certain recurring kinds or classes of problems. We thus have the notion of a personal style in art, consisting of both habitual tricks and type solutions" (Heath 1991). Such tricks, habits, and type characteristics make it possible to talk of an architect's repertoire or 'manner' both as a quality and as a methodology. Moreover, it may just be that *maniera* is all one's creative identity really is: "style is a way of stating who one is: politically, sexually, in terms of status and class. Style is a device of conformity, or of opposition. Style conveys mood. Style is a device by which we judge—and are judged by—others" (Ewen 1984:126).

COMMENTARY   Like beauty, style is not a word readily found in the indexes of recent books on architecture, although it is a topic that seems to fascinate architects. In nearly two hundred pages on the principles of architectural history, the art historian Paul Frankl (1914) mentions 'style' only about six times. Only three years later a new journal, *De Stijl*, espousing "the beauty in the new plasticism" (Jaffé 1967) was published in Leiden, Holland. Edited by Theo van Doesburg, around whom a movement formed, the ideas of the De Stijl movement remained inaccessible to the English-speaking world for half of the journal's fifteen-year existence. The International Style did not exist until 1932, when Henry-Russell Hitchcock and Philip Johnson gave their exhibition at the Museum of Modern Art that title, although it had by then been under way for seven years; it lasted another thirty-three, until Kunio Mayekawa finally declared it and everything it stood for an inhuman tragedy (Frampton 1980:261). The failure was one of confidence in architecture's self-image as healer of social conflict through liberal applications of style.

Masochistically, however, architects return to style again and again, just as a dog worries a bone, seeking and finding reassurance in doing what they do best—putting on the style. A colloquium held at the Royal Institute of British Architects (RIBA) in 1978 asked itself the question 'What is style?' After hearing that certain architects had it, others did it with, certain buildings had it, others had it added, the age and situation dictated it, modernism missed out on it because of lacking principles, and it was all that Piers Gough had going for him, the RIBA agreed to settle eventually for there being no easy answer (*Architects' Journal*, 29 November:1,028). In contradistinction to Charles Jencks, Philip Drew (1980) sees in postmodernism style rediscovered and rehabilitated, "a quite momentous recognition and acceptance of style as a positive factor in architecture, and acknowledgement that style is central to architecture . . . no longer taboo." In a long catalog of features, Drew parallels postmodernism with sixteenth-century mannerism in its use of multilayered space, spatial fragmentation, heterogeneity, ambiguity, dematerialization, perversity, iridescence, historical allusion, distortions of reality and scale, inherent estheticism, and the dominance of form over content.

Over the decade since Drew wrote this piece, architecture has witnessed a consolidation of anti-modern sentiment and a settling in of mannerist preoccupations that has superseded the self-conscious historical borrowings of postmodernism with an intense cultivation of style, regardless of attempts to dislodge it with declarations of 'Beyond Style' (Bucholtz and Monk 1984) or redirecting it away from buildings to the drawn representations of buildings as Luscombe and Peden (1992:4) do so successfully. Though they studiously avoid the word *style*, it gurgles under every line of Peter Cook and Rosie Llewellyn-Jones's *New Spirit in Architecture* (1991), an anthology of architects 'mentioned' among the plebs and architectural kingmakers and having the common characteristic "that they each display a certain [*je ne sais quoi*] spirit," in other words, *maniera*. Architecture is now an industry of awesome size. Architecture media and publishing interests, the marketing techniques of professional institutions and corporations, and keen competition for academic prestige, creative acceptability, and international recognition have transformed a profession into a style industry of tremendous potency whether most architects are prepared to admit it or not.

Among younger contemporary architects, modernist notions of style being decried in favor of architecture being a neutral and direct conduit for economic, social, and cultural expression or reform are now ignored. There are still pockets of concern for the user in architects' requesting a socially responsible architecture (Ghirardo 1991), but the postmodernist idea of responsibility is for a full-on architecture that intervenes and obliges rather than acquiesces in the lowest common denominator, an architecture that forges ahead with style and 'with (borrowed) styles' and drags everyone kicking and screaming with it.

It is intriguing how quickly a study such as that by Judith Blau (1984) dates, based, as it was, on surveys undertaken in 1974 and 1979. Even now, such a few years later, the study does not reflect the same kinds of concerns expressed in current letters to the professional journals. Under the subheading of "Ideas and Style," for instance, Blau reports the ideas of rank-and-file architects being "at fundamental odds with the prevailing style of built architecture and with the objectives evident in practice," the bland ideas of their pragmatic principals, the monumentalism and 'stylistic poverty' of late-modernism (by which is meant "the international style as the symbolic embodiment of monopoly capitalism and commercial imperatives"). Instead the younger architects argue for humanistic architecture and user concerns (137)—are these (now older) architects expressing the same concerns today? Blau taps seventies feelings rubbing up against sixties values; values that went down with the International Style, and which, by then already a decade old, were being replaced with newly assembled humanitarian concerns already rather dated. By the time the book was published, these values were a generation gone, and useless as examples of contemporary feeling in a profession almost thirty years on.

Even though corporate International Style modernism still lingers, nobody takes it seriously as a threat any more because the pursuit of style has made it irrelevant. It is impossible, for instance, to reconcile Blau's 'findings' with a firm like Morphosis, whose employees presumably feel no such dissonance with their principals' values and are not 'at odds' with the 'prevailing style' around them, whatever that might be. They are, of course, located in the potboiler of Los Angeles, where no one style prevails. And despite also the widely acknowledged failure of the modernist agenda in architecture generally arising from finding itself somewhere between the hell of economic production and the heaven of social ideals, certain contemporary industrial designers, while admitting a complicity with production, still see style properly harnessed as the panacea for social and cultural ills, as though a crisis never happened. Writes the Italian designer Matteo Thun:

> We in the Western industrialised nations have it constantly hammered into us by the marketing-men, who are seconded by the mass media, that we need to define ourselves by buying and consuming, the 'demonstrative consumer' being the ideal held up for emulation. Why then should this gospel concentrate on prestige products and avant-garde design? If equal energy were devoted to the stylistic enhancement of the mundane objects of everyday life, this life would be much more worth living (In Fischer 1989:211).

The assumption by Thun is that style at the hands of a (no doubt good) designer is something that can enhance life, a wondrous alchemy that transforms mundane existence into 'much more'. What this much more is nobody seems prepared to say, but it smacks of false consciousness, of designers actually believing their own advertising. I wonder how many architects still believe in transforming the world by design, as against those who are reconciled to the fact that style is all there is?

FURTHER SOURCES   Bucholtz and Monk 1984; Crook 1987; Oxman, Radford and Oxman 1987; Macleod 1971; Rykwert 1982.

4. Character as 'Evident Particularity'

In general whatever is productive of character in a building must be conspicuous and distinctive; and it should rather consist of one than many features. **J. C. Loudon.** 1833. *Encyclopedia of Cottage, Farm and Villa Architecture*:1,120.

When I define Beauty as the promise of Function; Action as the presence of Function; Character as the record of Function; I arbitrarily divide that which is essentially one. **Horatio Greenough.** 1853. "Relative and Independent Beauty." Cited in Rowe 1976.

In recalling the impressions we have received from the works of man, after a lapse of time long enough to involve in obscurity all but the most vivid, it often happens that we find a strange preeminence and durability in many upon whose strength we had little calculated, and that points of character which had escaped the detection of judgement, become developed under the waste of memory; as veins of harder rock, whose places could not at first have been discovered by the eye, are left salient under the action of frosts and streams. **John Ruskin.** 1855. "The Lamp of Power":§1.

. . . a truly significant building is preeminently a structure, organized according to *the principles of architectural composition* and infused with a symbolic content which is usually described as *character.* **Colin Rowe.** 1976:62.

Character is seldom, if ever, defined, but it is generally implied that it may be at once the impression of artistic individuality and the expression, either symbolic or functional, of the purpose for which the building was constructed. **Colin Rowe.** 1976:62

. . . attention to detail and to human scale creates that elusive quality of *character,* and every nationality has a subtle way of expressing it differently. **Charles, Prince of Wales.** 1989:117.

TRACE   Character derives from the Greek *charassein,* cut or engrave, and in its literal sense is variously a brand, stamp, or distinctive mark; a graphic symbol in writing or printing; or a cipher or magical symbol. In its figurative sense it is variously any feature, trait, or characteristic; an essential peculiarity, or the nature or sort of a person or thing; and the aggregate of peculiar qualities that constitutes personal or national individuality; and the mental or moral constitution. Commonly we use *in character* for that which is in harmony with an assumed part or role, or is appropriate, or is in keeping with a person's usual conduct or attitudes, or is dressed for the part.

In ancient Greek usage the word *ethos* referred "to the study of and representation of human character [of any kind whether good or bad] in art," which differs from its modern use as "loftiness of character" or "high moral bearing," meanings that arose from misinterpretations of passages from Aristotle and Pliny during the nineteenth century (Pollitt 1974:188–189). In France *character* formed part of architectural considerations from early in the eighteenth century, but in England it did not enter the architectural vocabulary until very late in the century, when suddenly it appeared in regular usage. Colin Rowe (1976) maintains that character in architecture is implied, if not defined, as "the impression of artistic individuality and the expression, either symbolic or functional, of the purpose for which the building is constructed."

COMMENTARY   The Prince of Wales (Charles 1989) opens his *A Vision of Britain* with a salute to character, "something rather special about Britain, about our landscape, about our villages and our towns, and about those aspects of our surroundings which provide us with what we rather loosely call character. This character, which is so evident in the local architectural styles of the buildings you see in each county, is part of an extraordinarily rich tradition we've inherited from our forbears" (17). A century of pages later Prince Charles refers to the 'elusive quality' of character; character had changed from something 'special' and 'so evident' that it was worth fighting for and preserving to something 'elusive' that was being sought among the details and through human scale. Something occurred over those hundred pages that caused character in such apparent abundance and vivacity to be lost, as though in reviewing the environmental degradation the text became contaminated and character in the end could summon only a weak plea for details and scale.

While the word *character* may be, and frequently is, used indifferently in everyday speech or writing, as certain of the above definitions indicate, it is clear that Prince Charles has a particular concept in mind, intimated in part by his own sketches and the 'mood' of many photographs throughout the book. Character for His Royal Highness is inherent in the landscape or place and in certain sorts of buildings (mainly vernacular), *and* is a quality that can be introduced by design. In this emphasis he is reiterating the sentiment of nineteenth-century picturesque landscape painters, gardeners, and theorists, who saw character as a 'congruity of mood', which, by the middle of the nineteenth century, had come to oppose the academic idealist tradition by seeking an 'evident particularity' in a work, a cult of distinctive characteristics, in Loudon's terms, that was anti-academic (Rowe 1976:66–67). The Modern Movement reimposed academic rules of design of a sort in which purity of expression was uppermost and character, if it was admitted as a quality at all, was a moralistic symbolic content consciously introduced by the designer in combination with 'rules' of composition (see 10A.5, Composition) if a building was to achieve success and significance (E. Pickering, cited in Rowe 1976). It is this prescription and the severity of its outcomes that galvanized the reaction by the Prince of Wales.

British nostalgia *cum* lifestyle magazines like *Country Life, In Britain,* and *This England* depend on the looseness of 'character' in trading on the inherent abundance of character in Britain, just as the tourist industry does in singling out the curiosities and the picturesque in its evocative photographs. Such magazines are the hallmarks of the 'character industry', the *Architectural Digest* being the nearest equivalent in the United States; to a certain extent the antique, history, and 'house and garden' magazines in many countries provide sufficient outlets for nostalgic yearnings. Furthermore, those sections of bookshops labeled 'Americana' or 'Australiana', or their localized variants, provide abundant stocks of works evidencing particularities that sum up—pictorially mostly—national, state, regional, or district 'characteristics'. The specifically architectural contribution to the character industry is the 'design guide', or any collation purporting to codify the distinctive architectural qualities of a place, especially those heritage studies that go beyond just building inventories.

One such heritage study is that on San Francisco's downtown, reported in *Splendid Survivors* (Corbett 1979) using a model and survey technique based on *The Evaluation of Historic Buildings* by Harold Kalman of 1978 (cited in Corbett). Under the primary evaluation category "Environment" are two criteria dealing specifically with character: Continuity and Setting. *Continuity* is the factor by which a building "contributes to the continuity or character of the street, neighborhood, or area" and holds character to be an existing evidential quality "of a distinguished area" that is either established, supported, or negated by a building. *Setting* is the reverse; the factor by which "setting and/or landscape contributes to the continuity or character of the street, neighborhood, or area," and holds character to be the quality that is discerned in a place and thereby dominates or distinguishes it. *Integrity* is another primary category, in which *Alterations* is a factor that evaluates the degree by which a building has been altered in relation to the 'overall character'. Here and there the survey uses phrases such as 'urban character', 'traditional character', and 'historic character', even though character is never clearly defined and in the case of historic character actually mixes evaluation categories. But we all know what they meant!

Turning to design guides, one of the earliest and most notable is that of the County Council of Essex, England, popularly called the *Essex Design Guide* (Essex 1973). Its planning policy calls for dwelling densities to be compatible with 'the general character of the area' (10), while its visual policy demands the creation of a 'visually satisfactory environment' by setting buildings within "a dominant landscape of a character indigenous with Essex," by using 'vernacular' materials "to perpetuate the unique building character of the county," and by detailing "to reinforce the character required by the design and its location" (15). In the Practice Notes portion supporting the policies, comprising the bulk of the *Guide*, attempts to demonstrate what character is are at best vague. Highly variegated spaces are intended to produce 'special character or identity', and individual spaces are to be emphasized by 'change in architectural character', yet 'regional character' is to be retained by a limited palette of local materials and colors and by fostering 'the local vernacular character', which accords directly with R. W. Brunskill saying that "the choice of walling material establishes the character of . . . vernacular architecture" (Brunskill 1971). Conversely, one would be hard-pressed to find the word 'character' in John Prizeman's *Your House: The Outside View* (London, Hutchison, 1975), yet its hundreds of photographs and drawings positively exude congruity of mood and everything to do with character referred to above. Confounding, but we know what they mean.

A key word used in the trace was 'appropriate', another of those terms whose meaning everyone thinks they know and yet is most elusive to pin down, even with a dictionary. It is a selfish word, describing the annexation and possession of qualities that the 'appropriator' deems suitable. In the spirit of professional selflessness, architects have described as appropriate those qualities *they* deem appropriated by a place or object viewed in a quasi-objective way. But any objectivity is specious, and what is or is not appropriate becomes a matter of opinion—architects appropriate 'appropriate' to their own ends. The combination 'appropriate character' produces the most charged of paradoxes imaginable, and highlights the pervasive difficulty in using 'character'—the confounding of its generality with its particularity. If 'appropriate' were expunged from architectural, planning, historical, and urban design discourse, would these disciplines be any the worse for it? And if 'appearance' were substituted for 'character', would you know what I mean?

FURTHER SOURCES   Brolin 1980; Germann 1972; Lavin 1992; Rykwert 1982; Vidler 1990.

5. Composition as Artful Arrangement

The whole force and rule of design, consists in a right and exact adapting and joining together the lines and angles which compose and form the face of the building. **Leon Battista Alberti.** 1755a:1.1.

. . . the whole matter of building is composed of lineaments and structure. All the intent and purpose of lineaments lies in finding the correct, infallible way of joining and fitting together those lines and angles which define and enclose the surfaces of the building. **Leon Battista Alberti.** 1755b:1.1.

Composition . . . should have its laws, or it would be only a fancy and a caprice. . . . Composition should have reference to two elements—the material made use of, and the processes that can be applied to it. **Eugène-Emmanuel Viollet-le-Duc.** *Learning to Draw.* 1879. Cited in Hearn 1990:170.

The role of composition pure is to link together, to make effective, to unite into a whole. It is primarily the agent of connection. It will create . . . a whole network of vestibules, of staircases, of covered or open courts, of corridors, all of which we designate by the word circulation. . . . It is the more or less graceful articulation of this network which to a great extent determines the building's appearance. Beaux-Arts Professor **Georges Gromort.** Cited in Drexler 1977:114–115.

Composition is dead that creation may live. **Frank Lloyd Wright.** 1931. *Modern Architecture.* Endpapers.

Composition is our stock-in-trade; it involves tasks of an exclusively physical order. Composition comprises choice of surface, division of the surface, co-modulation, relationships of density, colour scheme. **Le Corbusier** and **Amédée Ozenfant.** 1920. *Purism.* Cited in Benton, Benton and Sharp, 1975:90.

Just as building elements may be described . . . as 'the words, as it were, that form our architectural language', so the term 'composition', though now unfashionable in architectural circles, can be used to indicate the means of assembling those elements into an architectural whole. **Peter Collins.** 1965:179.

TRACE   Composition is quite simply and literally together-placing, from the Latin *com-positio* and *componere,* and implies both wholeness and order in the placement of parts. To compose in music is to *invent* as well as to assemble in proper form, and this is a meaning that applies also to architecture; in fact, just as an arrangement in music is composition, so it is in architecture. Indeed, the notion of positioning makes composition and disposition not altogether different in architecture, and Vitruvius uses *dispositio* for the Greek *diathesis,* in the sense of composition or arrangement, to mean the placement of individual parts within a whole (Pollitt 1974:166–167).

Vitruvius writes of a 'common ground' of theory that unites all scholarly activity and that in the visual sciences such as astronomy and geometry he calls the *logos optikos,* the 'subject of vision'. Tzonis and Lefaivre (1986) try to identify this logic in classical architecture as a formal system by analyzing classical buildings as compositions. The Latin architectural texts made the word *composition* quite familiar to classical architects, but the first appearance of composition as an architectural term in English was most likely in Robert Morris's *Lectures on Architecture* (1734); he writes "Architecture is an art useful and extensive, it is founded upon beauty, and proportion or harmony are the great essentials of its composition" (cited in Rowe 1976:63).

COMMENTARY   In classical architecture, as in classical thought, the coherence of the system is uppermost, and formal analysis provides one means of understanding how a building is made, of understanding the forms themselves, as against relying on emotional concepts or spatial qualities that can only describe the effects a building has. The formal conventions that make up the canonic system of classical architecture are three—*taxis, genera,* and *symmetry*—explained in 6A.1, Order, and together make up the canon or system of rules in classical composition. Composition in the classical formal sense has already been touched upon in other sections, for example, the whole and part (chapter 2B), order (chapter 6A), geometry, scale, and proportion (chapter 9A). What will be covered here is composition not so much in its formal canonic sense but as an architectural desire for system and cohesion and the conflicts generated in modernist attempts to avoid it.

It would be hard to find two more opposite modern views about composition than those by Frank Lloyd Wright and Le Corbusier and Amédée Ozenfant, above. Wright had earlier objected to composition in his essay "The Cause of Architecture" (1925), asserting that "we may no longer speak of 'composition'" claiming that a work of architecture should be regarded as a plastic thing modeled like a fluid, and not as something superimposed, aggregated, or composed. Yet in their work, Wright and Le Corbusier did not differ greatly; they each adopted compositional rules and utilized ordering systems for assembling a building right down to the finest detail. Le Corbusier developed and applied his Five Points, and later the Modulor, while Wright variously favored certain arrangements in his domestic work, such as the cruciform plan, the pinwheel plan, 'intersecting' spaces, the perimeter corridor and horizontal layering by roof planes, window lines and string courses, and banding of brickwork and timber, as well as certain motifs such as the stripping and framing of panels or elements, the 'captured' sphere, and interlacing patterns, which he echoed time and again (see Hitchcock 1942). Wright was criticizing the rule-bound compositional approach of academicism, not composition *per se;* in other words, he merely preferred his rules of composition to those of others, his art to that of lesser mortals.

Academic composition is said to restrict the 'play' of elements or parts by being both too prescriptive in its rules and too restrictive in the range of elements. Any modern composition that smacks of such rigidification is labeled academic, irrespective of whether it is the result of a classical prescription or not; it is this academic composition that Wright thought the enemy of creativity. Modern composition, on the other hand, is said to have a high degree of freedom, with room to 'play' untrammeled (to a degree) by fixed rules and with a widely varying repertoire of elements. Any academic composition that attempted such freedom was labeled baroque or mannerist or indicated a moment of decline or aberration. It is this 'free' composition that appealed to Le Corbusier and still does to most modern architects; unless that freedom denies any rules, as Deconstructivism appears to do.

In a bid to uncover how the two worlds connect or differ, Alan Colquhoun (1989) explores the dominance of composition in the academic tradition in relation to the dominance of functionalism in modern architecture wherein composition, if it mattered at all, was only one of many elements competing for attention. One conclusion he reaches is that it is in part the degree, not the absence, of composition that differentiates the modern way from the classical. In other words, composition continued to be a concern of modern architects, and Colquhoun points to early modern writers on composition like Howard Robertson, who attempted to reconcile the classical tradition with the modernist project by reaffirming universal principles in architecture but denying they have any particular stylistic outcome.

However, composition was eschewed by the avant-garde because rules for its application interfered with the progressive agenda of contemporary architecture, and gradually, the insistence of this view managed to largely discredit composition by the 1950s. But there was a vehemence in avant-garde criticism, enough to cause Colquhoun to ask, "Where should we look for the origins of the violent antagonism of the twentieth-century avant-garde to composition?" The answer lies in the emphasis the romantic movement gave to organicism, production, and growth, the in-dwelling of spirit (zeitgeist) and the 'principle of structuration' that eliminated the 'composer' in favor of 'mechanisms' of manifestation. It is this emphasis on *system* that gives Colquhoun the title "Classicism versus the Project" and enables him to declare in closing his essay that there are good reasons for reinterpreting the notion of composition for today. While he leaves this declaration hanging to await elaboration at another time, he implies it is a *lack* of system in contemporary architectural design and thinking that warrants another look at composition.

The difficulty with modernist denials of composition is that they force an opposition of the kind that Colquhoun discerns because they are conceived as *either/or* instead of *both/and.* For whatever differences there may seem to be between academic and 'free' composition, they disappear immediately when it is recognized that each is rule-bound; degrees suddenly are of no import, for composition is composition; there is no 'versus'—we have both composition *and* the project. The issue then becomes not whether composition should be acceptable, because it already is, but how composition fits, what rules we choose to abide by, in whatever mode of designing we happen to be. It is not that Deconstructivism or the 'new spirit' is nonsystematic, in compliance with a poststructural age in which being systematic is unacceptable. If this were so, composition could not be considered as Colquhoun suggests, but would also be unacceptable; indeed, some see it this way. On the contrary, composition already is involved in Deconstructivism and against the ideology of poststructuralism, which shows how awkwardly architecture sits in the literary world; *it is just different* from classical and modern composition. We are back with Frank Lloyd Wright.

A final pertinent point is whether Deconstructivism, in challenging the status of "ideal forms and traditional composition" upon which Johnson and Wigley (1988) remark in relation to Tschumi's Parc de la Villette (92) is not tacitly endorsing composition as a legitimate architectural activity. Tschumi's project may challenge traditional composition, but certainly does not disdain romantic composition; it just composes artfully.

FURTHER SOURCES   Collins 1965; Hearn 1990; Kaufmann 1955; Krier 1988; Rowe 1976.

B. Conventions of Communication

1. The Rule of Architectural Convention

The true antithesis of nature is not art but arbitrary conceit, fantasy, and stereotyped convention.
    Not but that there exist conventions which are vital and natural. The arts in certain times and places are controlled by conventions of rite and ceremony. Yet they do not then of necessity become barren and unesthetic, for the conventions themselves live in the life of the community. **John Dewey.** 1934:152.

There is no doubt that [in manners] a man at first learns simply to understand and use certain conventions, conventions which may vary between groups and communities, but which have in common the aim of creating settled expectations, against the background of which the true freedom of social intercourse may develop. But a man who remains punctiliously ruled by those conventions . . . is, socially speaking, a disaster. . . . The art of manners is the art of seeing what is apt before knowing exactly what success will consist in. **Roger Scruton.** 1979:228–229.

The idea of a "modern" architecture . . . stressed the need to remake the language of the art, to explode the conventions and out of the debris to construct a way of speaking adequate to the modern moment. **Anthony Vidler.** 1992:189.

TRACE   Convention is primarily to do with common agreement, its etymology deriving from the Latin *conventio,* for meeting or covenant. The adjective 'conventional' means being characterized by convention, not natural, original, or spontaneous (SOED), while in art it is applied to works considered artificial or stilted. Its correlate is conventionalism, the adherence to or regard for conventional conduct or thought. If adherence to convention is *merely* so regarded, the conventional person or thing is, architecturally speaking, a disaster, as Scruton alludes above. So goes 'normal' architectural thinking.

To talk of conventions in architecture is not to clarify them, although it *is* to suppose their existence. The question is, What are they? Under a consistent doctrine such as classicism this may be quite obvious, but under present conditions the question would involve interrogating the beliefs currently held by architects. Questioning how beliefs are acquired, changed, or administered, as Stanley Fish (1989) suggests, involves addressing "conventions of description, argument, judgement, and persuasion [which] operate in this or that profession or discipline or community" (116). Among such categories may presumably be found the communicative conventions of architecture. "When critics speak of 'convention' in art, they often have in mind organization, form, genre, cross-reference, certain patterns of conformity and departure," writes Roger Scruton (1983:21). The impact in architecture first of communications theory in the 1960s and of semiotics later has reinforced the idea of an architecture of conventions in the form of a system of codings.

COMMENTARY   Being conventional is not something architects like to contemplate let alone admit to, because it is tantamount to being ordinary, undistinguished, unimaginative, boring, unoriginal, uninspired, even banal. The pejorative overtones of the word are so strong that convention in architecture has been permanently tainted—to speak of it is to raise the specter of a moribund 'language' akin to that of classicism understood as a system of rules and motifs, classicism as a style, rather than the sensibility Porphyrios (1982) would have us believe it to be. "Words like 'tradition', 'convention', 'habit', and 'taste', all express forms that have no meaning outside a system," comments Christian Norberg-Schulz (1965:159), for whom, architecturally, convention "is generally used to express that the forms are conservative and exhibit a tendency to lag behind the needs they should serve." Convention therefore smacks of a style within a system of meaning that is somehow out of step with contemporary needs. Concomitantly, to suggest that a contemporary manner is in any way conventional is to spell the death of it as a light to the future.

Against such stylistic conventions may be placed the conventions of communication in architecture, be they the written and drawn kind that pass between architect and builder, the spoken and written kind between critic and architect, or the passive kind more open to interpretation between the work and the participant. Except in the case of the legally binding communication of construction documents, written and drawn communications become suspect if they too closely approach common understanding. Conventions of pictorial perspective are favored less than the more stylized axonometric; simulation of the real in model-making is favored less than exotic sculpting in brass or mahogany; plain words are favored less than jargon and pretentious allusions to literacy in critiques. What use are conventions then in architectural communication, if subversion of understanding is attempted by architects and critics at every turn? What system of architectural communication is there that has no fixity of convention in the signs it uses? Is communication of the kind architects imagine to occur possible at all?

Norberg-Schulz claims that "a *conventional sign* is by definition a whole whose own structure is irrelevant. It represents another whole whose structure is also semantically irrelevant. The conventional sign, therefore, acts formally as an *element* . . . [and] can also be a characteristic building type, a ground-plan, or a particular space-form, etc. We understand that it is linked with the symbol-milieu . . ." (1965:169). Norberg-Schulz, writing at the beginning of what was to become a semiotic fervor, is saying that architecture as a whole *may* be a structure that is irrelevant, that it or any part of it *may* stand for something else the structure of which too *may* be semantically irrelevant. In other words, if it communicates at all, architecture communicates only raw elemental properties or qualities within some system of symbols that are not necessarily architectural.

On this view, the form of the Sydney Opera House is a sign of the functions it houses, even though these are only vaguely hinted at by the shapes and placement of the shells, which is irrelevant to it as a sign of the resolve of government to foster an imaginative cultural artifact (or "Australia's break with colonial conformity and provinciality," as Jencks 1977 offers), which in turn is irrelevant to what it has become as a synecdochic sign for Sydney, Australia, and a "wonder of the world." If we examine the Opera House more closely, the roof forms are a sign of a visceral living organism inside a shell-like enclosure, which is irrelevant to the bifurcated disposition of the shells into opera theater and concert hall 'wings', which is irrelevant to their dramatic glazed walls being a sign for 'eyeballing' the harbor, which in turn is irrelevant to the audiences eyeballing the performances by facing away from the harbor in the auditoria; and the podium is a sign of a solid platform on which to gather, which is irrelevant to the actual disposition of spaces and the myriad circulation paths underneath it. In terms of conventional signs indicating 'entrance', the building is perverse in offering great steps to the upper and foyer concourses that do not admit entrance to the interior, and in offering a gaping cavity in the sides of the podium to the lower concourse, which is a sign for service and 'trade', but is actually the major entrance to the interior. Does all this make the building an unconventional sign?

The Sydney Opera House flaunts almost every architectural convention one can think of, and for that reason Sydney has a most remarkable building. The Opera House is the quintessential romantic work and the ultimate aspiration of all architects seeking not to be trammeled by convention. Because it is a sign for a special event in a special setting on Benelong Point, however, it is irrelevant to the architecture of the city, which is posing a problem for the redevelopment of East Circular Quay leading to the Opera House. To the great consternation of planners, architects, and concerned and informed citizens, the conventions of commercial city architecture, even the best, are unable to reconcile the nonconventions of the Opera House. The debate is a semiotic one, although it is not recognized as such, and is as charged as the one over the Venturi and Scott Brown extension to the National Gallery in London and the Graves extension to Breuer's Whitney Museum in New York.

The question persists as to whether architectural conventions have in common 'the aim of creating settled expectations' and of offering a setting for the 'true freedom' of which Scruton speaks above, or whether they must ever be repeatedly demolished for their debris, as Vidler suggests. Certainly, Utzon seems to have had no intention of 'exploding conventions', from which to construct 'a way of speaking adequate to the modern moment'; he just did the best he could with the best means he had.

The term 'conventionist' has been coined for the position that adopts an architecture of largely historical references and that relies on and has its appeal in certain widely held conventions developed over centuries. Typical are the adoption of building types and the reliance on "historical and historicist references, conventions, and rule structures for the palette of architectural expression" (Rowe 1987:130), of which the work described by Charles Jencks in his *Language of Post-Modern Architecture* (1977) is a representative selection. According to Rowe, "The foundational aspect is apparent in the conventionalist position's (implicit) belief that certain forms of architectural expression found in the historical record are worthy of emulation because they represent the touchstones of human experience with architecture" (Rowe 1987:142).

In discussing the literary professions, Stanley Fish remarks, "the convention is the way of acknowledging that we are engaged in a community activity in which the value of one's work is directly related to the work that has been done by others" (1989:164). Perhaps all that can be said of architecture is that conventions apply to conventional situations, and that breaking away from convention is acceptable if you wish to go it alone. We have come a long way.

FURTHER SOURCES   D. Lewis 1969; Hubbard 1980; Rykwert 1972; Vidler 1992.

2. The Violent Language of Architecture

Function has today an increasing variety of forms to choose from. New materials and new building methods constantly enlarge this wide range of choices. These can provide a more complete architectural vocabulary and great differences in the treatment of buildings. **James J. Sweeney** and **Josep L. Sert.** 1960:173.

Herder [1770] describes how primitive man, confronted with a lamb — "white, gentle, woolly" — exercises his capacity for reflection by seeking a characteristic of the animal. Suddenly the lamb bleats, and lo! man has found the distinguishing trait. . . . The notion that the visual characteristics of an object are incapable of being distinguished and remembered unless they are associated with sound and thus related to language, I propose to call the myth of the bleating lamb. **Rudolf Arnheim.** 1966:141.

Language, according to Saussure, is fundamentally (and not by accident or through depravation) an instrument of communication. One never finds in Saussure's writings the idea that language must represent a structure of thought that would exist independently of any linguistic formulation. **Oswald Ducrot** and **Tzvetan Todorov.** 1972:15.

I think that if interpretation becomes necessary, architecture may have failed. **Werner Duttmann.** In Emanuel 1980.

Moderns presuppose that the last word will be delivered in one unified language. Aristotle's sciences speak a bundle of languages with analogies between them. There is no one vocabulary for writing a report on all the facts. **David Kolb.** 1990:18.

TRACE   The word *language* has been used throughout this book, but is only now defined and examined. From the Latin *lingua,* tongue, language is both the whole panoply of words and their connections of a nation or people, and the same for the expression of thought. The goal of linguistics is to build a theoretical model of language (Fish 1989:3).

Leon Vaudoyer coined the term *l'architecture parlante* in 1852 to explain buildings, like a number of those by Ledoux, designed as three-dimensional metaphors *(Le Magasin Pittoresque XX,* 1852:388. Cited in Crook 1987). Architecture has never quite recovered from that remarkable declaration. It has been said of the Modern Movement: "If the new architecture was to make room for itself, it had first to extirpate what was called at the time 'the meaningless masquerade of out-worn conventions' (Frankl). But rather than a particular architectural language, it was the idea itself of linguistic communication in architecture that came under assault. This can be traced both in the writing and the work of the masters of the Modern Movement" (Bonta 1979:31).

COMMENTARY   Architecture as *both* a communication medium and as possessed of a 'language' has been the conventional wisdom of the profession for several generations now. Words like 'language', 'grammar', 'vocabulary', 'syntax', and many others insinuate themselves into architectural discussion, especially in design studio in considering an architect's or student's range and deployment of architectural elements. One of the most perplexing aspects of architecture is that we cannot avoid using linguistic terms in discussing it at almost any level. Putting aside the question of what is communicated by architecture as a language for the moment, how do we get around the language used to describe architecture as a language? Is architecture as language communication or structure—the communication of structure, or the structure of communication?

Denis Hollier (1989) argues that architecture pre-exists itself, that architecture is what architecture or anything becomes the moment it structures what it does without imitation.

To use the word 'architecture' presupposes its meaning and its actions and supersedes its etymology as *arche + tecton*, master builder. The sense of architecture in the description of God as the Great Architect of the Universe has a precedence over the universe itself; architecture pre-empts the universe! What hope have we of comprehending what architecture is if it precedes all comprehension; or of comprehending architecture as language if the concepts we have of it are already linguistic?

Michel Foucault has two suspicions about language. The first is that it "does not say exactly what it means...[it has] a lesser meaning that shields, restrains, and despite everything transmits another meaning, the meaning 'underneath' it. This is what the Greeks called *allegoria* and *hyponoïa*." The other is "that there are many things in the world that speak, and that not all are language. After all, it might be that nature, the sea, rustling trees, animals, faces, masks, crossed swords all speak. Perhaps there is some language articulating itself in a way that would not be verbal...the *semaïnon* of the Greeks" (in Ormiston and Schrift 1990:59). Perhaps architecture is this kind of language, which may explain its awkward fit to the standard linguistic model.

The standard idea of architecture as language has been presented most forcefully by Charles Jencks in *The Language of Post-Modern Architecture:*

> A Post-Modern building is ... one which *speaks* on at least two levels at once: to other architects and a concerned minority who care about specifically architectural meanings, and to the public at large, or the local inhabitants, who care about other issues concerned with comfort, traditional building and a way of life. Thus Post-Modern architecture looks hybrid and ... rather like the front of a Classical Greek temple. The architects can *read* the implicit *metaphors* and subtle meanings of the column drums whereas the public can respond to the explicit metaphors and *messages* of the sculptors. Of course, everyone responds somewhat to both *codes* of meaning ... and it is this discontinuity in taste cultures which creates both the theoretical base and *'dual coding'* of Post-Modernism" (emphasis added; Jencks 1977:6).

Jencks excludes from postmodern those designers whose buildings "do not communicate coherently because they are coded exclusively on an aesthetic level," and clarifies the term postmodern to cover "only those designers who are aware of architecture as a *language*." Thus, architecture is a language for architects who think architecture is language! For Jencks, architecture can only be a bleating lamb, or a flock whose chorus is thought to add up to complexity and subtlety instead of to more bleating lambs. Under 'Language' in the index to *Post-Modern*, Jencks lists *cliche, grammar, irony, malapropism, message, rhetoric,* and *simile,* while in a later work (Jencks 1980) he indexes most of these separately, along with *ellipsis, hyperbole, oxymoron, synecdoche,* and *vocabulary.* Also in Jencks's text and a selection of other architectural writers may be found the following linguistic or philological terms from grammatical and literary analysis: *antonym, asyndeton, elision, etymology, euphemism, metonymy, syllepsis, syndeton, synonym.*

This armory of terminology, however, does not make the speeches, readings, and codes of architecture that Jencks so assuredly walks among any more certain than a wish-list. Unless it can be explained why architecture is a good or even valid medium for communication when the print, film, and television media are so much more effective, efficient, and cheap, and can reach so many people, there seems no reason for architecture to be a medium. Also, languages don't just happen for their own sake; they happen because of a need to signify for cooperative reasons, for safety, ordering, understanding, and storytelling; they become imperative. An architectural language presupposes such cooperation, and unless this can be shown as essential, there seems no need for a language at all; language has a facilitating agenda, and those who advocate architecture as language may be proselytizing for unity of some kind.

Or they may be proselytizing for separation, as the Greek etymology (*proselytos*, stranger or resident foreigner) suggests. Certainly there is a substantial separation, a gulf even, between those who use linguistic terminology in relation to architecture and those who don't. It is arguable whether such fine discriminations as Jencks poses are in fact ways of separating out or creating strangers. "By no more instant means do we identify the stranger than by his alien language, his alien dialect, or his alien accent," writes Robert Ardrey. "Within a human society the speaking of a single language serves, as in any animal society, to integrate sub-groups. Yet so subtle is a single human tongue that differences of inflection, of connotation, of construction, of even vocabulary serve as well to separate sub-groups as to integrate them." Ardrey could well have been referring to architects. He continues: "The prime foundation for the future of civil violence must be the invention of strangers. And the prime ingredient for the invention of strangers must be non-communication between those who speak the same language" (1970:281). How else are the verbal clashes between reactionary and progressive forces in architecture to be interpreted if not as violence between strangers? Le Corbusier's notorious statement "Architecture or revolution: revolution can be avoided" might be reinterpreted as ". . . neither can be avoided."

In terms of architecture as a language system, if it is argued that architecture need not *necessarily* be saying anything cogent in order to communicate, or that it communicates *inescapably* anyway, no matter whether its messages are intelligible or not, or even that it only communicates *inadvertently*, then its 'language' is no more or less than the grunts of exertion or the intermittent clanking of a sloppy mechanism. Even on the most generous equation with words scrambled on a page, architecture is not a language; not even remotely does it approach *haiku* or the freest of poetry or the blankest of verse. Indeed, as a supposed language, architectural elements remain trapped at the level of Egyptian hieroglyphs as they were thought to be well into the Renaissance, symbolic and allegorical emblems, or at best the simple ideograms that many turned out to be. Architecture has neither the necessary determinate order of hieroglyphics as a language, nor the phonogram with which to assemble words, nor the determinatives with which to manipulate meaning. Charles Jencks cannot decipher architecture's Rosetta Stone.

If everyday use of simple linguistic terms like those outlined above does not at the same time bring to consciousness the full theoretical implications of such an emphasis for architecture as a system of communication, using more complex terms only confounds their necessary dependence upon an already unstable foundation. Such tacit acceptance of architecture as a language capable of transferring meaning is, to say the least (when architecture is presumed to be saying the most!), ironic. This is not to say that a language utilizing these terms cannot exist for architectural history, criticism, or theory; obviously it can and it does. It is just that the language of which architecture is supposed to consist does not operate as a critical language like history, criticism, or theory; it cannot be readily recognized as a language, or persuade as a living language does.

What is meant, then, when linguistic terminology is used in the design studio? Frequently it does not allude to an actual *language* of architecture, but attempts to persuade a student to develop, or to develop more of, a *repertoire* of architectural elements and to contrive and settle ways (rules?) to array them. And to speak of a repertoire, especially a visual repertoire, is to invoke something that, while not altogether different from a language in that it is learned and grows in range and sophistication with experience and maturity, operates in an entirely separate manner to a language. A repertoire is a stock of devices used by knowing designers to communicate to knowing observers through their familiarity with the devices. It is not a language in the sense of being capable of conveying new or original concepts using conventionalized elements or structures indifferent to the meaning being conveyed. Architecture as repertoire uses variations on known concepts, and communicates by virtue of its proximity or distance, familiarity or estrangement, in relation to these fixities, just as set pieces and their interpretation become the repertoire of the performances of repertory theater.

Finally, a parallel may be drawn between language and the point Stanley Fish makes concerning the presuppositions of speakers and hearers in relation to the meaning of verbal utterances: "If the presuppositions of an utterance vary with the beliefs of speakers and hearers . . . then 'every sentence can be analyzed with . . . as many different sets of presuppositions' as there are different possible contextualizations and there is no regular and predictable way to assign a meaning" (1989:1). Likewise, if the intentions of a building vary with the beliefs of designers and observers, then every building can be analyzed into as many sets of intentions as there are contextualizations, and there can be no regular and predictable way to assign meaning, hence no communication of any consequence and hence no language of any purpose. We are immediately confronted with the prospect of works of architecture that merely are, without any further rationale than that they exist, their intention and purpose mute testimonies to their existence, but their repertoires offering endless opportunities for engagement.

FURTHER SOURCES   10B.3, Mean; Benhabib 1992; Bonta 1979; Gombrich 1971; Hesselgren 1972; Hollier 1989; Kolb 1990; Lavin 1992; Oxman, Radford and Oxman 1987; Rowe 1987.

3. Can Architecture Mean Anything?

Better the rudest work that tells a story or records a fact, than the richest without meaning. There should not be a single ornament put upon great civic buildings, without some intellectual intention. **John Ruskin.** 1855. "The Lamp of Memory":§7.

The material of literature is *already* significant. Every particle of it has been organised in order to convey significance, and in order to convey the same significance to all. But for the material of architecture, no system of accepted meanings has been organised. If, therefore, we derive associative values from its forms, those values will be determined wholly by the accidents of our time and personality. Our readings will disagree. **Geoffrey Scott.** 1924:61.

A building has to be itself. A building wants to be a building. A building ought to show what it means. **Hans Hollein.** Lecture, 1962. In Klotz 1984.

. . . the meaning of an object consists in its relations to other objects, that is, in a structure. The meaning of an architectural element, therefore, also consists in its relations to the other elements (and to its own parts, i.e to its inner organization). . . . Meaning presupposes the repetition of a *limited* number of elements and relations, which, however, should allow all the combinations necessary to cover all important life-situations. **Christian Norberg-Schulz.** 1965:155–156.

Even cheap information beats expensive architectural form as a conveyor of meaning in the environment. **Martin Pawley.** 1990. Caption to plate 84, showing street signs.

TRACE   The verb *mean,* from the German *meinen,* is to have in mind as a purpose, to purpose, or to design. In relation to a remark it is to intend to have a particular reference and, in relation to things or words, to have a certain signification, to import, or to portend. *Meaning* is that which is intended or actually is expressed or indicated, although despite Pollitt's declaration above, meaning has an archaic sense of 'purpose'. More generally, from the late seventeenth century it had the sense of 'significance'. It was an ancient Greek intellectual tradition to seek a meaning behind any particular occurrence, to find the basic material or ontological substance for the pre-Socratics, or the *a priori* Form of the Platonists; for them, form and meaning were inseparable and codependent.

Meaning conveyed by a building was not an important consideration in architecture until Greco-Roman ways were rediscovered via Vitruvius in the fifteenth century, whereupon they *became* meaningful to the Renaissance mind. Vitruvius alluded to meaning when he wrote of 'significance': "In all matters, but particularly in architecture, there are these two points:—the thing signified, and that which gives it its significance. That which is signified is the subject of which we may be speaking; and that which gives significance is a demonstration on scientific principles. It appears, then, that one who professes himself an architect should be well-versed in both directions" (Vitruvius 1960:1.1.3).

COMMENTARY   It may seem odd that so near the end of this book a section is introduced on meaning while the term has been used throughout with little apparent difficulty. It is one indication of the parallel worlds we inhabit that 'meaning' can be used meaningfully in everyday life until it is questioned. I am reminded here of the well-known aphorism by Mrs. Edmund Craster: "The Centipede was happy quite, /Until the Toad in fun /Said 'Pray which leg goes after which?' /And worked her mind to such a pitch, /She lay distracted in the ditch /Considering how to run"; meaning too when questioned becomes distracted. "*Meaning* is ultimately an indefinable word, since it itself is the foundation on which all definition rests" writes art historian J. J. Pollitt (1974:25). The short answer to the question posed by the title to this section, "Can architecture mean anything?" is not a simple yes or no, but rather, of all the possible meanings (and nonmeanings) architecture can have, which are to be privileged and why?

An answer to the question of privileging resides in the psychoanalytical work of Freud and the existentialism of Sartre; they suggested that meaning is embedded in human consciousness, not in some externality. For Sartre, "consciousness is itself the fact, the signification, and the thing signified." On the Sartrean account, consciousness of 'architecture' would be its meaning, without distraction, without seeking attributes attaching to or even interpreted from a work. Just as in speaking of memory Sartre "distinguishes between the 'content' of one's past which is unchangeable, and the 'meaning' of the past in relation to one's total life, which is 'eminently variable'," Stuart Charmé maintains that "any 'compelling power' of the past to motivate present behavior is derived from a present choice or action that simultaneously 'chooses' a specific view of the past" (Charmé 1984:29–31). So it is with meaning; any compelling power of past attributes prompting present meaning is a choice from within a specific view of that past. But undistracted consciousness is not so easy.

Any purported meaning is also more than just a specific individual view; it is delimited by both the sum of views agreed within a community for the time being and expanded by the views brought in by other multiple and ongoing interpretations; it is this *inexhaustibility* that makes meaning a hermeneutical fact (Madison 1988:111–115). Despite Derrida's deconstruction of presence, it is therefore possible to argue for architectural meaning as a presencing (consciousness) that does not exist *necessarily* and independently as the truth of a work, the *final* meaning, or as an entirely subjective and relative understanding of the interpreter. Rather, if we assume a work to have meaning, we must do so knowing that its truth is unprovable because any truth is necessarily dependent on our present interpretation.

The recovery of 'lost' meaning attempted by George Hersey in *The Lost Meaning of Classical Architecture* (1988) can only ever be an interpretive archaeological fiction, for even if the lost meaning of classical architecture were recoverable, it would also require the recovery of classical culture and lived classical life for it to be meaningful—an impossibility for us, here and now. As it is, Hersey can recover a meaning lost only in relation to the value it is presumed to have had for ancient classical civilization. So any 'meaning' is already and always so heavily qualified as not to be meaning-as-truth at all but something else, meaning-as-application. As application, architectural meaning becomes what we wish to reconstruct it as in order to suit the use it serves in explicating it. For the historian, meaning is what the historian makes use of in explication; for the designer, meaning is what assists the designer in construing a design task; for the critic, meaning is what helps in situating a work in a milieu. Historical meanings, which embrace all existing works of architecture or past projects, become meaningful only for what we choose to make of them in our present interpretive circumstances.

Clearly, intentionality is uppermost in this explanation—not the originating intention, for that is an impossible task, only the interpretive intention. Of what import is it that classical architecture might have had sacrificial content in its forms if we now have no place for sacrifice except *with the intention* of writing a specific account of ancient classical architecture? Does having some angle on ancient classical meanings make for more 'meaningful' allusions if and when we see or use classical references? Only if the current *intention* is that there is leverage to be had by using classical allusion. Does historical meaning impact on the present use of similar repertoire or figures in contemporary architecture? Only if we *intend* to assimilate new work with historical precedent or continuity because we privilege types or influences or origins as generative forces. "The relation of words to their meaning is not natural but *intended,* and this intention is realized through a necessary body of conventions and rules," writes Roger Scruton (1979:159), and it is this agreement by convention for the time being that fixes the meanings of the concepts, themes, and practices whose traces head each section of this book.

The suggestion of 'levels' of meaning in current writing is no more than a pretension suggesting that readers recognize and align themselves with the author's perspicacity, no more than a display of taste. And lack of taste in our time is what Hersey refers to in claiming "we have been the heirs of a scientific philology that drains architecture of its poetry" and victims of "formalism: the repetition and variation of forms for their own sake, irrespective of their literary, associational, and poetic meanings, and irrespective also of their mythical origins." These comments mark his intention to set up an agenda to correct a deficiency in current architecture, for he goes on to declare "even in a purely formal world new architectural meanings can be generated" (1988:149, 152). Hersey's quest has been a quintessentially postmodern architectural project, his finding symbolic meaning among the remnants of classical detail and terminology is a first floor-slab offering to the new poetic architectural age—at least this much is clear. Well might it be asked of other key postmodern architects and theorists: What is *their* intention?

FURTHER SOURCES   Barthes 1985, "The Third Meaning"; Clarke 1984; Dewey 1934; Kolb 1990; Ogden and Richards 1947; Scott 1924; Snodgrass 1990.

4. Metaphor as Necessity and Difficulty

Weight and resistance, burden and effort, weakness and power, are elements in our own experience from feelings of ease, exaltation, or distress. But weight and resistance, weakness and power, are manifest elements also in architecture, which enacts through their means a kind of human drama. Through them the mechanical solutions of mechanical problems achieve an aesthetic interest and an ideal value. **Geoffrey Scott.** 1924:119.

The concrete spectacle has done what the mere idea could not: it has stirred our physical memory. . . . We have looked at the building and identified ourselves with its apparent state. *We have transcribed ourselves into terms of architecture.* . . The whole of architecture is, in fact, unconsciously invested by us with human movement and human moods. Here, then, is a principle complimentary to the one just stated. *We transcribe architecture into terms of ourselves.* This is the humanism of architecture. **Geoffrey Scott.** 1924:212–213.

A metaphor is, by definition, the transcription of one thing into terms of another, and this in fact is what the theory under discussion [the humanism of architecture] claims. It claims that architectural art is the transcription of the body's states into forms of building. **Geoffrey Scott.** 1924:216.

The house looms large, if not as a refuge, as a metaphor, live, dead and mixed. It is the repository of our wishes and dreams, memories and illusions. It is, or at least it ought to be, instrumental in the transition from being to well-being. **Bernard Rudofsky.** 1977.

I believe that a healthy architecture should represent today—should deal with the technology of today—and the technology of today is industrialized. But not all *That* industrialized. **Cesar Pelli.** In Suckle 1980.

TRACE   Metaphor is the technique of transferring or transporting a name or description to something as if it were that thing but clearly is not. It derives from the Old French *métaphore* and the Latin *metaphora,* which in turn come from the Greek (*meta*—with, after or beyond + *pherein*—to bear or carry). "When I say he *is* an ox, then I have used a metaphor, and what I say is inevitably false," writes the philosopher Roger Scruton, who would exclude *simile* as a rhetorical figure because it can be true. "A metaphor may be apt, appropriate, vivid or compelling, but it cannot be true. For many metaphors, there are corresponding similes which, as it were, creep in behind them with their literal meanings intact: the aptness of the metaphor consists merely in the truth of the corresponding simile . . . the central feature of every figure [of speech] . . . is that it is, when successful, false" (Scruton 1983:17). For an elaborate treatment of metaphor see William Empson's *The Structure of Complex Words* (1951:Chapter 18).

Metaphor is a rhetorical *figure* precisely because its abnormality dominates, unlike the 'figure' of architecture, which is more like 'shape', coming as it does from classical rhetoric and from music in which it is a grouping of elements that gives a single, complete, and distinctive impression. So, metaphor cannot be a figure in the architectural sense, and indeed is difficult to realize at all, despite Charles Jencks (1977, 1980) giving it extensive coverage.

COMMENTARY   It is a none-too-commonly-known fact that in Western culture the understanding of architecture is metaphoric in that it is rarely known for itself. It was argued in 8B.1, Abstraction, that the detachment of abstraction interfered with the reconstitution of architecture from its code under the sway of Modernism, unlike the Japanese 'concrete' tradition of Ando (unusual in the face of an enigmatic and largely abstract Japanese tradition), and in this circumstance metaphor is the mechanism of Western architectural assimilation and comprehension. Architecture is understood either as 'standing for' something else by virtue of interpreting meaning (the Western tradition), or in the relation effected between it and the participant or observer (the Zen, Eastern tradition). There are architects like Frank Lloyd Wright who have succeeded in melding these understandings, and there are a number at present who are trying to do the same; for example, Richard le Plastrier in Australia.

In short, Western architecture is primarily accessed through and currently obsessed with metaphor. Architecture either is or is not some statement of what it is or is not, as the literal metaphorists say, or it is the effect it has or the feeling it induces, as the figurative metaphorists would say. The many metaphors of what architecture *is* listed in 8A.3, Dictums, are examples of the first kind of metaphor. So forceful has the inclination to metaphor been that architecture has ceased 'to be' itself, leading to great consternation about what architecture actually is. There have been or are still only a few architects in the Western tradition content to say that "architecture is architecture," and then merely address what pertains to it alone, Alvar Aalto and Carlo Scarpa being notable among them. Why is architecture for so many architects and theorists presented in the guise of something else? This has already been answered in part in the section on dictums, and to extend it further here would take us further into the action of metaphor, a task too large for this short essay. Instead, the second aspect concerning the transference of metaphor will be examined.

Transference is a fact of perception and it inhabits every corner of language (metaphor!). We speak of loud colors and soft shades, rough language and smooth talk, light music and heavy metal, glaring errors and hidden meanings, dazzling repartee and somber tones, colorful character and abrasive personality. It is natural that transferences of some kind should inhabit architecture, not the least being architecture construed as social therapy correcting a wayward citizenry, affirmed principally by Jeremy Bentham's Panopticon in the eighteenth century and continuing to the architecture/health fanaticism of the twentieth, remnants of which are still around (see 'Dwelling Machines' in Sorkin 1991:187–202). From initially positive notions of the therapeutic potential of architecture, by the mid-twentieth century mostly negative prognoses dominated discourse, mainly concerning degeneration.

In roughly chronological order we have witnessed rampant sprawl and 'diseased' cities (air, water, and visual pollution); the 'sick' building syndrome (arising from the unhealthy effects of asbestos, plastics, air-conditioning, and radiation from fluorescent lighting, video screens, and portable telephones); concrete 'cancer', and anti-modern 'hysteria', generally culminating in Prince Charles's accusations of 'deformed monsters' and (monstrous) 'carbuncles' (1989).

While transference of health terminology might imply human assimilation with architecture once corrected, it is the sensate that actually effects closure, the sheer experience of architecture. Experiencing architecture used to be a major focus of writing in a nonintellectual way (Norberg-Schulz 1965; Rasmussen 1959), but has since the sixties either been ignored or become so intellectualized that it has been 'lost sight' of altogether (witness the shift to art and literary theory compilations issuing from a number of architectural presses), notwithstanding the many attempts to reclaim space as *the* central architectural experience (Von Meiss 1986; Trancik 1986; Tschumi 1990).

The nearest the Western architectural tradition has come to the fully sensorial and to Tadao Ando's *shintai* has been the metaphoric notion of 'empathy'. As a tradition, empathy may be traced back to Alberti, Francesco di Giorgio, and Filarete, but its modern usage is celebrated in Louis Sullivan's Bayard Building in New York, according to Vincent Scully (1959). Empathy was central to the concept of *Einfühlung,* "that is, an act of inner imitation, or the lending of our humanity to forms without souls; the reading of ourselves, as it were, into inorganic nature. Architecture, besides expressing the universal idea of matter and the individual characteristics of buildings, became symbolic of the movements of man and by extension of man himself. In the opinion of the day [mid-nineteenth century], this identification was the highest degree of poetry architecture could achieve" (Menocal 1981:64; 192, n70). It is the emotional and esthetic power of empathy that makes the transference of human feeling and sensation at once so necessary and yet so difficult for understanding architecture.

As long as three generations ago, Geoffrey Scott was clear on the play of human empathy in understanding buildings when he said "our capacity to realise the forces at work in a building *intellectually* is, to all intents, unlimited; but our capacity to realise them *aesthetically* is limited. We feel the value of certain curves and certain relations of pressure or resistance by an unconscious (or usually unconscious) analogy with our own movements, our own gestures, our own experiences of weight. . . . Our aesthetic reactions are limited by our power to recreate in ourselves, imaginatively, the physical conditions suggested by the form we see: to ascribe its strength or weakness into terms of our own life" (Scott 1924:115–116). What was skipped in this passage is the difficulty that the same 'power to recreate' presents in the case of modern materials and construction. Scott maintains rightly that human physical experience and hence empathy does not assist in reconciling the "exaggerated disparity between the visible bulk . . . and its capacity for resistance" of a material like steel, for instance. We might vaguely sense the tensile forces in a steel cable structure because of reaching and stretching, but we have no way of relating to the compressive forces in a steel stanchion or concrete reinforcement. The same may be said of shell, membrane, geodetic, bridge, and retention structures, and empathetic metaphors for them elude us just as they do for the high-rise tower, phallic comparisons in particular notwithstanding.

What should not be missed in what has been said is that while the application of metaphor to architecture *post-hoc* may be prevalent and legitimate, as Jencks's 'historical' writings have shown, in no way is the designing facilitated. The attempt here has been to reposition metaphor at the conceptual end of the spectrum, as architects do when they offer up retrospective dictums in the form "Architecture is . . ." for others to latch on to while designing. Regardless of the countless words uttered in support of metaphor in architecture, metaphor is hardest to manage. As one final illustration of the difficulty in bringing health notions to designing, the illness metaphor has been written about incisively by critic Susan Sontag, who pleaded in the prologue to *Illness as Metaphor* first published in 1979, "illness is not a metaphor, and the most truthful way of regarding illness—and the healthiest way of being ill—is one most purified of, most resistant to, metaphoric thinking" (Sontag 1991). Substitute architecture for illness and you have a fair statement of the agenda of the Modern Movement. Modernism ended for its critics when they metaphorically declared it an illness and eventually dead; it continues for its protagonists, who metaphorically proclaim any alternative to modernist ideology an illness and a dead-end! (Harry Seidler. In Frampton and Drew 1992). Where does metaphor go from here?

FURTHER SOURCES · Coyne and Snodgrass 1992; Hejduk 1985; Hersey 1988; Kolb 1990; Macormac 1985; Schon 1979; Snodgrass 1990; Sontag 1966.

5. Signature: Vanity, Necessity, or Insane Pedantry

In the city, we are barraged with images of the people we might become. **Jonathon Raban.** 1988:64.

. . . if we all keep on stamping our own personal mark or "signature" on each building we design, each city will end up having a fish building, a Meier building, a Jahn building, until each city will be a bit like a Woolworth's, with a sample of everything and with no character of its own. **Cesar Pelli.** In Tigerman, 1987.

One thing we have gotten good at, in our rectangular way, is preserving the legacy of what we haplessly destroy. I am thinking of a Plexiglas case at the Asia Society that contains a carved and painted wallaby, "attributed to George Ngallametta" (a delectably insane pedantry in context), that is the loveliest thing imaginable. **Peter Schjeldahl.** 1988. "Dreamings: The Art of Aboriginal Australia." *The 7 Days Art Columns 1988–1990* (New York, 1990:74).

TRACE   Definitions of signature, from the Latin *signatura,* sign manual, emphasize both *authentication* and *peculiarity.* A signature is a distinctive mark made by one's own hand as confirmation of authenticity. It is also a peculiarity noted about a natural object that sets it apart or acts as a sign for its special properties, especially plants for medicinal purposes. The signature is one of five sixteenth-century notions in an organized 'corpus of resemblance' (the others are convenience, sympathy, emulation, and analogy), which Michel Foucault revives to show the tradition of interpretation upon which the twentieth century is built: "The notion of *signatura,* the signature, which is the image of an invisible and hidden property among the visible properties of an individual" (in Ormiston and Schrift 1990:60).

The architect and Gothic historian John James (1979/1981) found certain marks or traces in the stonework of Chartres Cathedral, which for him became the signature of particular master masons by means of which he could identify the sequence and extent of their building activity. Architecture carrying the marks of individual architects has arguably always been a quality, architects being selected for their individual design ability. But idiosyncratic design traits became more acceptable from sixteenth-century Mannerism after Michelangelo onward through the baroque period, and reached a finesse with late-eighteenth century French architects before what was to become the free-for-all of the nineteenth. However, while Kenneth Frampton remarks of art, "after the medieval period, society covets the individual signature," architecture, he believed, "does not have the same iconic or fetishistic status as art, nor despite the emergence of the star architect, is it possible to give comparable status to the 'signature building'" (Ghirardo 1991:19). But signature buildings there were, nonetheless.

COMMENTARY   When Paul McCartney visited Australia in spring '93, he completed his first record shop signing since the sixties. His half hour done, the evening news showed McCartney about to step back into his limousine when rushed by a fan brandishing a guitar; Paul signed it, the fan retreated in a fuzz but was found a few minutes later by the TV reporter, who asked what he intends to do with the guitar: "He signed it. I'm never going to play it again. I'll lock it away in a cupboard." The story was the same for everyone whose mementos were signed; even the hand that was shaken was not to be washed.

This minor episode prompts another, an after-hours visit several years ago to the Australian National Gallery in Canberra with a group of architects to view selections from the art collection of the entrepreneur and sometime yachtsman Alan Bond. Passing through galleries of Australian tribal art, we reached the exhibition and its centerpiece, an unexciting oil painting by Van Gogh entitled 'Irises'. Worth x-million dollars, the work was in a select annex simply spot-lit, the signature glowing. I later heard we had probably been looking at a copy, the original apparently locked away in a vault. If this were so, *Van Gogh's signature was not authentic,* but the unsigned aboriginal artifacts that aroused only idle curiosity en route were. Late twentieth-century culture has become obsessed with the signature in Western art and architecture.

University campuses are occasionally the playground for architectural innovation and today a campus, whatever its achievements academically, is considered deficient until it has at least one 'signature' building by an architect of renown, an index that the institution has 'arrived' culturally. One notable recent example is the Wexner Center for the Visual Arts at Ohio State University, Columbus, won in open competition by Peter Eisenman and Trott Architects in partnership. Praised and awarded since it opened in 1989, as Eisenman's first major building it was described by one critic as "the most eagerly awaited building of the decade." As Ohio State's first signature building, in a mostly negative review it was faintly praised: "the design has artistic merit . . . a state-of-the-art facility that is more handsome than many campus buildings" (Jack L. Nasar. "Form follows gumption." *The Columbus Dispatch*, Nov. 12, 1989). But the visitor's guide leaflet lovingly regurgitates the architects' rhetoric; the signature is authentic, institutional vanity is rewarded. What is this mysterious 'best' that level-headed people seek by competition?

In a word, with a signature building you gain an *attitude*. Not just an architectural attitude as against any old attitude, but the peculiar attitude of an architectural star. Architectural theorizing attaching to a critical practice promoted with the right mix of seriousness and quirkiness makes for a star attitude; this is the architecture business. In the quotation in the trace above, Kenneth Frampton parenthesizes "It is an interesting coincidence that the terms for business [firm] and signature [firma] come from the same root." One might also compare *signatura* with the Latin etymology of 'design', *designo,* which is "to point out, mark, denote, designate, describe, represent, brand . . ." (Lewis, 1891). From this definition one can say that what is noticed in a designed artifact is the *mark* of the designer, the designer's signature. A work of art or architecture is the manifestation of its conception and of its doing, of choices made and not made within selected limits, all inextricably bound in its matrix; the surfaces of a work are in effect the boundaries of choice.

For the art historian Sir Ernst Gombrich it is knowledge of the choices made by the artist or architect within a limited structure, the tradition of the discipline, that makes for artistic expression. "The fully-expected is hardly registered," he writes, "and the wholly unexpected will seem meaningless. It is the right proportion between the expected and the unexpected which constitutes the charm and magic of artistic expression" (Gombrich 1980:19). Accepting Gombrich's term 'expression', something like 'right proportion' is at the core of everyday architectural expression, whereas 'signature' is an excess of the expected or unexpected or both. Put more simply, signature is the designer's 'enabling prejudices' (Rowe 1987:37).

Commenting on the arrival of British architects Stirling and Wilford on the American architectural scene, Michael Sorkin (1991) remarks of being disappointed by the "well-mannered" School of Architecture extension at Rice University, noting that "Sympathetic critics scramble to uncover Stirlingesque tokens in describing the work, like art authenticators judging an attribution." Critics and pilgrim architects alike find it difficult to locate Stirling's signature within the work itself and even from among the undistinguished buildings on campus, so the standard gag at Rice goes. Not so for some star architects, the most banal for Sorkin being Philip Johnson, whose art—"like Gloria Vanderbilt's or Betty Crocker's—is in forming his signature. He recognizes that the first rule in this kind of practice is to broaden the product line to the maximum, to place the valorizing imprimatur on everything" (1991:172–173). For Stirling and Johnson both, statements turning the ordinary into the extraordinary by being "by James Stirling" or "by Philip Johnson," or turning the extraordinary into the extra-extraordinary in the case of the Wexner by being "by Peter Eisenman," are 'delectably insane pedantry' in the context of the publicity that inevitably trumpets such buildings. But it is a pedantry diametrically opposite that attributes the wallaby to George Ngallametta; the wallaby is its own signature, even carved and painted, it needs no George to make it authentic; architecture, on the other hand, is worthless it seems without James/Michael, Philip, and Peter.

The moment a building is *celebrated* by privileging it as having been designed is the moment of rupture between simply being and being architecture, between continuity and peculiarity. And the moment a designed building is privileged by acknowledging the name of the designer, the signature, is the moment of rupture between simply being architecture and being a 'work' of architecture. This rupturing makes design always an individual affair, of creation and of being, as the German philosopher Martin Heidegger (1936) makes clear when he construes a 'work' of art as "the bringing forth of a being such as never was before and will never come to be again" and creation as "such a bringing forth." In contrast to what Heidegger calls the at-handness, or *readiness,* of equipment, the principle characteristic of design is that "its createdness is part of the created work"; he uses 'thrust' to describe this evidential quality. The signature of a work of architecture is thus the creative attitude the designer brings to it, that 'invisible and hidden property' to which Foucault refers behind the visible properties of the work. Architects survive only on the vanity by-line. Wallabies survive, even as effigies. For it to survive, must architecture become more vain or more wallaby-like?

FURTHER SOURCES   4B.3, Artist; Frascina and Harrison 1982; Hejduk 1985; Hughes 1990; Johnson 1991.

REFERENCES

AAM (Archives d'Architecture Moderne), ed. 1978. *Rational Architecture: The Reconstruction of the European City.* Brussels: AAM Editions.

Ackerman, James. 1991. *Distance Points: Essays in Theory and Renaissance Art and Architecture.* Cambridge, Mass.: MIT Press.

Agrest, Diana. 1991. *Architecture from Without: Theoretical Framing for a Critical Practice.* Cambridge, Mass.: MIT Press.

Alberti, Leon Battista. 1755a. *The Ten Books of Architecture.* Leoni edition. New York: Dover Publications, 1986.

Alberti, Leon Battista. 1755b. *On the Art of Building in Ten Books.* Translated by Joseph Rykwert, Neil Leach, and Robert Tavernor. Cambridge, Mass.: MIT Press, 1991.

Alexander, Christopher. 1979. *The Timeless Way of Building.* London: Oxford University Press.

Alexander, Christopher, *et al.* 1977. *A Pattern Language.* London: Oxford University Press.

Alexander, Christopher. 1992. *The Nature of Order: Draft Manuscript for Discussion.* New York: Oxford University Press.

Allsopp, Bruce. 1977. *A Modern Theory of Architecture.* London: Routledge & Kegan Paul.

Al-Sayed, M. *et al.,* eds. 1988. *Architecture and Body.* New York: Rizzoli International Publications.

Altman, Irving. 1975. *The Environment and Social Behavior: Privacy, Personal Space, Territory, Crowding.* California: Brooks/Cole Publishing.

Angelil, Marc M. 1989. "Technique and the metaphysics of science: The rational-irrational element of science-technology within the making of architecture." *Harvard Architecture Review: The Making of Architecture.* Vol. 7:62–75.

Antoniades, Anthony C. 1986. *Architecture and Allied Design: An Environmental Design Perspective.* Second edition. Dubuque, Iowa: Kendall/Hunt.

Antoniades, Anthony C. 1990. *Poetics of Architecture: Theory of Design.* New York: Van Nostrand Reinhold.

Antoniades, Anthony C. 1992. *Epic Space: Toward the Roots of Western Architecture.* New York: Van Nostrand Reinhold.

Archea, John. 1975. "Applied interdisciplinary research on environment and aging: Conceptual and methodological conflicts." In Windley, Buerts & Ermst (eds). *Theory Development in Environment and Aging*. Washington, D.C.: Gerontological Society, 1975.

Archer, John. 1987. "The architect and the mountain lake: Adolf Loos and the crisis of culture." *Midgård Journal of Architectural Theory and Criticism*, Vol. 1, no. 1:63–77.

Ardrey, Robert. 1970. *The Social Contract: A Personal Inquiry into the Evolutionary Sources of Order and Disorder*. London: Collins.

Arendt, Hannah. 1961. *Between Past and Future: Six Exercises in Political Thought*. New York: Meridian.

Aristotle. *The Ethics of Aristotle: The Nicomachean Ethics Translated*. Translated by J. A. K. Jackson. London: Penguin Books, 1955.

Aristotle. *Poetics*. Edited by G. M. Kirkwood. New York: Norton, 1982.

Aristotle. *The Politics*. Edited by Stephen Everson. Cambridge, England: Cambridge University Press, 1988.

Arnauld, Antoine. 1662. *The Art of Thinking: Port-Royal Logic*. Translated by James Dickoff and Patricia James. New York: Bobbs-Merrill, 1964.

Arnheim, Rudolf. 1954. *Art and Visual Perception*. Berkeley and Los Angeles: University of California Press, 1974.

Arnheim, Rudolf. 1966. *Towards a Psychology of Art: Collected Essays*. London: Faber & Faber.

Arnheim, Rudolf. 1977. *The Dynamics of Architectural Form*. Berkeley and Los Angeles: University of California Press.

Arnheim, Rudolf. 1982. *The Power of the Centre*. Berkeley and Los Angeles: University of California Press, 1984.

Arup, Ove. 1979. "Arup associations." *Architectural Review: AR '30s*. Special issue. Vol. 166, no. 993, November:315–321.

Ashe, Geoffrey. 1977. *The Ancient Wisdom*. London: Macmillan.

Ashihara, Y. 1983. *The Aesthetic Townscape*. Translated by Lynne E. Riggs, Cambridge, Mass.: MIT Press.

Ashley, Kathleen M. 1990. *Victor Turner and the Construction of Cultural Criticism: Between Literature and Anthropology*. Bloomington: Indiana University Press.

Association Francaise d'Action Artistique. 1985. *Architecture In India*. Paris: Electa Moniteur.

Attoe, Wayne. 1978. *Architecture and Critical Imagination*. Chichester, England: John Wiley & Sons.

Bachelard, Gaston. 1964. *The Poetics of Space*. Translated from the French by Maria Jolas. Boston: Beacon Press, 1969.

Bailey, Joe. 1975. *Social Theory for Planning*. London and Boston: Routledge & Kegan Paul.

Bandini, Micha. 1982. "Fashion and consumption: Notes on Aldo Rossi." *Transition*, Vol.3, no.1, March.

Banham, Reyner. 1962. *Theory and Design in the First Machine Age.* Second edition. London: Butterworth, 1988.

Banham, Reyner. 1969. *The Architecture of the Well-Tempered Environment.* London: Architectural Press, 1973.

Banham, Reyner. 1971. *Los Angeles: The Architecture of Four Ecologies.* Harmondsworth, England: Pelican Books, 1973.

Banham, Reyner. 1975. *Age of the Masters: A Personal View of Modern Architecture.* Revised edition; first published in 1962 as *Guide to Modern Architecture.* London: Architectural Press.

Banham, Reyner. 1976. *Megastructure: Urban Futures of the Recent Past.* London: Thames & Hudson.

Banham, Reyner. 1981. *Design by Choice.* Edited by Penny Sparke. London: Academy Editions.

Barker, Roger. 1968. *Ecological Psychology: Concepts and Methods for Studying the Environment of Human Behavior.* Stanford, Ca.: Stanford University Press.

Barthes, Roland. 1957. *Mythologies.* Translated by Annette Lavers. London: Paladin, 1989.

Barthes, Roland. 1985. *The Responsibility of Forms: Critical Essays on Music, Art, and Representation.* Translated by Richard Howard. Oxford, England: Basil Blackwell.

Bartley, William W. III. 1973. *Wittgenstein.* London: The Cresset Library, 1986.

Becherer, Richard. 1984. *Science Plus Sentiment: César Daly's Formula for Modern Architecture.* Ann Arbor, Mich.: UMI Research Press.

Beck, Haig, ed. 1988. *Parliament House Canberra: A Building for the Nation.* Sydney, Australia: Collins Publishers Australia.

Beck, Haig, and Jeffrey Turnbull, eds. 1987. *Critiques 1: Papers and Projects from the Programme of Studies for the Master of Architecture Examined by Design.* Melbourne, Australia: University of Melbourne, Department of Architecture and Building.

Beck, Haig, and Jeffrey Turnbull, eds. 1988. *Critiques 2: Raw Architecture.* Melbourne, Australia: University of Melbourne, Department of Architecture and Building.

Bell, David. 1990. "Inmediasres." *In Via 10.* See Capelli, Naprstek, and Prescott 1990.

Benedikt, Michael. 1987. *For an Architecture of Reality.* New York: Lumen Books.

Benedikt, Michael. 1991. *Deconstructing the Kimbell: An Essay on Meaning and Architecture.* New York: Lumen Books.

Benhabib, Seyla. 1992. *Situating the Self: Gender, Community and Postmodernism in Contemporary Ethics.* New York: Routledge.

Bennington, Geoff. 1987. "Complexity without contradiction in architecture." *AA Files.* No. 15, Summer:15–18.

Benton, Tim. 1987. *The Villas of Le Corbusier 1920–1930.* New Haven: Yale University Press.

Benton, Charlotte A., ed. 1975. *Documents: A Collection of Source Material on the Modern Movement.* Milton Keynes, England: Open University Press.

Benton, Charlotte A., Tim J. Benton, and Denis Sharp, eds. 1975. *Form and Function: A Source Book for the History of Architecture and Design 1890–1939.* London: Crosby Lockwood Staples.

Berkeley, Ellen P., and Matilda McQuaid, eds. 1989. *Architecture: A Place for Women.* Washington, D.C.: Smithsonian Institution Press.

Berlin, Isaiah. 1953. *The Hedgehog and the Fox: An Essay on Tolstoy's View of History.* London: Weidenfeld and Nicholson.

Betsky, Aaron. 1990. *Violated Perfection: Architecture and the Fragmentation of the Modern.* New York: Rizzoli International Publications.

Billings, Keith, and Samer Akkach. 1992. "A study of ideologies and methods in contemporary architectural design teaching." *Design Studies.* Vol. 13, no. 4, October:431–450.

Birkhoff, George D. 1933. *Aesthetic Measure.* Cambridge, Mass.: Harvard University Press.

Blackwell, W. 1984. *Geometry in Architecture.* New York: John Wiley & Sons.

Blake, Peter. 1960. *Le Corbusier: Architecture and Form.* Middlesex, England: Pelican Books.

Blake, Peter. 1963. *Frank Lloyd Wright: Architecture and Space.* Harmondsworth, England: England: England: Penguin Books.

Blake, Peter. 1974. "The folly of modern architecture." *The Atlantic.* Vol. 234, no. 3, September:59–66.

Blake, Peter. 1977. *Form Follows Fiasco: Why Modern Architecture Hasn't Worked.* Boston: Little, Brown.

Blau, Judith R. 1984. *Architects and Firms: A Sociological Perspective on Architectural Practice.* Cambridge, Mass.: MIT Press.

Bloomer, Kent C., and Charles W. Moore. 1977. *Body, Memory and Architecture.* New Haven: Yale University Press.

Bond, Frederick Bligh, and Rev. T. S. Lea. 1917. *Gematria: A Preliminary Investigation of the Cabala Contained in the Coptic Gnostic Books of a Similar Gematria in the Greek Text of the New Testament.* Great Britain: Research Into Lost Knowledge Organisation, distributed by Thorston Publishers, 1977.

Bonta, Juan P. 1979. *Architecture and Its Interpretation: A Study of Expressive Systems in Architecture.* London: Lund Humphries.

Bonta, Juan Pablo. 1990. "Reading and writing about architecture." *Design Book Review.* Issue 18, Spring:13–16.

Borges, Jorge Luis. 1970. *Labyrinths.* Harmondsworth, England: Penguin Books.

Borradori, Giovanna. 1988. "Towards an architecture of exile: A conversation with Jean-Francois Lyotard." In *Threshold.* See Diani and Ingraham 1988.

Borsi, Franco. 1987. *The Monumental Era: European Architecture and Design 1929–1939.* New York: Rizzoli International Publications.

Boudon, Philippe. 1969. *Lived-in Architecture: Le Corbusier's Pessac Revisited.* Translated by Gerald Onn. London: Lund Humphries, 1972.

Boulding, Kenneth. 1962. *Conflict and Defense.* New York: Harper & Row.

Boyd, Robin. 1961. *The Australian Ugliness.* Second edition. Melbourne, Australia: F. W. Cheshire.

Boyne, Roy. 1990. *Foucault and Derrida: The Other Side of Reason.* London: Unwin Hyman.

Bragdon, Claude. 1910. *The Beautiful Necessity: Architecture as "Frozen Music."* Wheaton, Ill.: Quest Books, 1978.

Bragdon, Claude. 1913. *A Primer of Higher Space (the Fourth Dimension).* New York: Manas Press.

Bragdon, Claude. 1916. *Four-Dimensional Vistas.* New York: Knopf.

Bragdon, Claude. 1932. *The Frozen Fountain: Being Essays on Architecture and the Art of Design in Space.* New York: Knopf.

Braham, A. 1980. *The Architecture of the French Enlightenment.* London: Thames & Hudson.

Brissenden, R. F., ed. 1973. *Studies in the Eighteenth Century II: Papers Presented at the Second David Nichol Smith Memorial Seminar, Canberra 1970.* Canberra, Australia: ANU Press.

Brissenden, R. F., and J. C. Eade, eds. 1976. *Studies in the Eighteenth Century III: Papers presented at the Third David Nichol Smith Memorial Seminar, Canberra 1973.* Canberra, Australia: ANU Press.

Broad, C. D. 1942. "Features in Moore's ethical doctrines." *In The Philosophy of G. E. Moore.* See Schilpp 1968.

Broady, Maurice. 1966. "Social theory in architectural design." *Architectural Association Quarterly.* Vol. 81, no. 88, January.

Broady, Maurice. 1968. *Planning for People: Essays in the Social Context of Planning.* London: National Council for Social Services.

Broadbent, Geoffrey H. 1973. *Design in Architecture: Architecture and the Human Sciences.* Chichester, England: John Wiley & Sons.

Broadbent, Geoffrey H. 1978. "A plain man's guide to the theory of signs in architecture." *Architectural Design.* Vol. 49, no. 8/9, July/August.

Broadbent, Geoffrey H. 1979. "Design and theory building." In *Developments in Design Methodology.* See Cross 1984.

Broadbent, Geoffrey H. 1990. *Emerging Concepts in Urban Space Design.* London: Van Nostrand Reinhold.

Broadbent, Geoffrey H., Richard Bunt, and Charles Jencks, eds. 1980. *Signs, Symbols, and Architecture.* London and New York: John Wiley & Sons.

Broadbent, Geoffrey H., and Anthony Ward. 1969. "Design methods in architecture." *Architectural Association Paper No. 4.* London: Lund Humphries.

Brogan, Hugh. 1985. *The Penguin History of the United States of America.* London: Penguin Books, 1990.

Brolin, Brent. 1976. *The Failure of Modern Architecture*. New York: Van Nostrand Reinhold.

Brolin, Brent. 1980. *Architecture in Context: Fitting New Buildings with Old*. New York: Van Nostrand Reinhold.

Brolin, Brent. 1985. *Flight of Fancy: The Banishment and Return of Ornament*. London: Academy Editions.

Bronowsky, Jacob. 1977. *A Sense of the Future: Essays in Natural Philosophy*. Selected and edited by Piero E. Ariotti in collaboration with Rita Bronowski. Cambridge, Mass.: MIT Press.

Brown, Denise Scott. 1989. "Room at the top? Sexism and the star system in architecture." *In Architecture*. See Berkeley and McQuaid 1989.

Brownlee, David B., and David G. De Long. 1991. *Louis I. Kahn: In the Realm of Architecture*. New York: Museum of Contemporary Art/Rizzoli International Publications.

Brunskill, Ronald W. 1971. *Illustrated Handbook of Vernacular Architecture*. London: Faber and Faber. Second expanded edition, 1978.

Bucholtz, Jeffery, and Daniel B. Monk, eds. 1984. *Precis: Beyond Style*. Journal of the Graduate School of Architecture and Planning, Columbia University. Volume 5, Fall.

Bullock, Alan. 1985. *The Humanist Tradition in the West*. New York: W. W. Norton.

Bunt, Richard, and Charles Jencks. 1980. *Signs, Symbols and Architecture*. Chichester, England: John Wiley & Sons.

Burke, Edmund. 1756. *A Philosophical Enquiry into the Origin of Our Ideas of the Sublime and the Beautiful*. Edited, introduction, and notes by J. T. Boulton. New York: Columbia University Press, 1958.

Burke, G. 1976. *Townscapes*. Harmondsworth, England: Pelican Books.

Callenbach, Ernest. 1978. *Ecotopia*. London: Pluto Press.

Calvino, Italo. 1986. *The Uses of Literature: Essays*. Translated by Patrick Creagh. San Diego: Harcourt Brace Jovanovich.

Camus, Albert. 1955. *The Myth of Sisyphus*. London: Penguin Books.

Cannon, John, ed. 1980. *The Historian at Work*. London: George Allen & Unwin.

Canter, David. 1977. *The Psychology of Place*. London: Architectural Press.

Canter, David, and Terence Lee, eds. 1974. *Psychology and the Built Environment*. London: Architectural Press.

Capelli, John, Paul Naprstek, and Bruce Prescott, eds. 1990. *Via 10: Ethics and Architecture*. Graduate School of Fine Arts, University of Pennsylvania. Distributed by Rizzoli International Publications, New York.

Carl, P. 1983. "Ancient Mesopotamia and the foundation of architectural representation." *Princeton Journal: Rituals*. Vol. 1:170–186.

Carr, Edward H. 1961. *What Is History?* Second edition. Edited by R. W. Davies. London: Penguin Books, 1987.

Carter, Paul. 1987. *The Road to Botany Bay: An Essay in Spatial History* London: Faber & Faber.

Center, Bella, Sara Hart, and Barbara Knecht. 1984. "Reflecting the Gaze." In *Precis*. See Bucholtz and Monk 1984.

Chambers Twentieth Century Dictionary (CTCD). 1972. A. M. Macdonald, ed. Edinburgh: W. & R. Chambers.

Chang, Amos Ih Tiao. 1956. *The Tao of Architecture.* Princeton, N. J.: Princeton University Press, 1981.

Charles, Prince of Wales. 1989. *A Vision of Britain: A Personal View of Architecture.* London: Doubleday.

Charmé, Stuart L. 1984. *Meaning and Myth in the Study of Lives: A Sartrean Perspective.* Philadelphia: University of Pennsylvania Press.

Chermayeff, Serge, and Christopher Alexander. 1963. *Community and Privacy: Toward a New Architecture of Humanism.* New York: Doubleday.

Ching, Francis D. K. 1979. *Architecture: Form, Space, and Order.* New York: Van Nostrand Reinhold.

Clarke, David. 1984. *Arguments in Favor of Sharpshooting.* Portland, Oregon: Timber Press.

Clark, Roger H., and Michael Pause. 1985. *Precedents in Architecture.* New York: Van Nostrand Reinhold.

Clark, S. 1985. "The *Annales* Historians." In *The Return of Grand Theory.* See Skinner 1985.

Collins, Peter. 1965. *Changing Ideals in Modern Architecture 1750–1950.* London: Faber & Faber Paperback 1967.

Collins, Peter. 1971. *Architectural Judgement.* Montreal: Queen's University Press.

Colomina, Beatriz. 1988. "On Adolf Loos and Josef Hoffmann: Architecture in the age of mechanical reproduction." In *Raumplan versus Plan Libre.* See Risselada 1988.

Colomina, Beatriz, ed. 1988. *Revisions 2: Architectureproduction.* New York: Princeton Architectural Press.

Colquhoun, Alan. 1981. *Essays in Architectural Criticism: Modern Architecture and Historical Change.* Cambridge, Mass.: Oppositions Books/MIT Press, 1986.

Colquhoun, Alan. 1989. *Modernity and the Classical Tradition: Architectural Essays 1980–1987.* Cambridge, Mass.: MIT Press, 1991.

Conrads, Ulrich. 1964. *Programmes and Manifestoes on 20th-century Architecture.* Translated by Michael Bullock, 1970. Cambridge, Mass.: MIT Press, 1971.

Cook, John W., and Heinrich Klotz. 1973. *Conversations with Architects.* New York: Praeger Publishers.

Cooke, John R. 1989. *Architects, Engineers and the Law: Commentary and Materials.* Sydney, Australia: Law Book Company.

Cooke, John R. 1991. "Architects and engineers: Practising in the public interest." *University of New South Wales Law Journal.* Vol. 14, no. 1:73–97.

Cook, Peter. 1969. *Architecture: Action and Plan.* London: Studio Vista.

Cook, Peter, and George Rand. 1989. *Morphosis: Buildings and Projects.* New York: Rizzoli International Publications.

Cook, Peter, and Rosie Llewellyn-Jones. 1991. *New Spirit in Architecture.* New York: Rizzoli International Publications.

Coomaraswamy, Ananda K. 1977. *Coomaraswamy.* 3 vols. Edited by Roger Lipsey. Princeton, N.J.: Princeton University Press.

Cooper, Clare C. 1975. *Easter Hill Village: Some Social Implications of Design.* New York: Free Press.

Corbett, Michael R. 1979. *Splendid Survivors: San Francisco's Downtown Architectural Heritage.* Prepared by Charles Hall Page & Associates, Inc. for The Foundation for San Francisco's Architectural Heritage. San Francisco: Living Books.

Cornford, R. M. 1937. *Plato's Cosmology: The Timaeus of Plato.* London: Routledge.

Coyne, Richard, and Adrian Snodgrass. 1991. "Is designing mysterious? Challenging the dual knowledge thesis." *Design Studies.* Vol. 12, no. 3:124–131.

Coyne, Richard, and Adrian Snodgrass. 1992. "Rescuing CAD from rationalism." *Design Studies.* Vol. 14, no. 2:100–123.

Coyne, Richard, Adrian Snodgrass, Tony Fry, and Paul Redding. 1991. *Gadamer Action & Reason. A Two-Day Conference on the Application of the Hermeneutic Philosophy of Hans-Georg Gadamer within the Human Sciences.* Sydney, Australia: Department of Architecture, University of Sydney.

Critchlow, Keith. 1969. *Order in Space.* London: Thames & Hudson.

Critchlow, Keith. 1976. *Islamic Patterns.* London: Thames & Hudson.

Critchlow, Keith, and Rod Bull. 1979. *Time Stands Still: New Light on Megalithic Science.* London: Gordon Fraser.

Crook, J. Mordaunt. 1987. *The Dilemma of Style: Architectural Ideas from the Picturesque to the Post-Modern.* London: John Murray.

Cross, John, ed. 1987. *The Oxford Book of Aphorisms.* Oxford, England: Oxford University Press.

Cross, Nigel, ed. 1984. *Developments in Design Methodology.* Chichester, England: John Wiley & Sons.

Cuff, Dana. 1991. *Architecture: The Story of Practice.* Cambridge, Mass.: MIT Press.

Cullen, Gordon. 1961. *Townscape.* London: Architectural Press.

Curtis, William J. R. 1982. *Modern Architecture Since 1900.* Oxford, England: Phaidon.

Curtis, William J. R. 1985. "The ancient in the modern." In *Architecture in India.* See Association Francaise d'Action Artistique, 1985.

Cuthbert, Alexander. 1985. "Politics, privilege and design: Place and placemaking in Hong Kong." In *Place and Placemaking.* See Dovey, Downton and Missingham 1985.

Dal Co, Francesco. 1954. *Figures of Architecture and Thought: German Architecture and Culture 1880–1920.* New York: Rizzoli International Publications, 1990.

Dal Co, Francesco, and Giuseppe Mazzariol. 1985. *Carlo Scarpa: The Complete Works.* New York: Rizzoli International Publications.

Daley, Janet. 1982. "Design creativity and the understanding of objects." In *Developments in Design Methodology.* See Cross 1984.

Dallery, A. B., and C. E. Scott, eds. 1989. *The Question of the Other: Essays on Contemporary Continental Philosophy.* Albany: State University of New York Press.

Darke, Jane. 1979. "The primary generator and the design process." In *Developments in Design Methodology.* See Cross 1984.

Davey, Peter. 1980. *Arts and Crafts Architecture: The Search for Earthly Paradise.* London: Architectural Press.

Davis, Mike. 1991. "The infinite game: Redeveloping Downtown L. A." In *Out of Site.* See Ghirardo 1991.

Dawkins, Richard. 1989. *The Selfish Gene.* New edition. Oxford, England: Oxford University Press.

Dean, Andrea Oppenheimer. 1983. *Bruno Zevi on Modern Architecture.* New York: Rizzoli International Publications.

Dean, John, and Bruce Judd, eds. 1983. *Medium-Density Housing in Australia.* Red Hill, ACT: RAIA National Education Division.

Dc Bono, Edward. 1969. *The Mechanism of Mind.* London: Jonathon Cape.

De Bono, Edward. 1971. *The Dog-Exercising Machine: A Study of Children as Inventors.* London: Penguin Books.

De Ménil, Dominique. 1968. *Visionary Architects: Boullée Ledoux Lequeu.* Houston: University of St. Thomas.

Derrida, Jacques. 1976. *Of Grammatology.* Baltimore: John Hopkins University Press.

Derrida, Jacques. 1978. *Writing and Difference.* Chicago: University of Chicago Press.

Derrida, Jacques. 1981. *Dissemination.* London: Athlone.

Derrida, Jacques. 1987. *The Truth in Painting.* Translated by Geoff Bennington and Ian McLeod. Chicago and London: University of Chicago Press.

Descartes, René. 1637. *Discourse on Method.* Translated by Arthur Wollaston. London: Penguin Books, 1960.

Dewey, John. 1934. *Art as Experience.* New York: Paragon Books, 1979.

De Wofle, Ivor, ed. 1971. *Civilia. The End of Sub Urban Man: A Challenge to Semidetsia.* London: Architectural Press.

Diamonstein, Barbralee. 1985. *American Architecture Now II.* New York: Rizzoli International Publications.

Diani, Marco, and Catherine Ingraham, eds. 1988. "Restructuring architectural theory." *Threshold.* Vol. IV, Spring. Republished in 1989 by Northwestern University Press, Evanston, Illinois.

Divry's New English-Greek and Greek-English Handy Dictionary. 1978. Revised edition. New York: D. C. Divry.

Doczi, György. 1981. *The Power of Limits: Proportional Harmonies in Nature, Art and Architecture*. Boulder, Colorado: Shambhala Publications.

Doty, William G. 1986. *Mythography: The Study of Myths and Rituals*. Tuscaloosa, Al.: University of Alabama Press.

Dovey, Kim. 1979. *The Dwelling Experience: Towards a Phenomenology of Architecture*. Melbourne, Australia: University of Melbourne Research Paper No. 55.

Dovey, Kim, Peter Downton, and Greg Missingham, eds. 1985. *Place and Placemaking*. Proceedings of the PAPER Conference. Melbourne, Australia: Association for People and Physical Environment Research.

Doxiadis, C. A. 1963. *Architecture in Transition*. London: Oxford University Press.

Doxiadis, C. A. 1972. *Architectural Space in Ancient Greece*. Translated and edited by Jacqueline Tyrwhitt. Cambridge, Mass.: MIT Press.

Drew, Philip. 1980. "Post modern: The renewal of style in architecture." *Transition*. No. 3. March:9–16.

Drew, Philip. 1985. *Leaves of Iron*. Sydney, Australia: Collins/Angus & Robertson, 1991.

Drexler, Arthur. 1977. *The Architecture of the Ecoles des Beaux Arts*. Cambridge, Mass.: MIT Press.

Dubos, René. 1981. *Celebrations of Life*. New York: McGraw-Hill.

Ducrot, Oswald, and Tzvetan Todorov. 1972. *Encyclopedic Dictionary of the Sciences of Language*. Translated by Catherine Porter. Oxford, England: Blackwell Reference, 1981.

Dundes, Alan. 1984. *Sacred Narrative. Readings in the Theory of Myth*. Berkeley: University of California Presss.

Dunster, David, ed. 1978. *Architectural Monographs 4: Alvar Aalto*. London: Academy Editions.

Eco, Umberto, and Thomas A. Seboek. 1983. *The Sign of Three: Dupin, Holmes, Peirce*. Bloomington: Indiana University Press, Midland Book edition, 1988.

Eliade, Mircea. 1954. *The Myth of the Eternal Return*. Translated by Willard R. Trask. New York: Pantheon Books.

Eliade, Mercia. 1959. *The Sacred and the Profane*. Translated by Willard R. Trask. San Diego: Harcourt Brace Jovanovich.

Elkner, Brian A. 1970. "Diderot and the Sublime: The artist as hero." In *Studies in the Eighteenth Century II*. See Brissenden 1973.

Emanuel, Muriel, ed. 1980. *Contemporary Architects*. New York: St. Martin's Press.

Emmons, Paul F. 1987. "Whole amidst part: Perceiving the architecture of Frank Gehry." *Midgård Journal of Architectural Theory and Criticism*. Vol. 1, no. 1:91–103.

Empson, William. 1951. *The Structure of Complex Words*. London: Hogarth Press, 1985.

Essex, County Council of. 1973. *A Design Guide for Residential Areas*. Tiptree, Essex, England: Anchor Press.

Etlin, Richard A. 1991. *Modernism in Italian Architecture 1890–1940*. Cambridge, Mass.: MIT Press.

Evans, M. 1980. "The geometry of the mind." *Architectural Association Quarterly.* Vol. 12, no. 4:32–55

Ewen, S. 1984. "The political elements of style." In *Precis.* See Bucholtz and Monk 1984.

Farber, J. C., and H. H. Reed. 1980. *Palladio's Architecture and Its Influence: A Photographic Guide.* New York: Dover.

Fathy, Hassan. 1973. *Architecture for the Poor.* Chicago, Ill.: University of Chicago Press.

Feyerabend, Paul. 1988. *Against Method.* Revised edition. London: Verso.

Fischer, Volker, ed. 1989. *Design Now: Industry or Art?* Translated by H. Brill. Munich: Prestel-Verlag.

Fish, Stanley. 1989. *Doing What Comes Naturally: Change, Rhetoric, and the Practice of Theory in Literary and Legal Studies.* Durham, N. C., and London: Duke University Press.

Fitch, James M. 1976. "Architectural criticism: Trapped in its own metaphysics". *Journal of Architectural Education.* Vol. 29, no. 4, April 1976:2–3.

Fleming, John, Hugh Honour, and Nikolaus Pevsner. 1972. *The Penguin Dictionary of Architecture.* Harmondsworth, England: Penguin Books.

Fleming, W. 1980. *Arts and Ideas.* Sixth edition. New York: Holt, Rinehart & Winston.

Flew, Antony. 1971. *An Introduction to Western Philosophy: Ideas and Argument from Plato to Sartre.* New York: Bobbs-Merrill Company.

Flew, Antony, ed. 1979. *A Dictionary of Philosophy.* London: Pan Books.

Foucault, Michel. 1966. *The Order of Things: An Archaeology of the Human Sciences.* London: Tavistock Publications, 1970.

Foucault, Michel. 1977a. *Discipline and Punish: the Birth of the Prison.* Translated by Alan Sheridan. New York: Pantheon Books.

Foucault, Michel. 1977b. *Language, Counter-Memory, Practice.* Donald Bouchard, editor. Oxford, England: Basil Blackwell.

Frampton, Kenneth. 1980. *Modern Architecture: A Critical History.* London: Thames & Hudson.

Frampton, Kenneth. 1982. *Modern Architecture and the Critical Present. AD Architectural Design Profile* 7–8. London: Architectural Design.

Frampton, Kenneth, and Philip Drew. 1992. *Harry Seidler: Four Decades of Architecture.* London: Thames and Hudson.

Frankl, Paul. 1962. *Gothic Architecture.* Translated by Dieter Pevsner. Harmondsworth, England: Penguin Books.

Frankl, Paul. 1914. *Principles of Architectural History: The Four Phases of Architectural Style, 1420–1900.* Translated and edited by J. F. O'Gorman. Cambridge, Mass.: MIT Press, 1982.

Frascari, Marco. 1988. "Maidens 'Theory' and 'Practice' at the sides of Lady Architecture." *Assemblage.* Vol.7:14–27.

Frascari, Marco. 1991. *Monsters of Architecture: Anthropomorphism in Architectural Theory.* Savage, Md: Ronman & Littlefield.

Frascina, Francis, and Charles Harrison, eds. 1982. *Modern Art and Modernism: A Critical*

Anthology. Published in association with The Open University. London: Paul Chapman Publishing, 1988.

Gallion, A., and S. Eisner. 1950. *The Urban Pattern: City Planning and Design.* Fifth edition. New York: Van Nostrand Reinhold, 1986.

Games, Stephen. 1985. *Behind the Façade.* London: Ariel Books/British Broadcasting Corporation.

Gandelsonas, Mario. 1991. *The Urban Text.* Cambridge, Mass.: MIT Press.

Garrigan, K. O. 1973. *Ruskin on Architecture: His Thought and Influence.* Madison, Wisconsin: University of Wisconsin Press.

Gehl, Jan. 1987. *Life Between Buildings.* New York: Van Nostrand Reinhold.

Germann, Georg. 1972. *Gothic Revival in Europe and Britain: Sources, Influences and Ideas.* London: Lund Humphries with the Architectural Association.

Ghirardo, Diane, ed. 1991. *Out of Site: A Social Criticism of Architecture.* Seattle, Washington: Bay Press.

Giedion, Siegfried. 1941. *Space Time and Architecture: The Growth of a New Tradition.* Fifth edition. Cambridge, Mass.: Harvard University Press, 1967.

Gilland, W., and D. Woodcock. 1984. *Architectural Values and World Issues: Proceedings of the 71st Annual Meeting of the Association of Collegiate Schools of Architecture 1983.* Washington, D. C.: Association of Collegiate Schools of Architecture.

Girouard, Mark. 1985. *Cities & People: A Social and Architectural History.* New Haven and London: Yale University Press.

Gleick, James. 1988. *Chaos: Making a New Science.* London: Cardinal/Sphere Books.

Goffman, Erving. 1959. *The Presentation of Self in Everyday Life.* Harmondsworth, England: Pelican Books, 1971.

Goldberger, Paul. 1983. *On the Rise: Architecture and Design in a Postmodern Age.* New York: Times Books.

Gombrich, Ernst H. 1971. *Meditations on a Hobby Horse.* London: Phaidon Press.

Gombrich, Ernst H. 1979. *The Sense of Order: A Study in the Psychology of Decorative Art.*

Gombrich, Ernst H. 1980. "Four theories of artistic expression." *Architectural Association Quarterly* 12(4):14–19.

Goodman, Robert. 1972. *After the Planners.* Harmondsworth, England: Penguin Books.

Gosling, David, and Barry Maitland, eds. 1984. *Urbanism.* AD Architectural Design Profile 15. London: Architectural Design.

Gowan, James, ed. 1975. *A Continuing Experiment: Learning and Teaching at the Architectural Association.* London: Architectural Press.

Grabow, Stephen. 1983. *Christopher Alexander: The Search for a New Paradigm in Architecture.* Stocksfield, England: Oriel Press.

Greenough, Horatio. 1852. *The Travels, Observations, and Experiences of a Yankee Stonecutter.* Gainesville, Florida: Scholars' Facsimiles and Reprints, 1958.

Gropius, Walter. 1956. *Scope of Total Architecture.* London: Allen & Unwin.

Gross, John, ed. 1987. *The Oxford Book of Aphorisms.* Oxford, England: Oxford University Press.

Grudin, Robert. 1990. *The Grace of Great Things: Creativity and Innovation.* New York: Tickner & Fields.

Guénon, René. 1942. *Crisis of the Modern World.* Translated by Marco Pallis and Richard Nicholson. London: Luzac & Company, 1975.

Guénon, René. 1953. *The Reign of Quantity and the Signs of the Times.* Translated by Lord Northbourne. London: Luzac & Company.

Guénon, René. 1958. *Symbolism of the Cross.* London: Luzac & Company.

Guiley, Rosemary E. 1991. *Harper's Encyclopedia of Mystical & Paranormal Experience.* San Francisco: HarperCollins.

Gutman, Robert, ed. 1972. *People and Buildings.* New York: Basic Books.

Gutman, Robert. 1981. "Architecture as a service industry." *Casabella.* No. 475, November:28–32; and no. 476, December:108–109.

Gutman, Robert. 1988. *Architectural Practice: A Critical View.* New York: Princeton Architectural Press.

Gwilt, Joseph. 1867. *The Encyclopedia of Architecture: Historical, Theoretical, and Practical.* Revised edition by Wyatt Papworth. Foreword by Michael Mostoller. New York: Crown Publishers, 1982.

Habraken, Nicolaas. 1971. *Supports: An Alternative to Mass Housing.* Translated by B. Valkenburg. New York: Praeger Publishers, 1972.

Hacking, Ian. 1975. *Why Does Language Matter to Philosophy?* Cambridge and New York: Cambridge University Press.

Harbison, Robert. 1991. *The Built, the Unbuilt and the Unbuildable: In Pursuit of Architectural Meaning.* Cambridge, Mass.: MIT Press.

Harrington, K. 1985. *Changing Ideas on Architecture in the* Encyclopedie. *1750–1776.* Ann Arbor, Mich.: UMI Research Press.

Harris, Errol. 1970. *Hypothesis and Perception: The Roots of Scientific Method.* London: George Allen & Unwin.

Harrison, J. F. C. 1984. *The Common People: A History from the Norman Conquest to the Present.* London: Flamingo, published by Fontana Paperbacks.

Harvey, David. 1973. *Social Justice and the City.* London: Edward Arnold, 1976.

Harvey, David. 1985. *The Urbanization of Capital: Studies in the History and Theory of Capitalist Urbanization.* Baltimore: Johns Hopkins University Press.

Hatje, Gerd, ed. 1963. *Encyclopaedia of Modern Architecture.* London: Thames & Hudson.

Hauser, Arnold. 1974. *The Sociology of Art.* Translated by Kenneth J. Northcott. London: Routledge & Kegan Paul, 1982.

Hays, K. Michael, ed. 1987. *Harvard Architectural Review: Patronage.* Vol. 6:4–174.

Hays, K. Michael. 1988. "Oggetti, testi e testi-oggetto: sulla recente svolta verso la testualita" (Objects, texts and object-texts: on the recent turn toward textuality). *Casabella.* Vol. 52, September:39–41.

Hays, K. Michael. 1990. "Rebuttal: Theory as a mediating practice." *Progressive Architecture.* November:100.

Hays, K. Michael, and Carol Burns. 1990. *Thinking the Present: Recent American Architecture.* New York: Princeton Architectural Press.

Hearn, M. F., ed. 1990. *The Architectural Theory of Viollet-le-Duc: Readings and Commentary.* Cambridge, Mass.: MIT Press.

Heath, Tom F. 1970. "The algorithmic nature of the design process." In *Emerging Methods.* See Moore 1970.

Heath, Tom F. 1971. *Experimental Aesthetics and Architecture.* New York: American Elsevier.

Heath, Tom F. 1974. "Should we tell the children about aesthetics, or should we let them find out in the street?" In *Psychology and the Built Environment.* See Canter and Lee 1974.

Heath, Tom F. 1984. *Method in Architecture.* Chichester, England: John Wiley & Sons.

Heath, Tom F. 1991. *What, if Anything, Is an Architect?* Melbourne, Australia: Architecture Media Australia.

Heidegger, Martin. 1926. *Being and Time.* Translated by J. Macquarrie and E. Robinson. Oxford, England: Basil Blackwell, 1962.

Heidegger, Martin. 1936. "The origin of the work of art." In *Martin Heidegger.* See Krell 1978.

Heidegger, Martin. 1953. "The question concerning technology." See Krell 1978.

Heidegger, Martin. 1971. *Poetry, Language, Thought.* Translated by A. Hofstadter. New York: Harper & Row.

Hejduk, John. 1985. *Mask of Medusa: John Hejduk Works 1947–1983.* Edited by Kim Shkapich. New York: Rizzoli International Publications, 1989.

Henderson, Linda Dalrymple. 1983. *The Fourth Dimension and Non-Euclidean Geometry in Modern Art.* Princeton, N. J.: Princeton University Press.

Herrmann, W. 1962. *Laugier and Eighteenth Century French Theory.* London: A. Zwemmer, 1985.

Herrmann, W. 1973. *The Theory of Claude Perrault.* London: A. Zwemmer.

Hersey, George. 1988. *The Lost Meaning of Classical Architecture: Speculations on Ornament from Vitruvius to Venturi.* Cambridge, Mass.: MIT Press.

Hesselgren, Sven. 1972. *The Language of Architecture.* London: Barking.

Hillier, Bill, and Julienne Hanson. 1984. *The Social Logic of Space.* Cambridge, England: Cambridge University Press.

Hillier, Bill, John Musgrove, and Pat O'Sullivan. 1972. "Knowledge and design." In *Developments in Design Methodology.* See Cross 1984.

Hitchcock, Henry-Russell. 1942. *In the Nature of Materials: The Buildings of Frank Lloyd Wright, 1887–1941.* New York: Da Capo Press, 1969.

Hofstadter, Douglas R., and Daniel C. Dennett, eds. 1981. *The Minds I: Fantasies and Reflections on Self and Soul.* New York: Basic Books.

Holl, Steven. 1989. *Anchoring: Selected Projects.* New York: Princeton Architectural Press.

Holl, Steven. 1991. " 'Nexus World' project." *Progressive Architecture.* August:61.

Hollier, Denis. 1989. *Against Architecture: The Writings of Georges Bataille.* Cambridge, Mass.: MIT Press.

Horwich, Paul. 1990. *Truth.* Oxford, England: Basil Blackwell.

Hoy, David. 1985. "Jacques Derrida." In *Grand Theory.* See Skinner 1985.

Hubbard, William. 1980. *Complicity and Conviction: Steps Toward an Architecture of Convention.* Cambridge, Mass.: MIT Press.

Hughes, J. Quentin, and Norbert Lynton. 1962. *Simpson's History of Architectural Development. Volume 4: Renaissance Architecture.* New York: McKay.

Hughes, Robert. 1990. *Nothing If Not Critical: Selected Essays on Art and Artists.* London: Harvill, 1991.

Hutchinson, Maxwell. 1989. *The Prince of Wales: Right or Wrong? An Architect Replies.* London: Faber & Faber.

Huxtable, Ada Louise. 1986. *Architecture, Anyone?* Berkeley: University of California Press.

Ingraham, Catherine. 1991. "Lines and linearity: Problems in architectural theory." In *Drawing/Building/Text.* See Kahn 1991.

Jacobus, Lee A., ed. 1986. *A World of Ideas: Essential Readings for College Writers.* New York: St. Martin's Press.

Jaffé, Hans L. C. 1967. *De Stijl.* Translated by R. R. Symonds and Mary Whitall. New York: Harry N. Abrams.

James, John. 1979. "Gothic pinnacles." *Architectural Association Quarterly.* Vol. 11, no. 3:55–59.

James, John. 1979. *The Contractors of Chartres.* 2 vols. Wyong, Australia: Mandoorla.

James, John. 1982. *Chartres: The Masons Who Built a Legend.* London: Routledge & Kegan Paul.

James, John. 1987. *A Traveller's Key to Medieval France: A Guide to the Sacred Architecture of Medieval France.* In conjunction with Francois Bucher, Jeanne Stage, and Hilary James. London: Harrap Columbus.

James, John. 1989. *The Template-makers of the Paris Basin: Toichological Techniques for Identifying the Pioneers of the Gothic Movement.* Leura, Australia: West Grinstead Publishing.

James, William. 1907. *Pragmatism.* Buffalo, N. Y.: Prometheus Books, 1991.

Jameson, Fredric. 1988. "Postmodernism and utopia." In *Utopia Post Utopia: Configurations of Nature and Culture in Recent Sculpture and Photography.* Cambridge, Mass.: Institute of Contemporary Art/MIT Press.

Jarzombek, Mark. 1989. *On Leon Baptista Alberti: His Literary and Aesthetic Theories.* Cambridge, Mass.: MIT Press.

Jencks, Charles. 1971. *Architecture 2000: Predictions and Methods.* London: Studio Vista.

Jencks, Charles. 1973. *Modern Movements in Architecture.* Harmondsworth, England: Pelican Books.

Jencks, Charles. 1975. *Le Corbusier and the Tragic View of Architecture.* London: Allen Lane Penguin Books.

Jencks, Charles. 1977. *The Language of Post-Modern Architecture.* London: Academy Editions, 1981.

Jencks, Charles. 1980. *Late-Modern Architecture.* London: Academy Editions.

Jencks, Charles. 1983. *Kings of Infinite Space: Frank Lloyd Wright & Michael Graves.* London: Academy Editions.

Jencks, Charles, and George Baird, eds. 1969. *Meaning in Architecture.* New York: George Braziller.

Jencks, Charles, and William Chaitkin. 1982. *Current Architecture.* London: Academy Editions.

Johnson, Paul-Alan. 1983a. "About face: Front/back perceptions of housing users." In *Conference Proceedings.* See Joiner *et al.* 1983.

Johnson, Paul-Alan. 1983b. "User-feedback and an evaluation of some medium-density housing in Sydney." In *Medium-Density Housing.* See Dean and Judd 1983.

Johnson, Paul-Alan. 1989. "Domestic space standards and performance in NSW public housing." In *Housing Issues.* See Judd and Bycroft 1989.

Johnson, Paul-Alan. 1990. "Mapmakers of the early New South Wales settlement." *The Globe. Journal of the Australian Map Circle.* No. 33:15–29.

Johnson, Paul-Alan. 1991. "Mythmaking: The polyhymn of architecture—or taking Barthes." In *Proceedings.* See Linzey 1991a.

Johnson, Philip C. 1979. *Philip Johnson Writings.* New York: Oxford University Press.

Johnson, Philip C., and Mark Wigley. 1988. *Deconstructivist Architecture.* New York: Museum of Modern Art.

Joiner, Duncan *et al.* eds. 1983. *Conference on People and Physical Environment Research Proceedings, 8–11 June.* Wellington, New Zealand: New Zealand Ministry of Works and Development.

Jones, J. Christopher. 1984. *Essays in Design.* Chichester, England: John Wiley & Sons.

Jones, J. Christopher, and D. G. Thornley. 1963. *Conference on Design Methods.* London: Pergamon Press.

Judd, Bruce, and Peter Bycroft, eds. 1989. *Housing Issues 4: Evaluating Housing Standards and Performance.* Red Hill, ACT: RAIA National Education Division.

Kahn, Andrea, ed. 1991. *Drawing/Building/Text: Essays in Architectural Theory.* New York: Princeton Architectural Press.

Kant, Immanuel. 1785. *Foundations of the Metaphysics of Morals* and *What Is Enlightenment?* Translated and with an introduction by Lewis White Beck. New York: Macmillan/The Library of Liberal Arts, 1987.

Kant, Immanuel. 1790. *The Critique of Judgement.* Translated and with analytical indexes by James Creed Meredith. Oxford, England: Oxford University Press, 1952.

Kaufmann, Emil. 1952. "Three Revolutionary Architects: Boullee, Ledoux and Lequeu." *Transactions of the American Philosophical Society.* Vol. 63, no. 3.

Kaufmann, Emil. 1955. *Architecture in the Age of Reason: Baroque and Post-Baroque in England, Italy, and France.* New York: Dover Publications, 1968.

Kenawell, W. W. 1965. *The Quest at Glastonbury: A Biographical Study of Frederick Bligh Bond.* New York: Garrett.

Kennedy, M. I. 1981. "Towards a rediscovery of 'feminine' principles in architecture and planning." *Women's Studies International Quarterly.* Vol. 4:75–81.

Kierkegaard, Søren. 1843. *Fear and Trembling.* Translated and with an introduction by Alastair Hannay. London: Penguin Books, 1985.

Kipnis, Jeffrey. 1990a. "Rebuttal: Theory used and abused." *Progressive Architecture.* November:98–100, 158.

Kipnis, Jeffrey. 1990b. *In the Manor of Nietzsche: Aphorisms Around and About Architecture.* New York: Calluna Farms Press.

Kirk, Stephen J., and Kent F. Spreckelmeyer. 1988. *Creative Design Decisions: A Systematic Approach to Problem Solving in Architecture.* New York: Van Nostrand Reinhold.

Kloos, Maarten, ed. 1991. *Architecture Now: A Compilation of Comments on the State of Contemporary Architecture.* Amsterdam: Architectura & Natura Press.

Klotz, Heinrich. 1984. *The History of Postmodern Architecture.* Translated by Radka Donnell. Cambridge, Mass.: MIT Press, 1988.

Knevitt, Charles, ed. 1986. *Perspectives. An Anthology of 1001 Architectural Quotations.* London: Lund Humphries.

Kockelmans, J. J. 1965. *Martin Heidegger: A First Introduction to his Philosophy.* Pittsburgh: Duquesne University Press.

Koestler, Arthur. 1967. *The Ghost in the Machine.* London: Hutchinson.

Kolb, David. 1990. *Postmodern Sophistications: Philosophy, Architecture, and Tradition.* London & Chicago: University of Chicago Press.

Kollar, L. Peter. 1972. *Symbolism in Christian Architecture.* Unpublished Ph.D. thesis. School of Architecture, University of New South Wales.

Kollar, L. Peter. 1980. "Ars sine scientia nihil: In praise of knowledge." *Transition.* No. 3, March:17–20.

Kollar, L. Peter. 1983. *On the Architectural Idea.* Sydney, Australia: privately published.

Kollar, L. Peter. 1985. *On the Whole and the Part.* Sydney, Australia: privately published.

Kollar, L. Peter. 1987. *Patterns of Delightful Architecture.* Sydney, Australia: privately published.

Kollar, L. Peter. 1990. "Foundations of a general theory of architecture." Manuscript. Sydney, Australia: August.

Kostof, Spiro. 1985. *A History of Architecture Settings and Rituals.* New York: Oxford University Press.

Kostof, Spiro, ed. 1977. *The Architect: Chapters in the History of the Profession.* New York: Oxford University Press.

Krell, D. F., ed. 1978. *Martin Heidegger. Basic Writings from* Being and Time *(1927) to* The Task of Thinking *(1964).* London: Routledge and Kegan Paul.

Krier, Leon. 1983. "Elements of Architecture." *Architectural Design.* Vol. 53, No. 9/10.

Krier, Rob. 1979. *Urban Space.* London: Academy Editions.

Krier, Rob. 1988. *Architectural Composition.* New York: Rizzoli International Publications.

Kroll, Lucien. 1986. *The Architecture of Complexity.* Translation and foreword by Peter Blundell Jones. London: B. T. Batsford.

Kuhn, Thomas. 1970. *The Structure of Scientific Revolutions.* Chicago: University of Chicago Press.

Kunze, Donald. 1987. *Thought and Place: The Architecture of Eternal Place in the Philosophy of Giambattista Vico.* New York: Peter Lang.

Lachterman, David R. 1989. *The Ethics of Geometry: A Genealogy of Modernity.* New York: Routledge & Kegan Paul.

Lakatos, Imre. 1978. *Philosophical Papers of Imre Lakatos,* Vols. 1 and 2. Edited by John Worrall and Gregory Currie. Cambridge, England: Cambridge University Press.

Lang, Jon. 1987. *Creating Architectural Theory: The Role of the Behavioral Sciences in Design.* New York: Van Nostrand Reinhold.

Lang, S. 1952. "The ideal city from Plato to Howard." *The Architectural Review.* Vol. 112, No. 668, August:91–101.

Langdon, Richard, *et al.,* eds. 1984. *Design Policy.* 6 vols. London: Design Council.

Langer, Susanne K. 1953. *Feeling and Form: A Theory of Art Developed From Philosphy in a New Key.* London: Routledge & Kegan Paul.

Larousse Encyclopedia of Music. 1971. Geoffrey Hindley, ed. London: Hamlyn Publishing Group.

Latour, Alessandra, ed. 1991. *Louis I. Kahn: Writings, Lectures, Interviews.* New York: Rizzoli International Publications.

Laugier, Marc-Antoine. 1753. *An Essay on Architecture.* Translated and with an introduction by Wolfgang Herrmann and Anni Herrmann. Los Angeles: Hennessey & Ingalls, 1977.

Lavin, Sylvia. 1990. "Essay: The uses and abuses of theory." *Progressive Architecture.* August: 113–114, 179.

Lavin, Sylvia. 1992. *Quatremère de Quincy and the Invention of a Modern Language of Architecture.* Cambridge, Mass.: MIT Press.

Lawlor, Robert. 1982. *Sacred Geometry: Philosophy and Practice.* London: Thames & Hudson.

Lawson, Bryan. 1980. *How Designers Think.* London: Architectural Press.

Le Corbusier. 1923. *Towards a New Architecture.* Translated by F. Etchells. London: Architectural Press, 1970.

Le Corbusier. 1930. *Precisions on the Present State of Architecture and City Planning.* Translated by Edith Schreiber Aujame. Cambridge, Mass.: MIT Press, 1991.

Le Corbusier. 1954. *The Modulor: A Harmonious Measure to the Human Scale Universally Applicable to Architecture and Mechanics.* Second edition. Translated by P. de Francia and A. Bostock. Cambridge, Mass.: MIT Press, 1968.

Le Corbusier. 1958. *Modulor 2.* Translated by P. de Francia and A. Bostock. Cambridge, Mass.: Harvard University Press, 1980.

Lesnikowski, Wojciech with Calli Spheeris. 1987. "Vitruvius to Venturi: On the changing nature of theories of architecture." *Inland Architect.* Vol. 31, no. 5, September/October: 28–39.

Lethaby, William R. 1891. *Architecture, Mysticism and Myth.* London: Architectural Press, 1974.

Lévi-Strauss, Claude. 1966. *The Savage Mind.* Chicago: University of Chicago Press.

Lévi-Strauss, Claude. 1969. *The Raw and the Cooked.* Translated by John and Doreen Weightman. New York: Harper & Row.

Lewis, Charlton T. 1891. *An Elementary Latin Dictionary.* Oxford, England: Oxford University Press, 1956.

Lewis, Clarence I. 1969. *Values and Imperatives: Studies in Ethics.* Edited by John Lange. Stanford, Ca.: Stanford University Press.

Lewis, David K. 1969. *Convention: A Philosophical Study.* Cambridge, Mass.: Harvard University Press.

Lewis, Roger K. 1985. *Architect? A Candid Guide to the Profession.* Cambridge, Mass.: MIT Press.

Linzey, Michael, coord. 1991a. *Proceedings: Myth, Architecture, History, Writing.* PAPER Conference. 12–14 July, 1991. Auckland, New Zealand: Association for People and Physical Environment Research.

Linzey, Michael. 1991b. "Speaking to and talking about: Maori architecture." *Interstices: A Journal of Architecture and Related Arts.* Vol. 1, February 1991:49–60.

Lip, Evelyn. 1979. *Chinese Geomancy: A Layman's Guide to Feng Sui.* Singapore, Times Books International.

Lipman, Alan. 1971. "Professional ideology: 'Community' and 'total' architecture." *Journal of Architectural Research and Teaching.* Vol. 1, no. 3:39–49.

Loos, Adolf. 1910. "Architecture." Translated by H. F. Mallgrave. *Midgård Journal of Architectural Theory and Criticism.* Vol. 1, no. 1, 1987:49–56.

Loos, Adolf. 1921. *Spoken into the Void.* Translated by Jane O. Newman and John H. Smith. Cambridge, Mass.: MIT Press, 1982.

Lorenz, Clare. 1990a. "Kicking against the pricks." *Building Design.* October 19:25–26.

Lorenz, Clare. 1990b. *Women in Architecture: A Contemporary Perspective.* London: Trefoil Publications.

Luscombe, Desley, and Anne Peden. 1992. *Picturing Architecture: Graphic Presentation Techniques in Australian Architectural Practice.* Sydney, Australia: Craftsman House.

Lynch, Kevin. 1960. *The Image of the City.* Cambridge, Mass.: MIT Press, 1965.

Lynch, Kevin. 1984. *Good City Form.* Cambridge, Mass.: MIT Press, 1989 (first published c1981 as *A Theory of Good City Form*).

Lyotard, Jean-Francois. 1984a. *Driftworks.* Edited by Roger McKeon. New York: Semiotext(e).

Lyotard, Jean-Francois. 1984b. *The Postmodern Condition: A Report on Knowledge.* Translated by G. Bennington and B. Massimi. Manchester, England: Manchester University Press.

Macarthur, John. 1991. "Seven doubts about urbanism." *Transition.* No. 34:83–94.

MacLeod, Robert. 1971. *Style and Society: Architectural Ideology in Britain 1835–1914.* London: RIBA Publications Ltd.

Macormac, E. R. 1985. *A Cognitive Theory of Metaphor.* Cambridge, Mass.: MIT Press.

Macrae-Gibson, Gavin. 1985. *The Secret Life of Buildings: An American Mythology for Modern Architecture.* Cambridge, Mass.: MIT Press.

Madison, Gary B. 1988. *The Hermeneutics of Postmodernity: Figures and Themes.* Bloomington: Indiana University Press, 1990.

Maitland, Barry, and David Gosling. 1984. *Concepts of Urban Design.* London: Academy Editions.

March, Lionel J., ed. 1976. *The Architecture of Form.* Cambridge, England: Cambridge University Press.

March, Lionel, and Philip Steadman. 1971. *The Geometry of Environment: An Introduction to Spatial Organization in Design.* London: RIBA Publications.

Marcus, Clare Cooper, and Wendy Sarkissian. 1986. *Housing as if People Mattered: Site Design Guidelines for Medium-Density Family Housing.* Berkeley: University of California Press.

Marcuse, Herbert. 1972. *An Essay on Liberation.* Harmondsworth, England: Pelican Books.

Marder, Tod A. 1985. *The Critical Edge: Controversy in Recent American Architecture.* Cambridge, Mass.: MIT Press.

Margolin, Victor, ed. 1989. *Design Discourse: History, Theory, Criticism.* Chicago: University of Chicago Press.

Marin, Louis. 1984. *Utopics: Spatial Play.* Translated by Robert A. Vollrath. Atlantic Highlands, N. J.: Humanities Press.

Markus, Thomas A. 1985. *Visions of Perfection: The Influence of Utopian Thought Upon Architecture from the Middle Ages to the Present Day.* Glasgow: Third Eye Centre.

Marquard, Odo. 1981. *Farewell to Matters of Principle.* Translated by Robert M. Wallace with the assistance of Susan Bernstein and James I. Porter. New York: Oxford University Press, 1989.

Marshall, Peter. 1992. *Demanding the Impossible: A History of Anarchism.* London: HarperCollins Publishers.

Martin, J. Leslie, Ben Nicholson, and Naum Gabo. 1937. *Circle: International Survey of Constructive Art.* New York: Praeger Publishers, 1971.

Marvel, Jonathon Jova, ed., and Margaret Reeve, curator. 1986. *Investigations in Architecture:*

Eisenman Studios at the GSD:1983–85. Cambridge, Mass.: Harvard University Graduate School of Design.

McLachlan, Noel. 1989. *Waiting for the Revolution: A History of Australian Nationalism.* Ringwood, Australia: Penguin Books.

Memmott, Paul. 1988. "Aboriginal housing: The state of the art (or non-state of the art)." *Architecture Australia: Discourse V.* Vol. 77, no. 4, June:34–47.

Menocal, Narciso G. 1981. *Architecture as Nature: The Transcendentalist Idea of Louis Sullivan.* Madison: University of Wisconsin Press.

Merquior, José G. 1985. *Foucault.* London: Fontana Press.

Meurant, Robert C. 1992. "The myth of perfection of the Platonic solids." In *Proceedings.* See Linzey 1991a.

Michell, G. 1977. *The Hindu Temple: An Introduction to its Meaning and Forms.* London: Paul Elek.

Michelson, William, ed. 1975. *Behavioral Research Methods in Environmental Design.* Stroudsburg, Pa.: Dowden, Hutchinson & Ross.

Middleton, Robin. 1982. "The Beaux-Arts tradition in France." *Transactions 1. The Record of Papers Presented to the RIBA.* Vol. 1, no. 1:62–72.

Missingham, Greg. 1985. "Ariadne's reinforcing rod: Conjectures on place and architectural archetypes." In *Place and Placemaking.* See Dovey, Downton and Missingham 1985.

Miller, Nory. 1987. *Helmut Jahn.* New York: Rizzoli International Publications.

Mitchell, William J., ed. 1972. *Environmental Design: Research and Practice.* Los Angeles: University of California.

Mitchell, William J. 1990. *Logic of Architecture: Design, Computation, and Cognition.* Cambridge, Mass.: MIT Press.

Moment, Gairdner B., and Helen M. Habermann. 1973. *Biology: A Full Spectrum.* Baltimore: Williams & Wilkin Company.

Moore, Charles. 1978. *The Work of Charles W. Moore. A + U Architecture and Urbanism 5.* Edited by Toshio Nakamura. Tokyo: A + U Publishing Co., May.

Moore, Charles, Gerald Allen, and Donlyn Lyndon. 1974. *The Place of Houses.* New York: Holt Rinehart & Winston.

Moore, Charles, and Gerald Allen. 1976. *Dimensions: Space, Shape and Scale in Architecture.* New York: Architectural Record Books.

Moore, Charles, William J. Mitchell, and William Turnbull. 1988. *The Poetics of Gardens.* Cambridge, Mass.: MIT Press.

Moore, Gary T., ed. 1970. *Emerging Methods in Environmental Design and Planning.* Cambridge, Mass.: MIT Press, 1973.

Morris, Meaghan. 1988. *The Pirate's Fiancee.* New York: Verso.

Muller, Peter. 1976. *Walter Burley Griffin Memorial Lecture: The Esoteric Nature of Griffin's Design for Canberra.* Typescript of the lecture delivered on the centenary of Walter Burley Griffin's birth. Canberra, Australia, 24 November.

Mumford, Lewis. 1922. *The Story of Utopias.* New York: The Viking Press, 1962.

Mumford, Lewis. 1938. *The Culture of Cities.* London: Secker & Warburg.

Mumford, Lewis. 1944. *The Condition of Man.* London: Harcourt Brace & World.

Mumford, Lewis. 1961. *The City in History.* Harmondsworth, England: Pelican Books.

Mumford, Lewis. 1970. *The Myth of the Machine: The Pentagon of Power.* New York: Harcourt Brace Jovanovich.

Murray, Alexander S. 1874. *Who's Who in Mythology: Classic Guide to the Ancient World.* London: Studio Editions, 1988.

Murray, Peter, ed. 1982. *Transactions 2. The Record of Papers Presented to the RIBA.* Vol. 1, no. 2.

Muschamp, Herbert. 1974. *File Under Architecture.* Cambridge, Mass.: MIT Press.

Muschamp, Herbert. 1983. *Man About Town: Frank Lloyd Wright in New York City.* Cambridge, Mass.: MIT Press.

Naylor, G. 1968. *the bauhaus.* London: Studio Vista.

Neale, R. S. 1973. "Bath: Ideology and Utopia, 1700–1760." In *Studies in the Eighteenth Century III.* See Brissenden and Eade 1976.

Neumeyer, Fritz. 1991. *The Artless Word: Mies van der Rohe on the Building Art.* Cambridge, Mass.: MIT Press.

Newman, Oscar. 1972. *Defensible Space: People and Design in the Violent City.* London: Architectural Press.

Nietzsche, Friedrich. 1870. *On Truth and Lie in an Extra-Moral Sense.* In *Nietzsche.* See Schacht 1982.

Nietzsche, Friedrich. 1878. *Human, All-Too-Human: A Book for Free Spirits.* Translated by R. J. Hollingdale, with an introduction by Erich Heller. Cambridge, England: Cambridge University Press, 1986.

Nietzsche, Friedrich. 1885. *Beyond Good and Evil: Prelude to a Philosophy of the Future.* Translated and with introduction and commentary by R. J. Hollingdale. Harmondsworth, England: Penguin Boooks, 1973.

Norberg-Schulz, Christian. 1965. *Intentions in Architecture.* Cambridge, Mass.: MIT Press, 1979.

Norberg-Schulz, Christian. 1971. *Existence, Space and Architecture.* New York: Praeger.

Norberg-Schulz, Christian. 1975. *Meaning in Western Architecture.* New York: Rizzoli International Publications, 1980.

Norberg-Schulz, Christian. 1980. *Genius Loci: Towards a Phenomenology of Architecture.* New York: Rizzoli International Publications.

Nowell-Smith, P. H. 1954. *Ethics.* London: Penguin Books.

Nuttall, Zelia. 1922. "Royal ordinances concerning the laying out of new towns." *Hispanic American Historical Review.* Vol. 5:245–254.

Ockman, Joan, ed. 1985. *Revisions 1: Architecture Criticism Ideology.* Princeton, N. J.: Princeton Architectural Press.

Ogden, Charles K., and Ivor A. Richards. 1947. *The Meaning of Meaning: A Study of the Influence of Language upon Thought and of the Science of Symbolism.* London: Routledge.

Oliver, Paul, ed. 1969. *Shelter and Society.* London: Barrie & Rockliffe/The Cresset Press.

Oliver, Richard, ed. 1981. *The Making of an Architect, 1881–1981: Columbia University in the City of New York.* New York: Rizzoli International Publications.

Onians, Richard B. 1951. *The Origins of European Thought About the Body, the Mind, the Soul, the World, Time, and Fate.* Cambridge, England: Cambridge University Press, 1988.

Ormiston, Gayle L., and Alan D. Schrift, eds. 1990. *Transforming the Hermeneutic Context: From Nietzsche to Nancy.* Albany: State University of New York Press.

Ortony, Andrew, ed. 1979. *Metaphor and Thought.* Cambridge, England, and New York: Cambridge University Press.

Oxford Dictionary of Quotations (ODQ). 1977. Second edition. Oxford, England: Oxford University Press.

Oxman, Robert, Antony Radford, and Rivka Oxman. 1987. *The Language of Architectural Plans: In which the principles, elements and operations of Architectural Planning are explored using computer graphics as a planning sketchbook.* Red Hill, ACT: RAIA National Education Division.

Padovan, R. 1986. Three-part series on Dom Hans van der Laan. In *Architect* from Vol. 93, no. 4, 1986:54–57, entitled sequentially: "A necessary instrument," "Measuring and counting," and "Theory and practice."

Pagels, Elaine. 1979. *The Gnostic Gospels.* London: Penguin Books.

Palladio, Andrea. 1570. *The Four Books of Architecture.* Translated by Isaac Ware, 1738. New York: Dover Publications, with a new introduction by Adolf K. Placzek, 1965.

Papageorgiou, Alexander. 1971. *Continuity and Change: Preservation in City Planning.* London: Pall Mall Press.

Papanek, Victor. 1972. *Design for the Real World: Human Ecology and Social Change.* Frogmore, St. Albans, Herts., England: Paladin, 1977.

Parrinder, Geoffrey, compiler. 1990. *Collins Dictionary of Religious & Spiritual Quotations.* Glasgow: HarperCollins Publishers.

Pawley, Martin. 1990. *Theory and Design in the Second Machine Age.* Oxford, England: Basil Blackwell.

Pennick, Nigel. 1980. *Sacred Geometry: Symbolism and Purpose in Religious Structures.* San Francisco: Harper & Row.

Pepchinski, Mary. 1991. "The landscape of memory." In *Drawing/Building/Text.* See Kahn 1991.

Pérez-Gómez, Alberto. 1984. *Architecture and the Crisis of Modern Science.* Cambridge, Mass.: MIT Press.

Perin, Constance. 1970. *With Man in Mind: An Interdisciplinary Prospectus for Environmental Design.* Cambridge, Mass.: MIT Press.

Pevsner, Nikolaus. 1943. *An Outline of European Architecture.* Seventh edition. Harmondsworth, England: Penguin Books, 1963.

Pevsner, Nikolaus. 1960. *Pioneers of Modern Design: From William Morris to Walter Gropius.* Harmondsworth, England: Pelican Books, 1972.

Pevsner, Nikolaus. 1968. *The Sources of Modern Architecture and Design.* London: Thames and Hudson.

Pevsner, Nikolaus. 1976. *A History of Building Types.* London: Thames & Hudson.

Philp, Mark. 1985. "Michel Foucault." In *Grand Theory.* See Skinner 1985.

Placzek, Adolf K., ed. *Macmillan Encyclopedia of Architects.* 1982. Vols. 1–4. New York: Free Press.

Plato. *The Republic.* Translated by H. D. P. Lee. Harmondsworth, England: Penguin Books, 1955.

Plattus, Alan J. 1983. "Passages into the city: The interpretive function of the Roman Triumph." *Princeton Journal: Rituals.* Thematic Studies in Architecture, Vol. 1. Princeton, N.J.: Princeton Architectural Press.

Plunz, Richard, ed. 1982. *Design and the Public Good: Selected Writings 1930–1980 by Serge Chermayeff.* Cambridge, Mass.: MIT Press.

Poe, Edgar Allan. 1844. *Essays and Reviews.* New York: The Library of America, 1984.

Pollitt, Jerry J. 1974. *The Ancient View of Greek Art: Criticism, History, and Terminology.* New Haven and London: Yale University Press.

Popper, Karl R. 1972. *Objective Knowledge.* Oxford, England: Oxford University Press.

Porphyrios, Demetri. 1978. "Heterotopia: A study in the ordering sensibility of the work of Alvar Aalto." In *Architectural Monographs 4: Alvar Aalto.* See Dunster 1978.

Porphyrios, Demetri, ed. 1982. *Classicism Is Not a Style.* London: Architectural Design and Academy Editions.

Porphyrios, Demetri, ed. 1984. *Leon Krier: Houses, Palaces, Cities. AD Architectural Design Profile 54.* London: Architectural Design.

Prak, Niels L. 1968. *The Language of Architecture.* The Hague, Mouton Publishers.

Prak, Niels L. 1984. *Architects: The Noted and the Ignored.* Chichester, England: John Wiley & Sons.

Prall, David W. 1929. *Aesthetic Judgement.* New York: Thomas Y. Crowell/Apollo Editions, 1967.

Prall, David W. 1936. *Aesthetic Analysis.* New York: Thomas Y. Crowell/Apollo Editions, 1964.

Preiser, Wolfgang F. E., ed. 1973. *Environmental Design Research.* Stroudsburg, Pa.: Dowden, Hutchinson & Ross.

Preiser, Wolfgang F. E., ed. 1978. *Facility Programming: Methods and Applications.* Stroudsburg, Pa.: Dowden, Hutchinson & Ross.

Preiser, Wolfgang F. E., ed. 1985. *Programming the Built Environment.* New York: Van Nostrand Reinhold.

Preiser, Wolfgang F. E., ed. 1989. *Building Evaluation.* New York: Plenum Press.

Preiser, Wolfgang F. E., Harvey Z. Rabinowitz, and Edward T. White. 1988. *Post-Occupancy Evaluation.* New York: Van Nostrand Reinhold.

Preiser, Wolfgang F. E., Jacqueline C. Vischer, and Edward T. White, eds. 1991. *Design Intervention: Toward a More Humane Architecture.* New York: Van Nostrand Reinhold.

Price, R. H., M. Glickstein, D. L. Horton, and R. H. Bailey. 1982. *Principles of Psychology.* New York: Holt Reinhart & Winston.

Proshansky, Harold M., William H. Ittelson, and Leanne G. Rivlin. 1970. *Environmental Psychology: Man and his Setting.* New York: Holt Rinehart & Winston.

Proust, Marcel. 1981. *Remembrance of Things Past.* Three vols. Translated by C. K. Scott Moncrieff and revised by Terence Kilmartin. London: Penguin Books, 1983.

Quantrill, Malcolm. 1974. *Ritual and Response in Architecture.* London: Lund Humphries.

Quine, Willard V. O. 1961. *From a Logical Point of View.* Cambridge, Mass.: Harvard University Press.

Raban, Jonathon. 1974. *Soft City.* London: Collins Harvill, 1988.

Radford, Anthony, and Garry Stevens. 1987. *CADD Made Easy: A Comprehensive Guide for Architects and Designers.* New York: McGraw-Hill.

Raglan, Lord. 1964. *The Temple and the House.* London: Routledge & Kegan Paul.

Rapoport, Amos. 1969. *House Form and Culture.* Englewood Cliffs, N. J.: Prentice-Hall.

Rapoport, Amos. 1982. *The Meaning of the Built Environment: A Nonverbal Communication Approach.* With a new epilogue by the author. 1990. Tucson: University of Arizona Press.

Raskin, Eugene. 1974. *Architecture and People.* Englewood Cliffs, N. J.: Prentice-Hall.

Rasmussen, Steen E. 1959. *Experiencing Architecture.* Cambridge, Mass.: MIT Press, 1991.

Rawls, John. 1971. *A Theory of Justice.* Cambridge, Mass., Harvard University Press.

Ricoeur, Paul. 1961. *Universal Civilisation and National Cultures: History and Truth.* Evanston, Ill.: Northwestern University Press.

Risselada, Max, ed. 1988. *Raumplan versus Plan Libre: Adolf Loos and Le Corbusier, 1919–1930.* New York: Rizzoli International Publications.

Robertson, D. S. 1945. *Greek and Roman Architecture.* Reprinted and corrected second edition. London: Cambridge University Press.

Robertson, Howard, and F. R. Yerbury. 1989. *Travels in Modern Architecture 1925–1930.* London: Architectural Association.

Rose, Steven. 1992. *The Making of Memory.* London: Bantam Press.

Rosenau, Helen. 1959. *The Ideal City in its Architectural Evolution.* Boston: Boston Book & Art Shop.

Rosenau, Helen. 1979. *Vision of the Temple: The Image of the Temple of Jerusalem in Judaism and Christianity.* London: Oresko Books.

Rosenau, Helen. 1983. *The Ideal City: Its Architectural Evolution in Europe.* London: Methuen & Co. Ltd.

Rossbach, Sarah. 1984. *Feng Shui.* London: Hutchinson/Rider.

Rossi, Aldo. 1981. *A Scientific Autobiography.* Cambridge, Mass.: MIT Press.

Rossi, Aldo. 1982. *The Architecture of the City.* Cambridge, Mass.: Oppositions Books/ MIT Press.

Rossi, Aldo. 1985. *Three Cities.* New York: Rizzoli International Publications. Translation of *Tre Citta: Perugia, Milano, Mantua.* Milan and New York: Electa Rizzola, 1984.

Rowe, Colin. 1976. *The Mathematics of the Ideal Villa and Other Essays.* Cambridge, Mass.: MIT Press, 1989.

Rowe, Colin, and Koetter, Fred. 1978. *Collage City.* Cambridge, Mass.: MIT Press.

Rowe, Peter G. 1987. *Design Thinking.* Cambridge, Mass.: MIT Press.

Rowe, Peter G. 1991. *Making a Middle Landscape.* Cambridge, Mass.: MIT Press.

Rudofsky, Bernard. 1977. *The Prodigious Builders: Notes toward a natural history of architecture with special regard to those species that are traditionally neglected or downright ignored.* London: Secker & Warburg.

Ruskin, John. 1851/1853. *The Stones of Venice.* Three vols. Orpington, Kent, England: George Allen, 1888.

Ruskin, John. 1854. *Lectures on Architecture & Painting.* London: George Allen, 1905.

Ruskin, John. 1855. *The Seven Lamps of Architecture.* Second edition. London: Ward Lock, 1911.

Ruskin, John. 1859. *Sesames and Lilies, The Two Paths and The King of the Golden River.* London and Toronto: J. M. Dent & Sons, Everyman's Library edition. No. 219, 1907.

Ruskin, John. 1862. *Unto This Last: Four Essays on the First Principles of Political Economy.* London: George Allen & Unwin, c1877.

Russell, Bertrand. 1952. *The Impact of Science on Society.* London: Unwin Paperbacks, 1976.

Rybczynski, Witold. 1989. *The Most Beautiful House in the World.* New York: Viking Penguin.

Rykwert, Joseph. 1972. *On Adam's House in Paradise: The Idea of the Primitive Hut in Architectural History.* New York: Museum of Modern Art.

Rykwert, Joseph. 1976. *The Idea of a Town: The Anthropology of Urban Form in Rome, Italy and the Ancient World.* London: Faber & Faber.

Rykwert, Joseph. 1982. *The Necessity of Artifice.* London: Academy Editions.

Rykwert, Joseph, Neil Leach, and Robert Tavernor, translators. 1991. *Leon Battista Alberti: On the Art of Building in Ten Books.* Cambridge, Mass.: MIT Press.

Saarinen, Thomas F. 1976. *Environmental Planning: Perception and Behavior.* Boston: Houghton Mifflin.

Sagan, Carl. 1981. *Cosmos.* London: Macdonald & Co (Publishers) Ltd.

Saint, Andrew. 1983. *The Image of the Architect.* New Haven: Yale University Press.

Santayana, George. 1896. *The Sense of Beauty Being an Outline of Aesthetic Theory.* New York: Dover Publications, 1955.

Sartre, Jean-Paul. 1949. *Existentialism as a Humanism.* Translated by Philip Mairet. New York: Philosophical Library.

Sartre, Jean-Paul. 1963. *Essays in Aesthetics.* New York: Philosophical Library.

Sarkissian, Wendy, and Terry Doherty. 1987. *Housing Issues 2: Living in Public Housing.* Red Hill, ACT: RAIA National Education Division.

Sarup, Madan. 1989. *An Introductory Guide to Post-Structuralism.* Athens, Ga.: University of Georgia Press.

Schacht, Richard. 1982. *Nietzsche: Arguments of the Philosophers Series.* London and Boston: Routledge & Kegan Paul.

Schilpp, P. A. 1968. *The Philosophy of G. E. Moore.* Evanston, Ill.: Northwestern University.

Schirmbeck, E. 1983. *Idea, Form, and Architecture: Design Principles in Contemporary Architecture.* Translated by Henry J. Cowan. New York: Van Nostrand Reinhold, 1987.

Scholfield, P. H. 1958. *The Theory of Proportion in Architecture.* London: Cambridge University Press.

Schön, Donald. 1979. "Generative metaphor: A perspective on problem-setting in social policy." In *Metaphor and Thought.* See Ortony 1979.

Schön, Donald. 1983. *The Reflective Practitioner: How Professionals Think in Action.* New York: Basic Books.

Schön, Donald. 1982. "Reflection in action." In *Transactions 2.* See Murray 1982.

Schön, Donald. 1985. *The Design Studio.* London: RIBA Publications.

Schön, Donald. 1987. *Educating the Reflective Practitioner.* San Francisco: Jossey-Bass.

Scott, Geoffrey. 1924. *The Architecture of Humanism: A Study in the History of Taste.* London: Architectural Press. Second edition, 1980.

Scruton, Roger. 1979. *The Aesthetics of Architecture.* Princeton: Princeton University Press. Second printing, 1980.

Scruton, Roger. 1983. *The Aesthetic Understanding.* London and New York: Methuen.

Scully, Vincent. 1959. "Louis Sullivan's Architectural Ornament." *Perspecta.* No. 5:73–80.

Semper, Gottfried. 1851. *The Four Elements of Architecture and Other Writings.* Translated by H. F. Mallgrave and W. Herrmann. Cambridge, England: Cambridge University Press, 1989.

Serlio, Sebastiano. 1611. *The Five Books of Architecture.* New York: Dover Publications, 1982.

Shapiro, G., ed. 1990. *After the Future: Postmodern Times and Places.* New York: State University of New York Press.

Sharp, Dennis. 1981. *Sources of Modern Architecture: A Critical Bibliography.* London: Granada Publishing.

Short, John R. 1987. *The Humane City: Cities as if People Matter.* Oxford and New York: Basil Blackwell.

Shorter Oxford English Dictionary on Historical Principles (SOED). 1973. Two vols. Third edition. Revised and edited by C. T. Onions with etymologies revised by G. W. S. Friedrichsen. Oxford, England: Clarendon Press, 1992.

Skinner, Quentin, ed. 1985. *The Return of Grand Theory in the Human Sciences.* Cambridge, England: Cambridge University Press (Canto edition, 1990).

Small, Harold H., ed. 1947. *Form and Function: Remarks on Art by Horatio Greenough.* Berkeley and Los Angeles: University of California Press.

Smith, Huston. 1989. *Beyond the Post-Modern Mind.* Wheaton, Ill.: Theosophical Publishing House.

Smith, Michael P. 1984. *Sydney Opera House: How it was built and why it is so.* Sydney, Australia: Collins.

Smith, Peter F. 1974. *The Dynamics of Urbanism.* London: Hutchinson Educational.

Snodgrass, Adrian. 1990. *Architecture, Time and Eternity: Studies in the Stellar and Temporal Symbolism of Traditional Buildings.* Vol. 1. Sat-Pitaka Series, Indo-Asian Literatures. Vol. 356. New Delhi: P. K. Goel for Aditya Prakashan.

Snodgrass, Adrian, and Richard Coyne. 1990. "Is designing hermeneutical?" Working paper. Faculty of Architecture, University of Sydney, October.

Snodgrass, Adrian, and Richard Coyne. 1992. "Models, metaphors and the hermeneutics of designing." *Design issues.* Vol. 9, No. 1:56–74.

Soleri, Paolo. 1973. *The Bridge between Matter and Spirit is Matter becoming Spirit: The Arcology of Paolo Soleri.* Cambridge, Mass.: MIT Press.

Solomon, Robert C. 1977. *Introducing Philosophy. Problems and Perspectives.* New York: Harcourt Brace Jovanovich.

Sontag, Susan. 1966. *Against Interpretation and Other Essays.* New York: Farrar, Straus and Giroux.

Sontag, Susan. 1991. *Illness as Metaphor and AIDS and Its Metaphors.* London: Penguin Books.

Sorkin, Michael. 1991. *Exquisite Corpse: Writing on Buildings.* London and New York: Verso.

Stace, Walter. 1937. *The Concept of Morals.* New York: Macmillan.

Stanislowski, D. 1946. "The origin and spread of the grid-pattern town." *The Geographical Review.* Vol. 36:105–120.

Steadman, Philip. 1979. *The Evolution of Designs: Biological Analogy in Architecture and the Applied Arts.* Cambridge, England: Cambridge University Press.

Steiner, George. 1967. *Language and Silence.* London: Faber and Faber.

Stevens, Garry. 1990. *The Reasoning Architect: Mathematics and Science in Design.* New York: McGraw-Hill.

Stern, Robert. 1986. *Pride of Place: Building the American Dream.* Boston: Houghton Mifflin Company.

Stern, Robert. 1988. *Modern Classicism.* New York: Rizzoli International Publications.

Stiny, George, and James Gipps. 1978. *Algorithmic Aesthetics.* Berkeley: University of Califonia Press.

Stirling, William. 1897. *The Canon: An Exposition of the Pagan Mystery Perpetuated in the Cabala as the Rule of all the Arts.* Foreword by John Michell. London: Research Into Lost Knowledge Organisation, distributed by Thorston Publishers, 1981.

St. John Wilson, Colin. 1992. *Architectural Reflections: Studies in the Philosophy and Practice of Architecture.* Oxford, England: Butterworth Architecture.

Stokes, Adrian. 1978. *The Critical Writings of Adrian Stokes.* Vols. 1–3. London: Thames & Hudson.

Stone, Christopher D. 1987. *Earth and Other Ethics: The Case for Moral Pluralism.* New York: Harper & Row.

Strasser, Steven. 1963. *Phenomenology and the Human Sciences: A Contribution to a New Scientific Ideal.* Duquesne Studies Psychological Series: Vol. 1, Duquesne University. Paperback reprint. Atlantic Highlands, N. J.: Humanities Press, 1980.

Strawson, P. F. 1971. *Logico-Linguistic Papers.* London: Methuen & Co. Ltd.

Suckle, Abby, ed. 1980. *By Their Own Design.* New York: Whitney Library of Design.

Sullivan, Louis H. 1918. *Kindergarten Chats and Other Writings.* New York: Dover Publications, 1979.

Summerson, John. 1957. "The case for a theory of modern architecture." *RIBA Journal.* Third series, Vol. 64, No. 8, June:307–310.

Summerson, John N. 1964. *The Classical Language of Architecture.* Cambridge, Mass.: MIT Press, 1966.

Sweeney, James Johnson, and Josep Lluis Sert. 1960. *Antoni Gaudí.* London: Architectural Press, 1970.

Tafuri, Manfredo. 1976a. *Theories and History of Architecture.* Translated by Giorgio Verrecchia. London: Granada Publishing, 1980.

Tafuri, Manfredo. 1976b. *Architecture and Utopia.* Translated by B. L. LaPenta. Cambridge, Mass.: MIT Press.

Tafuri, Manfredo. 1987. *The Sphere and the Labyrinth: Avant-Gardes and Architecture from Piranesi to the 1970s.* Translated by P. d'Acierno & R. Connolly. Cambridge, Mass.: MIT Press.

Tawa, Michael. 1982. "Unity and the idea." *Transition.* No. 9, March:32–37.

Tawa, Michael. 1989. "Theory and practice in building and architecture." *Architect S. A.* No. 3:7–9.

Tawa, Michael. 1991. *Sound, Music and Architecture: A study of the relationship between sound, number, space and time in sacred music and architecture according to the Vedic, Pythagorean and Platonic traditions.* Unpublished Ph.D. thesis. School of Architecture, University of New South Wales.

Taylor, Mark C. 1988. "Deadlines approaching anarchetecture." In *Threshold.* See Diani and Ingraham 1988.

Team 10. 1962. *Architectural Design 12: Team 10 Primer 1953–62.* Vol. 32, December. Later published as *Team 10 Primer.* Alison Smithson, ed. London: Studio Vista, 1968.

Teymur, Necdet. 1982. *Environmental Discourse: A critical analysis of 'environmentalism' in architecture, planning, design, ecology, social sciences, and the media.* London: ?uestion Press.

Thiis-Evensen, Thomas. 1987/1989. *Archetypes in Architecture.* Oxford, England: Oxford University Press/Norwegian University Press.

Thomas, John C., and John M. Carroll. 1979. "The psychological study of design." In *Developments in Design Methodology.* See Cross 1984.

Thompson, D'Arcy. 1968. *On Growth and Form.* Cambridge, England: Cambridge University Press.

Thorne, Ross, and Stuart Arden. 1980. *People and the Man Made Environment: Building, urban & landscape design related to human behaviour.* Collection of papers delivered at University of Sydney, May 19–23. Sydney: Department of Architecture, University of Sydney.

Tigerman, Stanley. 1982. *Versus: An American Architect's Alternatives.* New York: Rizzoli International Publications.

Tigerman, Stanley, ed. 1987. *The Chicago Tapes: Transcript of the conference at The University of Illinois at Chicago, November 7 and 8, 1986.* New York: Rizzoli International Publications.

Tigerman, Stanley. 1988. *The Architecture of Exile.* New York: Rizzoli International Publications.

Tindall, George B., and David E. Shi. 1992. *America: A Narrative History.* Third edition. New York: W. W. Norton & Company.

Torre, Susanna, ed. 1977. *Women in American Architecture: A Historic and Contemporary Perspective.* New York: Whitney Library of Design.

Torre, Susanna. 1991. *"Architecture: A Place for Women."* Review in *Design Book Review.* Issue 20, Spring 1991:74–76.

Trancik, Robert. 1986. *Finding Lost Space: Theories of Urban Design.* New York: Van Nostrand Reinhold.

Trefil, James. 1986. *Meditations at 10,000 Feet: A Scientist in the Mountains.* New York: Charles Scribner's Sons.

Tschumi, Bernard. 1981. *The Manhattan Transcripts.* London: Academy Editions/ St. Martin's Press.

Tschumi, Bernard. 1987. *Cinégramme Folie: Le Parc de la Villette.* Princeton, N. J.: Princeton Architectural Press.

Tschumi, Bernard. 1990. *Text 5. Questions of Space: Lectures on Architecture.* London: Architectural Association.

Tuan, Yi-Fu. 1977. *Space and Place.* Minneapolis: University of Minnesota Press.

Tuan, Yi-Fu. 1974. *Topophilia: A Study of Environmental Perception, Attitudes and Values.* Englewood Cliffs, N. J.: Prentice Hall.

Turnbull, Jeff, ed. 1989. *Critiques 3.* Melbourne, Australia: Department of Architecture and Building, University of Melbourne.

Twombly, Robert. 1986. *Louis Sullivan: His Life and Work.* Chicago: University of Chicago Press, 1987.

Tyng, Anne Griswold. 1975. *Simultaneous Randomness and Order: The Fibonacci-Divine Proportion as a Universal Forming Principle.* Unpublished Ph.D. thesis. Graduate School of Arts and Sciences, University of Pennsylvania,

Tzonis, Alexander. 1972. *Towards a Non-oppressive Environment: An Essay.* New York: I Press, distributed by George Braziller.

Tzonis, Alexander, and Liane Lefaivre. 1986. *Classical Architecture: The Poetics of Order.* Cambridge, Mass.: MIT Press.

Van Leeuwen, Thomas A. 1988. *The Skyward Trend of Thought: The Metaphysics of the American Skyscraper.* Cambridge, Mass.: MIT Press.

Van Pelt, Robert Jan, and Carroll William Westfall. 1991. *Architectural Principles in the Age of Historicism.* New Haven: Yale University Press.

Ventre, Francis T. 1990. "Regulation: A realization of social ethics." In *Via 10.* See Capelli, Naprstek, and Prescott 1990.

Venturi, Robert. 1966. *Complexity and Contradiction in Architecture.* New York: Museum of Modern Art, 1977.

Venturi, Robert, and Denise Scott Brown. 1984. *A View from the Campidoglio: Selected Essays 1953–1984.* New York: Harper & Row.

Venturi, Robert, Denise Scott Brown, and Steve Izenour. 1972. *Learning from Las Vegas.* Cambridge, Mass.: MIT Press.

Vesely, Dalibor. 1985. "Architecture and the conflict of representation." *AA Files.* No. 8, January:21–38.

Vesey, Godfrey, ed. 1974. *Philosophy in the Open.* Milton Keynes, England: Open University.

Vico, Giambattista. 1744. *The New Science of Giambattista Vico.* Revised translation of the third edition by Thomas Goddard Bergin and Max Harold Fisch. Ithaca and London: Cornell University Press, 1968.

Vidler, Anthony. 1977. "The idea of type: The transformation of the academic ideal, 1750–1830." *Oppositions* 8:95–115.

Vidler, Anthony. 1987. *The Writing of the Walls: Architectural Theory in the Late Enlightenment.* Princeton, Princeton University Press.

Vidler, Anthony. 1990. *Claude-Nicolas Ledoux: Architecture and Social Reform at the End of the Ancien Regime.* Cambridge, Mass.: MIT Press.

Vidler, Anthony. 1992. *The Architectural Uncanny: Essays in the Modern Unhomely.* Cambridge, Mass.: MIT Press.

Viollet-le-Duc, Eugène-Emmanuel. 1872. *Lectures on Architecture.* Translated by Benjamin Bucknall, 1877/1881. New York: Dover, 1987.

Vitruvius Pollio. 1486. *The Ten Books on Architecture.* Translated by M. H. Morgan, 1914. New York: Dover Publications, 1960.

Vivante, Leone. 1955. *A Philosophy of Potentiality.* London: Routledge & Kegan Paul.

Von Meiss, Pierre. 1986. *Elements of Architecture: From Form to Place.* London: Van Nostrand Reinhold (International), 1990.

Voyce, Arthur. 1949. *Russian Architecture: Trends in Nationalism and Modernism*. New York: Greenwood Press, 1969.

Wajcman, J. 1991. *Feminism Confronts Technology*. North Sydney, Australia: Allen & Unwin.

Ward, Barbara. 1976. *The Home of Man*. London: Andre Deutsch.

Watkin, David. 1977. *Morality and Architecture: The Development of a Theme in Architectural History and Theory from the Gothic Revival to the Modern Movement*. Chicago: University of Chicago Press.

Watkin, David. 1983. *The Rise of Architectural History*. London: Architectural Press.

Watson, David. 1990. *Rule-generated Architecture*. Geelong, Australia: Deakin University Press.

Weyl, Hermann. 1952. *Symmetry*. Princeton, Princeton University Press, 1980.

Weisman, Leslie K. 1992. *Discrimination by Design: A Feminist Critique of the Man-Made Environment*. Urbana, University of Illinois Press.

Whiffen, Marcus, ed. 1965. *The History, Theory and Criticism of Architecture*. Cambridge, Mass.: MIT Press.

Whiteman, John, Jeffrey Kipnis, and Richard Burdett, eds. 1992. *Strategies in Architectural Thinking*. Cambridge, Mass.: MIT Press.

Whittick, Arnold. 1974. *European Architecture in the Twentieth Century*. New York: Abelard-Schuman.

Wiebenson, Dora, ed. 1983. *Architectural Theory and Practice from Alberti to Ledoux*. Second revised edition. Chicago: Architectural Publications Inc. Distributed by the University of Chicago Press.

Williams-Ellis, Clough. 1929. *The Architect*. London: Geoffrey Bles.

Wittgenstein, Ludwig. 1945. *Philosophical Investigations*. Edited by G. E. M. Anscombe and Rush Rhees. Oxford, England: Basil Blackwell. 1953.

Wittkower, Rudolf. 1973. *Architectural Principles in the Age of Humanism*. London: Academy Editions.

Wolfe, Tom. 1981. *From Bauhaus to Our House*. London: Jonathon Cape, 1982.

Wotton, Sir Henry. 1624. *The Elements of Architecture*. Facsimile reprint of the first edition with introduction and notes by Frederick Hard. Published for The Folger Shakespeare Library. Charlottesville: University Press of Virginia, 1968.

Wright, Frank Lloyd. 1939. *An Organic Architecture. The Architecture of Democracy: The Sir George Watson Lectures of the Sulgrave Manor Board*. London: Lund Humphries.

Wright, Frank Lloyd. 1943. *An Autobiography*. New York: Duell, Sloan and Pearce.

Wright, Frank Lloyd. 1954. *The Natural House*. New York: Horizon Press.

Wright, Frank Lloyd. 1957. *A Testament*. New York: Horizon Press.

Xenophon. 1965. *Recollections of Socrates and Socrates' Defense Before the Jury*. Translated by Anna S. Benjamin. Indianapolis, Bobbs-Merrill.

Yates, Frances A. 1966. *The Art of Memory*. London: Routledge & Kegan Paul.

Yates, Frances A. 1972. *The Rosicrucian Enlightenment.* London: Ark Paperbacks, 1986.

Zambonini, Giuseppe. 1989. "Notes for a theory of making in a time of necessity." *Perspecta* 24:3–23.

Zevi, Bruno. 1948. *Architecture as Space: How to Look at Architecture.* Translated by M. Gendel, 1957. New York: Horizon Press, 1974.

Zevi, Bruno. 1978. *The Modern Language of Architecture.* Canberra, Australia: Australian National University Press.

Zimmer, Heinrich. 1960. *The Art of Indian Asia: Its Mythology and Transformations.* Two vols. Completed and edited by Joseph Campbell. Second edition, Princeton, Princeton University Press, 1983.

INDEX

Freud, Sigmund, 265
Fried, M., 124
front, 227, 228
Frugès, Henri, 59, 65, 123
Fry, Roger, 180
Fuller, R. Buckminster, 177, 185, 276
Fun Palace (Cedric Price), 72, 185
function, xi, 19, 40, 46, 49, 50, 55,
    90, 132, 151, 181, 200, 201, 207,
    226, 227, 246, 258, 272, 282,
    290, 294–297, 303–307, 317–319,
    323, 324, 327, 342, 347, 351,
    390, 395, 403, 410, 419, 420
functionalism, xiii, 9, 27, 28, 33, 39,
    49, 108, 119, 171, 182, 189, 224,
    271, 291, 293, 318, 326, 332,
    341, 342, 416
Futurist Movement, 90

Gadamer, Hans-Georg, 198
Gamble, John, 249
game, 56, 103–106, 127, 148, 256,
    297, 400
Games, Stephen, 128
Garnier, Tony, 52
Gaudí, Antoni, 58
Gautier, Théophile, 323
Geddes, Patrick, 52, 323
Gehry, Frank, 102, 334, 371
gematria (see also number, numerol-
    ogy), 366
gender, 54, 116, 119, 133, 153,
    168–172, 174, 306, 354, 356
genetics, 44, 104, 108, 213, 291, 329,
    340
genius, 96, 132, 165, 177, 180, 295,
    324, 328, 330, 391–394, 396
genius loci, 58, 391–394
geomancy, 367
geometry, 16, 36, 70, 81, 137, 184,
    238, 239, 254, 255, 271, 304,
    314, 330, 332, 333, 349, 350,
    357–362, 366–368, 370, 371,
    373, 374, 377, 378, 380, 387,
    389, 394, 415
Germann, Georg, 104
Gestalt psychology, 375, 386
Gestalten, 102, 245, 348
Ghirardo, Diane, 50, 55, 355, 409,
    432
Giedion, Siegfried, 9, 249, 382, 383,
    384
Giocondo, Fra, 30
Giurgola, Romaldo, 368, 369
Glastonbury Abbey, 314
Gleick, James, 112, 238, 239, 242,
    244
gnosis, 150, 159
Gnosticism, 150, 159, 233
Goad, Phillip, 122
God, 5, 6, 43, 48, 70, 92, 95, 104,
    114, 149, 150, 155, 158, 164,
    166, 187, 202, 207, 209–212,
    299, 329, 335, 358, 390, 422
    architect as, 172, 335
Godin, Jean-Baptiste, 52
Goffman, Erving, 173, 228
Gogh, Vincent van, 432
Goldberger, Paul, 41, 269, 270, 321
Gombrich, Ernst H., 227, 228, 433
good, 64, 105, 130, 139, 158, 193,
    194, 197, 198, 200–202, 209–213,
    219, 224, 226, 292, 303, 353
    and evil, 210, 223
    as built perfection, 211
    beginnings, 37
    common, 67, 142, 158, 214
    of consumer, 64, 65
    of greater number, 203
    public, 136, 140, 226–229
    will, 129, 183, 210, 211, 219, 220,
    300
Goodhue, Bertram, 129
Goodman, Nelson, 186, 401
Goodman, Robert, 125, 130, 136
goodness, 20, 27, 28, 105, 119, 192,
    196, 200, 202, 203, 210–212,
    214, 215, 224, 226, 283, 286,
    320, 322, 341, 351, 353, 373,
    399, 403
Goody, Joan, 120, 168, 171
Gough, Piers, 408
governance, xvi, xviii, 12, 18, 30, 32,
    43, 100, 107, 111, 193–195, 224,
    237, 265, 309–311, 316, 338,
    362, 378, 390
Grabow, Stephen, 98, 173, 182, 183,
    258
Graf, Douglas, 15
Graham Foundation (Harvard), 7
grammar, 13, 15, 55, 290, 346, 397,
    421, 422
Grand Architect of the Universe,
    104, 232
Grand Central Station, N.Y., 129
Grand Dispenser of Talents, 163
grand theory, xviii, 20, 33, 250, 352
grand vision, 113, 178
grandeur, 191, 284, 364, 396
Grassi, Georgio, 332
Graves, Michael, 143, 164, 167, 199,
    420
Green, David, 47
Greenough, Horatio, 305, 410
grid, 177, 236, 237, 306, 251, 333,
    358, 369, 380
Griffin, Walter Burley, 368, 369
Gromort, George R., 317, 414
Gropius, Walter, 21, 31, 66, 70, 85,
    97, 121, 135, 176, 185, 317, 405
growth, 91, 94, 108, 128, 135, 141,
    252, 277, 356, 372, 373, 396, 416
Guénon, René, xxii, 107, 108, 263,
    264, 316, 350, 351, 387, 389, 390

Guggenheim, Solomon R., 123, 180
Guggenheim Museum, New York,
    123, 167
Guiley, Rosemary E., 177, 289
Gutman, Robert, 19, 126, 134, 148,
    156, 157, 172, 175
Gwathmey Siegel and Associates,
    167
Gwilt, Joseph, 117, 184, 315, 358,
    399

habit, xix, 6, 35, 155, 188, 192, 198,
    200, 208, 224, 225, 272, 281,
    282, 294, 295, 301–303, 329,
    374, 408, 418
Habraken, Nicolaas John, 63, 115
Hadid, Zaha, 377
Halifax, Marquess of, 158
Hannay, Alastair, 299
Hare, R. M., 204
harmony, xiii, 34, 90, 91, 95, 96,
    107, 134, 145, 169, 171, 207,
    235, 247, 262, 271, 278, 316,
    352, 353, 369, 370–372, 377,
    378, 402, 403, 411, 415
    cosmic, 271, 352
    reasoned (Alberti), 402–404
Harrington, K., 44
Harris, Errol, 100
Harrison, J. F. C., 313
Harvey, David, 134, 145–147
Hatje, Gerd, 91
Hauser, Arnold, 134, 263, 264, 298,
    331
Häring, Hugo, 88, 328
Hawkes, Terence, 55
Hays, K. Michael, 6, 8, 9, 17, 35, 38
Hays and Burns, 8
Hearn, M. F., 277
Heath, Tom, 2, 46, 154, 161, 171,
    175, 189, 201, 203, 248, 251,
    253, 255, 269, 323–325, 334,
    344, 347, 364, 395, 399, 401, 408
Hegel, G. W. F., 5, 27, 51, 79, 105,
    169–171, 198, 273, 299, 329,
    338, 395, 397, 403
Heidegger, Martin, 49, 59, 151, 152,
    178, 189, 385, 387, 434
Heisenberg, Werner, 316
Hejduk, John, 72, 177, 333, 335, 359
Hellman, Louis, 286
Heraclitus, 99, 241
Herder, Johann G. von, 420
heritage, 22, 26, 195, 196, 412
hermeneutics, 17, 46, 109, 160, 253,
    261, 294, 303, 344, 346, 375,
    407, 426
Herron, Rod, 185
Hersey, George, 56, 169, 354, 426,
    427
Hertzberger, Herman, 54, 64, 115,
    338

Pythagoras, 247, 290, 357, 359, 365, 368
Pythius, 184

qualities, xviii, xx, 19, 23, 26, 27, 37, 51, 57–59, 64, 69, 80, 84–87, 91–94, 96, 98, 99, 101, 104, 107, 109, 113, 119, 122, 124, 131, 146, 151, 153, 155, 163–166, 170, 171, 175, 180, 191, 196, 201, 206–211, 218, 227, 229, 239, 242, 254, 274, 285–288, 304, 333, 337, 347, 348, 351–353, 358, 359, 367, 368, 371, 372, 375, 380, 381, 383, 390, 392, 396, 400, 401, 404, 406, 411, 413, 415, 419
   architectural, 8, 16, 25, 39, 50, 58, 68, 80, 83, 87, 96, 98, 109, 257, 262, 263, 266, 271, 305, 324, 330, 332, 334, 349, 351, 360, 361, 369, 396, 404, 412, 432
quality, xix, 39, 73, 82, 129, 136, 144, 153, 163–168, 208, 210, 214, 234, 269, 270, 287, 323, 333, 350, 361, 365, 371, 373, 395, 404
   assurance, 166, 327
   management, 61
   standards, 218
quantity, xix, 100, 163–165, 168, 204, 210, 324, 352, 365–368, 370, 375, 401
Quatremère de Quincy, Antoine Chrysostôme, 288, 289
Quine, Willard V. O., 267
Quinn, Patrick, 392
Quintilian, 403

Raban, Jonathon, 60, 66, 145, 324, 432
Raglan, Lord, 16
Rand, Ayn, 174
Rapoport, Amos, 16, 59–61
Raskin, Eugene, 179, 226
Rasmussen, Steen E., 430
ratio, 35, 48, 233, 234, 361, 362, 371, 373
ratiocinatio, 34, 35
rationalism, xx, 6, 7, 18, 90, 116, 172, 188, 206, 246, 248, 249, 252, 261, 298, 300, 315, 319, 324, 328, 329
rationality, xxii, 1, 3, 7, 9, 27, 33, 36, 39, 40, 43, 83, 90, 92, 108, 116, 137, 139, 159–161, 169, 177, 183, 184, 193, 196, 198, 199, 203, 205, 213, 214, 216, 217, 222, 225, 231, 248–250, 253–255, 258–260, 262, 264, 283, 284, 298–300, 313, 323–327, 329,

336, 340, 343, 360, 363, 365, 366, 373, 374, 393, 400, 407, 425
Rawls, John, 28, 139, 140, 162, 164, 194, 253
Read, Herbert, 333
reality, 43, 46
reason, 20, 42, 79, 84, 117, 149, 159, 160, 169, 180, 184, 197–199, 202, 205, 210, 211, 221, 231, 252, 288, 292, 313, 335, 362, 371, 402, 404
   Cunning of (Lakatos), 126, 127
   faith as Postulate of (Kant), 300
   sufficient (Leibniz), 316
reasoning, 3, 10, 46, 66, 69, 98, 166, 251, 260, 301, 316, 331–334, 359, 360, 371, 404, 405
   a posteriori, 6, 46, 108, 370
   a priori, 2, 5, 6, 46, 77, 99, 108, 197, 212, 232, 264, 265, 292, 316, 329, 337, 426
reductionism, 46, 79, 81, 89, 96, 242, 244, 261, 291, 310, 311, 337, 339
relativism, 27, 46, 194, 212–215, 273, 283, 347, 375, 427
Relativity, Einstein's Theory of, 357, 384
Relph, Edward, 392
Renaissance, 15
repertoire, 15, 307, 330, 408, 416, 424, 425, 427
revolt, xxiii, 266, 281
revolution, 32, 38, 54, 150, 176, 183, 189, 267, 268, 279, 331, 333, 334, 340, 347, 355, 423
   American, 168
   French, 131, 168
   industrial, 131, 141, 143, 145, 184
rhetoric, xvii, xviii, xx, 11–13, 20, 23, 48, 49, 53, 79, 96, 111, 113, 193, 200, 207, 208, 227, 228, 318, 324, 334, 341, 404, 423, 429, 433
Richards, J. M., 63
Richard Rogers and Partners, 186, 344
Ricoeur, Paul, 288
Riemann, Georg F. B., 357
Rietveld, Gerrit, 182
ritual, 47, 56, 87, 177, 188, 267, 268, 282, 295, 301, 302, 342, 351, 388, 393
Roark, Howard, 174
Rogers, Richard, 185, 274, 328, 338
Rogers and Piano, 344
Roget, Peter Mark, xxi, 348
role, xvii, 1, 5, 40, 41, 47, 52, 55, 57, 68, 91, 94, 102, 132, 134, 141, 150, 152, 153, 161, 170–176, 267, 295, 307, 328, 329, 351, 356, 357, 402, 405, 411, 414

of architects, 116, 131, 172–176, 179, 188
Ronchamp, Notre-Dame-du-Haut, 376
Rondelet, J. B., 184
rooftop remodelling, Vienna (Coop Himmelblau), 58
Root, Henry, 168
Rose, Steven, 342
Rosenau, Helen, 71
Rosicrucians (Rose Cross Fraternity), 72
Rossbach, Sarah, 367, 393
Rossi, Aldo, 30, 66, 174, 285, 288, 291, 297, 332, 343, 388
Rotondi, Michael, 324
Rousseau, Jean-Jacques, 194
Rowe, Colin, xvi, 70, 71, 411, 412
Rowe and Koetter, 70, 71, 172
Rowe, Peter, xvi, 16, 17, 18, 27–29, 31, 246, 256, 265, 393, 420, 434
Royal Australian Institute of Architects (RAIA), 135, 136
Royal Institute of British Architects (RIBA), 408
Royal Saltworks, Chaux, 51
Rudofsky, Bernard, 428
rule(s), 15, 23, 30, 31, 36, 57, 58, 61, 69, 77, 104, 105, 108, 114, 115, 124, 135, 154, 160, 161, 164, 180, 191, 194, 197, 200, 202, 206, 208–212, 224, 228, 229, 233, 234, 240, 242, 246, 251, 252, 254, 256, 258–260, 267, 272, 281, 285, 289, 296, 301–303, 307, 309, 316, 317, 320, 327, 333, 338, 346, 348, 349, 358, 360, 367, 370–372, 385, 397, 402, 404, 412, 414–420, 427, 434
   of thumb, xxii, 21, 161, 341
Rusch, Charles, W., 292
Ruskin, John, 5, 39, 52, 75, 84–86, 88, 92, 95, 111, 141, 179, 198, 205, 208, 245, 275, 276, 304, 361, 365, 370, 405, 411, 425
Ryan, Alan, 139, 162, 164
Russell, Bertrand, 105, 106
Rybczynski, Witold, 64
Rykwert, Joseph, xvi, 70, 85, 92, 305, 316, 339, 342, 366, 388, 389, 407
Rykwert, Leach, and Tavernor, xxiv, 91, 92, 117, 362, 370, 371, 383

Saarinen, Eero, 285, 286
Sagan, Carl, 241
St. Augustine, 289
St. Bartholomew's in New York, 129
St. John Wilson, Colin, 181, 202, 207, 220, 277, 401, 403

status (continued)
157, 166, 205, 227, 247, 257, 267, 268, 341, 408, 417, 432
status quo, 72, 267
Steiner, George, 38, 53, 54
stereometry, 357, 375
stereotomy, 357, 361
stereotype, 143, 174, 236, 289–292, 366, 417
Stieglitz, Alfred, 366
Stiny and Gipps, 402
Stirling, James, xiii, 434
Stirling, William, 366
Stirling and Wilford, 389, 433
Stokes, Adrian, 88
Stone, Christopher D., 193–197, 209, 224
story, 13, 47, 49, 254–257, 262, 273, 284, 423, 425
Strachey, Lytton, 45
Strasser, Steven, 7, 94
Strato of Lampsacus, 89
Strauss, Irwin, 329
Strawson, P. F., 64, 65
structuralism, xxiii, 16, 49, 188, 291
structure, xv, xvi, xix, xxi, 6, 15, 18, 46, 48, 52, 58, 69, 78, 83, 99, 100, 102, 103, 111, 113–116, 122, 124, 125, 138, 139, 150, 155, 170, 171, 187, 188, 207, 222, 233, 239, 242, 243, 253, 257, 259, 260, 268, 281, 285, 288, 310, 321, 323, 325, 328, 338, 340, 342, 343, 345, 376, 390, 419, 421, 424, 425, 433
  building, xiv, 17, 58, 69, 70, 72, 84, 91, 95, 103, 131, 169, 182–184, 186, 193, 208, 220, 344, 345
structuring, 233, 238, 249, 309, 313, 340, 348, 349, 358, 377, 380, 416, 421
style, xx, 1, 22, 30, 37, 38, 65, 76, 89, 96, 125, 174, 176, 184, 189, 198, 228, 245, 246, 272, 274–276, 279, 280, 304, 305, 318, 319, 326, 331, 332, 339, 340, 349, 365, 377, 379, 381, 383, 402, 404, 406–411, 412, 416, 418
subjectivity, 36, 46, 47, 55, 129, 165, 169, 170, 181, 214, 219, 221, 258, 283, 298, 300, 302, 335, 343, 356, 363, 370, 385, 396, 398, 403, 426
subject-object, xix, xxiii, 1, 4, 9, 31, 36, 39, 49, 101, 152, 251
Suckle, Abby, 338
Sullivan, Louis H., 9, 92, 169, 171, 179, 304, 305, 367, 430
Sulpitius, Fra Giovanni, 36
Summerson, John, 17, 21

Superstudio, 72
surplus, 108, 302, 369
Swedenborg, Emanuel, 5, 169, 350
Sweeney, James Johnston, 123, 420
Sweeney and Sert, 50
Sydney Opera House, 219, 359, 420
symbiosis, 89, 90, 108, 330, 346
symbol, 48, 58, 63, 69, 93, 131
  systems, 397, 401
symbolism, xxiii, 9, 14, 16, 47, 54, 56, 57, 109, 183, 264, 267, 291, 297, 312, 315, 319, 342, 354, 357, 358, 364, 366–369, 376–378, 387–389, 395, 397, 409, 411, 412, 419, 423, 427, 431
symmetry, 34, 35, 43, 95, 97, 104, 147, 235, 236, 238, 316, 340, 350, 361–364, 404, 415
  axial, 319, 359
  bilateral, 236, 237, 388
  rotational, 387
synchronicity, 177
syncretism, 107
syndicalism, 125
synecdoche, 100, 419, 422
synectics, 258
synergy, 89
syntagm, 17
syntalysis, 265
syntax, 55, 206, 249, 398, 401, 402, 421
synthesis, 19, 27, 35, 97, 179, 182, 253, 260–265, 282, 305–307, 309, 357
system(s), xxii, 19, 30, 31, 37, 43, 44, 50, 61, 71, 76, 115, 116, 125, 156, 161, 165, 169, 184, 185, 187, 189, 190, 192, 198, 207, 231, 235, 236, 239, 241–244, 248, 251, 252, 261, 266, 290–292, 302, 312, 321, 324, 338, 339, 343, 347, 352, 358, 362, 366, 369, 371, 373–375, 379, 390, 397, 415, 416, 418, 419, 423–425
  of traditional siting (Doxiadis), 362
systemics, 90, 291, 349, 373

taboo(s), 87, 143, 408
Tafuri, Manfredo, 52, 55, 176
talent, 65, 85, 120, 123, 124, 125, 129, 134, 142, 150, 155, 157, 162–166, 168, 180, 187, 313, 404
Talents, Parable of the Five, 162, 163
Taller de Arquitectura, 54
taste, xiv, 26, 28–30, 117, 122, 159, 180, 194, 203, 225, 227, 228, 271, 302, 306, 313, 380, 399, 401, 402, 404, 408, 418, 422, 427
Taut, Bruno, 90, 176, 177
Tawa, Michael, 338, 350, 366, 383
taxis, 235, 236, 415

taxonomy, 102, 132, 187–189, 249, 291, 305
Taylor, Charles, 198
Taylor, Mark C., 266
Team X/Team 10, 217, 234
Team Zoo, 297
technics, xvi, xx, 3, 9, 18, 31, 38, 76, 79, 126, 146, 147, 174, 175, 183–186, 188, 200, 211, 258, 279, 287, 317, 321, 324, 340, 344, 360
technocracy, 141, 175, 252, 321
technology, 27, 36, 50, 53, 61, 90, 116, 131, 154, 178, 182–187, 193, 198, 222, 252, 274, 275, 277, 282, 290, 331, 338, 344, 345, 358, 402, 403, 428
Technology Inc, 71
tectonics, xxv, 45, 58, 185, 200, 201, 233, 290, 310, 321, 382
teleology, 27, 101, 296, 345
text(s), 48, 49, 271, 276, 279, 285, 299, 350, 359, 363, 368, 378, 388, 392, 398, 401, 402, 405, 412, 415, 422
textuality, 6, 34, 36, 48, 59, 133, 276, 285
texture, 195, 285, 364, 401
Teymur, Necdet, xv, 37
Teyssot, Georges, 70
theory, xvi–xviii, xxii, 1, 2, 4, 6, 8–13, 15, 17–19, 21, 22, 30–50, 52, 62, 79, 120, 126, 127, 133, 139, 159, 164, 168, 169, 178, 187, 189, 191, 198, 202–204, 207, 209, 242, 245, 253, 258, 259, 261, 265, 266, 270, 274, 280, 286, 291, 295, 309, 312, 316, 319, 322–326, 333, 340, 346, 354–356, 366, 371, 403, 404, 407, 412, 415, 424, 428, 430
  and history, 22
  and practice, xxi, 3, 7, 8, 11, 12, 22, 23, 31, 33–38, 49, 52, 69, 130, 160, 178, 190, 240, 309
  espoused, 187, 189, 190, 345
  of pumpoids, 13, 256
theory of architecture, 1, 3–11, 13, 17, 18, 20–23, 28–32, 34–37, 40, 42, 43, 46, 49, 66, 83, 136, 139, 148, 171, 184, 190, 204, 215, 222, 291, 303, 312, 319, 333, 339, 352, 355, 376, 390, 407
theory-talk (see also design-talk, rhetoric), xvii, 10–13, 17, 190, 204, 205, 285, 341
Thiis-Evensen, Thomas, xii, 93, 290, 292, 376, 377
Third Man Argument, 7
Thiry, Paul, 226, 227
Thomas and Carroll, 258